I0879487

# ANCIENT RECORDS OF EGYPT

## VOLUME 4

*The Twentieth to the Twenty-sixth Dynasties*

# ANCIENT RECORDS OF EGYPT

## VOLUME 4

*The Twentieth to the Twenty-sixth Dynasties*

*Translated and Edited by*

JAMES HENRY BREASTED

UNIVERSITY OF ILLINOIS PRESS
*Urbana and Chicago*

FRONTISPIECE: James Henry Breasted, copying a hieroglyphic text in the Temple of Buhen, Egypt; Egyptian Expedition of the University of Chicago, Oriental Exploration Fund, Egyptian Section; photographed by Friedrich Koch, 1906. Courtesy of The Oriental Institute of the University of Chicago.

First Illinois paperback, 2001

Manufactured in the United States of America
P 6 5 4 3 2
∞ This book is printed on acid-free paper.

Library of Congress Cataloging-in-Publication Data
Ancient records of Egypt / translated and edited by James Henry Breasted ; introduction and supplementary bibliographies by Peter A. Piccione.
p. cm.
Originally published: Chicago : University of Chicago Press, 1906.
Includes bibliographical references and indexes.
Contents: v. 1. The first through the seventeenth dynasties — v. 2. The eighteenth dynasty — v. 3. The nineteenth dynasty — v. 4. The twentieth through the twenty-sixth dynasties — v. 5. Supplementary bibliographies and indices.
ISBN 978-0-252-06990-1 (vol. 1 : pbk. : alk. paper) — ISBN 978-0-252-06974-1 (vol. 2 : pbk. : alk. paper) —ISBN 978-0-252-06975-8 (vol. 3 : pbk. : alk. paper) —ISBN 978-0-252-06976-5 (vol. 4 : pbk. : alk. paper) — ISBN 978-0-252-06991-8 (vol. 5 : pbk. : alk. paper)
1. Egypt—History—To 332 B.C.—Sources.
I. Breasted, James Henry, 1865–1935.
DT83.A658 2001
932—dc21 00-053216

University of Illinois Press
1325 South Oak Street
Champaign, IL 61820-6903
www.press.uillinois.edu

# TABLE OF CONTENTS

## VOLUME I

---

## VOLUME II

LIST OF FIGURES



---

## VOLUME III

LIST OF FIGURES



## VOLUME IV

LIST OF FIGURES

# EXPLANATION OF TYPOGRAPHICAL SIGNS AND SPECIAL CHARACTERS

1. The introductions to the documents are in twelve-point type, like these lines.

2. All of the translations are in ten-point type, like this line.

3. In the footnotes and introductions all quotations from the documents in the original words of the translation are in *italics*, inclosed in quotation marks. *Italics* are not employed in the text of the volumes for any other purpose except for titles.

4. The lines of the original document are indicated in the translation by superior numbers.

5. The loss of a word in the original is indicated by —, two words by — —, three words by — — —, four words by — — — —, five words by — — — — —, and more than five by ———. A word in the original is estimated at a "square" as known to Egyptologists, and the estimate can be but a very rough one.

6. When any of the dashes, like those of No. 5, are inclosed in half-brackets, the dashes so inclosed indicate not lost, but uncertain words. Thus ⌈—⌉ represents one uncertain word, ⌈— —⌉ two uncertain words, and ⌈———⌉ more than five uncertain words.

7. When a word or group of words are inclosed in half-brackets, the words so inclosed are uncertain in meaning; that is, the translation is not above question.

8. Roman numerals I, II, III, and IV, not preceded by the title of any book or journal, refer to these four volumes of Historical Documents. The Arabic numerals following such Romans refer to the numbered paragraphs of these volumes. All paragraph marks (§ and §§, without a Roman) refer to paragraphs of the same volume.

9. For signs used in transliteration, see Vol. I, p. xvii.

# THE TWENTIETH DYNASTY

# REIGN OF RAMSES III

## BUILDING AND DEDICATION INSCRIPTIONS OF MEDINET HABU TEMPLE

1. This building is the most completely preserved temple of Egypt, antedating the Ptolemaic period. With its inscriptions and reliefs, it forms a vast record of the reign of Ramses III, parallel with the other record which he has left us in the great Papyrus Harris (§§ 151–412). It was dedicated by the king in his twelfth year, by the introduction of a new calendar of feasts, with richly endowed offerings (§§ 139–45). It was entirely built by Ramses III, as its inscriptions show. To this fact, as well as to its fine state of preservation, is due its importance. That imposing line of similar temples, of the Eighteenth Dynasty, which once extended eastward and northeastward from Medinet Habu, has now almost entirely vanished. The one exception is the ruined temple of Thutmose III, beside the Medinet Habu temple. The Nineteenth Dynasty temples, crowded into the same line, have likewise perished, leaving the wreck of the Ramesseum and the Kurna temple of Seti I. Each of these temples was, with slight exception (Kurna), the work of one king, and the scenes on the Ramesseum pylons, as well as those at Medinet Habu, indicate what an irreparable loss we have suffered in the destruction of these records of individual reigns. The Medinet Habu temple is therefore unique, and we must intensely regret that it was a Twentieth rather than an Eighteenth Dynasty temple which survived.

2. We shall first notice the inscriptions which concern the building (§§ 3–34); second, the historical records preserved on its walls (§§ 35–138); and, third, the great calendar of

feasts (§§ 139–45). The inscriptions of earliest date (year 5) are found farthest back, viz., in the second court; while the second pylon, which forms the front of this court, bears an immense inscription of the year 8. The first pylon, the final front of the temple, carries records of the eleventh and twelfth years; so that the gradual growth of the temple from rear to front is clear. At the same time, it must be remembered that the cutting of the scenes and inscriptions was sometimes delayed. Thus the door of the treasury in the oldest part of the temple bears a scene depicting events of the eighth year or later.

Besides the records of the building on its own walls, there is also a record of it in Papyrus Harris (§ 189).

**3.** In all the dedicatory inscriptions which follow, the traditional formula is introduced by the king's name, preceding the pronoun "*he*." This has been omitted in the translations throughout. Beginning at the rear, with the oldest portion of the building, we find a dedicatory inscription running around the holy of holies, which is as follows:

**4.** [a]He made (it) as his monument for his father, Amon-Re, king of gods, making for him a great and august temple of fine, white sandstone, its doors of genuine electrum; an august palace for his image, which is in his house. He made it for him in the sacred district by the side of "Lord of Life," the pure ground of the ruler of Thebes, the eternal resting-place, the accustomed court of the lord of Tazoser, the path of the leaders of the Nether World. I did not overturn the tombs of the lords of life,[b] the tomb-chambers of the ancestors, the glorious place

[a]"Paroi extérieure . . . . côté nord. . . . . Dernière partie du palais" (meaning temple), Champollion, *Notices descriptives*, I, 739 f.; but "Inschrift um die Cella," Lepsius, *Denkmäler*, III, 213, *d*.

[b]A euphemism for the dead; the king means that in locating his temple in the ancient Theban cemetery he did not appropriate the ground occupied by the old tombs. It is to the already ancient necropolis that the series of epithets (beginning "*sacred district*" and continuing to the end) refers.

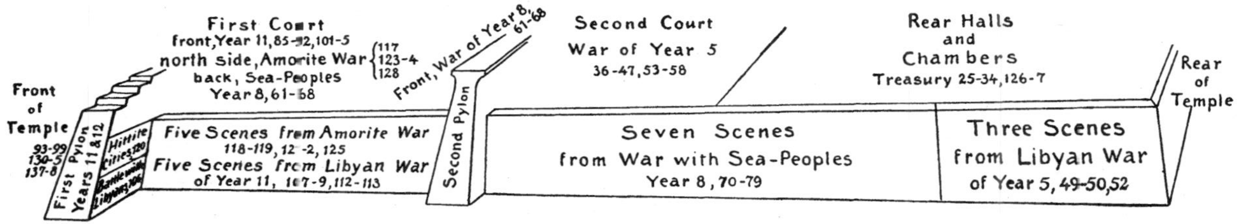


PLAN OF SCENES AND INSCRIPTIONS IN MEDINET HABU TEMPLE

The observer faces southward and looks against the outside of the north wall. The numerals indicate the paragraphs of the translations herein.

which was at the beginning, of the lord of Rosta, the divine way of the gods and the cavern-dwellers[a] to the revered dead.

5. On a chapel of Khonsu, in the heart of the oldest portion, is the following dedication:[b]

He made (it) as (his) monument for his father, Khonsu, residing in Thebes; making for him an august "Great Seat"[c] of fine white sandstone, the door of electrum, in "The-House (*ḥ·t*)-of-Usermare-Meriamon-Possessed-of-Eternity-on-the-West-of-Thebes;" that he may establish his son, Lord of Diadems, Ramses, Ruler of Heliopolis, as excellent sovereign upon the throne of Atum, like Re, forever.

6. What is now the second court, but originally the first court, was then built in front of the older structure. It contains inscriptions of the year 5; and its dedication is as follows:

7. [d]He made it as (his) monument for his father, Amon-Re, making for him "The-House (*ḥ·t*)-of-Usermare-Meriamon-Possessed-of-Eternity-in-the-House-of-Amon," like unto the great palace of the horizon; of fine sandstone. The "Great Seat" is of gold, its pavement of silver, its doors of gold and black granite;[e] the broad-hall of stone of Ayan, the doors thereof of copper in beaten work, the inlay-figures of electrum and every splendid costly stone. When the sun rises, he shines into its midst, his splendor envelops its house, the favorite seat of ⌜his⌝ father, Amon. When he sets, he touches its beauty, silver, electrum, and every costly stone. . . . . . . .

8. Another inscription[f] in the same court also refers to the building. We find among the epithets following the name of the king:

---

[a]Meaning the inhabitants of the nether world, the dead.

[b]"Troisième salle hypostyle," Rougé, *Inscriptions hiéroglyphiques*, 138.

[c]Or: "*a great place, an august shrine.*"

[d]Brugsch, *Thesaurus*, 1307=Champollion, *Notices descriptives*, I, 732 f. "Sur la frise de la seconde cour, à partir du milieu de la frise de la galerie ouest;" see also Mariette, *Voyage dans la haute Egypte*, II, 53.

[e]Or: "*black copper.*"

[f]Second court, "galerie de l'ouest;" Champollion, *Notices descriptives*, I, 738.

"..... mighty in making monuments in Victorious Thebes, making his august house like the horizon of heaven, like the great house of the All-Lord who is in heaven. ....."

**9.** During the festival of Min, on the walls of this same (second) court, the king recites to the god the building and equipment of the temple:

[a]3"...... Thou didst find me as a babe upon the breast, thou didst establish me, thou didst place (me) upon thy throne 4. . . . 5. . . I built for thee an august house in thy name, of 6fine white sandstone. Its form is like the horizon of heaven, over against Karnak [b]on the [⌜west of Thebes⌝].[b] 7Its doorposts are of fine gold, the inlay-figures of every splendid costly stone.[c] Its treasury [⌜overflow⌝]s 8with everything, even that which the hands of Tatenen (Ptah) made. I fashioned images of the gods and goddesses 9to rest in the midst of thy house. I made my image before thy front, the regalia 10of every splendid costly stone, in order to follow thee at thy every appearance, at thy every feast every day, when thou proceedest before its beautiful face. 11Thou multipliest for it the years in millions. Thou makest it like one among thy divine ennead, established before thee, forever. I bring 12to thee the tribute of every land, in order to flood thy treasury and thy storehouse. I multiply for thee feasts again, in order to provision thy temple. I multiply for thee wheat in heaps, thy granary[d] 13approaches heaven; cattle yards, oxen, bullocks, ⌜steers⌝; the sea bears galleys and transports; and poultry yards are supplied with thy divine offerings, the bird-pools are gathered in them. ......"

**10.** Forming the front of this court, the king erected a great pylon, which bears records of the year 5 on its back,

---

[a]Northern colonnade, second court; Brugsch, *Thesaurus*, 1307 f. = Champollion, *Notices descriptives*, I, 734, 735 (with considerable omissions); Rougé, *Inscriptions hiéroglyphiques*, 118–20; and better, Piehl, *Inscriptions*, I, CXLVIII, B–CL.

[b]Omitted by Brugsch.

[c]Brugsch stops here.

[d]In the tomb of the "*chief measurer of the granary of the house of Amon, Userhet,*" there is an inscription in which Ramses III is called: "*the great Nile, the great harvest-goddess of Egypt, making monuments with a loving heart for his father, Amon ...... making for him a very great granary, whose grain-heaps approach heaven*" (Naville, *Inscriptions historiques de Pinodjem* III, 6, n. 3).

facing the court, and of the year 8 on its front. It has also on its back the following dedication:

[a]He made (it) as his monument for his father, Amon-Re, king of gods; making for him a festive hall,[b] before his portal, surrounded by great, ⌜new⌝ monuments, like the horizon of heaven.

This, of course, refers to the erection of this addition[c] in front of the earlier portal.

**11.** [d]The dedication of the granite portal of this pylon (now the second pylon), once the entrance portal of the temple, is as follows:

He made a monument for his father, Amon-Re, making for him a great doorway of fine granite, the door of cedar, bound with copper, the inlay-figures of electrum. Its beautiful name is: "Usermare-Meriamon,-Amon-Rejoices-to-See-Him."

**12.** The present first court was then erected before this pylon; it bears records of year 8 and possibly year 12. Its dedication inscription is as follows:

[e]He made a monument as a great[f] benefaction from a heart of love for his father, Amon-Re-Iny,[g] ruler of Thebes, making for him a house of millions of years on the west of Thebes. Its beauty reaches Manu, like the heavens which bear the sun; the sun sails to — therein, his love pervades its house.

---

[a]Back of second pylon, over colonnade behind it; photograph, not very clear.

[b]Lit., "*the broad*" (*wsḫ·t*), indicating the shape of the hall.

[c]It would require examination on the spot to decide exactly what new portion is meant.

[d]Second pylon, doorposts of granite doorway facing first court; Champollion, *Notices descriptives*, I, 731 f.=Lepsius, *Denkmäler*, III, 210, *c*;=Brugsch, *Thesaurus*, V, 1308; Lepsius, *ibid.*, III, 210, *d*, is the same dedication on the other doorpost, but lacking the name of the portal.

[e]First court, "nordöstlicher Architrav," Lepsius, *Denkmäler*, III, 213, *c*.

[f]Duplicate shows *tnr*.

[g]Uncertain divinity here identified with Amon (cf. Lanzone, I, 62). Another dedication on the back of the second pylon, over the roof of the colonnade behind it, is verbatim the same as far as the name of Amon, to which it then merely appends a series of epithets (photograph).

13. Another dedication in the same court is the following:

[a]He made a monument for Amon, he made a house of millions of years, on the west of Thebes. It is the place of his heart's satisfaction, in the district of Manu, the pure ground of the lord of gods, the resting-place of his divine ennead, the divine adytum since the time of the god, for the king of gods. He is satisfied when he rests in it; when he reaches (it), he is joyful of heart.

14. The following is still another dedication of the same court:

[b]He made a monument for his father, Amon-Re, making for him "The - House - of - Usermare - Meriamon - Possessed-of-Eternity-in-the-House-of-Amon," west of Thebes, of good white [sand]stone; the "Great Seat" — of electrum, the doorways of gold, the doors of copper, in beaten work, the in[lay-figures of electrum] ————.

15. The great pylon which forms the front of this court has on its back inscriptions of the year 11, and on its front records of years 11 and 12. It has the following dedications:

[c]He made a monument for his father, Amon-Re, lord of Thebes, making for him a very great pylon, before his august house.

He made a monument for his father, Amon-Re, king of gods; erecting for him great flagstaves of real cedar of the royal domain.[d]

And again:

16. [e][He made a monument for his father], Amon-Re, king of gods;

---

[a]First court; Champollion, *Notices descriptives*, I, 730; "nordöstlicher Architrav," Lepsius, *Denkmäler*, III, 213, *b*.

[b]"An der östlichen Aussenwand des Vorhofes," Lepsius, *Denkmäler*, III, 213, *e*=Brugsch, *Thesaurus*, 1308.

[c]First pylon, left (southern) tower, by left flagstaff channel; photograph; the other channel was not included in the photograph.

[d]The variant on the other pylon (§ 16) has: "*of the best of the terraces, of the choicest of the Lord of the Two Lands,*" as parallel of this phrase; showing clearly that *ḫnt* is properly rendered by "*royal domain,*" and that this "*royal domain*" was located on the "*terraces*" of Lebanon, as under Thutmose III. (See my *New Chapter*, p. 28, where the examples from the Old Kingdom in note *b* should be omitted.)

[e]First pylon, right (northern) tower, on the right of the right flagstaff channel; photograph; the left channel was not included in this photograph. I have restored the lost beginnings from the parallel inscription on the other pylon.

erecting for him a colonnade at the double façade of his house, its ⌜roof⌝[a] of real electrum.

[He made a monument for his father, Amon-Re, lord of] Thebes; making for [him] great flagstaves of real cedar of the best of the terraces, of the choicest of the Lord of the Two Lands.[b]

**17.** The stone building in front of the Medinet Habu temple, known as the pavilion, was but the entrance of a great palace, which was considered as part of the temple, for it bore the same name.[c] It extended back to the second court of the temple, and the first pylon was apparently inclosed in its court. This palace served as the king's dwelling, at least during the celebration of great feasts in the Medinet Habu temple, and the doorway connecting the second court with this palace refers to this use, thus:[d]

The king appears like Re in the palace of his august broad-hall, to cause his father, Amon, to appear at his "Feast of the Valley;"

And again:

Ruler, beautiful in coming forth, like ⌜Horus⌝ at his appearance in heaven at early morning from his august palace which is in the horizon.

### *Silsileh Inscriptions*

**18.** The official who was taking out sandstone at the quarries of Silsileh, as the temple progressed, has left a record[e]

---

[a] I read *ḏ ͻ ḏ ͻ* or *tp*, "*head*," but the photograph is not clear; are the capitals meant?

[b] Further dedications of the usual form will be found in Piehl, *Inscriptions*, I, CLII f., I; CLIII f., M.

[c] Viz., "*The-House* (*ḥ·t*)-*of-Usermare-Meriamon-in-the-House-of-Amon*" (Lepsius, *Denkmäler*, Text, III, 167), which is the same as the name of the temple; see above dedications, *passim*.

[d] Daressy, *Recueil*, XX, 82; he thinks, however, that the pavilion was not connected with the palace, enveloping the front of the temple, and referred to in the above inscription. But the name and the location of the pavilion seem to me to exclude this view. The purpose of this building was already noted by Erman (*Aegypten*, 107, 108).

[e] Champollion, *Notices descriptives*, I, 256, 257 = Lepsius, *Denkmäler*, VI, 23, 8; Piehl, *Sphinx*, VI, 143–45 (transcription only).

of one of his expeditions thither which he had cut in hieratic on the wall of the quarry. It is especially interesting, because it gives the number of men engaged:

*First Inscription*

**19.** [1]Year 5,[a] first month of the third season (ninth month) under the majesty of King Ramses [2]III, L. P. H., beloved of all gods, given life forever and ever.

Expedition[b] which his majesty, L. P. H., made by the overseer of the White House, Setemhab, for "The-House (*ḥ·t*)-of-Millions-of-Years-of-King-Usermare-Meriamon-in-the-House (*pr*)-of-Amon,"[c] to do the work on the monuments in "The-House-of-Millions-of-Years-of-King-Usermare-Meriamon-in-the-House-of-Amon,"[c] in western Thebes.

| | |
|---|---|
| Men of the army who were under his command[d] | 2,000 men |
| Quarrymen | 500[e] men |
| Large transports (*wsḫ*) which were under his command[d] | 40 |
| ⌜—⌝ ships | 4 |
| ——— | 500[f] men |
| Total, various persons | 3,000 |

**20.** Two other inscriptions were left beside the above, by the same official at the same time:

[a]So both Lepsius, *Denkmäler*, and Champollion, *Notices descriptives;* Piehl has "year 2" (by misreading the month); but the second inscription (§ 20) corroborates the old publications, and the above reading is unquestionably correct.

[b]The determinative is uncertain in Lepsius, *Denkmäler*, and Champollion, *Notices descriptives;* Piehl gives the "legs;" if the determinative be the "roll," we should read "*command*," and supply "*to*" before the official's name instead of "*by*."

[c]This is the name of the Medinet Habu temple; see dedication inscriptions above.

[d]Lit., "*who were before him.*"

[e]Piehl has 300; but Lepsius, *Denkmäler*, shows clearly 500 (Champollion, *Notices descriptives*, 200, having overlooked three strokes). Lepsius, *Denkmäler*, is corroborated by the last number, which is in both Lepsius, *Denkmäler*, and Champollion, *Notices descriptives*, 500, and impossibly 700 (Piehl), which it would necessarily be, to make a total of 3,000. The numerals are, of course, like those in Papyrus Harris.

[f]Piehl, 700; but see preceding note.

*Second Inscription*[a]

[1]Year 5,[b] first month of the third season (ninth month), under the majesty of King Ramses III,[c] L. P. H., ——— [expedition] [2]which the king's-scribe, overseer of the White House —[d] made, (for) "The-House (*ḥ·t*)-of-Millions-of-Years-of-King-Usermare-Meriamon,-L.-P.-H.,-in-the-House (*pr*)-of-Amon."

*Third Inscription*[e]

He came, to do the work on the great and mighty monuments of his majesty, L. P. H., [⌈for⌉] "The-House-of-Millions-of-Years-of-King-Usermare-Meriamon,-L.-P.-H.-in-the-House-of-Amon," on the west of Thebes.

## HISTORICAL INSCRIPTIONS[f]

**21.** The walls of this temple, as we have said, form a vast record of the achievements of Ramses III. This record is chiefly devoted to his wars. Had these wars been reported in the sober and intelligible style of Thutmose III's Annals, we should have known much of them which it is now safe to say we shall never know. It is difficult to describe the character of these Medinet Habu inscriptions. Perhaps, under the influence of the Kadesh poem, it has now become impossible to narrate a war or a victory of the Pharaoh in

---

[a]Champollion, *Notices descriptives*, I, 255 = Lepsius, *Denkmäler*, VI, 23, No. 6.

[b]Champollion, *Notices descriptives*, has 1, having omitted the hook at the top of the stroke given by Lepsius, which converts the sign into 5, as in the first inscription (§ 19). As these inscriptions are together, from the same month and the same reign, and by an official with the same title, for the same building, there can be no doubt that Lepsius is correct.

[c]Double name in original. There is perhaps no loss before "*expedition*" at the end of l. 1.

[d]The official's name is omitted at the end, and the connection between the temple name and the preceding is wanting.

[e]Champollion, *Notices descriptives*, I, 255 = Lepsius, *Denkmäler*, VI, 23, No. 7.

[f]See Baedeker's *Egypt*, 1902, 297 ff., and *Notice explicative des ruines de Medinet Habu*, by Georges Daressy (Cairo, 1897).

any other than poetic style. The record must be a poem. This would not be an unmixed misfortune, if the poem were intelligible; but the style is such as to render not merely whole lines, but entire strophes and whole passages, utterly unintelligible. This is due to two facts: first, total lack of order or progress in the narrative; second, the figurative character of the language. The first fault renders the reader's impressions fragmentary and confused in the highest degree. The texts consist almost exclusively of praise of the king and exultation over the conquered foe. The court and priestly flatterers of the king either put all this in the mouths of the Egyptians, or the discomfited enemies are made to express their wonder and terror at the king's valor, mingled with lamentation at their own undoing. All this is mingled in rapid alternation, so that one is often in doubt which party is speaking; and deep in the midst of this confused mixture there may be a few connected phrases stating whether the enemy came by land or water, or where the battle took place, or what were the names of the hostile chiefs. This utter lack of progress or continuity is rendered still more troublesome by the second fault of these texts, viz., their figurative language. Like Arabic poetry, they contain so many epithets of a highly pictorial character as frequently to make even a common word unintelligible. When the text speaks of the "*full flame*," who could divine that it means the Egyptian fleet; or when it mentions the "*wall of metal*," who could infer that the Egyptian army is intended?[a] Just as some old Arabic poetry is unintelligible without a native commentator, who stood nearer the author than we do, so, much of these Medinet Habu texts is likely to remain unintelligible, without some obliging

[a]See inscription of the year 8, l. 23, § 66, note.

Egyptian familiar with their style, to explain their overdrawn metaphors and metonymies.

22. Fortunately, the temple contains, besides its vast quantity of historical inscriptions, also no less than forty important relief scenes depicting the achievements of the king, in the conventional style common since the days of Seti I. These reliefs are accompanied by the usual explanatory inscriptions, which are commonly couched in such general terms that the total of their historical content is small.

23. The fraction of this great mass of documents which has been published, was copied without any approach to accuracy. Champollion's publication overleaps whole lines, or transposes two successive lines; Rosellini is next to unreadable, so badly are the signs drawn. Chabas bewailed this condition of things thirty years ago,[a] but it is no better today. Over half of the historical reliefs which the temple contains are unpublished. One of the most pressing needs of Egyptology is an exhaustive publication of this entire temple. I was able to procure large-scale photographs of all of the unpublished scenes and inscriptions. Twelve of these were made for me through the courtesy of Baron von Bissing, by Mr. Arthur Weigall; and to both these gentlemen I would express my sincere thanks.

24. With slight exception, this historical material is distributed chronologically from the rear to the front of the temple, the oldest being in the rear. But in the following translations it is naturally arranged chronologically, irrespective of position in the temple, which will be found in the footnotes. The temple really faces southeast, but in locating scenes and inscriptions we have assumed that it

[a] *Etudes sur l'antiquité historique*, 227, 228.

faces east, for the sake of convenience, as is done in Baedeker's guide-book.

### I. TREASURY OF MEDINET HABU TEMPLE

25. This temple contains a group of treasure-chambers, five in number, the walls of which bear scenes and inscriptions indicative of the contents of the rooms. These are of some historical importance. The scenes themselves have not yet been published (except the weighing scene), but the accompanying inscriptions are as follows:[a]

**26.** [b]Utterance of King Ramses III to his father, Amon-Re, king of gods: "I have built for thee an august treasury[c] in my house in Thebes, which I fill with every real, costly stone, in order to brighten thy beauty therewith, forever.

[d]Utterance of King Ramses III to his father, Min-Amon: "I bring to thee myrrh for thy temple, a statue kneeling upon the ground,[e] my figure of gold and every costly stone, mounted in Asiatic gold, to make ointment for thy majesty in my house, which is in Thebes. I have put my name in its midst, like the heavens upholding the sun every day. It is an abiding horizon bearing thy name, supplied with provision, forever."

**27.** [b]Bringing a chest of silver and gold to his father, Amon-Re, king of gods.

[f]Presentation of native gold to his father, Amon-Re.

[f]Bringing every splendid costly stone to his father.

[g]Utterance of King Ramses III to his father, Amon-Re, king of gods: "I have gathered for thee monuments of gold and silver — as (my) ⌈image⌉ upon earth in the midst of thy treasury."

---

[a]Dümichen, *Historische Inschriften*, I, 30–34, and II, 47, *b;* Champollion, *Notices descriptives*, I, 365, 366.

[b]Dümichen, *Historische Inschriften*, I, 31.

[c]See Papyrus Harris, § 190.

[d]Dümichen, *Historische Inschriften*, I, 30.

[e]The neighboring reliefs show this statue; on a rectangular base with feet kneels a figure of the king, bearing in his outstretched hands an ointment jar; a similar statue is mentioned in Papyrus Harris, 28, 10, § 268.

[f]Dümichen, *Historische Inschriften*, I, 30. [g]*Ibid.*, I, 31.

**28.** [a]Utterance of King Ramses III to his father, Amon-Re, king of gods: "I present to thee monuments for thy temple, of electrum, of the mountains,[b] and native gold [of] —[c] from the workshop of Ptah, the impost of Retenu (*Rṯnw*) as tribute before thee, in order to supply thy temple; for thy treasury, being products of the choicest of every country. I fill thy house from the tribute of my sword, from my might in every land."

**29.** [d]Utterance of King Ramses III, to his father, Amon-Re, king of gods: "Take thou gold and silver like sand of the shore, I have produced them for thee from the waters and the mountains, that I might present them to thee by the measure,[e] the regalia of thy majesty everyday. I bring to thee lapis lazuli, malachite and every costly stone in chests, ⌜and⌝ electrum. I have made for thee many sacred eye amulets of every splendid, costly stone."

Over[f] each of two cow-form weights: "*Gum of God's-Land.*"

On[f] a heap between two trees: "*Gum of Punt.*"

**30.** Each[f] of the following eight on a sack:[g]

1. Gold of Kush.
2. Gold, 1,000 deben.
3. Gold of the mountain.[h]
4. Gold of the water, 1,000 deben.
5. Gold of Edfu.
6. Gold of Ombos, 1,000 deben.
7. Gold of Coptos.
8. Lapis lazuli of Tefrer.[i]

---

[a]Dümichen, *Historische Inschriften*, I, 31; "over vases of various forms."

[b]Electrum really occurred and occurs commonly in nature, which the artificial alloy then imitated. See Lepsius, *Metalle*, 44–48.

[c]The lost word has determinative of a land.

[d]Dümichen, *Historische Inschriften*, I, 31.

[e]*Ḏdmwt ḥr tꜣ*, an unknown measure; see also Harris, 17*a*, 10.

[f]Dümichen, *Historische Inschriften*, I, 32. See the expedition to Punt, Papyrus Harris (§ 407).

[g]See Lepsius, *Metalle*, 35; for a still fuller list of gold regions, see *Recueil*, 16, 51 f.

[h]Gold from the mountain mine, as distinguished from gold of the stream in the next sack.

[i]An unknown country; see Lepsius, *Metalle*, 73, 74, and Brugsch, *Geographie*, III, 61–63.

On[a] each of four heaps: "1. *Native gold;* 2. *Gold;* 3. *Silver;* 4. *Silver.*"

On[a] two piles of rectangular blocks: "1. *Lapis lazuli;* 2. *Malachite.*"

31. The[b] king and Thoth are before Amon; by the king:

I bring to thee silver, gold, copper, royal linen, gums of Punt. I fill thy treasury with every splendid costly stone, to brighten thy beauty therewith, forever and ever.

Over Thoth:

Utterance of Thoth: "I write for thee myriads of ten-thousands, united in a sum of millions, of silver, gold, copper, lapis lazuli, malachite of Reshet (*Rˀ-šˀ-ty*), fine gold of Emu (*ᶜˀmw*), before thy august father, Amon-Re, king of gods, that he may give to thee the jubilees of Re, the years of Atum."

32. On[c] three heaps:

1. Fine gold of the mountain; 2. Real lapis lazuli.
3. Real malachite.

[c]Utterance of King Ramses III to his father, Amon-Re, king of gods: "I bring to thee every real costly stone, silver and gold in sacks, I cause thy treasury to overflow, and provisions to flood in thy house."

On three piles of metal plates: "1. *Silver;* 2. *Copper;* 3. *Lead.*"

33. A[d] pair of balances, with the ape of Thoth at the top. Thoth, who presides over the weighing, says to Amon:

"I come to thee, to see thy beautiful face, bearing every splendid, costly stone, for the hills and mountains pay thee impost of gold and every costly stone."

The king then says to Amon:

"I come to thee, and I report to thee the statement of gold of the land of the Negro. It is thou, who makest the mountains, every costly stone, in order to brighten thy beauty. I bring them to thee in the accurate balances; I unite them for thee in myriads of millions."

---

[a]Dümichen, *Historische Inschriften*, I, 32.

[b]*Ibid.*, I, 33. [c]*Ibid.*, I, 34.

[d]*Ibid.*, II, 47, *b;* Champollion, *Notices descriptives*, I, 366.

The king bears a tray heaped with gold, and has before him the words: "*Bearing gold to his father, Amon-Re.*" On the scales is a pile of gold, bearing the words: "*Native gold.*"

**34.** One of the small rooms in the rear of the temple contains a relief, showing the gods of the South bringing their wealth to the king; they are accompanied by the words:[a]

> Utterance of the gods, the lords of the southern frontier, the gods who reside in the Southland, who bring the mountains with their costly stones, the trees with [their] fruit, [to] King Ramses III: "God's-Land, with every splendid costly stone, native gold of Emu (*ᶜm ᵓ w*), lapis lazuli, — —, malachite of Reshet (*R ᵓ -š ᵓ -ṯ*), added together in millions, we bring northward to thee; the dues (*ḥsb*) of Negro-land by water, after the northward voyage. All the products of the Southland are in the writings of Thoth; they are for thy house of millions of years, according as thou lovest Thebes."

The enumeration of the tribute of the North, "*the sea and the isles*" then follows, but is not completely published.

## II. FIRST LIBYAN WAR, YEAR 5

**35.** The materials for this war are extensive, but they are so unsatisfactory that we can only see in vague outlines a repetition of the conditions which led to Merneptah's Libyan war. The Libyans under their king, Themer, have made common cause with the roving sea robbers of the Thekel and the Philistines. Some of the latter joined the land forces of the Libyans; others entered the Nile mouths with their ships. The Libyans had improved the generation of laxity which preceded the rise of Ramses III's reign, to push eastward farther into the Delta, and, as in Merneptah's time, to settle on both banks of the "*great river,*" the Canopic branch of the Nile. They had plundered the

---

[a] *Recueil*, 19, 19.

towns of the western Delta from Memphis on the south to Kerben (probably in the vicinity of Canopus) on the north. This plundering had been going on for years unremittingly; but the invasion of the Libyan army forced Ramses III to act. He marched against the allies, met them in the western Delta at a town called "*Usermare-Meriamon-is-Chastiser-of-Temeh*" (§ 52), and completely defeated them, slaying 12,535 men and taking at least 1,000 prisoners. After a great triumph on the field, the captives and spoil were brought to the palace, where the king inspected them from the balcony, and the people rejoiced in their new-found security, as in the days of Merneptah.

The materials are these:

1. Great Inscription in the Second Court, Medinet Habu (§§ 36–47).

2. Relief Scenes in the Second Court and Outside North Wall, Medinet Habu (§§ 48–58).

3. Papyrus Harris, **76**, 11–**77**, 6 (§ 405).

### I. GREAT INSCRIPTION IN THE SECOND COURT (YEAR 5)[a]

**36.** This inscription is the longest in the Medinet Habu temple, filling seventy-five lines. It is also by far the most difficult in this collection of difficult texts. It represents the last extreme of those peculiarities mentioned above (§ 21),

[a]Occupying a large portion of the south wall, behind the columns of the southern colonnade in the second court of the Medinet Habu temple; in seventy-five vertical lines, not too well preserved. It was first published by Rosellini (*Monumenti Storici*, 139–41, but omitted by Champollion) and then by Burton (*Excerpta hieroglyphica*, 43–45); later by Dümichen (*Historiche Inschriften*, II, 46); de Rougé (*Inscriptions hiéroglyphiques*, 139–47); Brugsch (*Thesaurus*, 1197–1207), and extracts (including names of chiefs, ll. 47 and 48) by Lepsius (*Denkmäler*, Text, III, 178). Brugsch states that he used his own copy, and collated Burton, de Rougé, and a copy by Eisenlohr; but he inserts lacunæ at the ends of ll. 15–20, where they do not belong, and other slips show that we have still to await an adequate edition of this text. I collated the various editions for all questionable passages, and was able to use photographs of some portions.

so that whole passages are unintelligible. Nor would they, if translatable, furnish any new facts of importance concerning the war; for almost the entire inscription consists of praise of the king, mingled with exultation over the fallen foe and the lamentations of the conquered. Only here and there appear incidents of the campaign, or references from which its course and character may be inferred. They are chiefly four: the king's triumph as he views from the palace balcony the prisoners and the trophies of the slain (§ 42, ll. 36–41); the names of the hostile chiefs (§ 43, ll. 48 and 49); the brief mention of the northern sea-roving allies (§ 44, ll. 51–54); and the security of the people, even of a woman alone upon the road (§ 47, l. 73). Only portions of which the rendering would have been exceedingly uncertain have been omitted; but the entire text is of such peculiar difficulty that the following attempt at translation as a whole is exceedingly unsatisfactory to the author.[a]

*Introduction*

**37.** [1]Year 5 under the majesty of Horus: Mighty Bull, Extending Egypt, Mighty of Sword, Strong-Armed, Slayer of the Tehenu; Wearer of the Double Diadem; [2][⌈Mighty in Strength, like his father, Montu⌉], Overthrower of Tehenu in Heaps in their Place; Golden Horus: Valiant, Lord of all Might, Making the Boundary as Far as he Desires Behind his Enemies ——— [3]his Fear, his Terror is a Shield [⌈over⌉] Egypt; King of Upper and Lower Egypt: Lord of Day, Youthful and Bright, Shining like the Moon, he hath Repeated [his] Birth ——— [Usermare-Meriamon]; [4]Son of Re: Ramses (III), Ruler of Heliopolis, first in victory, appearing [in] Egypt, of whom Re has exacted that he return with offerings, whom the divine ennead has caused ———

[a]The entire inscription has been translated only once, viz., by Chabas, in the first edition of his *Etudes sur l'antiquité historique* (which I have not seen), and again in the second edition (228–33), only ll. 17–50). But he had only the entirely inadequate publications of Rosellini and Burton; this fact, and the state of knowledge of the language over thirty years ago, made an understanding of the text and a realization of its difficulties impossible.

[5]victory, lord of valor, warrior, having an image like the son of Nut, to make the whole earth like ——— [6]King Ramses III, ruler, great in love, lord of offerings, whose image is like Re at early morning.

*The King's Power and Goodness*

**38.** His terror ——— [7]— of his serpent-crest, established upon the throne of Re as king of the Two Lands. The land from front to rear is relieved,[a] the chiefs do honor ——— [8]gathered together in the lands, in the reign of King Ramses III, the brave and valiant king, who creates his —, when he sees ——— [9]raging, ⌜favorite⌝ protector, who has come in Egypt, long-armed, swift-footed, smiting every land; counselor, excellent in plans, skilled in laws, giving ——— [10]exultation. His name has penetrated all hearts as far as the limit of the darkness; he reaches his limits, he terrifies the ⌜ends⌝[b] of the earth, . . . . . . . . [countries] [11]which they knew not. Their lords come with fearful step to crave the breath of life which is in Egypt from Horus, the mighty Bull, great in kingship, King Ramses III, the great wall [12]of Egypt, protecting their limbs. His might is like Set in laying low the Nine Bows; youth, divine at his coming forth, like Harakhte. When he appears he seems like Atum, when he opens his mouth, with [13]breath for the people, to sustain alive the Two Lands with his sustenance every day; favorite son, champion of the divine ennead, for whom they overthrow the lands.

*Defeat of Amor?*

**39.** ⌜Gored⌝[c] is the chief of ⌜Amor⌝ (ʾ *-m-* —) in [⌜his⌝] blood[d] [14]his seed is not; all his people are taken captive, carried off, ⌜spoiled⌝.

---

[a]Lit., "*cooled*." [b]Or possibly: "*the isles*."

[c]This uncertain adjective (ʿ *b* ʿ *ty*) occurs several times in the texts of Ramses III, each time applied to the king. If this is the case here, it would leave "*the chief of Amor*" without a verb. I have supposed it to mean "*horned*," both possessing horns or gored with them. The paragraph certainly concerns some foreign chief, but the space in which he is abruptly introduced is very small; and the mention of Amor is a mere conjecture, based on the first two letters, the last letter (*r?*) being lost. Examination of the original would determine the matter in all probability. If Amor is correct, its desolation then refers to the invasion of the sea-peoples, by whom Amor was wasted, as narrated in the long inscription of year 8 (§ 64, l. 17). This fits well the mention of the sea-peoples as allies of the Libyans in the year 5 (below ll. 51 ff.). They had already reached Amor at that time, and some of their vessels had pushed on to Egypt in time to assist the Libyans in the war of the year 5.

[d]See Israel passage, III, 604, examples.

Everybody in his land comes with praise [15]that[a] the great sun of Egypt may look upon them, that the sun-disk may turn to them, the Sun ⌈—⌉, coming forth, [16]rising upon the earth, the warmth of Egypt, which is in heaven.

*Praise of the People*

**40.** They say: "Exalted is the Sun of our land! We were lost [17]in the land daily (⌈in⌉) the darkness, which King Ramses III has expelled. The lands and countries are stripped, [18]and brought to Egypt as slaves; gifts gathered together for her gods' satiety, provisions, supplies, are a flood [19]in the Two Lands. The multitude rejoices in this land, none is sad, (for) Amon has established his son upon his throne, all the circuit of the sun [20]is united in his grasp; the vanquished of the Asiatics and the Tehenu. Taken are those who [21]were spoiling the condition of Egypt. The land had been exposed in continual extremity, since the (former) kings. They were desolated, the gods as well as all people. There was no hero [22]to seize them when they retreated. Lo, there was a youth like a gryphon . . . . . . . . . .[b] [24]like a bull ready for battle — — — — — upon the field. His horses were like hawks.[c] ⌈———⌉ [25]roaring like a lion ⌈terrible⌉ in rage. The officers (*snn*) are mighty like Reshep, when they see ten thousands likewise. ⌈—⌉ — — like Montu. [26]His name is a flame, the terror of him is in the countries. The land of Temeh comes together in one place in Libya, —,[d] and Meshwesh (*M-š*ˀ*-w*ˀ*-š*ˀ), . . . . [31]. . . . .

*The Overthrow of the Enemy*

**41.** Lo, the heart of his majesty is violent with might, [⌈like a⌉] mighty [⌈lion⌉] [32]falling upon the sheep.[e] Equipped is he like a valiant bull, (his) two arms are sharp horns to tear open the mountains, behind

[a]Dümichen indicates no lacunæ at the lower ends of ll. 14–20, and the sense confirms this; but Brugsch has inserted lacunæ at the ends of all but l. 14, where the connection is very evident. The photograph shows that these lines are over a door which rises into the inscription at this point. The hieroglyphs extend to the very edge of the door, which would suggest that the door had been cut in after the inscription, but as no hieroglyph is cut through and the connection between lines is good, there is certainly no loss.

[b]Obscure and partially fragmentary epithets of the king.

[c]See the same comparison complete in the march to Zahi, year 8 (§ 72).

[d]Name of a foreign country of which only a pyramid (*Śpd?*) at the end is visible.

[e]Any small cattle.

⌜—⌝. The gods ⌜baffle⌝ [33]their plans which they who confront him ⌜lay⌝. As for those who shall invade his boundary, his majesty goes forth against them like a flame — — — in the dry herbage. [⌜They flutter⌝] like wild fowl [34]in the midst of the net, with legs struggling in the basket, made into a roast, laid low, prostrate on the ⌜ground⌝ — —. Their loss is heavy, [35]without number. Behold, evil is among them to the height of heaven.[a] Bound are their mighty men upon the place of slaughter, they are made into pyramids upon their [36]ground, by the might of the king, valiant in his limbs, the sole lord, mighty like Montu, King Ramses III.

### *The King's Triumphal Audience*

**42.** (They) come forth, carried off as captives to Egypt; the hands [37]and foreskins are without number; brought forward as captives, bound, under the balcony.[b] The chiefs of the countries are assembled, beholding their evil plight. The tens[c] [38]are conducted to the king, their arms extended, their praise reaching heaven, with hearts of love ⌜toward⌝ Amon-Re, the god who accords them the protection of the ruler. [39]The messengers of every land come, their hearts fluttering, and so transported that they (the hearts) are no longer in their bodies. Their faces behold the face of the king like Atum, protecting against the Temeh, in order to perfect the ⌜reign⌝ of his majesty. When their feet [40]trod Egypt, their leaders feared, and were made as common people in strength. (⌜Their⌝) names abide through the great name of his majesty. Their leaders — — — [41]fear; their mouths cannot mention the manner of Egypt.

### *The Discomfiture of the Enemy*

**43.** The land of Temeh is spread out, they flee. The Meshwesh (*M-š*ᵓ*-w*ᵓ*-š*ᵓ) are hung up [42]in their land, their plant is uprooted, there is not for them a survivor. All their limbs tremble for the terror, which protects against them. They say: "Behold, we are ⌜subject⌝ to Egypt, [43]its lord has destroyed our soul, forever and ever. . . . . [44]. . . . .

---

[a]A figure indicating the last extremity or excess.

[b]The balcony of the palace; see II, 982. This scene is depicted with all the details here narrated in the relief, § 52.

[c]A term for councilors, or nobles; see Maspero, *Etudes égyptiennes*, II, 197–204, and Brugsch, *Wörterbuch*, Supplement, 927–29.

Our feet find not a way to go; we traverse all the lands as their warriors, (⌈but⌉) they fight not with us in battle-array.[a] We kindled 45the fire for ourselves at our desire, (but) our own fire has taken (us), we cannot quench (it). Their lord is like Sutekh, beloved of Re, [his] roaring is heard — 46like a gryphon. He is behind us slaughtering, and he has no pity. He turns us back [⌈from the boundaries⌉] of Egypt, forever. . . . . . 47. . . . The fire has penetrated us, our seed is not. As for Ded (*Dy-dy*), Meshken (*M-š ᵓ -k-n*), Meryey[b] (*M-r˙ᵓ˙-y ᵓ -yw*) and Wermer (*Wr*[c]*-m-r ᵓ*), 48Themer (*Ṯ ᵓ -m-r ᵓ*), and every hostile chief who crossed the border of Egypt from Libya, he hath set fire from front to rear . . . . 49. . . . We know the great might of Egypt, for Re gives to her protection and victory when he appears shining 50like the sun, when he rises over the people (*rḫy˙t*). We come to him; we cry, 'Salâm' to him, we kiss the ground (to) his great might — — 51King Ramses III."

### *Defeat of the Northern Countries*

**44.** The northern countries are unquiet in their limbs, even the Peleset (*Pw-r ᵓ -s ᵓ -ty*), the Thekel (*Ṯ ᵓ -k-k*[*ᵓ -r ᵓ*]), 52who devastate their land. Their soul came, in the last extremity. They were warriors (*t-h-r ᵓ*) upon land, also[d] in the sea. Those who came[e] on [land] — — — 53Amon-

[a]This line may contain some reference to the Libyans doing mercenary service in the Egyptian army; meaning that these are not the ones who have defeated Libya, but the native Egyptians.

[b]Meryey is the Libyan king defeated by Merneptah, whose inscriptions mention Ded as his father (III, 579, l. 13). But the other Libyan kings above mentioned are new. They seem to be mentioned in chronological order. But as we know that Meryey was the son of Ded, Meshken is likely to have been the brother of Meryey. Themer was probably the contemporary of Ramses III, and Wermer reigned during the ephemeral kings of Egypt, between Merneptah and Ramses III, but survived into Ramses III's reign. Maspero thinks they are all contemporaries (*Struggle of the Nations*, 456).

[c]Brugsch gives *Wr* as the first sign of this name (evidently following Burton), but he first read "Za" (*Geschichte*, 597). This first sign is indicated as lost in all the other publications, including Lepsius (*Denkmäler*, Text, III, 178). Only Chabas (*Etudes sur l'antiquité historique*, 236) gives The (*Ṯ ᵓ*) as the first syllable. But as it is wanting in Rosellini and Burton, whose publications Chabas used (*ibid.*, 227 f.), the reading must be a restoration which has passed from Chabas into the histories without inquiry as to its source, e. g., lastly in Maspero's *Struggle of the Nations*, 459.

[d]See Müller, *Asien und Europa*, 360, n. 4.

[e]In view of the following: "*those who entered*" (*n ᵓ ᶜ ḳ*), we must certainly render here: "*those who came*" (*n ᵓ yy*), and not merely "nahend" (*n ᵓ yy*), as

Re was behind them, destroying them; those who entered into the river-mouths[a] were like wild fowl, creeping into the net, made ⸢—⸣ — — — — — [54]their arms. Their hearts fluttered, (so) transported (that) they were no longer in their bodies. Their leaders were carried off, slain, thrown prostrate. They were made captives — — — — [55]. . . . . .

### *Words of the Defeated Northerners*

**45.** "The only lord is in Egypt, no warrior is (so) accurate in shooting, none escapes him — — — [56]the ends of the Great Circle (Okeanos, *Šn-wr*), until they fear with one accord. We will beseech peace, coming with trembling step, for fear of him. . . . . . . . [57]. . . ."

### *The King's Valor*

**46.** He is like a bull standing in the field, his eye and his two horns ready and prepared to attack their rear with his head; a valiant warrior — — — — [58]roaring; a warrior lord of might, taking captive every land. They come bowing down for fear of him, the blooming youth, valiant like Baal, — — — — [59]the king effective in plans, possessed of counsel, not failing, but that which he does takes place instantly, Ramses III. . . . . . . [60]. . . . He is like the lion with deep (lit., heavy) [61]roar upon the mountain-tops, whose terror is feared from afar. A gryphon swift in every stride, whose two wings are iters of millions of years,[b] [62]like the — of the gait of the panther, knowing his prey, seizing upon his assailant, his two arms destroy the limbs of those who invade

Müller has rendered (*Asien und Europa*, 360). We have in the entire passage, first the approach both on land and water, and then the destruction of both parties on land and water. The passage is referred by Maspero (following Chabas) to the war of the year 8. But it is evident that in an inscription of the year 5 it can only refer to the Libyan war of that year; and that we must conclude that the sea-peoples already assisted the Libyans in this war. This is again rendered evident by the hands cut off as trophies as in the Libyan war of Merneptah. Had there been only Libyans in the battle, we should have had only phalli. Again, when we consider that the sea-peoples were already in the Libyan ranks in Merneptah's day, there is, of course, no reason why they should not be there now. Only the Thekel and the Peleset have not heretofore appeared in the South.

[a]*R*ᐣ*-ḥ*ᐣ*wt* occurs first in the Eighteenth Dynasty as "*river-mouths*," where the customs officers and frontier marine police were stationed by Amenhotep III (II, 916). In the war of the year 8 it is used also of "*harbor-mouths*" (§ 65, l. 20, and elsewhere).

[b]On "*iters*," see II, 965, l. 19, note; he means the distances attained with his wings would demand millions of years to cover with ordinary means of locomotion.

the boundary, raging — ⌜—⌝, whose right arm [63]is thrust into the fray, slaying hundreds of thousands in their place under his horses; he sees the thick of the multitude like grasshoppers, smitten, ground down, [64]crushed like ⌜—⌝; strong-horned, relying upon his strength, before whom hundred-thousands and ten-thousands are despised. His form is like Montu, [65]when he goes forth. Every land bows down for him, at the mention of him, the ruler excellent in plan like Osiris, equipping this whole land with — — [66]strong-armed, great in strength in the lands and countries; all that he hath done takes place as (if done by) Thoth.

*The King Egypt's Security*

**47.** King Ramses III is kind-hearted toward Egypt, bearing the protection of the land [67]on the height of his back[a] without trouble; a wall, casting a shadow for the people (*rḫy·t*). They dwell in his time, with heart relying upon the might of their [68]protection, the ⌜—⌝ of his two arms, saying: "A divine hawk, smiting and seizing!" He has made hosts by his victories, filling the storehouses [69]of the temples with the plunder of his sword, preparing the divine offerings from his excellent things . . . . [70]. . . . in that Amon, his august father, has given to him the lands, united together under the feet of King Ramses III. Lo, the golden Horus, rich in years, divine water [71]of Re, which came forth from his limbs, august living image of the son of Isis (Horus), who was born adorned with the royal diadem like Set, great in inundations bearing their sustenance for Egypt, [72]so that the people (*rḫy·t*) and the folk (*ḥnmm·t*) are possessed of good things; the sovereign, executing truth for the All-Lord, presenting it every day before him. Egypt and the lands are in peace in his reign, [73]the land is like ⌜—⌝ with untroubled heart. A woman goes about at her will, with her veil upon her head,[b] her going extending as far as she pleases. The countries come, bowing down to [74]the fame of his majesty, with their tribute and their children upon their backs. South as well as north [come] to him with praise, when they see him like Re at early morning. They — [75]the plans and stipulations of the victorious king, the ruler, effective in plan like the Beautiful-Faced (Ptah), the king, Lord of the Two Lands, lord of might, Ramses III, given life, like Re, forever.

[a]That is, bearing the burden of the land's defense upon his shoulders.

[b]That is, not hanging down over her face.

### 2. RELIEF SCENES IN SECOND COURT AND OUTSIDE NORTH WALL (YEAR 5)[a]

48. These scenes depict various incidents of the war, from the march to the frontier to the final triumphs, and probably furnish us with more information as to the character of the campaign than the long inscription devoted to it, which we have just studied.

*Scene*[b]

49. The king in his chariot, accompanied by troops, is marching against Libya. Before him is a chariot bearing the standard of Amon. Beside the king trots his tame lion. The inscriptions are these:

*Over the Amon Standard*

Utterance of Amon-Re, king of gods: "Lo, I am before thee, my son, lord of the Two Lands, Usermare-Meriamon, I give [to thee] all [⌈might and power⌉] among the Nine Bows; terror — — — their chiefs, I will open [for] thee the ways of the land of Temeh. I will trample them before thy horses."

*Over the King*[c]

The Good God, victorious king, rich in might, like Montu, lovely like Min, strong-armed like the son of Nut, great in strength, mighty in terror, whose roaring courses through the countries, a lion raging when he sees his opponent. None escapes — —. He rejoices among a hundred thousand, a valiant warrior in his own person, he looks upon untold myriads[d] as one. When he appears upon the battlefield like Baal, his flame consumes the Nine Bows.

[a]The publications are totally inadequate; they began in the days of Napoleon's expedition (*Description*, II, Pl. 12), and continued until Lepsius' day. Some scenes are still unpublished; for the publications, see note on each scene. I am indebted to Mr. A. H. Gardiner for a number of readings from photographs of the relief inscriptions.

[b]Exterior, north side, west end; Champollion, *Monuments*, 217 = Rosellini, *Monumenti Storici*, 124.

[c]This text also in Brugsch, *Recueil de monuments*, LV.

[d]Lit., "*hundreds of thousands of myriads.*"

*Scene*[a]

50. Ramses III, standing in his chariot with drawn bow, charges the fleeing Libyans, who are trampled by his horses. He is supported by mercenary archers and swordsmen, probably Sherden.

*Inscription*

Live the Good God, Montu, when he goes forth, beautiful upon the steed, charging into hundreds of thousands, mighty in valor, stretching the ⌈bow⌉ and shooting the arrows whither he will, fighting ——— piercing with sharp horns, overthrowing the Temeh, slain in their places in heaps before his horses, causing that they cease their opposition in their land, whose sword has overthrown their seed by the might of his father, Amon, in all lands together, Lord of the Two Lands, Ramses III.

*Scene*[b]

51. The king in his chariot charging the enemy in the conventional manner. The latter, represented as Libyans, are scattered to right and left or trampled beneath his horses' feet. Among the attacking Egyptians are their foreign auxiliaries, the Sherden.

*Inscription*[c]

Good God, in the form of Montu, great in strength, whose [heart] is glad when he sees the conflict, like a fire in —, firm on the right, stretching the bow, swift on the left, — — — with arrows, charging before him, conscious of his might, face to face, smiting hundreds of thousands, — the heart of the land of the Temeh; their lifetime, their

---

[a]Exterior, north side, west end; unpublished. Baedeker's *Egypt*, 1902, 303, "second scene." I had a photograph by Weigall.

[b]East wall, second court; Champollion, *Monuments*, 205 = Rosellini, *Monumenti Storici*, 136; see also Lepsius, *Denkmäler*, Text, III, 176.

[c]Behind the king there is a further inscription of one line, referring in the usual phrases to the enemy as "*overthrown before the horses of King Ramses III.*" The name of the royal horses is omitted in the publication.

souls are finished,[a] the strong-armed son of Amon is behind them like a young lion.[b] . . . . . .

*Scene*[c]

52. The king stands in a balcony with his waiting chariot below (behind him); he harangues his nobles, who are grouped before him. Behind them appoach five rows of captive Libyans and sea-peoples, each row headed by Egyptian officers and scribes, who throw down in five heaps severed hands and phalli, which the scribes record.

The accompanying inscriptions are these:

*Before the King*

Utterance of his majesty to the nobles and companions who are by his side: "Behold ye, the many good things, which Amon-Re, king of gods hath done for Pharaoh, his son, He hath carried captive the land of Temeh, Seped, and Meshwesh, who were robbers plundering Egypt every day, and overthrown them beneath my feet. Their plant is uprooted, so that not one survives. They have ceased all lying — —, forever, by the good counsels which his majesty has carried out, in order to cause — to be — ⸢— —⸣. Rejoicing and joy are yours to the height of heaven. My [majesty] raged like Set, extending Egypt, mighty ————, overthrowing the Nine Bows, through that which my father, lord of gods, Amon, lord of [⸢Thebes⸣], creator of my beauty, did for me."

*By the Palace*

City (*dmy*) of "Usermare-Meriamon-is-the-Chastiser-of-Temeh."[d]

*Over the Nobles*

Utterance of the nobles and companions, when they answered before the Good God: "Thou art Re ———— when thou risest, the people live.

---

[a]See Wadi Halfa stela of Sesostris, I, l. 16 (I, 512), and Breasted, *Proceedings of the Society of Biblical Archæology*, XXIII, 233.

[b]The usual epithets of the lion: "*heavy-voiced, roaring in the mountains, etc.*," follow here, but are badly copied.

[c]Exterior, north side, west end; Baedeker's *Egypt*, 1902, 303, "third scene;" unpublished. I had a photograph by Weigall.

[d]So Daressy, *Recueil*, 19, 18; but I was unable to find this inscription on my photograph. It is also given by Brugsch, *Geschichte*, 597.

⌜Thy heart⌝ is skilled in speech, and thy counsels are excellent. Thy fear hath repelled the Nine Bows; as for Temeh, their heart failed, coming that they might ⌜—⌝ Egypt. As for the lands and countries, their limbs tremble, the fear of thee is before them every day; but the heart of Egypt rejoices forever. . . . . . . ."[a]

Total[b] of foreskins (*k*ʾ-*r*ʾ-*n*ʾ-*ty*), [1][c]2,535.

Total of hands, 12,535.

Total of —[d] 12,758[e](+*x*).

Total of hands, 12,520 (+*x*).[f]

Total of hands, 12,635 (+*x*).[g]

*Scene*[h]

53. The king is seated in his chariot with his back to the horses, which are held by his officers, while three attendants hold sunshades over him. Beside him (below in the relief) was a line of officers, now mostly disappeared. Before him, his sons and the highest officials of the kingdom bring up four lines of captured Libyans, and at the head of the first three, the scribes throw down and count the hands cut off from the fallen Libyans, while at the head of the fourth line they are doing the same with the phalli severed from the slain.

---

[a]Four short lines more of conventional phrases.

[b]Each total is over a different heap, five heaps in all.

[c]There is just room for the 10,000-sign, which must have been here as in the other lines.

[d]The heap is one of phalli.

[e]The hundreds may be 9, and the arrangement would indicate 9.

[f]Only the tens and units are uncertain, and the total is probably the same as in the first two.

[g]The hundreds may be 9; if only 6, then the tens would be 3. As two of these five totals are identical (12,535), and a third is almost certainly the same, it is evident that the number 12,535 is the sum-total of dead; otherwise we should have over 60,000 dead, which is quite impossible.

[h]South wall, second court; Champollion, *Monuments*, 206=Rosellini, *Monumenti Storici*, 135; see also Lepsius, *Denkmäler*, Text, III, 177; Piehl, *Inscriptions*, I, CLVI, U–CLVIII; and part of inscription in Young, *Hieroglyphics*, 15; I had a photograph for some portions of the relief, especially the lowest row.

*Inscription over the King*

54. Utterance of the king, the lord of the Two Lands, Ramses III, to the king's-children, the king's-butlers, nobles, companions, and all the leaders of the infantry and chariotry: "Acclaim ye to the height of heaven! My sword has overthrown the Tehenu, who came, accoutered, their hearts determined to match themselves with Egypt. I went forth against them like a lion; I smote them, and they were made heaps. I was behind them like a divine Hawk when he has seen the birdlet in the — . . . . . . . . I laid low their soul, I took away their water, and my flame consumed their towns, I am like Montu in Egypt; my might overthrows the Nine Bows, (for) my august father, Amon, prostrates every land beneath my feet, while I am king upon the throne, forever."

*Inscription over Hands and Phalli*[a]

Bringing up the captured before his majesty, from the vanquished of Libya; making 1,000 men; making 3,000 hands; making 3,000 foreskins.

*Inscription over First Line*

55. Utterance of the king's-children, king's-butlers, and nobles, before the Good God: "Great is thy might, O victorious king. Thy roaring courses through the Nine Bows. Thou art the rampart, protecting Egypt; they dwell confident in thy strength, O Pharaoh, L. P. H., our lord."

*Inscription over Third Line*[b]

Utterance of the nobles and leaders (*ḥ ͗ w· tyw*): "Amon, the god, he has decreed the victory to the ruler, who carries off all lands, Ramses-Meriamon, ———."

[a]This inscription occurs four times, namely, over each of the four heaps, three of hands and one of phalli. Once (at the top) "*making 3,000 foreskins*" is omitted by Lepsius (*Denkmäler*, Text, III, 177); but the older publications (e. g., Rosellini, *Monumenti Storici*, 135), are correct in inserting it, as the photograph shows. Each time it thus records the capture of 1,000 and the slaying of 6,000 men. Taken together, they record a total of 28,000 men killed and captured. This is, of course, impossible. Moreover, the third relief on the north wall (outside, § 57) gives 12,535 as the number of slain. If we assume that only the two lower rows (one showing phalli and one hands) are different in our relief, we obtain a total of 12,000 slain (6,000 in each row), which roughly agrees with the other relief. The two upper rows are then mere duplicates of the third, added to fill up the space at the disposal of the artist. As such repetition is certain in § 57, this solution is very probable.

[b]Numbering from the top; the second line is without inscription.

*Inscription over Fourth Line*

Utterance of the king's-children, king's-butlers, and nobles: "Thou art the sun, when thou risest over Egypt, thy terror ——— O Pharaoh, L. P. H., child of Amon."

*Scene*[a]

56. The king in his chariot, accompanied by a pair of sunshade-bearers, and a body of soldiers, drives before him three lines of fettered Libyan prisoners.

*Inscription*

Ruler, beautiful as king, like Atum, mighty —, — the Tehenu, who come for f[ear of him]; he — him who invades his boundary. Amon, his august father, makes sound his limbs, King Ramses III, given life. Valiant —, great in strength like his father, Montu. . . . . . He hath overthrown his adversaries in their place. Those whom his sword captures, whose hands are bound before him, are living captives. He is like a mighty bull, he gores ——— beautiful, possessed of valor, ⌜which⌝ his father, Amon-Re, [⌜gave⌝] that he may give to him great victories, and a reign of jubilees like Re; the king, lord of might, Ramses III, given life like Re.

*Scene*[b]

57. At the left Amon is enthroned in a chapel, with Mut standing behind him. The king, approaching from the right, leads three lines of Libyan captives, whom he presents to the god.

*Inscription over Amon*

Utterance of Amon-Re, king of gods, to his son, King Ramses III: "Praise to thee! Thou hast captured thine adversaries; thou hast overthrown the invader of thy boundary. I give to thee my might in thy limbs, that thou mayest overthrow the Nine Bows. My hand is

---

[a]East wall, second court; Champollion, *Monuments*, 207 = Rosellini, *Monumenti Storici*, 137.

[b]East wall, second court; Champollion, *Monuments*, 208 = Rosellini, *Monumenti Storici*, 138; see also Lepsius, *Denkmäler*, Text, III, 176; Piehl, *Inscriptions*, I, CLV, P, Q, R–CLVI (only inscriptions with divinities and king).

the shield of thy body, warding off evil from thee. I give to thee the kingdom of Atum, shining upon the throne of Re."[a]

*Inscription before the King*

58. Utterance of King Ramses III before his father, Amon-Re, ruler of the gods: "How great is that which thou hast done, O lord of gods. Thy plans and thy counsels are those which come to pass throughout. Thou sentest me forth in valor, thy strength was with me. No land stood before me, at the mention of thee. I overthrew those who invaded my boundary, prostrated in their place. Their warriors (*pḥrr*) were — pinioned, slain in my grasp. I laid low the land of Temeh, their seed is not.[b] The Meshwesh (*M-š*ʾ*-w*ʾ*-š*ʾ), they crouch down for fear of me. It was ordained because of thy victory-bringing commands, it was given because of thy kingdom-bestowing ⌜power⌝."

*Inscription over Libyans*

Utterance of the leaders of the vanquished of Libya, who are in the grasp of his majesty: "Great is thy fame, O victorious king; how great the fear of thee and the terror of thee! Thou didst turn (us) back, when we went forth ⌜to⌝ fight, to ⌜invade⌝ Egypt, forever. Give thou to us the breath which we breathe, the life which is in thy hands, O lord, like the form ⌜of⌝ Amon-Re, king of gods."

## III. NORTHERN WAR, YEAR 8

59. Already in Ramses III's fifth year the tribes of the southern coast of Asia Minor and the maritime peoples of the Ægean had sent some of their advanced galleys to assist the Libyans in their war of that year against Egypt. Or, as in Merneptah's day, the plundering crews of their southernmost advance had incidentally joined the Libyan invasion. These were but the premonitory skirmishing-line of a more serious and more general movement. The peoples involved were the probably Cretan Peleset, a settlement of whom

[a]The short speech of Mut is of no historical consequence.

[b]See III, 604.

later became the biblical Philistines; the Thekel, who may be the Sikeli, later of Sicily;[a] the Shekelesh, the Denyen or Danaoi, and the Weshwesh (§ 64, l. 18), who are of uncertain origin.[b] Owing to pressure from uncertain sources without, large numbers of these peoples, accompanied by their wives, children, and belongings, in clumsy ox carts, left their homes, and moving eastward along the coast of Asia Minor, penetrated Syria. They were accompanied by a strong fleet also. In the author's opinion, this movement was really a "Völkerwanderung," not merely an invasion, with a few families of the chiefs. They were strong enough to hold all northern Syria at their mercy; from Carchemish, through the Syrian Hittite conquests to the coast, as far south as Arvad, and inland as far south as Amor, they plundered the country. They had a central camp somewhere in Amor

**60.** Ramses evidently still held the coast south of Arvad. Mustering his forces, he dispatched his war fleet to this coast, possibly with his motley army of various mercenaries and Egyptians on board, or in transports thus convoyed. At some point[c] on the coast he met the enemy; a land and naval action took place. Possibly the two battles were near together. In any case, Ramses, after the land victory, was able to station his archers on the strand and aid in the destruction of the hostile fleet. His victory over both forces seems to have been complete, for we do not hear of any further trouble from this source during the remainder of his reign.

---

[a]But see III, 570, note.

[b]See III, 306, and Müller, *Asien und Europa*, 360 ff. Papyrus Harris also adds the Sherden (§ 403), who probably were from Sardinia and associated with the Lycian tribes in common enterprises on the sea. On all these northern peoples, see also the discussion of Hall, *Earliest Civilization of Greece*, and *Annual of the British School at Athens*, VIII, 157.

[c]The land battle was certainly not south of Amor; the naval battle was in one of the harbors of the Phœnician coast.

The sources for this war are:

1. The Great Inscription on the Second Pylon (Medinet Habu, §§ 61–68).

2. The Relief Scenes on the North Wall and in the Second Court (Medinet Habu, §§ 69–82).

3. Papyrus Harris (§ 403).

### I. GREAT INSCRIPTION ON THE SECOND PYLON, YEAR 8[a]

61. Of the long inscriptions in the Medinet Habu temple, this is by far the most clear and intelligible, both in language and arrangement. After the date and the usual encomium of the Pharaoh, which occupies about one-third of the inscription (ll. 1–12), the king is introduced as addressing his court and the people of the land, in a speech very similar to that which concludes Papyrus Harris (Pls. 75–79). After reverting to Amon's choice of him for the throne, with which the Pharaohs so often introduce their addresses, he narrates the northern invasion of Syria (§ 64, ll. 16–18), his preparations to repel it (§ 65, ll. 18–23), and then, in highly figurative language, briefly describes the overthrow of the invaders by land and sea (§ 66, ll. 23–26). He closes with a song of triumph as long as the account of the war, occupying one-third of the inscription (§§ 67, 68, ll. 26–38). It is therefore only the middle third of the inscription (§§ 63–66, ll. 13–26) which contains narrative of historical importance.

---

[a]Occupying the entire front of the north tower of the second pylon in the Medinet Habu temple. It is published entire only in Greene, *Fouilles exécutées à Thèbes dans l'année* 1855 (Paris, 1855), Pls. I–III. Champollion noted and copied the parts containing foreign names (Champollion, *Notices descriptives*, I, 348, giving date incorrectly as year 9); similar fragments also by Lepsius (*Denkmäler*, Text, III, 175, parts of ll. 1, 2, 17, 18, 20, 24, and 35); the important passage, ll. 16 and 17, also by Chabas (*Etudes sur l'antiquité historique*, 2d ed., 260 ff., from a photograph); finally, ll. 16–25, by Brugsch (*Thesaurus*, 1207–10). Not much can be said for the accuracy of any of these texts. I collated Greene exhaustively with a series of large-scale photographs, which brought out scores of new signs and many new words; Brugsch was also useful, but a careful publication is very much needed.

*Introduction; Praise of Ramses*

**62.** [1]Year 8, under the majesty of Horus: mighty Bull, valiant Lion, strong-armed, lord of might, capturing the Asiatics; Favorite of the Two Goddesses: Mighty in Strength, like his father, Montu, destroying the Nine Bows, driving (them) from their land; Hawk, divine at his birth, [2]excellent and favorite egg of Harakhte, sovereign, excellent heir of the gods, fashioning their images on earth, doubling their offerings; King of Upper and Lower Egypt, Lord of the Two Lands: Usermare-Meriamon; Son of Re, Ramses (III), Ruler of Heliopolis; king, lord of valor, extending (his) two arms, and taking away the breath [3]from the countries by the heat of his limbs, great in the power of Montu, — the fray like Re, ⌜daily⌝ ——— valiant upon (his) horse, fighting hand to hand upon his feet, warrior like the shooting-stars in heaven, King [4]Ramses III; charging into the thick of the fray like ——— turning back the Asiatics, fighting in the territory of rebels who know not Egypt, who tell how they have heard [5]of his might, who come with praise, trembling in all their limbs ——— of the Asiatics. His form and his limbs are ⌜straight⌝, the equal of Baal, mighty in the multitude, without his like. He [6]smites millions, alone by himself; all lands are despised and contemptible before him, appearing ———. They come — [⌜to⌝] look upon Egypt, prostrate, bowing down before him. They say every day: "Montu is in his great form, which is in Egypt [7]among you, bearing his mighty sword. Let us all come, that we may make for him ——— him ⌜in⌝ his grasp, the King Ramses III." Beautiful is the appearance of the king, like the son of Isis [8]the defender, firstborn son of Re-Atum, ——— wearing the white crown, wearing the red crown, beautiful of face, wearing the double plume like Tatenen. His loveliness — — — — in the early morning, beautiful, sitting upon the throne like Atum, when he has assumed the regalia of Horus and Set; Nekhbet and Buto, the serpent-crown of the South and the serpent-crown of the North, they take [9]their place upon his head. His two hands grasp the crook-staff and hold the scourge, — conscious of strength — — ⌜among⌝ the Nine Bows —. Plentiful are fowl and provision in his reign, like his father, the Beautiful-Faced (Ptah), Nun, great in love as king, like Shu, son of Re. [10]When he appears, there is rejoicing over him, like Aton; strong and valiant, mustering the lands at [his] desire, — like ⌜Montu⌝, creating them like Ptah; ready and skilled in law, there is none like him; like Re when he took the land as a kingdom, King Ramses [11]III, — numerous in monuments, great in wonderful works, making festive the temples, — the son of Re, — who came forth from his limbs, — firstborn ⌜of⌝ the gods. He was appointed as a youth to be king of the Two Lands, to be ruler of every circuit of Aton, a shield protecting [12]Egypt in his time. They sit under the shadow of his might, the strong one ——— victorious hand laid upon their head; King Ramses III, the king himself, he saith:

### *Ramses' Speech; His Accession*

**63.** "Hearken to me [13]all the land, gathered in [⌜one place⌝], the court, the king's-children, the butlers, — living, the —,[a] the youth, all[b] the young men who are in this land. Give your attention to my utterance, that ye may know my plans for sustaining you alive, [14]that ye may learn of the might of my august father, Amon-Kamephis, creator of my beauty. His great might —, victorious against every fallen foe, beneath my feet. He decrees to me victory, and his hand is with me, so that every invader of my boundary is slain in my grasp; his chosen one [15]whom he found among hundreds of thousands,[c] who was established upon his throne for safety ⌜—⌝ ⌜when there was not a single man among them to rescue (them)⌝ from the Nine Bows. I surrounded her,[d] I established her by my valiant might. When I arose like the sun as king over Egypt, I protected her, [16]I expelled for her the Nine Bows."

### *Northern Invasion of Syria*

**64.** "The countries — —, the ⌜Northerners⌝ in their isles were disturbed, taken away in the ⌜fray⌝ — at one time. Not one stood before their hands, from Kheta (*Ḫtʾ*), Kode (*Ḳdy*), Carchemish (*Ḳ-rʾ-ḳʾ-m-šʾ*), Arvad (*ʾ-rʾ-ṯw*), [17]Alasa (*ʾ-rʾ-sʾ*), they were wasted. [The]y [⌜set up⌝][e] a camp in one place in Amor (*ʾ-m-rʾ*). They desolated his

---

[a]The determinative shows that the word designates young men (*rnp·w?*).

[b]"*All*" may apply to the whole series.

[c]Compare the selection of Thutmose III from among the priests of Karnak (II, 131–48) by oracle of the god.

[d]Egypt, as shown by the end of the line, compared with the beginning of l. 16.

[e]The lacuna is hardly large enough for a verb. The end of the plural suffix (*n* of *sn*) is visible before "*camp.*" If we read "*their*" (*pʾ ysn*), it would fill the lacuna, and we should necessarily render: "*Wasted was their camp, etc.*," meaning the camp of the allied Syrians, which was wasted by the Northerners. The series of names preceding as object of the preposition must in that case close the preceding sentence.

people and his land like that which is not. They came with fire prepared before them, forward[a] to Egypt. Their main support[b] [18]was Peleset (*Pw-r* ͗ *-s* ͗ *-t*), Thekel (*T̠* ͗ *-k-k* ͗ *-r* ͗), Shekelesh (*Š* ͗ *-k-rw-š* ͗), Denyen (*D* ͗ *-y-n-yw*, sic!), and Weshesh (*W* ͗ *-š* ͗ *-š* ͗),[c] (These) lands were united, and they laid their hands upon the land[d] as far as the Circle of the Earth. Their hearts were confident, full of their[e] plans."

*Ramses' Preparations*

**65.** "Now, it happened through[f] this god, the lord of gods, [19]that I was prepared and armed[g] to ⌈trap⌉ them like wild fowl. He furnished my strength and caused my plans to prosper. I went forth, directing these marvelous things. I equipped my frontier in Zahi, prepared before them. The chiefs, the captains of infantry, [20]the nobles, I caused to equip the harbor-mouths,[h] like a strong wall, with warships, galleys, and barges, ⌈—⌉. They were manned ⌈completely⌉ from bow to stern with valiant warriors bearing their arms, soldiers [21]of all the choicest of Egypt,[i] being like lions roaring upon the mountain-tops. The charioteers were warriors (*pḥrr*) ⌈— —⌉,[j] and all good officers (*snn*), ready of hand. Their horses were quivering in their every limb, ready to crush [22]the countries under their feet. I was the valiant Montu, stationed before them, that they might behold the hand-to-hand fighting[k] of my arms. I, King Ramses III, was made a far-striding hero, conscious of his might, valiant to lead his army [23]in the day of battle."

---

[a]The meaning of this important phrase, "*forward*" (*m ḥr*), with a verb of going, is established among others by the passage in the Kadesh battle (III, 308: Poem, l. 12), and Merneptah's Hymn of Victory (III, 609, l. 5); but the idiom is not infrequent; see also Griffith, *Proceedings of the Society of Biblical Archæology*, 19, 298. "*To*" may be rendered "*toward*" or "*against*."

[b]See Müller, *Asien und Europa*, 360, n. 2.

[c]On these peoples, see introduction to this war (§§ 59 ff.).

[d]Lit., "*Two Lands;*" it is doubtful whether we are to suppose that this is an error (as later) for "land." Some of the northern ships had already reached Egypt, as they had done in the year 5 (§ 44, ll. 51 f.).

[e]Text has "*our.*"

[f]That is, by his intervention.

[g]*Grg ḥry.*

[h]The same phrase (*r* ͗ *-ḥ* ͗ *·wt*) is used of the "*river-mouths,*" in the war of the year 5 (§ 44, l. 53).

[i]Possibly: "*of every land and of Egypt.*"

[j]See Papyrus Harris, 8, 10, note.

[k]Or possibly: "*the captures;*" the article is plural.

*Defeat of the Enemy*

**66.** "Those who reached my boundary, their seed is not; their heart and their soul are finished forever and ever. As for those who had assembled before them on the sea, the full flame was in their front, before the harbor-mouths, and a wall of metal [24]upon the shore surrounded them.[a] They were dragged, overturned, and laid low upon the beach; slain and made heaps from stern to bow[b] of their galleys, while all their things were cast upon the water. (Thus) I turned back the waters to remember Egypt;[c] when they mention my name in their land, [25]may it[d] consume them, while I sit upon the throne of Harakhte, and the serpent-diadem (*wr˙t-ḥkꜣ˙w*) is fixed upon my head, like Re. I permit not the countries to see the boundaries of Egypt to ⌜—⌝ ⌜among⌝ them. As for the Nine Bows, I have taken away their land and their boundaries; they are added to mine. [26]Their chiefs and their people (come) to me with praise. I carried out the plans of the All-Lord, the august, divine father, lord of the gods."

*Ramses' Song of Triumph*

**67.** "Rejoice ye, O Egypt, to the height of heaven, for I am ruler of the South and North upon the throne of Atum. The gods have appointed me to be king [27]over Egypt, to be victor, to expel them for her from the countries; they decreed to me the kingdom while I was a child, and my reign is full of plenty — — — Strength has been given to me, because of my benefactions to the gods and goddesses, from a heart of love. I have expelled your [28]mourning, which was in your heart, and I have made you to dwell in peace. Those whom I have overthrown shall not return, the tribute — — — their land, their detestation is the daily mention of my name, King Ramses III. [29]I have covered Egypt, I have protected her by my valiant might, since

[a]The "*full flame*" is the Egyptian fleet in the harbor, and the "*wall of metal*" is the Egyptian infantry ashore, as shown in the relief (§ 74). These highly figurative phrases, otherwise unintelligible, are rendered quite certain by the relief.

[b]Lit., "*from tail to head*," a phrase which occurs also where ships are not concerned (§ 90, year 11, l. 18). Hence we should perhaps put a full pause here and render thus: ". . . . . *made heaps from tail to head. As for their galleys, all their things, etc.*"

[c]Or: "*for a remembrance of Egypt*," meaning that they (the foe) may remember Egypt.

[d]Or: "*the thought consumes.*"

I assumed the rule of the kingdom ——— the might of my two arms, bringing terror among the Nine Bows. Not a land stays at hearing my name, 30(but) they leave their cities, starting in their places, forsaking ——— before them. I am a goring Bull, confident in his two horns. My hand is equal 31to my courage following my valor, when my heart says to me: 'Make —'— my office ——— in the bow of the morning-barque (*mskt·t*), I bring to you jubilation. 32Mourning is in the countries, trembling is in every land ——— which I wrought. My heart is filled as a god — — valiant, lord of the sword. I know that his might is greater 33than (that of) the gods. The ⌜lifetime⌝ which the gods who are in — decree ———. There is not a moment in your presence, which brings not plunder by the plans of the counsel 34which is in my heart, for the support of Egypt. Desolated is ——— the chief of their cities, wasted at one time. Their groves, and all their people are consumed by fire.[a] 35They lament in their hearts: 'We will ——— their — to Egypt.'"

**68.** "I am the strong and valiant one; my designs come to pass without fail. 36I have shown my excellence, since I ⌜know⌝ this god, the father of the gods ——— I have not ignored his temple, (but) my heart has been steadfast to double the feasts and food-offerings 37above what was before. My heart is filled with truth every day, my abhorrence is lying ——— the gods are satisfied with truth. Their hands are for me the shield of my body, to 38ward off evil and misfortune from[b] my limbs; the king, ruler of the Nine Bows, Lord of the Two Lands, Ramses III, given life, stability, satisfaction, like Re, forever and ever."

### 2. RELIEF SCENES OUTSIDE NORTH WALL AND IN SECOND COURT, YEAR 8

**69.** These scenes depict the war against the invading sea-rovers of Asia Minor with unusual interest. We see the equipment of the troops, the march to Syria, even possibly a lion[c] hunt on the march, the great battle, both on land and sea, furnishing the earliest known representation of a naval battle, and the final triumphs.

---

[a]Lit., "*have become ashes*" (*ssf*), used of a roast fowl.

[b]Lit., "*that are in*"(!), meaning "that might be in, etc."

[c]See § 74, note.

*Scene*[a]

70. Ramses III stands in a balcony, with two sunshade-bearers behind him. Before him are the standard-bearers of the army, who kneel in salute, followed by a trumpeter. Beside these appear lines of the new recruits levied for the coming war, to whom the officers are distributing bows and quivers of arrows. Spears, quivers, bows, and swords lie piled up beside them.

71. The inscriptions are these:

*Behind the King*

All the gods are the protection of his limbs, to give to him might against every country.

*Before the King*

——— king; he saith —— to the princes, every leader of the infantry and chariotry who are before his majesty: "Bring out the weapons ———. Let the archers march to destroy the enemies, who know not Egypt, with might."

*Over the Officials*

Utterance of the princes, companions, and leaders of the infantry and chariotry: "Thou art the king who shinest upon Egypt. When [thou] risest, the Two Lands live. Great is thy might in the midst of the Nine Bows. Thy roaring is as far as the circuit of the sun. The shadow of thy sword is over thy army. They march, filled with thy might. Thy heart is stout, (for) thy excellent plans are established. Amon-Re appears, leading thy way. He lays low for thee every land beneath thy feet; [thy] heart is glad — forever. ⌈Thou art⌉ the protection which comes forth without delay. The heart of the Temeh is [dis]turbed,[b] the Peleset (*Pw-*[*r*ᵓ]-*s*ᵓ-*ṯ*) are hung up, ⌈—⌉ in their towns, by the might of thy father, Amon, who has decreed to thee ———."

---

[a]Outside north wall of second court; Champollion, *Monuments*, 218 = Rosellini, *Monumenti Storici*, 125; cf. Champollion, *Notices descriptives*, I, 370.

[b]Read *tfy*.

*Over Officers by the Weapons*[a]

——— [Give] the weapons to the infantry, the chariotry and to the archers ———.

*Over Officers Distributing Weapons*

Take ye the [weapon]s of [King] Ramses III.

*Over Soldiers Receiving Weapons*

The infantry and chariotry who are receiving [weapons].

*Scene*[b]

72. Ramses III in his chariot, followed by two sunshade-bearers, and accompanied by Egyptian and Sherden infantry, departs for Zahi. The inscriptions are these:

*Over the King*

The king, rich in might, at his going forth to the North, great in fear, dread of the Asiatics (*St̤ᐧ ty*), sole lord, skilled in hand, conscious of his might, like Baal, valiant in strength, ready for battle against the Asiatics (ᶜ ᵓ *mw*), marching afar in his advance, ⌜confident⌝, —, smiting tens of thousands ⌜in heaps⌝ in the space of an hour. He overwhelms the combatants like fire, causing all those who confront him to become [ashes].[c] They are terrified at (the mention of) his name, while he is (yet) afar off, like the heat of the sun over the two (Nile) shores; a wall casting[d] a shadow for Egypt. They dwell [confident in] the might of his strength, King Ramses III.

*Over Horses*

Great first span of his majesty (named): "Amon-He-Giveth-the-Sword."[e]

---

[a]This and the following inscription have been omitted by Champollion, and Rosellini is very fragmentary. Still another address (below) among the officers has been omitted by Champollion, and is too fragmentary in Rosellini to be read.

[b]Outside north wall of second court; Champollion, *Monuments*, 219 = Rosellini, *Monumenti Storici*, 126.

[c]Read *ssf*, from parallel texts.

[d]Read *kh*, as in year 5, l. 67 (§ 47).

[e]Published also in Lepsius, *Denkmäler*, Text, III, 172.

*Behind King and over Sherden*

His majesty marches out in victorious might, to destroy the rebellious countries. His majesty [marches out] for Zahi, like the form of Montu, to crush every country that has transgressed his boundary. His infantry are like bulls, ready for battle upon the field. [His] horses are like hawks in the midst of the fowl before him. The Nine Bows are under (his) power. Amon, his august father, is for him a shield, King — —, Lord of the Two Lands, Ramses III.

*Scene*[a]

73. Ramses III in his chariot, with drawn bow, charges into the discomfited northern allies, chiefly Peleset, as shown by their high feathered head-dress. Their chariots are manned by two warriors armed with shield and spear, and a driver. On foot they fight by fours, each man with two spears and a shield. The native Egyptian troops and their Sherden auxiliaries are mingled in the thick of the fight, slaying the Northerners on every hand, and penetrating to the heavy two-wheeled ox carts in which are the enemy's wives, children, and supplies.

The inscriptions are these:

*Over the Battle*

———— [at] the sight of him, as when Set is enraged, overthrowing the enemy before the celestial barque (*mskt˙t*), trampling the lands and countries prostrate, crushed ⌜—⌝ before his horses. His heat consumes [them] like fire, desolating their gardens — —.

*Over King's Horses*

Great first span of his majesty (named): "Beloved-of-Amon."

*Scene*[b]

74. Five warships of the Northerners, manned by Peleset and Sherden, are hard pressed by four Egyptian warships,

[a]Outside north wall of second court; Champollion, *Monuments*, 220–220 *bis* = Rosellini, *Monumenti Storici*, 127, 128.

[b]Outside north wall of second court; Champollion, 222, 223 = Rosellini,

whose native bowmen are disabling the enemy with a severe archery discharge at long range, before the heavy swords and spears of the latter can be brought into play at close quarters. When the archery has nearly emptied the enemy's vessels, the Egyptians close in with sword and shield, and in the resulting mêlée one of the northern ships has capsized. In three of the Egyptian vessels are pinioned prisoners taken from the enemy, while those who swim ashore are seized and bound by the waiting Egyptian archers. The latter, led by the king, themselves augment the volleys of the Egyptian archers in the warships, and render still more disastrous the complete destruction of the northern fleet. Behind the king are his chariot and waiting attendants.

**75.** The inscriptions are as follows:

*By the King*

The Good God, Montu over Egypt, great in might, like Baal in the countries, mighty in strength, far-reaching in courage (lit., heart), strong-horned, terrible in his might, a — wall, covering Egypt, so that every one coming shall not[a] see it, King Ramses III.

*Over the Chariot*

Lo, the northern countries, which are in their isles, are restless in their limbs; they infest the ways[b] of the harbor-mouths. Their nostrils and their hearts cease breathing breath, when his majesty goes forth like a storm-wind against them, fighting upon the strand like a warrior (*pḥrr*). His puissance and the terror of him penetrate into their limbs.[c]

---

*Monumenti Storici*, 130, 131; Mariette, *Voyage dans la haute Egypte*, II, 55. I had also good photographs. At this point the order of the war reliefs is interrupted by the scene of a lion hunt, the inscriptions of which contain only conventional phrases in praise of the king. It has often been published; best by Mariette, *ibid.*, II, 54; also by Champollion, *ibid.*, 221; and Rosellini, *ibid.*, 129.

[a]Negative with a verb implying negation; lit., "*everyone coming shall not fail to see it.*"

[b]The word "*way*" (*w*ʾ*t*) is used by the Egyptians for a sea route as well as a land route.

[c]Champollion has here interchanged two lines, but they are correct in Rosellini.

Capsized and perishing in their places, their hearts are taken, their souls fly away, and their weapons are cast out upon the sea. His arrows pierce whomsoever he will among them, and he who is hit falls[a] into the water. His majesty is like an enraged lion, tearing him that confronts him with his hands (sic!), fighting at close quarters on his right, valiant on his left, like Set; destroying the foe, like Amon-Re. He has laid low the lands, he has crushed every land beneath his feet, the king of Upper and Lower Egypt, the Lord of the Two Lands, Usermare-Meriamon.

*Scene*[b]

76. The king, attended by sunshade- and fan-bearers, stands in a balcony.[c] Behind him waits the royal chariot, with numerous attendants and soldiers. A castle is depicted over the chariot. Before the king, the two viziers and other officers of high rank present to him Peleset prisoners. Other officials superintend the counting of the hands severed from the fallen of the enemy, the numbers being recorded by four scribes.

77. The inscriptions are these:

*By the King*

Utterance of his majesty to the king's-children, the princes, the king's-butlers, and the charioteers: "Behold ye, the great might of my father, Amon-Re. The countries which came from their isles in the midst of the sea, they advanced to Egypt, their hearts relying upon their arms.[d] The net was made ready for them, to ensnare them. Entering stealthily into the harbor-mouth, they fell into it. Caught in their place, they were dispatched, and their bodies stripped. I showed

[a]Lit., "*becomes one fallen into the water.*"

[b]Outside north wall of second court; Champollion, *Monuments*, 224 = Rosellini, *Monumenti Storici*, 132; the inscriptions are also in Dümichen, *Historische Inschriften*, II, 47; the castle and a few extracts, Lepsius, *Denkmäler*, Text, III, 171.

[c]This balcony is, of course, to be understood as belonging to the castle depicted over the chariot; but it has been detached by the artist, in order to enlarge it sufficiently to accommodate the king's figure represented with the usual heroic stature.

[d]Not weapons.

you my might which was in that which my majesty wrought while I was alone.[a] My arrow struck (lit., seized), and none escaped my arms nor my hand. I flourished like a hawk among the fowl; my talons descended upon their heads. Amon-Re was upon my right and upon my left, his might and his power were in my limbs, a tumult for you; commanding for me that my counsels and my designs should come to pass. Amon-Re established the — of my enemies, giving to me every land in my grasp."

*Over the Officials*

Utterance of the king's-children, the princes, and the companions; they reply to the Good God: "Thou art Re, shining like him. Thy might crushes the Nine Bows, every land trembles at thy name, thy fear is before them every day. Egypt rejoices in the strong-armed, the son of Amon, who is upon his throne, King Ramses III, given life, like Re."

*Over the Castle*

Migdol of Ramses, Ruler of Heliopolis.

*Over Horses*

Great first span of his majesty (named): "Strong-is-Amon."

*Over Grooms*

Live the Good God, achieving with his arms, making every country into something that exists not, strong-armed, mighty, skilful of hand, King Ramses III.

*Over Prisoners*[b]

Said the vanquished chieftains of Thekel (*Ṯ*ᵓ-*k*-*k*ᵓ-*r*ᵓ): "——— like Baal ——— give to us [the breath that thou givest] ———."

*Scene*[c]

78. In a small chapel sits Amon, with Mut and Khonsu behind him. The king standing before him leads by cords

[a]Champollion has here omitted an entire line, which will be found in Rosellini's and Dümichen's copies.

[b]Omitted by Rosellini and Champollion, and only noted by Lepsius (*Denkmäler*, Text, III, 171); the fragments he gives show that it contained the conventional phrases.

[c]Outside of north wall of second court; Champollion, *Monuments*, 226 = Rosellini, *Monumenti Storici*, 134; the inscriptions alone, Brugsch, *Recueil de monuments*, LV, 3, 4; and the words of the Thekel also, Dümichen, *Historische Inschriften*, II, 47, *a*.

two lines of foreign captives, above Thekel, below Libyans. The inscriptions are as follows:

*Over Amon*

Utterance of Amon-Re, lord of heaven, ruler of gods: "Come thou with joy, slay thou the Nine Bows, lay low every opponent. Thou hast cast down the hearts of the Asiatics, thou takest the breath from their nostrils, — — — by my designs."

*Before the King*

Utterance of King Ramses III before his father, Amon-Re, king of gods: "I went forth, that I might take captive the Nine Bows and slay all lands. Not a land stood fast before me, . . . . . . . . and my hands took captives in the van of every country, by the decrees which came forth from thy mouth, . . . . . . that I might overthrow my every opponent. The lands behold me with trembling, (for) I am like Montu, — — — him who relies upon thy designs, O protector, lord of might ———."

*Over the Thekel*

79. Said the fallen, the great ones of Thekel, who were in the grasp of his majesty, while praising this Good God, Lord of the Two Lands, Usermare-Meriamon: "Great is thy strength, victorious king, great Sun of Egypt. Greater is thy might than a mountain of gritstone, and thy terror is like Set. Give to us breath, that we may breathe it, the life that is in thy grasp, forever."

*Over the Libyans*

Said the fallen of Libya, who were in the grasp of his majesty: "Breath, breath! O victorious king, Horus, great in kingship."

*Scene*[a]

80. Amon, with Mut behind him, stands extending the sword to Ramses III. The latter, leading three lines of fettered captives, advances toward the god, to whom he stretches out his arm. The inscriptions are these:

[a]Second court, second pylon, left (southern) tower, front; published by Champollion, ***Monuments***, 332 (in publication, 331 *bis*, where it is located in the Ramesseum!); Rosellini, ***Monumenti Storici***, 144 (both omit divinities and accom-

*Before Amon*[a]

Utterance of Amon-Re, lord of heaven: "Come thou in peace! Thou hast taken captive thine adversary,[b] and slain the invader of thy border. My strength was with thee, overthrowing for thee the lands. Thou cuttest off the heads of the Asiatics (*ᶜ ͻ mw*). I have given to thee thy great might, I overthrow for thee every land, when they see thy majesty in strength like my son, Baal in his wrath."

*Before the King*

**81.** Utterance of King Ramses III to his father, Amon-Re, ruler of the gods: "Great is thy might, O lord of gods. The things which issue from thy mouth, they come to pass without fail. . . . . . Thy strength is behind as a shield, that I may slay the lands and countries that invade my border. Thou puttest great terror of me in the hearts of their chiefs; the fear and dread of me before them; that I may carry off their warriors (*pḥrr*), bound in my grasp, to lead them to thy ka, O my august father, — — — — —. Come, to ⌜take⌝[c] them, being: Peleset (*Pw-r ͻ -s ͻ -ṯ*), Denyen (*D ͻ -y-n-yw-n ͻ*), Shekelesh (*Š ͻ -k ͻ -rw-š ͻ*). Thy strength it was which was before me, overthrowing their seed, — thy might, O lord of gods. He who relies upon him whom thou hast entrusted with the kingship, and everyone that walks in thy way are in peace. Thou art the lord, strong-armed for him who leans his back upon thee,[d] a Bull with two horns, ready, conscious of his strength. Thou art my august father, who createdst my beauty, that thou mightest look upon me, and choose me to be lord of the Nine Bows. Let thy hand be with me, to slay him that invades me, and ward off every enemy that is in my limbs."

---

panying inscriptions); Lepsius, *Denkmäler*, III, 211 (inscription over prisoners, also *ibid.*, Text, III, 174); Sharpe, *Inscriptions*, II, 39; Mariette, *Voyage dans la haute Egypte*, II, 52 (one row only); de Rougé, *Inscriptions hiéroglyphiques*, 129 (upper ends of lines of king's speech, lower ends being covered by rubbish). I had a photograph by Schroeder & Cie., Zürich.

[a]The one before Mut contains only the conventional assurances of protection.

[b]Lit., "*the one reaching thee*" (*pḥ tw*); the phrase is common in these inscriptions, with varying pronoun ("*him, her*") for "*his, her adversary.*" Cf. the personal name, *Pḥ-sw-ḫr* = "*His adversary is fallen.*"

[c]Possibly: "*to number.*"

[d]Lit., "*thou art a strong-armed lord, for him who leans to him* (*his*) *back.*" The preposition "*to*" (*n*) is more often "*upon*" (*ḥr*).

*Over Captives*

**82.** Utterance of the leaders of every country, who are in the grasp of his majesty: "Great is thy might, victorious king, great sun of Egypt. Greater is thy strength than a mountain of gritstone; thy might is like Baal. Give to us the breath that we breathe; the life which is in thy hands."

*Over Middle Line of Captives*

Utterance of the vanquished of Denyen (*D ˀ -y-n-yw-n ˀ*): "Breath! Breath! O good ruler, great in might [like] Montu, residing in Thebes."

*Over Lower Line of Captives*

Utterance of the vanquished of Peleset (*Pw-r ˀ -s ˀ -ty*): "Give to us the breath for our nostrils, O king, son of Amon."

## IV. SECOND LIBYAN WAR

**83.** The disastrous defeat of the year 5 had doubtless too seriously weakened the Libyans for them again to attempt the invasion of Egypt during the reign of Ramses III. But in the year 11 they were themselves invaded by the Meshwesh, a related tribe living on their west, and the Meshwesh chieftains, Keper and Meshesher, father and son, laid waste the Libyan country. The Libyans were then forced to join the Meshwesh in an invasion of Egypt. The allies pushed eastward as far as the canal of Heliopolis, called the "*Water of Re*,"[a] doubtless at some point near its departure from the Nile. Here, at a place called Hatsho (*ḥ˙t-š ᶜ˙t*), in the early part of the twelfth month of his eleventh year, Ramses defeated them in a disastrous battle, in which Keper was captured and his son Meshesher killed. Ramses pursued the routed enemy over eleven miles[b]

[a]The name of the herd of Amon in Papyrus Harris, 10, 8 (§ 224), shows that the battle was fought near this canal.

[b]If the terminus of this eleven miles is the margin of the Libyan desert, the point on that margin must be well south in the narrow part of the Delta; otherwise it would be more than eleven miles from the canal of Heliopolis to the Libyan

westward as far as his own town, on a rise of ground called "*The-Town-of-Usermare-Meriamon-Which-is-upon-the-Mount*[a]*-of-the-Horns-of-the-Earth.*" He slew 2,175 men, and took 2,052 prisoners, of whom 558 were women and girls; among these were the survivors of the household of the hostile chief. Returning, flushed with victory, Ramses indulged in the usual triumphal celebrations. The prisoners were distributed throughout the country, and nearly a thousand of the Meshwesh were made herdmen in charge of a herd of Amon, named after this victory (Harris, 10, 8, § 224).

**84.** These wars, while they checked the aggressiveness of the tribes[b] on the west of the Delta during the remainder of reign of Ramses III, could only temporarily interrupt the tide of immigration into the Delta from the west. Still Ramses III could now style himself in his titulary: "*Protector of Egypt, guardian of the countries, conqueror of Meshwesh, spoiler of the land of Temeh.*"[c]

The sources for this war are:

1. Great Inscription of the First Pylon (Medinet Habu, §§ 85–92).
2. Poem on Second Libyan War (§§ 93–99).
3. Relief Scenes on First Pylon and Outside North Wall (Medinet Habu, §§ 100–114).
4. Papyrus Harris (76, 11–77, 6, § 405).

---

desert. The question of how the pursuit crossed the Nile branches is a difficult one. In the war of the year 5 the Libyans are stated to have been on both sides of the river; if the victory of year 11 took place on the Heliopolis canal, they must have been on both sides at this time also.

[a]This place also marked the limit of the pursuit of Merneptah; see Great Inscription of Karnak, l. 49, note (III, 588).

[b]Papyrus Harris (77, 3, § 405) gives a list of five of these unknown tribes, beside the Meshwesh and the Libyans.

[c]Lepsius, *Denkmäler*, Text, III, 170; left pylon, front of Medinet Habu temple; compare similar title of Thutmose IV (II, 822).

### I. GREAT INSCRIPTION ON THE FIRST PYLON[a]

**85.** The fifty long lines of this document, owing to their bad state of preservation, the lack of clear arrangement in the content, and that highly figurative style, extreme in this document even for Medinet Habu, are hardly less difficult than the long inscription of the year 5. Whole lines are so fragmentary that it would have served no practical purpose to introduce their mutilated words and phrases here; they have therefore been omitted wherever necessary, but the omission is always indicated. Under these circumstances the progress of the narrative can be but vaguely discerned. At the beginning it is fortunately more clear. The alliance, undoubtedly between the Meshwesh and the Tehenu of Libya (§ 86, ll. 1 and 2), although mentioned before the invasion of the Tehenu by the Meshwesh (§ 87, l. 2), of course preceded that invasion, which issued in the alliance. Then follow, in natural order, the invasion of Egypt by the allies (§ 88, ll. 3–5), the march of Ramses III (§ 89, ll. 6, 7), and the battle (§ 90, ll. 7–20). This last, as usual, is chiefly a song of praise to the Pharaoh's valor, which is brought out by depicting the ruin of Meshesher, the Meshwesh chief with his chiefs, his family, and his host. This leads to a long triumphal description of the discomfiture of the defeated (§§ 91, 92, ll. 20–41); and the document then concludes with a speech by the Pharaoh, glorifying himself in the conventional phrases.

---

[a]On the back of the southern tower of the first pylon facing the first court, in 50 vertical lines over the battle scene (§ 101). There are long and frequent lacunæ. It was published by Dümichen (*Historische Inschriften*, I, 20–25); partially by de Rougé (*Inscriptions hiéroglyphiques*, 111–113, ll. 19–30, lower ends wanting; wrongly attached to another inscription); and extracts by Lepsius (*Denkmäler*, Text, III, 174). A photograph shows that Dümichen's text is excessively incorrect; but unfortunately my photograph shows only the lower ends of a few lines.

*The Alliance*

**86.** [1][⌈The foe⌉][a] had allied themselves against Egypt, the god permitting that they should ⌈lead on to mount their horses⌉, (but) mighty was the valor of him who is the sole lord, and his talons ⌈made ready⌉ like a ⌈trap⌉ at their arrival, when they came with restless limbs[b] to lay [2]themselves like mice under his arms, the king, Ramses III.

*Invasion of Tehenu*[c]

**87.** As for the (chief of)[d] Meshwesh (*M-š*ˀ*-w*ˀ, sic!), since he appeared, he went to one place, his land with him, and invaded the Tehenu, who were made ashes, spoiled and desolated were their cities, their seed was not.

*Invasion of Egypt*

**88.** They ⌈disregarded⌉ the beauty of this god who[e] slays the invader of Egypt, saying . . . . .: "We will settle in Egypt." So spake they with one accord, and they continually entered the boundaries of Egypt. Then was prepared for them [4]death[f] . . . . . . . of the ⌈mighty⌉ god, —— [⌈who brightens⌉] the heaven more than the sun, ⌈mighty⌉ with their hands before him. They were numerous [5]. . . . . . . Amon was his protection, his hand was with him, to confound their faces, to destroy them.

*March of the Pharaoh*

**89.** [6]King Ramses III; his majesty went forth in ——— his heart [⌈confident⌉] in his father, the lord of gods. He was ——— seized herds of small cattle; his infantry and [7]his chariotry bearers of victory; the mighty men whom [he] trained [⌈as⌉] valiant warriors. He was a strong wall, firm in ——— King Ramses III.

---

[a]Some such words must be lost in the small lacuna (see Brugsch, *Hieroglyphisch-demotisches Wörterbuch*, Supplement, 568).

[b]Lit., "*showing restlessness in their limbs;*" the phrase is several times used of the northern peoples also, in the Medinet Habu inscriptions.

[c]That this is an invasion of Libya by the Meshwesh is unnoticed in any of the histories. It seems to have been noticed by Spiegelberg (*Zeitschrift für ägyptische Sprache*, 34, 23, [65]), though he draws no historical conclusions.

[d]The phrase below, "*his land with him,*" would indicate that the chief of the Meshwesh is designated here. He gathered all his people (called "*land*") in one place.

[e]Lit., "*when slaying, etc.*"

[f]Lit., "*Death was put round about for them,*" or: "*death surrounded them.*"

*The Battle*

**90.** His majesty was a hero, protecting — — [8]to fight hand to hand, his voice upraised, shouting like a gryphon ——— his beauty, undivided ——— his nostrils; his talons were — — — [9]his every — before him against his enemy; fearful in might like the shout ———, swift of foot, falling ——— horses — — — — arrows, — — [a10]slain in their place, their hearts and their souls are finished, perishing — — —. Their mouths have ceased contradiction in — —. Egypt ——— their souls — — — —. [11]His arms are against them like ⌜—⌝, his hand is upon them, he feels about, surrounding — — all — their limbs. Meshesher (*M-š*ᵓ*-š*ᵓ*-r*), son of Keper (*K*ᵓ*-pw-r*) ——— [12]laid low at the feet of his majesty. His chiefs, his family, his army are lost — completely. His eyes behold the hue[b] of the Sun, his warriors (*pḥrr*) fight ——— their —, their children — — — [13]their arms and their hearts, as living captives; their stuff and their children are borne [⌜upon⌝] their backs. Their herds, their horses, [their] wives ———. The god brings them and their — — — — [14]against them, a lesson for millions of years. All generations are desolated upon — ⌜women⌝, their —, stripped are their — — — — flourishing — — them, Amon-Re, with the ⌜hand⌝ of ——— mighty, confident ——— [15]to — extol him who repels her[c] assailant, — — King Ramses III, who moves quickly, bathing the sword in the slain ——— their food, fruitlessly looking while there is no — — [16]the way ⌜—⌝ before them. As for the land of Meshwesh (*M-š*ᵓ———), ⌜when they⌝ seize their people, their weapons fall from their hands, their hearts cannot ——— smelling fear at a single ⌜attack⌝ — — — — [17]they [⌜know⌝] who is lord of the [land] of Egypt, the great flame of Sekhmet ——— their hearts, consuming their bones, in the midst of their bodies; the —[d] — — — — them. The land re⌜joices⌝[e] and exults at the sight of his valor, the Lord of the Two Lands, Ramses III. [18]Every — is in his hand as far as the [⌜southern⌝] towns, as well as the northern marshes. — — — —

---

[a]The battle begins in ll. 9, 10, which are unfortunately almost entirely destroyed.

[b]Lit., "*skin of the sun!*" This remarkable phrase is applied to the shining appearance of the sun, in religious texts, and Horus is said to have a shining skin. "*The sun*" must here be a figure for the Egyptian king.

[c]Egypt's.

[d]The first lost word, as determinative shows, is some designation of the king.

[e]Read *wnf*.

fire, strong-armed, hurling flame, — to pursue their souls, to plunder their —, which are in their land. The excellent words of Thoth confound their faces; (from) tail to head among them, they are laid low in their place. 19[a]His hand clutches[b] the body of the invader of his border, the ⌜breath⌝ of [their] nostrils —— taken, perishing, — he leaves not, when enraged ————. His talons are over the head of the Meshwesh, the king, Ramses III, 20the kindly.

*Discomfiture of the Enemy*

**91.** The Meshwesh and the land of Temeh, who were bound ——— in Egypt. All lands bow themselves to him, like Set, — overthrowing ⌜—⌝, laying low. The Meshwesh and Temeh mourn and are cast down; they go . . . . . 21[c]Their eyes — the ways, looking behind them; ⌜flying⌝ far, fleeing in . . . . . . . 22The flame seizes them, destroying their name; their feet are weary upon the ground, (but) they wait not the great lord of Egypt. . . . . . . 23. . . . They say when they see the people:[d] "—— Montu is the form of the man who is behind us ——— . . . 24He is behind us like Set, [destroying] the foe. He beholds myriads like grasshoppers; behold, they are in an evil plight. . . . . 25. . . We are like the ⌜driven barque⌝ with the wind behind it. Our weapons are lost, cast away; our hands are ⌜weak⌝." Their soul and their heart are finished ——— . . 27victory from the time of the god to eternity. "Her[e] violence is that which courses in our limbs, her lord is he who is in heaven; his form is like him ——— Ramses III. 28He seems like the radiance of the sun; his reach, and the terror of him are like Montu . . . . . ——— 30. . tearing like a divine hawk, we are made ⌜impotent⌝, cut down ⌜——⌝. He sends arrow upon arrow like shooting-stars ———. 31The net was spread for us, while we were before [⌜him⌝]. Our ⌜hands⌝ and our feet were — in the palace. The god has taken us for himself, as ⌜prey⌝, like wild goats creeping into the trap. The fierce-eyed ——— 32. . . . He turns

[a]The upper two-thirds of ll. 19–30 are also published by de Rougé (*Inscriptions hiéroglyphiques*, 111–13).

[b]Lit., "*claws.*"

[c]The last third of ll. 21–31 is lost, except a word or two at the ends of ll. 22–27.

[d]Probably meaning, when they arrive at home and see their own people, they excuse their flight in this way.

[e]Meaning Egypt.

not back, he heeds not our pleadings. . . . .[33]. . . We are overthrown, our heart perishes ——— like trees. We have heard since those things[a] from our grandfathers, ⌈our repulse in their time⌉ . . . . [34]from Egypt . . . . . . and we desired to take to our heels,[b] ⌈fleeing⌉ from the flame. Libya has misled us like —. We hearkened to their counsels,[c] the fire — seized [35]——— making for us a warning forever and ever, a chastisement for those whom the boundary of Egypt beholds."[d] He shall tread upon ⌈—⌉ ⌈as far as⌉ Tazoser; Montu, strong in arm, he [36]who takes — [⌈in⌉] the fray with you, his assailant, King Ramses III. The land of Meshwesh is desolated at one time, the Libyans and the Seped are destroyed, their seed is not [37]. . . . their ⌈arms⌉ hanging over their heads;[e] their children do not ——— whom fear has seized, weeping and [lamenting] in their hearts: "The fame of thy majesty [38]——— them like fire" . . . . . . [40]. . . . . . bearing [their] tribute — — — [to] laud and to praise [41]the Good God, Lord of the Two Lands, making [his] boundary as far as he desires in all lands.

*Speech of Ramses*

**92.** Lo, Horus, rich in years, who came forth from Re, from his very limbs, [42]to whom he decreed —, abiding upon his throne[f] . . . . . . [44]. . . . . . King Ramses III; he says to the king's-children, the great princes, the leaders [45]of the infantry and chariotry: "Give to me your attention — — — complete. I will tell you, I will inform you; I am the son of Re, I came forth from his limbs, I sit [46]upon his throne in rejoicing, since I have been established — —. I give to this land my good counsels, (my) plans are carried out. I am the hero of Egypt, I defend her, placing her — — — [47]lord. I overthrow for [her] every one who invades [her] boundary, I am an abundant Nile, supplying her —, overflowing with good things. I am the excellent sovereign who fills [48]—, giving breath to the nostrils of all people. I have laid low the Meshwesh, and the land of Temeh by the might of my sword. I have caused their overthrow. Behold, [49]ye [⌈know⌉] that there is no

---

[a]Of course, meaning former defeats.

[b]On hearing the stories of their earlier defeats, they were reluctant to invade Egypt again, and wished to flee.

[c]The Meshwesh now blame the Libyans for their defeats.

[d]When they would invade it.

[e]The arms of the prisoners were often so bound, over their heads.

[f]Here follow nearly three lines of conventional epithets of the king.

contradiction in [⌜my speech⌝]. It was the might of Amon which carried them off, that he might give myriads of jubilees to his son, the Lord of the Two Lands, Ramses III."

50[a]The king, like the form of Re, of ⌜abiding⌝ — — —. His heart is stout, like his father, Montu. [b]He takes as living captives the Meshwesh and the land of Temeh bound before him, taxed with their impost for the [⌜treasury⌝] ————.

## 2. POEM ON THE SECOND LIBYAN WAR[c]

93. Over two-thirds of the poem are taken up by the date, and the laudation of the Pharaoh appended to it. The narrative then begins with the invasion of Egypt (§ 95, ll. 23, 24), followed by Ramses' attack (§ 96, ll. 24–27), the capture of Keper, the father of the Meshwesh chief (§ 97, ll. 27–30), the defeat of the enemy (§ 98, ll. 30–32); and the poem concludes with Ramses' victorious return (§ 99, ll. 33, 34).

### *Date*

94. [1]Year 11, second month of the second season (sixth month), seventh day[d] under the majesty of Horus: Mighty Bull, Great in Kingship; Wearer of the Double Diadem, [Great in Jubilees, like Ptah]; Golden Horus: Rich in Years, like Atum, Sovereign, Protector of [Egypt, Binder of the Coun]tries; [2]King of Upper and Lower Egypt: Usermare-Meriamon; Son of Re, Lord of Diadems: Ramses (III), Ruler of Heliopolis. . . . . . . .[e]

---

[a]This line has no connection with the preceding, but belongs to the figure of the king.

[b]Or: "*His captivity as living prisoners, the Meshwesh, etc., are bound, etc.*"

[c]On the face of the first pylon, Medinet Habu, right hand (northern tower), beside the right-hand doorpost of the central portal; published by Champollion (*Notices descriptives*, I, 728 f.; extracts only); relief and list at the top, Lepsius, *Denkmäler*, III, 209, *d* (see also *ibid.*, Text, III, 170); list only in Champollion, *ibid.*, I, 345; complete by Dümichen, *Historische Inschriften*, I, 13–15, and de Rougé, *Inscriptions hiéroglyphiques*, 121–26; de Rougé gives much the better text. The list was also published by Daressy (*Recueil*, 20, 119).

[d]The date is some six months after the victory.

[e]The fivefold titulary is followed by seventeen lines of which only fragments have survived. They contained only a long succession of the conventional laudatory epithets applied to the king, constituting merely an expansion of the titulary. References to the defeat of the enemy begin in l. 19, introducing the poetic account of the invasion.

### *Conclusion of Introductory Triumph*

The flame ——— [20]their bones, boiling and scorching in their limbs. They tread the land like those who come into the trap; slain are their [21]heroes on the spot they tread, and their speech is taken away forever. They are overthrown at one time, seized upon are their leaders who were before them. [22]They are bound like fowl before the hawk whose every step is concealed in the midst of the thicket, sitting in[a] — —. [23]They are laid low, doing obeisance.

### *The Invasion*

**95.** The hostile foe had taken counsel again, to spend their lives in the confines of Egypt, that they might take the hills and plains as their (own) districts.[b] [24]The foe set their faces toward Egypt, coming on foot themselves[c] to —,[d] which is in the [e]fire of the ⌜lowlands⌝ with its mighty heat.[e]

### *Ramses' Attack*

**96.** The heart of [25]his majesty was wroth like Baal in heaven, all his limbs were endowed with strength and might. He betook himself — — a goodly ⌜charge⌝, to fight hand to hand multitudes on his right hand and on his left, [26]meeting their very selves, advancing like an arrow against them, to slay them. His — strength was mighty like [27]his father, Amon.

### *Capture of Hostile Chief*

**97.** Keper (*K*ᵓ*-pw-r*ᵓ) came to salâm, like ⌜—⌝;[f] he laid down his arms, together with his soldiers. He [28]cried to heaven, to beseech his son;[g] his feet and his hands were ⌜paralyzed⌝, he stood still in his place,

---

[a]The king is the hawk; the picture is that of the fowler sitting behind a screen, or in the bushes, waiting to pull together the open net, as often seen in tomb reliefs. But the introduction of the hawk mixes the figures.

[b]Dümichen has numbered 23 twice.

[c]Or: "*on their own feet,*" being perhaps contrasted with those who went riding, or by water?

[d]The determinative indicates a building.

[e]An overdrawn figure for the dangerous proximity of the king in the Delta or lowland.

[f]*T̠*ᵓ*k* with determinative of an eye.

[g]For help; "*to heaven*" is merely idiomatic for "*at the top of his voice,*" and does not indicate the place to which his cry was directed. The word "cry" is here *d̠*ᶜ*ḳ*, Hebrew, צעק.

while the god,[a] who knew his [29]reins, (even) his majesty, fell upon their[b] heads like a mountain of granite.

*Defeat of Enemy*

**98.** They were scattered, overturned, brought to the ground; their blood was[c] [30]like a flood, their bodies ⌈crushed on⌉ the spot, trampled ————. The army was slain [31]———— to take them, slaying those whom his arms had taken, bound like fowl, laid low upon the ⌈—⌉ [32]under the feet of his majesty. He was like Montu the victorious, with his feet upon his[d] head. His[e] leaders are before him, slain in his grasp.

*Victorious Return*

**99.** [33]Happy are his counsels, his designs have come to pass. He returns to his palace, his heart gratified. He is like a plundering lion, terrifying the [34]goats, in his ⌈coat of mail⌉, King Ramses III. As for Egypt, their hearts rejoice at seeing his victories; they acclaim with one accord over the flight ————.

### 3. RELIEF SCENES ON FIRST PYLON AND OUTSIDE NORTH WALL[f]

**100.** These scenes are of the conventional order, but furnish some facts that are new, regarding the campaign. Some of the accompanying inscriptions also are of the greatest importance; e. g., the short line over the battle scene, giving the limits of the pursuit (§ 102). The long inscription over the same scene (§§ 103, 104) is almost exclusively laudation of the Pharaoh for his prowess, but mentions

[a]Meaning the Pharaoh.

[b]Meaning doubtless Keper and his son; the latter is mentioned (§ 90, l. 11), and his name given as Meshesher. Our narrative describes the capture of his old father, who afterward appears in the list of captives as "*chief of the Meshwesh, 1 man*," but without name appended (§ 111). In the inscription belonging to the battle the son is said to have been killed (§ 90, ll. 11, 12), and the father driven pinioned before the Pharaoh's horses. He is depicted so pinioned in the line of foreign chiefs on the pavilion (§ 114, No. 6).

[c]De Rougé's copy here inserts the words: "*in their place.*"

[d]The head of the conquered foe, perhaps the Libyan chief.

[e]The Libyan chief's leaders.

[f]Also one relief from the front of the pavilion (§ 114).

the capture of Keper and adds the important fact that his son (Meshesher) was slain (ll. 11, 12). The closing section (§ 105, l. 24) also furnishes the date of the battle, between the tenth and twentieth of the twelfth month in the year 11. The date of the Poem (§§ 93–99) is some six months later. The final triumph (§§ 110, 111) furnishes the exact numbers of captured and slain.

*Scene*[a]

**101.** In the conventional manner the king is shown charging the enemy in his chariot, in which he stands with drawn bow. Two lines of Egyptian chariots accompany him, with occasional bodies of infantry; and the enemy, driven before them, or falling pierced by the king's arrows, are scattered in the wildest confusion, as the king drives over the fallen.

**102.** The inscriptions are these:

*Over the Charge*[b]

[⌈The pursuit⌉][c] trom Hatsho[d] (*Ḥ·t-š c· t*) to the town of Usermare-

---

[a]First pylon, inside, southern tower; unpublished; I had a photograph by Schroeder & Cie., Zürich.

[b]Fragments of the name of the king's steeds may be discerned over the horses, but large pieces have fallen off, carrying it nearly all away.

[c]Some such words must have begun this title of the charge; but some six or eight words have really been lost, for some early vandal has cut out a large rectangle here, carrying away a third of this little inscription. This important line was overlooked by Dümichen in his first publication; but appeared in his *Photographische Resultate* (Pl. 26), too small to be read. It was used by Brugsch in his *Geographie* (35, 36), where he misunderstood the portion he published (Pl. IV, No. 242). He then published it entire in the *Wörterbuch* (Supplement, 164), and in *Aegyptologie* (472); again by Levy, *Recueil,* 15, 171.

[d]This town, the name of which means "*House of Sand,*" is depicted on the north wall (§ 107). It was a stronghold on the western road, 8 iters from the edge of the plateau. The name is misread by Brugsch as *Ḥ·t-ḫ c·t;* but it is clearly *Ḥ·t-š c·t* in § 107, and I have verified the reading on both walls carefully in the photographs. It must have been near Perire, where Merneptah's pursuit of the Libyans began (III, 579, 600), if not identical with it. There is a *Ḥ·t-š c·t* mentioned on a late stela at Coptos (Petrie, *Coptos,* XXII). See also Daressy, *Recueil,* 19, 19.

Meriamon, which is upon the "Mount of the Horns of the Earth,"[a] making eight iters[b] of butchery among them.

*Over Battle*[c]

**103.** Horus, strong bull, mighty-armed, strong-armed, lord of terror in the lands and countries, desolating the Temeh[d] and Meshwesh, who are made heaps, crushed, destroyed before [his horses]. ²Live the Good God, son of Amon, brave, valiant, like Montu, residing in Thebes, great ruler, by whose name one adjures, beautiful upon the steed, ³brave in the fray, strong-horned among multitudes, ⌜experienced in⌝ charging among them like ⁴one rejoicing in heart, hero ⌜slaying⌝ his ⌜assailing⌝ enemies, seizing the aggressor, confronting the invader of ⁵his boundary, great in fame in the land of Meshwesh, great in terror, lord of might, destroying the name of the Asiatic lands, sending ⁶his fire as a flame into their limbs, like Re, when he rages, in order to extend the confines of Egypt, by the great victories ⁷of his sword, despising a million, holding in contempt two millions, firm-hearted, charging into hundred-thousands, the youthful Bull, mighty in ⁸slaughter, like Set when he is enraged, the valiant warrior, achieving with his two arms, planning in heart, like Shu, son of Re, ⁹great in victory among the lands and countries, planting terror in the heart of the Meshwesh, their people and their heirs upon the earth have vanished,[e] ¹⁰their — has perished forever, the countries — their soul —, they mention his every name in dread, King

[a]Also the limit of Merneptah's pursuit of the Libyans (III, 600, ll. 1 and 9), *q. v.* Ramses III otherwise uses this word for the far south, the commoner application. At Karnak he applies it as a gentilic parallel with the people of Upper Nubia (*Annales*, IV, 5, l. 2). His new town or fortified station, not mentioned in the first Libyan war, was doubtless founded at the close of that war as a safeguard against Libyan aggression. In Papyrus Harris (51, *a*, 5) it is again mentioned and shown to be on the "*western canal*," perhaps "*The Water of Re*" of 10, 8, and **62***a*, 2.

[b]This is, of course, parallel with the pursuit measured in iters by Thutmose III (II, 479, l. 18). On the length of the iter, see II, 965, note, and Levy, *Recueil*, 15, 161–171.

[c]This inscription has been published by Dümichen (*Historische Inschriften*, I, 18, 19, and *Photographische Resultate*, 26), and de Rougé (*Inscriptions hiéroglyphiques*, 114–17); see also Lepsius, *Denkmäler*, Text, III, 173.

[d]This line is longer than the rest, and the lower end was covered in de Rougé's day. His publication therefore omits the end from here on, but makes no note of the loss.

[e]Lit., "*are not.*" This phrase is thus parallel with the much-discussed phrase applied to Israel: "*his seed is not.*" (III, 604.)

of Upper and Lower Egypt, Lord of the Two Lands, Usermare-Meriamon, [11]victorious king, conscious of his might, ruler treading ⌜—⌝, repelling the Nine Bows, taking captive the Meshwesh, who are made heaps; their chief[a] [12]is fettered before his (Pharaoh's) horses, his son, his wife, his family are slain, their children and their stuff upon their backs [13]while coming, subjecting themselves to his valor; like a bull with ready horn, he thrusts, becoming that which his father, Amon-Re grants him, destroying [14]his —, King Ramses III, ruler, giving breath to Egypt, so that they sit under the shadow [15]of his might, beautiful when appearing upon the throne of Atum; his [⌜form⌝] is like Re over the shadows, great in might, the rampart of this land, it acclaims and it jubilates [16](over) his valor.

**104.** Lo, this Good God, the august, divine youth, who came forth from Re, beautiful as a child, like the son of Isis, [17]Sutekh, valiant, strong-armed, like [his] f[ather], Montu, the white and red crown, and the etef-crown are upon his head . . . . . . . [18]. . mighty of arm in drawing the bow.[b] When he beholds millions before him like a flood, (he) charges into the multitude, [19]repelling the invader; they are laid low on his right and his left; overthrowing the Temeh, desolating the Meshwesh, [20]causing them to cease trampling the boundaries of Egypt, King Ramses III, sole lord, making his boundary as far as he desires, putting [21]fear and terror in the heart of the Asiatics, mighty Lion, plundering his every adversary, taking captive the lands of the Nine Bows, overthrowing them; a — tempest, [22]he comes up behind his adversaries; they ⌜hear⌝ his roaring like Baal in heaven; his august father, Amon-Re gives [23]the lands of the Nine Bows to him . . . . lord of strength, destroying the name of the Meshwesh forever and ever, King Ramses III, given life, like Re, forever.

**105.** [24]Year 11, fourth month of the third season (twelfth month), day $10(+x)$,[c] of King Ramses III. Beginning[d] of the victory of Egypt, [25]which the victorious king established;[e] who receives acclamation, who exercises the kingship of Re, enlarging Egypt, repelling

---

[a]This chief, Keper by name, is counted in the enumeration, § 111; see also § 97, note.

[b]Lit., "*in drawing (stretching out) when bearing the bow.*"

[c]Not more than 20.

[d]The form is not the usual one here, and another rendering is possible.

[e]Or: "*recorded.*"

the Nine Bows, setting terror in every land. It was [26]the sole lord who made heaven and earth from the origin of the world, Amon-Re, king of gods, the mighty Bull, with ready horns. Lo, the heart of this god who created the earth, inclined to establish [27]the boundaries of Egypt, with great power. He chose a lord, whom he created, [28]begotten, the issue of his limbs, a divine boy, an august youth, [29]great in might, strong-armed, full of plans, brave, lord of counsels, firm-hearted, ready in [30]designs, wise in life, like Thoth, taking account like Shu, son of Re, Usermare-Meriamon, [31]egg that came forth from Re, Ramses, Ruler of Heliopolis, youthful, valiant lord, to whom was assigned [32]victory from birth, the hero of great — like Montu, who has commanded him to crush [33]the lands, to lay them low, to repel them from Egypt. Montu and Sutekh are with [him in] [34]every fray, Anath (*ᶜnṯ*) and Astarte (*ᶜ-s-ṯy-r ᵓ-ṯ*) are his[a] shield. Amon judges [35]his speech, he turns not himself back, bearing the sword of Egypt over the Asiatics. He is the example of every land to[b] ———.

*Scene*[c]

**106.** Battle with the Libyans. The Egyptian heavy infantry, with sword and shield, preceded by the archers, all in faultless line, have thrown into confusion the Libyans, among whom Egyptian officers leap forward for the hand-to-hand fray. Ramses III has dismounted from his chariot and binds Libyan captives;[d] by his waiting chariot are his officers and bodyguard.

The inscriptions are the following:

*Before the King*

Good God, [great] in victory, lord of might, seizing every land, encompassing the lands, — — — to seek them that transgress his bound-

[a]The ancient artist has inserted the pronoun in the wrong place, as belonging to Astarte.

[b]Both Dümichen and de Rougé have omitted something at the end of the line, or more probably omitted the last line.

[c]First pylon, rear (west) side of projection, outside of north wall, lowest row; Baedeker's *Egypt*, 1902, 303; unpublished; I had a photograph by Weigall and another by Beato.

[d]This portion will be found summarily published from Beato's photograph in Maspero, *Struggle of the Nations*, 473.

ary, charging into —, slaying hundreds of thousands; before whom none stands; he is like Baal in his hour (of wrath). He rages like a hawk among the birdlets and the ⌜doves⌝ (*šfw*); valiant upon the battlefield, fighting hand-to-hand upon his feet, seizing the chiefs with his two hands; (even) King Ramses III.

*Over Captives*

Barbarians (*Ḫ ᵓ š· tyw*), whom his majesty took as living captives, 2,052. Slain in their place, 2,175.[a]

*Over the King's Horses*

Great first span of his majesty (named): "Beloved-of-Amon," of the great stable of Usermare-Meriamon (Ramses III).

*Over Officers*

Charioteers — —[b] of his majesty, who are favorites of the Good God.

*Scene*[c]

**107.** Ramses in his chariot, supported by his chariotry, charges the discomfited Libyans. The Egyptians are supported by archers, who shoot the Libyans from the walls of two neighboring Egyptian fortresses.

The inscriptions, which are badly weathered and broken, are these:

*Over the King*

King . . . . . . great in might, slaying the Meshwesh, smitten and overthrown before his horses . . . . . .[d]

*Over the Horses*

Great first span of his majesty (named): "Victory-in-Thebes."

---

[a]These numbers are corroborated by § 111, where they are itemized.

[b]Determinative of men.

[c]East half of north wall, outside of first court, lower row; unpublished; Baedeker's *Egypt*, 1902, 303. I had a photograph by Weigall.

[d]The remainder (seven short lines) is badly weathered and not wholly legible on the photograph, but all that is clear consists solely of the conventional epithets of the Pharaoh.

*Over Fortresses*

— of the Meshwesh who came into Egypt ⌜—⌝ ⌜before⌝ . . . . . .[a]

*In One Fortress*

Hatsho (*Ḥ ꜣ t-š ꜥ t*[b]).

*Scene*[c]

**108.** Ramses III steps into his chariot, dragging Libyan captives, whom he grasps by the hair.

An inscription[d] over the horses reads:

The Good God, Set, when he appears . . . . . He hath — the hearts of the Meshwesh, their mighty men are —, ⌜seized⌝ —, pinioned before his horses. His terror ⌜—⌝ diffuses through their limbs, and his fear penetrates their members. Amon-Re is with him ⌜against them⌝, to lay them low, overthrown at the fame of him, (even) Ramses III.

*Scene*[e]

**109.** Ramses III, accompanied by two sunshade-bearers and an adjutant officer, inspects three lines of captives brought up by three Egyptian officers.

The inscriptions are these:

*Before Middle Row*

[Utterance of Pharaoh to the —], commander in chief of the army, king's-son: "Say to the vanquished chief of the Meshwesh: 'See how thy name is obliterated forever and ever. Thy mouth hath ceased con-

---

[a]The remainder (consisting of as much again) is broken by a joint in the masonry along which the horizontal line of text runs.

[b]See § 102. The determinative is a small circle, both here and in § 102; ignoring the *t*, which does not mean much in this period (other late examples of "*sand*" written with *t* are known), we should have a "*House of Sand*." It is evident that the Meshwesh invasion had reached and invested this fortress, which Ramses III is here pictured as relieving.

[c]East half of north wall, outside of first court, lower row; unpublished; Baedeker's *Egypt*, 1902, 303. I had a photograph by Weigall.

[d]Unpublished.

[e]East half of north wall, outside of first court, lower row; unpublished; Baedeker's *Egypt*, 1902, 303. I had photograph by Weigall.

tradiction at the mention of Egypt, by the might of my father, the lord of gods. . . . . . . .'"

*Over Officer*

"See how Pharaoh hath obliterated thy name forever. Thy mouth hath ceased contradiction at the mention of Egypt."[a]

*Scene*[b]

110. King Ramses III, enthroned, with two sunshade-bearers behind him, addresses a prince of rank and his two viziers, the court and leaders of the army, while two lines of captive Meshwesh, preceded by the collected hands severed from the slain, are presented to him. Over the whole is the long inscription of fifty lines translated above (§§ 103–5). The other inscriptions are these:

*Before the King*

Utterance of his majesty to the hereditary prince, and the two viziers: "Behold ye, the many good things which Amon-Re, king of gods, has done for Pharaoh, L. P. H., his child, ——— [his] dues, his possessions, his cattle, the plunder which Egypt carried away, slaying — — — — —." The Pharaoh [⌜recorded⌝] them victoriously in his own handwriting.

*Over the Viziers*

Utterance of the hereditary prince and the two viziers who are in the presence of his majesty, praising this Good God, Lord of the Two Lands, Usermare-Meriamon (Ramses III): "Thou art Re, shining like him. When thou risest, the people live. Thy strength is mighty, overthrowing the Nine Bows; kindly disposed toward Egypt, bringing victory. The might of Montu is mingled with thy limbs. Thy counsels abide, thy designs come to pass, for whom Amon finds — —, establishing the throne of Egypt, — — whom his heart loves, ruler, enduring in monuments — — he — for thee the kingdom. He hath made — — — as far as the Great Bend, beneath thy feet."

---

[a]The officer, who is the king's son, thus carries out the instructions of his father.

[b]First pylon, inside, facing first court, north tower. Published partially, but with the inscriptions complete, by Dümichen (*Historische Inschriften*, I, 26, 27).

*Over the Hands*

**111.** Total, 2,175[a] hands.

*Over the Libyans*

The captivity which the mighty sword of Pharaoh, L. P. H., carried away from the vanquished of the Meshwesh:

| | |
|---|---|
| Chiefs of the Meshwesh | 1 man[b] |
| Chieftains (ᶜ ᵓ) of the — enemy | 5 men |
| Meshwesh | 1,20[5][c] men |
| Youths | 152 |
| Boys | 131 |
| Total | 1,494 |
| Their wives | 342 women |
| Maids (*nfr·t*) | 65 |
| Girls | 151 |
| Total | 558 |

(Total) of the mighty sword of Pharaoh, as living captives: 2,052[d] various persons.

Those whom his majesty slew in their place were 2,175.

Their possessions:

| | |
|---|---|
| Cattle: bulls | 119(+*x*) |
| Swords of 5 cubits (length) | 115 |
| Swords of 3 cubits (length) | 124 |
| Bows | 603 |
| Chariots | 93[e] |
| Quivers | 2,310 |
| Spears | 92 |
| Horses of the Meshwesh, and asses | 183 |

---

[a]Corroborated by § 106, on the back of the first pylon, outside the first court.

[b]There is a reference to this "*chief*" (*wr*) in the inscription over the battle (§ 103, ll. 11, 12).

[c]The units are restored by calculating from the total given. The bulk of these prisoners, viz., 971, were enslaved, to care for herds in the vicinity of the battle (see Harris, 10, 8).

[d]This number is the correct sum-total of prisoners, male and female, above enumerated, and is corroborated by § 106.

[e]The units are uncertain, and may be increased; but 93 is a minimum, and 99 is a maximum.

*Scene*[a]

**112.** Ramses III, riding in his chariot, drives before him two lines of Libyan captives, and is greeted by a group of priests. Beside the horses trots the king's tame lion.

The inscriptions are the following:

*By the King*

Live the Good God, plenteous in valor, lord of might, confident in his strength . . . . . . . .[b]

*Over Upper Line*

Utterance of the leaders of the land of Meshwesh, who are pinioned before his majesty: "Great is thy might, O victorious king, Sun of Egypt . . . . . ."[b]

*Over Lower Line*

Utterance of the vanquished of Meshwesh, who are before his majesty: "Breath! Breath! O ruler, good and beautiful as king of Egypt."

*Over Priests*

Utterance of the prophets ————: ". . . . . . ."[c]

*Scene*[d]

**113.** Ramses III leads two lines of captive Libyans and presents them to Amon, who is seated in a chapel, with Mut standing behind him. The inscriptions before the divinities contain only the conventional promises usual in such scenes. The king boasts that in the strength of Amon, "*the* (singular) *Meshwesh was overthrown.*" Over the prisoners are the words: "*Utterance of the fallen of Meshwesh who are in the grasp of his majesty: . . . . . . . .*"[e]

---

[a]East half, north wall, outside of first court; lower row; unpublished; Baedeker's *Egypt*, 1902, 303. I had a photograph by Weigall.

[b]Only similar epithets.

[c]The usual epithets, without a single specific allusion.

[d]East half of north wall, outside of second court, lower row; unpublished; Baedeker's *Egypt*, 1902, 303. I had a photograph by Weigall.

[e]The usual prayer.

*Scene*[a]

**114.** A line of seven kneeling chiefs (one lost), with arms pinioned behind them; they are recognizable in features and costume, and by accompanying inscriptions, as follows:

1. Negro.

The chief of Kush the wretched.

2. Lost.

3. Negro. Inscription lost.

4. Libyan.

The chief of Libya.

5. Negro.

The chief of Terses (*Tw-r* ͗ *-ss*).

6. Libyan.

The chief of Meshwesh.

7. Negro.

The chief of Terew (*Ty-r* ͗ *y-w* ͗).

### V. THE SYRIAN WAR

**115.** The materials for this war are solely relief scenes, which are too meager to afford us more than a hint of its extent or character. The invasion from Asia Minor had broken the strength of the North-Syrian peoples. Ramses III therefore improved the opportunity to invade them. The reliefs show him storming no less than five strong cities. One of them is called "*the city of Amor*," with perhaps the name of the city lost at the end; two others are defended by Hittites; a fourth is surrounded by water, and is, therefore. thought to be Kadesh; the fifth stands on high ground, but offers no other characteristic by which it might be identified.

---

[a]Relief on the façade of the left wing of the pavilion; published by Champollion, *Monuments*, 202 = Rosellini, *Monumenti Storici*, 142 = Lepsius, *Denkmäler*, III, 209, *a;* pendant to the similar relief on the other wing (§ 129).

116. It is clear that Ramses III pushed down the Orontes as far as the Hittite frontier, and Shabtuna just south of Kadesh is mentioned in his geographical list (§ 131). But he apparently made no permanent conquests, and the campaign was evidently little more than a plundering expedition, though it may have been necessary for the preservation of the Pharaoh's Syrian possessions. The question of the date of this campaign will be found discussed in §§ 132, 133.

*Scene*[a]

117. The king assaults a Syrian fortress on foot; he has left his chariot, and shoots with the bow as he advances; before him are his bodyguard and Sherden mercenaries. The fortress rises in four successive battlements to a lofty citadel or tower in the middle, from which waves a triangular banner. Here stands the chief and his companions. The walls are manned with bearded Semites, one of whom offers incense to Ramses from the lowest battlement.

*Inscriptions*[b]

In the city: "*Amor*" (ʾ*-m-r* —); by a chief beseeching mercy: "*Utterance of the chief of the city of Amor.*" By the king, only the conventional phrases descriptive of his valor.

*Scene*[c]

118. The king standing in his chariot with uplifted sword, charges the chariotry of the Syrian enemy; before him Egyptian archers and heavy Sherden infantry are

---

[a]First court, north wall, behind pillars, lower row; unpublished; Baedeker's *Egypt* (German edition, 1897), 301. I had a photograph by Weigall.

[b]Unpublished, except the name of the city and the title of the chief, by Müller (*Asien und Europa*, 226, from notes by Eisenlohr). In my photograph the inscription in the city is concealed by a pillar.

[c]East half of north wall, outside of first court, upper row; first scene from east end; published by Champollion, *Monuments*, 228; the city also by Müller, *Asien und Europa*, 226.

assaulting a fortified city surrounded by water, evidently a moat. The scaling-ladders are up, and while some of the assaulting party attack the gate with axes, others have climbed the ladders, gained a footing on the ramparts, and are slaying the defenders. From the top of the wall an Egyptian trumpeter sounds the victory.[a]

*Scene*[b]

**119.** The king, having left his chariot, charges the Syrian enemy on foot, spear in hand. Behind him follow the chariotry and heavy infantry. The enemy are defending a walled city, which stands upon a hill. The short inscription (mutilated and very incorrectly published) contains the usual epithets of the king. It refers to enemy as "*Asiatics*" (*S*ṯ*ʾtyw*).

*Scene*[c]

**120.** The king in his chariot, with drawn bow, storms two fortresses. Behind him are his bodyguard and adjutants. The defenders of the strongholds, who fall in numbers before his attack, are Hittites. The scene, therefore, commemorates the capture of at least two Hittite walled towns in Syria. The name of one of the fortresses is given as "*Ereth*" (ʾ-*r*ʾ-ṯʾ).[d] The inscription over the king contains only the customary epithets extolling the king's valor. The name of the chariot horses is recorded as "*Victory-in-Thebes*."

---

[a]The two short inscriptions contain the usual epithets of the king, but they are excessively incorrect as published, and also fragmentary.

[b]East half of north wall, outside of first court, upper row; second scene from east end; published by Champollion, *Monuments*, 227; the city also by Müller, *Asien und Europa*, 225.

[c]First pylon, rear (west) side of projection outside of north wall, upper row; unpublished; Baedeker's *Egypt*, 1902, 303. I had a photograph by Weigall.

[d]So Daressy, *Recueil*, 19, 18; I could not discern the name on the photograph.

*Scene*[a]

121. The king, standing alone, receives three lines of Syrian (Semitic) prisoners, each headed by an Egyptian officer. The only inscription, that before the king, reads:

The king himself, he said to the hereditary prince, king's-scribe, commander in chief of the army, king's-son — —:[b] "Collect the captives whom the valor of Pharaoh, L. P. H., has taken, and place them [in] the offices in the house (*pr*) of Amon-Re, king of gods; (for) it was his hand which captured them."

*Scene*[c]

122. Riding in his chariot, with his tame lion trotting beside the horses, Ramses III drives before him two lines of Syrian (Semitic) captives. The inscriptions are these:

*Over King*

Good God, beautiful in his appearance, like Re, ———, coming in triumph — — —. His valor is mighty, he hath taken captive the lands of the Asiatics (*Sṯ·tyw*). . . . . . . .[d]

*Over Captives*

Utterance of the vanquished of every country who are before his majesty: "Breath from thee! O lord of Egypt, Sun of the Nine Bows! Thy father, Amon, hath put us beneath thy feet forever, that we may see and breathe the breath of life; that we may hail (*brk·n*)[e] his temple. Thou art our lord forever, like thy father, Amon. Every land is beneath thy feet, like Re, forever, O Lord of the Two Lands, Usermare-Meriamon."

---

[a]North wall, east end, outside, first court, upper row, third scene from east end (Baedeker's *Egypt*, 1902, 303); unpublished. I had a photograph by Weigall.

[b]Left vacant by the scribe; who was to be crown prince was not certain at this time!

[c]North wall, east end, outside first court, upper row, fourth scene from east end (Baedeker's *Egypt*, 1902, 303); unpublished. I had a photograph by Weigall.

[d]Customary epithets of the king.

[e]See also § 127.

*Scene*[a]

**123.** "Triumphal return of the king in his chariot, followed by two sunshade-bearers and his bodyguard; he drives before him three rows of prisoners—Libyans, Syrians, Peleset, etc.—whom he holds by cords, and is received by the rejoicing Egyptian grandees." The inscription over the king refers to "*the chiefs of the countries pinioned before him,*" but otherwise contains only the usual epithets. The horses are called: "*Great first span of his majesty (called): 'Repulser-of-the-Nine-Bows,' of the great stable of Usermare-Meriamon (Ramses III).*"

*Inscriptions over Grandees*[b]

Utterance of the —, the nobles, and the [lead]ers: "[Come] in peace, victorious king, Horus, rich in years. Thou hast seized the lands, the Nine Bows are fettered before thy horses, for thy father, Amon, hath assigned to thee [all lands] beneath thy feet."

*Scene*[c]

**124.** "The king stands in a balcony; behind him two sunshade-bearers, two fan-bearers, officers, and priests; Syrian captives are led before him in three rows," preceded by Egyptian officers and a group of nobles.

The inscriptions are these:

*Before the King*

Utterance of King Ramses III to the king's-children, magnates, ⌜—⌝ and attendants: "Hear ye my words, that I may cause you to know of the might of Amon, lord of eternity, since he crowned me as king, as

---

[a]First court, north wall, behind pillars, lower row; unpublished; Baedeker's *Egypt* (German edition, 1897), 302. I had a photograph by Weigall, but the speech of the grandees was cut off by a pillar.

[b]Only this greeting of the grandees is published by de Rougé, *Inscriptions hiéroglyphiques*, 127.

[c]First court, north wall, behind pillars, lower row; unpublished; Baedeker's *Egypt* (German edition, 1897), 301. I had a photograph by Weigall.

a divine youth, while I sat upon his throne victoriously. His hand abode with me, destroying ——— [those who invaded] my boundary were slain in their place. . . . . . . ."[a]

*Over the Nobles*[b]

Utterance of the king's-children, nobles, and leaders in praising this Good God, Lord of the Two Lands, Ramses III: "Thou art like Re when he [riseth], and thy dawning is like him at early morning. Mighty art thou, valiant in overthrowing the Nine Bows. The heart of Egypt is happy in possession of —. The might of Montu is diffused in thy limbs. . . . . . . ."[c]

*Scene*[d]

**125.** Ramses III leads two lines of Syrian (Semitic) captives; before him is an array of elaborate metallic vessels. He presents all to Amon, seated, with Khonsu standing behind him in a chapel.

The inscriptions with the gods are as usual and contain no reference to the character of the captives. The king's speech alludes to the war thus: "*I took captive the peasant-serfs of* —;" but the name of the land is lost. The captives are designated as "*The chiefs of every country who are in the grasp of his majesty.*"

*Scene*[e]

**126.** Before Amon enthroned with Mut and Khonsu behind him, the king leads by cords two bearded chiefs. A rich display of splendid vessels stands before the king. The inscriptions are these:

---

[a]Here follows only a long series of the usual epithets describing the king's valor.

[b]The first of the group is the king's eldest son. In the photograph I discern before him the words: "*Hereditary prince* (*rpˁ·ty*), *king's-scribe, commander* [*in chief of the army*] ———."

[c]Similar adulation continues, with no specific allusions to the nature of the event.

[d]North wall, east end, outside first court, upper row, fifth scene from east end (Baedeker's *Egypt*, 1902, 303); unpublished. I had a photograph by Weigall.

[e]At the door of the treasury of the temple; published by Dümichen, *Historische Inschriften*, I, 28, 29; and *Photographische Resultate*, 28, 29.

*Over Amon*

Utterance of Amon, lord of Thebes, to his son, Lord of the Two Lands, Usermare-Meriamon: "Come thou in peace, O Good God, lord of might, captor of the Nine Bows, at thy return having crushed the countries. Thou hast slain their chiefs, who were beginning to trespass thy boundaries, they fell by thy blade. The countries that knew not Egypt come to thee, (with) their tribute upon their backs, from the victories which I have decreed to thee forever."

*Before the King*

The king himself, presenting the tribute to Amon from the great chiefs of every country, being: silver, gold, lapis lazuli, malachite, all (kinds of) costly stones without limit, from the booty which his majesty carried off, from that which his valiant sword captured; placed before (his) august father, Amon-Re, lord of Thebes, according as he gave to [him] all valor.

*Over the Chiefs*

**127.** Utterance of the wretched chief of Amor (*ʾ-m-r ʾ*), and the wretched, vanquished chief of Libya: "Breath! O Good ruler, strong-armed, great in might. Thou art verily the son of Amon, thy form is like him. He has assigned to thee every land, together overthrown beneath thy feet. Thou art like the sun, when he rises; men live at thy appearance. Give to us the breath, which thou givest, that we may hail[a] thy double serpent-diadem, that we may speak of thy might to our sons' sons. They are brought low through the fear of thee, of which we tell them; O thou Sun over Egypt, like the one which is in heaven, King Ramses III."

*Scene*[b]

**128.** "The king leads two rows of prisoners, before the Theban triad."

*Inscription over King*[c]

Utterance of the king, Lord of the Two Lands, Usermare-Meriamon, before his father, Amon-Re, lord of heaven, ruler of gods: "I went upon

[a]*B ʾ-r ʾ-k ʾ*=Semitic, ברך, "bend the knee;" see Bondi, *Lehnwörter*, 40, 41. See also § 122.

[b]First court, north wall, behind pillars, lower row; Baedeker's *Egypt* (German edition, 1897), 302.

[c]Only the inscriptions over the king and prisoners are published; Rougé, *Inscriptions hiéroglyphiques*, 127, 128; letter by Piehl, *Inscriptions*, I, CXLVII, f. A.

thy way, I came at thy command, all thy designs come to pass, thou causest the — of the countries to — for fear[a] of me, overthrown in their place. I cut [them] down, slain at the fame of me. I carried off their people, all their possessions, all the splendid costly stone of their country; they are placed before thee, O lord of gods. Give to thy beloved, grant thou the participation of thy divine ennead in the might of thy sword.[b] I have carried them away: the males thereof to fill thy storehouse; their women to be subjects of thy temple. Thou causedst that I make my boundary as far as I desired. My hand was not repulsed; behold, the lands praised my might like a strong-armed one before them, by the might of thy sword, O my august father. Thy terror and thy — overthrew —."

*Over Prisoners*

Utterance of the chiefs of all countries who are in the grasp of his majesty: "Thou art Re. . . . . . ."[c]

*Scene*[d]

**129.** A line of seven captive chiefs kneeling with arms pinioned behind them. Their racial peculiarities are clearly depicted in features and costumes, and also indicated by accompanying inscriptions.

*Inscriptions*

1. Hittite.

The wretched chief of Kheta as living captive.

2. Amorite.

The wretched chief of Amor.

3. Asiatic.

Chieftain (ᶜ ᵓ) of the foe of Thekel (*Ṯ*ʾ ᵓ *-kw-r* ᵓ).

---

[a]Or possibly: "*because I was ready for battle.*"

[b]The other gods are to receive only as much of the booty of Amon's sword as he permits.

[c]Here follow the conventional epithets of praise.

[d]Relief on the façade of the right wing of the pavilion of Medinet Habu; published by Champollion, *Monuments*, 203 = *Notices descriptives*, I, 720, 721 (see also *ibid.*, I, 709) = Rosellini, *Monumenti Storici*, 143 = Lepsius, *Denkmäler*, III, 209, *b;* Mariette, *Voyage dans la haute Egypte*, II, 51; pendant to the similar relief on the other wing (§ 114).

4. Sherden.

Sherden (*Š*ꜣ*-r*ꜣ*-d*ꜣ*-n*ꜣ) of the sea.

5. Bedwi.[a]

Chieftain (ᶜꜣ) of the foe of Sha[⌜su⌝] (*Š*ꜣ-—).

6. Teresh.

Teresh (*Ty-w-r*ꜣ*-š*ꜣ) of the sea.

7. Head lost.

Chieftain of the Pe[leset] (*Pw* ————).

*Scene*[b]

130. Amon standing at the right extends to the king the sword, and leads to him 126 captives of the conventional form, each bearing an oval containing the name of a conquered city or country. The king smites with the war-mace a group of the enemy, whom he holds by the hair.

The inscriptions are these:

*Over Amon*

Utterance of Amon-Re, lord of Thebes: "O my son, of my body, my beloved, Lord of the Two Lands, Usermare-Meriamon, rich in years like Atum — overthrowing his enemies. Thou hast slain every land that began to trespass thy borders, in thy grasp. Thou hast taken every land. . . . . . Thou hast — him on the north of him; the great fame of thee, it has encompassed every land; the fear of thee, it has penetrated the countries. Thou art like Horus over the Two Lands, the son of the bow-peoples. I magnify[c] thy victories, I set the fear of thee in the hearts of the lands of Haunebu. Thy mighty blade is in

---

[a]See Müller, *Asien und Europa*, 139 and 393. This chieftain is therefore to be connected with the war against the Seirites (§ 404).

[b]First pylon, left hand (southern) tower, front, left half; published by Dümichen (*Historische Inschriften*, I, 11, 12), but with only the upper portion of the geographical list, and omitting the king's figure; list entire by Daressy (*Recueil*, XX, 116–119, and *ibid.*, XXI, 30–39) and partially by Maspero (*Zeitschrift für ägyptische Sprache*, 1882, Pl. VI). A similar scene at Karnak shows Ramses III receiving from Amon the countries of "*Retenu*" and the "*southern countries*," while he "[*cuts off*] *the heads of the rebels*" before the god.

[c]Dümichen's lacuna is not in the text (photograph).

their limbs, thy majesty strikes[a] them down, thy hands cut off the head of thy enemy. I make ⌜thee⌝ lord of —, the Sand-dwellers [⌜come⌝], bowing down to thy name. Dreadful is thy serpent-crest among them; the war-mace in thy right hand, the — in thy left hand. Thou hast subdued the hearts of the rebels; the chiefs come to thee, bearing tribute —, every good product of their countries. I give to thee Egypt with good things, the bow-peoples as subjects of thy palace. The South comes to thee in fear, and the North bowing down to thy fame. I open for thee the ways of Punt, with myrrh and incense for thy serpent-diadem. I lead thee, and my strength is in thy limbs, to destroy the lands that invade thee. . . . ."[b]

*By the Victims*

Smiting the chiefs of all countries.

131. The geographical names borne by the captives (who are alternately Semite and Hittite in features)[c] are largely taken from the list of Ramses II at Karnak. In the portions not so borrowed[d] such a name as Shabtuna (*S*ᵓ*-bw-dw-n*ᵓ, No. 75)[e] indicates the Amorite valley, as we should expect.[f] The insertion of such names as Carchemish, Mitanni, and Arrapachitis[g] shows clearly the decorative character of the list. The most interesting name is Levi-El (*R*ᵓ*-wy-*ᵓ*-r*ᵓ), which is parallel with Jacob-El and Joseph-El, which Daressy would identify with Shiloh.[h]

---

[a]Read the *f* as determinative, misunderstood from the hieratic. "*Majesty*" is perhaps to be read "*mace*."

[b]The conclusion contains only the conventional promises.

[c]Except 8 (at the ends of the rows) who are Negroes; and the names they bear are taken from the list on the other pylon (§ 138).

[d]The entire list of Ramses II at Karnak is not yet excavated, or, if now excavated during the recent work at Karnak, is not yet published, so that the extent of the borrowing is not yet certain. See Daressy, *Recueil*, XX, 119.

[e]See III, 310, note.

[f]We might expect some places from the Edomite war (§ 404) also, but there is not space here for such discussion.

[g]See Müller, *Asien und Europa*, 227.

[h]See Daressy, *Recueil*, XXI, 37, 38; on the list as a whole, see Müller (*Asien und Europa*, 227 f.), who had only Dümichen's incomplete publication, and Sayce, *Bulletin de la Société Khédiviale de Géographie*, 1892, 661.

### BLESSING OF PTAH[a]

132. This document is the pendant of the one of the year 11 (§§ 93–99). It is dated in the year 12, and the presence of the date would indicate that it records some specific occurrence; but it is difficult to determine what this occurrence was from our inscription, as it is copied from that of Ramses II at Abu Simbel (III, 394–414).

133. This brings up the whole question of the date of the Amorite war. The arrangement of the records in the Medinet Habu temple in chronological order from rear to front is so evident that the location of those reporting the Amorite war is of the first importance. We find them all (with one exception) on walls in front of—that is, later than—the second pylon (bearing records of the year 8), and among records of the Libyan war of the year 11. Had the Amorite campaign immediately followed the defeat of the sea-peoples in the year 8, it is certain that the very full records of that year would have contained some reference to it. But the long row of scenes depicting the campaign of the year 8 (outside north wall) contains nothing from the Amorite war, and the arrangement[b] of the whole wall clearly indicates that the Amorite war is at least as late as the year 11. But as the second Libyan war occurred in that year, the Amorite war would have probably been later. We have to remember,

[a]Inscription at Medinet Habu temple of Ramses III, cut into the front of the first pylon, on the south (left) tower, just at the left of the entrance. It exactly matches in form and size the inscription of year 11 (§§ 93–99) on the right of the entrance. Published: relief at top and list, by Champollion, *Monuments*, 204; Rosellini, *Monumenti Storici*, 123; Lepsius, *Denkmäler*, III, 209, *c* (see also, *ibid.*, Text, III, 170); complete by Dümichen (*Historische Inschriften*, I, 7–10); and Rougé (*Inscriptions hiéroglyphiques*, II, 131–38, but without the relief at the top). The geographical list at the top also, by Daressy (*Recueil*, XX, 120).

[b]The reliefs begin at the rear with three scenes from the war of year 5; proceed toward the front with seven scenes from the war of year 8; and conclude at the front with a group of scenes from the Libyan war of year 11, and the Amorite war.

however, that on the treasury in the rear of the temple interior (that is, the oldest portion of the building) there is a relief (§§ 126, 127) showing the king of Amor as a captive. But he is here in company with a Libyan king, and as we cannot suppose that the Amorite war occurred as early as the year 5 (first Libyan war), it is evident that this Libyan king was taken in the Libyan war of year 11, when Ramses III actually did capture a Libyan king (§ 97), whereas no such capture is mentioned in the records of the year 5. Thus this relief on the treasury again connects the Amorite war with the Libyan war of year 11. They must thus have occurred close together, from the testimony of the reliefs.

**134.** Returning now to our monument, copied, as we have stated, from an Abu Simbel stela of Ramses II, we find that the slight changes in it, necessary to suit the times of Ramses III, are not in favor of the above conclusion. Especially is this true in one case, where Ramses II's stela refers to the Hittites thus, (Ptah speaks): "*I have made for thee the land of Kheta into subjects of thy palace*" (III, 410). Here Ramses III's redactor has changed "*Kheta*" into "*every land;*" although, according to the reliefs and the lists, Ramses III must have fought the Hittites. The relief at the top of our stela contains a list of names of three African and ten Syrian towns, accompanying thirteen Asiatic (sic!) prisoners, and Müller[a] refers the latter without hesitation to the Amorite war. The presence of the African names with Asiatic figures would lead one to suspect this list to be nothing more than decorative. Against this stela one must now weigh the evidence of the reliefs, which seems to me conclusive for dating the Amorite war in or shortly after the year 11. This conclusion is thus reached rather in spite of than because of our stela.

[a]Müller, *Asien und Europa*, 394 ("S. 227").

**135.** All changes in the version of Ramses II have been indicated in the footnotes to the translation of the Abu Simbel stela (III, 394–414), which may therefore serve in place of a repetition of the document here.

The relief at the top shows Ramses III, "*smiting the chiefs of all countries*" in the presence of Ptah-Tatenen, who presents to him a sword, and leads up thirteen Asiatic captives, represented in the conventional form with ovals, the first three of which contain the names of African places.

## VI. THE NUBIAN WAR

**136.** The materials for this war, like those of the Amorite war, are solely relief scenes. These permit no definite conclusions regarding it. Nubia had now been so thoroughly Egyptianized that Ramses III's war or wars there were doubtless confined to quelling unimportant insurrections on the extreme southern frontier, or to expeditions against the outlying tribes on the east of Nubia.

Besides the material below, see also the Nubian chiefs represented with the Meshwesh chief captured in the year 11, on the pavilion (§ 114). There are also unpublished scenes from this war on the rear (west) side of the temple (Baedeker's *Egypt*, 1902, 302).

### SLAYING OF PRISONERS BEFORE AMON-RE[a]

**137.** This relief shows Ramses III "*slaying the chiefs of all countries*" in the presence of Amon-Re, who extends to him a sword at the same time leading to him a list of 124 captives, depicted in the usual form, each with an oval con-

[a]Relief scene on the façade of the Medinet Habu temple, right (northern) tower, front, first pylon; published by Champollion, *Notices descriptives*, I, 725–28 (list partially); Dümichen (*Historische Inschriften*, I, 16–18, without king's figure, the victims and accompanying inscriptions) and Rougé (*Inscriptions hiéroglyphiques*, 109, 110, with same omissions and without list). Rougé has incorrectly appended to the long inscription in this scene twelve lines, from the back of the same pylon-tower, belonging to the war of the eleventh year, ll. 19–30; Dümichen

taining the name of each place or country symbolized.[a] Over the god is a poetic inscription of eighteen lines, taken from the similar scene among the Karnak reliefs (III, 116) of Seti I, who appropriated it from the Building Inscription of Amenhotep III (II, 891, 892). It had meantime been expanded by Seti I (III, 113–18); his version was now slightly elaborated by Ramses III.[b] His additions, however, contain nothing of historical importance. Under the god's arm is an inscription, which has now become stereotyped in this position. Each strophe begins: "*I cause them to see thy majesty, etc.;*" and the whole is taken from Thutmose III's Hymn of Victory (II, 658 ff.), following the example of Seti I and Ramses II.

**138.** The list of 124 geographical names is largely a compilation from the lists of Thutmose III, and other earlier sources, and therefore of little historical importance, save in restoring the earlier lists where they are fragmentary. They are chiefly African countries;[c] but some names repeated on the other pylon (§131) are evidently Asiatic.[d]

---

(*Historische Inschriften*, I, 22, 23); also by Lepsius (*Denkmäler*, III, 210, *a;* see also *ibid.*, Text, III, 171). None of these publications has the complete geographical list, which has been published by Daressy (*Recueil*, XX, 113–16). I also had a good photograph by Schroeder & Cie., Zürich.

[a]An unpublished scene on the left (south) tower of the pavilion shows the king "presenting two rows of captives before Amon" (Baedeker's *Egypt*, 1902, 298). The lower row are Libyans, but, according to the inscriptions (Champollion, *Notices descriptives*, I, 722 f.), they also include Nubians, for the king says: "*Thou givest to me the land of Kush.*" Otherwise the inscriptions contain nothing of historical importance.

[b]The beginning of the same inscription is used again by Ramses III accompanying a duplicate of this scene in the great Karnak temple (Lepsius, *Denkmäler*, III, 207, *d*). The geographical list, however, is limited to fifteen names, chiefly the Nine Bows.

[c]The arrangement in Karnak places the southern countries on the southern pylon-tower; but this arrangement was not retained by Ramses III, who places this African list on the northern pylon-tower.

[d]The inscription over the god says: "*I cause to come to thee the chiefs of the southern countries, with their tribute and their children upon their backs, every good product of their country.*" This would indicate that the list should be African; but see the further content of the poem (III, 116).

## MEDINET HABU TEMPLE CALENDAR[a]

**139.** This, the most elaborate temple calendar which has survived from the pre-Ptolemaic age, contains a number of historic data of the greatest interest. It begins with a long speech[b] by Ramses III, addressed to Amon. The king offers the usual praise to the god, and continues with an enumeration of his own good works for him in Thebes. These are in general those which we have more in detail in Papyrus Harris. In mentioning the feasts it is evident that the Medinet Habu temple was their center rather than Karnak. Of the property of the Medinet Habu temple, the king says to Amon:

**140.** I have put its possessions into writing, that I might inclose them in thy grasp. I made for thee thy property lists, that they might be [17]forever and [ever] in thy name. I offered to thee the Two Lands as thy portion, according as thou gavest them to me since I was born.

**141.** This is followed by matters of historical importance:

I built strongholds (*bḫn·w*) in thy name in Egypt [18]and [⌜all⌝] lands, likewise the land of Asia. I taxed them for their impost every year, every town by its name, gathered together, bearing their tribute, to bring them [to] thy ka, O lord of gods [19]. . . . . . . I made these things by my might, from that which my ka created,[c] from my captures [20]in the land of the Negroes, and in the land of Zahi (*Ḏ*ˀ*-hy*). There was naught therein for any (other) god, but I gave them to thy ka, that thou mightest be satisfied therewith, for thou art my divine father, heir of eternity, traversing everlastingness as lord of gods. [21]Set me in thy heart at all times, let the land abide like Thebes, thine accustomed house. . . . . . [22]Let thy provision be brought into its midst and all plenty into the chapel . . . . . . multiplying its children, that they may be prophets and divine fathers for thee, to call [⌜for⌝] thee for thy food, [23]to praise thee;

---

[a]On the outside of the south wall; it has never been properly or exhaustively published; the publications will be found in the notes on §§ 139–45.

[b]Daressy, *Recueil*, XIX, 15–17.

[c]The "*generations*" or "*classes*" of youth and captives classified for service are constantly said to be "*created*" (*sḫpr*) by the king. So Papyrus Harris often. The exact meaning is often "*brought up, trained, educated*," and again, "*organized*."

others ⌈for⌉ the administration ⌈of⌉ the work, in order to supply all daily offerings. I have collected for the herds of all small cattle, fields, domains of high land [24]⌈— —⌉ gardens of — — wild fowl descending into the pool; in order to make festive thy oblations, with plenty. . . I — all — the captivity of my sword. Every land overflowed [25]⌈————⌉ gold, silver, and the possessions of all lands went into it, that my house might be for thee an august sanctuary, with thy majesty in the midst thereof — forever.

The king's speech then concludes with further praise and prayer.

142. Following this inscription is the act of establishment[a] of the festal offerings of the temple. It begins:

Year 12, first month of the third season (ninth month) [twenty-sixth[b] day, the day] of the king's [coronation] upon the Horus-throne, when he received the regalia of his father, Re.

143. The new calendar of feasts was thus introduced on the anniversary of the king's coronation in his twelfth year at the completion of the temple of Medinet Habu and the termination of his wars. The act mentions several new feasts founded by Ramses III, to one of which are appended the words:

Which Ramses III founded for his father, Amon-Re, king of gods, from the [victories] which the — might of Pharaoh won, among the fallen of — in the year —,[c] third month of the third season (eleventh month) [day] —.

144. Now follows the great calendar[d] enumerating all

[a]So Daressy (*Recueil*, XIX, 17), but the act itself is very mutilated; he publishes only the opening line, as above, and the names of two feasts mentioned by the document.

[b]The day is known from the calendar following.

[c]Evidently the numeral 11 is to be inserted, as he was out on the campaign of that year in the eleventh month.

[d]Dümichen, *Aegyptische Kalender-Inschriften*, Taf. I–XXXIV; and *Die kalendarischen Opferfestlisten im Tempel von Medinet Habu;* Brugsch, *Thesaurus*, II, 364; Greene, *Fouilles à Thèbes*, IV–VI.

the old and new annual feasts of Amon, and to each feast is attached a list of the various offerings to be presented at that feast. These are so elaborate and extensive that they cover a large part of the southern wall of the temple. The particular treasury or source of income from which each offering or group of offerings shall be taken is also indicated. It begins with the daily offerings for each of the 365 days, followed by the eight "*feasts of heaven,*" which were at monthly, half-monthly, or shorter intervals. This introduces the chief section of the calendar, the portion which treats of the annual feasts. As of prime importance to the king, the feast of his coronation on the twenty-sixth of Pakhons (ninth month) heads the list. It lasted one day, but was later lengthened by the king to no less than twenty days.[a] All the other annual feasts which now follow are in proper chronological order, beginning with the rising of Sirius on New Year's Day, and proceeding with the other three traditional feasts[a] of the first month. On the nineteenth of the second month (Paophi) began the next feast, that of Opet, the greatest in the Theban calendar. It continued under Ramses III till the twelfth of the third month, a total of twenty-four days.[c] The list is preserved only as far as the seventeenth or eighteenth of the fifth month, but, besides the above, it contains seventeen more annual feast days, making in all no less than forty-five annual feast days during the first 138 days of the year; that is, almost one annual feast every three days, or more than 120 in the year,

[a]See Papyrus Harris, § 237.

[b]Wag, Thoth, and the "*Great Going Forth of Osiris.*

[c]In Thutmose III's day it was eleven days long (see my remarks, *Zeitschrift für ägyptische Sprache*, 37,126), so that it has been prolonged thirteen days since his reign; in Papyrus Harris it is twenty-seven days long, so that it was extended at least three days by Ramses III.

at the same rate.[a] This is not including the minor "*feasts of heaven*" which were connected with each month.

**145.** Among the names of the new feasts there is one of historical importance in the fifth month (the day is not given), called: "*Slaying-of-the-Meshwesh*."[b]

The lists of objects offered are precisely those enumerated in Papyrus Harris, and an exhaustive comparison would throw much light on the lists in the papyrus.

---

## ACT OF ENDOWMENT OF THE TEMPLES OF KHNUM[c]

**146.** To Sethe's arguments that this document was issued by Ramses III, may be added the remark of de Rougé that the neighboring fragment,[d] containing the name of Ramses III, is of the same style. Sethe has shown[e] that the "*field*," regularly referred to is the "dodekaschoinos," the field of twelve schoinoi belonging to Khnum, which extended from Assuan to Takompso.[f] This land is by this document of

---

[a]The rate for the remainder of the year is not likely to have decreased much, for Ramses III later prolonged the feast of his coronation to twenty days; it fell in the ninth month.

[b]Dümichen, *Aegyptische Kalender-Inschriften*, XXXIII.

[c]Blocks built into the quay on the island of Elephantine; published by de Rougé, *Inscriptions hiéroglyphiques*, 256–58; de Morgan, *Catalogues des monuments*, I, 118, *c*, 119, *d;* see Spiegelberg, *Studien und Materialen*, 94–98; also translated by Sethe, *Untersuchungen*, II, 27, 28. I have mostly followed Sethe in the above translation, with some few additions from Rougé's copy, which was not used by Sethe.

[d]This fragment bearing the name of Ramses III (Rougé, *Inscriptions hiéroglyphiques*, 258), records his command "*to cleanse all the temples of the South from all abomination . . . . . to inspect the treasuries and granaries, to protect the people and herds, to double* ———, *to bring in truth and to banish falsehood, to cause lying to be an abomination; to build* ———."

[e]Sethe, *Untersuchungen*, II, 28.

[f]According to an inscription in Maharraka, found by Sethe in one of Lepsius' notebooks, Takompso must be at least as far south as the former town, so that Sethe's ably defended thesis confining the dodekaschoinos to the cataract between Assuan and Philæ is thus disproved for the Græco-Roman age at least, and probably also for the earlier time. See Sethe, *Zeitschrift für ägyptische Sprache*, 41, 60, 62.

Ramses III conveyed for all time to Khnum. That this was a new gift the late copy of Zoser's donation of the same land shows to be impossible. Hence we here see Ramses III confirming an old possession of the god, which confirmation he, of course, viewed as a gift, precisely as we find him doing in Papyrus Harris (§ 222). The enactments of the document, making the land given, as well as its inhabitants and products, free from taxation by the crown, or any government requisition by the vizier, are most important. They confirm the statements in Genesis (47:21–26) that the priests were not taxed.

*Date*

**147.** [1]———— . . . . . . . .[a]

[3]Decree issued at the court on this day to the vizier, the princes, the companions, the courts of justice,[b] the mayors commanding settlements [⌜and all royal officers; that the inhabitants of this [4]field be not taken for enforced labor⌝] by an officer of the royal estate or any people sent on a commission to the field; that their ships be not stopped by any patrol; that their ships be not taken by (lawful) seizure, in order to carry out any commission of the Pharaoh, by any people sent on a commission [to the field] ———— [5]———— [⌜that there be not taken⌝] any ⌜—⌝[c] belonging to them by (lawful) seizure, by robbery, or ⌜—⌝, by any mayor, any inspector, any officer sent on a commission to the field. As for anyone who shall do it, the ⌜—⌝[c] which he took shall be collected from him ———— [6]————.

**148.** [As for the] fishermen, fowlers, natron-gatherers, salt-gatherers, all who pursue their callings for the temples of the father[d] of all gods and goddesses, there shall be no ⌜procedure⌝ against them by [any] one ———— [7]————.

**149.** [As for] — — — — — [any] honey-collectors, any one belonging to a temple, against whom some one shall transgress, and he shall

[a]That the lost beginning contained the date is evident from the mention of "*this day*" in l. 3.

[b]Lit., "*the courts that hear (cases)*."

[c]Sethe suggests "Stück Vieh."

[d]Khnum.

say: "A certain inspector or a certain officer is the one who has transgressed against me," he shall ⸢see to it⸣ that the damage accruing shall be made good, that the first, which shall be secretly taken from the temple, shall be made good to the god. And there shall not be collected ——— 8——— [⸢but there shall be taken⸣] all that they have, ⸢besides⸣ what they cultivate for themselves, for their divine offerings.[a]

150. And no overseer of cattle, nor any one shall take a beast of the herd, to give it to another as ⸢food⸣ or by robbery ——— 9——— to ⸢—⸣ it from him secretly likewise ⸢— —⸣. And no future vizier shall make requisition upon any prophet of these temples, for silver, gold, leather, clothing, ointment ——— 10——— but all people shall stand and abide in these temples, following their callings [for] their gods therein ———.

## PAPYRUS HARRIS[b]

151. The invaluable treasure of facts and statistics preserved to us in this remarkable document has, with the exception of one section at the end, never been exhaustively studied until recently. The closing section, which is a short historical account of Ramses III's reign, has received much

[a]Temple income.

[b]Found by the natives at Thebes in 1855. It lay with four other rolls in a hole in the floor of a common cliff-tomb near Der el-Medineh, beneath a pile of mummies which filled the tomb. Together with some twenty other rolls, found by the Arabs at the same time, it was offered for sale to Mr. A. C. Harris, of Alexandria, who purchased it; hence its name. The other papyri, not purchased by him, seem to have belonged to the series of court records containing the prosecution of tomb-robbers under Ramses IX. Papyrus Harris is now in the British Museum, where it was admirably published by Birch, *Facsimile of an Egyptian Hieratic Papyrus of the Reign of Ramses III, now in the British Museum* (London, 1876). It is practically in a perfect state of preservation, there being only a small piece of three lines torn out of Pl. 1. The *Dictionnaire du Papyrus Harris* (Vienna, 1882), by Piehl, is invaluable as a concordance, to which I express my general obligation here.

[Since finishing my study of the Papyrus Harris, I have received Professor Erman's admirable essay, "Zur Erklärung des Papyrus Harris" (*Sitzungsberichte der Königlichen Preussischen Akademie, der Wissenschaft*, 1903, XXI, 456–74). Additional observations drawn from his study are severally acknowledged in the notes.]

attention, but the apparently uninteresting gifts and lists, which occupy 95 per cent. of the space in the document, have never, until recently, been carefully examined for historical purposes.[a] The following discussion and translation are not offered as an exhaustive monograph on the papyrus; they purpose no more than to enable the reader to employ the invaluable data furnished by the document, for historical purposes. The numerous metrological, botanical, and archæological questions[b] suggested by the lists do not fall within our province in the present treatise, and no attempt has been made to settle them.

**152.** This remarkable manuscript is the largest papyrus extant, being no less than 133 feet long, and containing 117 columns,[c] usually of twelve or thirteen lines. Written in a magnificent hand, it is the most sumptuous manuscript left us by ancient Egypt. The content of the document is not less remarkable than its external form. It is a detailed statement of Ramses III's benefactions to gods and men during his entire reign of over thirty-one years. It was compiled at his death by his son, to be placed in the king's tomb, and is distinctly mortuary in its character and pur-

---

[a]Professor Erman's essay, mentioned above (p. 87, n. b).

[b]For the metrology involved in the historical discussion, I have followed Griffith. For the reader's convenience, I append the following equivalents:

1 deben = about 1,404 grains, or 2.925 troy ounces.

1 kidet = about 140.4 grains ($\frac{1}{10}$ of a deben).

1 sixteen fold heket = about 2.10 to 2.16 imp. bushels.

1 heket = about 292 to 300 cubic inches (1 bushel = about 7.39 to 7.59 heket).

1 hin = about 29.2 to 30 cubic inches.

1 stat = about $\frac{2}{3}\frac{7}{0}$ of an acre.

But most of the units of measure employed are unknown, and I have simply transliterated. Where I have translated botanical names, I have been dependent for the most part upon Loret's very useful investigations; but in cases of doubt I have usually transliterated the term without comment. As to the metals involved, this papyrus uses *ḥm·t* for both bronze and copper, and unless the alloy is indicated, I have regularly rendered copper (see 14*a*, note).

[c]Published in seventy-nine plates.

pose. It was intended to secure to the departed Pharaoh the favor of all the gods in the hereafter, by showing them his numerous benefactions in all their temples, and his great deeds among men. Prayers for the king's well-being in the world beyond continually appeal to these good works as ground for the favor of the gods, on whose good-will the king's happiness after death depends. Ramses IV, the son to whom the document clearly owes its preparation, does not forget to put into his deceased father's mouth long prayers in his own (the son's) behalf, entreating for him from the gods, whose companion the departed king now is, a long and prosperous reign. So prominent are these prayers for Ramses IV that they must also have formed a strong motive for the preparation of the document by him.[a]

**153.** The document is dated on the day of the king's death,[b] as will be evident from the following considerations: The long lists of gifts cover thirty-one years; all annual traditional feasts of all the temples recorded were celebrated thirty-one times. It is thus evident that Ramses III died so early in the year 32 that the small fraction of gifts presented during the beginning of that year were not considered; nor did the king survive long enough in the year 32 to celebrate any of its feasts. To this last observation there is one exception: a certain feast founded by Ramses III himself was celebrated in the year 32. It began on the

[a]In precisely the same way the deceased Seti I prays for his son, Ramses II (III, 280); and we find the latter petitioning his deceased father to pray to the gods, whose companion he (the father) now is, for his (the son's) welfare (III, 279).

[b]This was long ago recognized by Birch (*Zeitschrift für ägyptische Sprache*, 1872, 119 ff.), although his data, as he took them from the papyrus, were seriously in error. But, this conclusion of Birch has since been entirely overlooked, or it has been generally held that the papyrus was written and dated some time before the king's death, although it over and over again, with all the euphemisms known to the Egyptians, states that he was already dead. [Later: See also Erman on this point (*op. cit.*).]

twenty-sixth of Pakhons, and lasted twenty days. This feast must therefore have fallen early in the year 32, and the king lived at least twenty days of that year. Now, in Ramses III's calendar of feasts at Medinet Habu the feast of the anniversary of his coronation is recorded as beginning on the twenty-sixth of Pakhons[a] (ninth month), so that the twenty-day feast in our papyrus is the celebration of the coronation anniversary; its first day, the twenty-sixth of Pakhons, is the first day of each year of the reign. This feast, which began the year 32, the old king celebrated in that year; but no more. When the Feast of the Nile-god,[b] which fell just ninety-five days after the close of the Feast of Coronation, was celebrated, the Pharaoh had been gathered to his fathers, for the papyrus records this feast no later than the year 31. We have thus fixed the date of the king's death within ninety-five days, and the papyrus is dated on the sixth of Epiphi, which falls within that period.

**154.** When, furthermore, we remember that the papyrus continually represents the king as stating that he is deceased, it is evident that the date at the head of the document is that of the king's death, the last date which could be recorded in his reign. The papyrus thus furnishes us the exact length of his reign, thirty-one years and forty days, or more exactly, forty-one days, if we include the day of his death.[c]

---

[a]§§ 142, 143.

[b]The date of this feast is not given in the papyrus, but is to be found on Ramses III's stela at Silsileh (Lepsius, *Denkmäler*, III, 218, *d*, l. 15).

[c]That Ramses III ruled in round numbers thirty-one years is also shown by the Papyrus Mallet (*Recueil*, I, Pl. I, ll. 2, 3), which contains a statement of payments made "*from year 31 to year 3, making 4 years.*" Had Ramses III ruled far into year 32, the above limits would have included more than four years; but the scribe ignores the forty days of year 32. There is no coregency with Ramses IV here (Maspero, *Struggle of the Nations*, 480); and the dates as they stand are clear proof that there was never any coregency at all. Still less is there a shadow of proof that the coregency lasted four years (Maspero, *Struggle of the Nations*, 481), making Ramses III reign thirty-six years. The document on which this

155. The document was evidently put together as rapidly as possible after the king's death, and the sections furnished by the three main temples—Thebes, Heliopolis, and Memphis—were written by three different scribes, as the varying hand and orthography clearly show.[a] The Theban scribe wrote also the general introduction, but a fourth scribe had to do with the records from the smaller temples, while a fifth furnished the concluding or historical section. One of these scribes was perhaps also the artist of the three vignettes. The haste with which the document was compiled is evident both from the fact that some of the greatest of the minor temples are entirely omitted, and from the numerous errors in the footings of the lists, as well as some glaring omissions. It is evident, also, that the scribes at Heliopolis and Memphis were unable to render as full reports as that of the Theban scribe; doubtless owing to the shorter time allowed them because of the delay involved in the journey from Thebes with their instructions, and the return thither with the finished report, before the day of the king's funeral. The entire omission of many of the more important smaller temples is probably to be accounted for in the same way; their reports failed to arrive in time.[b]

156. The material in the great papyrus is, in the main, very systematically arranged. To the three great gods of Egypt—Amon of Thebes, Re of Heliopolis, and Ptah of Memphis—the major portion of the space is naturally devoted. Besides these three great sections is another, of

---

last conclusion is based contains an encomium of the reign of Ramses V, copied by a scribe in the year 4. Its attribution to Ramses IV (*ibid.*, 481) is an oversight, for it was formerly correctly assigned by Maspero to Ramses V (*Momies royales*, 664).

[a]See Erman (*Sitzungsberichte der Königlichen Preussischen Akademie*, 1903, XXI, 459–62) for a table of these differences.

[b]This will not, however, explain the absence of such temples as Erment and Dendera, which were but a few miles away from Thebes.

general scope, devoted to the other temples, followed by a summary of all the temples of Egypt, and a concluding historical section, reciting the king's great deeds in war, commerce, and the like.

**157.** The following table will render this arrangement clear:[a]

I. Introduction (**1**; §§ 182, 183).
II. Theban Section (**2–23**; §§ 184–246).
III. Heliopolitan Section (**24–42**; §§ 247–304).
IV. Memphite Section (**43–56**; §§ 305–51).
V. General Section (**57–66*b***; §§ 352–82) (small temples).
VI. Summary (**67–74**; §§ 383–96).
VII. Historical Section (**75–79**; §§ 397–412).

Each of these sections, except the first and last, is arranged on the same general plan. At the beginning of each of the sections II, III, and IV is a vignette, showing the king worshiping the gods to whom the following section is devoted. The text of each section is then introduced by a prayer, which merges into a recital of the king's buildings and other benefactions for the god, concluding with an appeal to him, calling attention to the following lists. These lists contain six different classes of material: (1) the god's estate; (2) his income; (3) the king's new gifts to him; (4) grain for the old feasts; (5) offerings for new feasts founded by him; and (6) offerings to the Nile-god.

**158.** The statement that the first class of material constitutes the god's estate will need some demonstration. It is clear that the papyrus enumerates old income of the god merely confirmed to him by Ramses III, in the offerings of grain for the old annual feasts like that of Southern Opet at Thebes (**16*b***, 13–15); for these are not only separated

[a] Bold figures indicate the plates of the papyrus.

by a rubric from the new feasts founded by Ramses III (e. g., **17***a*–**21***b*), but they refer distinctly to "*that* (*income*) *which was before*" (**16***b*, 14), which is included in them. If this be true, we may expect to find old possessions of the god elsewhere in the lists. Thus among the king's gifts we find the statement that he "*made*" for Amon the great vineyard called "*Kanekeme*" (**8**, 5). Had we no other information regarding this vineyard, we must have supposed that it was a new possession of Amon, equipped and given him by Ramses III. But we know that it was in existence long before Ramses III's time, and in possession of Ramses II's mortuary temple, the Ramesseum, also a temple of Amon at Thebes.[a] We thus see that Ramses III enumerates as his own gifts, property long in the possession of the god before Ramses III was born, evidently viewing his confirmation of it to the god as the conveyance of a gift.[b] To us it is indifferent whether such confirmation really did constitute a gift; it is enough for us to know that all property so confirmed was an old possession belonging to the earlier estate of the god. With this fact in mind, let us see if such property as enumerated can be distinguished from the new donations actually given by Ramses III.

**159.** The first list in each of the Theban, Heliopolitan, and Memphite sections is headed thus:

> List of things, cattle, gardens, lands, galleys, workshops, and towns, which Pharaoh[c] gave to the house (*pr*, estate) of the god X, as property forever and ever (**10**, 1 ff.; **31**, 1 ff.; **51***a*, 1 ff.; **61***a*, 1 ff.).

**160.** The second section of the lists is clearly the god's annual income or a part of it; it is headed each time[d] thus:[e]

---

[a]See **8**, 5, and note.

[b]He does the same in his Elephantine act of endowment (§§ 146–50).

[c]So Thebes; the rest use Ramses III's name.

[d]The scribe has omitted the heading by mistake in the general section.

[e]So the summary; the others give the various temples, etc., by name.

Things exacted, impost of the people and all the serf-laborers of the houses, temples, and estates which he gave to them as their yearly dues (**12***a*, 1 ff.; **32***a*, 7 ff.; **51***b*, 3 ff.; **68***b*, 4 ff.).

Yet it is stated that Ramses III "*gave*" this income to the gods, although it is evident that it is income which they must long before have enjoyed.

**161.** The third section of the lists is five times so headed:

Gold, silver, etc.,[a] which Ramses III gave as gifts of the king, in order to provision the house of the god X, from the year 1[b] to the year 31.[b]

**162.** We see that these "*gifts*" are distributed through thirty-one years, while the "*property*"[c] of the first heading is, as far as the heading is concerned, each time merely once given, and is never called "*gifts of the king*." On looking at the lists themselves, under the first and third headings, we find, for example at Heliopolis, lands under both; while at Thebes we find cattle under both. Why were these not put together? Evidently because some of the land was former "*property*" of the god, while the rest was a "*gift of the king*." Now, the estate of the god, as Erman has noticed, is of course given as it was found at the king's death, using the names then in vogue; hence we find the keepers of a herd named after Ramses III's victory over the Meshwesh (**10**, 8) included in the estate. Evidently the 971 Meshwesh slaves who kept this herd were a gift of Ramses III, and other gifts of his, not discernible because not accidentally so distinguished, are thus, of course, included in the estate. This made no difference to Ramses

[a]Long series of portable property.

[b]The summary has for this phrase, "*while he was king upon earth.*"

[c]The word employed (*ymy-pr*) is the usual term, both for the document by which property is conveyed by mortmain, and for such property itself. The term is therefore of itself sufficient to determine the character of the property to which it is applied.

III, while claiming, as he did, to have given the whole estate to the god.

**163.** The important point for us is, that we have here an inventory of the whole estate, and that we can now determine from the great papyrus the total wealth held by the three great temples of Egypt—an economic datum till recently unknown in the study of ancient Egypt or of any other oriental country of the time. If we thus leave the total amount of Ramses III's new gifts somewhat uncertain, such uncertainty is of little importance, for it is evident in any case that the bulk of his alleged donations to the gods were old and traditional possessions, for a large share of which the priesthoods were doubtless indebted to the Eighteenth Dynasty.[a]

**164.** The classification of the property of the temples in the document is shown in the appended table (p. 96).

**165.** We can now proceed to determine what proportion of the wealth of the country was in possession of the temples of the land. To do this, we must compile a condensed summary of their property, taking first the temple estates (see table, p. 97).

**166.** With these data we can safely deal only in the case of people and land. The cattle are lumped together without showing what proportion of sheep, goats, etc., the numbers contain. We do not know the size of the gardens and groves, or towns; nor the size and value of the ships and workshops. But with the people belonging to the temples, and the lands, we can operate with tolerable precision, as compared with our former total lack of data. The population of Egypt up to within the last five or six years was reckoned at toward six millions, but the latest census places

[a]For example, Amon owns but nine Syrian towns, and we know that Thutmose III alone gave Amon three Syrian towns (II, 557).

## CLASSIFICATION OF THE PROPERTY OF THE TEMPLES

| | II. Theban Section | III. Heliopolitan Section | IV. Memphite Section | V. General Section (Small Temples) | VI. Summary |
|---|---|---|---|---|---|
| 1. Introductory Vignette | **2**; § 184 | **24**; § 247 | **43**; § 305 | None | None |
| 2. Prayer to the God and Recital of the King's Benefactions in Buildings and Gifts | **3–9**; §§ 185–221 | **25–30**; §§ 248–79 | **44–50**; §§ 306–36 | **57–60**; §§ 352–63 | None |
| 3. The God's Estate | **10–11**; §§ 222–26 | **31–32***a*, 6; §§ 280–82 | **51***a*–**51***b*, 2; §§ 337–39 | **61***a*–**62***a*, 10; §§ 364–70 | **67–68***b*, 3; §§ 383–85 |
| 4. The God's Income | **12***a*–**12***b*; §§ 227–30 | **32***a*, 7–**32***b*; § 283 | **51***b*, 3–**52***a*, 3; §§ 340, 341 | **62***a*, 11–13; § 371 | **68***b*, 4–**70***a*, 2; §§ 386, 387 |
| 5. The King's Gifts to the God | **13***a*–**16***b*, 12; §§ 231–35 | **33***a*–**34***b*, 5; §§ 284–88 | **52***a*, 4–**53***b*, 11; §§ 342–45 | **62***b*–**66***a*; §§ 372–81 | **70***a*, 3–**74** §§ 388–96 (for 5–8) |
| 6. Grain for the Old Feasts | **16***b*, 13–15; § 236 | **34***b*, 6–9; § 289 | **53***b*, 12–**54***a*, 1; § 346 | None | |
| 7. Offerings for New Feasts Founded by Ramses III | **17***a*–**21***b*, 10; §§ 237–44 | **34***b*, 10–**37***a*; §§ 290–95 | None | None | |
| 8. Offerings for the Nile-god | None | **37***b*–**41***b*; §§ 296–303 | **54***a*, 2–**56***a*; §§ 347–50 | None | |
| 9. Private Statues of Amon | **21***b*, 11–16; § 245 | None | None | None | Above in the estates |
| 10.[a] Concluding Prayer of Ramses III | **22, 23**; § 246 | **42**; § 304 | **56***b*; § 351 | **66***b*; § 382 | None |

[a]These numbers do not wholly conform with those found in the translation, because of the absence of some of the heads in certain sections. Thus No. 8 of this table is wanting in the Theban section, and hence in the translation No. 9 has become No 8.

TEMPLE ESTATES

| | [a]THEBES | HELIOPOLIS | MEMPHIS | GENERAL (SMALL TEMPLES) | SUMMARY |
|---|---|---|---|---|---|
| People | 86,486[b] | 12,364[c] | 3,079 | 5,686[d] | 107,615[e] |
| Large and Small Cattle | 421,362 | 45,544 | 10,047 | 13,433 | 490,386 |
| Gardens and Groves | 433 | 64 | 5 | 11 | 513[f] |
| Lands | 864,168¼ stat | 160,084¾ stat | 10,154 stat | 36,012 stat | 1,070,419[g] stat |
| Ships | 83 | 3 | 2 | None | 88 |
| Workshops | 46 | 5½ (sic!) | None | 2 | 53½ (sic!) |
| Towns of Egypt | 56 | 103 | 1 | None | 160 |
| Towns of Syria and Kush | 9 | None | None | None | 9 |
| Total Towns | 65 | 103 | 1 | None | 169 |

[a]To the fortune of Amon (Thebes) must also be added the 2,756 statues, of which the materials are enumerated (**68***a*, 3–**68***b*, 3).

[b]The papyrus gives the correct total in this case.

[c]The papyrus gives 12,963.

[d]The papyrus gives 5,811.

[e]The papyrus gives 113,433.

[f]The papyrus gives 514.

[g]The papyrus gives 1,071,780.

it above nine millions. It is much to be doubted whether in its ancient state the land could support as large a population as modern improved conditions have produced. Granting this, we see that one person in about eighty-five of the population was temple property; or, accepting the lower figure for the ancient population (Diodorus gives six million as the population in Roman times), one person in about fifty-five. But, remembering that the list of smaller temples is incomplete, we may say that one person in from fifty to eighty of the population belonged to the temples. In no case were more than 2 per cent. of the people temple property.

**167.** Turning to the consideration of the land, we find the temples in possession of a total of 1,070,419 stat, or about 722,533 acres. The archives of modern Egypt contain a registration of about five millions of acres,[a] whence it will be seen that the temples owned nearly one-seventh, or over 14½ per cent., of the land. Including the smaller temples[b] omitted by the papyrus, probably over 15 per cent. of the land belonged to the religious foundations. This was distributed as follows:

| | |
|---|---|
| Thebes | 583,313.57 acres |
| Heliopolis | 108,057.2 " |
| Memphis | 6,853.95 " |
| Small Temples | 24,308.1 " |
| Total | 722,532.82 acres |

**168.** The income of the temples is also very instructive when tabulated.

[a] *Reports by His Majesty's Agent and Consul-General on ..... Egypt and the Soudan,* in 1902 (published April, 1903), 24, 25.

[b] The scribe does not itemize the land by temples (**62***a*, 8), but as he does not include Khnum of Elephantine among the list of temple-slaves, he may be omitting the entire dodekaschoinos, which we know was the property of Khnum under Ramses III (§§ 146–50).

TEMPLE INCOMES FOR THIRTY-ONE YEARS

| | Thebes | Heliopolis | Memphis | General (Small Temples) | Summary |
|---|---|---|---|---|---|
| Gold | 569 d.,[a] $6\frac{1}{2}$ k. or 138.852 lb. | None | None | None | 559[b] d., $6\frac{1}{2}$ k. or 138.852 lb. |
| Silver | 10,964 d., 9 k. or 2,672.694 lb. | 586 d., $3\frac{11}{12}$ k. or 142.933 lb. | 98 d., $3\frac{11}{12}$ k. or 23.983 lb. | None | 11,649[b] d., $6\frac{5}{6}$ k. or 2,839.61 lb. |
| Copper | 26,320 d. or 5,279.04 lb. | 1,260 d. or 252.72 lb. | None | None | 27,580 d. or 5,531.76 lb. |
| Garments | 3,722 | 1,019 | $133\frac{1}{2}$ | None | $4,874\frac{1}{2}$[c] |
| Yarn | 3,795 d. or 761.17 lb. | None | None | None | 3,795 d. or 761.17 lb. |
| Incense, Honey, and Oil | 1,047 various jars[d] | 482 various jars | None | None | 1,529 various jars |
| Shedeh[e] and Wine | 25,405 various jars[d] | 2,385 various jars | 390 various jars | None | 28,180[f] various jars |
| Silver received in Exchange for Objects of Impost Sold by the Temples | 3,606 d., 1 k. or 878.987 lb. | 456 d., $3\frac{1}{2}$ k. or 111.235 lb. | 141 d., $3\frac{1}{10}$ k. or 34.444 lb. | None | 4203, d., $7\frac{3}{5}$ k.[g] or 1,024.666 lb. |

[a]d. stands for deben = about 1,404 grains (91 grammes); k. stands for kidet, which is $\frac{1}{10}$ of a deben. Precious metals are in lbs. troy.

[b]These two numbers are totally wrong as given by the papyrus, see note **68**$b$, 6.

[c]Papyrus has 4,575.

[d]Content unknown.

[e]Perhaps a wine of pomegranates, perhaps must.

[f]Papyrus has 28,080.

[g]Papyrus has 4,208 deben, $7\frac{3}{5}$ kidet.

TEMPLE INCOMES FOR THIRTY-ONE YEARS—*Continued*

| | Thebes | Heliopolis | Memphis | General (Small Temples) | Summary |
|---|---|---|---|---|---|
| Grain | 309,950[a] measures | 77,100[a] measures | 37,400[a] measures | 73,250[a] measures | 497,700[b] measures |
| Vegetables | 24,650 bundles[c] | 4,800 bundles[c] | 600 bundles[c] | 3,300 bundles[c] | 33,350[d] bundles |
| Flax | 64,000 bales[c] | 4,000 bales[c] | None | 3,000 bales[c] | 71,000 bales |
| Water-fowl | 289,530 | 37,465 | None | None | 326,995[e] |
| Cattle | 866 head | 98 head | 15½ head | None | 979½[f] |
| Geese | 744 head | 540½ head | 135 head | None | 1,419½[g] |
| Ships | 82 | 8 | None | None | 90 |
| Products of the Oasis | Numb'rs not given | Numb'rs not given | Numb'rs not given | None | Numb'rs not given |
| Products of God's-Land, Syria, and Kush | Included above | Included above | Numb'rs not given | None | Numb'rs not given |

[a]Sixteenfold heket.

[b]Papyrus has 460,900, having evidently omitted Memphis.

[c]Size unknown.

[d]Papyrus has 32,750.

[e]Papyrus has 100,000 more!

[f]Papyrus has 980.

[g]Papyrus has 1,920.

169. The above table shows the total income for thirty-one years, so that all numbers must be divided by thirty-one to obtain the annual income. Egypt's wealth has from the most ancient times consisted chiefly of grain and cattle, but especially the former. Yet of cattle the annual income of all temples was less than thirty-two head a year, and so great a temple as Memphis is charged with only half a beef each year. There is no gold in the income of either Heliopolis or Memphis, nor in that of the latter any incense, honey, oil, or flax. Other items are so small that it is impossible to believe that these lists contain the total income of any temple. The numbers would indicate that this entire list may be the income exclusively from Ramses III's new endowments.[a] Having already credited himself with giving the hereditary estate of each temple, when he comes to the income, he probably omits the annual receipts from the hereditary estate, which formed an old and standing income, and lists only the income from his own new endowments.

170. This income is annually as follows:

[a]Erman has also expressed his doubt as to the possibility that this list represents the entire income of the temple (*op. cit.*, 471), but thinks them possibly "nur nebensächliche Steuern."

ANNUAL INCOME

| | Thebes | Heliopolis | Memphis | General (Small Temples) | Summary |
|---|---|---|---|---|---|
| Gold | 18 d., 3⅘ k. or 4.48 lb. | None | None | None | 18 d., 3⅘ k. or 4.48 lb. |
| Silver | 353 d., 7 k. or 86.214 lb. | 18 d., 9⅕ k. or 4.612 lb. | 3 d., 1⅘ k. or 0.775 lb. | None | 375 d., 8 k. or 91.601 lb. |
| Copper | 849 d. or 170.285 lb. | 40 d., 6 k. or 8.143 lb. | None | None | 889 d., 6 k. or 178.428 lb. |
| Garments | 120 | 33 | 4 | None | 157 |
| Yarn | 122 d. or 24.47 lb. | None | None | None | 122 d. or 24.47 lb. |
| Incense, Honey, and Oil | 34 various jars | 15 various jars | None | None | 49 various jars |
| Shedeh and Wine | 819 various jars | 77 various jars | 13 various jars | None | 909 various jars |
| Silver received in Exchange for Objects of Impost Sold by the Temples | 116 d., 3⅕ k. or 28.353 lb. | 14 d., 7⅕ k. or 3.588 lb. | 4 d., 5⅗ k. or 1.111 lb. | None | 135 d., 6 k. or 33.052 lb. |
| Grain | 9,998 measures | 2,487 measures | 1,207 measures | 2,363 measures | 16,055 measures |
| Vegetables | 795 bundles | 155 bundles | 20 bundles | 106 bundles | 1,076 bundles |
| Flax | 2,064 bales | 129 bales | None | 97 bales | 2,290 bales |
| Water-fowl | 9,340 | 1,208 | None | None | 10,548 |
| Cattle | 28 | 3 | ½ | None | 31½ |
| Geese | 24 | 17 | 4 | None | 45 |
| Ships | About 8 every 3 years. | About 1 every 4 years | None | None | 3 |
| Products of Oasis | No numbers | No numbers | No numbers | None | No numbers |
| Products of God's-Land, Syria, and Kush | Included above | Included above | No numbers | None | Uncertain |

171. The political significance of these lists largely attaches to the question of Amon's share in them. The estate of the god embraced over 10 per cent. of the lands of Egypt,[a] and at most about 1½ per cent. of the population, or perhaps even a little less than 1 per cent. This meant a fortune in land of over five times that of Heliopolis, and over nine times that of Memphis, while in people the disproportion was still greater. That this disproportion was due solely to Ramses III is impossible. If we are correct in concluding that the above income was derived from Ramses III's new endowments, there is nothing in these figures which would indicate that Amon's vast wealth was due to Ramses III alone. Amon's annual income in gold, of which the other temples received none, is something less than 26,000 grains. Of other items Amon received roughly: 17 times as much silver; 21 times as much copper; 3 times as many garments; 2 times as much incense, honey, and oil; 9 times as much shedeh and wine; 1⅔ times as much grain; 10 times as much flax; 8 times as many waterfowl; 7 times as many cattle; about the same number of geese; 10 times as many ships; as all the other temples combined. This disproportion, if maintained through the Eighteenth and Nineteenth Dynasties, would account for the enormous wealth of Amon;[b] but that wealth was not the result of the donations of one reign.

172. At this point we must examine the list explicitly stated to contain Ramses III's gifts to the temples.

---

[a]See table, p. 98.

[b]It is to be supposed that the old fortune of Amon, if confiscated or depleted by Amenhotep IV, was restored by Harmhab.

RAMSES III'S GIFTS TO THE GODS DURING THIRTY-ONE YEARS

| | Thebes | Heliopolis | Memphis | General (Small Temples) | Summary |
|---|---|---|---|---|---|
| Gold | 183 d., 7 k. or 44.777 lb.[a] | 1,479 d., $3\frac{1}{6}$ k. or 360.583 lb. | 265 d., $5\frac{1}{2}$ k. or 64.728 lb. | 1,719 d., $8\frac{1}{4}$ k. or 419.207 lb. | 3,648 d., $3\frac{1}{12}$ k. or 889.295 lb. |
| Silver | 827 d., $1\frac{1}{4}$ k. or 201.612 lb. | 2,285 d., $\frac{1}{2}$ k. or 549.668 lb. | 516 d., 6 k. or 125.921 lb. | 2,428 d., $5\frac{1}{6}$ k. or 591.951 lb. | 6,027 d., $2\frac{1}{12}$ k. or 1,469.152 lb. |
| Lapis lazuli | 14 d., $\frac{1}{2}$ k. or 3.425 lb. | 1 d., 1 k. or 0.268 lb. | 3 d., 2 k. or 0.780 lb. | 10 d., 6 k. or 2.583 lb. | 28 d., $9\frac{1}{2}$ k. or 7.056 lb. |
| Copper and Bronze | 822 d. or 164.87 lb. | 1,883 d., 7 k. or 377.816 lb. | 2,018 d. or 404.753 lb. | 14,130 d., 3 k. or 2,834,134 lb. | 18,854 d. or 3,781.573 lb. |
| Myrrh | 5,140 d. or 1,252.875 lb. 3 heket, 20 hin | 1,787 d. or 435.581 lb. 2 heket | 1,046 d. or 254.962 lb. | | 7,973 d. or 1,943.418 lb. 5 heket, 20 hin |
| Garments | 9,116 | 18,793 | 7,026 | 2,947 | 37,882 |
| Incense, Honey, Oil, and Fat | 9,105 various jars | 3,740 various jars | 1,046 various jars | 2,574 various jars | 16,485 various jars |
| Shedeh and Wine | 22,566 various jars | 103,550 vari'us jrs. | 25,978 various jars | 3,287 various jars | 155,381 vari'us jrs. |
| Grain | None | 5 heket | 40 heket | 2,231[b] measures | 35,741 heket |
| Cattle | 297 | None | 979 | 1,142 | 2,418 |
| Geese | 8,160 | None | 419 | 194 | 8,773 |
| Water-fowl | 126,300 | None | 576 | 2,073 | 128,949 |
| Land | None | $54\frac{1}{4}$ stat and 2 gardens | None | 1,361 stat and 4 gardens | $1,415\frac{1}{4}$ stat and 6 gardens |

[a]All conversions are in lbs. troy except copper and bronze, which are avoirdupois.

[b]Sixteenfold heket.

173. This list shows immensely more gold, silver, copper, garments, cattle, grain, and land given to the other temples than to Amon, while it is only in a few less valuable commodities that Amon is in the lead. Even including Amon's income with the above gifts, Heliopolis was yearly receiving twice as much gold as Thebes from all sources. Amon's superiority is, however, in the aggregate decidedly maintained, as a combination of the income and the gifts shows. It is evident also that, while the gifts of land to other temples have been enumerated in this list, the lands given to Amon are not included here, but are counted in Amon's estate, as it was also clear from the names of the herds that the cattle given Amon were to some extent included in the estate. In using the list of gifts, therefore, it must not be forgotten that in the items of land and cattle it is incomplete, and that it is impossible to determine exactly the extent of Ramses III's gifts in these two forms of property. But, judging from those gifts of which we are able to determine the amount, the wealth of Amon in Ramses III's day, was not due to his donations, nor can we aver that the fortune of Amon of necessity constituted such a menace to the state as alone to threaten its overthrow—a conclusion now current, and everywhere accepted.

174. An important question suggested by these lists is the relation of income and expenditure. The following tables indicate the total income of three great temples in grain:

GRAIN FOR OLD FEASTS DURING THIRTY-ONE YEARS

| | | | |
|---|---|---|---|
| Thebes | 2,981,674 | 16-fold | heket |
| Heliopolis | 1,097,624 | " | " |
| Memphis | 947,688 | " | " |
| Small temples | Not given | | |

The total annual income in grain was therefore as follows:

| | | | |
|---|---|---|---|
| Thebes | For the old feasts | 96,183 | 16-fold heket |
| | Income (from Ramses III) | 9,998 | " " |
| Total | | 106,181 | " " |
| Heliopolis | For the old feasts | 35,407 | " " |
| | For the offerings to the Nile | 3,598[a] | " " |
| | Income (from Ramses III) | 2,487 | " " |
| Total | | 41,492 | " " |
| Memphis | For the old feasts | 30,570 | " " |
| | For the offerings to the Nile | 1,211[b] | " " |
| | Income (from Ramses III) | 1,207 | " " |
| Total | | 32,988 | " " |

**175.** From these figures it will be seen how far the income of Ramses III was from furnishing enough grain for the old feasts. They must have been drawn from the old income, which, in view of the vast extent of the temple lands, was greatly in excess of these amounts contributed to the offerings. Erman suggests that the surplus was used in building Ramses III's temples,[c] like that at Medinet Habu, Karnak, and other places. But the question arises whether it was not consumed in the maintenance of the other temples of the Eighteenth and Nineteenth Dynasties. We know that some of the Eighteenth Dynasty Theban temples, like that of Amenhotep III behind the Memnon colossi, had already perished at the vandal hands of the Nineteenth Dynasty kings. We can understand, too, how the mortuary temples, which were so largely the personal sanctuaries of earlier Pharaohs, might be desecrated. Yet, if their offerings were in some cases maintained, Ramses III would

[a]Only during the last seventeen years of the reign.

[b]Only during the last three years of the reign.

[c]*Op. cit.*, 474.

have been likely to include them in the totals given in the papyrus, without any remark as to their employment; for he does not itemize by temples the grain and other offerings given for the feasts.

176. This brings up the question: What Theban temples are known to the papyrus as sharing in Amon's income and Ramses III's bounty? They are referred to in three different places: the narrative of buildings and good works (§§ 189–214), the list of people (§§ 223, 224), and the income (§ 227); and they include six different temples:

| No. 1. Temples Built or Improved[a] | No. 2. People Attached to | No. 3. Income |
|---|---|---|
| Medinet Habu temple. | Medinet Habu temple. | Medinet Habu temple. |
| Small Karnak temple. | Small Karnak temple. | Small Karnak temple. |
| Southern Karnak temple. | Luxor temple. | Luxor temple. |
| Great Karnak temple. | Southern Karnak temple. | Southern Karnak temple. |
| Khonsu-temple. | | Khonsu-temple. |

177. From this it is evident that the income and the people of the great Karnak temple must be included elsewhere. When we notice that the Medinet Habu temple is credited with 62,626 people (**10**, 3), or three-fourths of all the people belonging to Amon, it is evident where the people belonging to the Karnak temple are to be found. Again, when we see that the people attached to the Khonsu-temple

[a]The Luxor temple is omitted, and yet Ramses III built a chapel on the river side of this temple. The lower part of a sandstone stela (*Recueil*, 16, 55, 56), used in antiquity to prop a falling statue of Ramses II at Luxor, contains a record of building by Ramses III in the same temple: "*Ramses III, doubling offerings in Luxor . . . . . . maker of monuments, profitable to him that begat him . . . . . building a house in Luxor on the right of his august father, Amon-Re. . . . . . It is like the horizon of heaven, made of fine sandstone; it shall endure as long as heaven endures, a place for the promenade of the lord of gods at his beautiful feast of Opet. . . . . . . He made (it) as [his] monument for his father, Amon-Re, presider over his Yp·t; making for him a great and august chapel of the front, of marvelous great blocks.*" The omission of this building in the Theban section is another evidence of the hastiness with which the document was prepared, and the resulting incompleteness.

are also included somewhere else, we are led to conclude that the fortunes of the different Amon-temples are not always kept apart by the papyrus; in other words, the fortunes of all might be comprehended under one head as the estate of Amon.

**178.** Indeed, this common estate is unequivocally mentioned, for we find the five herds belonging to the five temples of No. 3 spoken of as "*the five herds made for this house*" (12*a*, 3, 4). "*This house,*" therefore, comprised the property of five different temples, and beyond doubt designates the estate of Amon, irrespective of the different temples among which it was divided. That other temples besides the five of No. 3 above may be included under one head is indicated by a record of restoration in the small Eighteenth Dynasty temple by Ramses III, which reads thus:[a]

**179.** He made it as a restoration of the monument of his father, "Amon-Re-of-Splendid-Seat,"[b] who rests in his temple in the precinct[c] of "The-House-of-Millions-of-Years-of-King-Usermare-Meriamon-Possessed-of-Eternity-in-the-House-of-Amon"[d] on the west of Thebes, when his majesty found it beginning to fall to ruin.

**180.** This small Medinet Habu temple is nowhere mentioned in the inscriptions; yet it was clearly restored and maintained by Ramses III, and is here included in the precincts of Ramses III's great temple, which stood beside it. Its people were, of course, also included in the 62,626 people of the great temple. Clearly, Ramses III made

---

[a]Sharpe, *Egyptian Inscriptions*, II, 60; again, less accurately, Lepsius, *Denkmäler*, Text, III, 163. The inscription occurs twice with unimportant variants.

[b]This is the name of the Amon of the Eighteenth Dynasty temple of Medinet Habu. It literally reads: "*Amon-Re-Splendid-of-Seat;*" compare a similar Amon on a bronze axe in Alnwick Castle (Birch, *Catalogue*, Pl. B): "*Amon-Splendid-of-Horizon,*" in the record of a foundation ceremony by Thutmose III.

[c]*Mr.*

[d]The name of Ramses III's Medinet Habu temple; see building inscriptions (§§ 1–20), where a shorter form is also in use.

his temple of Medinet Habu the administrative head of Amon's estate, and counted as belonging to it the property of the Karnak temple, that of the small Medinet Habu temple, and doubtless of others also, like that of Mut, who is mentioned in the headings, but whose fortune is nowhere listed. This fact once established for Thebes, the same may be true of Heliopolis and Memphis; and the vast income of these great sanctuaries, which we may compute from the temple lands, may have been distributed among far more temples than those mentioned in the papyrus. This distribution of income we cannot control (even if it were all counted in each case as income of the chief sanctuary alone), because the income lists evidently contain only a part of the income, as we have already shown; and the outgo covers only the maintenance of feasts, not the support of the great army of priests and officials.[a]

This discussion of the lists might be carried much farther, but doubtless the subject is above sufficiently introduced to make the importance and proper significance of the lists evident.

**181.** The historical section at the end furnishes a valuable supplement to the records of Ramses III's wars in his Medinet Habu temple. It is especially instructive, despite its obscurity, in its account of the anarchy preceding the rise of Ramses III's father. This paragraph, with its description of civil war and famine, reads like a chapter from the rule of the Mamlukes in Egypt. The section further furnishes accounts of an Edomite war, a new well in the Ayan desert, expeditions to Punt and the Sinaitic Peninsula,

[a]Certain things consumed by the priests are included in the great Medinet Habu Calendar, but only during feasts, like that of Opet, to the offerings of which is appended a list of the grain, beer, oil, etc., consumed by the priests during the twenty-four days of the feast. Such expenses may therefore be included in the lists of festal offerings in our papyrus, and evidently are so, e. g., in § 238, Pl. **17*b***.

besides new details regarding the wars already known to us from the Medinet Habu temple. It finally closes with a brief statement of Ramses III's philanthropic measures for his whole realm, followed by a prayer for the prosperity of his son, whom all are exhorted to obey.

## I. INTRODUCTION

### *Pl. 1. Date and Introduction*

**182.** [1]Year 32, third month of the third season (eleventh month), sixth day;[a] under the majesty of the King of Upper and Lower Egypt: Usermare-Meriamon, L. P. H.; Son of Re: Ramses (III), Ruler of Heliopolis, L. P. H., beloved of all gods and goddesses; [2]king, shining in the White Crown like Osiris; ruler, brightening the Nether World[b] like Atum; ⸢ruler⸣ of ⸢—⸣ of the great house in the midst of the cemetery, traversing eternity forever as king of the Nether World; King of Upper and Lower Egypt; Usermare-Meriamon; Son of Re: Ramses (III), Ruler of Heliopolis, L. P. H., the Great God.

### *Content and Purpose of the Document*

**183.** [3]He tells, in praise, adoration, and laudation, the many benefactions and mighty deeds, which he did as king and as ruler on earth, for:

#### *Gods of Thebes*[c]

1. The house (*pr*) of his august father, Amon-Re, king of gods, [4]Mut, Khonsu, and all the gods of Thebes;

#### *Gods of Heliopolis*

2. The house (*pr*) of his august father, Atum, lord of the Two Lands of Heliopolis; Re-Harakhte; Saosis (*Yws-ʿꜣ-st*), mistress of Hotepet and all the gods of Heliopolis;

---

[a]All words in spaced type are in red in the original.

[b]Because he is dead, as this and the following phrases show.

[c]The following five paragraphs are the heads of the five great sections of the papyrus, II, III, IV, V (VI, a summary, is not noted), and VII.

*Gods of Memphis*

3. The house of his august father, [5]Ptah, the great, South-of-His-Wall, lord of "Life-of-the-Two-Lands;"[a] Sekhmet, the great, beloved of Ptah; Nefertem, defender of the Two Lands and all the gods of Memphis;

*All Gods*

4. The august fathers, all the gods and goddesses of South and North;

*Men*

5. As well as the good benefactions [which he did for] the people of the land of Egypt and every land, to unite them[b] all together; [6]in order to inform the fathers, all the gods and goddesses of South and North, and all [foreigners],[c] all citizens, all (⸢common⸣) folk, and all people, of the numerous benefactions and many mighty deeds, which he did upon earth as great ruler of Egypt.[d]

## II. THEBAN SECTION

### 1. INTRODUCTORY VIGNETTE

*Pl. 2. Vignette*

**184.** Ramses III stands praying before Amon-Re, Mut, and Khonsu. The accompanying notes are:

*Over Amon*

Amon-Re, king of gods, lord of heaven, ruler of Thebes.

---

[a]Name of a sacred district in Memphis in which the chief Ptah-temple stood.

[b]Viz., his benefactions, etc., that is, to make a list of them, as contained in this document.

[c]This list is almost a repetition of that in 78, 13; hence it probably began, as that does, with foreigners. The whole list would then be: [*kꜣwy*], *pʿ·t*, *rḫy·t*, *ḥnmm·t*, and differs from 78, 13, only in the order of *pʿ·t* and *rḫy·t*, which are there reversed. The exact meaning and relations of these different terms are unknown except of the first, and the above renderings are purely arbitrary. We only know that they are all commonly used, with no obvious distinctions in meaning, for the people of Egypt.

[d]This long sentence may be epitomized thus: In the year 32, etc., of Ramses III, deceased (ll. 1, 2), he tells the benefactions and mighty deeds which he did while king for the gods of Thebes, Heliopolis, Memphis, and of South and North, as well as for all men, in order to inform gods and men of these deeds (ll. 3–6). It will be seen that this introduction epitomizes the content of the entire papyrus.

*Over Mut*

Mut, the great, mistress of Ishru.

*Over Khonsu*

Khonsu in Thebes, beautiful rest.

*Before the King*

I tell the prayers, praises, adorations, laudations, mighty deeds and benefactions which I did for thee, in thy presence, O lord of gods.

### 2. PRAYER TO AMON,[a] AND RECITAL OF THE KING'S BENEFACTIONS

*Pl. 3. Introduction*

**185.** [1]Praises, prayers, brave deeds and benefactions which he did for the house (*pr*) of his august father, Amon-Re, king of gods; Mut, Khonsu, and all the gods of Thebes.

*Prayer of Ramses III*

**186.** [2]Said King Ramses III, L. P. H., the Great God, in praising this god, his august father, Amon-Re, king of gods, the primordial, who was at first, [3]the divine god, the self-begetter, who sustains the arm and exalts the etef-crown, maker of what is, creator of what exists, hiding himself from men and gods:

*His Decease*

**187.** Give to me thy ears, O lord of gods; [4]hear my prayers which I make to thee. Lo, I come to thee, to Thebes, thy mysterious city. Thou art divine among the gods who are in thy image. Thou hast gone to rest in "Lord-of-Life,"[b] thy glorious seat, [5]before the august front of thy court;[c] (so) I have mingled with the gods, the lords of the nether world, like my father, Osiris, lord of Tazoser. Let my soul (*bˀ*) be like the souls of the gods who rest at thy side [6]in the eternal

[a]Although all three of the great gods of Thebes are mentioned in the introduction, the following prayer is really addressed to Amon only. In the other two sections (Heliopolis and Memphis) the same is true; that is, the prayer is actually addressed to the great god, although the other gods are mentioned in the beginning.

[b]*Nb-ˁnḫ*, a euphemism for the place of the dead, often applied to the west side at Thebes.

[c]Lit., "*forecourt,*" a metonymy for sanctuary, referring to Karnak, which faces west.

horizon. Give breath for my nostrils and water for my soul (*b* ᵓ). Let me eat the oblations, the provisions of thy divine offerings. Make my majesty to be noble, abiding in thy presence 7like the great gods, the lords of the nether world. May I go in and go out in thy presence as they do. Command thou that my fame be like theirs against my enemies; establish my offerings presented to my 8ka, abiding daily unto eternity.

*Retrospect*

**188.** I was king upon earth, ruler of the living; thou settedst the crown upon my head, as thou didst; I was inducted in peace into the august palace; 9I sat upon thy throne with joy of heart. Thou it was, who didst establish me upon the throne of my father, as thou didst for Horus on the throne of Osiris. I did not oppress, I did not deprive 10another of his throne.[a] I did not transgress thy command, which was before me. Thou gavest peace and contentment of heart among my people (*ḥnmm·t*), and every land was in adoration before me. I know of the excellent things 11which thou didst as king, and I multiplied for thee many benefactions and mighty deeds.

*Pl. 4. Medinet Habu Temple*[b]

**189.** I made for thee an august house of millions of years, abiding upon the mountain of "Lord-of-Life,"[c] before thee, 1built of sandstone, gritstone, and black granite; the doors of electrum and copper in beaten work. Its towers were of stone, towering to heaven, 2adorned and carved with the graver's tool,[d] in the great name of thy majesty. I

---

[a]I am not sure that this is correct. The difficulty is one of interpretation. He may merely mean: "*I did not oppress, I did not plunder another in his place;*" as the word "*throne*" may equally well mean "*seat, place,*" as commonly. The above rendering, however, connects logically with the preceding. "*Oppress*" (ᶜᵓ-*š*ᵓ-*ḳ*) is Hebrew, עשׁק.

[b]See Peuillet, *Recueil*, XVIII, 166 ff.; also Daressy, *ibid.*, XX, 133 ff.

[c]A general name for the west, which was localized at Medinet Habu; it is opposite Karnak, Amon's great temple, hence "*before thee.*" An inscription in the temple itself places it on the same mountain; Amon speaks of "*the great house of Atum, established before me forever, upon the mountain of 'Lord-of-Life'*" (Champollion, *Notices descriptives*, I, 736). On the later name, see Maspero, *Struggle of the Nations*, 507, n. 3.

[d]See Brugsch, *Zeitschrift für ägyptische Sprache*, 1876, 146–48; and for correct reading (*bsn·t*), Brugsch, *Hieroglyphisch-demotisches Wörterbuch*, Supplement, *s. v.*

built a wall around it, established with labor, having ramps and ⸢towers⸣[a] of sandstone. [3]I dug a lake before it, flooded with Nun,[b] planted with trees and vegetation like the Delta.[c]

### *Temple Endowment and Equipment*

**190.** I filled its treasury[d] with the products of the lands of Egypt: [4]gold, silver, every costly stone by the hundred-thousand. Its granary was overflowing with barley and wheat; (its) lands, its herds, their multitudes were like the sand of the shore. I taxed for it the [5]Southland as well as the Northland. Nubia and Zahi [came][e] to it, bearing their impost. It was filled with captives, which thou gavest to me among the Nine Bows, (and with) classes[f] which I trained by the ten-thousand. [6]I fashioned thy great statue[g] resting in its midst; "Amon-Endowed-with-Eternity" was its august name; it was adorned with real costly stone like the horizon.[h] When it appeared, there was rejoicing to see it. [7]I made for it table-vessels, of fine gold; others of silver and copper, without number. I multiplied the divine offerings presented before thee, of bread, wine, beer, and fat geese; [8]numerous oxen, bullocks, calves, cows, white oryxes, and gazelles offered in his slaughter yard.

### *Accessory Monuments*

**191.** I dragged great monuments like mountains of alabaster and hus stone,[i] [9]sculptured with labor, and resting on the right and the left of its portal,[j] carved with the great name of thy majesty forever;

---

[a]These words (*ʿ˒-r˒-ty* and *ṯ˒-k˒-r˒*) occur five times together in this papyrus, each time as the accessories of an inclosure wall. The first is the Hebrew עליה, and hence here an ascent or ramp; see Bondi, *Lehnwörter*, 36, 37. The second is perhaps a Hebrew סגור, as Bondi suggests (*ibid.*, 88), and means inclosed towers or strong closures of the gates and windows.

[b]Celestial water; see II, 888, l. 20. [c]Lit., "*Northland.*"

[d]See inscriptions in this treasury, which is still in a perfect state of preservation (§§ 25–34).

[e]The verb has clearly been omitted by error of the scribe.

[f]See 76, 5, 6, § 402.

[g]This is the cultus statue; as it was light enough to be carried in procession, the adjective "*great*" is only conventional.

[h]Or the horizon-god. [i]*Ḥws*, an uncertain stone.

[j]These are the colossi which were placed on each side of a temple entrance. They have now disappeared at Medinet Habu.

other statues of granite and gritstone; [10]scarabs[a] of black granite, resting in its midst. I fashioned Ptah-Sokar,[b] Nefertem and all the gods of heaven and earth, resting in its chapel, wrought with fine gold, [11]and silver in beaten work, with inlay of real costly stones, beautified with labor.

*Pavilion and Connected Buildings*[c]

**192.** I made for thee an august palace of the king in its midst, like the great house of Atum which is in heaven. The columns, [12]door-posts, and doors were of electrum; the great balcony for the (royal) appearances was of fine gold.

*Pl. 5. Temple Ships*

**193.** I made for it[d] ships laden with barley and wheat for transport to [1]its granary without cessation. I made for it great treasure-ships upon the river, laden with a multitude of things for its august treasury.

*Temple Lands*

**194.** [2]It was surrounded with gardens and arbor-areas,[e] filled with fruit and flowers for the two serpent-goddesses. I built their ⌜châteaux⌝[f]

---

[a]Like the colossal scarab in black stone, discovered in Constantinople and now in the British Museum.

[b]This statue doubtless stood in the first court by the first pylon, where there is a votive text to "*Ptah, residing in 'The-House-Usermare-Meriamon-Possessed-of-Eternity-in-the-House-of-Amon' on the west of Thebes*" (Lepsius, *Denkmäler*, Text, III, 173).

[c]This is the palace connected with the Medinet Habu temple, of which the so-called "pavilion" formed the monumental entrance. The "pavilion" being of stone, has survived, but the bulk of the building, being of sun-dried brick, has perished. It ran at least as far back on the south side of the temple as the middle of the first court, with which its balcony was connected by a stairway still partially surviving. See Daressy (*Recueil*, XX, 81–83), who separates the pavilion from the building at its rear, to which the stairway belongs; but it is evident that the pavilion, the temple, and connected buildings formed one whole, designated by the same name; for the pavilion and the temple bear the same name (Lepsius, *Denkmäler*, Text, III, 167): "*The (ḥ·t)-House-of-Usermare-Meriamon-in-the-House-of-Amon.*"

[d]This "*it*" (feminine in Egyptian) refers to the temple (fem.), and not to the palace (masc.).

[e]Lit., "*places of chambers of trees;*" cf. § 264.

[f]See III, 588, l. 49.

having [3]⌜windows⌝; I dug a lake before them, supplied with lotus flowers.

*Small Karnak Temple*

**195.** [4]I made for thee a mysterious horizon in thy city of Thebes over against thy forecourt,[a] O lord of gods, (named): "House (*pr*)-of-Ramses-Ruler-of-Heliopolis,-L.-P.-H.,-in-the-House-of-Amon," abiding like the heavens bearing the sun. [5]I built it, I laid it in sandstone, having great doors of fine gold. I filled its treasury with the things which my hands carried off, to bring them [6]before thee every day.

*Southern Karnak Temple*

**196.** I adorned[b] for thee Southern Opet[c] with great monuments; I built for thee a house therein like the throne of the All-Lord (named): "Temple-of-Ramses-Ruler-of-Heliopolis,-L.-P.-H.,-[7]Possessed-of-Joy-in-Karnak."

---

[a]Used here by metonymy as often for sanctuary as a whole. This small temple is in front of the great Amon-temple of Karnak, and the later Bubastite extension inclosed it partially within the said temple. It is identified by Ramses III with the great Karnak temple, and bore the same name given above, as is shown by the following inscriptions in the first court of the small Karnak temple (Champollion, *Notices descriptives*, II, 12–14; Brugsch, *Recueil de monuments*, 57, 1; Lepsius, *Denkmäler*, III, 207, *c*): "*(Ramses III). He made (it) as his monument for his father, Amon-Re, king of gods; making for him the 'House (pr)-of-Ramses-Ruler-of-Heliopolis-in-the-House-of-Amon,' anew of fine white sandstone, established as an eternal work,* ⌜*wherein*⌝ [⌜*Amon*⌝] *appears, to give a multitude* —— [⌜*to*⌝] *King Ramses III.*" On the other side of the court it reads: "*Ramses III, maker of the monument, establishing (it) for him that formed him, in the great and splendid seat, on the divine ground before Karnak, illuminating Thebes wherein Amon rests, his heart glad, and his great divine ennead follows him, rejoicing to see the beautiful pure monument of King Ramses III, beloved of Khonsu-Neferhotep.*" The great Karnak temple bore the same name as this small temple, as is seen by comparing 5, 7 and 6, 3 with above inscriptions in the small temple. The latter was already finished in his sixteenth year, as new offerings are recorded on the wall as founded in Pauni of that year (Brugsch, *Recueil de monuments*, I, Pl. 40; Champollion, *Monuments descriptives*, II, 15, 16).

[b]Lit., "*made festive.*"

[c]Southern Opet is usually the name for Luxor, but the temple was counted as in Karnak (*Yp·t-ys·wt*), as its name shows. It stood, however, on the south of the great temple, by the temple of Mut, and hence could be spoken of as in Southern Opet.

### *Works in Great Karnak Temple*[a]

**197.** I again established thy monuments in "Victorious Thebes,"[b] the place of thy heart's rest, beside thy face (named): "House (*pr*)-of-Usermare-Meriamon-in-the-House-of-Amon," [8]like the shrine of the All-Lord; built of stone, like a marvel established as an eternal work; the doorways upon them were of granite, doors and [9]doorposts of gold. I supplied it with classes which I trained, bearing offerings by the hundred-thousand.

### *Monolithic Shrine*

**198.** [10]I made for thee a mysterious shrine in one block of fine granite;[c] the doors upon it were of copper in hammered work, engraved with thy divine name. [11]Thy great image rested in it, like Re in his horizon, established upon his throne unto eternity in thy great and august court.

### *Cultus Utensils*

**199.** [12]I made for thee a great sacrificial tablet of silver in hammered work, mounted with fine gold, the inlay-figures being of Ketem[d]-gold, bearing statues of the king, L. P. H., of gold in hammered work, an offering-tablet bearing thy divine offerings, offered before thee.

### *Pl. 6*

[1]I made for thee a great vase-stand,[e] for thy forecourt, mounted with fine gold, with inlay of stone; its vases were of gold, containing wine and beer, in order to present them before thee every morning.

---

[a]This temple is not said to have been built by him, but "*beautified*" (*smnḫ*, or "*established*"), which indicates embellishment. As to the name of the great Karnak temple under Ramses III, it must have contained his name, as above. The word "*built*" (in l. 8) is not finite, but a participle referring to the temple or the embellishments added. The work is also referred to (l. 8) as "*them*," showing clearly that accessory monuments of some sort are meant. Moreover, the following works are for the Karnak temple, as is shown by 6, 3. Ramses III, however, did some building, though not extensively, in the great Karnak temple.

[b]A name for the east side, or a part of the east side of Thebes, probably Karnak (see II, 329).

[c]Cf. Inscription of Ineni, l. 1 (II, 45; *Recueil*, XII, 106).

[d]The Hebrew כֶּתֶם, "gold;" see Dümichen, *Zeitschrift für ägyptische Sprache*, 1872, 44 f.

[e]The gift of a similar stand is recorded in the Khonsu-temple, thus: "*I made a great vase-stand of gold for thy oblations*" (from a photograph by Borchardt).

### *Feast of the Appearance*

**200.** [2]I made for thee a storehouse for the "Feast of the Appearance,"[a] with male and female slaves. I supplied them with bread, beer, oxen, fowl, wine, incense, fruit, vegetables, flowers, pure offerings before thee every day, being an increase of the daily offering which was before.

### *Ornaments of Cultus Statue, Etc.*

**201.** [3]I made for thee a splendid amulet[b] of gold, with inlay; great collars and tassels of Ketem-gold complete, to bind them to thy body, every time thou appearest in thy great and splendid seat in Karnak. [4]I made for thee a statue of the king, of gold, in hammered work, resting in the place which he knows,[c] in thy august shrine.

### *Record Tablets*

**202.** [5]I made for thee great tablets of gold, in beaten work, engraved with the great name of thy majesty, bearing my prayers. [6]I made for thee other tablets of silver, in beaten work, engraved with the great name of thy majesty, with the decrees of the house. [7]I made for thee great tablets[d] of silver, in beaten work, engraved with the great name of thy majesty, carved with the graver's tool, bearing the decrees and the inventories of the houses and temples which I made in Egypt, [8]during my reign on earth; in order to administer them in thy name forever and ever. Thou art their protector, answering for them.[e] [9]I made for thee other tablets of copper in beaten work, of a mixture of six

---

[a]A feast at which the god appeared and was carried in procession, as its name implies (*wn-ḥr*=lit., "*opening or showing the face*").

[b]In the form of the sacred eye (*wḏ* ᵓ).

[c]Only the king and the High Priest were admitted to the holy of holies, and "*knew*" it. Such statues of the king may be seen standing beside the cultus image of the god at Medinet Habu (Lepsius, *Denkmäler*, III, 212, *a*).

[d]This word (ᶜ *nw*) is different from the one (ᶜ *wt*) used in the two preceding cases, and was larger. It was upon an ᶜ *nw* that Ramses II's treaty of peace with the Hittites was engraved. The golden tablets are not mentioned in the lists later on, but the silver tablets are mentioned (13*b*, 13, 14), and their weights given, showing that an ᶜ *wt* weighed about 19⅓ deben, while an ᶜ *nw* was over 143½ deben.

[e]The Karnak temple was thus the place of deposit for temple archives of all Egypt, and the sanctuary of Amon the ecclesiastical capital.

(⌜parts⌝),[a] of the color of gold, engraved and carved with the graver's tool with the great name of thy majesty, with the house-regulations of the temples; likewise [10]the many praises and adorations which I made for thy name. Thy heart was glad at hearing them, O lord of gods.

*Cultus Sieve*

**203.** [11]I made for thee a great vase of pure silver, its rim of gold, engraved with thy name. A sieve was upon it of beaten work, of pure silver, a great sifting-vessel of silver, having a sieve and feet.[b]

*Golden Statues*

**204.** [12]I wrought upon the portable images of Mut and Khonsu, fashioned and made anew in the gold-houses, made of fine gold in thick overlay, with inlay of every costly stone which Ptah made, having collars before and behind, [13]and tassels of Ketem-gold. They rest with heart satisfied at the mighty deeds which I did for them.

*Pl. 7. Stelæ*

**205.** [1]I made for thee great stelæ for thy portal, overlaid with fine gold, with inlay-figures of Ketem-gold; large bases were under them, overlaid with silver, bearing inlay-figures in gold, to the pavement line.

*Grain*

**206.** [2]I gave to thee ten ten-thousands of measures of grain, to provision thy divine offerings of every day, to convey[c] them to Thebes every year, in order to multiply thy granaries[d] with barley and wheat.

*Foreign Revenues*

**207.** [3]I brought to thee the captives of the Nine Bows, the gifts[e] of the lands and countries for thy court. I made the road to Thebes like a ⌜foot⌝ to lead[f] before thee, bearing much provision.

---

[a]Lit., "*a mixture of a hexad*," evidently referring to the proportions of the alloy; but the term is not clear. The weight of these tablets is given in the lists (14*a*, 3) as 205½ deben; there were four of them, weighing together 822 deben.

[b]The weight of these sieve-vases, etc., is given in 13*b*, 6–8 (§ 231).

[c]Lit., "*row them*."

[d]On the granaries of Amon, see § 9.

[e]*B*ɔ-*r*ɔ *k*ɔ=a Semitic ברך, with the connected idea of kneeling in homage (Bondi, *Lehnwörter*, 41, 42).

[f]"*Lead*" lacks an object, and the whole passage is obscure.

*Periodic Offerings*

**208.** [4]I founded for thee oblations at the feasts of the beginnings of the seasons, to make offering before thee at thy every appearance. They were supplied with bread, beer, oxen, fowl, wine, incense, and fruit without number. They were levied anew upon the princes and inspectors as an increase of all the benefactions which I did for thy ka.

*Sacred Barge*

**209.** [5]I hewed for thee thy august ship "Userhet" of 130[a] cubits (length) upon the river, of great cedars of the (royal) domain, of remarkable size, overlaid with fine gold to the water line, like the barge of the Sun, when he comes from the east, and everyone lives at [6]the sight of him. A great shrine was in the midst of it, of fine gold, with inlay of every costly stone like a palace; rams' heads[b] of gold from front to rear, ⌜fitted⌝ with uraeus-serpents wearing etef-crowns.

*Products of Punt*

**210.** [7]I led to thee Punt with myrrh, in order to encircle thy house every morning, I planted incense sycamores in thy court; they had not seen (it) before since the time of the god.

*Mediterranean Fleet*

**211.** [8]I made for thee transports, galleys, and barges, with archers equipped with their arms, upon the sea. I gave to them captains of archers and captains of galleys, manned with numerous crews, without number, in order to transport the products of the land of Zahi (*Ḏ*ʾ*-h*) and the countries of the ends of the earth to thy great treasuries in "Victorious Thebes."[c]

*Cattle and Fowl*

**212.** [9]I made for thee herds in the South and North containing large cattle, fowl,[d] and small cattle by the hundred-thousand, having

---

[a]Nearly 224 feet. See II, 32, and p. 222, n. c.

[b]There is usually a ram's head at bow and stern of these barges, but here they were evidently also on the cabin shrine.

[c]See 5, 7, note.

[d]The word for "*herd*" (*mnmn*) is more inclusive in Egyptian than English, and includes also fowl.

overseers of cattle, scribes, overseers of the horns,[a] inspectors, and numerous shepherds in charge[b] of them; having cattle-fodder; in order to offer them to thy ka at all thy feasts, that thy heart may be satisfied with them, O ruler of gods.

### *Vineyards, Trees, Etc.*

**213.** [10]I made for thee wine-gardens in the Southern Oasis, and the Northern Oasis likewise without number; others in the South with numerous lists; they were multiplied in the Northland by the hundred-thousand. I manned them with gardeners from the captives of the countries; having lakes ⌈of my digging⌉, [11]supplied with lotus flowers, and with shedeh (*šdḥ*)[c] and wine like drawing water,[d] in order to present them before thee in "Victorious Thebes." [12]I planted thy city, Thebes, with trees, vegetation, isi-plants, and menhet flowers for thy nostrils.

### *Khonsu-Temple*

**214.** [13]I built a house[e] for thy son, Khonsu in Thebes, of good sandstone, red gritstone, and black stone (granite). I overlaid its doorposts and doors with gold, (with) inlay-figures of electrum, like the

*Pl. 8*

horizon of heaven. [1]I worked upon thy[f] statues in the gold-houses, with every splendid costly stone which my hands brought.

### *Sanctuary in Residence City*

**215.** [2]I made for thee an august quarter in the city of the Northland, established as thy property forever; "House (*pr*)-of-Ramses-

[a]See Piehl, *Zeitschrift für ägyptische Sprache*, 1885, 60, 61.

[b]Lit., "*behind them.*"

[c]An intoxicating drink of uncertain character. See p. 101, n. e.

[d]See II, 461, l. 5. Same figure again in **8**, 6.

[e]This is Ramses III's well-known temple of Khonsu at Karnak. It was not completed by him, but was continued by his successors until the accession of the high priests of Amon. The dedication in the hypostyle reads: "*He made (it) as his monument for Khonsu in Neferhotep (Thebes), making for him (the hall called): 'Exaltation-of-Brightness' for the first time of fine white sandstone, making high his great seat, with electrum, adorned with every splendid costly stone*" (Brugsch, *Thesaurus*, VI, 1310). But Brugsch does not give the name of the king, and the dedication may belong to Ramses IV, who also built in this hall.

[f]Doubtless referring to Khonsu, as the papyrus marks a paragraph at the end of l. 1, as we have indicated.

Ruler-of-Heliopolis,-L.-P.-H.,-Great-in-Victory," it is called,[a] forever. 3I conveyed to it Egypt with its[b] tribute; the people of every land were gathered in its midst. It was furnished with large gardens and places for walking about, with all sorts of date groves, bearing 4their fruits, and a sacred[c] avenue, brightened with the flowers of every land,[d] isi-plants, papyrus, and dedmet flowers, like sand.

### *Its Vineyard and Olive Garden*

**216.** 5I made for it Kanekeme,[e] inundated like the Two Lands, in the great olive-lands; bearing vines; surrounded by a wall around them by the iter;[f] planted with great trees 6in all their many paths, wherein was oil more than the sand of the shore; in order to bring them to thy ka, to "Victorious Thebes;" wine like drawing water[g] without measure, 7to present them before thee as a daily offering. 8I built for thee thy temple in the midst of its ground,[h] established with labor, excellent in stone of Ayan (*ᶜ yn ͻ*). Its door and its doorposts were of gold, mounted with copper; the inlay-figures were of every costly stone, like the double doors of the sky.

### *Cultus Image*[i]

**217.** 9I fashioned thy august image, wherewith the "Appearance" is made,[j] like Re when he brightens the earth with his beams; "Amon-of-Ramses-Ruler-of-Heliopolis" was its great and august name. I filled its house with male and female slaves, whom I carried off from the lands of the Bedwin (*Sty·w*). 10The lay priests of the temple were ⌜— —⌝[k] children of great men, whom I trained. Its treasury was overflowing with products of every land; its granaries approached

---

[a]Lit., "*is said to it for a name.*"

[b]Text has "*their,*" referring to Egypt as plural.

[c]The avenue leading up to the temple door.

[d]Compare the flowers of Syria, brought to Egypt by Thutmose III (II, 451).

[e]Name of an important vineyard of Amon in the Delta; it existed in the days of Ramses II, from whose cellars at the Ramesseum many sherds from broken wine-jars have been found, bearing the name of this vineyard (Wiedemann, *Zeitschrift für ägyptische Sprache*, 1883, 33 ff.; Spiegelberg, *Ostraca*, Pls. XIX–XXXIV).

[f]See II, 965, note. [g]See 7, 11. [h]The ground of Kanekeme.

[i]This must have been the cultus image in the Tanis temple, the equipment of which he has above enumerated.

[j]With which the god appears in processions and feasts.

[k]*Ṯ ͻ -tkmw* (or possibly *mṯ ͻ -tkmw*) occurs also in the inscription, year 8 (§ 65, l. 21), where it applies to charioteers.

heaven, its herds [11]were multiplied more than the sand;[a] cattle yards, offered to his ka, (as) divine offerings daily, full and pure before him; fattening-houses containing fat geese; poultry yards containing wild fowl; [12]gardens with wine, provided with their fruit, vegetables and all kinds of flowers.

### *Temple in Nubia*

**218.** [13]I made for thee an august house in Nubia (*T*ʾ-*pd·t*), engraved with thy august name, the likeness of the heavens (named): "House-of-Ramses-Ruler-of-Heliopolis,-L.-P.-H.,-Great-in-Victory," abiding, bearing thy name forever.

### *Pl. 9. Temple in Zahi*

**219.** [1]I built for thee a mysterious house in the land of Zahi (*Ḏ*ʾ-*h*ʾ), like the horizon of heaven which is in the sky, (named): "The-House-(*ḥ·t*)-of-Ramses-Ruler-of-Heliopolis,-L.-P.-H.,-in-Pekanan,"[b] [2]as the property of thy name. I fashioned thy great statue resting in the midst of it (named): "Amon-of-Ramses-Ruler-of-Heliopolis,-L.-P.-H." The Asiatics of Retenu (*Rtnw*) came to it, [3]bearing their tribute before it, for it was divine.

### *Miscellaneous*

**220.** I brought the earth, united for thee, bearing their imposts, to convey them to Thebes, thy mysterious city. [4]I made for thee statues in the districts of Egypt; they were for thee (⌈and⌉) the gods who preserve this land. I built for them temples, gardens containing their groves, [5]lands, small cattle, large cattle, many slaves; they are thine forever, thine eye is upon them, thou art their protector unto eternity. [6]I wrought upon thy great and grand statues which are in their districts in the lands of Egypt. I restored their temples [7]which were in ruin. I multiplied the divine offerings presented to their ka's as an increase of the daily offerings which were formerly

### *Lists*

**221.** [8]See, I have listed[c] all that I did before thee, O my august, divine father, lord of gods, that men and gods may know of my benefactions, [9]which I did for thee in might, while I was upon earth.

---

[a]From here to the end of the section the enumeration is simply a list without syntactical connection with the preceding.

[b]Lit., "*the Canaan.*"

[c]Lit., "*collected;*" the noun is the common word for list, as on the next plate (10, 1).

### 3. AMON'S ESTATE

*Pl. 10*

**222.** [1]List of things, cattle, gardens, lands, galleys, workshops, and towns, which Pharaoh, L. P. H., gave to the house (*pr*) of his august father, [2]Amon-Re, king of gods, Mut, Khonsu, and all the gods of Thebes, as property forever and ever:[a]

*People Attached to Temples, Etc.*

*Medinet Habu Temple*

**223.** [3]"The-House (*ḥ·t*)-of-King-Usermare-Meriamon,-L.-P.-H.,-in-the-House-of-Amon,"[b] in the South and North, under charge of the officials (*sr*) of the temples of this house (*pr*), equipped with all its things: heads 62,626

*Small Karnak Temple*

[4]"House (*pr*)-of-Usermare-Meriamon,-L.-P.-H.,-in-the-House-of-Amon," in the South and North, under charge of the officials, equipped with all its things: heads 970

*Luxor Temple*

[5]"House (*pr*)-of-Ramses-Ruler-of-Heliopolis,-L.-P.-H.,-in-the-House-of-Amon," in the South and North, under charge of the officials, equipped with all its things: heads 2,623

*Southern Karnak Temple*

[6]"The House (*ḥ·t*)-of-Ramses-Ruler-of-Heliopolis,-L.-P.-H.,-Possessed-of-Joy-in-the-House-of-Amon," under charge of the High Priest; equipped with all its things: heads 49

---

[a]The list now follows, and the first series of items is a statement of the numbers of people ("*heads*") attached to the various temples, to herds, etc. This list of people runs to **11**, 4.

[b]This name of the Medinet Habu temple is often found in the temple itself. Its full form there is: "*House-of-Usermare-Meriamon-Possessed-of-Eternity-in-the-House-of-Amon-on-the-West-of-Thebes*" (Lepsius, *Denkmäler*, Text, III, 173); but "*on-the-West-of-Thebes*" is sometimes omitted (*ibid.*, 179 and 185), as well as "*Possessed-of-Eternity*" (*ibid.*, 182, 183, 184, 185).

### *Five Herds of the Theban Temples*

**224.** [7]Herd[a] of "Usermare-Meriamon,-L.-P.-H.,-in-the-House-of-Amon," which is (called): "Usermare-Meriamon,-L.-P.-H.,-Captor-of-Rebels-is-a-Great-Nile:"[b] heads[c] 113

[8]Herd (called): "Usermare-Meriamon,-L.-P.-H.,-is-the-Conqueror-of-the-Meshwesh-at-the-Water-of-Re,"[d] under charge of the steward Pay (*Py*ᵓ *y*); Meshwesh: heads 971

[9]Herd (called): "Ramses-Ruler-of-Heliopolis,-L.-P.-H.,-in-the-House-of-Amon-is-a-Great-Nile:" heads 1,867

[10]Herd (called): "Usermare-Meriamon,-L.-P.-H.,-in-the-House-of-Amon,[e] ⌈————⌉," under charge of the Vizier of the South: heads 34

[11]Herd of "Ramses-Ruler-of-Heliopolis,-L.-P.-H.,-in-the-House-of-Amon," under charge of the cattle-overseer Key (*K*ᵓ *y*): heads 279

### *Royal Residence*

**225.** [12]"House (*pr*)-of-Ramses-Ruler-of-Heliopolis,-L.-P.-H.,-Great-in-Victory," the city which the Pharaoh, L. P. H., made for thee in the North, in the ownership of

[a]The following five herds, as the names show, belonged one to each of the preceding four temples, and the Khonsu-temple, as is shown by 12*a*, 1–4, where they follow these five temples in a group.

[b]This herd still existed under Ramses IV; see Hammamat Inscription, l. 14 (§ 466).

[c]These are not "*heads*" of cattle, but the people in charge of the herd.

[d]This canal on which Ramses III defeated the Meshwesh in the year 11, can only have been in the western Delta. That it was so located is shown by its occurrence in a list of Delta localities just after Busiris, "*the western river, the great river* (*Canopic branch*), *the 'Water of Re'*" (Golénischeff Papyrus, *Zeitschrift für ägyptische Sprache*, 40, 105). It is called the "*western canal*" in § 340 (see also § 370). It was the canal passing out of the Fayûm northward as the continuation of the Bahr Yusuf. It is mentioned in Saitic times on a stela in Berlin (No. 15393), recording the gift of a building by Apries (seventeenth year), located "*on the west of the canal named 'North,' which is between the highlands and Memphis.*" In Ptolemaic times it connected Heracleopolis with Alexandria (see § 831, note).

[e]The rest of the name is uncertain; possibly: "*Made:* (=*called*)-'*the-People-Are-a-Great-Nile*(?).'"

the house of Amon-Re, king of gods, saying: "As thou art mighty, thou shalt cause it to abide forever and ever:" heads 7,872

*Khonsu-Temple*

[13]House (*pr*)-of-Ramses-Ruler-of-Heliopolis,-L.-P.-H.,-in-the-House-of-Khonsu: heads 294

*Ramses III's Gifts of People*

[14]People whom he gave to the house of "Khonsu in Thebes, Beautiful Rest," Horus, lord of joy: persons[a] 247

[15]Syrians, and Negroes of the captivity of his majesty, L. P. H., whom he gave to the house (*pr*) of Amon-Re, king of gods, the house (*pr*) of Mut, and the house (*pr*) of Khonsu: persons[a] 2,607

[16]Bows[b] of "Usermare-Meriamon,-L.-P.-H.,-Establisher-of-His-House-in-the-House-of-Amon;" people settled, whom he gave to this house: heads 770

*Pl. 11. Private Statues in Great Karnak Temple*

[1]The processional images, statues, and figures, to which the officials, standard-bearers, inspectors, and people of the land pay impost, [2]which the Pharaoh, L. P. H., gave; in the ownership of the house of Amon-Re, king of gods, to protect them and answer for them forever and ever;

[3]2,756 gods,[c] making: heads 5,164

[4]Total heads 86,486

*Miscellaneous Property*

**226.** [5]Large and small cattle, various 421,362

[6]Gardens and groves 433

---

[a]Lit., "*times*" (*sp*).

[b]Meaning foreign archers settled in a temple district.

[c]It is difficult to determine the exact nature of these statues; they appear here in the god's estate; the materials of which they were made (?) appear independently following the king's gifts (**21***b*, 11–16); and finally in the general summary (**68***a*, 3–**68***b*, 3) they are again included in the sacred estates. Erman suggests votive statues of the god donated by the king's subjects.

| | |
|---|---|
| [7]Lands, stat | 864,168¼ |
| [8]Transports and galleys | 83 |
| [9]Workshops of cedar and acacia | 46 |
| [10]Towns of Egypt | 56 |
| [11]Towns of Syria ($Ḫ$ ᵓ-*rw*) and Kush | 9 |
| Total | 65 |

### 4. AMON'S INCOME

*Pl. 12a*

**227.** [1]Things exacted, the impost of all the people and serf-laborers of "The-House (*ḥ·t*)-of-King-Usermare-Meriamon,-L.-P.-H.,-in-the-House-of-Amon" (Medinet Habu temple), [2]in the South and North under charge of the officials; the "House (*pr*)-of-Usermare-Meriamon,-L.-P.-H.,-in-the-House-of-Amon" (small Karnak temple), in the (residence) city; the "House (*pr*)-of-Ramses-Ruler-of-Heliopolis,-L.-P.-H.,-in-the-House-of-Amon" (Luxor temple); [3]the "House (*ḥ·t*)-of-Ramses-Ruler-of-Heliopolis,-L.-P.-H.,-Possessed-of-Joy-in-the-House-of-Amon-of-Opet" (southern Karnak temple); the "House-of-Ramses-Ruler-of-Heliopolis,-L.-P.-H.,-in-the-House-of-Khonsu" (Khonsu-temple); the five herds[a] [4]made for this house,[b] which King Usermare-Meriamon, L. P. H., the Great God, gave to their treasuries, storehouses and granaries [5]as their yearly dues:

| | | | | |
|---|---|---|---|---|
| **228.** [6]Fine gold | 217 | deben, | 5 | kidet |
| [7]Gold of the mountain, of Coptos | 61 | " | 3 | " |
| [8]Gold of Kush | 290 | " | 8½ | " |
| [9]Total, fine gold, and gold of the mountain | 569 | " | 6½ | " |
| [10]Silver | 10,964 | " | 9 | " |
| [11]Total, gold and silver | [c]11,546 | " | 8 | " |
| [12]Copper | 26,320 | " | | |

[a]These are the five herds enumerated in **10**, ll. 7–11 (§ 224).

[b]"*House*" is here used, as frequently, in the sense of estate, and means the estate of Amon, divided among the five preceding temples, there being one herd for each of the five temples.

[c]Incorrect; correct total is 11,534 deben, 5½ kidet.

[13]Royal linen, mek-linen, fine southern linen, colored southern linen, various garments 3,722
[14]Yarn, deben 3,795
[15]Incense, honey, oil, various jars (ᵓ c c) 1,047

*Pl. 12b*

[1]Shedeh and wine, various jars (ᵓ c c) 25,405
[2]Silver, being things of the impost of the people (*rm·t*) given for the divine offerings[a] 3,606 deben, 1 kidet

**229.** [3]Barley ⌜—⌝ of the impost of the peasants (*yḥwty*), 16-fold heket 309,950
[4]Vegetables, bundles 24,650
[5]Flax, bales 64,000
[6]Water-fowl from the impost of the fowlers and fishermen 289,530
[7]Bulls, bullocks of the bulls, heifers, calves, cows, cattle of ⌜—⌝, cattle of ⌜—⌝, of the herds of Egypt 847
[8]Bulls, bullocks of the nege-bulls, heifers, calves, cows, being impost of the lands of Syria (*Ḫ*ᵓ*-rw*) 19

Total 866

[9]Live geese of the exactions 744
[10]Cedar: tow-boats and ferry-boats 11
[11]Acacia: tow-boats, ⌜canal⌝-boats, boats for the transportation of cattle, warships,[b] and kara-boats: 71
[12]Total, cedar and acacia: boats 82
[13]Products of the Oasis[c] in many lists for the divine offerings.

## 5. THE KING'S GIFTS TO AMON

*Pl. 13a*

**230.** [1]Gold, silver, real lapis lazuli, real malachite, every real costly stone, copper, garments of royal linen, mek-linen, [2]fine southern linen, southern linen, colored garments, jars, fowl, all the things which King Usermare-Meriamon, L. P. H., the Great God, gave, [3]as gifts of

[a]Silver received from sale of articles delivered to the temples as taxes from the people.

[b]*Ṯ*ᵓ*-r*ᵓ*-ty;* see Spiegelberg, *Rechnungen*, 35.

[c]The Northern Oasis (*wt*), see Karnak Inscription of Merneptah (III, 580, l. 20).

the king, L. P. H., in order to provision the house of his august fathers (sic!), Amon-Re, king of gods, Mut, and Khonsu, from [4]the year 1 to the year 31, making 31 years.

| | | | | |
|---|---|---|---|---|
| **231.** [5]Fine Ketem-gold; 42 ⸢—⸣ (*dmḏ·t*), making | 21 | deben | | |
| [6]Fine gold in ⸢raised work⸣;[a] 22 finger rings, making | 3 | " | 3 | kidet |
| [7]Fine gold in inlay; 9 finger rings, making | 1 | " | 3½ | " |
| [8]Fine gold in ⸢raised work⸣,[a] and in inlay of every real, costly stone; a ⸢ring⸣ of the column of Amon, making | 22 | " | 5 | " |
| [9]Fine gold in hammered work; a tablet, making | 9 | " | 5½ | " |
| [10]Total, fine gold in ornaments | 57 | " | 5[b] | " |
| [11]Gold of two times; in ⸢raised work⸣, and in inlay; 42 finger rings, making | 4 | " | 5½ | " |
| [12]Gold of two times; 2 vases | 30 | " | 5 | " |
| [13]Total, gold of two times | 35 | " | ½ | " |
| [14]White gold: 310 finger rings, making | 16 | " | 3½ | " |
| *Pl. 13b* | | | | |
| [1]White gold: 264 beads, making | 48 | " | 4 | " |
| [2]White gold in beaten work: 108 finger rings for the god, making | 19 | " | 8 | " |
| [3]White gold: 155 amulet cords, making | 6 | " | 2 | " |
| [4]Total, white gold | 90 | " | 7½ | " |
| [5]Total, fine gold, gold of two times and white gold | 183 | " | 5[c] | " |
| [6]Silver: a vase[d] (with) the rim of gold, in ⸢raised work⸣, making | 112 | " | 5 | " |
| [7]Silver: a sieve for the vase, making | 12 | " | 3 | " |
| [8]Silver: a sifting-vessel for the vase, making | 27 | " | 7 | " |
| [9]Silver: 4 vases, making | 57 | " | 4½ | " |
| [10]Silver: 31 large panniers with lids, making | 105 | " | 4 | " |

[a] *Šʿḥʿ*.

[b] There should be 7 kidet, an error of 2; but the correct total of 57 deben, 7 kidet was employed in obtaining the grand total (13*b*, l. 5).

[c] See preceding note.

[d] This and the following are the vases for the sieve, etc., mentioned in 6, 11.

| | | | | |
|---|---|---|---|---|
| [11]Silver: 31 caskets with lids, making | 74 | deben | 4 | kidet |
| [12]Silver: 6 measuring-vases (ᶜ*rḳ*), making | 30 | " | 3 | " |
| [13]Silver: in hammered work, a tablet (ᶜ*wt*), making | 19 | " | 3½ | " |
| [14]Silver: in hammered work, 2 tablets[a] (ᶜ*nw*), making | 287 | " | ½ | " |
| [15]Silver in scraps | 100 | " | | |
| [16]Total, silver in vessels and scraps | 827[b] | " | 1¼ | " |

*Pl. 14a*

| | | | | |
|---|---|---|---|---|
| [1]Total, gold and silver in vessels and scraps | 1,010 | " | 6¼ | " |
| [2]Real lapis lazuli: 2 blocks, making | 14 | " | ½ | " |
| [3]Bronze,[c] in hammered work: 4 tablets (ᶜ*nw*), making | 822 | " | | |

| | |
|---|---|
| **232.** [4]Myrrh: deben | 51,140 |
| [5]Myrrh: heket | 3 |
| [6]Myrrh: hin | 20 |
| [7]Myrrh wood: logs | 15 |
| [8]Myrrh fruit in measures (*yp˙t*) | 100 |
| [9] Royal linen: garments (*dw*) | 37 |
| [10] " " upper garments (*dw*) | 94 |
| [11] " " hamen-garments | 55 |
| [12] " " mantles | 11 |
| [13] " " wrappings of Horus | 2 |
| [14] " " —[d] garments | 1 |
| [15] " " garments (*ydg*ᵓ) | 690 |
| [16] " " tunics | 489 |
| [17] " " garments for the august ⌈statue⌉ of Amon | 4 |

*Pl. 14b*

| | |
|---|---|
| [1]Total, royal linen, various garments | 1,383 |
| [2]Mek-linen: a robe | 1 |

[a]These are mentioned in 6, 7.

[b]The exact total is 826 deben, 4½ kidet.

[c]These tablets are mentioned in 6, 9, showing that the material was bronze, though the designation both here and there is *ḥmt*, the usual word for copper.

[d]Reading unknown.

| | |
|---|---|
| [3]Mek-linen: a mantle | 1 |
| [4] " " in a ⸢cover⸣[a]: a garment for the august ⸢statue⸣ of Amon | 1 |
| [5]Total, mek-linen: various garments | 3 |
| [6]Fine southern linen: garments (*dw*) | 2 |
| [7] " " " —[b] garments | 4 |
| [8] " " " upper garments (*dw*) | 5 |
| [9] " " " garments (*ydg* ͗) | 31 |
| [10] " " " tunics | 29 |
| [11] " " " kilts | 4 |
| [12]Total, fine southern linen, various garments | 75 |
| [13]Colored linen: mantles | 876 |
| [14] " " tunics | 6,779 |
| [15]Total, colored linen, various garments | 7,125[c] |
| [16]Total, royal linen, mek-linen, fine southern linen, southern linen, colored linen, various garments | 8,586[c] |

*Pl. 15a*

| | |
|---|---|
| **233.** [1]White incense: (*mn*)-jars | 2,159 |
| [2]White incense: (*mn*)-jars[d] | 12 |
| [3]Honey: (*mn*)-jars | 1,065 |
| [4]Oil of Egypt: (*mn*)-jars | 2,743 |
| [5]Oil of Syria (*Ḫ* ͗ *-rw*): (*m-s* ͗ *-ḫy*)-jars | 53 |
| [6]Oil of Syria (*Ḫ* ͗ *-rw*): (*mn*)-jars | 1,757 |
| [7]White fat: (*mn*)-jars | 911 |
| [8]Goose fat: (*mn*)-jars | 385 |
| [9]Butter: (*mn*)-jars | 20 |
| [10]Total, filled jars (͗ ᶜ ᶜ) | 9,125[e] |

[a]*K* ͗*-ṯ* ͗*-ty* = כֶּסֶת (Bondi, *Lehnwörter*, 82, and 51).

[b]Same as 14*a*, 14.

[c]530 short.

[d]An uncertain hieratic sign after *mn* indicates that it is different from that of l. 1.

[e]The correct total is 9,105.

| | |
|---|---|
| [11]Shedeh: colored (*mn*)-jars | 1,377 |
| [12]Shedeh: (*k* ͗ *-bw*)-jars | 1,111 |
| [13]Wine: (*mn*)-jars | 20,078 |
| [14]Total, shedeh and wine: jars (*mn* and *k* ͗ *bw*) | 22,556[a] |
| [15]Hirset (*ḥrst*) stone: sacred eye amulets | 185 |
| [16]Lapis lazuli: sacred eye amulets | 217 |

*Pl. 15b*

| | |
|---|---|
| [1]Red jasper: scarabs | 62 |
| [2]Malachite: scarabs | 224 |
| [3]Bronze and Minu (*mynw*) stone: scarabs | 224 |
| [4]Lapis lazuli: scarabs | 62 |
| [5]Various costly stones: sacred eye amulets | 165 |
| [6]Various costly stones: seals as pendants | 62 |
| [7]Rock-crystal: seals | 1,550 |
| [8] " " beads | 155,000 |
| [9] " " cut: hin-jars | 155 |
| **234.** [10]Wrought wood: seals[b] | 31 |
| [11]Alabaster: a block | 1 |
| [12]Cedar: *bp* ͗ *-ny-ny* | 6 |
| [13]Cedar: *tp*ʿ*t* | 1 |
| [14]Neybu (*N* ͗ *y-bw*) wood: 3 logs, making (deben) | 610 |
| [15]Cassia wood: 1 log, making (deben) | 800 |
| [16]Reeds: bundles | 17 |

*Pl. 16a*

| | |
|---|---|
| [1]Cinnamon: measures (*msty*) | 246 |
| [2]Cinnamon: bundles | 82 |
| [3]Grapes: measures (*msty*) | 52 |
| [4]⸢Rosemary⸣ (*nkp* ͗ *ty*): measures (*msty*) | 125 |
| [5]Yufiti (*Yw-fy-ty*)-plant: measures (*msty*) | 101 |
| [6]⸢Dom-palm fruit⸣ of Mehay (*M-h* ͗ *-yw*): measures (*msty*) | 26 |
| [7]Fruit: heket | 46 |
| [8]Grapes: crates | 1,809 |
| [9]Grapes: bunches | 1,869 |

[a]The correct total is 22,566.

[b]Thebes, Heliopolis and Memphis each received one a year of these objects.

| | |
|---|---|
| [10]⌜Pomegranates⌝: crates | 375 |
| [11]*B*ᵓ-*k*ᵓ-*y*ᵓ-plant, in measures (*yp*˙*t*) | 1,668 |
| **235.** [12]Various cattle | 297 |
| [13]Live geese | 2,940 |
| [14]Live turpu (*Tw-r-pw*)-geese | 5,200 |
| [15]Live water-fowl | 126,300 |

*Pl. 16b*

| | |
|---|---|
| [1]Fat geese from the ⌜flocks⌝ | 20 |
| [2]Natron: bricks | 44,000 |
| [3]Salt: bricks | 44,000 |
| [4]Palm-fiber: ropes | 180 |
| [5]Palm-fiber: loads | 50 |
| [6]Palm-fiber: ⌜—⌝ | 77 |
| [7]Palm-fiber: cords | 2 |
| [8]Sebkhet (*sbḫ*˙*t*)-plants | 60 |
| [9]Flax (*pš*˙*t*): bekhen (*bḫn*) | 1,150 |
| [10]Ideninu (*Ydnynyw*) | 60 |
| [11]Hezet (*hḏ*˙*t*)-plant: measures (*msty*) | 50 |
| [12]Pure ⌜—⌝, deben | 750 |

### 6. GRAIN FOR THE OLD FEASTS

**236.** [13]Clean grain for the divine offerings of the feasts of the sky,[a] and the feasts of the first of the seasons, which King Usermare-Meriamon L. P. H., the Great God, founded for [14]his father, Amon-Re, king of gods, Mut, Khonsu, and all the gods of Thebes, as an increase of the divine offerings,[b] as an increase of the daily offerings,[b] in order to multiply that which was before, [15]from the year 1 to the year 31, making 31 years: 2,981,674[c] 16-fold heket.

---

[a]The offerings for these and the following feasts of 6 and 7 are recorded likewise in the Great Calendar of Medinet Habu (§§ 139–45), from which the scribe could copy them, though with some changes. Thus for twenty-one years the Coronation feast was only one day long, as shown in the calendar (made in year 12), but in year 22 it was made 20 days long. Similarly in year 12 the calendar gives the Feast of Opet as 24 days long, but our papyrus treats it as 27 days long for 31 years! The scribe evidently reckoned with these changes, for his numbers are even multiples of 31, as so commonly with the other temples.

[b]These words are incorrectly repeated in the text by a dittography.

[c]This amounts to 6,360,908 bushels, or 205,190 bushels annually.

### 7. OFFERINGS FOR NEW FEASTS FOUNDED BY RAMSES III

*Pl. 17a*

**237.** [1]Oblations of the festivals which King Usermare-Meriamon, L. P. H., the Great God, founded for his father, [2]Amon-Re, king of gods, Mut, Khonsu, and all the gods of Thebes, during the 20 days of offering, of the festival (called): [3]"Usermare-Meriamon,-L.-P.-H.,-Making-Festive-Thebes-for-Amon," from the first month of the third season, (ninth month), day 26,[a] to the second month of the third season (tenth month), day 15; [4]making 20 days; from the year 22 to the year 32,[b] making 11 years; together with the oblations of the [5]feast of Southern Opet (Luxor), from the second month of the first season (second month), day 19, to the third month of the first season (third month), day 15, making 27 days;[c] [6]from the year 1 to the year 31, making 31 years.

| | |
|---|---|
| **238.** [7]Fine bread: large oblation-loaves | 1,057 |
| [8]Fine bread: large loaves (*syd*) | 1,277 |
| [9] " " large loaves (*bḥ*) | 1,277 |
| [10] " " loaves (*ḏdmt-ḥr-t* ᵓ) | 440 |
| [11]Bread: large oblation-loaves | 43,620 |
| [12]Papyrus ⌈rind⌉ of the house of incense[d] | 685 |
| [13]Beer of the beer-cellar: 4,401 (jars), making | ——[e] |

[a]This is the coronation day of Ramses III, the twenty-sixth of Pakhons, being so recorded in the festival calendar on the south wall of the Medinet Habu temple (Greene, *Fouilles*, Pl. IV, ll. 9 and 10, twice): "*The first month of the third season, day 26, the day of the royal coronation (ḫᶜ stny) of King Ramses III.*" (See also § 153.) This feast was at first only one day long, but in the year 22 it was made twenty days long.

[b]As this feast fell within the 40 days during which Ramses III survived in his thirty-second year, it was, therefore, celebrated in that year also; but none of the old feasts, as he did not survive to celebrate them in the thirty-second year.

[c]This feast was not 27 days long, throughout the reign, but only 24 at first (see Breasted, *Zeitschrift für ägyptische Sprache*, 37, 126, where this passage in Harris was not yet noted). Under Thutmose III it lasted only 11 days (*ibid.*); it was an old feast, but because Ramses III lengthened it he includes it among feasts founded by himself. As he lengthened it from 24 to 27 days, it is not likely that the lengthening from 11 to 24 days was also due to him. If lengthened further in later times, it was prolonged at the end, for in the Twenty-first Dynasty it still began on the nineteenth. (*Inscriptions historiques de Pinodjem*, l. 13, below.)

[d]The numeral must refer to the separate pieces.

[e]The scribe has omitted the amount in hins.

| | |
|---|---|
| 14 Fine bread, meat, rahusu[a] (*r* ͗ -*ḥw-sw*)-cakes: measures[b] (*ḥtp*) for show | 165 |
| 15 Fine bread, meat, rahusu-cakes: measures[c] (*ḥtp*) of gold | 485 |

*Pl. 17b*

| | |
|---|---|
| 1 Fine bread, meat, rahusu-cakes: measures (*ḥtp*) for eating[c] | 11,120 |
| 2 Fine bread, meat, rahusu-cakes: measures (*ṯ* ͗ *y*) for the mouth of the eater[c] | 9,845 |
| 3 Fine bread, meat, rahusu-cakes: vases (*g* ͗ *y*) of the prince | 3,720 |
| 4 Fine bread of the divine offerings: vases (*dny* ͗) of gold, equipped | 375 |
| 5 Fine bread of the divine offerings: loaves (*by* ͗˙ *t*) | 62,540 |
| 6 " " " " " loaves (*pr-sn*) | 106,992 |
| 7 " " " " " white loaves | 13,020 |
| 8 Fine bread: large loaves (ᶜ *ḳ*) for eating[d] | 6,200 |
| 9 " " sweet loaves (*s* ᶜ *b*)[e] | 24,800 |
| 10 " " loaves (ᶜ *ḳ*) of the fire | 16,665 |
| 11 " " large loaves (ᶜ *ḳ*) | 992,750 |
| 12 " " loaves (*pws* ͗ -ᶜ *ḳ*) of grain | 17,340 |
| 13 " " white oblation-loaves | 572,000 |
| 14 " " pyramidal loaves | 46,500 |
| 15 " " kyllestis-loaves | 441,800 |

*Pl. 18a*

| | |
|---|---|
| 1 " " loaves (*wdnw-nt*) | 127,400 |
| 2 Kunek (*ḳwnk*)-bread: white loaves (*t* ͗) | 116,400 |
| 3 Fine bread: loaves (*p* ᶜ˙ *t*) | 262,000 |
| 4 Total of fine bread: various loaves (ᶜ *ḳ*) | 2,844,357[f] |

---

[a]Connected by Bondi (*Lehnwörter*, 62 and 86), with מרחשת, "pan."

[b]Or: "*baskets*" or "*vessels.*"

[c]These phrases evidently apply only to the loaves, in any case "*for eating*" occurs often with loaves alone; see 17*b*, l. 8, and the lists in Spiegelberg's "Geschäftsjournal" (*Recueil*, 17, 143 f.).

[d]Probably these terms indicate that these things were eaten at the feast. Thus in l. 3, each vessel or vase of food was eaten by a noble; the more plentiful supplies that follow were then eaten by the people.

[e]See Piehl, *Zeitschrift für ägyptische Sprache*, 1886, 80 ff.

[f]The real total is 2,806,407, not counting 25,710 "*measures,*" etc. (17*a*, 14–17*b*, 4). Even including the fine bread of 17*a*, ll. 7–10, which make 4,051 loaves, the scribe is still nearly 34,000 in excess of the real sum. The difference must lie in the "*measures,*" etc. (17*a*, 14–17*b*, 4).

| | |
|---|---|
| [5]Rahusu-cakes: measures (*ṯmṯm*) | 344 |
| [6]Cakes: measures (*yp˙t*) | 48,420 |
| [7]Rahusu (*Rʾ-ḥw-sw*): measures (*yp˙t*) | 28,200 |
| [8]Flour: vessels (ʿ) | 3,130 |
| **239.** [9]Shedeh: jars (*mn*) | 2,210 |
| [10]Shedeh: jars (*kʾ-bw*) | 310 |
| [11]Wine: jars (*mn*) | 39,510 |
| [12]Total, shedeh and wine: jars (*mn* and *kʾ-bw*) | 42,030 |
| [13]Beer: various jars | 219,215 |
| [14]Sweet oil: jars (*mn*) | 93 |
| [15]Sweet oil: hin | 1,100 |

*Pl. 18b*

| | |
|---|---|
| [1]White incense: jars (*mn*) | 62 |
| [2]Incense: various measures (*yp˙t*) | 304,093[a] |
| [3]⌈Inflammable⌉ incense: jars (*mn*) | 778 |
| [4]Red oil (*bḳ*): jars (*mn*) | 31 |
| [5]Oil (*nḥḥ*): jars (*mn*) | 93 |
| [6]Oil (*nḥḥ*): hin | 110,000 |
| [7]Honey: jars (*mn*) | 310 |
| [8]White fat: jars (*mn*) | 93 |
| [9]Olives: jars (*mn*) | 62 |
| [10]Southern linen: garments (*dw*) | 155 |
| [11]Southern linen: garments (*rdw*) | 31 |
| [12]Colored linen: garments (*yfd*) | 31 |
| [13]Colored linen: tunics | 44 |
| Total | 261 |
| **240.** [14]Wax: deben | 3,100 |
| [15]All (kinds of) fine fruit: measures (*kʾ-bw-sʾ*) | 620 |
| [16]All (kinds of) fine fruit: measures (*ṯʾy*) | 620 |

*Pl. 19a*

| | |
|---|---|
| [1]Fruit: measures (*ḥtp*) | 559,500 |
| [2]Fruit: measures (*dny˙t*) | 78,550 |

[a]The scribe has written "*making*" after this numeral, intending to add the weight in deben, but forgot it, as in 17*a*, 13.

| | |
|---|---|
| [3]Figs of the impost: measures (*yp·t*) | 310 |
| [4] " " " weights (*mḫ ͗*) | 1,410 |
| [5] " " " measures (*msty*) | 55 |
| [6]Figs: in measures (*yp·t*) | 15,500 |
| [7]Figs: measures (*ṯ ͗ y*) | 310 |
| [8]Mehiwet (*Mhywt*):[a] ⌜cakes⌝ (*s ͗ -t ͗*) | 3,100 |
| [9]Cinnamon: measures (*ḥtp*) | 220 |
| [10]Cinnamon: measures (*msty*) | 155 |
| [11]Semu (*s ͗ mw*)-plant: measures (*ḥtp*) | 1,550 |
| [12]⌜Cabbage⌝ (*Š ͗ wt*): heket | 620 |
| [13]Khithana (*Ḫy-ṯ ͗ -n ͗*)-fruit: heket | 310 |
| [14]Khithana (*Ḫy-ṯ ͗ -n ͗*)-fruit: ⌜bundles⌝ (*ᶜ nbw*) | 6,200 |
| [15]Grapes: measures (*msty*) | 117 |
| [16]Grapes: measures (*ṯ ͗ y*) | 1,550 |

*Pl. 19b*

| | |
|---|---|
| [1]Southern fruit: heket | 8,985 |
| [2]Enbu (*ᶜ nbw*): measures (*d ͗ mw*) | 620 |
| **241.** [3]Papyrus sandals: pairs | 15,110 |
| [4]Salt: 16-fold heket | 1,515 |
| [5]Salt: bricks | 69,200 |
| [6]Natron: bricks | 75,400 |
| [7]Thick stuff: garments (*dw*) | 150 |
| [8]Flax (*pš*): measures (*sbḫ·t*) | 265 |
| [9]⌜Tamarisk⌝(*y ͗ sr*): bundles | 3,270 |
| [10]Reed-grass: bundles | 4,200 |
| [11]Leather sandals: pairs | 3,720 |
| [12]⌜Dom-palm fruit⌝(*Ḥw-ḳw-ḳw*): in measures (*yp·t*) | 449,500 |
| [13]⌜Pomegranates⌝: in measures (*yp·t*) | 15,500 |
| [14]⌜Pomegranates⌝: crates (*pdr*) | 1,240 |
| [15]Olives: jars (*g ͗ y*) | 310 |
| [16]Jars and vessels of the mouth of the Heliopolitan canal[b] | 9,610 |

*Pl. 20a*

| | |
|---|---|
| [1]Papyrus ⌜rind⌝: measures (*yp·t*) | 3,782 |
| [2]Nebdu (*nbdw*): measures (*yp·t*) | 930 |

[a]Unknown fruit.

[b]Perhaps the place of the workshop where the jars were made.

| | |
|---|---|
| **242.** [3]Bulls | 419 |
| [4]Bullocks of the bulls | 290 |
| [5]Oxen (*ngʾ*) | 18 |
| [6]Heifers | 281 |
| [7]Two-year-olds (cattle) | 3 |
| [8]Calves | 740 |
| [9]Bullocks (*Tpw*) | 19 |
| [10]Cows | 1,122 |
| [11]Total, various cattle | 2,892 |
| [12]Male of the white oryx | 1 |
| [13]White oryxes | 54 |
| [14]⸢Male gazelle⸣ (*nrʾw*) | 1 |
| [15]Gazelles | 81 |
| [16]Total | 137 |
| [17]Total, various cattle (*yʾ·t*) | 3,029 |

*Pl. 20b*

| | |
|---|---|
| [1]Live geese (*rʾ*) | 6,820 |
| [2] " fowl (*ḥt-ʿʾ*) | 1,410 |
| [3] " turpu (*twrpw*)-geese | 1,534 |
| [4]Cranes | 150 |
| [5]Live hatching-fowl | 4,060 |
| [6]Live water-fowl | 25,020 |
| [7]Pigeons (*mny·t*) | 57,810 |
| [8]Live pedet (*pʿd·t*)-birds | 21,700 |
| [9]Live sesha (*sʾ-ʿšʾ*) birds | 1,240 |
| [10]Doves | 6,510 |
| [11]Total, various fowl | 126,250[a] |
| **243.** [12]Jars ⸢of the canal⸣ filled with fish, having wooden ⸢lids⸣ | 440 |
| [13]White fish | 2,200 |
| [14]Dressed shene (*šnʿ*)-fish | 15,500 |
| [15]Fish cut up | 15,500 |

*Pl. 21a*

| | |
|---|---|
| [1]Fish, whole | 441,000 |

[a]Lacking four of being correct.

| | |
|---|---|
| **244.** ²Blossoms[a] of the impost of flowers: sunshades[b] | 124 |
| ³Blossoms:[a] tall bouquets | 3,100 |
| ⁴Blossoms[a] of the impost of flowers: "garden fragrance"[c] | 15,500 |
| ⁵Isi-plant: measures (*yp·t*) | 124,351 |
| ⁶Flowers: garlands | 60,450 |
| ⁷Flowers: ⌜strings⌝ (*k ͻ -r ͻ -ḥw-ty*) | 620 |
| ⁸Blue flowers: ropes | 12,400 |
| ⁹Flowers for the hand | 46,500 |
| ¹⁰Flowers: measures (*ḏdm·t*) | 110 |
| ¹¹Lotus flowers for the hand | 144,720 |
| ¹² " " bouquets | 3,410 |
| ¹³ " " for the hand[d] | 110,000 |
| ¹⁴Papyrus flowers: bouquets | 68,200 |
| ¹⁵Papyrus: ⌜stems⌝ (ᶜ) | 349,000 |

*Pl. 21b*

| | |
|---|---|
| ¹Large bouquets of the impost of flowers | 19,150 |
| ²Dates: measures (*mḏ ͻ yw*) | 65,480 |
| ³Dates: ⌜cut branches⌝ | 3,100 |
| ⁴Vegetables: measures (*ḏdm·t*) | 2,170 |
| ⁵Vegetables: bundles | 770,200 |
| ⁶Isi-plant for the hand | 128,650 |
| ⁷Corn: bouquets | 11,000 |
| ⁸Ears of grain for the hand | 31,000 |
| ⁹Blossoms: bouquets | 1,975,800 |
| ¹⁰Blossoms: measures (*ḥtp*) | 1,975,800 |

### 8. PRIVATE STATUES OF AMON[e]

**245.** ¹¹The amount belonging to the 2,756 statues and figures which are above:[f]

---

[a]*Rnpy;* it probably means blossoms or flowers here, but in some passages it may mean vegetables; see **37***a*, 8, 9.

[b]The sunshades were made of green plants and flowers.

[c]Name of a plant or kind of bouquet?

[d]L. 11 has *sšn* for lotus, while l. 13 has *sšnyny*, indicating some difference.

[e]See **II**, 1–3, and note.

[f]See **II**, 1–3. In the final summary (**68***a*, 3–6) the proportions of gold and silver are given, viz., 7,205 deben, 1 kidet of gold, and 11,047 deben, ¼ kidet of silver, being roughly two parts gold to three parts silver, the usual proportion for electrum, of which the statues were therefore probably made.

| | | | |
|---|---|---|---|
| [12]Fine gold and silver | 18,252 deben, | $1\frac{1}{4}$ kidet | |
| [13]Real costly stones: various blocks | 18,214 " | 3 " | |
| [14]Black copper, copper, lead, ⌜tin⌝ | 112,132 " | | |
| [15]Cedar: various logs | | | 328 |
| [16]⌜Mastic tree⌝ (*šʾ-wʾ-bw*): various logs | | | 4,415 |

### 9.[a] RAMSES' CONCLUDING PRAYER TO AMON

*Pl. 22*

**246.** [1]How happy is he who depends upon thee! O god, Amon, Bull of his mother, ruler of Thebes. Grant thou that I may arrive in safety, landing in peace, [2]and resting in Tazoser like the gods. May I mingle with the excellent souls of Manu, who see thy radiance at early morning. [3]Hear my petition! O my father, my lord, I am alone among the gods who are at thy side. Crown my son as king upon the throne of Atum, establish him [4]as mighty Bull, lord, L. P. H., of the two shores, King of Upper and Lower Egypt, Lord of the Two Lands: Usermare-Setepnamon, L. P. H.: Son of Re, Lord of Diadems: Ramses (IV)-Hekma-Meriamon, L. P. H., emanation [5]that came forth from thy limbs. Thou art the one who didst designate him to be king, while he was a youth. Appoint thou him to be ruler, L. P. H., of the Two Lands over the people. Give to him a reign of millions of years, [6]his every limb being whole, in prosperity and health. Place thy crown upon his head, seated on thy throne; and may the serpent-goddess[b] alight upon his brows. Make him divine [7]more than any king, and great like thy reverence, as lord of the Nine Bows. Make his body to flourish and be youthful daily, while thou art a shield behind him [8]for every day. Put his sword and his war-mace over the heads of the Bedwin (*Sṯ·tyw*); may they fall down in fear of him like Baal. Extend for him the boundaries as far as he desires; [9]may the lands and countries fear in terror of him. Grant for him that Egypt may rejoice,

---

[a]This numbering does not conform with the scheme in the Heliopolitan section, where No. 8 is devoted to the offerings to the Nile-god, which were not given at Thebes. This is another evidence of the late origin of Theban power. The official offerings of the king to the Nile became a fixed custom in the days when Heliopolis was the seat of power and Thebes was an obscure village of Upper Egypt. The offerings to the Nile-god at Memphis were not old, but were founded by Ramses III in his twenty-ninth year.

[b]The uraeus serpent-crest.

ward off all evil, misfortune and destruction. [10]Give to him joy abiding in his heart, jubilation, singing and dancing before his beautiful face. Put love of him in the hearts of the gods and goddesses; his kindness and his terror [11]in the hearts of men. Complete the good things of which thou hast told me on earth for my son, who is upon my throne. Thou art the one who didst create him, confirm his [12]kingdom to the son of his son, thou being to them a protector, answering for them and they being to thee servants with their eyes upon thee doing benefactions

*Pl. 23*

for [1]thy ka, forever and ever. The things that thou ordainest, they come to pass, abiding and established; the things that thou sayest, they endure like gritstone. [2]Thou didst adjudge to me a reign of 200[a] years; establish them for my son who is (still) upon earth; make [3]his life longer than (that of) any king, in order to repay the benefactions which I have done for thy ka. Let him be king by reason of thy command; [4]even thine, who crownest him; let him not ⌜reverse that which thou hast done⌝, O lord of gods. Give great and rich Niles in his time, in order [5]to supply his reign with plentiful food. Give to him the princes who have not known Egypt, with loads [6]upon their backs for his august palace, King of Upper and Lower Egypt, Lord of the Two Lands: Usermare-Setepnamon, L. P. H.; Son of Re, Lord of Diadems: Ramses (IV)-Hekma-Meriamon, L. P. H.

## III. HELIOPOLITAN SECTION

### I. INTRODUCTORY VIGNETTE

*Pl. 24. Vignette*

**247.** Ramses III stands praying before Harakhte, Atum, Saosis, and Hathor. The accompanying notes are:

*Over Harakhte*

Harakhte, great god, lord of heaven.

*Over Atum*

Atum, lord of the Two Lands of Heliopolis.

[a]This must refer to some priestly oracle, attributed to Amon, in which he had promised Ramses III a reign of 200 years. The deceased king prays for the fulfilment of this promise to his son.

*Over Saosis*

Saosis, mistress of Heliopolis.

*Over Hathor*

Hathor, mistress of Hetep (*Ḥtp*).

*Before the King*

I tell the prayers, praises, adorations, and laudations, mighty deeds, benefactions, which I did for thee, in thy presence, O great prince.

### 2. PRAYER TO RE AND RECITAL OF THE KING'S BENEFACTIONS

*Pl. 25. Introduction*

**248.** [1]The prayers, praises, laudations, mighty deeds, and benefactions which King Usermare-Meriamọn, L. P. H., the Great God, did [2]for his father, Atum, lord of the Two Lands of Heliopolis, Re-Harakhte, Saosis, the mistress of Hetep (Hathor), and all the gods of Heliopolis.

*Prayer*

**249.** Said the King Usermare-Meriamon, L. P. H., the Great God, [3]in praising his father, this august god, Atum, lord of the Two Lands of Heliopolis, Re-Harakhte:

Praise to thee, Re-Atum, All-lord, creator of that which is, rising [4]in heaven, illuminating this land with his rays. The hidden ones, dwelling in the West,[a] turn their faces to thee; they rejoice to behold thy beauty. All people jubilate at [5]the sight of thee. Thou it is who madest heaven and earth; and thou didst appoint me to be king over the Two Lands, and Ruler, L. P. H., on thy great throne. Thou didst assign to me all the lands as far [6]as the circuit of the sun. They feared, and fell down to my name, as they do to thy name. I was diligent in pursuit of benefactions and numerous great deeds [7]for thy house

*Buildings and Temple Gifts*

**250.** I extended thy wall in the house of Re, I filled his treasury with the products of the lands of Egypt; I loaded his granaries with barley and spelt, [8]which had begun to stand (empty) since the (former)

---

[a]The dead.

kings. I made great designs for thy ⌜—⌝,[a] I caused them to rest in the shrines of thy temple; I made the regulations for [9]the priests ($w^c b$) in the house of Re. I made him more divine than formerly, [10]I cleansed Heliopolis for his divine ennead. I built his temples, which were gone to ruin, I fashioned their gods in their mysterious forms of gold, silver, and every costly stone, as everlasting works.

### *Sanctuary in the Heliopolis Temple*

**251.** [12]I made for thee an august house in the midst of thy temple, like the heavens, abiding and bearing the sun, before thee, founded

*Pl. 26*

with gritstone, laid with limestone, established [1]with good work, enduring in thy name. It is the great and mysterious horizon of Harakhte, the "Great Seat" is of gold, the double doors of Ketem-gold, while thy mother rests [2]in the midst of it, rejoicing and satisfied at seeing it. I equipped it with the classes[b] which I trained, personal property, lands, and herds without number.

### *Colossi in the Heliopolis Temple*

**252.** [3]I made for thee great monuments in the house of Re, of gritstone, which Atum shaped into great images, sculptured with toil, dragged up, and [4]resting in their places forever and ever, in thy great, august and lovely forecourt, carved with thy divine name like the sky.

### *Amulets for the Statue of Re*

**253.** [5]I made for thee august amulets of fine gold, with inlay of real lapis lazuli and real malachite. I attached them to thy body in the great house of thy protection and thy magnificence, [6]in thy splendid seat, that they might protect the august limbs as ⌜perennial⌝ amulets for thy great, grand and lovely form.

---

[a]The word (*rḫ'nf*) is plural, as shown by the possessive article; it must indicate divine statues, and literally translated means "*that which he knows*," perhaps an esoteric priestly term for statue. Compare a similar expression in **29**, 4.

[b]"*Classes*" (*ḏ ᵓ m*), a word later meaning "generations," and here referring to the successive "classes" into which the youth were divided as they became of age liable to conscription for enforced service. See **76**, 5, note, § 402.

### *Granite Shrine*

**254.** [7]I made for thee a mysterious shrine of granite, wherein Atum and Tafnut rest. The double doors upon it were of copper, mounted [8]with gold, engraved with the great name of thy majesty, forever and ever.

### *Stelæ with Temple Regulations*

**255.** [9]I made for thee great decrees for the administration of thy temple, recorded in the hall of writings of Egypt; stelæ were made, with outlined figures,[a] carved with the graver's tool, [10]abiding for thee forever, nor is there destruction for them.

### *Temple Balances*

**256.** [11]I made for thee splendid balances of electrum;[b] the like of which had not been made since the time of the god. Thoth sat upon it as guardian of the balances, [12]being a great and august ape[c] of gold in beaten work. Thou weighest therein before thee, O my father, Re, when thou ⌈measurest⌉ of gold and silver by the hundred-thousands,

*Pl. 27*

brought as tribute [1]before thee from their coffers, and given to thy august treasury in the house of Atum. I founded for it[d] daily divine offerings, in order to supply its altar at early morning.

### *Storehouses for Feasts*

**257.** [2]I made for thee a storehouse for the "Feast of the Appearance," being built upon pure ground, on the land of Heliopolis, divine in workmanship. I filled it with beautiful slaves of the choicest, and clean grain by the ten-thousand, in order to supply them.

### *Storehouse for Temple Income*

**258.** [3]I made for thee a pure storehouse containing divine offerings more than were before me, since (former) kings. I equipped it with

---

[a]The decrees were drawn with the pen upon stone stelæ, and then cut into the stone.

[b]The amount of gold and silver which went into these balances will be found in § 285.

[c]The ape was the sacred animal of Thoth, and a figure of this ape was regularly mounted upon the balances, of which Thoth was the presiding god.

[d]Namely, for the balances; evidently offerings were made to it.

everything, it suffered no lack; in order to supply thy offerings at early morning.

*Special Oblation-Storehouse*

**259.** [4]I made an oblation-storehouse for thy forecourt, filled with divine offerings, and plentiful food, and containing great oblations of gold and silver, in order to offer them to thy ka, O lord of gods. I equipped them, [5]I completed them with barley and wheat, filled with the spoil which I carried away from the Nine Bows. They were for thy ka, O sole lord, maker of heaven and earth, that the feasts of the first of the seasons might be doubled before thee.

*Cattle and Poultry Yards*

**260.** [6]I made thee cattle yards, equipped, containing bulls, and bullocks; fattening-houses anew, containing fat geese.

*Cleansing of Sacred Lakes*

**261.** [7]I cleansed the sacred[a] lakes of thy house, I removed all the filth that was in them, which had been the fashion of them formerly since the earth began. Thy divine ennead was satisfied in heart and rejoiced over them.

*Vineyards and Shedeh Gardens*

**262.** [8]I gave shedeh and wine as daily offerings, in order to present the land of Heliopolis in thy splendid and mysterious seat; groves, and verdure, with their plants anew. The lords of the land of life are satisfied therewith. [9]I made for thee great gardens, equipped, containing their groves, bearing shedeh and wine in the great house of Atum; and the divine ennead of Heliopolis rejoice in feasts to satisfy thy beauty daily.

*Olive-Lands*

**263.** [10]I made for thee olive-lands in thy city of Heliopolis, I equipped them with gardeners and numerous people, to make pure oil, the best of Egypt, in order to light[b] the flame in thy august house.

[a]Text has "*goddesses*" (*ntry·t*), which would read "*lakes of the goddesses of thy house*," which is probably an error for (*ntry*) "*sacred, divine.*"

[b]Lit., "*send up.*"

*Groves and Flower Gardens*

**264.** [11]I made for thee groves and arbors,[a] containing date trees; lakes supplied with lotus flowers, papyrus flowers, isi flowers, the flowers of every land, dedmet flowers, myrrh, and sweet and fragrant woods for thy beautiful face.

*New Temple Domains*

**265.** [12]I made for thee domains anew, with pure barley; I doubled their lands which had been waste, in order to double the divine offerings

*Pl. 28*

in numerous lists, for thy great, august and lovely name. [1]I made for thee numerous lands in the New Isles, in the southern and northern districts, by the ten-thousand. There were made for them stelæ[b] engraved with thy name, abiding for thee, bearing decrees forever.

[2]I made for thee a poultry yard[c] containing wild fowl; I conducted[d] the pools to thy city, Heliopolis, in order to present them to thy ka, O my father, conducted to thee and to thy divine ennead which follows thee.

*Officials, Servants, and Slaves*

**266.** [3]I appointed for thee archers and collectors of honey, bearing incense to deliver[e] their yearly impost into thy august treasury. [4]I appointed for thee hunting archers to capture white oryxes, in order to offer them to thy ka at all thy feasts. [5]I made for thee boatmen and tax-officials (*m-š ͗ -k ͗ -bwy*)[f] of the people, whom I created to collect the impost of the Two Lands, the taxes and the exactions, in order to transport them to thy treasury in the house of Re, in order to double thy divine offerings more than a million times. [6]I appointed slaves as watchmen of thy harbor, in order to watch the harbor of the Heliopolitan canal in thy splendid place.[g] [7]I made door-keepers of the slaves,

---

[a]See § 1021 for the same phrase (*ᶜ*·*t nt ḫt*); also § 194.

[b]Boundary stelæ, demarking the lands.

[c]See Spiegelberg, *Rechnungen*, 34, 35.

[d]Lit., "*I caused that the pools should be drawn to thy city,*" not referring to water-supply, but meaning that the fowl of the pools were thus brought.

[e]*F ͗ y.* See Spiegelberg, *Rechnungen*, 53.

[f]See Spiegelberg, *Recueil*, XV, 143 f.

[g]This is the temple, so that the canal probably passed close by the temple inclosure.

manned with people, in order to watch and ⸢protect⸣ thy court. [8]I made slaves as watchmen of the canal-administration, and the watchmen of the pure barley, for thee likewise.

*Granaries Restored*

**267.** [9]I made for thee granaries filled with grain, which had begun to fall to waste, and they became millions.

*Golden Statues*

**268.** [10]I made for thee statues of gold in beaten work, kneeling upon the ground[a] before thee, bearing divine offerings. I made others likewise, of pure silver, in order to satisfy thy two serpent-goddesses at every time.

*Vessels of the Temple Cult*

**269.** [11]I made a great vase-stand in thy forecourt, bearing vases of gold and silver, containing shedeh, supplied with divine offerings in numerous lists, in order to offer to thy ka, O great prince. [12]I made for thee table-vessels without number, of silver and gold with inlay, engraved with thy name; a censer, nemset (*nms˙t*)-vases, great denya (*dny*ᵓ)-vases, enkhy (ᶜ *nḫy*)-vases, hesy (*ḥsywt*)-vases, and numerous bowls (ᶜ *wy*), in order to convey them into [13]thy presence with libations of wine; thy divine ennead was satisfied in heart and rejoiced over them.

*Pl. 29. Temple-Ships*

**270.** [1]I made for thee transports, and galleys manned with people, in order to transport the products of God's-Land to thy treasury and thy storehouse.

*Restoration of Horus-Chapel and its Grove*

**271.** [2]I restored the "House-of-Horus-Presider-over-Temples;" I built his walls, which were in ruins. [3]I made to grow the august grove, which was in its midst; I planted it with papyrus in the midst of the Delta marshes, (though) it had begun to decay[b] formerly.

[a]Such a statue is depicted in the Medinet Habu treasury (Dümichen, *Historische Inschriften*, II, 30), and described in § 26, note.

[b]Lit., "*to rest.*"

*Temple Grove*

**272.** [4]I made to grow the pure grove of thy temple, I put it in its accustomed condition when it had gone to waste; I equipped it with gardeners to cultivate it, to make libations of shedeh in the "Place-Which-He-Knows."[a]

[5]I made for thee great festival oblations for thy court, as an increase of that which was done formerly since (former) kings, supplied with bulls, bullocks, mountain cattle,[b] oil, incense, honey, [6]shedeh, wine, gold, silver, royal linen, numerous garments, plants, and all flowers for thy beautiful face.

*Offerings in Hapi Temple*

**273.** [7]I made for thee great festival oblations in the house of Hapi, and all the gods of Khereha (*Ḫr-ᶜ ḥ ᵓ*) were in festivity.

*Temple of Re North of Heliopolis*

**274.** [8]I made for thee an august house north of Heliopolis, established as an everlasting work, engraved with thy name, viz.: "The-House-(*ḥ˙t*)-of-Millions-of-Years-of-Ramses-Ruler-of-Heliopolis-L.-P.-H.-in-the-House-of-Re-on-the-North-of-Heliopolis."[c] I equipped it with people and property, in order to convey into thy house gardens, containing flowers for thy forecourt.

*Temple Herds*

**275.** [9]I made for thee a herd (called): "Doer-of-Benefactions," supplied with plentiful cattle without number, in order to present them to thy ka at all thy feasts. I doubled those who belonged to them in classes,[d] belonging to thy name. [10]I made for thee another herd for thy august house, in order to supply thy temple with plentiful provisions (called): "Herd-of-Ramses-Ruler-of-Heliopolis,-L.-P.-H.,-Doubling-Offerings-in-the-House-of-Re." I filled it with cattle, and herdmen likewise. They shall not pass away, forever, belonging to thy ka.

---

[a]A name for the place of the cultus. See also p. 143, n. a.

[b]Small cattle, goats, and the like.

[c]This is probably the beautiful incrusted temple at Tell-el-Yehudiyeh.

[d]See **26**, 2, note.

### *Restorations*

**276.** [11]I made thee works, with workmen, builders, and stonecutters, in order to fashion thy house, in order to restore thy house.

### *Temple of Re*[a]

**277.** [12]I made for thee the "House (*pr*)-of-Ramses-Ruler-of-Heliopolis,-L.-P.-H.,-in-the-House-of-Re," equipped with people and property, like the sand.

### *Pl. 30. New Saosis Temple*

**278.** [1]I made for thee an august house, west of the Heliopolitan canal, for thy mother, Saosis (*Yws-*ᶜ ͻ *s*), mistress of Heliopolis.

### *Settlement of Foreign Captives*

[2]I made for thee a pure settlement of numerous classes;[b] whose sons I brought into thy house (called): "Taking-of-the-Foreigners."

### *Sacred Bulls*

[3]I raised the black cattle[c] and great bulls, purified from every evil in their fields.

### *Barge of Saosis*

[4]I hewed a large barge for thy great daughter, Saosis, mistress of Hetep (⌜called⌝): "Sep-in-Heliopolis;"[d] [5]of cedars of ⌜—⌝, the best of the royal domain, which were covered with gold like the barge of millions of years.

### *Lists*

**279.** [6]Behold, the list of them[e] is before thee, O my father, my lord, in order to inform thy divine ennead of my benefactions.

---

[a]This is evidently the chief temple at Heliopolis, to which Ramses III could have done no more than make some additions or restorations. It is probably the second in the list, **31**, 4; as the first (**31**, 3) is called a *Ḥ ˙ t*, and this temple is a *Pr*.

[b]See **26**, 2, note.

[c]See Spiegelberg, *Zeitschrift für ägyptische Sprache*, 1891, 81, 82.

[d]Or the barge may also have been for the god Sep, as a second object of the preposition.

[e]Ramses III's pious deeds.

### 3. RE'S ESTATE

*Pl. 31*

**280.** [1]List of things, cattle, gardens, groves, lands, galleys, workshops, and towns which King Usermare-Meriamon, L. P. H., the Great God, gave to [2]his august father, Atum, lord of the Two Lands of Heliopolis, Re-Harakhte, as property, forever and ever.

*People Attached to Temples, Etc.*

| | | |
|---|---|---|
| **281.** [a][3]"The-House (*ḥ·t*)-of-Ramses-Ruler-of-Heliopolis,-L.-P.-H.,-in-the-House-of-Re," under charge of the "Great Seer"[b] and the officials, with all possessions: | heads | 1,485 |
| [4]People whom he gave to the house of Atum, lord of the Two Lands of Heliopolis, Re-Harakhte, who were in the ownership of the house, under his charge: | (heads) | 4,583 |
| [5]Those belonging to "The-House-of-Ramses-Ruler-of-Heliopolis,-L.-P.-H.,-in-the-House-of-Re-North-of-Heliopolis," under charge of the scribe, and chief inspector, Perehotep (*P ˀ -R ᶜ -ḥtp*), equipped with its possessions: | heads | 2,177 |
| [6]The ⌈château⌉ of Pharaoh, L. P. H., which is in this place[c] under charge of the chief scribe, Thutmose and the officials: | heads | 1,779 |
| [7]"The ⌈—⌉[d]-of-Ramses-Ruler-of-Heliopolis,-L.-P.-H.,-Sustaining-Alive-the-Two-Lands," under charge of the scribe, and chief inspector, Hori: | heads | 247 |
| [8]Orderlies, children of chiefs, nobles, epru (ᶜ*-pw-r* ˀ),[e] and people of the settlement,[f] which is in this place: | heads | 2,093 |
| [9]Total | heads | [g]12,963 |

[a]A list of people like that in **10**, 3–11, 4, *q. v.*

[b]Title of the High Priest of Heliopolis.

[c]"*This place*" can only mean the temple just mentioned on the north of Heliopolis; on the château, see III, 588, l. 49. It must here have been attached to the Re-temple, as was the palace at Medinet Habu with the temple there; otherwise, the personnel would not have belonged to the god.

[d]*M ˀ wt*, with the determinative of land, is perhaps some temple estate.

[e]These are the people supposed by Chabas to have been Hebrews, a theory long since exploded.

[f]See **30**, 2.

[g]The correct total is 12,364.

*Pl. 32a. Miscellaneous Property*

| | |
|---|---|
| **282.** [1]Various cattle | 45,544 |
| [2]Gardens and groves | 64 |
| [3]Lands: stat | 160,084½ ¼ |
| [4]Workshops of cedar and acacia | 5½[a] |
| [5]Transports and galleys | 3 |
| [6]Towns of Egypt | 103 |

4. RE'S INCOME

**283.** [7]Things exacted, impost of the people of "The-House (*ḥ·t*)-of-Ramses-Ruler-of-Heliopolis,-L.-P.-H.,-in-the-House-of-Re;" [8]those of "The House (*ḥ·t*)-of-Ramses Ruler-of-Heliopolis,-L.-P.-H.,-in-the-House-of-Re-on-the-North-of-Heliopolis," the temples (*r ͗-pr*) and herds of this house (*pr*), [9]under charge of the officials, as their yearly dues:

| | |
|---|---|
| [10]Silver | 586 deben, 3⅔ ¼ kidet |

*Pl. 32b*

| | |
|---|---|
| [1]Copper | 1,260 deben |
| [2]Royal linen, mek-linen, double-fine southern linen, fine southern linen, southern linen, colored linen: various garments | 1,019 |
| [3]Incense, honey, oil: various jars (͗ ᶜᶜ) | 482 |
| [4]Shedeh, wine: various jars (͗ ᶜᶜ) | 2,385 |
| [5]Silver[b] from the things of the impost of the people for the divine offerings: | 456 deben, 3½ kidet |
| [6]Clean grain of the impost of the peasants: 16-fold heket | 77,100 |
| [7]Vegetables: bundles | 4,800 |
| [8]Flax: bales | 4,000 |
| [9]Water-fowl from the impost of the fowlers and fishermen | 37,465 |
| [10]Bulls, bullocks of the bulls, heifers, calves, cows, cattle of ⌜—⌝, cattle[c] of ⌜—⌝ of the herds | 98 |
| [11]Live geese of the exactions | 540½ (sic!) |
| [12]Cedar: a ferry-boat | 1 |
| [13]Acacia: transports and kara (*k ͗-r ͗*)-boats | 7 |

[14]Products of the oasis in numerous lists for the divine offerings

[a]The fraction applied to such an object is quite inexplicable, unless the noun be read as singular and 5½ be measures of timber.

[b]See **12***b*, 2. [c]Corrected from **12***b*, 7.

### 5. THE KING'S GIFTS TO RE

*Pl. 33a*

**284.** [1]Gold, silver, real lapis lazuli, real malachite, every splendid, costly stone, black copper, garments, [2]of royal linen, mek-linen, fine southern linen, southern linen, colored garments, jars of everything, [3]which King Usermare-Meriamon, L. P. H., the Great God, gave, as gifts of the king, L. P. H., [in order to provision the house of his august father],[a] Atum, lord of the Two Lands of Heliopolis, Re-Harakhte, [4]from the year 1 to the year 31, making 31 years:

| | | | | |
|---|---|---|---|---|
| **285.** [5]Fine mountain gold and gold for the balances[b] | 1,278 | deben, | 9⅔ | kidet |
| [6]Fine gold, gold of two times, and white gold in vessels and ornaments: | 198 | " | 3½ | " |
| [7]Total, gold | 1,479 | " | 3[c] | " |
| [8]Crude silver for the balances and silver in vessels | 1,891[d] | " | ½ | " |
| [9]Silver in beaten work: 1 tablet, making | 394 | " | | |
| [10]Total, silver | 2,255[e] | " | ½ | " |
| [11]Total, gold and silver | 3,734 | " | 3½ | " |
| [12]Real lapis lazuli: 1 block, making | 1 | " | 1 | " |
| [13]Lapis lazuli and malachite: a great scarab | | | 36 | " |
| [14]Black copper for the balances | 67 | " | 3 | " |
| [15]Copper in beaten work: 2 tablets, making | 400 | " | 3 | " |

*Pl. 33b*

| | |
|---|---|
| [1]Copper in vessels | 1,416 deben, 1 kidet |
| [2]Total copper | 1,819 deben, --(sic!)[f] kidet |
| **286.** [3]Royal linen, mek-linen, fine southern linen, southern linen, colored linen; various garments | 18,793 |
| [4]Myrrh: deben | 1,787 |

[a]Something has fallen out here, by error of the scribe; the restoration is from the parallel passage 13*a*, 3.

[b]Meaning the balances above mentioned in **26**, 11–**27**, 1 (§ 256). The gold amounts to some 311¾ pounds, troy.

[c]The fraction (⅙) is ignored.

[d]Nearly 461 pounds, troy.

[e]Thirty short.

[f]The scribe has omitted the number; the real total is 1,883 deben, 7 kidet.

| | |
|---|---|
| [5]Myrrh: heket | 2 |
| [6]Myrrh wood: logs | 20 |
| [7]Myrrh fruit in measures (*yp·t*) | 100 |
| [8]Incense, oil, honey, fat: various jars (ᶜ ͻ ͻ) | 3,740 |
| [9]Shedeh and wine: various jars (ᶜ ͻ ͻ) | 103,550 |
| [10]Incense: kararuti (*ḳ ͻ -r ͻ -rw-ty*)[a] | 530 |
| [11]Incense: large measures (*yp·t*) | 62 |
| [12]Good manna of Punt: deben | 300 |
| **287.** [13]Ubat (*wb ͻ t*) stone: seals mounted in gold | 11 |
| [14]Hirset (*ḥrs*) stone: deben | 50 |

*Pl. 34a*

| | |
|---|---|
| [1]Green feldspar[b]: deben | 50 |
| [2]Red jasper: deben | 200 |
| [3]Marvelous[c] stone: offering-table | 1 |
| [4]Ubat (*wb ͻ· t*) stone: seals | 200 |
| [5]Rock-crystal, and costly stones: various pendants | 2,195 |
| [6] " cut: hin | 10 |
| [7] " beads | 22,450 |
| [8]Sticks[d] of cinnamon: measures (*msty*) | 17 |
| [9]Reeds:[e] deben | 2,000 |
| [10]Syrian barley: heket | 5 |
| [11]Cumin: heket | 5 |
| **288.** [12]Wrought wood: seals | 31 |
| [13]Meru (*mry*) wood, with ebony: a ⌜staff⌝ | 1 |
| [14]Hewn wood: a block (for) the balances | 1 |
| [15]Carob wood: a log of 4 cubits (length)[f] | 1 |

*Pl. 34b*

| | |
|---|---|
| [1]Persea tree cut: (a log) of 2 cubits | 1 |
| [2]Mera (*mr ͻ*) wood: a post for the balances of 3 cubits, 4 palms | 1 |

---

[a]Probably a weight.

[b]*Nšm·t*, see *Catalogue Alnwick Castle*, 230.

[c]*N-by ͻ y·t*, apparently not gritstone (*by ͻ y·t*).

[d]Lit., "*reeds*," meaning the reedlike pieces of curled bark.

[e]This is perhaps also some similar aromatic bark in curled sticks or reeds; otherwise it would not be weighed by the deben.

[f]Probably for the beam of the balances, as we have the post in **34***b*, 2.

| | |
|---|---|
| [3]Wood and ⸢bark: handle⸣ of a ⸢—⸣ | 1 |
| [4]Olive land, equipped, one (grove), making | 54¼ stat |
| [5]Gardens of all (kinds of) trees, equipped | 2 |

### 6. GRAIN FOR THE OLD FEASTS

*The Old Feasts*

**289.** [6]Clean grain of the divine offerings, of the feasts of heaven and the feasts of the beginnings of the seasons, which [7]King Usermare-Meriamon, L. P. H., the Great God, founded for his august father, Atum, lord of the Two Lands of Heliopolis, Re-Harakhte, [8]being an increase of the divine offerings, and an increase of the daily offerings, in order to double that which was before me, L. P. H., [9]from the year 1 to the year 31, making 31 years: 16-fold heket, 1,097,624.

### 7. OFFERINGS FOR NEW FEASTS FOUNDED BY RAMSES III

**290.** [10]Oblations of the festival offerings which King Usermare-Meriamon, L. P. H., the Great God, founded for this house, [11]as an increase of the festival offerings of former time, year by year, from the year 9 to the year 31, making 23[a] years:

| | |
|---|---|
| **291.** [12]Fine bread: large oblation-loaves of gold | 460 |
| [13]Fine bread: loaves (*bḥ*) | 4,600 |

*Pl. 35a*

| | | | |
|---|---|---|---|
| [1]Fine bread: | | large oblation-loaves | 23,000 |
| [2] " | " | oblation-measures (*ḥtp*) | 80,500 |
| [3] " | " | loaves (ᶜ *ḳ*) of the fire | 920 |
| [4] " | " | large loaves (ᶜ *ḳ*) | 460,000 |
| [5] " | " | tall white loaves | 80,500 |
| [6] " | " | white oblation-loaves | 920,000 |
| [7] " | " | white pyramidal loaves | 103,500 |
| [8] " | " | kyllestis-loaves | 34,500 |
| [9] " | " | loaves (*wdnw-nt*) | 80,500 |
| [10]Kunek (*ḳwnk*)-bread: | | white loaves | 80,500 |
| [11]Total, fine bread: | | various loaves (ᶜ *ḳ*) | 2,760,420[b] |

[a]Hence the following quantities are all evenly divisible by 23. This division, carried through the entire list, furnishes a complete list of the annual offerings presented at this feast.

[a]Real total is 1,868,980.

| | |
|---|---|
| 12 Cakes: ⌜—⌝ | 69,000 |
| 13 Cakes: loaves (*by˙t*): | 11,500 |

*Pl. 35b*

| | |
|---|---|
| 1 Rahusu (*r*ʾ-*ḥw-sw*)-cakes: round loaves | 2,875 |
| 2 Rahusu (*r*ʾ-*ḥw-sw*)-cakes: measures (*ṯmṯm*) | 46 |
| **292.** 3 Beer: measures (*ṯrf*) | 198,260 |
| 4 Shedeh: colored jars (*mn*) | 1,380 |
| 5 Shedeh: jars (*k*ʾ*bw*) | 2,990 |
| 6 Wine: jars (*mn*) | 16,100 |
| 7 Total, shedeh and wine: jars (*mn* and *k*ʾ*bw*) | 20,470 |
| **293.** 8 Bulls | 966 |
| 9 Bullocks of the bulls | 1,886 |
| 10 Oxen (*ng*ʾ) | 703 |
| 11 Heifers | 1,242 |
| 12 Calves | 1,242 |
| 13 Cows | 5,911 |
| 14 Total, various cattle | 11,960 |
| 15 Males of the white oryx | 230 |

*Pl. 36a*

| | |
|---|---|
| 1 Live geese | 1,150 |
| 2 Live hatching-fowl | 2,300 |
| 3 Live water-fowl | 13,800 |
| 4 Total, live water-fowl | 17,250 |
| **294.** 5 Honey: jars (*g*ʾ*y*) | 92 |
| 6 Incense: jars (*k*ʾ-*ḥr-k*ʾ) | 9,200 |
| 7 " food-jars (*ṯbw*) | 4,600 |
| 8 " white loaves | 1,150 |
| 9 " measures (*ḥtp*) | 34,500 |
| 10 " measures (*dny˙t*) | 126,500 |
| 11 " jars (ʾʿʿ*bw*) | 26,500 |
| 12 Papyrus ⌜rind⌝, worked into incense: various measures (*yp˙t*) | 34,500 |
| 13 Fruit: measures (*ḏdmt*) | 690 |
| 14 " " (*ṯ*ʾ*y*) | 23,000 |
| 15 " " (*ḥtp ḥr* ⌜*nmtt*⌝) | 34,500 |

*Pl. 36b*

| | |
|---|---:|
| [1]Fruit: various measures (*ḥtp*) | 1,150,000 |
| [2] " measures (*d*ˀ-*w*ˀ-*r*ˀ) | 4,600 |
| [3] " measures (*dny*) | 23,000 |
| [4]Papyrus ⌜rind⌝: various measures (*yp˙t*) | 23,000 |
| [5]⌜Dom-palm fruit⌝: measures (*ḥtp*) | 4,600 |
| [6]Figs: ⌜pyramids⌝ (*s*⌜*d*⌝*f*) | 4,600 |
| [7]Katha[a] fruit and katha flowers: heket | 23,000 |
| **295.** [8]Lotus flowers for the hand | 46,000 |
| [9]Isi-plant: various measures (*yp˙t*) | 483,000 |
| [10]Isi-plant: for the hand | 231,500 |
| [11]Flowers: garlands | 46,000 |
| [12]Papyrus (flowers): bouquets | 483,000 |

*Pl. 37a*

| | |
|---|---:|
| [1]Papyrus: large pools[b] | 6,900 |
| [2]⌜Flax⌝: measures (*dydy*) | 92,000 |
| [3]Isi-plant: ⌜measures⌝ (*dydy*) | 69,000 |
| [4]Menhet (*mnḥ*)-plant in measures (*yp˙t*) | 26,500 |
| [5]Dates: measures (*mḏ*ˀ) | 241,500 |
| [6]Milk: measures (*gs-r*ˀ) | 8,600 |
| [7]Clusters of ⌜berries⌝ for the hand | 92,000 |
| [8]Blossoms:[c] bouquets | 1,150,000 |
| [9]Blossoms:[c] measures (*ḥtp*) | 1,150,000 |
| [10]Herbs: bundles (*ḥtp˙t*) | 4,600 |
| [11]Sehetep (*sḥtp*) of carob-pods | 92,000 |
| [12]Fire wood: (⌜logs⌝)[d] | 11,500 |
| [13]Charcoal: measures (*gs-r*ˀ) | 2,300 |

### 8. OFFERINGS FOR THE NILE-GOD

*Pl. 37b. Old Offerings*

**296.** [1]Oblations for the "Books of the Nile-God,"[e] which he founded anew in the house of the Nile-god, father of gods; [2]together with the "Books of the Nile-God" which are presented in the Pool of

---

[a]*K*ˀ˙*ṯ*ˀ. [b]Perhaps papyrus-producing pools? [c]See **21***a*, 2–4.

[d]Or some measure implied as a matter of course; cf. Maspero, *Recueil*, I, 59.

[e]The "*Books of the Nile-God*" were lists of the offerings presented to him twice a year. The first record of such offerings is under Ramses II, who established a

Kebeh (*Ḳbḥ*) in the house of Re-Harakhte; [3]the "Books of the Nile-God," which are presented in the house of Anubis, lord of designs in Neru (*Nr*ᵓ*w*), being an increase of their (offerings) that were formerly, [4]year by year, from the year 1 to the year 31, making 31 years.

### *Offerings Founded by Ramses III*

**297.** [5]"Books of the Nile-God," which King Usermare-Meriamon, L. P. H., the Great God, founded 48 years, making 31 years:[a] [6]272 "Books of the Nile-God," making:

| | |
|---|---|
| [7]Fine bread of the divine offerings: various loaves (*by*ᵓ*ʿt*) | 470,000 |
| [8]Fine bread of the divine offerings: persen (*pr-sn*)-loaves, white loaves, and seshu (*sšw*)-loaves | 879,224 |
| [9]Cakes: various measures (*ypʿt*) | 106,910 |
| [10]Kunek (*ḳwnk*)-bread: loaves (*wdnw-nt*) | 46,568 |
| [11]Beer: various jars | 49,432 |
| Making | ———[b] |
| [12]Clean grain: 16-fold heket | 61,172½ |
| **298.** [13]Bulls | 291 |
| [14]Bullocks of the bulls | 17 |

*Pl. 38a*

| | |
|---|---|
| [1]Calves | 51 |
| [2]Cows | 2,564 |
| Total | 2,923 |

semiannual feast of the Nile-god at Silsileh and recorded the fact, together with a fine hymn to the god, on the rocks at Silsileh (Stern, *Zeitschrift für ägyptische Sprache*, 1873, 129–35). These were renewed by Merneptah, and again by Ramses III, both of whom had duplicates of Ramses II's stela carved beside it. The "*Books*" were thrown into the stream, and doubtless also the offerings themselves, of which the "*Books*" contained the lists. Ramses III's stela is dated in Phamenoth of the sixth year, and, like Ramses II, he celebrated the two feasts on the fifteenth of Thoth and the fifteenth of Epiphi (Lepsius, *Denkmäler*, III, 218, *d*, l. 15).

[a]I am unable to explain this addition: "*making 31 years*," unless it is a dittography from the end of the l. 4. Evidently the 48 years is a total of annual offerings obtained by adding 31 years of old offerings and 17 years of Ramses' newly founded offerings, for the 272 books of l. 6 are exactly divisible by 17 (sixteen times). Hence the list beginning l. 6 refers to the 17 years of Ramses' new foundation, as all such lists in this papyrus refer to his new foundations, e. g., **34***b*, 10 ff. The items of the list following (**37***b*, 7, to **41***b*, 6) are almost all even multiples of 17.

[b]The scribe has omitted the number of hins which these jars make.

| | |
|---|---:|
| [3]Goats | 1,089 |
| [4]Fat geese | 192 |
| [5]Live geese and fowl (*ḫt*-ʿꜣ) | 3,938 |
| [6]Hatching-fowl | 364 |
| [7]Water-fowl | 2,653 |
| [8]Pigeons | 68 |
| [9]Sesha (*s*ꜣ-ʿ*š*ꜣ)-birds | 19,928 |
| [10]Total, various fowl | 27,143 |
| **299.** [11]Shedeh: jars (*k*ꜣ*-bw*) | 209 |
| [12]Wine: jars (*mn*) | 7,154 |
| [13]White fat: 3,513 jars (ʿ), each one ¼ hin, making: hins | 627½[a] |
| [14]Onions: measures (ʿ) | 12,712 |

*Pl. 38b*

| | |
|---|---:|
| [1]Salt (*spr*): jars (ʿ) | 12,712 |
| [2]Natron: jars (ʿ) | 12,712 |
| [3]Dried dates: jars (ʿ) | 11,872 |
| [4]Dried myrrh: jars (ʿ) | 11,872 |
| [5]Uz (*wḏ*)-mineral: jars (ʿ) | 11,872 |
| [6]Eye-paint: jars (ʿ) | 11,872 |
| [7]Incense: censerfuls | 848 |
| [8] " measures (*spr*) | 424 |
| [9] " 87,344 jars (ʿ), making incense: deben | 23,008 |
| [10] " measures (*dny·t*) | 6,420 |
| [11] " jars (ʿ) | 2,568 |
| [12] " jars (ʿꜣꜣ *bw*) | 1,304 |
| [13]White incense: hin | 85 |
| [14]Oil: hin | 85 |
| **300.** [15]Fruit: measures (*mḥ·tt*) | 254,240 |

*Pl. 39*

| | |
|---|---:|
| [1]Fruit: measures (*dny·t*) | 2,672 |
| [2]Fruit: jars (ʿ) | 154,672 |
| [3]Berries: jars (ʿ) | 11,872 |
| [4]Raisins:[b] jars (ʿ) | 11,872 |

[a]The scribe has made a bad miscalculation, 3,513 quarter-hin jars = 878¼ hin.

[b]Lit., "*raisin-berries,*" meaning the individual grapes, plucked from the stem.

| | |
|---|---|
| [5]Best fruit: jars (*gᵓy*) | 9,600 |
| [6]Honey: 20,800 jars (*pw-gᵓ*), each one ¼ hin, making: hin | 5,200 |
| [7]Honey: 1,040 jars (*mḥ·tt*), each one 1 hin, making: hin | 1,040 |
| [8]Honey for cakes: hin | 7,050, halves 25 |
| [9]White fat for cakes: hin | 1,419, halves 25 |
| [10]Cinnamon: logs | 3,036 |
| [11]Best oil: 848 jars (*bpᵓ*), each one ½ hin, making: hin | 424 |
| [12]Best oil: 3,036 jars (ᶜ), each one ¼ hin, making: hin | 758 |
| **301.** [13]Shelled beans: jars (ᶜ) | 11,998 |

*Pl. 40a*

| | |
|---|---|
| [1]Raisins: jars (ᶜ) | 11,872 |
| [2]Raisins in measures (*yp·t*) | 106,000 |
| [3]Carob-pods in measures (*yp·t*) | 106,000 |
| [4]Herbs:[a] bundles (*ḫrš*) | 159,000 |
| [5]Herbs:[a] bundles (*ḥtp·t*) | 11,872 |
| [6]Cyperus of the shore, for the hand | 71,200 |
| [7]Palm-fiber: measures (*msty*) | 43,900 |
| [8]White fruit: jars (*gᵓy*) | 4,240 |
| [9]Live "garden fragrance"[b] | 106,000 |
| [10]Seneb (*snb*)-berries: jars (ᶜ) | 11,872 |
| [11]Butter: jars (*nms·t*) | 12,040 |
| [12]Milk: jars (*nms·t*) | 12,040 |
| [13]Milk: jars (*mhn*) | 198 |
| [14]⌈Pomegranates⌉ in measures (*yp·t*) | 96,000 |
| [15]Apples (*dpḥ·t*): baskets (*kᵓ-rᵓ-ḥw-ty*) | 848 |

*Pl. 40b*

| | |
|---|---|
| [1]Isi-plant: measures (*ḏdmt*) | 848 |
| [2]Isi-plant: for the hand | 8,480 |
| [3]Flowers: garlands | 43,640 |
| [4]Clusters of grapes for the hand | 74,000 |
| [5]Blossoms:[c] bouquets | 114,804 |
| [6]Blossoms:[c] clusters (*ḥtp·t*) | 114,804 |
| **302.** [7]Gold: a statue of the Nile-god, nusa (*nwsᵓ*) | 6,784 |
| [8]Silver: a statue of the Nile-god, nusa (*nwsᵓ*) | 6,784 |
| [9]Real lapis lazuli: a statue of the Nile-god, nusa (*nwsᵓ*) | 6,784 |

---

[a]Or vegetables. [b]See **21***a*, 4. [c]See **21***a*, 2–4.

| | |
|---|---|
| [10]Real malachite: a statue of the Nile-god, nusa (*nws* ᵓ) | 6,784 |
| [11]⌜Iron⌝: a statue of the Nile-god, nusa (*nws* ᵓ) | 6,784 |
| [12]⌜Raised⌝ copper: a statue of the Nile-god, nusa (*nws* ᵓ) | 6,784 |
| [13]Lead: a statue of the Nile-god, nusa (*nws* ᵓ) | 6,784 |
| [14]⌜Tin⌝:[a] a statue of the Nile-god, nusa (*nws* ᵓ) | 6,784 |
| [15]Menit-uz (*mny·t-wḏ*):[b] a statue of the Nile-god, nusa (*nws* ᵓ) | 6,784 |

*Pl. 41a*

| | |
|---|---|
| [1]Minu (*mynw*) stone: a statue of the Nile-god, nusa | 6,784 |
| [2]Shesmet (*šsm·t*) stone: a statue of the Nile-god, nusa | 6,784 |
| [3]Green feldspar (*nšm·t*): a statue of the Nile-god, nusa | 6,784 |
| [4]Alabaster: a statue of the Nile-god, nusa | 6,784 |
| [5]Red jasper: a statue of the Nile-god, nusa | 6,784 |
| [6]Hirset (*ḥrs·t*) stone: a statue of the Nile-god, nusa | 6,784 |
| [7]Kenmet (*knm·t*) stone: a statue of the Nile-god, nusa | 6,784 |
| [8]Mesdemet (*msdm·t*) stone: a statue of the Nile-god, nusa | 6,784 |
| [9]Seher (*shr*): a statue of the Nile-god, nusa | 6,784 |
| [10]Tur (*twr*): a statue of the Nile-god, nusa | 6,784 |
| [11]Bronze: a statue of the Nile-god, nusa | 6,784 |
| **303.** [12]Various costly stones: a statue of the Nile-god, nusa | 13,568 |
| [13]Rock-crystal: seals | 10,196 |
| [14] " " bracelets | 10,196 |
| [15] " " ⌜armlets⌝ | 10,196 |

*Pl. 41b*

| | |
|---|---|
| [1]Sycamore wood: statues of the Nile-god | 5,096 |
| [2]Sycamore wood: statues of the Nile-goddess | 5,098 |
| [3]Southern linen: kilts | 10,196 |
| [4]Stone: ubas (*wb* ᵓ) | 31,650 |
| [5]Fire wood: (⌜logs⌝)[c] | 510 |
| [6]Charcoal: measures (*gs-r* ᵓ) | 17 |

### 9. RAMSES' CONCLUDING PRAYER TO RE

*Pl. 42. Ramses III's Prayer for His Son*

**304.** [1]Complete thou for me the mighty deeds, which I did for thee, O father. I have reached the West[d] like Osiris; grant that I may

[a]See Brugsch, *Zeitschrift für ägyptische Sprache*, 1892, 110 ff.

[b]Some unknown metal.

[c]See **37***a*, 12, note.

[d]The place of the dead (*ymy wr·t*).

receive offerings,[a] which come forth before thee; that I may smell [2]incense and myrrh like thy divine ennead. Grant that thy radiance may bathe[b] my head daily; that my soul may live, that he may behold thee at early morning. Do thou the [3]desire of my heart, O august father, for I was a benefactor of thy ka, while I was upon earth. Hear my petition, do that which I say, which gods as well as [4]men announce to thee. Establish my son to be king, as lord of the Two Regions, that he may rule the Two Lands, like thee, as sovereign, L. P. H., in Egypt: [5]Usermare-Setepnamon, L. P. H., whom thou hast chosen for thyself, to be heir, to magnify thy name. Set the white crown and the divine double crown upon his head, like as thou wert crowned [6]upon earth, as Horus, wearer of the double diadem. Make sound his every limb, make to flourish his bones and his eyes, flourishing in beholding the love of millions.[c] Make his duration [7]upon earth like the Pole Star; ready, like a mighty Bull, seizing the Two Lands. Give to him the Nine Bows, united under his two feet, saluting[d] [8]his name, while his sword is over them. Thou art the one who createdst him, when he was a child; thou didst appoint him to be hereditary prince upon the double throne of Keb; thou didst say: "Let him become king [9]upon the throne of him who begat him." The things which thou ordainest, they come to pass, abiding, and established. Give to him a great and prolonged reign, and jubilees great and mighty, like Tatenen; [10]King of Upper and Lower Egypt, Lord of the Two Lands: Usermare-Setepnamon, L. P. H.; Son of Re, Lord of Diadems: Ramses (IV)-Hekma-Meriamon, L. P. H.

## IV. MEMPHITE SECTION

### I. INTRODUCTORY VIGNETTE

*Pl. 43. Vignette*

**305.** Ramses III stands praying before Ptah, Sekhmet, and Nefertem. The accompanying notes are these:

---

[a]The word (*ḥtp*) is determined with a flower like the word *ḥtp·t*, "*bouquet, cluster,*" but *ḥtp*, "*offering,*" is meant. The same error is found in 44, 9.

[b]Lit., "*anoint.*"

[c]Lit., "*millions of love.*"

[d]Lit., "*in the posture of salâm to his name.*"

*Over Ptah*

Ptah the great, "South-of-His-Wall." lord of "Life-of-the-Two-Lands."

*Over Sekhmet*

Sekhmet the great, beloved of Ptah.

*Over Nefertem*

Nefertem, protector of the Two Lands.

*Before the King*

I tell the prayers, praises, adorations, laudations, mighty deeds, and benefactions, which I did for thee in thy presence, O Resi-inebef.[a]

### 2. PRAYER TO PTAH AND RECITAL OF THE KING'S BENEFACTIONS

*Pl. 44. Introduction*

**306.** [1]The prayers, praises, adorations, laudations, mighty deeds and benefactions, which King Usermare-Meriamon, L. P. H., the Great God, did for [2]his father, Ptah, the great, "South-of-His-Wall," lord of "Life-of-the-Two-Lands;" Sekhmet, the great, beloved of Ptah; Nefertem, protector of the Two Lands; and all the gods of Memphis.

*Prayer of Ramses III*

**307.** Said King Usermare-Meriamon, the Great God, [3]to his father, this august god, Ptah, the great, "South-of-His-Wall," lord of "Life-of-the-Two-Lands," Tatenen, father of the gods, lofty-plumed, ready-horned, beautiful-faced, upon the great throne:

*Praise of Ptah*

**308.** "Hail to thee! Great art thou, revered art thou, [4]O Tatenen, father of the gods, great god of the first time, former of men, maker of gods, beginning that became the first primeval being, after whom happened all that came to pass, who made the sky after[b] the conception of his mind, [5]who suspended it by the elevation of the atmosphere,[c]

---

[a]The epithet of Ptah; "*South-of-His-Wall.*" [b]Or: "*by.*"

[c]*Šwt.* It has the determinative of "heaven" (Piehl gives "ciel"), but the context demands "air or atmosphere," and I render it so, by connecting it with *Šw*, the air-god, who according to the myth crept between heaven and earth, separated them, and lifted the heavens.

who founded the earth by that which he himself did, who surrounded it with Nun,[a] and the sea; who made the nether world, who satisfied the dead, and caused the sun to come to prosper them, [6]as ruler of eternity, lord of everlastingness; lord of life, who fills the throat and gives breath to every nostril; who preserves alive all men by his sustenance. Lifetime, destiny and bringing up are under his authority, men live by that which comes out of his mouth; maker of [7]offerings for all the gods, in his form as Nun, the great; lord of eternity, everlastingness is under his authority; breath of life for all people; leading the king to his great throne in his name: King of the Two Lands. I am thy son whom thou hast installed as king [8]in the place of my father in peace. I ⌜follow⌝ thee, thy plans are before me.

*The King's Decease*

**309.** Thou didst multiply good things for me, while I was upon earth, thou hast led me to rest by thy side in the western heavens like all the mysterious gods of the Nether World, and I am associated [9]with thy divine ennead in thy mysterious seat, like Apis, thy august son, who is by thy side. Grant that I may eat food[b] of thy divine offerings, of

*Pl. 45*

bread, incense, beer, shedeh, and wine. Grant that [1]I may live again in Tazoser, seeing thee every day like thy divine ennead.

*The King's Benefactions*

**310.** While I was ruler, L. P. H., upon earth as lord of Egypt, did I not incline my heart mightily to thee, [2]in order to seek all benefactions for thy august house, in order to present them before thee in thy city of Memphis?

*New Ptah-Temple*

**311.** [3]I made for thee a house[c] anew in thy court, the place of thy heart's rest at thy every appearance (called): "The-House *(h·t)*-of-

---

[a]The primeval ocean. [b]See 42, 1.

[c]So little of Memphis has survived that this temple of Ramses III has disappeared. See a fragment in Brugsch, *Recueil de monuments*, I, Pl. IV, 2, 4; and another in *Annales*, III, 26, 27. A mortuary temple of Ramses III at Memphis called: "*House-of-Ramses,-Ruler-of-Heliopolis,-of-the-Temple-of-Memphis*," in Ptolemaic times (British Museum Stela, Young, *Hieroglyphics*, 77, 78; Brugsch, *Thesaurus*, 908; the same temple on Berlin sarcophagus, No. 18, *ibid.*, 910). On our passage, see Naville, *Transactions of the Society of Biblical Archæology*, VII, 134 f.

Ramses-Ruler-of-Heliopolis,-L.-P.-H.,-in-the-House-of-Ptah," in the 4great and mysterious court of "Him-Who-is-South-of-His-Wall,"[a] founded in granite, laid in limestone. Its great doorposts bore lintels of Elephantine granite; the doors upon it[b] were of copper in a mixture of six (⌈parts⌉).[c] The great doorways were of gold, with inlay of stone; the bolts[d] of black copper, overlaid with gold, bearing figures of Ketem-gold, with gold in inlay. Its monuments were sculptured and established with labor. Its towers were of stone, approaching 7heaven. Its "Great Seat" was enlarged like a "Great House," having a door of gold like the double doors of heaven.

### *Divine Image*

**312.** I wrought upon thy image, 8resting in its shrine, in gold, silver, and real, costly stone, established with labor.

### *Endowment*

**313.** I equipped it with serf-laborers in numerous lists, having lands and herds in South and North.

### *Pl. 46*

1Its storehouses were overflowing with numerous possessions, naval archers, collectors of honey, delivering incense and delivering silver, 2merchants without number, deliveries of clean grain by the ten-thousand; numerous gardens, plentiful in shedeh and wine; cattle yards, bulls, bullocks, and 3fattening-houses; the products of Egypt, God's-Land, Syria and Kush. I made them more numerous than the sand, in its august storehouse, the magazine containing divine offerings, supplied 4with food, without lack in any of its places. They were for thy ka, O sole lord, maker of what is, Ptah, "South-of-His-Wall," ruler of eternity. 5I gave to thee 20,000 16-fold heket of grain, to convey them to thy house each year, in order to provision thy temple with divine offerings, in addition to the daily offerings which were before me.

---

[a]See § 305 (last word).

[b]Masculine, referring to the lintel, not to the temple, which is here feminine. The doors were mounted in lintel and threshold, and not from the doorposts.

[c]See 6, 9, note.

[d]Or possibly all the mountings, including hinges.

### *Older Ptah-Temple*

**314.** [6]I restored the house of Ptah, thy great seat, I caused it to be like the horizon, wherein Re is. I filled its storehouses with numerous possessions. I loaded its granaries with barley and spelt.

### *Cultus Image and its Portable Shrine*

**315.** [7]I made a design for thy processional image, in the gold-house anew, of thy temple, wrought[a] of gold, native silver, real lapis lazuli, malachite, and every splendid costly stone. [8]I made its august shrine like the horizon of heaven, in[b] thy barque in the midst of it, resting upon it. I set up its great ⌈—⌉. [9]The shrine was with a ⌈roof⌉, two columns, and an upper ⌈cornice⌉ of the ⌈roof⌉; they were of gold in ⌈raised work⌉, in real, costly stone. I wrought upon its great carrying-

*Pl. 47*

poles, [1]overlaid with fine gold, engraved with thy name. When thou appearest with glad heart in Ineb-Sebek (*Ynb-Sbk*)[c] in thy great and mysterious form of "Him-Who-is-South-of-His-Wall (Ptah)," thou fillest thy city of Memphis with the radiance of thy limbs, and the people rejoice to see thy beauty.

### *Restoration of Hatkeptah*

**316.** [2]I cleansed Hatkeptah,[d] thy splendid seat; I built its temples, which had gone to ruin; I fashioned its gods in their august forms, of gold, silver, every costly stone in the gold-houses.

### *Silver Tablets*

**317.** [3]I made for thee great tablets of silver in hammered work, engraved and carved with the graver's tool, in the great name of thy majesty, with the adorations and prayers which I offered before thee, and bearing the decrees for the administration of thy house forever.

---

[a]Adjective, referring to the image.

[b]The shrine stood in the center of the model of a Nile boat, and the whole was borne on poles, supported on the shoulders of the priests.

[c]Lit., "*Wall-of-Sebek*," a sanctuary in Memphis, whence the god is carried in the shrine, amid rejoicing multitudes.

[d]Lit., "*House-of-the-Ka-of-Ptah*," an ancient name of the Ptah-temple of Memphis, frequently also applied to the city itself.

*Bronze Tablets*

**318.** [4]I made for thee two tablets of a mixture of six (⌜parts⌝),[a] being of the color of fine mountain gold, engraved and adorned with thy name, carved with the graver's tool, with the excellent praises which I offered to thy ka.

*Amulets*

**319.** [5]I made for thee august amulets for thy body, of fine Ketem-gold, and of silver, in beaten work, in ⌜raised work⌝ with inlay of real lapis lazuli, in order to put them upon thy limbs in thy "Great Seat," and all the gods of the house of Ptah were contented therewith.

*Monolithic Shrine*

**320.** I made for thee a mysterious shrine of Elephantine granite, established with work forever, of a single block, having double doors of bronze, of a mixture of six (⌜parts⌝),[a] engraved with thy august name, forever. [7]Ptah, Sekhmet, and Nefertem rest in it, while statues[b] of the king are by their side, to present offerings before them. I founded for them divine offerings presented before them, enduring for thee forever, before thy beautiful face.

*Temple Regulations*

**321.** [8]I made for thee great decrees with secret words, recorded in the hall of writings of Egypt, made into stelæ of stone engraved with the graver's tool, for the administration of thy august house, forever; and the administration of thy pure settlement of women. I brought their children who were forsaken, being people of the serf-laborers, (⌜in⌝) the hands of others. I put them for thee into the offices in the house of Ptah, and there were made for them decrees forever.

*Storehouses for the Feasts*

**322.** [10]I made for thee storehouses for the "Feasts of the Appearance" in thy divine house. They were built upon the (temple) soil, and established with labor. I filled them with slaves whom I had carried off as captives, to serve for thy divine offerings, full and pure, in order

[a]Alloy of bronze, see 6, 9.

[b]Such statues are shown in the reliefs at Medinet Habu (Lepsius, *Denkmäler*, III, 212, *a*).

[11]to provision the house of Ptah with food and provisions, in order to double that which was before thee, O Resi-inbef (Ptah); and thy divine ennead was glad of heart, and rejoiced over them.

*Pl. 48. Cattle and Poultry Yards*

**323.** [1]I made for thee cattle yards, filled with bulls and bullocks; fattening-houses likewise, containing fat geese; poultry yards ⸢of the exactions⸣ containing wild fowl, in order to offer to thy ka every day.

*Collectors*

**324.** [2]I made for thee archers and collectors of honey, delivering incense; I established for them tax-officials (*mš ᵓ kᵓ ḥwy*) to conduct them and to collect their annual impost for thy august storehouse, in order to fill the magazines of thy house with numerous possessions, in order to double thy divine offerings, for presentation to thy ka.

*Granaries*

**325.** [3]I made for thee granaries filled with barley and spelt, containing many grain-heaps, towering to heaven, in order to provision thy temple every day, before thy lovely face, O maker of heaven and earth.

*Statues of the King*

**326.** [4]I made for thee statues of the king, L. P. H., of gold in beaten work; others of pure silver in beaten work likewise, kneeling upon the ground before thee,[a] bearing a vase and an offering-tablet, containing divine offerings of bread and beer, in order to offer them before thee every day.

*Cultus Implements*

**327.** [5]I made for thee a great vase-stand for thy court, overlaid with fine gold, with labor; its vases were of gold and silver, carved with thy name, supplied with divine offerings and with every good thing, in order to offer (them) before thee at early morning.

*Red Sea and Mediterranean Ships*

**328.** [6]I made for thee transports and galleys[b] in the midst of the sea, manned with galley-crews in numerous lists, in order to transport the

[a]See **28**, 10, note.

[b]According to **51***a*, 13, there were but two ships: evidently one on the Mediterranean and one on the Red Sea.

products of God's-Land, and the impost of the land of Zahi (*Ḏ* ᵓ-*h* ᵓ) to thy great storehouses in thy city of Memphis.

*Festival Oblations*

**329.** [7]I made for thee great festival oblations as new foundations, in order to offer (them) to thy ka at each of thy appearances. They were supplied with bread, beer, oxen, fowl, incense, fruit, vegetables, shedeh, wine, royal linen, plentiful mek-linen, fine southern linen, [8]oil, incense, honey, dried myrrh, every good aromatic wood, sweet in fragrance, before thy lovely face, O lord of gods.

*Feast of the "First-of-the-Flood"*

**330.** [9]I made for thee a great festival oblation of the "First-of-the-Flood"[a] for thy great, august and lovely name, Ptah-Nun, the great, father of the gods. They were supplied with food like water in thy great and august court of Ineb-Sebek,[b] [10]for all thy images, and the gods of the deeps. They ⌜were paid⌝ dues and ⌜—⌝ from the storehouses, magazines, granaries, cattle yards, and poultry yards each year, in order to satisfy the great council of Nun, so that they are satisfied and rejoicing in the feast at the sight of them.

*Sacred Barge*

**331.** [11]I hewed thy august barge, O lord of eternity, of 130[c] cubits length upon the river; of great new[d] cedars, of the best of the royal domain. Its "Great House" was of gold, and of real costly stones, as far as the water; and of gold on each side of it. Its bow

*Pl. 49*

[1]bore a pair of hawks of fine gold, with inlay of every costly stone, more beautiful in work than the evening-barque. The stern was of fine gold, its two steering-oars ⌜wrought⌝ in fine gold. Ptah, the beautiful of face, South-of-His-Wall, appeared, [2]in order to rest in its "Great House," like the horizon-god, while his heart was satisfied and glad at

---

[a]A feast (*tp-nwy*) on the canal of Memphis. Compare the feast of the "*First-of-the-River*" (*tp-ytr*) at Thebes, e. g., on the Lateran obelisk (II, 838).

[b]See 47, 1.

[c]About 217 feet.

[d]Text has "*real*" (*m* ᵓ ᶜ *w*), which must be an error for the usual adjective, "*new*" (*m* ᵓ *w*).

the sight of it, making his beautiful voyage upon the flood, to his daughter, the mistress of the sycamore (Hathor), [3]on the south of Memphis. The people[a] rejoice at the sight of him, and there is jubilee before him to[b] his august house.

*Sacred Cattle*

**332.** [4]I protected the sacred cattle of Apis, male and female, which had been neglected in the herds of every house. I made them all more divine than their[c] sacred cattle. [5]I extended their boundaries to their accustomed places, which others had taken from them for fields. Their landmarks were set up, engraved with thy name; and there were made for them decrees for administering them on earth.

*Supplies of Incense*

**333.** [6]I brought to thee plentiful tribute of myrrh, in order to go around thy temple with the fragrance of Punt for thy august nostrils at early morning. [7]I planted incense and myrrh-sycamores in thy great and august court in Ineb-Sebek,[d] being those which my hands brought from the country of God's-Land, in order to satisfy thy two serpent-goddesses every morning.

*Cultus Vessels*

**334.** [8]I made for thee table-vessels for thy "Great Seat," being censers, vases (*nms˙t*), altar-vessels bearing gen (*gn*)-vases, heset (*ḥsyw˙t*)-vases, ekhu (*ᶜḫw*)-vessels, enkhi (*ᶜnḫy˙w˙*)-vases, and great altar-vessels for oblations, [9]bearing divine offerings. They were of fine gold and silver, in beaten work, with inlay of every costly stone without number, in order to present them to thy ka every day, O Ptah, father of gods, former of men.

*First Jubilee*

**335.** [10]I celebrated for thee the first jubilee (*ḥb-s*[*d*]) of my reign,[e] as a very great feast of Tatenen. I doubled for thee that which was done in the midst of the court, and there was offered to thee [11]a festival offering, consisting of numerous oblations of bread, wine, beer, shedeh, vegetables, bulls, bullocks, calves by the hundred-thousand, cows by

---

[a]Original has two words for "people," *rḫy˙t* and *ḥnmm˙t*.

[b]Till he reaches his house.

[c]To whom "*their*" refers is not evident.

[d]See **47**, 1.

[e]See §§ 413–15.

the ten-thousand, without number: the products of [12]the lands of Egypt like the sand of the shore. The gods of South and North were gathered in the midst of it.[a] I restored thy temple, the jubilee-houses

*Pl. 50*

[1]which were before in ruins, since the (former) kings. I wrought upon[b] thy divine ennead, the lords of the jubilee (*ḥb-st*), in gold, silver, and costly stones, as formerly. [2]I made for them clothing of royal linen and mek-linen; I mixed for them ointment for their serpent-crests. I founded divine offerings, [3]offered to their ka's, abiding as daily offerings for their ka's forever.

*Lists*

**336.** [4]Behold, I have, listed[c] the benefactions which I did before thee, O Ptah-South-of-His-Wall, lord of the White Wall (Memphis), that the gods of the house of Ptah may know of my benefactions.

### 3. PTAH'S ESTATE

*Pl. 51a*

**337.** [1]List of the things, cattle, gardens, lands, galleys, workshops, and towns, which [2]King Usermare-Meriamon, L. P. H., the Great God, gave to his august father, Ptah, the great, "South-of-His-Wall," lord of "Life-of-the-Two-Lands," as property forever and ever.

*People Attached to Temples, Etc.*

**338.** [3]"The-House (*ḥ·t*)-of-Ramses-Ruler-of-Heliopolis,-L.-P.-H.,-in-the-House-of-Ptah," under charge of the officials: 09

[4]"Herd-of-Ramses-Ruler-of-Heliopolis,-L.-P.-H.,-in-the-House, of-Ptah," under charge of the overseer of herds, Huy: heads 1,361

[5]"House (*pr*)-of-Usermare-Meriamon,-L.-P.-H.," the town[e] upon the western road and western canal, under charge of the steward, Penithtowe (*Pn-yṯt-t᾽wy*): heads 40

---

[a]This exactly accords with the record of the vizier Ta's visit to the South, "*to take the gods of the South*" (§§ 413, 414).

[b]Upon their images. [c]See **9**, 8. [d]See **10**, 2, note.

[e]This is the town mentioned as the limit of the pursuit of the Libyans (§ 102). The "*western canal*" is probably the "*Water of Re*" (**10**, 8). It is mentioned again in § 340.

| | | |
|---|---|---|
| "House (*pr*)-of-Ramses-Ruler-of-Heliopolis,-L.-P.-H.,-in-the-House-of-Ptah," under charge of Huy, who is chief of the house | heads | 16 |
| 7 People whom he gave to the house of Ptah, the great, "South-of-His-Wall," lord of "Life-of-the-Two-Lands," who were on account of the house, under charge of the High Priest and the officials: | heads | 841 |
| 8 "Ptah-of-Ramses-Ruler-of-Heliopolis,-L.-P.-H.,-Finding-Place-in-the-House-of-Ptah,"[a] under charge of the deputy, Ptahmose: | heads | 7 |
| 9 Syrians and Negroes of the captivity of his majesty, L. P. H., whom he gave to the house of Ptah: | persons[b] | 205 |
| 10 Total, heads | | 3,079 |

*Miscellaneous Property*

| | |
|---|---|
| **339.** 11 Various cattle | 10,047 |
| 12 Gardens and groves | 5 |
| 13 Transports and galleys[c] | 2 |

*Pl. 51b*

| | |
|---|---|
| 1 Lands: stat | 10,154 |
| 2 Town | 1 |

### 4. PTAH'S INCOME

**340.** 3 Things exacted, impost of the people of "The-House (*ḥ·t*)-of-Ramses-Ruler-of-Heliopolis,-L.-P.-H.,-in-the-House-of-Ptah;" 4 "Herd-of-Ramses-Ruler-of-Heliopolis,-L.-P.-H.,-in-the-House-of-Ptah;" "House (*pr*)-of-Usermare-Meriamon,-L.-P.-H.,-the-Town-5 on-the-Western-Canal;" "House (*pr*)-of-Ramses-Ruler-of-Heliopolis-in-the-House-of-Ptah;" and the temples (*r*ᵓ-*pr*) of this house; which[d] was delivered into 6 their treasuries as their dues:

| | |
|---|---|
| **341.** 7 Silver | 98 deben, 3⅔ ¼ kidet |
| 8 Fine southern linen, southern linen, colored linen: various garments | 133½ |
| 9 Wine: jars (*mn*) | 390 |

[a] The name of some particular statue of Ptah.

[b] See 10, 14 and 15.

[c] See **48**, 6.

[d] The antecedent of this pronoun is "*impost*," in l. 3.

| | |
|---|---|
| [10]Silver, in things of the impost of the people, for the divine offerings: | 141 deben, $3\frac{1}{10}$ kidet |
| [11]Clean grain of the impost of the peasants: 16-fold heket | 37,400 |
| [12]Vegetables: bundles | 600 |
| [13]Bulls, bullocks, calves, cows, cattle of ⌜—⌝, and cattle of ⌜—⌝ of the herds | $15\frac{1}{2}$ |

*Pl. 52a*

| | |
|---|---|
| [1]Live geese of the exactions | 135 |

[2]Products of Egypt, products of God's-Land, products of Syria, products of Kush [3]and of the oasis,[a] for the divine offerings in numerous lists.

### 5. THE KING'S GIFTS TO PTAH

**342.** [4]Gold, silver, real lapis lazuli, real malachite, every splendid, costly stone, copper, black copper, [5]garments of royal linen, mek-linen, fine southern linen, southern linen, colored garments, jars,[b] cattle, fowl, and everything, [6]which King Usermare-Meriamon, L. P. H., the Great God, gave as gifts of the king, L. P. H., to [7]the house of Ptah, the great, "South-of-His-Wall," lord of "Life-of-the-Two-Lands," and (to) the temples in his ownership, from the year 1 to the year 31, making 31 years:

| | | | |
|---|---|---|---|
| **343.** [8]Fine gold, gold of two times, white gold in vessels and ornaments | 263 deben, | $5\frac{1}{2}$ kidet | |
| [9]Gold: ornaments of the prince | 2 | " | |
| [10]Silver in vessels and scraps | 342 | " | $7\frac{1}{6}$ " |
| [11]Silver in beaten work: a great tablet of 1 cubit, 6 palms' length, 1 cubit, 1 palm, 3 fingers' width: 1, making | 173 | " | $8\frac{2}{3}\ \frac{1}{6}$ " |
| [12]Total, silver in vessels and ornaments | 516 | " | 6 " |

*Pl. 52b*

| | |
|---|---|
| [1]Total, gold and silver in vessels, ornaments and scraps | 780 deben, $1\frac{1}{2}$ kidet |
| [2]Real lapis lazuli, mounted in gold and ⌜fastened⌝ with 2 strings of ⌜beads⌝: 1, making | 3 " |

---

[a]See 12*b*, 13.

[b]Jars of oil, wine, shedeh, honey, etc.

| | |
|---|---|
| [3]Real lapis lazuli | 3 deben, 2 kidet |
| [4]Real malachite | 2 " |
| [5]Green feldspar (*nšm·t*) | 10 " |
| [6]Lapis lazuli, and real malachite: scarabs mounted and pivoted in gold | 36 |
| [7]Lapis lazuli: large scarabs | 46 |
| [8]Malachite: large scarabs | 46 |
| [9]Bronze in hammered work, of a mixture of 6 (⌈parts⌉): a great tablet, making | 245 deben |
| [10]Bronze in beaten work, of a mixture of 6 (⌈parts⌉): a great tablet, making | 65 " |
| [11]Bronze in vessels and scraps | 1,708 " |
| [12]Total, bronze in vessels and scraps | 2,018 " |
| **344.** [13]Royal linen, mek-linen, double-fine southern linen, fine southern linen, southern linen, and colored linen, various garments | 7,026 |
| [14]Myrrh: deben | 1,034 |
| [15]White incense, honey, oil, fat, butter: various jars (ʾʿʿ) | 1,046 |
| [16]Shedeh, and wine: various jars (ʾʿʿ) | 25,978 |

*Pl. 53a*

| | |
|---|---|
| [1]Total, various jars (ʾʿʿ) | 27,024 |
| [2]Ivory: tusks | 1 |
| [3]Nenybu (*N-n-y-bw*) wood: deben | 725 |
| [4]Cassia: deben | 894 |
| [5]Cinnamon wood: bundles | 45 |
| [6]Sticks[a] of cinnamon: measures (*msty*) | 28 |
| [7]Syrian barley: heket | 40 |
| [8]⌈Rosemary⌉: measures (*msty*) | 40 |
| [9]Yufiti (*Yw-fy-ty*)-plant: measures (*msty*) | 80 |
| [10]Semu (*sʿmw*)-plant: measures (*msty*) | 11 |
| [11]Fruit: heket | 14 |
| **345.** [12]Cedar: planks | 8 |
| [13]Mesdemet (*msdm·t*) stone: deben | 50 |
| [14]Dedmet (*ddm·t*) flowers: measures (*dmʾw*) | 50 |
| [15]Natron: deben | 14,400 |

[a]See **34***a*, 8.

*Pl. 53b*

| | |
|---|---|
| [1]Rock-crystal: beads | 31,000 |
| [2] " " cut: hin | 441 |
| [3] " " seals | 3,200 |
| [4]Wrought wood: seals | 31 |
| [5]Bulls, bullocks, heifers, calves, and various cattle | 979 |
| [6]Live geese | 269 |
| [7]Live turpu (*twrp*)-geese | 150 |
| [8]Live urdu (*wrdw*)-birds with golden beaks | 1,035 |
| [9]Live urdu (*wrdw*)-birds | 41,980 |
| [10]Live water-fowl | 576 |
| [11]Total, various fowl | 44,010 |

### 6. GRAIN FOR THE OLD FEASTS

**346.** [12]Clean grain of the divine offerings of the feasts of heaven and the feasts of the beginnings of the seasons, which [13]King Usermare-Meriamon, L. P. H., the Great God, founded for his father, Ptah, the great, "South-of-His-Wall," lord of "Life-of-the-Two-Lands," [14]as increase of the divine offerings, and as increase of the daily offerings, doubling that which was before me, L. P. H.

*Pl. 54a*

[1]from the year 1 to the year 31, making 31 years: 16-fold heket: 947,688

### 7. OFFERINGS TO THE NILE-GOD

**347.** [2]"Books of the Nile-God," which King Usermare-Meriamon. L. P. H., the Great God, founded for his august father, [3]Ptah, the great, "South-of-His-Wall," lord of "Life-of-the-Two-Lands," from the year 29 to the year 31, making 3 years:

| | | |
|---|---|---|
| [4]Fine bread of the divine offerings: | loaves (*by*ᵓ·*t*) | 73,800 |
| [5] " " " " " | loaves (*pr-sn*) | 191,142 |
| [6] " " " " " | pyramidal loaves | 6,150 |
| [7]Cakes: pyramidal loaves | | 14,760 |
| [8]Beer: jars (*ds*) | | 1,396 |
| [9]Dried dates: jars (ᶜ) | | 2,396 |
| [10]Dates: measures (*mḏ*ᵓ) 2,396, making | | ——[a] |

[a]Omitted by the scribe.

| | |
|---|---|
| 11 Clean grain ⌜—⌝: 16-fold heket | 3,633½ $\frac{1}{16}$ |
| 12 Bulls | 41 |
| 13 Cows | 164 |
| Total | 205 |

*Pl. 54b*

| | |
|---|---|
| 1 Various goats | 205 |
| 2 Live geese | 574 |
| 3 Live fowl (*ḫt*ʿʾ) | 84 |
| 4 Live hatching-fowl | 164 |
| 5 Live water-fowl | 287 |
| 6 Sesha (*s*ʾ-ʿ*š*ʾ)-birds | 3,025 |
| 7 Total, various fowl | 4,339[a] |
| **348.** 8 Wine: jars (*mn*) | 820 |
| 9 Wine: jars (ʿ) | 2,366 |
| 10 Onions: measures (ʿ) | 2,366 |
| 11 Salt (*spr*): measures (ʿ) | 2,366 |
| 12 Incense: censerfuls | 164 |
| 13 " measures (*spr*) | 82 |
| 14 " jars (ʿ) | 19,892 |
| 15 " deben | 4,469 |

*Pl. 55a*

| | |
|---|---|
| 1 Best oil: jars (⌜*bp*ʾ⌝) | 164 |
| 2 Best oil: jars (ʿ) | 574 |
| 3 Cinnamon: logs | 574 |
| 4 Myrrh: jars (ʿ) | 2,396 |
| 5 Eye-paint: jars (ʿ) | 2,396 |
| 6 Uz (*wḏ*)-mineral: jars (ʿ) | 2,396 |
| **349.** 7 Gold: statues of the Nile-god | 656 |
| 8 Gold: nusa | 656 |
| 9 Gold: nusa[b] | 656 |
| 10 Silver: statues of the Nile-god | 656 |

[a]The correct total is 4,134.

[b]This is evidently a dittography; for the silver statues are followed only by the same number of nusa of silver (l. 11), so that the repetition of the gold (l. 9) is superfluous.

| | |
|---|---:|
| [11]Silver: nusa | 656 |
| [12]Every real, costly stone: statues of the Nile-god | 15,744 |
| [13]Every real, costly stone: nusa | 15,744 |
| [14]Sycamore wood: statues of the Nile-god | 984 |
| [15]Sycamore wood: statues of the Nile-goddess | 984 |
| [16]Rock-crystal: bracelets | 2,968 |
| [17]Rock-crystal: seals | 2,968 |

*Pl. 55b*

| | |
|---|---:|
| **350.** [1]Southern linen: kilts | 2,968 |
| [2]Honey for cakes: hin | 66 |
| [3] " jars (*mḥtt*) | 164 |
| [4] " jars (*pw-gᵓ*) | 3,280 |
| [5]White fat for cakes: hin | 250 |
| [6]White fat: jars (ʿ) | 574 |
| [7]Shelled beans: jars (ʿ) | 2,396 |
| [8]Natron: jars (ʿ) | 2,396 |
| [9]Seneb (*snb*)-berries: jars (ʿ) | 2,396 |
| [10]Every fine fruit: jars (ʿ) | 22,960 |
| [11]Milk: jars (*nms't*) | 2,396 |
| [12]Butter: jars (*nms't*) | 2,396 |
| [13]Best fruit: jars (*gᵓy*) | 2,396 |
| [14]Fruit: jars (*gᵓy*) | 2,396 |
| [15]Fruit: jars (*mḥtt*) | 45,100 |

*Pl. 56a*

| | |
|---|---:|
| [1]Raisins in measures (*yp't*) | 21,000 |
| [2]Carob-pods in measures (*yp't*) | 21,000 |
| [3]Herbs: bundles (*ḥtp*) | 2,396 |
| [4]Cyperus of the shore, for the hand | 14,350 |
| [5]⌈Pomegranates⌉ in measures (*yp't*) | 21,000 |
| [6]Live "garden fragrance"[a] | 21,000 |
| [7]Isi-plant, for the hand | 1,640 |
| [8]Flowers: garlands | 2,970 |
| [9]Blossoms:[b] bouquets | 21,000 |
| [10]Blossoms:[b] clusters (*ḥtp't*) | 21,000 |
| [11]Stone: uba (*wbpᵓ*) | 15,150 |
| [12]Palm-fiber: measures (*msty*) | 15,150 |

[a]See **21***a*, 4.

[b]See **21***a*, 2.

### 8. CONCLUDING PRAYER OF RAMSES III

*Pl. 56b*

**351.** [1]Give to me thy eyes and thy ears, O lord, Ptah, father of fathers, former of the gods; and hear [2]my plea, which I make before thee. I am thy beloved son, great in benefactions. Install [3]my son to be king, establish him upon thy throne as ruler of every land over the people, Usermare-Setepnamon, L. P. H., the child [4]who came forth from thy limbs. Grant that he may be crowned upon earth like the son of Isis (Horus), when he took the etef-crown, bearing the ⌜—⌝. Grant [5]that he may rest upon thy throne as king of the Two Lands, as Horus, the mighty Bull, beloved of Mat. Give to him my kingdom [6]according as thou makest his life happy upon earth, possessed of joy. Make his sword victorious, while the lands and countries fall [7]beneath his feet forever. Let him take possession of Egypt as ruler, L. P. H., of the Two Lands; let him be divine [8]before thee, possessed of thy favor. Extend for him the boundaries of the Nine Bows; let them come because of his might, that they may do obeisance to him. [9]Give satisfying life, united with his limbs, and health for his members at every season, [10]King of Upper and Lower Egypt, Lord of the Two Lands; Usermare-Setepnamon, L. P. H., Son of Re, Lord of Diadems; Ramses (IV)-Hekma-Meriamon, L. P. H.

## V. GENERAL SECTION

(SMALL TEMPLES)

### I. PRAYER TO THE GODS AND RECITAL OF THE KING'S BENEFACTIONS

*Pl. 57. Introduction*

**352.** [1]The praises, prayers, adorations, laudations, mighty deeds, and numerous benefactions, which King Usermare-Meriamon, L. P. H., the Great God, did for his fathers (sic!), all the gods and goddesses of South and North.

*Prayer of Ramses III*

**353.** [2]Said King Usermare-Meriamon, L. P. H., the Great God, in praising and magnifying all the gods of South and North:

*Praise of the Gods*

[3]Hail to you, gods and goddesses, lords of heaven, earth, and the Nether World, great of foot in the barque of millions of years, by the

side of your[a] father, Re. His heart is satisfied when he sees their beauty, in order to make prosperous the land of Egypt, bringing a Nile that overflows from their mouth, [4]leading it from their mouth, that the lords of eternity and everlastingness may eat. Under their charge is the breath of life, and the term of life is (under) their seal, which their father made, on coming forth from their mouth. He rejoices, and flourishes at the sight of them, the great in heaven, the mighty [5]in earth, giving breath to nostrils that were stopped up. I am your son whom your hands created, whom ye crowned as ruler, L. P. H., of every land. Ye wrought for me good things upon earth, that I might assume my office in peace.

### *Benefactions to the Gods*

**354.** Was not my heart constant in seeking out mighty benefactions, [6]for your temples? I equipped them with great decrees, recorded in every hall of writings; with their people, their lands, their herds; with their galleys and ships upon the Nile. I restored their [7]temples which formerly were in ruin. I founded for you divine offerings, as an increase of that which was before you. I wrought for you in the gold-houses, in gold, silver, lapis lazuli, and malachite. I made plans for your storehouses. I completed them with numerous possessions. [8]I filled your granaries with barley and spelt, in heaps. I built for you houses and temples, carved with your name forever. I provided their serf-laborers, I filled them with numerous people. I did not take people as a tithe, [9]from the temples of any gods, since those kings;[b] doing it in order to appoint them to the infantry and chariotry. I made edicts for administering them upon earth, for the kings who shall be after me. I presented to you oblations before you, [10]supplied with every good thing. I made for you storehouses for the "Feast of the Appearance;" I filled them with plentiful food. I made for you table-vessels of gold, silver, and copper by the hundred-thousand. I hewed your barges upon the Nile, [11]bearing a "Great House,"[c] overlaid with gold.

---

[a]Original has "*their*," as usual in such constructions in Egyptian.

[b]He means that he did not levy upon the people presented to the temples by former kings, in order to secure troops.

[c]Shrine.

*Temple of Onouris at Thinis*

**355.** I made an august [house][a] of stone of Ayan (ʿ*yn*ʾ) in the house of my father, Onouris-Shu, son of Re (called): "The-House (*ḥ·t*)-of-Ramses-Ruler-of-Heliopolis,-L.-P.-H.,-the-Judge-in-the-House-of-Onouris." I filled it with people and slaves of the choicest. [12]Its storehouse contained plentiful possessions; the granaries contained grain. I founded for it daily divine offerings, in order to offer them to thy ka, O Shu, son of Re. I surrounded the house (*pr*) of Onouris with a wall, built with 20 ⌜courses⌝ in the ground foundation, and a height of 30 cubits; having [13]ramps, ⌜towers⌝,[b] and battlements on its every side. Its doorposts and lintels were of stone of Ayan (ʿ*yn*ʾ), bearing doors of cedar mounted with copper, excluding[c] the Asiatics and Tehenu who transgressed their limits of old.

*Pl. 58. Temple of Thoth at Hermopolis*

**356.** [1]I did numerous benefactions in Hesret (*Ḥsr*ʾ) for my father Thoth, dwelling in Hermopolis. I built for him a house anew in his court; it was [2]a mysterious chapel for the All-Lord. I made for him another house as a dwelling-house; it was the horizon of heaven before him. When he appeared, he was contented in heart, to rest in them; [3]he rejoiced and was glad to see them. I supplied them with food and provisions, containing the products of every land; numerous slaves whom I brought into the offices over them. I doubled the divine offerings presented before him from the storehouse of the "Feast of the Appearance," containing provisions. I made for him festal offerings, and oblations of the feasts of the first of the seasons, in order to satisfy his two serpent-goddesses [5]at every season. I surrounded the house of Thoth with a wall, built with twenty ⌜courses⌝ in the ground foundation, and a height of 30 cubits, having ramps, ⌜towers⌝[b] and battlements on its every side. [6]Its doorposts and lintels were of stone of Ayan (ʿ*yn*ʾ), bearing doors of cedar, mounted with copper, in order to exclude the Asiatics and Tehenu, who trod their limits from of old.

---

[a]Some similar word has been omitted by the scribe.

[b]See **4**, 2.

[c]See **58**, 6.

*Temple of Osiris at Abydos*[a]

**357.** 7I restored Abydos, the district of Osiris, by benefactions[b] in Towêr. I built my house[c] of stone in the midst of his temple, like Atum's great house 8of heaven. I settled it with people bearing numerous offices, rich and ⌜poor⌝ of all that exist. I made for it divine offerings, the gifts of its altar, O my father, 9Osiris, lord of Tazoser. I made for him a statue of the king, L. P. H., presenting monuments and table vessels likewise, of gold and silver.[d] I surrounded the house (*pr*) of Osiris 10and Harsiese with a great wall, towering like a mountain of gritstone, with ⌜ramps⌝ and ⌜towers⌝;[e] bearing battlements, and having doorposts of stone and doors of cedar. 11I hewed a great barge for Osiris, like the evening-barque which bears the sun.

*Temple of Upwawet at Siut*

**358.** 12I restored the walls in the house of my father, Upwawet, of the South, lord of Siut (*S ͗ yw ͘ t*). I built my house therein, of stone of Ayan (*ᶜ yn ͗*), inscribed and engraved with the graver's tool in his

*Pl. 59*

august name. 1I completed it with the good things of every land. I assigned to it serf-laborers in numerous lists. I made for it a storehouse anew containing divine offerings, in order to present them to his ka daily. I hewed for him 2a great barge of the "First-of-the-River," like the morning-barque of Re which is in heaven. I walled about his house with a wall, established with labor, with twenty ⌜courses⌝ in the ground foundation, and with a height of 30 cubits; having ramps, 3⌜towers⌝[e] and battlements in its whole circumference; great doorposts of stone, and doors of cedar, fitted with mountings (of bronze) of a mixture of six (⌜parts⌝),[f] engraved with the great name of thy majesty, forever.

*Temple of Sutekh at Ombos*

**359.** 4I restored the house of Sutekh, lord of Ombos; I built its walls which were in ruin, I equipped the house in its midst in his divine

---

[a]See Mariette, *Abydos*, I, 4, 5, 10, for the name of this temple, of which only fragments have survived.

[b]Lit., "*examples of benefaction.*"

[c]His palace, as at Medinet Habu.

[d]The statue bore sacrificial vessels, etc.

[e]See 4, 2.

[f]See 6, 9.

name, built with excellent work, [5]forever. "House-of-Ramses-Ruler-of-Heliopolis,-L.-P.-H.,-in-the-House-of-Sutekh-of-Ombos," was its great name. I equipped it with slaves, the captives and people, whom I created. I made for him herds in the North, in order [6]to present them to his ka as a daily offering. I made for him divine offerings anew, being an increase of the daily offerings which were before him. I gave to him lands, high and low, and islands, in the South [7]and North, bearing barley and spelt. His treasury was supplied with the things which my hands brought, in order to double the feasts before him every day.

*Temple of Horus at Athribis*[a]

**360.** [8]I did numerous benefactions among the great sacred cattle before my father, Harkhentikhet. I restored the walls of his temple, built and made anew, smoothed and polished. The divine offerings were doubled for him as daily offerings before his lovely face every morning. I brought for him tribute of male and female slaves, silver, gold, royal linen, fine southern linen, oil, [10]incense, honey, bulls, and bullocks. I made for him a herd[b] anew with numerous cattle, in order to present (them) to his ka, the great prince. I arranged the administration of his august house on water and land; it was made [11]into great great decrees[c] in his name, forever. I set the prophets and inspectors of his house over them, to administer its serf-laborers, and to offer to his house.

*Deposition of the Rebellious Vizier in Athribis*

**361.** I cast out the vizier who had entered [12]into their midst, I took away all his people who were with him. I made it like the great temples in this land, protected and defended, forever and ever.[d] I brought

*Pl. 60*

(back again) all its people [1]who had been cast out, with every man and every inspector, appointed to carry on their administration in his august house.

---

[a]See the rare titles of the priests of Athribis, Brugsch, *Thesaurus*, VI, 1,414.

[b]See **62***a*, 4.

[c]The adjective would indicate that the stelæ containing the decrees are meant.

[d]Read *ḥnᶜ ḏt;* so Piehl and others.

### *Temple[a] of Sutekh in the Residence City*

**362.** [2]I made a great temple, enlarged with labor, in the house of "Sutekh-of-Ramses (II)-Meriamon,-L.-P.-H.," built, laid, smoothed, and inscribed with designs; having doorposts of [3]stone, and doors of cedar. "House-of-Ramses-Ruler-of-Heliopolis,-L.-P.-H.,-in-the-House-of-Sutekh," its name was called forever. I assigned to it serf-laborers of the people whom I created, male and female slaves whom I carried off as captives of [4]my sword. I made for him divine offerings, full and pure, in order to offer them to his ka every day. I filled his treasury with possessions without number, with granaries of grain by the ten-thousand, herds with cattle [5]like the sand, in order to offer them to thy ka, O thou great in might.

### *Good Works for All Gods and Goddesses*

**363.** [6]I did mighty deeds and benefactions, a numerous multitude, for the gods and goddesses of South and North. I wrought upon their images in the gold-houses, I built that which [7]had fallen to ruin in their temples. I made houses and temples in their courts; I planted for them groves; I dug for them lakes; I founded for them divine offerings of barley [8]and wheat, wine, incense, fruit, cattle, and fowl. I built the "Shadows of Re"[b] for their districts, abiding, with divine offerings for every day. I made great decrees for the administration of their temples, [9]recorded in the hall of writings forever. [10]Behold, the list is before you, O gods and goddesses, that ye may know of the benefactions which I did for your ka's.

## 2. THE GODS' ESTATES

### *Pl. 61a*

**364.** [1]List of things, cattle, gardens, lands, galleys, workshops, towns, and everything, [2]which King Usermare-Meriamon, L. P. H., the Great God, gave[c] to his fathers (sic!), the gods and goddesses, the lords of South and North:

---

[a]This temple was in the residence city of Ramses II (as is shown by **62*a*, 3**).

[b]See II, 1017, and my remarks in *Zeitschrift für ägyptische Sprache*, 40, 111.

[c]The designation "*as property, etc.*," which is found in the other headings (§§ 280, 337, etc.), is omitted here.

*People Attached to the Temples, Etc.*

**365.** [3]"The-House (*ḥ˙ t*)-of-Ramses-Ruler-of-Heliopolis,-L.-P.-H.,-the-Judge-in-the-House-of-Onouris:" heads 457

[4]People whom he gave to the house of Onouris of the tall plumes, residing in Thinis: heads 160

[5]"The-House (*ḥ˙ t*)-of-Ramses-Ruler-of-Heliopolis,-L.-P.-H.,-in-the-House-of-Osiris," lord of Abydos: heads 682

[6]People whom he gave to the house of his august father, Osiris, lord of Abydos: heads 162

[7]"House (*p˙ r*)-of-Ramses-Ruler-of-Heliopolis,-L.-P.-H.,-in-the-House-of-Sutekh-of-Ombos:" heads 106

[8]People whom he gave to the house of Min-Horus, Isis, and all the gods of Coptos: heads 39

**366.** [9]People whom he gave to the house of Hathor, mistress of Aphroditopolis: heads 12

[10]People whom he gave to the house of Sebek, lord of Neshit-Crocodilopolis: heads 22

[11]People whom he gave to the house of Min, Horus, Isis, and the gods of Panopolis:[a] heads 38

[12]"The-House (*ḥ˙ t*)-of-Ramses-Ruler-of-Heliopolis-in-the-House-of-Min," lord of Panopolis, under charge of Inu-shefenu (*Ynw-šfnw*), who is a commander of the army: heads 203

[13]People whom he gave to the house of ⌈Zebui⌉,[b] lord of Aphroditopolis: heads 38

[14]People whom he gave to the house of Khnum, lord of Sheshotep (*Š* ͗ *s-ḥtp*): heads 17

[15]People whom he gave to the house of Upwawet, leader of the Two Lands: heads 4

*Pl. 61b*

**367.** [1]"The-House (*ḥ˙t*)-of-Ramses-Ruler-of-Heliopolis,-L.-P.-H.,-Appearing-at-the-Jubilee-in-the-House-of-Upwawet," under charge of Thutemhab, who is a commander of the army: heads 157

---

[a] *Ypw*.

[b] God of the Antæopolite nome. The reading (*ḏb* ͑ *wy*) is uncertain (see Brugsch, *Dictionnaire géographique*, 889–91).

[2]"The-House ($ḥ·t$)-of-Ramses-Ruler-of-Heliopolis,-L.-P.-H.,-in-This-House," under charge of Inushefenu (*Ynw-šfnw*), who is a commander of the army: heads 122

[3]"The-House ($ḥ·t$)-of-Ramses-Ruler-of-Heliopolis,-L.-P.-H.,-in-the-House-of-Thoth," lord of Hermopolis: heads 89

[4]"House (*pr*)-of-Ramses-Ruler-of-Heliopolis,-L.-P.-H.,-in-This-House:" 66

[5]People whom he gave to this house: persons[a] 484

[6]People whom he gave to the house of Khnum Hatweret (*Ḥ·t-wr·t*): heads 34

**368.** [7]People whom he gave to the house of Amon-Re, lord of Yered (*Yʾ-rd*): heads 44

[8]People whom he gave to the house of Thoth of Pauzy (*Pʾ-wḏy*): heads 65

[9]People whom he gave to the house of Amon of Mewetkhent (*Mʾwt-ḫnty*): heads 44

[10]People whom he gave to the house of Sebek, lord of Mesha (*Mšʾ*): heads 38

[11]People whom he gave to the house of Anubis, lord of Sep: heads 78

[12]People whom he gave to the house of Set, lord of Oxyrhyncus: heads 99

[13]People whom he gave to the house of Hrishefyt (*Ḥry-šfyw*), King of the Two Lands: heads 103

**369.** [14]People whom he gave to the house of Sebek of Shedet, Horus, dwelling in the Fayûm: heads 146

[15]People whom he gave to the house of Set of ⸢Sesu⸣ (*Sssw*): heads 35

[16]People whom he gave to the house of Amon-Re, lord of "Thrones-of-the-Two-Lands," of the back-lands (Fayûm): heads 62

[17]People whom he gave to the house of Hathor, mistress of Aphroditopolis: heads 124

*Pl. 62a*

[1]"The-Herd-of-Ramses-Ruler-of-Heliopolis,-L.-P.-H.,-Doer-of-Benefactions-for-his-Mother-Bast:" heads 1,533

---

[a]See **10**, 14 and 15.

| | | |
|---|---|---|
| [2]People whom he gave to the house of Bast, mistress of Berset, on "The-Water-of-Re:"[a] | heads | 169 |
| [3]"House (*pr*)-of-Ramses-Ruler-of-Heliopolis,-L.-P.-H.,-in-the-House-of-Sutekh," in the "House[b] (*pr*)-of-Ramses (II)-Meriamon,-L.-P.-H.:" | heads | 106 |
| [4]"The-Herd-of-Ramses-Ruler-of-Heliopolis,-L.-P.-H.,-the-Benefactor-of-His-Father-Harkhentikhet (*Ḥr-ḫnt-ḫty*)-of-Athribis:" | heads | 124 |
| [5]People whom he gave to the house of Mut-Khent-ebui-enteru (*Ḫnt-ᶜ bwy-ntrw*): | heads | 24 |
| [6]Total | heads | 5,811[c] |

*Miscellaneous Property*

| | |
|---|---|
| **370.** [7]Various cattle | 13,433 |
| [8]Lands: stat | 36,012 |
| [9]Gardens | 11 |
| [10]Workshops | 2 |

3. THE GODS' INCOMES

| | |
|---|---|
| **371.** [11][d]Clean grain ⌈—⌉: 16-fold heket | 73,250 |
| [12]Vegetables: bundles | 3,300 |
| [13]Flax: bales (*n ᶜ ḥ*) | 3,000 |

4. THE KING'S GIFTS TO THE GODS

*Pl. 62b*

**372.** [1]Gold, silver, real lapis lazuli, real malachite, every real, costly stone, [2]copper, garments of royal linen, fine southern linen, southern linen, and colored linen; myrrh, cattle, fowl, and everything [3]which

[a]Cf. **10**, 8. Berset (*Bp ͗ -r ͗ -ys˙t*) has nothing to do with Belbeis.

[b]This means the city of Ramses (II).

[c]Real total is 5,686.

[d]That the following three items belong to the income will be seen by comparing the other lists, e. g., **32*b***, 7–9. Furthermore, they are in the proper place between the estate and the royal gifts; but the scribe has given them neither title nor rubric; and he has recorded no gold, silver, etc., which we find in the other sections (e. g., **32*a***, 7–**32*b***). Erman (*op. cit.*, 465) is certainly correct in inferring that the scribe's memoranda were too incomplete for him to insert here the usual rubric, as, e. g., **32*a***, 7.

King Usermare-Meriamon, L. P. H., the Great God, gave to them,[a] as gifts of the king, L. P. H., [4]from the year 1 to the year 31:

| | |
|---|---|
| **373.** [5]Gold in vessels, ornaments and scraps | 1,719 deben, 8¼ kidet |
| [6]Silver in vessels and scraps | 2,428 " 5⅙ " |
| [7]Total, gold and silver | 4,148 deben, 3½ kidet |
| [8]Gold combined with rock-crystal: collars | 4 |
| [9]Gold combined with rock-crystal: tassels[b] | 4 |
| [10]Gold garlands for the head | 1 |
| [11]Silver overlaid with gold: a sacred eye amulet[c] for Thoth | 1 |
| [12]Real lapis lazuli | 10 deben, 6 kidet |
| [13]Real malachite | —[d] " ⅓ ⅙ " |
| [14]Timhy (*Tymḥy*) stone of Wawat | 3 " |
| [15]Black copper overlaid with gold: ⸢corselets⸣ | 2 |
| [16]Black copper | 260 deben, 6 kidet |

*Pl. 63a*

| | |
|---|---|
| [1]Copper in vessels and scraps | 14,130 deben, 3 kidet |
| [2]Lead | 2,130 " |
| [3]Incense | 782 " |
| **374.** [4]Royal linen: garments (*dw*) | 17 |
| [5]Royal linen: upper garments (*dw*) | 25 |
| [6] " " wrappings of Horus | 3 |
| [7] " " mantles | 5 |
| [8] " " —[e] garments | 30 |
| [9] " " garments (*ḫnky*) | 2 |
| [10] " " garments (*yd*[*g* ᵓ]) | 179 |
| [11] " " tunics | 168 |
| [12] " " various garments | 10 |
| [13]Total, royal linen : various garments | 439 |
| [14]Fine southern linen: upper garments (*dw*) | 2 |
| [15] " " " large tunics | 2 |
| [16] " " " garments (*dw*) | 234 |
| [17] " " " —[e] garments | 29 |

[a]The gods.

[b]Hung down the back as counterpoises for the four collars.

[c]See **68***b*, 10. [d]Number omitted by the scribe. [e]See **14***a*, 14.

*Pl. 63b*

| | |
|---|---|
| 1Fine southern linen: garments (*yd*[*g* ʾ]) | 428 |
| 2 " " " garments (*h* ʾ *w-mn*) | 1 |
| 3 " " " tunics | 399 |
| 4 " " " kilts | 37 |
| 5 " " " various garments | 44 |
| 6Total, fine southern linen, various garments | 1,216[a] |
| **375.** 7Southern linen: mantles | 23 |
| 8Southern linen: —[b] garments | 1 |
| 9 " " garments (*dw*) | 218 |
| 10 " " garments (*yd*[*g* ʾ]) | 181 |
| 11 " " tunics | 43 |
| 12 " " garments (*ḳ* ʾ *-ḏ* ʾ *-m-r* ʾ) | 49 |
| 13 " " kilts | 23 |
| 14 " " garments (*yfd*) | 40 |
| 15Total, southern linen, various garments | 556[c] |
| 16Colored linen: mantles | 60 |
| 17Colored linen: —[a] garments | 12 |

*Pl. 63c*

| | |
|---|---|
| 1Colored linen: garments (*dw*) | 1 |
| 2 " " garments (*yfd*) | 4 |
| 3 " " tunics | 567 |
| 4 " " various garments | 92 |
| 5Total, colored linen: various garments | 736 |
| 6Total, royal linen, fine southern linen, southern linen, colored linen: various garments | 3,047[d] |
| 7Yarn: deben | 900 |
| 8Yarn: various hanks | 19 |
| **376.** 9White incense: jars (*mn*) | 601 |
| 10Honey: jars (*mn*) | 567 |
| 11Oil (*nḥḥ*) of Egypt: jars (*mn*) | 513 |

[a]Real total, 1,176.

[b]See 14*a*, 14.

[c]Real total, 578.

[d]One hundred and eighteen too much.

| | |
|---|---|
| [12]Oil (*nḥḥ*) of Syria: jars (*mn*) | 542 |
| [13]Oil (*bḳ*): jars (*mn*) | 1 |
| [14]Red oil (*bḳ*): jars (*mn*) | 1 |
| [15]White fat: jars (*mn*) | 273 |
| [16]Goose fat: jars (*mn*) | 44 |
| [17]Butter: jars (*mn*) | 31 |

*Pl. 64a*

| | |
|---|---|
| [1]Oil (*sft*): jars (*mn*) | 1 |
| [2]Total, filled jars | 2,688[a] |
| [3]Shedeh: jars (*mn*) | 134 |
| [4]Shedeh: jars (*k* ͗ *-bw*) | 287 |
| [5]Wine: jars (*m* ͗ *dydy*) | 2 |
| [6]Wine: jars (⸢*mrsw*⸣ and *mn*) | 2,864 |
| [7]Total, shedeh and wine: various jars (͗ ͑ ͑) | 3,247[b] |
| [8]Total, various jars | 4,975 |
| **377.** [9]Babay (*b* ͗ *-b* ͗ *-y* ͗): ⸢rings⸣ mounted in gold | 124 |
| [10]Various costly stones: sacred eye amulets | 5,673 |
| [11] " " " scarabs | 1,562 |
| [12] " " " seals as pendants | 1,643 |
| [13] " " " images of the king, L. P. H. | 557 |
| [14] " " " ⸢naophors⸣[c] | 62 |
| [15]Malachite: finger rings | 331 |
| [16]Ubat (*wb* ͗ *ͭ t*) stone: seals | 6,278 |

*Pl. 64b*

| | |
|---|---|
| [1]Rock-crystal: bracelets | 62 |
| [2] " " seals | 4,185 |
| [3] " " scarabs | 930 |
| [4] " " sacred eye amulets | 6,583 |
| [5] " " beads | 825,840 |
| [6] " " beads: clusters | 31 |
| [7] " " finger rings | 4,247 |

[a]Real total, 2,574.

[b]Real total, 3,287.

[c]Lit., "*bearers of the house of the arm.*"

| | |
|---|---|
| 8[a]⌜Sparkling⌝ lapis lazuli | 73 deben, 3 kidet |
| 9⌜Sparkling⌝ malachite | 34 " 3 " |
| 10Red jasper: finger rings | 31 |
| 11 " " scarabs | 93 |
| 12 " " deben | 19 |
| 13Uz (*wḏ*)-mineral: deben | 17 |
| 14Irer (*Yrr*) stone: semdets (*smd·t*) | 35 |
| 15Rock-crystal: semdets | 136 |
| 16Hirset (*ḥrs·t*) stone: semdets | 28 |
| 17Red jasper: semdets | 7 |

*Pl. 64c*

| | |
|---|---|
| 1Hukamu (*ḥw-ḳˀ-mˀ-mw*) stone: semdets | 160 |
| 2All costly stones: semdets | 160 |
| **378.** 3Meru (*mry*) wood: baskets and measures (*ṯˀy*) | 496 |
| 4Reeds: measures (*msty*) | 3 |
| 5Cinnamon: measures (*msty*) | 30 |
| 6Cinnamon: bundles | 37 |
| 7Yufiti (*ywfyty*)-plant: measures (*msty*) | 2 |
| 8⌜Rosemary⌝: measures (*msty*) | 2 |
| 9Semu (*sˀmw*)-plant: measures (*msty*) | 4 |
| 10Incense: measures (*ḳˀ-tˀ-rw-ty*) | 100 |
| 11Mehiwet[b] (*mhywt*): ⌜cakes⌝ (*sˀ-tˀ*) | 100 |
| 12Manna: measures (*msty*) | 10 |
| 13Grapes: measures (*msty*) | 22 |
| 14Various fruit: heket | 212 |
| 15Ibenu (*ybnw*): measures (*msty*) | 3 |

*Pl. 65a*

| | |
|---|---|
| 1Gums: heket | 2 |
| 2⌜Minium⌝: jars (*mn*) | 3 |
| 3Khenti (*ḫnty*): jars (*sny*) | 380 |
| 4Shesa (*šsˀ*): measures (*msty*) | 72 |
| 5Shesa (*šsˀ*): deben | 32,500 |
| 6⌜Dom-palm⌝ fruit: ⌜clusters⌝ | 2,548 |
| 7Palm leaves: bundles | 46,040 |
| 8Palm leaves: measures (*psˀ*) | 320 |

[a]See Annals, year 31, l. 15 (II, 473). [b]See 19*a*, 8.

| | |
|---|---|
| [9]Banu (*b* ᵓ *nw*): ⌜in⌝ cubes (*s* ᵓ *s*) | 351 |
| [10]Clean grain ⌜—⌝: 16-fold heket | 2,231 |
| [11]Fruit of the South: 16-fold heket | 95 |
| **379.** [12]Various cattle | 1,142 |
| [13]Cow-hides | 37 |
| [14]Cedar wood: various logs | 336 |
| [15]Mera (*mr* ᵓ) wood: poles | 2 |
| [16]Cassia wood: deben | 100 |

*Pl. 65b*

| | |
|---|---|
| [1]Natron: bricks | 3,842 |
| [2]Natron: 16-fold heket | 62 |
| [3]Salt: bricks | 4,242 |
| [4]Salt: 16-fold heket | 166 |
| [5]Olive: heket | 1,352 |
| [6]Dedmet (*ddm·t*) flowers: measures (*dm* ᵓ *mw*) | 97 |
| [7]Enbu (ᶜ *nbw*)-plant: measures (*dm* ᵓ *mw*) | 99 |
| [8]Grapes: crates | 253 |
| [9]Grapes: garlands | 80 |
| [10]⌜Pomegranates⌝: crates | 66 |
| [11]Fruit: heket | 87½ |
| [12]Flax (*pš*): measures (*sbḫ·t*) | 93 |
| [13]Ideninu (*ydnynw*)-plants | 118 |
| [14]Flax (*pš*): bekhen | 198 |
| [15]Tamarisk: bundles | 390 |

*Pl. 65c*

| | |
|---|---|
| [1]Southern flax: measures (*ḥtp*) | 46 |
| [2]Palm-fiber: ropes | 37 |
| **380.** [3]Fat geese from the ⌜flocks⌝ | 4 |
| [4]Live geese | 190 |
| [5]Live water-fowl | 153 |
| [6]Water-fowl, cut up | 1,920 |
| [7]Fish, cut up | 6,500 |
| [8]Fish, whole | 13,100 |
| [9]Beni (*b* ᶜ *ny*)-plant in measures (*yp·t*) | 2,300 |
| [10]Date-palm fiber[a] | 2,300 |

[a]Unit of measure?

| | |
|---|---|
| 11 Fire wood: (logs) | 200 |
| 12 Charcoal: measures (*gsr* ?) | 50 |
| 13 Vine gardens | 2 |
| 14 Sycamore gardens | 2 |
| 15 House, equipped with timbers (*ḥty*)[a] | 1 |
| 16 Lands: stat | 1,361 |

*Pl. 66a*

**381.** 1 Clean grain, ⌜—⌝ for the divine offerings of the feasts of heaven 2 and the feasts of the first of the seasons, which he gave to them[b] as increase of 3 the divine offerings, and as increase of the daily offerings, in order to double that which was before, 4 from the year 1 to the year 31, making 31 years: 16-fold heket: 250,326.

### 5. CONCLUDING PRAYER OF RAMSES III

*Pl. 66b*

**382.** 1 Hear ye, O great divine ennead, ye gods and goddesses! Put in your hearts the benefactions which I did, while I was king upon earth 2 as ruler of the living; grant that I may be divine like one of the divine ennead, that I may go in and out among you in Tazoser, 3 that I may proceed, while I am with you, before Re, that I may behold the radiance of his disk every morning. Grant that I may breathe the 4 air like you, that I may receive bread upon the offerings before Osiris. Let my heart be glad, hear that which I say, 5 establish my son as king on the throne of Horus, he being ruler, L. P. H., on the earth as Lord of the Two Lands, set the diadem upon his head like the All-Lord, 6 join to him the uraeus like Atum. Let him celebrate jubilees like Tatenen, having a reign as long as the Beautiful-Faced (Ptah). 7 May his sword be victorious against all lands, may they come for fear of him, bearing their tribute. Put the love of him 8 in the hearts of the people, may the whole land acclaim over him at the sight of him, may Egypt rejoice over him 9 with jubilation, united under his feet, forever; (even) the King of Upper and Lower Egypt, Lord of the Two Lands; Usermare-Setepnamon, L. P. H., 10 Son of Re, Lord of Diadems, like Amon: Ramses (IV)-Hekma-Meriamon, L. P. H.

---

[a] Compare *ḥty* in the building inscription of the High Priest, Amenhotep (§ 489, l. 8).

[b] The gods and goddesses in general.

## VI. SUMMARY

### 1. TOTAL OF THE GODS' ESTATES

*Pl. 67*

**383.** [1]List of the things of the gods and men:[a] gold, silver, real lapis lazuli, real malachite, all real, costly stones, [2]cattle, gardens, lands, galleys, workshops, towns, festal offerings,[b] oblations, "Books of the Nile-God," and all the things, which [3]King Usermare-Meriamon, L. P. H., the Great God, did for his august father, Amon-Re, king of gods; Atum, lord of the Two Lands of Heliopolis, Re-Harakhte; [4]Ptah, the great, "South-of-His-Wall," lord of "Life-of-the-Two-Lands," and all the gods and goddesses of South and North; while he was king upon earth:

**384.** [5]The processional images, statues, and figures of Amon-Re, king of gods: being 2,756 gods:[c] [6]heads 113,433[d]

| | |
|---|---:|
| [7]Various cattle | 490,386 |
| [8]Lands: stat | 1,071,780 |
| [9]Gardens and groves | 514 |
| [10]Transports and galleys | 88 |

*Pl. 68a*

| | |
|---|---:|
| [1]Towns of Egypt | 160 |
| [2]Towns of Syria[e] | 9 |
| Total | 169 |

**385.** [3]The amount belonging to the 2,756 statues[f] and figures:

| | | | | |
|---|---:|---|---:|---|
| [4]Fine gold | 7,205 | deben, | 1 | kidet |
| [5]Silver | 11,047 | " | $\frac{1}{4}$ | " |
| [6]Total, gold and silver | 18,252 | " | $1\frac{1}{4}$ | " |

[a]The portion referring to men is the narrative in Pls. 75–79, *q. v.*

[b]The scribe has here incorrectly inserted some of the income in this heading, but he has properly not included any of such items in the list following.

[c]The scribe has here inserted one of the minor items from the Amon-temple, where he should have given a general head, as the number following is the total of all people held by all the temples recorded in the papyrus. His total should be 108,338, not correcting earlier errors.

[d]For the correct numbers in the summary, see the table on p. 97.

[e]These all belonged to Amon, and are given (11, 11), as also in Kush.

[f]See 21*b*, 11, note, and 11, 1–3.

| | |
|---|---|
| 7Real lapis lazuli | 47 deben, 6 kidet |
| 8Black copper | 10,001 " 8 " |
| 9Copper in vessels and scraps | 97,148 " 3 " |
| 10Lead | 4,896 " |
| 11⌈Tin⌉ | 95 " |

*Pl. 68b*

| | |
|---|---|
| 1Various costly stones ⌈—⌉[a] | 18,168 [deben],[b] 1 kidet |
| 2Cedar: various logs | 328 |
| 3Persea: various logs | 4,415 |

## 2. TOTAL OF THE GODS' INCOMES

**386.** 4Things exacted, impost of the people and all the serf-laborers of the houses, temples, and estates, 5which he gave to them as their yearly dues:

| | |
|---|---|
| 6Fine mountain gold and gold of two times in vessels, ornaments, and scraps | 2,289 deben, 4½ kidet[c] |
| 7Silver [in] vessels and scraps | 14,050 " ½ " |
| 8Total, silver and gold in vessels, ornaments, and scraps | 16,339 " 6½ " |
| 9Gold combined with costly stones: collars, tassels, and cords | 9 |
| 10Silver overlaid with gold: sacred eye amulet of Thoth | 1 |
| 11Copper: deben | 27,580 |
| **387.** 12Royal linen, mek-linen, fine southern linen, southern linen, colored linen: various garments | 4,575 |

[a]*Yp·t.*

[b]Omitted by the scribe, or else he has incorrectly inserted *yp·t* for *dbn*.

[c]The only temple with gold in the income was Thebes, which received yearly 569 deben, 6½ kidet. Hence this total is incorrect by over 1,700 deben. As a mistake in addition is impossible where only one item is concerned, the scribe has added items which do not belong here in the income. Adding the 1,719 deben, 8¼ kidet, from the king's gifts to the small temples (**62***b*, 5), we obtain the scribe's total of gold here. Hence he has incorrectly inserted here in the income the gold and silver of the king's gifts to small temples. So also ll. 9 and 10, which are taken from **62***b*, 9–11. The copper is correct.

*Pl. 69*

| | |
|---|---|
| 1Yarn: deben | 3,795 |
| 2Incense, honey, oil: full jars (ᵓᶜᶜ) | 1,529 |
| 3Shedeh and wine: various jars (ᵓᶜᶜ) | 28,080 |
| 4Silver in things of the impost of the people | 4,208 deben, $7\frac{1}{2}$ $\frac{1}{10}$ kidet |
| 5Clean grain of the impost of the peasants: 16-fold heket | 460,900 |
| 6Vegetables: bundles | 32,750 |
| 7Flax: bales | 71,000 |
| 8Water-fowl of the impost of the fowlers and fishermen | 426,995 |
| 9Bulls, bullocks of the bulls, heifers, calves, cows, cattle of ⌜—⌝ cattle of ⌜—⌝ of the herd: (cattle) of Egypt | 961 |
| 10Bulls, bullocks of the bulls, oxen, heifers, calves, and cows of the impost of the lands of Syria | 19 |
| Total | 980 |
| 11Live geese of the exactions | 1,920 |
| 12Cedar: tow-boats and ferry-boats | 12 |
| 13Acacia: tow-boats, ⌜canal⌝-boats, boats for the transportation of cattle, warships,[a] and kara (*k*ᵓ-*r*ᵓ)-boats | 78 |

*Pl. 70a*

| | |
|---|---|
| 1Total, cedar and acacia: boats | 90 |

2Products of Egypt, products of God's-Land, products of Syria, Kush and the Oasis, for the divine offerings in numerous lists.

### 3. TOTAL OF THE KING'S GIFTS TO ALL GODS[b]

**388.** 3Gold, silver, real lapis lazuli, real malachite, all real, costly stones, copper, garments of 4royal linen, mek-linen, fine southern linen, southern linen, garments of colored linen, jars,[c] fowl, and everything which he gave to them, 5as gifts of the king, L. P. H.; festal offerings, oblations, and "Books of the Nile-God," while he was king upon earth:

[a]See 12*b*, 11.

[b]This section includes also the offerings, as the scribe was unable to separate them. The totals contain the most incredible errors in addition, which can be controlled for the most important items by comparing with table of the king's gifts, § 172.

[c]This means the wine, oil, incense, etc., which were put into jars.

| | | | |
|---|---|---|---|
| **389.** [6]Fine gold, gold of two times, and white gold in vessels, ornaments, and scraps | 1,663 deben | | |
| [7]Silver in vessels and scraps | 3,598 | " | 8 kidet |
| [8]Total, gold and silver in vessels and scraps | 5,261 | " | 8 " |
| [9]Real lapis lazuli, real malachite, real green feld-spar (*nšm·t*) stone | 30 | " | 9⅙ " |
| [10]Real lapis lazuli, real malachite: scarabs | | | 72 |
| [11]Timhy (*Tymḥy*) stone of Wawat | | | 3 kidet |

*Pl. 70b*

| | |
|---|---|
| [1]Black copper | 327 deben, 9 kidet |
| [2]Black copper overlaid with gold: corselets | 2 |
| [3]Copper in vessels and scraps | 18,786 deben, 7 kidet |
| [4]Lead: deben | 2,130 |
| **390.** [5]Myrrh: deben | 7,709 |
| [6]Myrrh: heket | 5½ |
| [7]Wood of the myrrh tree: (logs) | 1,059 |
| [8]Fruit of the myrrh in measures | 200 |
| [9]Royal linen, mek-linen, fine southern linen, southern linen, colored linen: various garments | 50,877 |
| [10]Incense, honey, oil (*nḥḥ*), oil (*bḳ*ʾ); various jars (ʾᶜᶜ) and measures (*yp·t*) | 331,702 |
| [11]Incense: ⌜—⌝ in measures (*yp·t*) | 35,130 |
| [12]Incense: large measures (*yp·t*) | 62 |
| [13]Shedeh and wine: jars (*mn* and *k*ʾ *bw*) | 228,380 |
| [14]Fine manna of Punt: deben | 300 |
| [15]Manna: measures (*msty*) | 10 |
| [16]All costly stones: sacred eye amulets, scarabs, and seals of various measures | 1,075,635 |

*Pl. 71a*

| | |
|---|---|
| [1]Alabaster: a block | 1 |
| [2]Yarn: deben | 700 |
| [3]Yarn: hanks | 19 |
| **391.** [4]Wrought wood: cases and seals | 92 |
| [5]Meru (*mry*) wood and ebony: ⌜staves⌝ | 497 |
| [6]Wrought wood: block for the scales | 1 |
| [7]Carob wood: a log | 1 |

| | |
|---|---|
| [8]Persea, a log of 2 cubits | 1 |
| [9]Mera (*mr* ͗) wood: post for the scales | 1 |
| [10]Mera (*mr* ͗) wood: poles | 2 |
| [11]Cedar: various logs | 351 |
| [12]Nenybu (*N-n-y-bw*) and cassia: deben | 3,129 |
| [13]Reeds: bundles and measures (*msty*) | 37 |
| [14]Cinnamon: 843 measures (*msty*) and bundles: deben | 2,000 |

*Pl. 71b*

| | |
|---|---|
| [1]Barley of Syria: heket | 45 |
| [2]Ivory: a tusk | 1 |
| [3]Eye-paint: deben | 50 |
| **392.** [4]⌈Rosemary⌉: measures (*msty*) | 167 |
| [5]Yufiti (*Ywfyty*)-plant: measures (*msty*) | 183 |
| [6]Mehiwet (*Mhywt*):[a] ⌈cakes⌉ (*s* ͗ *-t* ͗) | 3,100 |
| [7]Semu (*s* ͨ *mw*)-plant: measures (*ḥtp*) | 1,664 |
| [8]⌈Dom-palm⌉ fruit, grapes, figs, ⌈pomegranates⌉ and various fruit: crates of various measure (*yp˙t*) | 2,382,650 |
| [9]Bulls, bullocks of the bulls, oxen, heifers, calves, cows, goats, | 20,602 |
| [10]White oryxes, ⌈male gazelles⌉, gazelles | 367 |
| [11]Fat geese, live geese, various water-fowl | 353,919 |
| [12]Salt and natron: 16-fold heket | 1,843 |
| [13]Salt and natron: bricks | 355,084 |
| [14]Palm-fiber: various ropes | 345 |
| [15]Sebkhet (*sbḫ˙t*)-plant, flax (*pš*) and ideninu (*ydnynw*): 16-fold heket | 1,944 |

*Pl. 72*

| | |
|---|---|
| [1]Tamarisk and reed-grass: bundles | 7,860 |
| [2]Southern flax: measures (*ḥtp*) | 46 |
| **393.** [3]Fine bread: large oblation-loaves, *syd*-loaves, and *bḥ*-loaves of various measures | 161,287 |
| [4]Fine bread, meat, rahusu (*r* ͗*-ḥw-sw*)-cakes: large measures (*ḥtp*) of the ⌈court⌉ (*m* ͗), measures (*ḥtp*) of gold, measures (*ḥtp*) for eating, and measures (*ṯ* ͗ *y*) for the mouth of the eater[b] | 25,335 |

---

[a]See **19***a*, 8.

[b]See **17***b*, 1 and 2, note.

| | |
|---|---|
| [5]Fine bread: large loaves (ʿ ḳ) for eating, ⌜sweet⌝ loaves (ʿ ḳ), and loaves of every size | 6,272,421 |
| [6]Rahusu-cakes of every baking, measures (*yp·t*) | 285,385 |
| [7]Beer: various vessels (*ḥnw*) | 468,303 |
| [8]Olives: jars (*mn* and *g ʾ y*) | 1,726 |
| [9]Wax: deben | 3,100 |
| [10]⌜Cabbage⌝, khithana-fruit, southern fruit, measures (*yp·t*), and ⌜bundles⌝ (*ʾ nbw*) | 390,215 |
| [11]Dedmet flowers and enbu (*ʿnbw*): measures (*d ʿ mw*) | 866 |
| [12]Papyrus sandals: pairs | 15,110 |
| [13]Papyrus rind: measures (*yp·t*) | 26,782 |
| [14]Storea: measures (*yp·t*) | 930 |
| **394.** [15]Thick stuff: garments (*dw*) | 150 |

*Pl. 73*

| | |
|---|---|
| [1]Leather sandals: pairs | 3,720 |
| [2]Jars and vessels of the mouth of the Heliopolitan canal[a] | 9,610 |
| [3]Various fish | 494,800 |
| [4]Jars ⌜of the canal⌝ filled with fish, having wooden ⌜lids⌝[b] | 440 |
| [5]Blossoms, flowers, isi-plant, papyrus, and herbs: measures (*ḏdm·t*), bouquets, and for the hand | 10,130,032 |
| [6]Olive-lands equipped: 1, making, stat | 53¼ |
| [7]Gardens of all (kinds of) trees, equipped | 6 |
| [8]House equipped with timbers[c] | 1 |
| [9]Fire wood: (⌜logs⌝) | 3,260 |
| [10]Charcoal: measures (*gsr ʾ*) | 3,367 |
| [11]Incense, honey, oil (*nḥḥ*), best oil, fat, fruit, every costly stone, cinnamon, vegetables, and milk: measures (ʿ) of various capacity | 2,933,766 |
| **395.** [12]Gold, silver, every real costly stone: statues of the Nile-god: nusa | 48,236 |
| [13]Real lapis lazuli, real malachite, every costly stone, copper, lead, ⌜sparkling⌝ costly stone: statues of the Nile-god | 193,370 |
| [14]Sycamore wood: statues of the Nile-god, and statues of the Nile-goddess | 12,158 |
| [15]Stone: uba (*wb ʾ*) | 31,650 |
| [16]Ibenu (*ybnw*): measures (*msty*) | 60 |

[a]See **19***b*, 16, and note. [b]From **20***b*, 12. [c]See **65***c*, 15.

*Pl. 74*

| | |
|---|---|
| [1]⸢Minium⸣: jars (*mn·t*) | 3 |
| [2]Khenti (*Ḫnty*): jars (*sny*) | 380 |
| [3]Shesa (*šsᵓ*): measures (*msty*) | 72 |
| [4]Shesa (*šsᵓ*): deben | 32,500 |
| [5]Palm leaves: bundles | 46,040 |
| [6]Palm leaves: pesa (*psᵓ*) | 310 |
| [7]Banu (*bᵓnw*): cubes (*sᵓs*) | 351 |
| [8]Cow-hides | 37 |
| [9]Beni (*bᶜny*)-plant | 23,000 |
| [10]Date-palm fiber | 23,000 |

**396.** [11]Clean grain, ⸢—⸣ for the divine offerings of the feasts of heaven and the feasts of the first of the seasons, which he gave to these gods, [12]as an increase of the divine offerings, and as an increase of the daily offerings, in order to double that which was before me:

| | |
|---|---|
| 16-fold heket | 5,279,552 |

## VII. HISTORICAL SECTION

### *Pl. 75. Introduction*

**397.** [1]Said King Usermare-Meriamon (Ramses III), L. P. H., the Great God, to the princes, and leaders of the land, the infantry and chariotry, the Sherden (*Šᵓ-rᵓ-dᵓ-nᵓ*), the numerous archers, [2]and all the citizens[a] of the land of Egypt:

### *Former Anarchy*

**398.** Hear ye,[b] that I may inform you of my benefactions which I did while I was king of the people (*rḫy·t*). The land of [3]Egypt was ⸢overthrown[c] from without⸣, and every man was (⸢thrown⸣ out) of his right; they had no chief mouth (*rᵓ-ḥr*) for many years formerly until other times. The land of Egypt was [4]in the hands of chiefs[d] and of

[a](*ᵓnḫ·w*). These are the same as the "*ᶜnḫ·w of the army*," e. g., already in the Middle Kingdom (I, 681), and in the Eighteenth Dynasty, especially in the Decree of Harmhab (III, 45–67).

[b]Text has "*we!*" which is, of course, an error.

[c]*Ḫ ᶜ ᵓ*; on the meaning "*banish*," see Brugsch, *Oase*, 85; same usage in *Recueil*, XVII, 147, ll. 13, 14?

[d]The hieratic sign is that for "*chief*" (*wr*), not "*prince*" (*sr*), which occurs quite differently written in l. 1 of this same plate.

rulers of towns; one slew his neighbor, great and small. Other times having come after it, with empty years, Yarsu,[a] a certain Syrian (*Ḫ ᵓ -rw*) [5]was with them as chief.[b] He set the whole land tributary before him together; he united his companions and plundered their[c] possessions. They made the gods like men, and no offerings were presented in the temples.

*Rule of Setnakht*

**399.** [6]But when the gods inclined themselves to peace, to set the land (⌈in⌉)[d] its right according to its accustomed manner, [7]they established their son, who came forth from their limbs, to be Ruler, L. P. H., of every land, upon their great throne, (even) Userkhare-Setepnere-Meriamon, L. P. H., Son of Re, Setnakht-Mererre-Meriamon, L. P. H. [8]He was Khepri-Set, when he is enraged; he set in order the entire land, which had been rebellious; he slew the rebels who were in the land of Egypt; he cleansed [9]the great throne of Egypt; he was Ruler, L. P. H., of the Two Lands, on the throne of Atum. He gave ⌈ready faces, which had been turned away⌉.[e] Every man knew his brother who had been walled in.[f] [10]He established the temples in possession of divine offerings, to offer to the gods (*psḏ· t*) according to their customary stipulations.

*Rise of Ramses III and Death of Setnakht*

**400.** He appointed me to be hereditary prince in the place of Keb, I was the great chief mouth (*r ᵓ -ḥr*)[g] of the lands of Egypt, and com-

[a]The words (*ᵓ yr-sw*), read as a proper name, of which Arisu or Arsu have become current forms, means "*made himself.*" Hence Spiegelberg has proposed to render them so, explaining the foreign determinative which follows them by supposing that the name of the Syrian, to whom the determinative belongs, has fallen out. We should then render: "*X, a certain Syrian with them, made himself chief.*" The preposition before "*chief*" fits this rendering well (see Spiegelberg, *Orientalistische Litteraturzeitung*, II, 263–65).

[b]Not "*prince,*" but "*chief,*" as in l. 4; see above, note a.

[c]The Egyptians.

[d]The preposition (*ḥr* in *rdy ḥr ᶜ ḳ ᵓ*) seems to have fallen out.

[e]Or: "*turned back;*" perhaps meaning that those who had formerly been in hiding now came forth, and accepted service with him, that is, were "*ready of face;*" see inscription of Amenemhet (Ameni) l. 10 (I, p. 251, n. d).

[f]Staying within fortified walls during the previous hostilities, when each town was against its neighbor.

[g]The same office as that also claimed by Ramses II as crown prince, in the Kubbân Stela, l. 17 (III, 288).

*Pl. 76*

mander (*sḥn*) of [1]the whole land united in one. He went to rest in his horizon,[a] like the gods; there was done for him that which was done for Osiris; he was rowed in his king's-barge upon the river,[b] [2]and rested in his eternal house west of Thebes.[c]

*Accession of Ramses III*

**401.** Then my father, Amon-Re, lord of gods, Re-Atum, and Ptah, beautiful of face,[d] crowned me as Lord of the Two Lands on the throne of him who begat me; I received the office of my father [3]with joy; the land rested and rejoiced in possession of peace, being joyful at seeing me as ruler, L. P. H., of the Two Lands, like Horus when he was called to rule the Two Lands on the throne of Osiris. I was crowned [4]with the etef-crown bearing the uraeus; I assumed the double-plumed diadem, like Tatenen. I sat upon the throne (*tnṯᵓ·t*) of Harakhte. I was clad in the regalia, like Atum.

*Internal Organization*

**402.** [5]I made[e] Egypt into many classes,[f] consisting of: butlers of the palace, great princes, numerous infantry, and chariotry, by the hundred-thousand; Sherden (*Šᵓ-rᵓ-dᵓ-nᵓ*), [6]and Kehek (*Ḳhḳ*), without number; attendants by the ten-thousand; and serf-laborers of Egypt.

---

[a]Poetic for the death of the king; cf. similar phrases for the death of Thutmose I and of Thutmose II in the inscription of Ineni (II, 108, and 118, l. 16), and of Thutmose III in the inscription of Amenemhab (II, 592, ll. 35–37).

[b]The funeral procession crosses the river.

[c]His tomb in the Valley of the Kings' Tombs, No. 14 (Baedeker's *Egypt*, 270). He appropriated it from Queen Tewosret, wife of King Siptah. It had already been appropriated by Seti II, who finally had not used it. Setnakht took it, and enlarged it for his purpose (Lepsius, *Denkmäler*, III, 209–14; *Mêmoires de la mission française au Caire*, III, 137 ff.). He had been unable to finish his own tomb (No. 11, Baedeker's *Egypt*, 268), which was then taken over and completed by his son, Ramses III.

[d]The three great gods and the three great priesthoods, viz., of Thebes, Heliopolis, and Memphis, are here introduced. "*Father*" ought to be in the plural.

[e]Or: "*I trained*" (*šḫpr*).

[f]Not classes in the sense of castes of society, but classes for successive service in the army or civil offices, or state works or royal estates; with which meaning this word (*ḏᵓm·w*, Coptic, "*generations*") is common in the historical texts. See also **26**, 2, note.

### *War with Northern Asiatics*

**403.** I extended all the boundaries of Egypt; I overthrew those who invaded them from[a] their [7]lands. I slew the Denyen (*Dʾ-yn-yw-nʾ*) in[b] their isles, the Thekel (*Ṯʾ-k-rʾ*) and the Peleset (*Pw-rʾ-sʾ-ty*) were made ashes. The Sherden and the Weshesh (*Wʾ-š-š*) of the sea, [8]they were made as those that exist not, taken captive at one time, brought as captives to Egypt, like the sand of the shore. I settled them in strongholds, bound in my name. Numerous [9]were their classes like hundred-thousands. I taxed them all, in clothing and grain from the storehouses and granaries each year.

### *Edomite War*

**404.** I destroyed the people of Seir (*Sʾ-ʿʾ-rʾ*), of the tribes of [10]the Shasu (*Šʾ-sw*);[c] I plundered their tents of their people, their possessions, their cattle likewise, without number. They were pinioned and brought as captive, as tribute of Egypt. [11]I gave them to the gods, as slaves into their house[s].

### *Libyan Wars*[d]

**405.** Behold, I will inform you of other things, done in Egypt since my reign. The Libyans [1]and the Meshwesh (*M-šʾ-wʾ-šʾ*)

*Pl.* 77

were dwelling[e] in Egypt, having plundered the cities of the western shore,[f] from Memphis to Kerben (*Ḳʾ-rʾ-bʾ-nʾ*).[g] They had reached

---

[a]Or: "*in*."

[b]Meaning "who are in;" not that the victory took place in their isles.

[c]See the Bedwi chief as prisoner on the front of the pavilion (§ 129) with the chiefs of Asia Minor.

[d]The Libyan aggressions are here naturally treated as one subject, and the long continuance of the struggle to expel them, extending through two wars, must be drawn from the other sources.

[e]Lit., "*sitting*" (*snḏm*).

[f]Merneptah also makes use of the same rare word (*rwd*), "*shore*," in his Libyan campaign (Karnak Inscription, l. 30, III, 583).

[g]Identified by Brugsch, with some probability, as the place near Abukir, called by the Greeks, Heracleum (Brugsch, *Dictionnaire géographique*, 854 ff.). It is the place called Karbaniti in the annals of Ashurbanipal, to which Tirhaka marched from Memphis.

the great river[a] on both its banks.[b] [2]They it was who plundered the cities of Egwowe (*G-wt-wt*)[c] during very many years, while they were in Egypt. Behold, I destroyed them, slain at one time. I laid low [3]the Meshwesh, the Libyans, the Esbet (*ˀ-sˀ-bˀ-tˀ*),[d] the Keykesh (*Ḳˀ-y-ḳˀ-šˀ*), the Shai (*Šˀ-y*),[e] the Hes (*Hˀ-sˀ*) and the Beken (*Bˀ-ḳˀ-nˀ*); they were overthrown in their blood and made heaps. I turned them back [4]from trampling the border of Egypt. I carried away those whom my sword spared, as numerous captives, pinioned like birds before my horses,[f] their wives and their children by the ten-thousand, [5]their cattle in number like hundred-thousands. I settled their leaders in strongholds in my name. I gave to them captains (*ḥry·w*) of archers, and chief men of the tribes, branded and made into [6]slaves, impressed with my name; their wives and their children were made likewise.[g] I led their cattle into the house (*pr*) of Amon; they were made for him into herds[h] forever.

### *Well in Ayan*

**406.** I made a very great well [7]in the country of Ayan (*ᶜynˀ*). It was surrounded by a wall like a mountain of gritstone, with 20

[a]The *μέγας ποταμὸς* of Ptolemy, called by Strabo the Canopic branch of the Nile (Brugsch, *Dictionnaire géographique*, 856). See occurrence in exactly same connection in Merneptah's Libyan war (III, 580, l. 19).

[b]Lit., "*on its every side*" (*rwyˀ·t*); this word is used by Ramses II for the bank or side of the Orontes (III, 311, l. 21).

[c]This is possibly Canopus (*Pr-g-wˀ-ty*), as Brugsch thinks (*Dictionnaire géographique*, 820 ff.).

[d]Possibly to be read *M-sˀ-bˀ-tˀ*; this and the following are Libyan tribes of uncertain location. Petrie has attempted to find these names among the place-names still surviving in north Africa (*Proceedings of the Society of Biblical Archæology*, XXVI, 40, 41).

[e]Or: *Šˀ-y-tp?*

[f]Compare the reliefs of the return from the Libyan wars (§§ 56 and 112).

[g]A further indication of the occupation and employment of these captives is contained in an inscription behind Medinet Habu, referring to various negroes, Peleset(?), and Shekelesh (Lepsius, *Denkmäler*, III, 218, *c*): "*He causes that they cross the river, brought to Egypt, they are placed in strongholds of the king* ———. *When they reach the district of the king they are made chariot-drivers, charioteers, attendants, sunshade-bearers, attending the king.*"

[h]It is doubtless one of these herds which is mentioned in 10, 8, and given a name commemorating the victory over the Meshwesh.

⌜courses⌝ in the ground foundation, and a height of 30 cubits, having battlements. Its doorposts and doors 8were hewn of cedar, their bolts were of copper, with mountings.

*Punt Expedition*

**407.** I hewed great galleys with barges before them, manned with numerous crews, and attendants in great number; their 9captains of marines[a] were with them, with inspectors and petty officers, to command them. They were laden with the products of Egypt without number, being in every number[b] like ten-thousands. They were sent forth into the great sea of 10the inverted water,[c] they arrived at the countries of Punt, no mishap overtook them, safe and bearing terror.[d] The galleys and the barges were laden with the products of God's-Land, 11consisting of all the strange marvels of their country: plentiful myrrh of Punt,[e] laden by ten-thousands, without number. Their chief's children of God's-Land went before their tribute 12advancing to Egypt. They arrived in safety at the highland of Coptos;[f] they landed in safety, bearing the things which they brought. They were loaded, on the land-journey, upon asses and upon men; and loaded into 13vessels upon the Nile, (at) the haven of Coptos. They were sent forward down-stream[g] and arrived amid festivity, and brought (some) of the tribute into the (royal) presence like marvels. Their chief's

[a]Lit., "*galley-archers.*"

[b]Probably meaning that "*every number*" in the lists was a large one.

[c]"*The inverted water*" is the Euphrates (see Tombos Stela, l. 13, II, 73); hence "*the great sea of the inverted water*" is the Indian Ocean, of which the Persian Gulf (into which the Euphrates flows) is a part. The Egyptians doubtless counted the Red Sea as a part of this "*great sea of the inverted water,*" for the antique maps even far down into Arab times show the vaguest knowledge of the proper relations of these waters. It is possible to infer from this passage that Punt extended beyond the straits of Bab el-Mendeb.

[d]For all who might oppose them; it is a military expression, meaning that they were in efficient condition.

[e]See the trees of Punt in the Medinet Habu treasury, § 29.

[f]The "*highland or desert of Coptos*" here refers to the Red Sea end of the Coptos route, where the cargoes are unloaded from the vessels, and the land transport to the Nile begins.

[g]Showing that Ramses III did not live at Thebes (which is up-stream from Coptos), but in the north, in the Delta.

*Pl. 78*

children were in adoration before me, [1]kissing the earth, prostrate before me. I gave them to all the gods of this land, to satisfy the two serpent-goddesses every morning.

*Expedition to Atika*

**408.** I sent forth my messengers [2]to the country of the Atika (ᶜ ͗ *-ty-ka*),[a] to the great copper mines which are in this place. Their galleys carried them;[b] others on the land-journey were upon their [3]asses. It has not been heard before, since kings reign.[c] Their mines were found abounding in copper; it was loaded by ten-thousands into their galleys. [4]They[d] were sent forward to Egypt, and arrived safely. It was carried and made into a heap under the balcony,[e] in many bars[f] of copper, like hundred-thousands, being of the color of [5]gold of three times. I allowed all the people to see them, like wonders.

*Sinai Expedition*

**409.** I sent forth butlers and officials to the malachite-country, to my mother, Hathor, mistress of the malachite. There were brought for her silver, gold, royal linen, mek-linen, and many things [7]into her presence, like the sand. There were brought for me wonders of real malachite in numerous sacks, brought forward into my presence. They had not been seen before, [8]since kings reign.

*Ramses III's Good Works at Home*

**410.** I planted the whole land with trees and verdure, and I made the people dwell in their shade. I made [9]the woman of Egypt to go ⌜— —⌝[g] to the place she desired, (for) no stranger nor any one upon the

---

[a]Uncertain region, accessible both by sea and land from Egypt, hence probably in the Sinaitic Peninsula, where so much copper was obtained. See Müller, *Asien und Europa*, 133 and 393.

[b]Lit., "*were laden with them;*" meaning, of course, the messengers.

[c]Lit., "*since the reign;*" viz., "*since the reign of kings began.*"

[d]Or: "*it,*" the copper.

[e]The copper is piled up under the palace balcony.

[f]Lit., "*bricks.*"

[g]The two words literally mean: "*her ears being extended,*" but the significance of this statement is obscure. It may refer to the fact that her head and ears were uncovered; compare the similar statement in the inscription of the year 5, l. 73 (§ 47).

road molested her. I made the infantry and chariotry to dwell (at home) [10]in my time; the Sherden (*Š ꜣ -r ꜣ -d ꜣ -n ꜣ*) and Kehek (*Ḳhḳ*) were in their towns, lying the ⸢length⸣[a] of their backs; they had no fear, (for) there was no enemy [11]from Kush, (nor) foe from Syria. Their bows and their weapons reposed in their magazines, while they were satisfied and drunk with joy. [12]Their wives were with them, their children at their side; they looked not behind them,[b] (but) their hearts were confident, (for) I was with them as the defense and protection of their limbs. [13]I sustained alive the whole land, whether foreigners, (⸢common⸣) folk, citizens, or people, male or female.[c] I took a man

*Pl. 79*

out of his misfortune and I gave to him breath; [1]I rescued him from the oppressor, who was of more account than he.[d] I set each man in his security, in their towns; I sustained alive others in the hall of petition.[e] [2]I equipped the land in the place where it was laid waste. The land was well satisfied in my reign. I did good to the gods, as well as the men, [3]and I had nothing at all belonging to any (⸢other⸣) people. I exercised my sovereignty over the land as ruler of the Two Lands, while ye were my servants under my feet, without ⸢—⸣. Ye were [4]well pleasing to my heart, for ye did excellently, and ye were zealous for my commands[f] and my commissions.

### *Ramses III's Death*

**411.** Behold, I have gone to rest in the Nether World, like (my) father Re, [5]I have mingled with the great gods in heaven, earth and, the Nether World. Amon-Re has established my son on my throne; he has taken my office in peace, as ruler of the Two Lands, sitting on the throne [6]of Horus as lord of the two shores. He has assumed the

---

[a]Lit., "*the height of their backs.*"

[b]In fear.

[c]An enumeration which seems to begin at the bottom; *k ꜣ wy, rḫy·t, p ꜥ·t, ḥnmm·t;* but see Pl. 1, 6, note.

[d]Lit., "*the mighty who was weightier* (*or heavier*) *than he;*" compare the Hebrew, קל and כבד.

[e]Or: "*the hall of the Nether World*" (*dw ꜣ·t*); referring to his mortuary oblations?

[f]Lit., "*Ye were filled with my commands, etc.*"

etef-crown, like Tatenen, as: Usermare-Setepnamon, L. P. H., first-born son of Re, the self-begetter: Ramses (IV)-Hekma-Meriamon; [7]the child, son of Amon, who came forth from his limbs, shining as Lord of the Two Lands; he is like a true son, praised for his father's sake.

*Faithfulness to Ramses IV Urged*

**412.** Be ye attached to his sandals, [8]kiss the earth in his presence, bow down to him, follow him at all times, adore him, praise him, magnify his beauty as ye do [9]to Re every morning. Present to him your tribute (in) his august palace, bring to him the gifts[a] of the lands and countries. Be ye zealous for his commissions, [10]the commands which are spoken among you. ⌜Obey⌝ his behests, that ye may prosper under him. Labor for him as one man in every work; drag for him monuments, dig for him [11]canals, do ye for him the work of your hands, that ye may enjoy his favor, in possession of his provision every day. Amon has decreed to him his reign upon earth; he has doubled to him his lifetime [12]more than (to) any king; (even) the King of Upper and Lower Egypt, Lord of the Two Lands; Usermare-Setepnamon, L. P. H.; Son of Re, Lord of Diadems: Ramses (IV)-Hekma-Meriamon, L. P. H., given life forever:

---

## RECORD OF THE ROYAL JUBILEE

**413.** Ramses III commissioned his vizier, Ta, to take charge of the jubilee in the year 29, and it perhaps took place in that year. In that case he was made crown prince a year[b] before his father Setnakht's death.[c] Accepting this, it could not have been long before the celebration that the vizier left the capital (Tanis?) and went south to make preparations for it, as the following paragraph[d] shows:

Year 29, month [one] of the third season, day 28. The vizier Ta sailed north, after he had come to take the gods of the South for the Sed Jubilee.

---

[a]See § 207. [b]See § 400 on Ramses III's relations with his father.

[c]This accords with the only date of Setnakht's reign, "*year 1*" (Papyrus Sallier, I, 6).

[d]Spiegelberg, *Recueil*, 68, 69; from Papyrus Turin 44, 18 f.

**414.** At El Kab the High Priest of Nekhbet, Setau, recorded in his tomb, as one of the great events of his life, the visit of the vizier on the occasion of the latter's southern voyage (as above) and his visit there, as follows:[a]

[⌜Year 29⌝ under the majesty] of King Ramses III; first occurrence of the Sed Jubilee. His majesty commanded to commission the governor of the (residence) city, the vizier, Ta, to carry out the customary regulations[b] in the houses of the Sed Jubilee, to go to the "House-of-Ramses-Meriamon (Ramses II),-the-[Good-God]." Reception of the bow of the barque of the Divine[c] Hand by the king himself, when ⌜he⌝ was [in] the Southern City.[d]

**415.** This same Setau, in whose tomb the above occurs, was still High Priest of Nekhbet at El Kab in the year 4 of Ramses IX, when his tomb was decorated;[e] so that one man's tenure of a high office (attained, at the earliest, in middle life) includes the period from year 29 of Ramses III to year 4 of Ramses IX. Accepting thirty years for Setau's tenure of the office we have left, after deduction of the known dates of other kings, some fifteen years for the three Ramses, VI, VII, and VIII.[f]

---

[a]Brugsch, *Recueil de monuments*, II, Pl. 72, No. 2 (attributed to Ramses II); Brugsch, *Thesaurus*, V, 1129 (properly attributed); Champollion, *Notices descriptives*, I, 271; Lepsius, *Denkmäler*, Text, IV, 49.

[b]There is a feminine singular possessive with this word, "*her regulations*," but the Sed Jubilee is masculine.

[c]Same as Divine Votress, a kind of high priestess of Amon.

[d]This disconnected conclusion is preserved only by Champollion, and it reads as if it surmounted a scene depicting the king receiving the barque.

[e]Lepsius, *Denkmäler*, IV, Text, 50; Spiegelberg, *Recueil*, 24, 185; Maspero's date for the construction of this tomb, as under Ramses III (*Momies royales*, 667), must be modified in accord with this new datum.

[f]

| | |
|---|---|
| Remainder of Ramses III's reign | 2 years. |
| Ramses IV | 6 years. |
| Ramses V | 4+$x$ years. |
| Ramses IX (last date in Setau's term) | 4 years. |
| Total | 16 years. |

Leaving some fifteen years to insert between Ramses IV and Ramses IX.

## RECORDS OF THE HAREM CONSPIRACY[a]

**416.** Fragmentary and brief as these documents are, they afford a glimpse into the court intrigues and conspiracies of the Orient three thousand and two hundred years ago, which is as picturesque and interesting as it is important. Here are all the materials for a novel or a drama, with the full *dramatis personae* all present. The first question which arises is: Against whom was the conspiracy, here unfolded, directed? The king who empowers the prosecuting court to try the conspirators is called "*ruler of Heliopolis*" (§ 423), a term applied to several kings, but especially to Ramses III. One of the conspirators, in the course of their machinations, secured a "*magic roll of Ramses III . . . . his lord.*" It is clear, then, that the conspiracy was directed against this king, and, as we shall see, toward the close of his reign. One of his queens,[b] named Tiy, plots to make way with the old king and to place her son Pentewere[c] upon the throne.

---

[a]These records are contained in two documents: (*a*) the Judicial Papyrus of Turin; and (*b*) Papyrus Lee and Papyrus Rollin, both parts of one document. The Judicial Papyrus of Turin is a magnificent document, containing six columns, the first being but a mere fragment of the ends of all the lines. The papyrus roll is about twenty inches high, the letters about an inch to an inch and a quarter high, and the horizontal lines are two inches apart. It was published, and for that time well treated, by Devéria in the *Journal asiatique*, in 1865–68, (but see Chabas' valuable corrections, *Mélanges d'archéologie égyptienne*, 3[me] sér., Tome I, 5–47), and again revised by the author, as a "*tirage à part*" in 1868. The last was republished in the author's collected works (*Bibliothèque égyptologique*, V). Papyrus Lee contains the lower part of two columns, published by Sharpe (*Egyptian Inscriptions*, II, 47, 48) in 1855; shortly after by Lee (Hartwell House Catalogue, Pl. II); by Chabas, *Papyrus Magique*, Harris, 169–74; and *Mélanges d'archéologie égyptienne*, I, 9, 10; by Devéria, *op. cit.;* and by Newberry (*Amherst Papyri*, Pl. II and III, and pp. 19–22); Papyrus Rollin (No. 1888) in the *Bibliothèque Nationale* at Paris contains one short but complete column, published by Chabas, *op. cit.*, by Devéria, *op. cit.*, and by Pleyte, *Les Papyrus Rollin*, Pl. XVI.

[b]She may have been the mother or stepmother of Ramses III; see Erman, *Aegypten*, 87 (Mariette, *Catalogue général d'Abydos*, 1170).

[c]This was not his name, but a name given him in the court records, which call him "*Pentewere, who bore that other name.*" The chief conspirators are given assumed names by the records, as we shall see.

The "*chief of the chamber*," Pebekkamen, and a royal butler, named Mesedsure, were her chief coadjutors. The former procured from the overseer of the royal herds, Penhuibin, a number of magic wax figures of gods and men, which were able, in the belief of the owner, to disable or enfeeble the limbs of people. Two other men furnished similar materials, which were smuggled into the harem, and by such agencies the conspirators were empowered, as they thought, to disable or evade the people of the guard, who might otherwise have discovered and betrayed the plot.

**417.** Pebekkamen and Mesedsure secured the co-operation of ten harem officials of various ranks, four royal butlers, an overseer of the treasury named Pere, a captain of archers in Nubia named Binemwese, who was inveigled by the influence of a sister of his in the harem; Peyes, a commander of the army, three royal scribes in various offices, Pebekkamen's assistant, and several subordinate officials. As most of these people were in the personal service of the Pharaoh, the dangerous character of the complot is evident. Six wives of the officers of the harem-gate were used in securing the transmission of messages, and outside relatives of the inmates, not mentioned by name, are clearly implicated. Binemwese's sister sent him a letter urging him to incite the people to hostility against the king, and such was the purport of all the messages which left the harem. Evidently a revolution outside of the palace was intended to accompany their own coup within it. That the latter involved the assassination of the king is nowhere stated, but is self-evident.

**418.** Before their plans could be carried out, the conspirators were, in some way, betrayed, and ample evidence of their guilt was obtainable. The king ordered their prosecution, but before they came to trial he died.[a] It would almost appear that he knew his days were numbered when he gave instructions for the prosecution of the conspirators, for at the close of the commission constituting the special court therefor, he uses the remarkable words: (Go on with the prosecution, etc.), "*while I am protected and defended forever, while I am* ⌜*among*⌝ *the just kings who are before Amon-Re . . . . and before Osiris, ruler of eternity;*" that is, while I am among my deceased fathers. That the plot went so far that the king was injured, and survived his injuries only long enough to direct the prosecution of his assassins, is improbable, in view of a remark in the records, that Re did not permit the hostile plans to succeed;[b] but we may easily believe that it hastened the old king's end, even if he escaped unscathed.

**419.** The court commissioned to try the conspirators received its instructions directly from the king, and was given not only full discretion as to the verdict, but also final power to execute punishment, which was otherwise usually fixed by the Pharaoh after trial (§ 541). At the same time Ramses cautioned the judges to be certain of guilt, by the usual procedure in every case, and to punish none but the guilty. The court, thus constituted with such unusual powers, consisted of fourteen officials, viz., two overseers of the treasury, two standard-bearers of the army, seven royal butlers, a royal herald, and two scribes. Among them were a Libyan, a Lycian, a Syrian named Maharbaal ("*Baal hastens*"), and another foreigner, Kedendenna by name, of uncertain nationality. The unhealthy character of the conditions at the court of Ramses III are thus patent. Foreign

[a]He is called "*the Great God*" in the records of the trial, a term applied at this time only to deceased kings. See Papyrus Lee, col. 1, l. 3 (§ 455).

[b]Rollin, l. 3, § 454; but see note.

stewards and butlers, whose fidelity is purchased, are now the reliance of the Pharaoh. Their flaccid character and the dangerous persistence of the conspirators are shown by the fact that two of the judges, the butler Pebes and the scribe Mai, after their[a] appointment, together with two officers having the prisoners in charge, received in their dwelling some of the women conspirators and the general Peyes, with whom they caroused. These two judges, together with the two officers and another judge, Hori, the standard-bearer, were immediately put on trial for their indiscretion, and the first four were condemned to lose their noses and ears. On the execution of the sentence, Pebes committed suicide; Hori was found to be innocent.

420. The fate of the queen, Tiy, is unknown, as the records preserved do not contain her trial. The records of four different prosecutions are preserved. The judges were not all present at these four prosecutions. Six of them carried on the first, and condemned twenty-two persons, including the arch-conspirators Pebekkamen and Mesedsure, Binemwese, the captain of archers in Nubia, and Pere, overseer of the treasury; besides the six wives of the officers of the harem-gate. The penalty is not defined, but it was certainly death. The second prosecution, the judges for which are not mentioned, resulted in the condemnation of six persons, including Peyes, the army commander. All were permitted to commit suicide without leaving the court. Three butlers alone conducted the prosecution of the third group of four conspirators, among whom was the guilty young prince Pentewere. All four were found guilty, and were allowed to take their own lives. These three prosecutions disposed of

[a]That their indiscretion occurred only after their appointment is, of course, evident. They never would have been appointed had their intimacy with the conspirators occurred before. The object of Peyes and the women could only have been the corruption of the judges in their own interest.

the capital cases.[a] The fourth prosecution was that of the indiscreet judges and their two companions.

**421.** In the documents containing the above facts, the chief conspirators are given fictitious names, indicative of the abhorrence in which they were held. Thus Mesedsure means "*Re hates him*," and Binemwese is "*Wicked in Thebes*." Pentewere, the name applied to the guilty prince, who was in all probability only an unfortunate tool, is not a term of opprobrium, but is not his real name (Col. V, l. 7, § 447).

**422.** As to the character of the following records, the first document (Turin) omits the evidence, and is, therefore, not a full record of the trials, but forms merely an abstract of the proceedings, evidently for filing in the royal archives. The second document (Lee and Rollin), far less imposing in appearance, is fuller, and may have been part of the original scribal record of the prosecution.

### I. APPOINTMENT OF THE COURT.

*Col. 1. Introduction*

**423.** [1]——— Ruler of Heliopolis ———[b] [2]——— t[he] wh[ole] land ——— [3]——— the whole land ——— [4]——— their cattle ——— [5]——— to bring them ——— [6]——— all — before them ——— [7]——— for them; the — are ———

*Col. 2.*

[8]——— people saying ——— [9]——— they are ⌜the abhorred of the land.

*Commission of the Court*

I commission:

The overseer of the White House, Mentemtowe (*Mntw-m-tꜣwy*);

[a]For the three people tried and executed for practicing magic, whose names are lost in the full account of their trial (§§ 454–56), are probably included in the list of capital prosecutions without designation of their crime as magic. "*Collusion*" is a quite sufficient definition of their guilt in the abstract (Turin).

[b]The loss at the ends of the lines is of uncertain length; the last line joins Col. 2 without break, but it is perhaps a short line.

The overseer of the White House, Pefroi (*Pʾ yf-rʾ wy*);
[2]The standard-bearer, Kara (*Kʾ -rʾ*);
The butler, Pebes (*Pʾ y-Bʾ -sʾ*);
The butler, Kedendenna (*Kdndnnʾ*);
The butler, Maharbaal[a] (*M-hʾ -rʾ -b-ᶜ -rʾ*);
[3]The butler, Payernu (*Pʾ -yr-nw*);
The butler, Thutrekhnefer (*Dḥwty-rḫ-[n]fr*);
The king's-herald, Penrenut (*Pn-rnwt*);
The scribe, Mai (*My*);
[4]The scribe of the archives, Peremhab (*Pʾ -Rʾ -m-ḥb*);
The standard-bearer of the infantry, Hori; [5]saying:

*Instructions to the Court*

**424.** "As for the words which the people have spoken, I know them not. Go ye and examine them. [6]When they[b] go out, and they[b] examine them, they[b] shall cause to die by their own hand, those who should die, [7]without [my] knowing it. They shall execute the punishment [upon] the others, likewise without my knowing it. When [⌜ye⌝] ⌜go⌝ [⌜see to⌝ it] that ye give heed, and have a care lest ye execute punishment [9]upon — — — — unjustly[c] ⌜— — —⌝. Now, I say to you[d] in

*Col. 3*

very truth, [1]as for all that has been done, and those who have done it, let all that they have done fall upon their (own) heads; [3]while I am protected and defended[e] forever, [4]while I am ⌜among⌝[f] the just kings, who are before [5]Amon-Re, king of gods, and before Osiris, ruler of eternity."

II. THE CONDEMNED OF THE FIRST PROSECUTION

*Col. 4. First Prosecution*

**425.** [1]Persons brought in because of the great crimes which they had committed, and placed in the court[g] of examination before the great nobles of the court of examination, that they might be examined by:

---

[a]מהר בעל [b]We should expect "ye."

[c]*Gwš*, "*to bend, crook, break;*" it has also been thought to refer to torture.

[d]Text has "*them.*"

[e]See same phrase, I, 768, and IV, 528, l. 7.

[f]*Ḫr*, "*under,*" local. [g]Lit., "*seat or place of examination.*"

*Composition of the Court*

**426.** The overseer of the White House, Mentemtowe;
The overseer of the White House, Pefroi;
The standard-bearer, Kara;
The butler, Pebes;
The scribe of the archives, Mai;
The standard-bearer, Hori.

They examined them; they found them guilty; they brought their punishment upon them; their crimes seized them.

*The Condemned and Their Crimes*

**427.** ²The great criminal,[a] Pebekkamen (*Pᵓ y-bᵓ ky-kᵓ mn*), formerly chief of the chamber.

He was brought in because of his collusion with Tiy and the women of the harem. He made common cause with them, and began bringing out their words to their mothers and their brothers who were there, saying: "Stir up the people! Incite enemies to hostility against their lord." He was placed before the great nobles of the court of examination; they examined his crimes; they found that he had committed them. His crimes seized him; the nobles who examined him brought his punishment upon him.

**428.** ³The great criminal, Mesedsure (*Msd-sw-R*ᶜ),[b] formerly butler.

He was brought in because of his collusion [with] Pebekkamen, formerly chief of the chamber, and with the women, to stir up enemies to hostility against their lord. He was placed before the great nobles of the court of examination; they examined his crimes; they found him guilty; they brought his punishment upon him.

**429.** ⁴The great criminal, Peynok (*Pᵓ-ynywk*),[c] formerly overseer of the king's ⌜—⌝ of the harem, ⌜in the suite⌝.[d]

He was brought in because of his making common cause with Pebekkamen and Mesedsure, to commit hostility against their lord.

---

[a]This word (*ḫrw*) literally means "*fallen, miserable,*" and is the term regularly applied to rebels, foreign foes, and criminals. Chabas' objections (*Mélanges d'archéologie égyptienne,* 3me sér., I, 14) to translating "*criminal*" seem to me rather pedantic and unfair to Devéria.

[b]Meaning "*Re hates him;*" see introduction, § 421.

[c]"*The serpent.*"

[d]Lit., "*while following*" (the king?).

He was placed before the great nobles of the court of examination; they examined his crimes; they found him guilty; they brought his punishment upon him.

**430.** [5]The great criminal, Pendua (*P-n-dwꜣ w*), formerly scribe of the king's ⌈—⌉ of the harem, ⌈in the suite⌉.[a]

He was brought in because of his making common cause with Pebekkamen and Mesedsure, the other criminal, formerly overseer of the king's ⌈—⌉, and the women of the harem, to make a conspiracy with them, to commit hostility against their lord. He was placed before the nobles of the court of examination; they examined his crimes; they found him guilty; they brought his punishment upon him.

**431.** [6]The great criminal, Petewnteamon (*Pꜣ-tꜣ w mdy-Ymn*), formerly inspector of the harem, ⌈in the suite⌉.[a]

He was brought in because of his hearing the words which the people discussed with the women of the harem, without reporting them. He was placed before the great nobles of the court of examination; they examined his crimes; they found him guilty; they brought his punishment upon him.

**432.** [7]The great criminal, Kerpes (*Kꜣ-rꜣ-pw-sꜣ*), formerly inspector of the harem, ⌈in the suite⌉.[a]

He was brought in because of the words which he had heard and had concealed. He was placed before the nobles of the court of examination. They found him guilty; they brought his punishment upon him.

**433.** [8]The great criminal, Khamopet (*Ḥꜥ-m-yp·t*), formerly inspector of the harem, ⌈in the suite⌉.[a]

He was brought in because of the words which he had heard and had concealed. He was placed before the nobles of the court of examination. They found him guilty; they brought his punishment upon him.

**434.** [9]The great criminal, Khammale (*Ḥꜥ-m-mꜣꜣ-n-rꜣ*), formerly inspector of the harem, ⌈in the suite⌉.[a]

He was brought in because of the words which he had heard and had concealed. He was placed before the nobles of the court of examination; they found him guilty; they brought his punishment upon him.

**435.** [10]The great criminal, Setimperthoth (*Sty-m-pr-Dḥwty*), formerly inspector of the harem, ⌈in the suite⌉.[a]

---

[a]Lit., "*while following*" (the king ?).

He was brought in because of the words which he had heard and had concealed. He was placed before the nobles of the court of examination; they found him guilty; they brought his punishment upon him.

**436.** [11]The great criminal, Setimperamon (*Sety-m-pr-Ymn*), formerly inspector of the harem, ⸢in the suite⸣.

He was brought in because of the words which he had heard and had concealed. He was placed before the nobles of the court of examination; they found him guilty; they brought his punishment upon him.

**437.** [12]The great criminal, Weren (*W*ˀ*-r*ˀ*-n*ˀ), who was butler.

He was brought in because of his hearing the words from the chief of the chamber, and when he had ⸢withdrawn from⸣ him, he concealed them and did not report them. He was placed before the nobles of the court of examination; they found him guilty; they brought his punishment upon him.

**438.** [13]The great criminal, Eshehebsed (*ᶜš*ˀ*-ḥb-šd*), formerly assistant of Pebekkamen.

He was brought in because of his hearing the words from Pebekkamen; and when he had left him, he did not report them. He was placed before the nobles of the court of examination; they found him guilty; they brought his punishment upon him.

**439.** [14]The great criminal, Peluka (*P*ˀ*-rw-k*ˀ),[a] formerly butler and scribe of the White House.

He was brought in because of his collusion with Pebekkamen, having heard the words from him, without reporting them. He was placed before the nobles of the court of examination; they found him guilty; they brought his punishment upon him.

**440.** [15]The great criminal, the Libyan, Yenini (*Y-ny-ny*), formerly butler.

He was brought in because of his collusion with Pebekkamen, having heard the words from him, without reporting them. He was placed before the nobles of the court of examination; they found him guilty; they brought his punishment upon him.

*Col. 5*

**441.** [1]Wives of the people of the harem-gate, who united with the men, when the things were discussed; who were placed before the

---

[a]Lit., "*the Lycian.*"

nobles of the court of examination; they found them guilty; they brought their punishment upon them: six women.

**442.** [2]The great criminal, Pere (*P ͗ y-yry*), son of Ruma (*Rw-m ͗*), formerly overseer of the White House.

He was brought in because of his collusion with the great criminal, Penhuibin (*Pn-ḥwy-byn*), making common cause with him to stir up enemies to hostility against their lord. He was placed before the nobles of the court of examination; they found him guilty; they brought his punishment upon him.

**443.** [3]The great criminal, Binemwese (*Byn-m-W ͗ s·t*),[a] formerly captain of archers in[b] Nubia.

He was brought in because of the letter, which his sister, who was in the harem, ⌈in the suite⌉, had written to him, saying: "Incite the people to hostility! And come thou to begin hostility against thy lord." He was placed before Kedendenna,[c] Maharbaal,[c] Pirsun (*P ͗ -yr-swn*), and Thutrekhnefer;[d] they examined him; they found him guilty; they brought his punishment upon him.

## III. THE CONDEMNED OF THE SECOND PROSECUTION

**444.** [4]Persons brought in because of their crimes and because of their collusion with Pebekkamen, Peyes (*P ͗ y-yś*), and Pentewere (*Pn-t ͗ -wr*). They were placed before the nobles of the court of examination in order to examine them; they found them guilty; they[e] left them in their[f] own hands in the court of examination; they[f] took their[f] own lives; and no punishment was executed upon them.

**445.** [5]The great criminal, Peyes, formerly commander of the army.

The great criminal, Messui (*Ms-swy*), formerly scribe of the house of sacred writings.

The great criminal, Perekamenef (*P ͗ -R ͑ -k ͗ mn· f*), formerly chief.

The great criminal, Iroi (*Yy-r ͗ y*), formerly overseer of the ⌈—⌉ of Sekhmet.

---

[a]Meaning: "*Wicked in Thebes.*"

[b]Lit., "*of Nubia;*" he was probably in Nubia at the time. The phrase, "*of Nubia,*" may possibly belong to "*archers,*" but such a rendering is against the usual custom.

[c]See col. 2, l. 2.

[d]*Ibid.*, l. 3.

[e]The judges.

[f]The condemned.

The great criminal, Nebzefai (*Nb-ḏf ͗ w*), formerly butler.

The great criminal, Shedmeszer (*Š ͑ d-mśḏr*), formerly scribe of the house of sacred writings.

Total, 6.

### IV. THE CONDEMNED OF THE THIRD PROSECUTION

**446.** [6]Persons who were brought in, because of their crimes, to the court of examination, before Kedendenna, Maharbaal, Pirsun, Thutrekhnefer, and Mertusamon (*Mrty-wsy-Ymn*).[a] They examined them concerning their crimes; they found them guilty; they left them in their place; they took their own lives.

**447.** [7]Pentewere, who bore that other name.

He was brought in because of his collusion [with] Tiy, his mother, when she discussed the words with the women of the harem, being hostile against his lord. He was placed before the butlers, in order to examine him; they found him guilty; they left him in his place; he took his own life.

**448.** [8]The great criminal, Henutenamon (*H ͗ n-wtn-Ymn*), formerly butler.

He was brought in because of the crimes of the women of the harem; having been among them and having heard (them), without reporting them. He was placed before the butlers, in order to examine him; they found him guilty; they left him in his place; he took his own life.

**449.** [9]The great criminal, Amenkha (*Ymn-ḫ ͑ w*), formerly deputy of the harem, ⌜in the suite⌝.

He was brought in because of the crimes of the women of the harem; having been among them, and having heard (them), without reporting them. He was placed before the butlers, in order to examine him; they found him guilty; they left him in his place; he took his own life.

**450.** [10]The great criminal, Pere, formerly scribe of the king's ⌜—⌝ of the harem, ⌜in the suite⌝.

He was brought in because of the crimes of the women of the harem; having been among them, and having heard (them), without reporting them. He was placed before the butlers, in order to examine him; they found him guilty; they left him in his place; he took his own life.

---

[a]According to l. 7, these are all butlers.

## V. THE CONDEMNED OF THE FOURTH PROSECUTION

*Col. 6*

**451.** [1]Persons upon whom punishment was executed by cutting off their noses and their ears, because of their forsaking the good testimony[a] delivered to them. The women had gone; had arrived at their[b] place of abode, and had there caroused[c] with them and with Peyes. Their crime seized them.[d]

**452.** [2]This great criminal, Pebes (*P*ᵓ *y-b*ᵓ *-s*ᵓ), formerly butler. This punishment[e] was executed upon him; he was left (alone); he took his own life.

[3]The great criminal, Mai, formerly scribe of the archives.

[4]The great criminal, Teynakhte (*T*ᵓ *y-nḫt·t*), formerly officer[f] of infantry.

[5]The great criminal, Oneney (ᶜᵓ *-n*ᵓ *-n*ᵓ *y*), formerly captain[f] of police.

## VI. THE ACQUITTED

**453.** [6]Person[g] who had been connected with them; they had contended with him, with evil and violent words; he was dismissed; punishment was not executed upon him:

[7]The great criminal,[h] Hori, who was standard-bearer of the infantry.

---

[a]The king's instructions. [b]The condemned.

[c]Lit., "*made a beer-hall*" (ᶜ·*t-ḥḳ·t*); the same word in Piankhi, l. 134 (§ 880).

[d]The constitution of the court is not given.

[e]Cutting off nose and ears; mentioned in l. 1; afterward in despair he kills himself. The others lived and endured the disgrace. Pebes and Mai, the following prisoners, were judges appointed on this trial by the king.

[f]The question arises why these men (not judges) are implicated. The analogy of the case of the two judges shows that they must have had something to do with the trial. Looking at their titles, one a military officer and the other a captain of police, it becomes exceeding probable that we have in them the explanation of another difficulty. How could Peyes and the women, already in custody and awaiting trial, gain their freedom to go to the dwelling of one of their judges? The two officers Teynakhte and Oneney must have been in charge of them; and they secretly went with their charges to the judge's house. They were thus equally guilty with the two judges.

[g]As the rubric shows, this is the title of the following list, consisting of one person.

[h]So-called, although innocent, his name being here cited from the court docket where it appeared with the above words before it. He bears the same name and title as one of the judges (col. 2, l. 4). If he be the same man, then we may doubtless understand the language of l. 6 above as indicating an altercation in court, in which the prisoners had attempted to implicate one of the judges, an attempt which was thwarted by putting him on trial, and acquitting him.

## VII. THE PRACTICERS OF MAGIC

### *First Case of Magic*

454. [a]1He began to make magic rolls for ⸢hindering⸣ and terrifying, and to make some gods of wax, and some people, for enfeebling the limbs of people; 2and gave them into the hand of Pebekkamen, whom Re made not to be chief of the chamber, and the other great criminals, saying: "Take them in;" and they took 3them in. Now, when he set himself to do the evil (deeds) which he did, in which Re did not permit that he should succeed,[b] he was examined. Truth was found in every crime 4and in every evil (deed), which his heart had devised to do. There was truth therein, he had done them all, together with all the other great criminals. They were great crimes 5of death, the great abominations of the land, the things which he had done. Now, when he learned[c] of the great crimes of death which he had committed, he took his own life.

### *Col. 1. Second Case of Magic*

455. [d]"——— 1the king, L. P. H., for provisioning ⸢———⸣ ——— 2any — of my place of abode, to any person in the world." Now, when Penhuibin (*Pn-ḥwy-byn*), formerly overseer of herds, said to him: "Give to me a roll for enduing me with strength and might," 3he gave to him a magic roll of Usermare-Meriamon (Ramses III), L. P. H., the Great God,[e] his lord, L. P. H., and he began to

---

[a]Papyrus Rollin begins here, but the beginning of the case is lost, so that the name and office of the accused are unknown.

[b]It is not quite certain whether this remark refers to the failure of the whole conspiracy or only to this man's part in it. The former is more probable.

[c]That is, when he learned of what crimes he was charged with. The pronoun is *sw*, which is possibly for *se*, "*they*," viz., the judges; though the papyrus does not contain another example of such an error.

[d]Here Papyrus Lee begins; the beginning (top of the column) of the report is lost, and it is uncertain who is speaking. The name and office of the accused are also unknown.

[e]"*The Great God*" is applied at this time only to deceased kings, though it is used in the Old Kingdom of living kings. It regularly designates the deceased king in Papyrus Harris (*passim*), but is never applied to him in the vast inscriptions of Medinet Habu made during his life. In Papyrus Abbot, of the same age, the term always designates a deceased king; see also § 471 and commonly. A living king as presiding god of a distinct region or temple may receive the words "*great god*" in his formal cultus titulary (e. g., II, 894), but not otherwise. At the time

[a]⌈employ the magic powers of a god⌉[a] upon people. He arrived at the side [4]of the harem, this other large, deep place.[b] He began to make people of wax, inscribed,[c] in order that they might be taken in by the inspector, Errem (ʾ*-ry-m*),[d] [5]⌈hindering⌉ one troop and bewitching the others, that a few words[e] might be taken in, and others brought out. Now, when he was examined [6]concerning them, truth was found in every crime and in every evil (deed), which his heart had devised to do. There was truth therein, he had done them all, together with the [7]other great criminals, the abomination of every god and every goddess all together. The great punishments of death were executed upon him, of which the gods have said: "Execute them upon him."

*Col. 2. Third Case of Magic*

**456.** [f] [1]——— in the — — upon the measure. He went away ——— his hand enfeebled[g] — —. Now, when [2][he was examined concerning] them, truth was found in every crime and in [every] evil (deed), which his heart had devised to do. There was truth [3][therein, he had done them all, together with the othe]r great criminals, the abomination of every god and every goddess all together. They were great crimes of death, the great abominations of [4][the land, the things which he had done. Now, when he[h] learned of the] great [crim]es of death, which he had committed, he took his own life. Now, when the nobles, who examined him, learned that he had taken his own life [5]——— Re, altogether, of which the sacred writings say: "Execute it upon him."

---

this court record was made, then, the king was dead; but at the time when the roll was procured he was still living; hence the addition "*his lord*," meaning "his then lord." The king therefore lived to give the instructions for these prosecutions.

[a]While the rendering is doubtful in details, there is no doubt about the meaning in general, that he began to use the charms in the book.

[b]Some retired place by the wall of the harem, mentioned before in the lost portion of the papyrus, as the demonstrative shows.

[c]With the names of the persons represented, and the necessary charms.

[d]אל־רם.

[e]He evidently was thought to have bewitched the watch, that the intercourse with the harem might not be discovered.

[f]The second column of Papyrus Lee begins here; the name and office of the accused are lost with the missing top of the column.

[g]This is some official who has been the victim of the magical arts of the condemned; see Papyrus Rollin, l. 1 (§ 454).

[h]See § 454, l. 5.

# REIGN OF RAMSES IV

## HAMMAMAT STELA

457. These records on the rocks in the Wadi Hammamat bring us knowledge of the only considerable achievement of Ramses IV known to us.

### I. THE FIRST STELA

In the first stela[a] the king narrates how, by direct revelation of the god, he has been guided in a personal visit to the quarries of the Wadi Hammamat, which lie three days' journey from the Nile, on the road from Coptos to the Red Sea. In commemoration of this visit the first stela was then cut in the rocks. Its date shows that the king undertook this arduous desert journey only a little over a year and three months after his accession. The document is as follows:

458. At the top is a relief, in two fields, showing Ramses IV offering an image of Mat, the goddess of truth, to "*Amon-Re, lord of Thebes, lord of the highlands and mountains;*" "*Min, lord of the highlands;*" and "*Isis, mistress of heaven.*" Behind him stands Mat. Below this, in the second field, the king appears, making the same offering to Onouris, Osiris of Coptos, Isis, and Harsiese. Behind him is Thoth, writing.

459. Below the reliefs is the following inscription:

[1]Year 2, second month of the first season (second month), day 12[b] under the majesty of . . . . . .[c] [2]King Ramses IV. . . . . . . . . . . . . . . . . . . . . . . . . . . . . . . . . . . . . . [11] . . . .[d]

---

[a]Lepsius, *Denkmäler*, III, 223, *e*.

[b]He succeeded his father on the sixth of the eleventh month (§ 182), just 1 year, 3 months, and 11 days before this date.

[c]Full fivefold titulary; see following stela (§ 463).

[d]I have omitted the usual epithets following the king's titulary, as they contain purely conventional reference to the Pharaoh's power, mentioning Retenu and the Asiatics (ᶜ ʾ *mw*).

**460.** Lo, this Good God, excellent in wisdom, like Thoth, he has entered into the annals ⌜— [12]—⌝, he has perceived the records of the house of sacred writings, his divine heart does excellent things for the lord of gods, his understanding conceives pleasing things like ⌜—⌝, [13]which Re has repeated to him in his heart, that he might find the place of truth, (⌜where⌝)[a] this monument is founded, forever, hereafter.[b] He gave command to the king's-companions, those who enter in[c] to his majesty, the princes, [14]and the great authorities of the South and North, all of them; the scribes and wise men of the house of ⌜sacred writings⌝, to make this monument for the place of eternity in this mountain of Bekhen, [15]before God's-Land. King Ramses IV, beloved of Amon-Re, Harakhte, Min, lord of the desert, Horus, son of Osiris, and Eswere (Isis, the great); given life.

### II. THE SECOND STELA[d]

**461.** The king's personal investigation of the quarries early in the year 2 was followed by an expedition of his officers thither, over a year and nine months later, toward the close of the year 3. The second stela was erected by this expedition which, according to the statements of the stela, was the second largest expedition of the kind in ancient Egypt, of which we have any knowledge.[e] It contained no less than 8,362 men, not including 900 who died from the hardships incident to such a desert journey, and the labor of the quarry in the fierce heat of the desert.

**462.** After the date and introduction (§ 463) the stela naturally reverts to the king's visit (§ 464) and the preliminary search for suitable monumental blocks (§ 465). It then records in full the personnel of the expedition. It was led

---

[a]Or: "*the true place of this monument, founded, etc.*"

[b]To mark the place.

[c]*ḳ ḥr,* lit., "*enter upon;*" compare Arabic دجل على. It probably is not connected with *ᶜḳ ḥr,* Sethe, *Untersuchungen,* I, 46, note 1.

[d]Lepsius, *Denkmäler,* III, 219, *e.*

[e]The largest expedition was that of Mentuhotep IV (I, 442).

by the High Priest of Amon, Ramsesnakht, whose son Amenhotep succeeded to the same great office (§§ 486 ff.). He had under him 9 civil and military officers of rank (Nos. 2–10), 362 subordinate officers (Nos. 11–16, 18, and 21), 10 trained artificers and artists (Nos. 23, 24, 26, and 27), 130 quarrymen and stonecutters (No. 25), 50 gendarmes as police and overseers (No. 22), 2,000 slaves (No. 20), 5,000 infantry (No. 17), who, of course, assisted in the work, and 800 men of Ayan (No. 19). Their supplies were brought from Egypt by a train of ten carts and many pack-bearers.

*Date and Introduction*

463. The relief at the top shows Ramses IV offering Mat to the Theban triad and Bast. Behind him stand Min, Harsiese, and Isis. Below are the following twenty-two lines:

[1]Year 3, second month of the third season (tenth month), day 27, under the majesty of Horus: Mighty Bull, Living Truth, Lord of Jubilees, like his father, Ptah; Favorite of the Two Goddesses: Protector of Egypt, Binder of the Nine Bows; Golden Horus: Rich in Years, Great in Victory, Sovereign, Born of the Gods, [2]Creator of the Two Lands; King of Upper and Lower Egypt, Ruler of the Nine Bows, Lord of the Two Lands, Lord of Might: Hekmare[a]-Setepnamon; Son of Re, Lord of Diadems: Ramses (IV)-Meriamon, beloved of Amon-Re, king of gods, Harakhte, Ptah-South-of-His-Wall, lord of "Life-of-the-Two-Lands," Mut, Khonsu, Min, and Harsiese; given life. . . . . . . . . . . . . . . . . . . . . . . . . . . . . . . . [8]. . . . . . . . . . . . . . . . . . . . . .[b] His heart is vigilant in the pursuit of benefactions for his father, the creator of his body, who opens for him [9]the way to God's-Land. No one who lived (lit., was) before knew it, (for) its way is far before the ⌜people⌝, and they had no desire to enter it.

[a]The first half of this name is usually Usermare, as regularly in Papyrus Harris.

[b]The omitted portion (ll. 3 to beginning of 8) contains only conventional epithets in praise of the king. It is highly improbable that any of these refer to specific occurrences, as stated by Brugsch (*Geschichte*, 620). This praise merges gradually (l. 8) into specific reference to the Hammamat expedition.

### *King's Journey*

**464.** Lo, his majesty took account in his heart like his father Harsiese, and he led[a] the way to the place he desired. [10]He went around the august mountain, in order to make marvelous monuments for his father[b] and his fathers, all the gods and goddesses of Egypt. He set up a stela[c] upon this mountain, engraved with the great name of King Ramses IV,[d] given life like Re.

### *Preliminary Search*[e]

**465.** [11]Lo, his majesty gave command to the scribe of the house of sacred writings, Ramses-eshehab (*Rᶜ-ms-sw-ᶜš ͗-ḥb*); the scribe of ⌈crown possessions⌉, Hori; the prophet of the house of Min-Harsiese in Coptos, Usermare-nakht, to seek the ⌈—⌉ for [12]the "Place of Truth,"[f] in the mountain of Bekhen (*Bẖn*), after — — — — which were very good, being great and marvelous monuments.

### *The Expedition*

**466.** Then his majesty commanded to commission: 1. the first prophet of Amon, the chief of works, [13]Ramses-nakht, triumphant, to bring them to Egypt. The butlers and nobles who were with him, were:[g]

2. The king's-butler, Usermare-sekhepersu.
3. The butler, Nakhtamon.
4. The deputy of the army, Khamtir (*Ḫᶜ-m-ty-r ͗*).

---

[a]Or: "*that he might lead, etc.*" The rendering of Brugsch: "how he might lay out a road, etc." (*Geschichte*, 621), cannot be gotten out of the text.

[b]Either Amon or Horus (Harsiese) of Coptos.

[c]This is probably the stela of the year 2 above (§§ 459, 460).

[d]Double name.

[e]It is probable that this search took place on the first expedition at the time of the king's visit.

[f]A common name of the Theban cemetery, where the building for which the materials were intended may have been located. But the reference in the stela of the year 2 (above, § 460, l. 13) would indicate that the phrase is rather a designation of some spot in the mountain at Hammamat. The uncertain word (*wp*) preceding the phrase occurs in the same connection in a short inscription left by the same expedition near our stela (Lepsius, *Denkmäler*, III, 222, *i*): "*Year 3, second month of the third season (tenth month); his majesty commanded to bring the unknown ⌈—⌉ of the 'Place of Truth;' King Ramses IV.*"

[g]On the following list, see Brugsch, *Aegyptologie*, 228 ff.

5. The overseer of the White House, Khamtir.[a]

6. [14]The chief of the quarry-service, mayor, Amonmose, of the city (Thebes).[b]

7. The chief of the quarry-service, overseer of herds of "The-House-of-Usermare-Meriamon,"[c] Beknekhonsu.

8. The charioteer of the court, Nakhtamon.

9. The scribe of the army-lists, Sule (*Sw-n-r*ᵓ).

10. [15]The scribe of the deputy of the army, Ramses-nakht.

11. Scribes of the army — 20 men

12. Chiefs of the court stables — 20 men

13. The chief of the commandants of the army, Khamale (*Ḫ*ᵓ*-m-m*ᵓᵓ*-n-r*ᵓ) — (1 man)

14. Commandants of the infantry — 20 men

15. Charioteers [16]of the chariotry — 50 men

16. Chiefs of prophets, overseers of herds, prophets, scribes, inspectors — 50 men

17. People of the infantry — 5,000 men

18. Officers of the divisions of the court fishermen — [17]200 men

19. Eper (ᶜ*pr*) of the foreigners of Ayan (ᶜ*nw*) — 800 men

20. People of the ⌜crown possessions⌝[d] of the house of Pharaoh — 2,000 men

21. A chief deputy — 1 man

22. Mazoi gendarmes (*Md̠*ᵓ*y*) — 50 men

23. Chief artificer, Nakhtamon — (1 man)

24. Master workmen of the works of the [18]quarrymen — 3 men

25. Quarrymen and stonecutters — 130 men

26. Draughtsmen — 2 men

27. Sculptors — 4 men

28. The dead who are excluded from this list[e] — 900

Total — 8,368[f]

---

[a]This treasurer is mentioned also in a letter in Papyrus Mallet (*Recueil*, I, 51, Planches V, l. 5) from the fourth year of Ramses IV.

[b]Whether it is meant that he was mayor of Thebes, or merely belonged in Thebes, is not to be determined from the text; but there probably was not a mayor of all Thebes, which had a city governor, a mayor of the east, and a mayor of the west.

[c]This is the temple of Ramses III at Medinet Habu; the herd is mentioned in Papyrus Harris, 10, 7.

[d]Brugsch, *Aegyptologie*, 230, note; it is possible to render "*temples.*"

[e]See Spiegelberg, *Recueil*, XXI, 49.

[f]The correct total, including the ten important officials at the head (the leader

*Supplies*

**467.** [19]There were transported for them supplies[a] from Egypt in ten carts, there being six yoke of oxen to (each) cart, drawing (them) from Egypt to the mountain of Bekhen. [20][There were] many colporteurs laden with bread, meat, and cakes, without number.

*Offerings*

**468.** There were (also) brought the oblations for the satisfaction of the gods of heaven and earth from the Southern City (Thebes). They were pure with great purity, they were ⌈—⌉ [21]— — — — ⌈commanded⌉ the chief[b] ⌈that the priests might⌉ give ⌈—⌉. Bulls were slaughtered; calves were smitten; incense, it ⌈streamed⌉ to heaven; shedeh and wine, like a flood; beer ⌈overflowed⌉[c] in this place; the ritual priest, his voice ⌈presented⌉ the pure offering to Min, Horus, Isis, [22][Amon, Mut, Khonsu][d] and all the gods of[e] this mountain. Their hearts were glad, they received the oblations, that they might requite with myriads of jubilees, for their beloved son, King Ramses IV, given life forever.

---

## ABYDOS STELA[f]

**469.** This document, while it contains no important historical facts from the reign of Ramses IV, is of great psychological interest, and gives us, furthermore, one invaluable

---

and 9 subordinates), is 8,362. The 900 dead, as stated in the monument, are not included in this total. The scribe has made an error of 6 in the addition. Spiegelberg makes the discrepancy only 4 (*Recueil,* XXI, 49), but this is due to an error of 3 which has crept into his figures; *viz.,* he inserts among the items two 3's, whereas there is but one 3 in the entire list. He also excludes the leader, which reduces his error to 2, making his discrepancy 4 instead of 6.

[a]Whether this word (*ḥr˙t*) refers to food supplies or equipment in tools and the like is not evident. The colporteurs may have carried the food, and the ox carts the heavy tools.

[b]Chief (*mt*) of a priestly order or phyle (*s*ͻ). [c]*B*ᶜ*ḥ*?

[d]Restored from the relief at the top of the stela; so also Brugsch (*Geschichte,* 623).

[e]Brugsch emends so, or reads from a better copy; Lepsius' text is quite unintelligible.

[f]Stela now in Cairo, found by Mariette in Abydos; Mariette, *Abydos,* II, Pls. 34, 35 = Rougé, *Inscriptions hiéroglyphiques,* 156 ff. The stela is badly weathered, and the copy of Mariette is excessively inaccurate and incomplete; Rougé is much better. I had a collation of the original by Schaefer, which he kindly placed at my disposal.

datum, the length of Ramses II's reign, sixty-seven years. The petition of Ramses IV is that he may reign as long as did Ramses II, and the manner in which he reasons with Osiris regarding his desire is of unique interest.

**470.** [1]Year 4, third month of the first season (first month), day 10, under the majesty of King Ramses IV[a] . . . . . . . . .[b] [15]And thou shalt give to me health, life, long existence, a prolonged reign, endurance to my every member, sight to my eyes, hearing to my ears, pleasure to my heart daily. [16]And thou shalt give me to eat until I am satisfied; and thou shalt give me to drink until I am drunk; and thou shalt establish my issue (as) kings in the land, forever and ever. [17]And thou shalt grant me contentment every day, and thou shalt hear my voice in every saying, when I shall tell them to thee, and thou shalt give them to me with a loving heart. And thou shalt give to me [18]high and plenteous Niles, in order to supply thy divine offerings, and to supply the divine offerings of all the gods and goddesses of South and North; in order to preserve alive the [19]divine bulls;[c] in order to preserve alive the people of all thy lands, their cattle and their groves, which thy hand has made. [20]For thou art he who has made all, and thou canst not forsake them to carry out other designs with them; (for) that is not right.

**471.** And thou shalt be pleased with the land of Egypt, t[hy] [21]land, in my time; and thou shalt double for me the long duration, the prolonged reign of King Ramses II, the Great God; for more are the [mighty] [22]deeds, and the benefactions which I do for thy house in order to supply thy divine offerings, in order to seek every excellent thing, every sort of benefaction to do them for thy sanctuary [23]daily during these four years,[d] than those things which King Ramses II, the Great God, did for thee in his sixty-seven years. And thou shalt give to me the long existence [24]with the prolonged reign which thou gavest [him] as

[a]Full fivefold titulary.

[b]The remainder of the first fourteen lines contains only conventional prayers of mortuary character, addressed to Osiris.

[c]Of Athribis (*kmr* [sic!] *wr ntry*); see Spiegelberg, *Zeitschrift für ägyptische Sprache*, 1891, and Papyrus Harris, 30, 3 (§ 278).

[d]The four years which he has thus far reigned.

[⌈king⌉] — — upon — his[a] child[b] — while I sit upon his throne. For thou art he, who hast said it with [25]thy own mouth, and it shall not be reversed ———.[c] For thou art the great lord of Heliopolis, for thou art the [26]great lord of Thebes, for thou art the great lord of Memphis. Thou art he in whom is might, and that which thou doest is that which shall come to pass. Give to me [27]the reward of the great deeds which I have done for thee, even life, prosperity and health, long existence, and a [prolonged] reign; and thou shalt make — the limbs and preserve the members, [28]being with me as my good guardian and excellent protector. And thou shalt ⌈give to⌉ me every [⌈land⌉] and every [⌈country⌉] — — — — — — that I may present their tribute to thy ka and to thy name.

## BUILDING INSCRIPTION OF THE KHONSU-TEMPLE

**472.** Ramses III left the Khonsu-temple at Karnak, for the most part, incomplete. The chambers in the rear were then finished by Ramses IV,[d] including the smaller hypostyles, which contain the following dedication:[e]

Lord of the Two Lands: Hekmare-Setepnamon; Son of Re, Lord of Diadems: Ramses-Meriamon (Ramses IV); he made (it) as his monument for his father, Khonsu; making for him a temple, excellent, beautiful, enduring forever.

---

[a]Mariette has "thy;" Rougé, "his."

[b]This passage is now lost as far as "*sit,*" inclusive.

[c]Traces.

[d]See Lepsius, *Denkmäler*, Text, III.

[e]Champollion, *Notices descriptives*, II, 239; ceiling in the "galerie de droite" of the inner hypostyle. The remains of a sandstone obelisk found in Cairo, and now in the museum there, contain a dedication by Ramses IV, as follows: "*He made (it) as a monument for his father, Re, making for him a great obelisk, the name of which is 'Ramses-is-a-Child-of-the-Gods'*" (Daressy, *Annales*, IV).

# REIGN OF RAMSES V

## TOMB DEDICATION

473. Of the nine Ramessids who ruled after Ramses III the tombs of six[a] in the Valley of the Kings' Tombs are known. As a specimen of the dedication inscriptions the following of Ramses V may serve:[b]

Live Horus: Mighty Bull, Great in Victory, Sustaining Alive the Two Lands; Favorite of the Two Goddesses: Mighty in Strength, Repulser of Millions; Golden Horus: Rich in Years, like Tatenen (Ptah), Sovereign, Lord of Sed Jubilees, Protector of Egypt, Filling Every Land with Great Monuments in His Name; King of Upper and Lower Egypt, Lord of the Two Lands: Nibmare-Meriamon; Son of Re, of His Body, His Beloved, Lord of Diadems: Amonhirkhepeshef-Ramses (V)-Neterhekon, given life, like Re, forever. He made (it) as his monument for his fathers, the gods of the Nether World, making for them a new title,[c] in order that their names might be renewed; that they may give very many jubilees upon the Horus-throne of the living, every country beneath his feet, like Re, forever.

---

[a]According to Baedeker (1902), these are numbered as follows: Ramses IV (Hekmare), No. 2; Ramses VI (Nibmare), No. 9; Ramses IX (Neferkere), No. 6; Ramses X (Yetamon-Neterhekon), No. 1; Ramses XI (Khepermare), No. 18; Ramses XII (Menmare), No. 4. In Baedeker's list the name of Ramses XII (given as Neferkere) is to be corrected to Menmare.

[b]Lepsius, *Denkmäler*, III.

[c]*Syp·t* (see I, 178), meaning a title to land.

# REIGN OF RAMSES VI

## TOMB OF PENNO[a]

474. This official of the Pharaoh lived at Derr in Nubia, where there was a temple to Re or Horus built by Ramses II.

Penno was "*deputy of Wawat,*" as his chief office; but he was also "*chief of the quarry-service, steward of Horus, lord of Miam*" (*Myᶜ t*),[b] so that he had charge of the quarry operations in Wawat, as well as the administration of the property of the Horus-temple at Derr, called at that time Miam (*Myᶜ m*).

His relatives filled important local offices at Ibrim: two of them were "*treasurer of the Lord of the Two Lands in Miam (Ibrim);*"[c] another was "*scribe of the White House and mayor of Ibrim.*"[c] They thus had charge in the local administration of the treasury, which we see was organized in Nubia just as in Egypt at this period. The inscriptions in the tomb furnish a valuable glimpse of the life of the local Egyptian official in Nubia, as well as of the organization of the country and the conditions under Egpytian rule.

475. Penno had erected a statue of Ramses VI, which stood in the temple of Ramses II at Derr; and as a reward the Pharaoh sent him two vessels of silver. This great distinction is portrayed by Penno in his tomb.[d] He shows there, not merely his own reception of the two vessels from the viceroy of Kush, but the latter also, in the act of receiving the vessels from the Pharaoh, to be conveyed to Nubia.

---

[a]Hewn in the cliff at Ibrim, in Nubia; published by Lepsius, as indicated below. I am also indebted to Steindorff for a collation of Lepsius' plates with the original.

[b]Lepsius, *Denkmäler*, III, 229, *b*. [c]*Ibid.*, 231, *a*. [d]*Ibid.*, 230.

*Relief Scenes*

476. Before Ramses VI enthroned, stands the king's-son of Kush, and the accompanying inscriptions record the the following:

*Inscriptions*

Said his majesty to the king's-son of Kush: "Give the two silver vessels (*ṯbw*) of ointment of gums, to the deputy."

To which the king's-son of Kush replies:

"I will do (so); lo, the happy day shall be celebrated in every land."

*Relief Scene*

477. We now see the viceroy, after his arrival in Ibrim, presenting the two vases to Penno. The viceroy stands before the statue of Ramses VI, of which Penno has charge. Behind him is his steward, bearing a roll of papyrus. Penno, accompanied by two priests, stands before them, bearing in his uplifted hands two bowls containing cakes of ointment, which must be the vessels referred to in the inscriptions. The viceroy addresses Penno as follows:

*Inscriptions*

May Amon-Re, king of gods, favor thee! May Montu, lord of Hermonthis, favor thee! May the ka of Pharaoh, L. P. H., thy good lord, favor thee, who caused thee to fashion the statue of Ramses VI, son of Amon, lovely like Horus, lord of Miam (*My*ᶜ*m*) ———.[a]

Hearken, O deputy of Wawat, Penno, to Amon in Karnak. These things were spoken in the court of Pharaoh, thy good lord: "May Amon-Re, king of gods, favor thee! May Harakhte favor thee! May Montu favor thee! May the ka of Pharaoh, L. P. H., thy good lord, favor thee, who is satisfied with that which thou doest in the countries of the ⌜Negroes⌝[b] and in the country of Akati (ᵓ*-k*ᵓ*-ty*). Thou causest

[a]Here the artist has neglected to engrave the signs of nearly an entire line, leaving them only painted. They have now disappeared, leaving at the bottom of the line the isolated words: "*he slays the rebellious.*"

[b]*Nḥy.*

to bring them as captives before Pharaoh, L. P. H., thy good lord, in giving thy payment ⌜—⌝." Behold, I give to thee thy two vessels (*ṯbw*) of silver, that thou mayest anoint thyself with gums. Increase thou ⌜— — — —⌝ in the land of Pharaoh, L. P. H., wherein thou art.

**478.** The response of Penno, which is very brief, is badly preserved, but contained only a greeting "*for Pharaoh, L. P. H., my good lord.*"

The lands furnishing the income for the maintenance of the offerings presented to Ramses VI's statue were also recorded by Penno in his tomb, the inscription[a] doubtless being a copy of the official records regarding them. The lands comprised five different parcels, each of which is carefully demarked by four boundaries, enumerated as East, South, North, and West.

*Title*

**479.** [1]Domain of the statue of Ramses VI,[b] which rests in Miam (*My*ᶜ·*t*).[c]

*First District*

District north of "Ramses-Meriamon-[2]in-the-House-of-Re,"[d] the town; opposite the house of Re, lord of the eastern bend.[e]

*Boundaries*

The South is the lands of the domain of the [3]King's-Wife, Nefretiri, which rests in Miam (*My*ᶜ·*t*).

---

[a]Lepsius, *Denkmäler*, III, 229, *c;* I was able to control Lepsius' copy and to fill up some of the lacunæ from a photograph by Graf Grünau, but it was too small to establish a final text in badly preserved places.

[b]Full name given is: "*Amonhirkhepeshef-Ramses-Nuter-Ruler-of-Heliopolis.*"

[c]Unquestionably identical with the form *My*ᶜ*m* (Lepsius, *Denkmäler*, III, 115, tomb of Huy; cf. II, 1037). See also Brugsch, *Zeitschrift für ägyptische Sprache*, 1882, 31.

[d]This is the name of Ramses II's temple at Derr (see III, 503, and Brugsch, *Dictionnaire géographique*, 247); the words, "*the town*," are added to distinguish it from the temple. The scribe means the town, and not the temple.

[e]The Nile makes an immense bend to the east just below Derr; the "*House-of-Re*" may be the temple of l. 1, or some small, now vanished chapel of the local Re.

The East is the desert.
The North is the flax fields of Pharaoh, L. P. H.
The West is the Nile.

*Area*

Three khet.

*Second District*

**480.** [4]District of the ⌜—⌝ behind the land of Miyu (*My-yw*) in the lands of the deputy of Wawat.[a]

*Boundaries*

The South is the lands [5]of the domain of the statue under charge of the first prophet, Amenemopet.
The East is the great mountain.
The North is the flax fields [6]of Pharaoh, L. P. H., which are in the lands of the deputy of Wawat.
The West is the Nile.

*Area*

Two khet.

*Third District*

**481.** [7]District of the house of the goddess, east of the lands which are ⌜—⌝, and east of the great mountain.[b]

*Boundaries*

The South is the lands [8]of the domain of the statue under charge of the deputy of Wawat, Meri.
The East is the great mountain.
The North is the lands [9]of the herdman, Bahu (*Bꜣ-ḥw*).
The West is the Nile.

*Area*

Four khet.

*Fourth District*

**482.** District of the domain of Tehenut (*Tyḥnwt*) [10]at the western limit of the nome of Tehenut, in the flax fields of Pharaoh, L. P. H., together with [11]the lands which are ⌜—⌝.

---

[a]Meaning among the lands rented by or under charge of the deputy; the same in l. 6.

[b]This datum seems a contradiction of the one in l. 8, that the mountain was the eastern boundary of the land.

*Boundaries*

The East is the great mountain.

The South is the flax fields of Pharaoh, L. P. H., east [12]of the great mountain.

The North is the field of the Arasa (*ʾ-rʾ-sʾ*).

The West is the Nile.

*Area*

Six khet.

*Summary*

Total lands [13]given ⌜to⌝ it:[a] fifteen khet,[b] which makes ⌜—⌝ upper fields. The scribe ⌜of⌝ its domain, the deputy, Penno (*Pn-nwʿt*), [14]son of Herunofer (*Hrw-nfr*) of Wawat, has ⌜—⌝ (them), as fields ⌜rented⌝ to him, to pay[c] [15]to it one ox, slaughtered yearly.

*Fifth District*

**483.** District in the ⌜—⌝ fields which are under control of [16]the deputy of Wawat, not on the roll (above).

*Boundaries*

Its West is in ⌜front⌝[d] of the gravelly ground of the deputy, Penno.

[17]The South is the gravelly ground of the deputy, Penno.

The North is the ⌜—⌝ fields which are in the ⌜domain⌝ of the Pharaoh, L. P. H.

[18]The East is in front of the gravelly [ground] of the deputy, Penno.

*Area*

⌜Eight⌝ khet.

*Curse on Violator*

As for anyone who [19]shall disregard it, Amon, king of gods, shall pursue him, Mut shall pursue his wife, Khonsu shall pursue [20]his children; he shall hunger, he shall thirst, he shall faint and sicken.

---

[a]The statue.

[b]Mr. Griffith's statement (*Proceedings of the Society of Biblical Archæology*, 14, 418), that the "spaces between the notches" are to be counted, seems to be an oversight, for the total amounts to 19 by so counting. The notches themselves, however, amount to 15.

[c]On *fʾ*, "*pay*," see Spiegelberg, *Rechnungen*, 53.

[d]Steindorff has a sign like *grg*, which may be *ḥʾʿt*, "*front*."

# REIGN OF RAMSES VII

## STELA OF HORI[a]

484. This little stela records a commission intrusted by this almost unknown Pharaoh to Hori, his personal scribe, who is dispatched from Busiris to Abydos to pray at the great temple of Osiris, that the king may be given a long reign.

Above is a mortuary prayer in the name of Osiris of Abydos, Onouris of Thinis, Osiris of Busiris, Harendotes, and Eswere on behalf of King Usermare-Ikhnamon, Ramses (VII)-Menthirkhepeshef-Meriamon, who is also represented offering in a relief at the top. Then follows Hori's statement.

485. The scribe of Pharaoh, L. P. H., Hori, triumphant; he says: "I am a servant of thy[b] city (*nw˙t*), Busiris, thy city (*dmy*), which is in the Northland (Delta). I am the son of a servant of thy house, the scribe of Pharaoh, L. P. H., the favorite of Abydos, Pakauti (*P*ʾ-*k*ʾ*wtyw*), son of Seny (*Sny*), thy servant. I have been brought from my city of the Northland to thy city, Abydos, being a messenger of Pharaoh, L. P. H., your[c] servant. I have come to worship before you[c] and to beseech for him jubilees. Ye will hear his prayers, according as he is profitable to your ka's, and ye will accept me from the hand of Pharaoh, L. P. H., and my lord, L. P. H., and ye will give to me favor before him daily. ⌈Make your designs, I will cherish (them)⌉. It is said: 'Who can reverse your plans?' Ye are the lords of heaven, earth, and the Nether World, and men do as ye say. And ye will give mortuary offerings of bread and beer, and a sweet north wind for my father, Pakauti, and his son, the scribe of Pharaoh, Hori, triumphant."[d]

---

[a]Unpublished stela in the Berlin Museum, No. 2081 (*Ausführliches Verzeichniss des Berliner Museums*, 133). I had my own copy of the original.

[b]Meaning Osiris, whom he addresses.

[c]Plural.

[d]Names of other relatives follow.

## REIGN OF RAMSES IX

### INSCRIPTIONS OF THE HIGH PRIEST OF AMON AMENHOTEP

**486.** The high priests of Amon continued to extend their power and influence under Ramses IX. This process was sometimes accompanied by violence and insurrection. A woman testifying in a case which occurred in this reign, and desirous of dating a theft in her father's house, refers very significantly to the occasion when the theft took place:

[a]Examination: the Theban woman, Mutemuya, the wife of the sacred scribe, Nesuamon, was brought in; the oath of the king, L. P. H., not to lie, was administered to her. She was asked: "What hast thou to say?" She said: "When the revolt of the High Priest of Amon took place, this man stole some things of my father."

**487.** This may have been our High Priest Amenhotep, or possibly the affair belongs before his time. The records left by this powerful official significantly continue those of the High Priest of Amon, Roy, at the close of the Nineteenth Dynasty (III, 618–29). No connection can be traced between Roy and the high priests of the Twentieth Dynasty, unless we find it in the fact that the second prophet, who accompanies Roy on the Karnak wall, was named Beknekhonsu (§ 620), while the High Priest of Amon under Ramses III was also a Beknekhonsu.[b] The latter must have been succeeded by Ramsesnakht, whose father, Meribast, was not High Priest, and must have belonged to a collateral branch of the family. Ramsesnakht was the father

---

[a]Papyrus, British Museum, No. 10053; Spiegelberg, *Recueil*, 19, 91.

[b]See his statue found in the Mut-temple (Benson and Gourlay, *The Temple of Mut in Asher*, 343–47).

of our High Priest Amenhotep (§ 489, ll. 23, 24). He lived under Ramses III and IV, appearing as High Priest in year 3 of Ramses IV (§ 466), and was succeeded in the high priesthood by his son Nesuamon, whose brother, our Amenhotep, a second son of Ramsesnakht, followed Nesuamon in the great office.[a]

## I. BUILDING INSCRIPTIONS

**488.** In continuance of the privilege already gained by the high priests of Amon under the Pharaohs of the end of the Nineteenth Dynasty, Amenhotep, High Priest under Ramses IX, undertook the rebuilding of the High Priest's dwelling, connected with the Karnak temple of Amon. It had been erected by Sesostris I, some eight hundred years earlier. The kitchen, or refectory, had been solidly rebuilt by Roy, nearly a hundred years before, but the dwelling itself was now in a ruinous state. It stood on the south of the sacred lake (l. 7), east of the southern pylons, and its scanty remains were found there by Mariette.[b] At the east end of the neighboring pylon (VIII), by the similar record of Roy (III, 619–26), Amenhotep inscribed the following record[c] of his building:

---

[a]See Legrain, *Recueil*, 27, 71.

[b]See Mariette, *Karnak*, 11. This must be the strange building south of the lake (Mariette's plan, Pl. 2, R), the purpose of which was left uncertain by Mariette. He afterward (*op. cit.*, 62, 63) suggests this building as the one meant in our inscription, but strangely states that our inscription furnishes no indication of the location of the building, although it clearly states that the building overlooked the southern lake (l. 7). See also the following note, and Maspero's remarks (*Momies royales*, 670, 671).

[c]Mariette, *Karnak*, Pl. 40; Rougé, *Inscriptions hiéroglyphiques*, 202, 203; Brugsch, *Thesaurus*, 1322–24; Maspero, *Momies royales*, 669, 670 (partially); the inscription is on the inside (west) of the wall connecting pylons VII and VIII, at the point marked *h* on Mariette's plan (*Karnak*, Pl. 2). Other references to the High Priest Amenhotep's buildings have recently been discovered (by Legrain, *Annales*, V, 21) in which he refers to "*bringing artificers in every great work, that I might build the great place south of the* [⌜*lake*⌝] —. *I built this* ⌜—⌝ (determina-

**489.** [1]The assistant[a] whom his majesty taught, the High Priest of Amon-Re, king of gods, Amenhotep, triumphant, made it; to wit: I found this pure dwelling of the high priests [2]of Amon of former time, which is in the house of Amon-Re, king of gods, beginning to fall to ruin, while that which had been made in the time of King [3]Kheperkere, Son of Re, Sesostris (I), was ⌜(still) complete⌝. ⌜Then I⌝ built it anew with fine work and excellent workmanship. [4]I made thick its walls from its rear to its front. I built thoroughly upon it, I made its columns [5]and doorposts of great stones of excellent workmanship. I set up great doors of cedar, bound. I built thoroughly upon its [6]great lintel of stone which looks ⌜outward⌝, built — ⌜high —⌝ the High Priest of Amon, who is[b] in the house of Amon. I ⌜mounted⌝ its great door of —, [7]with bolts of copper and inlay-figures of fine gold and [⌜silver⌝] — —. I built its great ⌜courses⌝[c] (*ḏ*ˀ *ḏ*ˀ *w*) of stone, which opens toward the southern lake, upon the pure — [8]of the house of Amon. I surrounded [⌜it with a wall⌝] of brick. I erected its great ⌜carvings⌝[d] of stone ⌜at the doorposts⌝ — [9]doors of cedar. I — — — of great stones, dragged and cut as ⌜— — —⌝ — with [10]the royal titulary in the great name of Pharaoh, my [lord. I] built a treasury of ⌜brick⌝ anew in the great hall, the name of which is ——— [11]——— columns of stone, and doors of cedar, inscribed with ⌜—⌝ ——— [12]——— his majesty; it was the rear of the storehouse of the dues of Amon ——— [13]——— the great and august court, each High Priest of Amon ——— [14]——— every[thing] good and pure. I appointed its chiefs ——— [15]——— ⌜———⌝ ——— [16]——— taking the ———[e] [17]——— of stone, doors of cedar. I ——— [18]——— Ishru, they were [⌜planted with⌝] trees ——— [19]——— [20]— — — Pharaoh, my lord, to cause them to be given to Mut, the great, the —, that she might receive them, — — — — [21]——— as benefactions for Amon-Re, king of gods, my lord. I know that he is great, that he ⌜teaches

tive, two houses) *of the House of Amon anew; I made its double doors, wrought of meru wood, the inlay-figures of fine gold* ———." The "*great place*" must be the refectory, and its location is probably indicated as south of the lake.

[a]See the same phrase, II, 28.

[b]Or: "*shall be.*"

[c]See § 355, l. 12.

[d]*Ḥty;* see § 380, l. 15.

[e]Three lines are here lacking, not noted by Mariette (Maspero, *Momies royales*, 670, n. 1); but according to Rougé four lines are here lost (Rougé, *Inscriptions hiéroglyphiques*, 203); for convenience I have retained Mariette's numbering.

— —⌝ [22]saying: "Thou art the Lord of the Two Lands, Lord of [Diadems] ⌜Ramses (IX)⌝, L. P. H., a long term of life ⌜—⌝ for King Ramses IX, and may he grant to me life, health, a long term of life, [23]an old age of favor before Pharaoh, my lord. The High Priest of Amon-Re, king of gods, Amen-[24]hotep, son of the High Priest of Amon, Ramses-nakht, made (it)."

**490.** Another building inscription,[a] which almost certainly belongs to our High Priest, records works in the mortuary temples of the Ramessids, especially those of Ramses III and Ramses VI. Fragmentary as the inscription is, it shows that the High Priest's title, "*chief of all the works of the king*," gave him full charge of the building connected with the old temples.

**491.** [1]——— his way, doing excellent things in the house [⌜of Amon⌝] his [⌜father⌝] [2]——— myriads of — after old age ⌜———⌝ ——— [3]——— Amon-Re, king of gods — of "The-House-of-Millions-of-Years-of-King-Ramses VI" [4]——— ["The-House-of Millions-of-Years]-of-King-Usermare-Meriamon (Ramses III)-in-the-House-of-Amon" — — — — — repeating [5]——— ["The-House-of-Millions-of-Years-of-King] — -in-the-House-of-Amon-on-the-West-of-Thebes." His majesty repeated — — — — — [6]——— the [⌜place⌝] of rest which my father made on the west of Thebes in — — — — of Pharaoh [7]——— within of fine gold, genuine lapis lazuli and malachite — — — — marvels [8]——— great and august amulets which I made for Amon-Re, king of gods, the [9]——— likewise, in the name of Amon-Re, king of gods, correct ⌜— —⌝ [10]——— great ⌜works⌝ which I made, established[b] in — forever [11]——— ⌜I⌝ am he who gives ⌜oil⌝, incense, honey, — garlands [12]——— giving ⌜—⌝ to his ⌜every temple storehouse⌝ — — — — [13]——— ⌜— — —⌝ I ⌜finish⌝ it, praise [⌜to⌝] Re — — — — — [14]———. It is for the gold-house of Amon-Re, king of gods, in order to give — — — — — [15]——— which they made. The high priests of Amon-[Re, king of

[a]Found by Mariette in the chapel of the high priests, east of the sacred lake at Karnak (*g* on his plan, *Karnak*, Pl. 2); published by Mariette, *Karnak*, Pl. 39; corrections by Maspero, *Momies royales*, 668.

[b]*Smnḫ* is probable from the photograph.

gods] have not [⌜done the like⌝] — — — [16]——— ⌜which I have⌝ done during five years that Amon-Re, king of gods, my lord, might give to me, life, health, long existence, and a good old age [17][⌜as reward for⌝] the many benefactions and ⌜—⌝ fatigues which I have made for him in his house [18]——— it. He spends eight months of days therein, while I ⌜carry⌝ it ⌜around⌝, bearing him excellently —. I [19]——— [⌜Thou art my⌝] lord, I am thy servant, while I endure fatigues for thee — — — [20]——— Amon-Re, king of gods, hear my voice ⌜draw near⌝, let him not turn back — ⌜—⌝ [21]——— the transgressor,[a] I will report to Pharaoh, my lord, [⌜who⌝] will give [22]——— ["The-House-of]-King —[b]-in-the-House-of-Amon," "The-House-of-Usermare-Meriamon (Ramses III)-in-the-House-of-Amon-on-the-West-of-Thebes," — — the place [23]——— the high priests of Amon who shall come after me. Do not do this [c][24]——— transgressing against it, the transgressor who shall come, he shall not hinder [25]——— many generations in his house ⌜———⌝ — — — [26]—[30]. . . . . . . . . [31]——— of the gods of Ramses (II)-Meriamon [in] Memphis, king's-scribe, steward — ⌜—⌝ — —.

### II. RECORDS OF REWARDS[d]

**492.** As a reward for his pious work of rebuilding in the Karnak temple, Amenhotep was summoned by the king to the temple court, where, at the hands of the nobles and the chief treasurer, by the personal orders of the king, he was decorated with gold collars in the conventional manner. Splendid vessels of gold and silver, costly unguents, food and drink were also given him. In the king's address of praise

---

[a]Or: "*he* (*him*) *who transgresses against me.*"

[b]The vertical cartouche shows an *n* at the bottom.

[c]Or: "*who shall come after me in doing these things*" (the duties of the office).

[d]Karnak temple, wall scene by Pylon VIII, on east side of wall, connecting east ends of Pylons VII and VIII; published by Dümichen, *Historische Inschriften*, II, Pl. 42; the inscriptions alone; Rougé, *Inscriptions hiéroglyphiques*, 200, 201; Brugsch, *Thesaurus*, 1318, 1319. None of the publications shows the lower portions, only recently excavated. For these I had a photograph by Borchardt (Berlin, No. 5461), which was on too small a scale to insure certain readings, but enabled me to trace the drift of the newly uncovered portion.

to the first prophet, certain dues formerly paid to the palace are now to be paid to the High Priest. Unfortunately this, the most important portion of the document, is so obscurely worded that it is difficult to discern its exact purport. But it probably refers to the portion of the royal impost which, when collected by the king's officers and paid into his treasury, had then formerly been paid to Amon. Such impost is now placed directly in the hands of the High Priest, who can collect it from the people into the temple treasury, without its passing through the royal treasury. This enactment was either twice recorded, or it was repeated and made more sweeping in its scope; for Amenhotep has twice represented the scene of his royal rewards on the temple walls, each time accompanied by this enactment of the king, though in varying language.[a] In both scenes, contrary to the immemorial custom that the representations of the king should show him of heroic stature, towering far above his court and officers; the High Priest is here represented with the same heroic figure as the king. The high priests are gradually rising to equal the power and state of the Pharaoh. In keeping with this is the special mention by Amenhotep, in both scenes, of the fact that he inherited his office from his father, Ramsesnakht.

*Scene*

493. King Ramses IX[b] stands, scepter in hand, addressing two officials, who are supposed to be hanging golden collars upon the neck of the High Priest of Amon, Amenhotep.

---

[a]I have not given the duplicate separate treatment, but the variants from it have been inserted in the notes indicated by "variant." The inscriptions are published by Brugsch, *Thesaurus*, 1319 f. For the lower portions, not accessible in Brugsch's day, I had a photograph (Berlin, No. 5462), which was too small to insure certain readings everywhere.

[b]His throne-name, *Nfr-k* ᶜ *R* ᶜ *-Stp-n-R* ᶜ, is engraved over his head.

The latter is represented, however, with the same heroic stature as the king,[a] and is, therefore, so tall that the two officials are able to reach but a short way above his waist. Before the king are six stands, bearing sacks of gold, metal vessels, collars, etc. The inscriptions are these:

*Before the King*

**494.** [1]The king himself, he said to the princes and companions who were at his side: [b]"Give many favors and numerous rewards of fine gold, silver, [2]and myriads of all good things, to the High Priest of Amon-Re, king of gods, Amenhotep, triumphant, because of the many excellent monuments which he has made in the house of Amon-Re, king of gods, in (*ḥr*) the great name of the Good God."[c]

*By the High Priest*

**495.** Hereditary prince,[d] count, High Priest of Amon-Re, king of gods, Amenhotep, triumphant, is in the place of his father, the High Priest of Amon-Re, king of gods, in Karnak, Ramsesnakht, triumphant.

*Over the High Priest*

[1]Year 10, third month of the first season (third month), nineteenth day, in the house of Amon-Re, king of gods. The High Priest of Amon, king of gods, Amenhotep, triumphant, was conducted to[e] the great forecourt of [2]Amon, called: "One-Tells-His-Praise,"[f] in order to praise him with goodly and choice speech.[g] The nobles who came forth to praise him were:[h]

The treasurer of Pharaoh, [3]the king's-butler, Amenhotep, triumphant.

---

[a]Dümichen wrongly represents him as smaller than the king.

[b]Variant inserts: "*May Amon-Re, king of gods, favor thee.*"

[c]The concluding words were not read by Brugsch in the first relief, but Dümichen has as above. The variant confirms it, as the photograph shows "*his majesty.*"

[d]The second relief inserts: "*favorite of his lord.*"

[e]*Ḥr;* variant, *r.* [f]*Ḥrtw ḥsw·t-f;* Brugsch's *ḫrtw-f* is incorrect.

[g]Variant connects the preceding and the following, and had a different list of persons, thus: "——— *goodly and choice* [*speech*], *by the scribe, Khonsu* ———."

[h]These are the same officials whom we find in Papyrus Abbott (§ 511).

The king's-butler, Nesuamon.

The scribe of Pharaoh, the king's-butler, Neferkere-em-Per-Amon, [4]the herald of Pharaoh.

**496.** The things said to him as favor and praise on this day, in the great court of [5]Amon-Re, king of gods, saying:

"May Montu favor thee! May the ka of Amon-Re, king of gods, Pere-Harakhte, [6]Ptah, the great, "South-of-His-Wall," lord of "Life-of-the-Two-Lands," Thoth, lord of divine words, the gods of the heaven, and the gods of the earth favor thee! [7]May the ka of Ramses IX favor thee, the great ruler of Egypt, the beloved child [8]of all the gods,[a] because of the ⌈completion⌉ of every work!"

**497.** [b]"The harvests, the exactions of the impost [9]of the people of the house of Amon-Re, king of gods, shall be under thy charge, and thine shall be the tribute in full according to their sums.[c] Thou shalt give[d] [10]their —, causing that they should form ⌈part⌉[e] of the court of the treasuries, storehouses, and granaries of the house [11]of Amon-Re, king of gods; thus from the tribute of the heads and hands ⌈shall be⌉ the sustenance of Amon-Re, king of gods, [12]which thou didst (⌈formerly⌉) cause to be delivered to[f] Pharaoh, thy lord, the deed of a good servant, profitable [13]to Pharaoh, his lord; he being mighty to do benefactions for Amon-Re, king of gods, [14]the great god; and to do benefactions

---

[a]From here on, variant was evidently quite different. It has: "——— *the beloved child of* [*all*] *the* [*gods*] ——— *gold, the vessels* ——— *gold, the* ——— *the deed of a* [*good*] *servant* ———" cf. l. 12 below); while in the context of l. 12 (below) were the words: "——— *thy completion* ———." The praise in l. 8 has, in the variant, been partially transferred to l. 12; and that in l. 12 has, in the variant, been partially transferred to l. 8.

[b]Variant, "*The harvests and exactions of the house of Amon* ———."

[c]Or: "*heaps.*"

[d]The variant of this passage was not uncovered in Brugsch's day; the photograph is very indistinct, but it will be seen that the variant shows important divergencies here; and has transferred this passage to the end. It has: "——— *He fills the ⌈breweries⌉ with all his things, ⌈he being the lord of⌉ heaps of things, together with the gifts* — — — *⌈which⌉ Pharaoh, thy lord, makes in the house of the ⌈great⌉ god* — —. *Thus from the tribute of* [*the heads and hands*] *⌈shall be⌉ the sustenance, which thou didst (⌈formerly) cause⌉ to be delivered into the halls of the king's-house. The many, mighty deeds, the many, many benefactions, which thou doest in the house of the great god* ⌈— — — —⌉."

[e]The uncertain word represents two in the original, viz., "*the side;*" their connection here is quite obscure.

[f]Variant, "——— *Pharaoh, for his treasuries and storehouses* ———."

for Pharaoh, his lord — [15]— which thou doest. Now, behold, command has been given to the overseer of the White House, the butler of Pharaoh,[a] [16]and all [⌈the princes⌉],[b] to give to thee praise, to anoint thee with sweet oil of gums, and to give [⌈to thee⌉] the ⌈vessels⌉ of gold and silver, [⌈the reward of⌉] the servant of Pharaoh, thy lord, given to him as a favor [⌈of the king's-presence⌉] — the — of Amon on this day ———.

*Below the Scene*[c]

**498.** Given as a favor of the king's-presence to the great favorite of the Lord of the Two Lands, the High Priest of Amon, king of gods, Amenhotep, triumphant:

| | |
|---|---|
| Fine gold in ——— | — |
| ——— | — |
| Total, fine gold | — |
| Sweet beer ⌈—⌉ — ⌈jars⌉ | 40 |
| Sweet oil of gums: hin | 2 |

That which was said to him: one (viz., the king) spake to cause the Pharaoh's scribe of rolls to come forth. One spake [⌈to⌉] the overseers of the granaries of Pharaoh ——— in — of this — by Amenhotep, triumphant, — — —.

## THE RECORDS OF THE ROYAL TOMB-ROBBERIES

**499.** The papyrus records which inform us of the robberies among the royal tombs of this period, while they are strictly legal documents, afford so many valuable glimpses into the historical conditions under the later Ramessids that

[a]Here follow two lines below the uplifted arm of the High Priest, of which Brugsch saw only the first three words, now appearing at the end of his copy, in the wrong place.

[b]The legs of the figure for "*prince*" (*sr*) are probable in the photograph. "*Thy lord*" (following "*Pharaoh*") is impossible, owing to lack of determinative after it (*nb*), as regularly in this inscription.

[c]This inscription of three lines is unpublished. It is badly mutilated, and from the small-scale photograph little can be made of it. The variant also shows three similar lines below the scene, which contain a list of the gifts; but it is badly mutilated and not readable in the photograph. It begins quite differently from the above list.

they cannot be omitted from this historical series. The riches lying in the royal tombs, in the form of splendid regalia adorning the dead, rich coffins, and elaborate furniture, which had been accumulating for five hundred years, furnished an irresistible motive for the violation of such tombs. How far the corrupt officials, by indirect connivance, may have been involved in such robberies we cannot now determine. In our first document there are indications that all was not as it should have been among the officials of the government. Their apparent helplessness, and total inability properly to protect the necropolis, however interpreted, are clear evidence of the decadence in government now in progress. A coffin in the British Museum, doubtless of this age, furnishes significant evidence of the conditions in the Theban necropolis, as shown by the following remark,[a] recorded upon it by a scribe:

Year 3, fourth month of the first season, day 15; day of renewing the burial of Osiris, Tesitnakht (*T*ʾ-*s*ʾ·*t-nḫt*); after it had been found, the children of the cemetery having taken its coffins and violated the name thereof. They were restored again.

**500.** While Thebes as a whole was under the vizier as its governor, the main city, on the east side, was under a mayor; at this time a noble, named Peser. The west side was, likewise, under the control of a second mayor, who was also responsible for the necropolis. Under Ramses IX he was a certain Pewero. Peser, mayor of the east side, had in some way gained information of robberies among the royal tombs and he promptly handed in his information to the vizier, as

[a]British Museum coffin, No. 15659; Budge, *Catalogue of the Egyptian Collection in the Fitzwilliam Museum,* Cambridge, 1893, 18. An inspection of a file of court documents recording prosecution of tomb-robbers took place in year 6, of an unknown king, and the scribe's report on the inspection of the two jars containing the file is preserved in a papyrus in Vienna (Brugsch, *Zeitschrift für ägyptische Sprache,* 1876, Taf. 1; Erman, *Aegypten,* 167).

was his duty. The duty was probably not an unwelcome one, for he seems to have had no love for his rival, Pewero, whose administration of the necropolis he was thus able to compromise.

501. Pursuant to this information, the vizier sent a commission to inspect the cemetery, on the eighteenth of Hathor, in the sixteenth year of Ramses IX. Their report covered ten royal tombs, four tombs of the singing-women of the Amon-temples, and a number of tombs of the nobles and people, the exact number of which is not stated. The last were all found to have been plundered; two of the four tombs of the singing-women were in the same condition; but of the royal tombs, only one, that of Sebekemsaf, had been robbed, although two had been unsuccessfully mined into by the robbers. The part of the royal cemetery visited was the district of Drah abu-'n-Neggah, on the northern margin of the western plain of Thebes, and the royal tombs inspected were those of the Eleventh, Thirteenth, Seventeenth, and early Eighteenth Dynasties. The report on them, besides being historically valuable, affords a most interesting glimpse into the royal cemetery at this time. Perhaps the most remarkable reference in it is the description of the stela of Intef I's pyramid, bearing in relief the figure of the king, with his hound Behka between his feet (§ 514, ll. 9–11). This very stela was found by Mariette still bearing the figure of the king, and the hound with the name Behka inscribed beside it (I, 421 ff.), as described in the report of three thousand years ago.

502. Luckily for Pewero, he was able to locate the thieves, in any case he handed in to the vizier a list of their names. The next day, the nineteenth of Hathor, the vizier, Khamwese, and the Pharaoh's secretary, Nesuamon, examined the eight men accused of robbing the tomb of Sebekemsaf.

They confessed, and their story of the robbery is one of the most remarkable documents surviving from ancient Egypt (§ 538). To make the matter certain, the vizier and the Pharaoh's secretary crossed the river with them and made them show where the tomb of Sebekemsaf was located (§ 517). A similar test applied to a coppersmith who had confessed to robbing the tomb of Queen Isis, wife of Ramses III, indicated that the man knew nothing of this queen's tomb, and had evidently confessed that he might be momentarily relieved of the torture. As a matter of fact, the tomb of Queen Isis had been robbed by eight thieves, who can hardly be any other than the eight robbers of Sebekemsaf's tomb, although this fact was not discovered until the next year (§§ 542, 543). Then followed an inspection of "*The Place of Beauty*," a portion of the cemetery where the families of the Pharaohs were buried; they were found to be uninjured. Regarding the royal tombs as the most important, the officials of the necropolis considered the fact that nine of the ten reported robbed were found uninjured, as a great victory for the administration of the necropolis. They therefore sent the whole body of the necropolis employees over to the east side as an embassy of triumph. Some of these rejoicing subordinates went to the house of the mayor of the east side, Peser, who had furnished the information against them to the vizier, and loudly exulted before his door. Meeting three of them in the streets in the evening, Peser was unable to control his anger and, in the presence of witnesses, quarreled with them, told them their inspection of the necropolis was a farce, and accused them vaguely in grave charges, of which he said he was about to send notice to the Pharaoh. This was irregular, as all such charges could legally be reported only to the vizier.

**503.** Hearing of his enemy's charges immediately, Pewero

was quick to see the opportunity of again humiliating Peser. He reported the whole affair in a long letter to the vizier, dated the next day, the twentieth of Hathor. The vizier called the case the following morning, the twenty-first of Hathor, and, incensed at Peser's reflections upon an inspection which had been sent out from his office and partially conducted by him, the vizier quickly brought the proceedings to a close by summoning the three coppersmiths whom Peser had accused of robbing the ten royal tombs, and placed them at the disposition of the court; at the same time introducing the evidence of his own personal knowledge, gained on his visit to the necropolis. The unhappy Peser, who was himself a judge, and sitting on the bench with his colleagues in this case, was obliged to see the coppersmiths acquitted in their examination, which now followed. Whether he suffered any penalty for his indiscretion is not evident, but his allegations regarding the cemetery were all declared untrue, while the vague charges which he had threatened to make to the Pharaoh were ignored, as they had no legal status at all, unless presented in writing before the vizier.

504. It is clear that the state of affairs in the cemetery was sufficiently bad to justify charges against the officials of the necropolis, and although all the tombs indicated by Peser had not been robbed, the investigation had overlooked the robbery of at least one tomb, that of Queen Isis, so that the action of the vizier in completely exonerating Pewero was not justifiable, and arouses the suspicion that there was some reason for such action not apparent on the surface. It certainly was not calculated to preserve the royal burials from similar depredations in the future.

505. The results were, therefore, what might have been anticipated. Three years later, in the nineteenth year of

Ramses IX, just after he had associated with himself his son Ramses X as coregent, Pewero, the mayor of the West, who had learned wisdom, handed in to the vizier a list of sixteen people to be tried for robbery in the necropolis; while less than two months later he reported twenty-nine more, whom we find on the docket. Twenty days later six[a] of these men were convicted of robbing the tombs of Seti I and Ramses II. This robbery, therefore, carries us for the first time[b] from the western plain of Thebes to the Valley of the King's Tombs behind the western cliffs. The robberies were, therefore, spreading from the modest pyramids of the kings just before and after the Twelfth Dynasty in the plain, to the magnificent and, of course, more richly equipped cliff-tombs of the great emperors in the valley behind. Five more men were tried two days later and found innocent.

**506.** Eight months now elapsed without apparent disturbance among the royal tombs; but the usual contingent of tomb-robbers then appears on the court docket, this time numbering twenty-two persons (two women), who had robbed "*the tomb of Pharaoh.*" Which royal tomb is thus designated we do not know, but a thief, whose confession follows the above list of names, states that he robbed the tomb of a Queen Nesimut, and also that of Queen Bekurel, wife of Seti I. Twenty-seven days later a long list of robbers, the wives of eleven of whom were also implicated, and imprisoned, fills the docket, and a fragmentary record of uncertain date refers to the robbery of the tomb of Amenhotep III.

**507.** It is evident from these facts that not only the mortuary furniture, but also the very bodies of the greatest kings of Egypt were threatened with destruction. The robberies

[a]Mayer Papyri (§§ 544 ff.), from which all the following is taken.

[b]But see III, §§ 32A–32C.

had demonstrably now been going on for more than five years at least, and probably much longer. When Pharaohs like Ramses II and Merneptah were guilty of wholesale appropriation of the mortuary equipment of their great ancestors, the officials were naturally not above conniving at similar robberies for their own profit. The occasional prosecution and conviction of the "small fry" were, therefore, of no avail. Such were the conditions under the last three Ramessids in the royal cemetery at Thebes. The pious, and evidently sincere, efforts put forth on behalf of the royal bodies at the close of the Twentieth and the beginning of the Twenty-first Dynasties (§§ 595 ff., 636 ff.) saved them from destruction only after they had been bereft of their splendid furniture and stripped of their rich regalia, by the thieves whose prosecution is narrated in the following documents. So persistent and thorough was their work of plunder that of all the Pharaohs buried at Thebes, only one, Amenhotep II, has been found still in his sarcophagus in his own tomb. But his body had, in ancient times, already been stripped of all valuables. The tomb was securely closed with an iron grating and locked door by the modern government of Egypt, and the body of the great king left undisturbed in its ancient resting-place, where it had slept 3,400 years.

508. Hearing rumors of fabulous wealth on the person of their great ancestor, the tomb-robbers of modern Thebes, doubtless with the connivance of the necropolis guard, forced the tomb door, entered, and subjected the body of Amenhotep II, after an interval of three thousand years, to a second rifling, which was to all appearances entirely fruitless. Perhaps we shall be inclined to judge more charitably the government of Ramses IX and his successors, when it is added that Mr. Howard Carter, the efficient inspector of the government, after having identified and arrested the

guilty parties by tireless zeal in their pursuit, was unable to secure their conviction and punishment at the hands of the modern government. Mr. Carter's official report[a] on the whole matter is a striking modern commentary on the ancient conditions exposed in the following documents, and forms the last chapter in the long and dramatic history of the royal tombs at Thebes.

### I. PAPYRUS ABBOTT[b]

509. This document is really the vizier's abstract, taken from his files, recording the case between the two mayors, Peser and Pewero, as narrated above (§§ 499–504). The condition of the royal necropolis is, therefore, only incidental to the demonstration of the truth or falsity of Peser's charges against the necropolis administration. The whole case is concluded with the defeat of Peser, recorded at the end. The conditions in the necropolis, revealed in the document, led the scribe to consult it again after it had been lying for three years in the vizier's files, and on this occasion he recorded upon the back of the roll a list of tomb-robbers then awaiting trial, which had been handed in by Pewero, the mayor of the West. Nearly two months later he took down this same roll, to record a similar list beside the first (§ 535).

*Pl. 1. Date*

510. [1][Year 16,[c] third month of the first season, day 18], under the majesty of the King of Upper and Lower Egypt, the Lord of the

[a]*Annales.*

[b]A papyrus found at Thebes (?), and acquired by the British Museum in 1857 by purchase from Dr. Abbott, of Cairo. The roll is 17 inches high, and contains on the recto 7 columns from 10 to 14 inches wide. Two columns on the verso (8 and 9), containing only hastily written lists of thieves, are 6 to 7 inches wide. It is published in facsimile by the British Museum authorities in *Select Papyri* (London, 1860), Part II, Pls. I-VIII.

[c]All spaced words are rubrics.

Two Lands: Neferkere-Setepnere, L. P. H., Son of Re, Lord of Diadems: [2][Ramses (IX)-]Meriamon, L. P. H., beloved of [Amon]-Re, king of gods, and of Harakhte; given life forever and ever.

*First Commission of Inspection*

**511.** [3][There were sent] the inspectors of the great and august necropolis, the scribe of the vizier and the scribe of the overseer of the White House of Pharaoh, L. P. H., [4][in order to inspect the] sepulchers of former kings, the tombs and resting-places of the nobles, [5][located on] the west of the city; by: (1) the governor of the city and vizier, Khamwese; (2) the king's-butler, Nesuamon ([*Ns-sw-*] *Ymn*), the scribe of [6][Pharaoh]; (3) the major-domo of the house of the Divine Votress, L. P. H., of Amon-Re, king of gods, king's-butler, Neferkere-em-Per-Amon,[a] the herald of Pharaoh, L. P. H., [7][because of the] thieves [on] the west of the city, concerning whom the mayor, the chief of police of the great and august necropolis [8][of] Pharaoh [on] the west of Thebes, Pewero (*P*ͻ *-wr-*ͻ ͨ), had reported to the vizier, the nobles and butlers of Pharaoh, L. P. H.

*List of Members of the Commission*

**512.** [9][People] sent on this day:

The mayor and chief of police of the necropolis, Pewero;

[10a][Chief of polic]e of this house, Beknurel (*Bk-n-Wr-n-r*ͻ).

[11a]——— of the [necropolis].[b]

[12a]——— of this house.

[13a]——— of this house.

[14a]——— -amon.

[10b]Chief of police of this house, Menthirkhepeshef (*Mntw-*[*ḥr*]*-ḫpš-f*).

[11b]The scribe of the vizier, Penebik (*P*ͻ *-* ͨ *-n-bywk*).[c]

[12b]Chief scribe of the magazine of the overseer of the White House, Paynofer (*P*ͻ *y-nfr*).

[13b]Prophet of the House of (King) Amenhotep, L. P. H., Peͻenkhew (*P*ͻ *-* ͨ *n-ḫ* ͨ *w*).

---

[a]This official and Nesuamon (No. 2 above) also figure in the relief scene showing the reward of the High Priest Amenhotep (§ 495).

[b]Determinative preserved. N. B.—Letters a and b with line numbers are not to be confused with letters of footnotes.

[c]This man's name means "*the claw of the hawk.*"

[14b]Prophet of the wine-cellar of the house of Amon, Uramon (*Wr-Ymn*).

[15]The police of the cemetery, who were with them.

*Pl. 2. List of Tombs Inspected*

**513.** [1]The pyramids, sepulchers, and tombs, investigated on this day, by the inspectors:

*Tomb of Amenhotep I*

[2]The eternal horizon of King Zeserkere, L. P. H., son of Re, Amenhotep (I), L. P. H., which is 120 cubits [3]deep[a] (measured) from its superstructure, which is called: "The-High-⌜Ascent⌝," north of the "House[b]-of-Amenhotep,-L.-P.-H.,-of-[4]the-Garden," concerning which the mayor of the city, Peser (*P ͗-sr*), had reported to the governor of the city and vizier, Khamwese; [5]the king's-butler, Nesuamon, the scribe of Pharaoh, major-domo of the house of the Divine Votress, L. P. H., of Amon-Re, king of gods; [6]the king's-butler, Neferkere-em-Per-Amon, the herald of Pharaoh, L. P. H., and the great nobles, saying: "The thieves have broken into it." Inspected on this day; it was found uninjured by the inspectors.

*Pyramid of King Intef I*

**514.** [8]The pyramid of the king, the son of Re, Intefo (*Yn-[tf-]* ͑ ͗), L. P. H., which is on the north of the "House-of-Amenhotep,-L.-P.-H.,-of-the-Court (*wb* ͗)," [9]upon which the pyramid is destroyed, before which

[a]This can only be the depth of the passage into the mountain, measured from the building at its front. This passage has never been found, but its entrance was certainly located on the plain, by the tombs of the Eleventh and Thirteenth Dynasties here investigated. A temple of Amenhotep I was found here by Spiegelberg (*Zwei Beiträge*, 1–5). The tomb of Amenhotep I was the last to be located on the front of the western cliffs; his successor, Thutmose I, excavated his tomb in the valley behind, thus for the first time separating sepulcher and chapel. Hatshepsut's terraced temple, piercing into the cliff, brought her temple and her tomb behind it again close together; but those of following kings were again widely separated.

[b]This is not the mortuary temple of Amenhotep I, which was called "*House-of-Zeserkere (Amenhotep I)-on-the-West-of-Thebes*" (Lepsius, *Denkmäler*, Text, III, 238). With "*Amenhotep-of-the-Garden*" compare "*Amenhotep,-the-Image-upon-*⌜—⌝" (*mt*) (*ibid.*, 282), and "*Amenhotep-of-the-Court,*" in II, 8, of our document. These are doubtless all different Amenhoteps. See Sethe (*Götting'sche Gelehrte Anzeigen*) and Spiegelberg (*Zwei Beiträge*, 3).

its stela (still) stands; the [10]figure of the king stands[a] upon this stela, his hound being between his feet, [11]named[b] Behka (*Bḥ-ḥw-k*ʾ). It was inspected on this day; it was found uninjured.

*Pyramid of King Nubkheprure-Intef*[c]

**515.** [12]The pyramid of King Nubkheperre (*Nb-ḫpr-R*ᶜ), L. P. H., Son of Re, Intef, L. P. H., it was found in course of [13]being tunneled into by the thieves; they had tunneled 2½ cubits into its ⌜masonry⌝ (*ḏrw*), 1 cubit (distant) [14]from the outer chamber of the tomb of the chief of the oblation-bearers of the House of Amon, Yuroi (*Yw-r*ʾ*-y*), which is in ruins. It was uninjured; the thieves had not been able to enter it.

*Pyramid of King Sekhemre-Intef*

**516.** [16]The pyramid of King Sekhemre-Upmat (*Sḫm-R*ᶜ*-Wp-m*ʾᶜ*·t*), L. P. H.; Son of Re, Intefo (*Yntw·f-*ᶜʾ), L. P. H. It was found [17]in course of being tunneled into by the thieves, at the place where its stela of its pyramid was set up. [18]Inspected on this day; it was found uninjured; the thieves had been unable to enter it.

*Pl. 3. Pyramid of King Sebekemsaf*

**517.** [1]The pyramid of King Sekhemre-Shedtowe (*Sḫm-R*ᶜ*-Šd-t*ʾ*wy*), L. P. H., Son of Re, Sebekemsaf (*Sbk-m-s*ʾ*·f*), [2]It was found, that the thieves had broken into it by mining work through the base[d] of its pyramid, from the outer chamber of the tomb of the overseer of the granary of King Menkheperre (Thutmose III), L. P. H., Nebamon. The burial-place of the king was found void of its lord, L. P. H., as well as the burial-place of the great king's-wife, [5]Nubkhas (*Nb-ḫ*ᶜ*s*), L. P. H., his royal wife; the thieves having laid their hand upon them. The vizier, [6]the nobles, and the inspectors made an examination of it, and the manner in which the thieves had laid their hands [7]upon this king and his royal wife, was ascertained.

---

[a]Engraved in relief upon the stela, which still survives (I, 421 ff.), showing not only this dog with name as above, but also five others, which the scribe has not taken time to note.

[b]The name of the dog; the disconnected order of words is also in the original.

[c]Of the Thirteenth Dynasty; see I, 773 ff.

[d]*Nfrw;* see Petrie, *Medum*, Pl. VIII.

*Pyramid of King Sekenenre-Tao*

**518.** [8]The pyramid of King Sekenenre (*Śḳn(y)˙n-Rᶜ*), L. P. H., Son of Re, Tao (*T*ᵓ-ᶜᵓ), L. P. H. Inspected on this day [9]by the inspectors; it was found uninjured.

*Pyramid of King Sekenenre-Taoo*

[10]The pyramid of King Sekenenre, L. P. H., Son of Re, Taoo (*T*ᵓ-ᶜᵓ-ᶜᵓ), L. P. H., the second King Tao, L. P. H., II. [11]Inspected on this day by the inspectors; it was found uninjured.

*Pyramid of King Kemose*

**519.** [12]The pyramid of King Uzkheperre (*Wᵓḏ-ḫpr-Rᶜ*), L. P. H., Son of Re, Kemose (*Kᵓ-ms*), L. P. H. Inspected on this day; it was uninjured.

*Pyramid of King Ahmose-Sepir*

[13]The pyramid of King Ahmose-Sepir (*Yᶜḥ-ms-sᵓ-pᵓ-yr*), L. P. H. Inspected; found uninjured.

*Pyramid of Mentuhotep II*

**520.** [14]The pyramid of King Nibhepetre (*Nb-ḥp˙t-*[a]*Rᶜ*), L. P. H., Son of Re, Mentuhotep (II), L. P. H., which is in Zeseret (*Ḏsr-⌈t⌉*); it was uninjured.[b]

*Summary*

[15]Total of pyramids of the former kings, inspected on this day by the inspectors:

| | |
|---|---|
| Found uninjured | 9 pyramids |
| Found broken into | 1 |
| Total | 10 |

[a]This is now known to be the reading of this word, formerly read *ḫrw* (see Naville and Hall, and *Proceedings of the Society of Biblical Archæology*, 1905).

[b]On a Mentuhotep tomb at Thebes, see Carter, *Annales*, II, 201 ff. The tomb designated in our document was, of course, connected with the mortuary temple of Mentuhotep III, found by Naville and Hall at Der el-Bahri (*Egypt Exploration Fund Archæological Report*, 1903–4, 1 ff.); and Hall, *Proceedings of the Society of Biblical Archæology*, XXVII, 173–83. Its name was *yᶜḫw-yś˙t* (or *yś˙wt*). Zeseret was the name of the immediate locality in the Theban cemetery.

*Tombs of Queens and Noble Families*

**521.** [17]The tombs of the singing-women of the house of the Divine Votress, L. P. H., of Amon-Re, king of gods:

| | |
|---|---|
| Found uninjured | 2 |
| Found broken into by the thieves | 2 |
| Total | 4 |

*Pl. 4*

[1]These are the tombs and sepulchers in which the nobles, the ⌜—⌝, the Theban women, and the people of the land rest, [2]on the west of the city; it was found that the thieves had broken into them all, that they had pulled out their occupants [3]from their coverings and coffins, they (the occupants) being thrown upon the ground; and that they had stolen their articles of house-furniture, which [4]had been given them, together with the gold, the silver, and the ornaments which were in their coverings.[a]

*Report of the Commission*

**522.** [5]The mayor and chief of police of the great and august necropolis, Pewero, together with the chiefs of police, and [6]the inspectors of the necropolis, the scribe of the vizier, and the scribe of the overseer of the White House, who were with them, made a report upon them (the tombs) to:

[7]The governor of the city and vizier, Khamwese;

The king's-butler, Nesuamon;

The scribe of Pharaoh, L. P. H., the major-domo of the house of the Divine Votress, L. P. H., of [8]Amon-Re, king of gods, king's-butler, Neferkere-em-Per-Amon, the herald of Pharaoh, L. P. H.;

And the great nobles. [9]The mayor of the West, chief of police of the necropolis, Pewero, handed in the names of the thieves in writing [10]before the vizier, the nobles and butlers. They were seized and imprisoned; they were examined, and confessed the facts.

*Vizier's Inspection*

**523.** [11]Year 16, third month of the first season, day 19; day on which there went to inspect the great seats[b] of the king's-children,

[a]Evidently the scribe has forgotten the statement of the number, as given at the close of the preceding paragraph.

[b]Tombs.

the king's-wives, [12]and the king's-mothers, which are in "The-Place-of-Beauty:"[a]

The governor of the city and vizier, Khamwese; and the king's-butler, Nesuamon, the scribe of Pharaoh, L. P. H., [13]after the coppersmith,[b] Pekharu,[c] of the west of the city, son of Kharu, his mother, being Mitshere[d] (*My˙t-šry*), a serf of [14]"The-House-of-Usermare-Meriamon (Ramses III),-L.-P.-H.,-in-the-House-of-Amon," under charge of the High Priest of Amon-Re, king of gods, Amenhotep, (being) the man[e] who was found there [15]and arrested, while he was with the three people of the (said) temple, beside the tombs, whom the vizier, Nibmare-nakht, had [16]examined[f] in the year 14, had told, saying: "I was in the tomb of the king's-wife, Isis,[g] L. P. H., of King Usermare-Meriamon (Ramses III), L. P. H.; I carried off a few [17]things from it; I took possession of them."

*Examination of the Coppersmith*

**524.** Then the vizier and the butler had the coppersmith taken

*Pl. 5*

before them to [1]the tomb, while he was blindfolded as a man ⌜— —⌝. He was permitted to see[h] (again), when he had reached them.[i] The officials[j] [2]said to him: "Go before us to the tomb, from which you said: 'I carried away the things.'" The coppersmith went before the nobles[3] to one of the ⌜—⌝ tombs of the king's-children of King Usermare-Setepnere (Ramses II), L. P. H., the Great God, in which no one was buried, which was left open, [4]and (to) the hut of the workman of

[a]The name of a part of the necropolis.

[b]"*The coppersmith*" is the subject of the verb "*had told*" (l. 16). All that follows "*the coppersmith*" is merely the usual identification of such a serf, as found in the invoices of temple property.

[c]Lit., "*The Syrian;*" a very common name from the Eighteenth Dynasty on.

[d]Lit., "*Little Cat.*"

[e]Apposition with "*the coppersmith.*"

[f]He was therefore an old criminal, who had been tried ("*examined*") two years before, under a different vizier, the predecessor of Khamwese.

[g]It is highly probable that this tomb, although unknown to the coppersmith, had been robbed by the eight thieves of Sebekemsaf's tomb (see §§ 538, 539).

[h]Lit., "*his eye was given to him.*"

[i]The tombs.

[j]The vizier and the butler.

the necropolis, Amenemyenet (*Ymn-m-yn·t*), son of Huy, which was in this place, saying: "Behold, the tombs in which I was." The nobles examined the coppersmith with a ⌜severe⌝[a] examination in the great valley, (but) he was not [6]found to know any place there, except the two places upon which he had laid his hand. He took an oath[b] of the king, L. P. H., that he should be mutilated (by cutting off) his nose [7]and his ears and placed upon the rack (if he lied), saying: "I know not any place here among these tombs, except this tomb which is open, [8]together with the hut upon which I have laid your hands."

*Conclusion of Inspection*

**525.** The officials examined the tombs of the great seats which are in "The-Place-of-Beauty," in which the king's-children, king's-wives, king's-mothers, the goodly fathers and mothers of Pharaoh, L. P. H., rest. They were found uninjured. The great officials caused the inspectors, the administrators,[c] the workmen of the necropolis, the chiefs [11]of police, the police, and all the serf-laborers of the necropolis of the west of the city to go around as a great deputation[d] to the city.

*The Indiscretion of the Mayor of the City (East Side)*

**526.** [12]Year 16, third month of the first season, day 19; on this day, at the time of evening, beside the House of Ptah, lord of Thebes there came along the king's-butler, [13]Nesuamon, the scribe of Pharaoh, L. P. H.; and the mayor of the city, Peser; and they came upon the chief workman, Userkhepesh (*Wsr-ḫpš*); the scribe, Amennakht; [14]and the workman of the necropolis, Amenhotep. The mayor of the city spoke to the people of[e] the necropolis in the presence of the (said) butler of Pharaoh, [15]saying: "As for this deputation which ye have

[a]The bastinade, or some form of torture, is certainly meant; compare the examinations in Papyrus Mayer (§§ 544–557).

[b]Involving the name of the king, and hence the royal salutation.

[c]This is probably the same word (*ḥwtyw*) which occurs in the long inscription of Paynozem II (§ 671, l. 8), and the stela of Sheshonk (§ 676, l. 3), where it applies to dishonest necropolis officials.

[d]To celebrate the triumph of the mayor of the west side.

[e]This shows that the first designation "*of the necropolis*" (in l. 14) belongs to all three of the preceding names.

made this day, it is no deputation at all.[a] It is (only) your jubilation, which [16]ye have made?" So spake he to them. He took an oath of the king, L. P. H., in the presence of the (said) butler of Pharaoh, L. P. H., saying: "The scribe of the necropolis,[b] Horishere (*Ḥry-šry*), son of Amennakht, [17]and the scribe of the necropolis, Pebes, have told me five very serious accusations worthy of death against you. [18]Yea, I am writing concerning them to Pharaoh, L. P. H., my lord, L. P. H., that a man of Pharaoh, L. P. H., may be sent to take you all in charge." So spake he.

### *Pewero's Letter of Complaint*

**527.** [19]Year 16, third month of the first season, day 20. Copy of the letter which the mayor of the west of the city, the chief of police of the necropolis, Pewero, sent to the vizier, [20]concerning the words, which the mayor of the city, Peser, spoke to the people of the necropolis, in the presence of the butler of Pharaoh, L. P. H., and of the scribe of the overseer of the treasury, Paynozem.

**528.** [21]That which the mayor of the west of the city, Pewero, said, to wit:

[c]"The king's-butler, Nesuamon, the scribe of Pharaoh, L. P. H., happened by, when the mayor of the city, Peser, [22]was with him, while he (the mayor) stood quarreling with the people of the necropolis, beside the House of Ptah, lord of Thebes. The mayor of the city spoke

*Pl. 6*

to the people [1]of the necropolis, saying: 'Ye exult over me at the door of my house! Oh, indeed! Although I am the mayor who makes report[d] to [2]the ruler, L. P. H., and ye therefore exult over him. Ye were there; it[e] was inspected; ye found it uninjured! Broken into

---

[a]Here and on § 528, l. 8, see Gardiner, *Zeitschrift für ägyptische Sprache*, 41, 131.

[b]This necropolis is given a special designation (*n-ḥny-ḥny*), and is therefore distinguished from the ordinary necropolis to which the second scribe is attached.

[c]All the titles and conventional forms regularly introducing such a letter are here omitted and only the actual facts communicated are quoted by the recording scribe.

[d]Perhaps meaning that he only did his duty in reporting the robberies in the cemetery.

[e]The necropolis.

were (the tomb of) [3]Sekhemre-Shedtowe, L. P. H., Son of Re, Sebekemsaf, L. P. H., and (that of) Nubkhas, L. P. H., his royal wife; one great ruler, L. P. H., while he [4]makes ten reports. (I invoke) the ⸢severity⸣ of Amon-Re, king of gods, this great god, on behalf of his monuments, standing in his hall this day.'[a] [5]Then spake the workman, Userkhepesh, who is under the hand of the chief workman of the necropolis, Nakhtemhet, saying: 'But all the kings, together with their [6]king's-wives, king's-mothers, and king's-children, who rest in the necropolis, together with those who rest in "The-Place-of-Beauty," they are uninjured, [7]they are protected and defended forever.[b] It is the goodly designs of Pharaoh, L. P. H., their son, which protect them and examine them [8]⸢closely⸣.' The mayor of the city spake to him, saying: 'Are thy deeds as great as thy speech?' For this is indeed no little word which this [9]mayor of the city spake.

**529.** "This mayor of the city spake to him again, a second word, saying: 'The scribe of the necropolis,[c] Horishere, son of Amennakht, [10]came to the chief side[d] of the city, to my place of abode, and he told me three very serious accusations. [11]My scribe and the scribe of the two districts of the city put them in writing. Moreover, the scribe of the necropolis, Pebes, told me two other [12]matters; in all five. They were put in writing likewise. He that hath them cannot keep silence. Forbid, for they are great and capital crimes, [13]worthy of bringing to the block, and of executing every penalty because of them. Now, I shall write concerning them to Pharaoh, my lord, L. P. H., [14]that a man of Pharaoh, L. P. H., may be sent to take you all in charge.' So spake he to them, this mayor of the city. He made ten oaths of the king, L. P. H., saying: [15]'So will I do.'

**530.** "[e]I heard these words which the mayor of the city spoke to the people of the great and august necropolis of millions of years, of [16]Pharaoh, L. P. H., on the west of Thebes; and I report them to my lord, for it were a crime for one like me [17]to hear (such) words and conceal them. But I was not able to apprehend[f] the very serious words which

[a]The meaning of this last sentence is very uncertain. It may be that he calls upon Amon to protect the other monuments of Sebekemsaf, thus indicating the danger in which he thinks they are.

[b]The same words used of a cemetery in I, 768.

[c]Again defined as above.

[d]That is, the east side.

[e]"*I*" is Pewero, the writer of the letter.

[f]For myself.

the mayor of the city spoke; [18]the scribes of the necropolis[a] who stood among the people told me them, (but) my [19]feet were not present with them. I report them to my lord, that my lord may bring in one who apprehended[b] the words, which the mayor of the city spake, [20]and the scribes of the necropolis told me. 'I am writing of them to Pharaoh, L. P. H.,' said he. This is a crime [21]of these two scribes of the necropolis, that they should have applied to this mayor of the city, to report to him; for their fathers did not report to him, [22]but they reported to the vizier when he was in the South. When he was in the North, however, the necropolis-police of the suite of [23]his majesty, L. P. H., went North to the place where the vizier was, bearing their writings. ⸢I have⸣ made (this) deposition in the year 16, third month of the first season, day 20, [24]of the words which I have heard from the mayor of the city. I put them in writing before my lord, that those who apprehended them may be summoned for tomorrow."[c]

### *Pl. 7. Hearing of Peser's Accusations*

**531.** [1]Year 16, third month of the first season, day 21; on this day in the great court[d] of the city, beside the two stelæ of —— the forecourt of Amon in the gate (called): "Praise."

#### *Composition of the Court*

[2]People and nobles who sat in the great court of the city on this day:

1. [3]Governor of the city and vizier, Khamwese.
2. The High Priest of Amon-Re, king of gods, Amenhotep.
3. The prophet of Amon-Re, king of gods, ⸢scribe⸣ of "The-House-of-Millions-of-Years-[4]of-King-Neferkere-Setepnere,-L.-P.-H.," Nesuamon.
4. The king's-butler, Nesuamon, the scribe of Pharaoh, L. P. H.
5. The major-domo of the house of the Divine Votress, L. P. H., of Amon-Re, king of gods, [5]king's-butler, Neferkere-em-Per-Amon, the herald of Pharaoh, L. P. H.

---

[a] *Ḫr-n-ḫny.*

[b] Lit., "*one who reached* (*pḥ*) *the words.*"

[c] Conclusion of Pewero's letter to the vizier. The closing greetings, etc., are omitted. As will be seen by the following date, the case really came on the next day.

[d] Of justice (*ḳnb·t ꜥꜣ·t*).

6. The deputy of ⸢—⸣, Hori.
7. The standard-bearer of [6]the marines, Hori.
8. The mayor of the city, Peser.[a]

**532.** The governor of the city and vizier, Khamwese, had brought in the coppersmith, Pekharu, son of Kharu; [7]the coppersmith, Tharoy (*Ṯ*ˀ-*r*ˀ-*y*), son of Khamopet; and the coppersmith, Pekamen, son of Tharoy, of "The-House-of-Usermare-Meriamon (Ramses III),-L.-P.-H.," under charge of the High Priest of Amon.

**533.** [8]Said the vizier to the great nobles of the great court of the city: "This mayor of the city said a few words to the [9]inspectors and workmen of the necropolis, in the year 16, third month of the first season, day 19, in the presence of the king's-butler, Nesuamon, the scribe of Pharaoh, L. P. H., [10]delivering himself of slanders concerning the great seats,[b] which are in 'The-Place-of-Beauty.' Now, I, the vizier of the land, have been there, [11]with the king's-butler, Nesuamon, the scribe of Pharaoh, L. P. H. We inspected the tombs, where the mayor of the city said that the coppersmiths [12]of 'The-House-of-Usermare-Meriamon (Ramses III),-L.-P.-H.,-in-the-House-of-Amon,' had been. We found them uninjured; and all that he[c] said was found to be untrue. Now, behold, [13]the coppersmiths stand before you; let them tell all that has occurred." They were examined. It was found that the people [14]did not know any place in the seat[d] of Pharaoh, L. P. H., of which the mayor had spoken the words. He was found wrong[e] therein.

**534.** [15]The great nobles granted life to the coppersmiths of "The-House-of-Usermare-Meriamon,-L.-P.-H.,-[in-the-House-of]-Amon." They were reassigned to the High Priest of Amon-Re [king of gods], [16]Amenhotep, on this day.

The documents thereof are: one roll; it is deposited in the office of the vizier's archives.

*Later Dockets*

*Pl. 8*

**535.** [1]Year 1, first month of the first season, day 2, corresponding to the year 19. Copy of the records of the necropolis-thieves, [2]the

---

[a]The mayor thus belonged to the court which was to try his case.

[b]Tombs. [c]The mayor of the city. [d]The necropolis.

[e]Both here and above (l. 12) the word used (ᶜ*ḏ*ˀ) literally means "*guilty*," in a criminal case, and in a suit "*defeated*."

thieves of the tombs, which was placed before Pharaoh, L. P. H., by the mayor of the west of the city, Pewero:

Here follow the names of sixteen people, forming the list of thieves, of which the above is the title.

19Year 1, second month of the first season, day 25, corresponding to the year 19. Copy of the records of the necropolis-thieves, 20which was laid before the vizier, Nibmare-nakht,[a] by the mayor of the west of the city, Pewero:

Here follow the names of twenty-nine people, forming the list of which the above is the title.

## II. PAPYRUS AMHERST[b]

**536.** This fragment, unlike the Abbott papyrus, is part of the court record of the prosecution of the tomb-robbers guilty of the robbery of the tombs on which Peser had reported. It contains the remarkable confession of the eight men who robbed the tomb of Sebekemsaf and his queen, Nubkhas, and the record of their identification of the tomb, on being conducted to it, in the presence of the vizier. All this is omitted in Papyrus Abbott, and only the trial of the innocent coppersmiths is there recorded. A list of prisoners awaiting trial is also appended.

**537.** Column 1 is too fragmentary to yield any connected content; but it would appear that someone is mentioning

---

[a]This vizier is mentioned as having been in office in the fourteenth year of Ramses IX (Abbott, 4, 15), while in the year 16 we have the vizier Khamwese. Here we find Nibmarenakht as vizier again in the nineteenth year, and he appears also in Papyrus Mayer in the same year. We must either suppose that there were two viziers of the South, or that Nibmarenakht's term of office was interrupted for a time.

[b]Part of a roll containing three columns and part of a fourth, now in the collection of Lord Amherst of Hackney. Published by Chabas (*Mélanges d'archéologie égyptienne*, 3me sér., Tome II, Pls. I-IV), and by Newberry, *The Amherst Papyri* (London, 1899), Pls. IV-VII.

"*thieves ——— with thee*," perhaps admonishing one of the culprits to confess the names of his companions; for we next find someone speaking in the first person, referring to people of the High Priest of Amon (l. 3), and especially to "*quarrymen ——— who were with me when I was———*." The next two lines continue the mention of people who are known to be implicated in the robbery: Hapi and Setnakht, and reference is made to the "*year 13*," perhaps the date of some earlier theft.

**538.** In the next column (2) the common confession of all is in progress, having begun in the lost upper portion. It is as follows:

*Col. 2*

[a]1"——— King's-Wife, Nubkhas, L. P. H., his royal wife in the place of 2his —, it[b] being protected — its — with mortar, covered with blocks. We penetrated them ⸢all⸣, we found her 3resting likewise. We opened their coffins and their coverings in which they were. We found this 4august mummy of this king ⸢— — —⸣. There was a numerous list of amulets and ornaments of gold at its throat; 5its head had a ⸢mask⸣ of gold upon it; the august mummy of this king was overlaid with gold throughout. Its 6coverings were wrought with gold and silver, within and without; inlaid with every splendid costly stone. We stripped off the gold, which 7we found on the august mummy of this god, and its amulets and ornaments which were at its throat, and the coverings wherein it rested. 8[We] found the King's-Wife likewise; we stripped off all that we found on her likewise. We set fire to their coverings. 9We stole their furniture, which we found with them, being vases of gold, silver, and bronze. We divided, 10and made the gold which we found on these two gods, on their mummies, and the amulets, ornaments and coverings, into eight parts."

---

[a]The number of lines lost above is uncertain, but, judging from the next column, there were at least four.

[b]The place.

*Col. 3. List of Thieves*

**539.** [a] [1] [⌜List of the thieves⌝]:

[2] ——— (Lost name, etc.)

[3] ——— (Lost name, etc.)

[4] ——— (Lost name, etc.)

[5] The stonecutter of the "House-of-Amon-Re,-King-of-Gods," Hapi, under charge of the High Priest of Amon.

[6] The artisan of the "House-of-Amon-Re,-King-of-Gods," Iramon, of the master of the hunt, Nesuamon.

[7] The peasant, Amenemhab, of the house of Amenopet, who administers in the district of Amenopet, under charge of the High Priest of Amon.

[8] The water-carrier, Kemwese (*Kᵓ-m-Wᵓs·t*) of the shrine of King Menkheprure (Thutmose IV), L. P. H., under charge of ———.[b]

[9] Ehenefer (*ᶜḥᵓ-nfr*), son of Nakhtemmut (*Nḫt-m-Mw·t*), formerly in the hand of Telamon (*Ty-n-rᵓ-Ymn*), the negro slave of the High Priest of Amon.

[10] Total of the people who were in the pyramid of this great god: eight men.

*Examination of the Robbers*

**540.** Their examination was held, by beating with a double rod, smiting their feet [11] and their hands. They told the same story. The governor of the city and vizier, Khamwese; the king's-butler, Nesuamon, the scribe of Pharaoh, L. P. H., caused the thieves to be taken before them, [12] to the west of the city, in the year 16, third month of the first season, day 19;[c] and that the thieves should put hand upon the pyramid of this god, in whose sepulcher-chamber they had been. Their examination and their ⌜—⌝ were put into writing; and the vizier, the butler, the herald, and the mayor of the city reported to Pharaoh concerning it.

---

[a] The confession of the thieves is perhaps concluded here. If so, the next column began with a list of the thieves, of which the title occupied one line, and the three lost names, three more lines (each name with its titles occupying a line), making a total loss, at the top of the column, of four lines at least.

[b] Omitted by the scribe.

[c] This is the date of the expedition of the vizier and Nesuamon, as also related in Papyrus Abbott (col. 4, ll. 11, 12, above § 523); but no mention is there made of bringing out the robbers of Sebekemsaf's tomb, to make them identify it.

*Col. 4*

[a]———

| | |
|---|---|
| ——— | 3 men |
| Thief ⌜———⌝ | 1 man |
| Total | 4 |

*Thieves Awaiting Punishment*

**541.** Thieves of this pyramid of this god, who took to flight,[b] having been delivered to the High Priest of Amon-Re, king of gods, to have them taken and placed among the prisoners at the gate of the "House-of-Amon-Re-King-of-Gods," with their companions secretly,[c] that Pharaoh might determine their punishment:

The artisan of "The-House-of-Usermare-Meriamon (Ramses III),-L.-P.-H.,-in-the-House-of-Amon," Setnakht, son of Penanuket, under charge of the High Priest of Amon-Re, king of gods, the sem priest of "The-House-of-Usermare-Meriamon,-L.-P.-H.,-in-the-House-of-Amon," Nesuamon.

## III. TURIN FRAGMENT[d]

**542.** The coppersmith Pekharu, accused of robbing the tomb of Queen Isis (§§ 523, 524) was found to know nothing about it. It was hence supposed to be uninjured. But in the year 17 our fragment shows that it was found to have been robbed by eight thieves. These can hardly have been any other than the eight thieves of Sebekemsaf's tomb, who must have robbed the tomb of Isis before their arrest in the year 16. Hence it had been robbed when the vizier's inspection was made (§ 523), but he failed to discover the fact. Hence it would appear that Peser's charges against Pewero

[a]The number of lines lost is uncertain, but at least three-fourths of the page is lost.

[b]Whether this flight took place before the trial, or some of them escaped afterward, is uncertain.

[c]*n ṯ ͗ wt* for *m ṯ ͗ wt*.

[d]A fragment of hieratic papyrus in the Turin Museum, published in transcription by Spiegelberg, with translation (*Zwei Beiträge*, 12, 13).

were later gradually being verified, and that further examination was being made.

**543.** Year 17, third month of the second season, day 22. The workmen of the necropolis ceased work, and the butler, governor of the city, and vizier, Khamwese; the workmen of the necropolis and their overseers, went up to the ⸢place⸣ of the (female) singers,[a] to inspect (the tomb of) the king's-daughter, king's-wife, Isis, L. P. H. They opened her tomb, they found the granite block,[b] the eight thieves having done damage in the ⸢—⸣. They had wrought evil destruction on all that was therein; and they had damaged [its] owner.[c]

## IV. MAYER PAPYRI[d]

**544.** These two documents are the court records of the prosecution of the tomb-robbers, whose names are recorded on the back of the Papyrus Abbott, in the first year of Ramses X (nineteenth of Ramses IX), and of others in the next year, eight months later. The contents of the document will be found sufficiently indicated above (§§ 505 ff.) without further summary here.

### *Trial of Robbers of Ramses II and Seti I's Tombs*

**545.** [1]Year 1, of Uhem-mesut (*Whm-mś·wt*),[e] fourth month of the third season, day 15. On this day occurred the examination of the

---

[a]Queens. [b]The sarcophagus, as Spiegelberg has seen.

[c]The mummy.

[d]These two documents are in the Free Public Library Museum of Liverpool, in the Mayer collection. They are called Mayer A and Mayer B. Mayer A has twelve columns varying from 20 to 27 lines; B has but one column (in a different hand) of 14 lines. Many years ago Goodwin published some notes on the two (*Zeitschrift für ägyptische Sprache*, 1873, 39 ff.; *ibid.*, 1874, 63 ff.), but both are still unpublished. I was unable to use them when I visited the Mayer collection, as they were then in London; hence I owe a great debt to Spiegelberg, who without reserve placed his transcription of the original at my disposal. Spiegelberg has also published a translation of the documents (*Free Public Library Museum, Mayer Collection, . . . . Liverpool, Museum Report, No. 5. Mayer Collection Report, No. 1. Translation of Hieratic Papyri Mayer A and B, Liverpool, 1891*), which I found very useful.

[e]Lit., "*Repeating birth,*" and meaning "*Born again,*" a name often applied to the king, as Goodwin already saw. It is here Ramses X who is meant.

thieves of the tomb[a] [2]of King Usermare-Setepnere (Ramses II), L. P. H., the great god; and the tomb[b] of King Menmare, L. P. H., Seti (I), L. P. H., which are ⌜recorded⌝ in the treasury of [3]"The-House-of-King-Usermare-Meriamon (Ramses III),-L.-P.-H.," concerning whom the chief of police, Nesuamon, had reported, in this roll of [4]names; for he was there, standing with the thieves, when they laid their hands upon the tombs; [5]who were tortured at the examination on their feet and their hands, to make them tell the way they had done exactly.

*Composition of the Court*

**546.** [6]By the governor of the city and vizier, Nibmarenakht;

Overseer of the White House and overseer of the granary, Menmarenakht;

Steward and king's-butler, ⌜Ini⌝, the ⌜herald⌝ of Pharaoh, L. P. H.;

[7]Steward of the court, king's-butler, Pemeriamon (*P ᵓ-mry-Ymn*), the scribe of Pharaoh.

*Testimony of the Prisoner, Paykamen*

**547.** [8]Examination. The *X*,[c] Paykamen (*P ᵓ y-k ᵓ mn*), under charge of the overseer of the cattle of Amon, was brought in; the oath of the king, L. P. H., was administered to him, not to tell [9]a lie. He was asked: "What was the manner of thy going with the people who were with thee, [10]when ye robbed the tombs of the kings which are ⌜recorded⌝ in the treasury of 'The-House-of-King-Usermare-Meriamon,-L.-P.-H.?" [11]He said: "I went with the priest Teshere (*T ᵓ -šry*), son of the divine father, Zedi, of 'The House;' Beki, son of Nesuamon, of this house; [12]the *X*, Nesumontu of the house of Montu, lord of Erment; the *X*, Paynehsi of the vizier, formerly prophet of Sebek of Peronekh (*Pr ᶜ nḫ*); Teti (*T ᵓ -ty*) ⌜—⌝ [13]who belonged to Paynehsi, of the vizier, formerly prophet of Sebek of Peronekh; in all six."[d]

---

[a]Lit., "*house of the corridor.*"

[b]Judging from the connection, this word must mean "*tomb,*" but it is otherwise unknown to me; it is written with the *gs*-sign and the determinative for a building or tomb.

[c]This is a title (ᵓ ᶜ ᶜ) common among the people of the necropolis, and often occurring in these prosecutions. We have no hint as to its meaning, and I indicate it by *X*.

[d]Counting the speaker.

*Testimony of the Chief of Police*

548. The chief of police, Nesuamon, was brought in. [14]He was asked: "How didst thou find these men?" He said: "I heard that these men had gone to [15]rob this tomb. I went and found these six men. That which the thief, Paykamen, has said is [16]correct. I took testimony from them on that day . . . . . . . . [17]The examination of the watchman of the house of Amon, the thief, Paykamen, under charge of the overseer of the cattle of Amon, was held by beating with a rod, [18]the bastinade was applied to his feet. An oath was administered to him that he might be executed if he told a lie; he said: 'That which I did is [19]exactly what I have said.' He confirmed it with his mouth, saying: 'As for me, that which I did is what [they] did; I was w[ith the]se six men, I stole [20]a piece of copper[a] therefrom, and I took possession of it.'"

*Testimony of the Prisoner, Nesumontu*

549. [21]The *X*, the thief, Nesumontu, was brought in; the examination was held by beating with a rod; the bastinade was applied on (his) feet and his hand(s); [22]the oath of the king, L. P. H., was administered to him, that he might be executed if he told a lie. He was asked: "What was the manner of thy going to rob [23]in the tomb with thy companions?" He said: "I went and found these people; I was the sixth. I stole a [24]piece of copper[b] therefrom, I took possession of it."

*Col. 2. Testimony of Karu*

550. [1]The watchman of the house of Amon, the *X*, Karu (*Ḳ* ᵓ *-rw*), was brought in; he was examined with the rod, the bastinade was applied to his feet and his hands; [2]the oath of the king, L. P. H., was administered to him, that he might be executed if he told a lie. He was asked: "What was the manner of thy going [3]with the (sic!) companions when ye robbed in the tomb?" He said: "The thief, [4]the *X*, Pehenui, he made me take some grain. I seized a sack of grain, and [5]when I began to go down, I heard the voice of the men who were in this storehouse. I [6]put my eye to the passage, and I saw Paybek and Teshere, who were within. I [7]called to him, saying, 'Come!' and he came out to me, having two pieces of copper in his hand. He [8]gave them to me, and I

---

[a]*M* ᵓ *y w*, with determinative of metal.

[b]Same as in l. 20.

gave to him $1\frac{1}{2}$ measures of spelt to pay for them. I took one of them, and I [9]gave the other to the *X*, Enefsu (*ᶜ n·f-sw*).

*Testimony of Nesuamon*

**551.** [10]The priest, Nesuamon, son of Paybek, was brought in, because of his father. He was examined by beating with the rod. [11]They said to him: "Tell the manner of thy father's going with the men who were with him." He said: "My father was truly there. I was (only) a little child, and I know not how he did it." [13]On being (further) examined, he said: "I saw the workman, Ehatinofer (*ᶜ ḥ ᵓ ty-nfr*), while he was in the place where the tomb is, [14]with the watchman, Nofer, son of ⌈Merwer (*Mr-wr*)⌉, and the artisan, ⌈—⌉, in all three (men). They are the ones I saw [15]distinctly. Indeed, gold was taken, and they are the ones whom I know." On being (further) examined with a rod, he said: "These three men are the ones I saw distinctly."

*Testimony of Wenpehti*

**552.** [17]The weaver of "The House," Wenpehti (*Wn-pḥty*), son of ⌈—⌉, was brought in. He was examined by beating with a rod, the bastinade was applied to his feet and his hands. [18]The oath of the king, L. P. H., was administered, not to tell a lie. They said to him: "Tell what was the manner of thy father's going, [19]when he committed theft in the tomb with his companions." He said: "My father was killed when I was a child. [20]My mother told me: 'The chief of police, Nesuamon, gave some chisels of copper to thy father; then the captains of the archers and the *X* [21]slew thy father.' They ⌈held⌉ the examination, and Nesuamon took the copper and gave it to ⌈me⌉. It remains ⌈in the possession of⌉ my mother."

*Col. 3. Testimony of Enroy*

**553.** [1]A Theban woman, Enroy (*Yn-n-r ᵓ -y*), the mistress of the priest, Teshere, son of Zedi, was brought in. She was examined [2]by beating with a rod; the bastinade was applied to her feet and her hands. The oath of the king, [3]L. P. H., not to tell a lie, was administered to her; she was asked: "What was the manner of thy husband's going [4]when he broke into the tomb and carried away the copper from it?" She said: "He carried away some [5]copper belonging to this tomb; we sold it and devoured it."

*Second Trial*

**554.** [6]Fourth month of the third season, day 17; was held the examination of certain of the thieves of the cemetery.

Here follows the trial of five men, with the usual formulæ, only slightly varied from those used above. The tomb which they were accused of robbing is not mentioned. All five were found innocent. The prosecutions which follow (Columns 5–6), do not refer to any particular tombs, but they are followed in turn by a list (Col. 7), headed: "*Year 2, first month of the first season, day 13; the names of the robbers of the tomb of Pharaoh.*" This list contains the names of twenty-two persons (two women), among whom are some of those above prosecuted.

**555.** After a gap of a few lines Column 8 proceeds with an important trial, of which the beginning is lost in the gap.

*Col. 8*

He was again examined by beating with a rod. [2]They said to him: "Tell what were the other places which thou didst break into." He said: "I broke into the tomb of the King's-[3]Wife, Nesimut." He said: "It was I who broke into the tomb of the King's-Wife, Bekurel (*Bk-wr-n-r*ᵓ), wife of [4]King Menmare (Seti I), L. P. H., in all, three (tombs)."

**556.** After enumerating some of the things stolen, in response to a question of the vizier, the examination of the next man shows him to have been innocent. The fisherman who carried the thieves over to the west side is next examined (Column 9) and discharged; and of the three men whose trial follows, one was innocent. A list of twenty-five thieves fills the next column (10) which is headed: "*The thieves of the cemetery whose examination was held, concerning whom it was found that they had been in the tombs.*" Column 11 contains a similar list entitled: "*The thieves of the tomb, in* *the second month, tenth day,*" while the margin bears a list of "*the women who were imprisoned,*" being eleven of the wives of the thieves. The document then closes with proceedings in which some of the accused in the first trial reappear.

The second document (Papyrus Mayer B) is in a different hand, but records proceedings of the same sort. In a connection which is not entirely clear, the tomb of "*Amenhotep III, the Great God,*" is mentioned, and it is evident that it had been robbed.

# REIGN OF RAMSES XII

## THE REPORT OF WENAMON[a]

557. This unique document is our most important source for the position of Egypt in Syria at the close of the Twentieth Dynasty. It belongs to the fifth year of the last of the Ramessids, when he is but the shadow of a king. Hrihor, the High Priest of Amon, although not called king, is in control at Thebes, and Nesubenebded (Smendes), afterward the first king of the Twenty-first Dynasty, living at Tanis, rules the Delta. Under these circumstances Hrihor dispatches one of his officials, named Wenamon, to procure cedar from the Lebanon forests, for the construction of a new sacred barge for Amon. In accordance with an oracle of Amon, the messenger was intrusted with a certain image of the god called "*Amon-of-the-Way*," which he was to take with him as an embassy to the prince of Byblos. As the envoy met with extraordinary difficulties in the execution of his commission, he made out an elaborate report[b] on his return home to explain the long series of accidents which

---

[a]Papyrus found in 1891 by fellahin at el Khibeh, opposite Feshn in Upper Egypt, now in the possession of M. W. Golénischeff, of St. Petersburg. It consists of a part of one column, and another almost complete. It was published in transcription by M. Golénischeff in a collection of essays in honor of Baron V. de Rosen's jubilee, with a facsimile of the first twenty-one lines; and again by Golénischeff in revised transcription (*Recueil*, XXI), with translation. It was translated without alteration of Golénischeff's arrangement of the fragments, by W. M. Müller (*Mittheilungen der Deutschen Vorderasiatischen Gesellschaft*, 1900, 1); and by Erman (*Zeitschrift für ägyptische Sprache*, 38, 1–14) with a rearrangement of the fragments which seems to me unquestionably correct. The following translation, based largely on Erman, I published first in the *American Journal of Semitic Languages and Literatures*, 1905.

[b]That our document is Wenamon's authentic report there seems to me, after a study of its characteristics, not the slightest doubt; but there is not space here to discuss the question. See Erman (*Zeitschrift für ägyptische Sprache*, 38, 2), who reaches the same conclusion.

had interfered with the success of his mission. Although a large fragment is lacking from the middle of the first column, and the loss of another fragment at the end leaves the narrative unfinished, yet this report is, nevertheless, one of the most interesting and important documents yet discovered in Egypt.

558. On the sixteenth of the eleventh month, in the fifth year, probably of Ramses XII, Wenamon left Thebes and, presenting his credentials to Nesubenebded at Tanis, he was kindly received. Fifteen days after leaving Thebes (on the first of the twelfth month), he sailed from Tanis (?) into the Mediterranean in a merchant ship, commanded by a Syrian. Arrived at Dor, the gold and silver which he had brought with him as payment for the timber was stolen from him. Dor was now a petty kingdom of the Thekel, who, with the Peleset-Philistines, had begun entering Syria under Ramses III seventy-five or eighty years before. They had constantly pushed southward after their defeat by Ramses III in his eighth year, and had settled along the eastern coast of the Mediterranean as subjects of the Pharaoh. After the death of Ramses III they must have soon gained their independence. The Thekel chief of Dor gives Wenamon little satisfaction for the loss of his valuables, and after waiting nine days he sails northward to Tyre.

559. The account of the voyage from Dor to Tyre is lost in a lacuna. On the way from Tyre to Byblos he in some way met some of the Thekel with a bag (?) of silver. It weighed thirty deben, and, as he had lost thirty-one[a] deben of silver, he seized it as security. He arrived at Byblos four months and twelve days after his departure from Thebes, but, as he came in an ordinary merchant ship, and not in a

[a]About 7½ lbs., troy.

special ship of Nesubenebded, and was without rich gifts and the customary externals of former Egyptian envoys, Zakar-Baal, the prince of Byblos, would not receive him, and ordered him to leave. After nineteen days, one of the noble youths in attendance upon the prince fell into a prophetic frenzy and demanded that Wenamon and his god, "Amon-of-the-Way," be summoned and honorably treated.

**560.** About to return to Egypt, Wenamon was summoned to Zakar-Baal's palace, but, being without money and without credentials, which he had foolishly left with Nesubenebded at Tanis—having only the above-mentioned image of Amon, supposed to confer "*life and health*," but not likely to impress the Syrian—he was treated with scant respect. The claims of Hrihor and of Amon upon the Lebanon were scouted, and Zakar-Baal proved from his records that his fathers had been paid for their timber. Wenamon therefore sends to Nesubenebded for money, and the prince shows his good-will by dispatching to Egypt at once the heavy timbers of the hull. The messenger returned from Nesubenebded within forty-eight days (perhaps only nineteen or twenty days) with partial payment of the timber desired, whereupon Zakar-Baal sent three hundred men and three hundred oxen to fell and bring the rest of the timber.

**561.** Some eight months after Wenamon left Thebes the timber was ready. Zakar-Baal delivers it to him, and with grim humor tells him that he has been better treated than the last envoys from Egypt, who were detained at Byblos seventeen years and died there. The prince charges an attendant to conduct Wenamon to their tomb and show it to him. But Wenamon demurs and takes his leave, promising to see that the balance due on the timber is paid. As he is about to sail, a number of Thekel ships appear, for the purpose of arresting him, doubtless for his seizure of the silver. The unlucky Wenamon sits down upon the beach and weeps, while Zakar-Baal, hearing of his plight, sends him reassuring messages, with food, drink, and a female singer. In the morning the prince interviews the Thekel and sends Wenamon to sea. In some way he evades the Thekel, but is driven by a contrary wind to Cyprus (Alasa), where he is about to be killed by the Cyprians, when he finds someone who speaks Egyptian, succeeds in gaining the favor of the Cyprian queen, and is spared.

562. Here the remarkable report is broken off, and how Wenamon reached Egypt we do not know. It will be seen that in the Lebanon region, once conquered and controlled by the Pharaohs, they are no longer feared. Thus, at the close of the Twentieth Dynasty Egypt, while respected as a source of civilization (§ 579), cannot secure even ordinary protection and civility for her messengers in Syria, and this state of affairs had already existed, probably as early as the reign of Ramses IX, a generation earlier.

Besides the earliest known instance of prophetic ecstasy known to us, the document contains also another significant datum, viz., the princes of Byblos had, for two generations, been keeping their daily business records in a book or roll ($^{c}$*r*). Moreover, among the gifts brought to the prince of Byblos from the Delta were five hundred rolls of papyrus paper. Of course, the Phœnician did not write cuneiform with pen and ink upon these rolls; for a script worse suited to such writing materials than cuneiform can hardly be imagined. It is evident that he wrote upon papyrus the hieratic hand customarily written upon it in Egypt, the only method of writing then known which contained alphabetic signs for the whole alphabet. It thus becomes clear that by 1100 B. C. the cuneiform had been displaced in Phœnicia, and before the tenth century the Phœnician scribes, discarding the innumerable syllabic signs of the Egyptian hieratic, had accustomed themselves to employ only its alphabetic signs.

*Pl. 1. Departure from Thebes*

**563.** [1]Year five,[a] third month of the third season (eleventh month), day 16, day of the departure of the "eldest of the hall," of the house of Amon, [2][the lord of the] lands, Wenamon, to bring the timber for the great and august barge of Amon-Re, king of gods, which is on [⌜the river⌝] ——— (called): "Userhet"[b] of Amon.

*Arrival at Tanis*

**564.** On the day of my arrival at Tanis (*Ḏ*ᶜ*n*), at the [4]place of abode of Nesubenebded (*Ns-sw-b*ꜣ*-nb-dd*)[c] and Tentamon, I gave to them the writings of Amon-Re, king of gods, which they [5]caused to be read in their presence; and they said: "I will do (it), I will do (it) according to that which Amon-Re, king of gods, our [6]lord, saith." I abode until the fourth month of the third season,[d] being in Tanis.

*Voyage to Dor*

**565.** Nesubenebded and [7]Tentamon sent me with the ship-captain, Mengebet (*M-n-g-b-ty*), and I descended into [8]the great Syrian (*Ḫ*ꜣ*-rw*) sea, in the fourth month of the third season, on the first day. I arrived at Dor, a city of [9]Thekel (*Ṯ*ꜣ*-k*ꜣ*-r*ꜣ), and Bedel (*B*ꜣ*-dy-r*ꜣ), its king, caused to be brought for me much bread, a jar of wine, [10]and a joint of beef.

*The Robbery at Dor*

**566.** Then a man of my ship fled, having stolen:

| | |
|---|---|
| —[e] [vessels] of gold, [11][amounting to] | 5 deben |
| 4 vessels of silver, amounting to | 20 deben |
| A sack of silver | 11 deben |
| [12][Total of what] he [stole] | 5 deben of gold |
| | 31 deben of silver[f] |

[a]That this date must refer to Ramses XII was shown by Erman (*Zeitschrift für ägyptische Sprache*, 38, 2).

[b]The name of the barge of Amon; see, e. g., Papyrus Harris (§ 209).

[c]Greek Smendes; part of the name is here broken out, and the reading is taken from l. 6.

[d]Fourteen days after his departure from Thebes.

[e]The names of the articles of gold are broken out.

[f]About 1⅛ lbs. of gold and about 7½ lbs. of silver.

In the morning then I rose and went to [13]the abode of the prince, and I said to him: "I have been robbed in thy harbor. Since thou art the king of this land, [14]thou art therefore its investigator, who should search for my money. For the money belongs to Amon-Re, [15]king of gods, the lord of the lands; it belongs to Nesubenebded, and it belongs to Hrihor, my lord, and the other [16]magnates of Egypt; it belongs also to Weret (*Wʾrty*), and to Mekmel[a] (*M-kʾ-m-rw*), and to Zakar-[17]Baal (*Ṯʾ-kʾ-rw-B-ʿ-rʾ*),[b] the prince of Byblos,"[c] He said to me: [d]"To thy honor and thy excellence! but, behold, I know nothing [18]of this complaint which thou hast lodged with me. If the thief belonged to my land, he who went on board[e] [19]thy ship, that he might steal thy treasure, I would repay it to thee from my treasury till they [20]find thy thief by name; but the thief who robbed thee belongs to [21]thy ship. Tarry a few days here with me, and I will seek him." When I had spent nine days, moored [22]in his harbor, I went to him, and said to him: "Behold, thou hast not found my money [23][⌈therefore let me depart⌉] with ⌈the⌉ ship-captain, and with those who go — — — — —."[f]

————.[g]

*Pl. 3*

[1]———— the sea. He said to me, "Be silent. . . . . . . . ."[h]

*Departure from Tyre for Byblos*

**567.** [5]———— the harbor ———— [6]— — — [⌈I arrived at⌉] Tyre.[i] I went forth from Tyre at early dawn ———— [7]— — — — Zakar-Baal (*Ṯʾ-kʾ-rʾ-B-ʿ-r*), the prince of Byblos[j] ————.

---

[a]We have here given first the Egyptians who sent the valuables, and then the Syrians, to whom it was to be paid.

[b]זכר־בעל, as Müller and Erman have noted.

[c]This indicates the locality where Wenamon expects to purchase the timber.

[d]Something like "I am beholden to" is to be understood.

[e]Lit., "*descended into*."

[f]Four lines are lost here and an uncertain amount more.

[g]The total loss between the two parts of Pl. 1 is some twenty-three lines. The bulk of this loss precedes Pl. 3, and only a small portion follows it.

[h]Three lines containing but a few broken words; among them a reference to searching for the thieves, which shows that Fragment 3 belongs in this place. The journey from Dor to Tyre is somewhere in these lacunæ.

[i]Only the *r* of Tyre is preserved, but as he is just leaving there, it can hardly be the *r* of Dor.

[j]This is not the arrival, but merely the mention of his intended destination.

*Seizure of Security from Thekel Travelers*

**568.** ——— [8]the ——— I found 30 deben of silver therein. I seized [it, ⌜saying to them: "I will take⌝] [9]your money, and it shall remain with me until ye find [my money. ⌜Was it not a man of Thekel⌝] [10]who stole it, and no thief [⌜of ours⌝]? I will take it ———."[a] [11]They went away, while I ⌜—⌝ — ⌜—⌝ —.

*Arrival at Byblos*

**569.** [I] arrived ———— the harbor of Byblos. [⌜I made a place of concealment, [12]I hid⌝] "Amon-of-the-Way," and I placed his things in it. The prince of Byblos sent to me, saying: "Be[take thyself] (from) [13]my harbor." I sent to him, saying: "———. [x+1] ———[b] if they sail, let them take ⌜me⌝ to Egypt." —— I spent nineteen days in his [harbor], and he continually sent to me daily, saying: "Betake thyself away from my harbor."

*A Prophet of Byblos*

**570.** Now, when he sacrificed to his gods —, the god seized one of his noble youths (*ᶜ ḏd*), making him frenzied, so that he said: "Bring [the god] hither![c] Bring the messenger of Amon who hath him. [x+5]Send him, and let him go."

*Wenamon's Departure Prevented*

**571.** Now, while the frenzied (youth) continued in frenzy during this night, I found a ship bound for Egypt, and I loaded in all my belongings into it. I waited for the darkness, saying: "When it descends I will embark the god also, in order that no other eye may see him."

*Wenamon is Summoned*

**572.** The harbor-master came to me, saying: "Remain until morning by the prince." I said to him: "Art not thou he who continually came to me daily, saying: 'Betake thyself away from my harbor'?

[a]A few fragments of words for about one-third line.

[b]The lacuna here doubtless includes several lines, but it is not so large as the one before Pl. 3; see notes, p. 279. Of the uncertain line numbering I have inserted only every five lines for this fragment.

[c]Lit., "*up*." In ecstasy the youth demands the summoning of Wenamon and his image of Amon, and that they be honorably treated and dismissed.

Dost thou not say, 'Remain in the [⌈land'⌉], x+10in order to let depart the ship that I have found? that thou mayest come and say again, 'Away!'? He went and told it to the prince, and the prince sent to the captain of the ship, saying: "Remain until morning by the king."

*Wenamon Visits Zakar-Baal*

**573.** When morning came he sent and had me brought up, when the divine offering occurred in the fortress wherein he was, on the shore of the sea. I found him sitting in his upper chamber, leaning his back against a window, while the waves of the great Syrian sea beat against the — x+15behind him. I said to him: "⌈Kindness⌉ of Amon!" He said to me: "How long is it until this day since thou camest (away) from the abode of Amon?" I said: "Five months and one day until now."[a]

*Zakar-Baal Demands Wenamon's Papers*

**574.** He said to me: "Behold, if thou art true, where is the writing of Amon, which is in thy hand? Where is the letter of the High Priest of Amon, which is in thy hand?" I said to him: "I gave them to Nesubenebded and Tentamon." Then he was very wroth, and he said to me: "Now, behold, the writing and the letter are not in thy hand! Where is the ship of cedar, which Nesubenebded gave to thee? Where is x+20its Syrian crew? He would not deliver thy business to this ship-captain ⌈— —⌉ to have thee killed, that they might cast thee into the sea. From whom would they have sought the god then? And thee, from whom would they have sought thee then?" So spake he to me. I said to him: "There are indeed Egyptian ships and Egyptian crews who sail under Nesubenebded, (but) he hath no Syrian crews." He said to me: "There are surely twenty ships here in my harbor,

*Pl. 1*

which are in connection with Nesubenebded; and at this Sidon, 1whither thou also ⌈wouldst go⌉, there are indeed 10,000 ships also which are in connection 2with Berket-el[b] (*W*ˀ*-r*ˀ*-k*ˀ*-ty-r*ˀ) and sail to his house."

---

[a]This would be the twelfth of the fourth month.

[b]Erman thinks this must be some great Phœnician merchant resident in Tanis, and the parallelism certainly points clearly to someone in Tanis.

### *Wenamon Declares His Business*

**575.** Then I was silent in this great hour. [3]He answered and said to me: "On what business hast thou come hither?" I said to him: "I have come [4]after the timber for the great and august barge of Amon-Re, king of gods. Thy father did it, [5]thy grandfather did it, and thou wilt also do it." So spake I to him.

### *Zakar-Baal Demands Payment as of Old*

**576.** He said to me: "They did it, truly. [6]If thou give me (something) for doing it, I will do it. Indeed, my agents transacted the business; [7]the Pharaoh, L. P. H., sent six ships, laden with the products of Egypt, and they were unloaded into their [8]storehouses. And thou also shalt bring something for me." He had the journal of his fathers brought in, [9]and he had them read it before me. They found 1,000 deben of every (kind of) silver, which was in his book.

### *Zakar-Baal Declares His Independence*

**577.** [10]He said to me: "If the ruler of Egypt were the owner of my property, and I were also his servant, [11]he would not send silver and gold, saying: 'Do the command of Amon.' It was not the payment [12]of ⌜tribute⌝[a] which they exacted of my father. As for me, I am myself neither thy [13]servant nor am I the servant of him that sent thee. If I cry out to the [14]Lebanon, the heavens open, and the logs lie here on the shore of the sea."

### *Wenamon has no Equipment*

**578.** "Give [15]me the sails which thou hast brought to propel thy ships which bear thy logs to [Egypt]. [16]Give me the cordage [⌜which thou hast brought to bind⌝] the trees which I fell, in order to make them [⌜fast⌝] for thee [17]——— I make them for thee ⌜into⌝ the sails of thy [18]ships, and the tops are (too) heavy and they break, and thou die in the midst of the sea [19]when Amon thunders in heaven, and puts Sutekh in his time."

### *Egypt the Home of Civilization*

**579.** "For Amon [20]equips all lands; he equips them, having first equipped the land of Egypt, whence thou comest. [21]For artisanship

[a] *Mrk* for *brk? Fꜣ* = "*pay*" is common. Erman suggests that *mrk* is connected with *melek*, "*king*," but *f*ꜣ seems to me, to make this interpretation difficult.

came forth from it, to reach my place of abode; and teaching came forth [22]from it, to reach my place of abode. What (then) are these miserable journeys which they have had thee make?"

*Wenamon Claims Lebanon for Amon*

**580.** I said to him: [23]"O guilty one! They are no miserable journeys on which I am. There is no ship upon the river, [24]which Amon does not own. For his is the sea, and his is Lebanon of which thou sayest, 'It is mine.' It[a] [25]grows for 'Userhet' (the barge) of Amon, the lord of every ship. Yea, so spake Amon-Re, king of gods, saying to [26]Hrihor, my lord: 'Send me,' and he made me go, bearing this great god. But, behold, thou hast let [27]this great god wait twenty-nine[b] days, when he had landed [in] thy harbor, although thou didst certainly know he was here. He is indeed (still) what [28]he (once) was, while thou standest and bargainest for the Lebanon with Amon, its lord. As for what thou sayest, that the [29]former kings sent silver and gold, if they had given life and health, they would not have sent the valuables; [30](but) they sent the valuables [to] thy fathers instead of life and health. Now, as for Amon-Re, king of gods, he is the [31]lord of life and health, and he was the lord of thy fathers, who spent their lifetime offering [32]to Amon.[c] And thou also, thou art the servant of Amon. If thou sayest to Amon, 'I will do (it), I will do (it),' and thou executest his [33]command, thou shalt live, and thou shalt be prosperous, and thou shalt be healthy, and thou shalt be pleasant to thy whole land and thy people. Wish not [34]for thyself a thing belonging to Amon-Re, [king of] gods. Yea, the lion loves his own."

*Wenamon will Secure Payment*

**581.** "Let my scribe be brought to me, that I may send [35]him to Nesubenebded and Tentamon, the rulers whom Amon hath given to the North of his land, [36]and they will send all that of which I shall write to them, saying: 'Let it be brought;' until I return to the South and [37]send thee all, all thy trifles again." So spake I to him.

---

[a]Lebanon.

[b]This was four months and twelve days after leaving Thebes; he must therefore have reached Byblos three months and thirteen days after leaving Thebes.

[c]Ramses III built a temple of Amon in Syria (§ 219); Thutmose III gave three cities of the southern Lebanon district to Amon (II, 557); Zakar-Baal had a butler named Penamon, and there is no doubt that Wenamon's statement was correct.

### *Timber is Shipped; Messenger Brings Payment*

**582.** He gave my letter into the hand of his messenger. He loaded in the ⌈keel⌉,[a] [38]the head of the bow and the head of the stern, with four other hewn timbers, together seven; and he had them taken to Egypt. [39]His messenger went to Egypt, and returned to me, to Syria in the first month of the second season.[b] Nesubenebded and Tentamon sent:

[40]Gold: 4 *Ṯb*-vessels, 1 *K*ᵓ*k-mn*-vessel;
Silver: 5 *Ṯb*-vessels;
Royal linen: 10 garments, 10 ⌈*ḥm-ḫrd*⌉;
Papyrus: [41]500 rolls;
Ox-hides: 500;
Rope: 500 (coils);
Lentils: 20 measures;
Fish: 30 measures (*mšt*ᵓ);
She[c] sent me:
Linen: [42]5 ⌈—⌉, 5 ⌈*ḥm-ḫrd*⌉;
Lentils: 1 measure;
Fish: 5 measures (*mst*ᵓ).

### *More Timber Felled*

**583.** The prince rejoiced, and detailed [43]300 men and 300 oxen, placing overseers over them, to have the trees felled. They spent the second season therewith [44]⌈—⌉. In the third month of the second season[d] (seventh month) they dragged them [to] the shore of the sea. The prince came forth and stood by them.

### *Timber Delivered to Wenamon*

**584.** He sent to me, [45]saying: "Come." Now, when I had presented myself before him, the shadow of his sunshade fell upon me. Penamon, [46]a butler, he stepped between me, saying: "The shadow of

---

[a]*Pypy·t*, determined with a piece of wood. The three principal timbers of the ship are undoubtedly mentioned here.

[b]Within forty-eight days of the date of his departure (twelfth of the fourth month).

[c]Tentamon sent him a personal present.

[d]Some eight months after he left Thebes.

Pharaoh, L. P. H., thy lord, falls upon thee." He[a] was angry [47]with him, saying: "Let him alone!" I presented myself before him, and he answered and said to me: "Behold, the command which my [48]fathers formerly executed, I have executed, although thou for thy part hast not done for me that which thy fathers did for me. Behold, there has arrived [49]the last of thy timber, and there it lies. Do according to my desire and come to load it, for they will indeed give it to thee."

*Fate of a Former Embassy*

**585.** [50]"Come not to contemplate the terror of the sea, (but) if thou dost contemplate the terror of the sea, thou shalt (also) contemplate [51]my own. Indeed, I have not done to thee that which they did to the messengers of Khamwese,[b] when they spent seventeen years [52]in this land. They died in their place."[c] He said to his butler: "Take him, and let him see their tomb, wherein they [53]sleep."

*Zakar-Baal's Great Distinction*

**586.** I said to him: "Let me not see it! As for Khamwese, (mere) people were the messengers whom he sent to thee; but people [54]— — there was no [god among] his messengers. And yet thou sayest, 'Go and see thy companions.' Lo, art thou not glad? [55]and dost thou not have made for thee a tablet, whereon thou sayest: 'Amon-Re, king of gods, sent to me "Amon-of-the-Way," his [56][divine] messenger, and Wenamon, his human messenger, after the timber for the great and august barge of Amon-Re, king of gods? I felled it, [57]I loaded it, I supplied him (with) my ships and my crews, I brought them to Egypt, to beseech for me [58]10,000 years of life from Amon, more than my ordained (life), and it came to pass.' Then in future days when a messenger comes

[a]The chief of Byblos.

[b]Who this Khamwese was is not entirely certain. Erman recalls the occurrence of Khamwese as part of the name in the cartouche of Ramses IX, and it is not improbable that he is meant, for as the messengers have been some time dead, and this document is dated in the fifth year of Ramses XII, they must have left Egypt some twenty-five years earlier, which would certainly carry us back into the reign of Ramses IX.

[c]This phrase "*in their place*" in connection with dying must have some particular meaning. It is frequently so used in the inscriptions of Ramses III, and of the conspirators against him, who committed suicide; but its idiomatic force is not clear.

[59]from the land of Egypt, who is able to write, and reads thy name upon the stela, thou shalt receive water in the West, like the gods who are [60]there." He said to me: "It is a great testimony which thou tellest me."

*Payment of Balance Promised*

**587.** I said to him: "As for the many things which thou hast said to me, when I reach [61]the place of abode of the High Priest of Amon, and he shall see thy command in thy command,[a] [he] will have something delivered to thee."

*Thekel Ships Lie in Wait*

**588.** [62]I went to the shore of the sea, to the place where the timbers lay; I spied eleven ships [63]coming from the sea, belonging to the Thekel, saying:[b] "Arrest him! Let not a ship [64]of his (pass) to Egypt!" I sat down and began to weep. The letter-scribe of the prince came out to me, [65]and said to me: "What is the matter with thee?" I said to him: "Surely thou seest these birds which twice descend upon Egypt. [66]Behold them! They come to the pool, and how long[c] shall I be here, forsaken? For thou seest surely those who come [67]to arrest me again."[d]

*Zakar-Baal Reassures Wenamon*

**589.** He went and told it to the prince. The prince began to weep at the evil words which they spoke to him. [68]He sent out his letter-scribe to me, he brought me two jars of wine and a ram. He sent [69]to me Tentno (*Tynt-nw·t*), an Egyptian singer (feminine), who was with him, saying: "Sing for him; let not his heart feel apprehension." He sent to me, [70]saying: "Eat, drink, and let not thy heart feel apprehension. Thou shalt hear all that I have to say in the morning."

*Interview with the Thekel*

**590.** Morning [71]came, he had (the Thekel) called into his ⌈—⌉, he stood in their midst and said to the Thekel: "Why have ye come?"

---

[a]The text is translated verbatim; but it is perhaps corrupt.

[b]The report, otherwise, so full, abbreviates here; he means that they were under orders, of which he introduces the purport by the word "*saying*."

[c]Lit., "*until what comes.*"

[d]This word points to earlier trouble with the Thekel, and doubtless explains the "*twice*" above.

[72]They said to him: "We have come after the stove-up ships which thou sendest to Egypt with our ⌜—⌝ comrades." [73]He said to them: "I cannot arrest the messenger of Amon in my land. Let me send him away, and ye shall pursue him, [74]to arrest him."

*Escape to Alasa*

**591.** He loaded me on board, he sent me away — to the harbor of the sea. The wind drove me to the land of [75]Alasa (*ʾ-rʾ-sʾ*); those of the city came forth to me to slay me. I was brought among them to the abode of Heteb (*Ḥʾ-ty-bʾ*), [76]the queen of the city. I found her as she was going forth from one of her houses and entering into her other. I [77]saluted her, I asked the people who stood about her: "There is surely one among you who understands Egyptian?" One [78]among them said: "I understand (it)." I said to him: "Say to my mistress: 'I have heard as far as Thebes, the abode of Amon, that [79]in every city injustice is done, but that justice is done in the land of Alasa; (but), lo, injustice is done every day here." She said: "Indeed! What is [80]this that thou sayest?" I said to her: "If the sea raged and the wind drove me to the land where I am, [81]thou wilt not let them take ⌜advantage of⌝ me to slay me; I being a messenger of Amon. I am one for whom they will seek [82]unceasingly. As for the crew of the prince of Byblos whom they sought to kill, their lord will surely find [83]ten crews of thine, and he will slay them, on his part." She had the people called and stationed (before her); she said to me: "Pass the night ——."

---

## RECORDS OF THE RESTORATION OF THE ROYAL MUMMIES

**592.** We have already seen (§ 545) that the tombs of Ramses II and Seti I had been broken into in the first year of Ramses X (the nineteenth of Ramses IX). Under Ramses XII, in his sixth year, the High Priest of Amon, Hrihor, sent some of his people to restore the bodies, and to place them again in their coffins and sarcophagi. They left a record of this pious work on the coffins:

*Coffin of Seti I*

593. [a]Year 6, second month of the first season, day 7, day when the vizier, the High Priest of Amon-Re, king of gods, Hrihor, sent [to renew the bur]ial of King Menmare, L. P. H.; Son of Re: Menmare (sic!), L. P. H.; Son of Re: Seti (I)-Merneptah; by the hand of the inspector, Hirmamonpene (*Ḥr-m-Ymn-pnᶜ*), and the officer (*mnḥ*) Perepewyot (*Pꜣ-Rᶜ-pꜣ yw-yt*).

*Coffin of Ramses II*

594. [b]Year 6, third month of the second season, day 15, day when the noble of —— the High Priest of Amon-Re, king of gods, Hrihor, — sent ———.

## LETTER TO THE VICEROY OF KUSH[c]

595. This letter, the content of which is in itself of slight consequence, is important because of the person to whom it is addressed, the viceroy of Kush. Already in the Nineteenth Dynasty the gold-lands of Nubia had passed into the hands of Amon, though they were administered by the viceroy of Kush (III, 640). The next step was the administration of these Nubian gold-lands and the assumption of the office of viceroy of Nubia by the High Priest of Amon. This was done by Hrihor (§ 615), but the following letter shows that he had not yet done so in Ramses XII's seventeenth year, at which time the king still exercises his authority over the viceroy, and sends him after a tardy butler, who needs prodding in the execution of the king's commission to collect building materials, and to finish a shrine.

*Titulary*

596. [1][Horus: Mighty Bull, Beloved of Re; Favorite of the Two Goddesses: Mighty in Strength], Repulsing Hundreds of Thousands;

---

[a]Written with black ink in hieratic on the lid of the coffin; published: Maspero, *Momies royales*, Pls. XI A, XII; p. 553.

[b]Like the preceding; published by Maspero, *Momies royales*, Pl. XI B; 557.

[c]Turin papyrus, Pleyte et Rossi, Pls. 66, 67.

Golden Horus: Great in Strength, Making the Two Lands to Live, [2]Sovereign, L. P. H., Satisfied in Heart, Just, Pleasing the Two Lands; King of Upper and Lower Egypt, Lord of the Two Lands: [3]Menmare-Setepneptah, L. P. H.; Son of Re, Lord of Diadems: Ramses (XII)-Khamwese-Meriamon-Nuterhekon, L. P. H.

### *Introduction*

**597.** [4]Royal command to the king's-son of Kush, king's-scribe of the army, overseer of the granary, Paynehsi, the leader of [5]the archers of Pharaoh, L. P. H.; saying: "This royal command is brought to thee, to wit:

### *The Butler*

**598.** "Go forth ⌜— after⌝ [6]the major-domo, the butler of Pharaoh, L. P. H., and cause him to proceed with the business of Pharaoh, L. P. H., his lord, [7]which he was sent to do, in the southern region. When the writing[a] of Pharaoh, thy lord, reaches thee, [8]thou shalt join thyself to him, to cause that he do the business of Pharaoh, L. P. H., [9]his lord, whereon he was sent."

### *The Shrine*

**599.** "And thou shalt look to this portable shrine of this great goddess, [10]and thou shalt ⌜complete⌝ it, and thou shalt bear it to the ship, and thou shalt have it brought before him to my place of abode."[b]

### *Artisans' Supplies*

**600.** [11]"And thou shalt have brought ⌜for⌝ it khenmet stone, inkhu (*yn-n-ḫw*) stone, ⌜emory⌝ (*ys-m ᵓ -r ᵓ*), flowers of the katha-plant, [12]and many blue flowers, — to my place of abode; in order to fill the hand of [13]the artisans therewith. Do not neglect this business which I send to thee. [14]Behold, I write for thy testimony.[c] It is a letter to inform thee[d] of the king's well-being.

[15]"Year 17, fourth month of the first season, day 15."

---

[a]The present letter.

[b]Tanis?

[c]A formula used to indicate to the recipient that the matter is in writing, to serve as his testimony in case of future misunderstanding.

[d]Among other things.

## BUILDING INSCRIPTIONS IN THE TEMPLE OF KHONSU[a]

**601.** The temple of Khonsu is the only monument in which we can clearly trace the fall of the last Ramessid and the succession of the High Priest of Amon, Hrihor. This transition will be found briefly discussed in connection with Hrihor's inscriptions (§ 608). The dedications occupying the official place on the architraves of the hypostyle are all in the name of Ramses XII, as if he were in full enjoyment of the usual powers of the Pharaoh; while those around the base of the wall in the same hall (§§ 609, 610) contain but the scantiest reference to the king. On the rôle played by the king in the wall scenes in the same hall, see §§ 611–13.

The architrave dedications are as follows:

**602.** [b]Live Horus: . . . . . .[c] Ramses XII; he made (it) as his monument for his father, "Khonsu-in-Thebes-Beautiful-Rest;" which Ramses XII made for him.

[d]Live the Good God, maker of monuments in the house of his father, Khonsu, lord of Thebes, builder of his temple as an eternal work in fine white sandstone, increasing — — — —.[e]

[f]Live Horus: . . . . . . .[c] Ramses XII; he made (it) as his monument for his father, "Khonsu-in-Thebes-Beautiful-Rest," making for him (the hall called) "Wearer-of-Diadems" for the first time, of fine white sandstone, making splendid his temple as a beautiful monument,[g] forever, which the Son of Re, Ramses XII, made for him.

**603.** [h]. . . . . . Ramses XII, mighty king, great in monuments in

[a]Champollion, *Notices descriptives*, II, 233–35; Lepsius, *Denkmäler*, III, 238, *d*, Text, III, 65; Brugsch, *Recueil de monuments*, 59, 3–5.

[b]Architraves on both sides of central aisle of hypostyle, on sides facing aisle.

[c]Partial titulary

[d]Architraves on right of central aisle, side facing small columns.

[e]"Lacune de quelques signes et légende royale du même" (as above).

[f]Architraves over small columns on the right.

[g]Or: "*with beautiful monuments.*"

[h]Begins the same as the preceding.

the house of his father, Khonsu, lord of Thebes, building for him his house, made for the first time as an excellent, eternal work; the great gods are satisfied in heart over his monument, which the Son of Re, Ramses XII, made for him.

[a]Live the Good God, doing benefactions, the monument-builder, plentiful in wonders, whose every design comes to pass ⌜immediately⌝ like his father, Ptah-South-of-His-Wall. He has illuminated Thebes with great monuments ⌜of⌝ the king, which King Ramses XII, beloved of Khonsu, made for him.

[a]Only Brugsch, *Recueil de monuments*, 59, 3.

# THE TWENTY-FIRST DYNASTY

## THE TWENTY-FIRST DYNASTY

**604.** While these volumes are not intended to furnish discussions and reconstructions of the dynasties, the Twenty-first Dynasty is, nevertheless, so unusual in character, that it is impossible to classify the brief and fragmentary documents which it has left us, without some indication of its peculiarities.

**605.** Already under the last Ramessid (before his fifth year) we have seen, in the report of Wenamon, that a local dynast of Tanis, Nesubenebded, had assumed the sovereignty of the Delta. When Ramses XII died and the Twentieth Dynasty was ended, Nesubenebded became king of Lower Egypt, and the founder of the Twenty-first Dynasty of Manetho. At Thebes, the High Priest of Amon, Hrihor, became king of Upper Egypt. Of the Tanite kings we know next to nothing; but we are at least able to follow the high priests at Thebes from generation to generation without a break. They form the only connected thread along which we can trace the course of the dynasty. At Hrihor's death they were not able to maintain their royalty, and Nesubenebded ruled the whole country for a time. Hrihor's grandson, Paynozem I, having, while High Priest, married Makere, the daughter[a] of Pesibkhenno I of Tanis, likewise became sole king for a long reign. Otherwise the Tanites were dominant; but probably not on hostile terms with the high priests, who remained powerful princes, more or less independent, and boasting many of the titles of royalty.

**606.** Possessing only a few names of Tanite kings in northern monuments of their own, we are obliged to turn to Thebes for the materials with which to reconstruct the dynasty. The difficulty with these materials is that they

[a]See Maspero, *Momies royales*, 692–98.

frequently, indeed prevailingly, record royal dates with only the year, omitting the name of the Tanite king to whom the year belongs. From such documents[a] it is now possible to reconstruct the following table of the dynasty.[b] Space and the purpose of these volumes do not permit its discussion here, but some explanations will be found with the inscriptions upon which it is based. An asterisk with a number indicates that the king's name accompanies it in the original document; and the dagger, that the name of the High Priest occurs with it. It will be seen that there are only three dates with both. The numbers show that the Twenty-first Dynasty lasted 134+6$x$ years. As one $x$ is the entire reign of Hrihor (Nesubenebded), we must credit it with not less than 145 years.

**607.**

| PHARAOHS[c] | YEARS | HIGH PRIESTS |
|---|---|---|
| Nesubenebded | | Hrihor (high priest and king)<br>Payonekh (his son) |
| Akheperre-Setepnamon-Pesibkhenno I<br>17 years+$x$ | 6†<br>9†<br>10†<br>13†<br>17† | Paynozem I (his son) |

[a]They will be found, with one exception, in the following translations (§§ 608-92).

[b]The former discussions, as well as an exhaustive treatment of the Twenty-first Dynasty, will be found in Maspero's *Momies royales* (*Mémoires de la mission française au Caire*, I, 640–730). A modification of Maspero's reconstruction was proposed by Petrie, who proved that Hrihor and Siamon were distinct (*Proceedings of the Society of Biblical Archæology*, XVIII, 59, 60). New material found on the priestly mummies discovered in 1891 confirmed this conclusion. This material was published by Daressy (*Revue archéologique*, 28, 75–78), who furnished further modifications of Maspero's reconstruction, but did not employ all the available material. Another modification was proposed by Torr (*Revue archéologique*, 28, 296–98), who added a new High Priest. The above table agrees in the main with Daressy, but employs all the material and adds some corrections. No comparison with the data of Manetho is here necessary, as his account of the dynasty is almost worthless.

[c]The order of these kings is certain, but the connections between them are very loose, so that there is room for an ephemeral king who may be inserted somewhere in the second half (especially between Amenemopet and Siamon or Siamon and Pesibkhenno II), to make up the seven kings given by Manetho in this dynasty.

| PHARAOHS[a] | YEARS | HIGH PRIESTS |
|---|---|---|
| | 7 | Zekhonsefonekh (son of King Paynozem)[b] |
| | 8* | |
| Paynozem I 40 years+$x$ | 16† | Masaheret (son of King Paynozem) |
| | 25ǀ | |
| | 40† | Menkheperre-Pesibkhenno[c] (son of King Paynozem) 48 years+ $x$ |
| | 6† | |
| | 7† | |
| Amenemopet 49 years+$x$ | | Nesubenebded (his son) |
| | 22(?)*† | |
| | 49* | |
| | 1† | |
| | 2† | |
| | 3† | |
| | 5† | |
| | 7*† | Paynozem II (son of Menkheperre) |
| Siamon 16[d] years+$x$ | 8* | |
| | 9† | |
| | 10† | |
| | 13[e] | |
| | 14*†[f] | |
| | 16† | |

[a]See note c, p. 296.

[b]Noticed by Mr. Cecil Torr on a now missing coffin, on which the deceased calls himself: "son of the High Priest Zekhonsefonekh, son of King Paynozem" (*Revue archéologique*, 1896, 28, 298). His position above is not quite certain, but as we do not know who was High Priest in Paynozem I's seventh and eighth years, he may well fall in that gap.

[c]As Torr (*Revue archéologique*, 1896, 28, 296 ff.) has noticed, Paynozem II as High Priest under King Amenemopet calls himself in several places both son of the High Priest Menkheperre and son of King Pesibkhenno, showing that both the latter names belong to the same man. As Menkheperre occurs in a cartouche, e. g. (*Revue archéologique*, 28, 75), and likewise Pesibkhenno in a cartouche is once called High Priest, there is no doubt that Torr is correct in supposing that Menkheperre is the prenomen of Pesibkhenno. He thus assumed royal honors, and may possibly have ruled for a while alone. As he would not assume the throne-name till he had gained the throne, that is, until after Paynozem I's death, the High Priest Pesibkhenno whom we find in a fourth and twelfth year must be a different man. Hence I cannot agree with Torr that this Pesibkhenno is the same as Menkheperre, whose father regularly has the cartouche, while this Pesibkhenno is called simply son of Paynozem (without cartouche).

[d]A graffito at Karnak records year 17 of a king Siamon who may be our above king (*Recueil*, 22, 51 ff., No. 3 B).

[e]Maspero, *Momies royales*, 725.

[f]*Recueil*, 22, 61, No. 33; a graffito at Karnak; the king's name is almost broken away. It began with Amon, and, as it can hardly be Amenemopet, it must be Siamon.

| PHARAOHS[a] | YEARS | HIGH PRIESTS |
|---|---|---|
| Pesibkhenno II[b]<br>12 years + $x$ | 4†<br>5<br>10<br>12† | Pesibkhenno (his son) |
| TWENTY-SECOND DYNASTY | | |
| Reign of Sheshonk I | 5*†<br>10*†<br>11*†<br>etc. | Yewepet (son of Sheshonk I) |

The following inscriptions are arranged, for the most part, under the High Priest in whose term of office they fall, as this is, in the majority of cases, stated in the document.

[a]See note c, p. 296.

[b]Menkheperre-Pesibkhenno may never have governed all Egypt; hence I do not put him in the Pharaonic line, but number the last Pesibkhenno as II. Manetho is our only evidence for his position here.

## REIGN OF HRIHOR

### INSCRIPTIONS OF THE TEMPLE OF KHONSU

**608.** The inscriptions and reliefs in the temple of Khonsu at Karnak form the chief source for tracing the rise of Hrihor as High Priest of Amon, until his usurpation of the kingship, and they clearly establish the early contentions of Rougé,[a] so ably supplemented by Maspero,[b] as against those of Lepsius, regarding the close of the Twentieth and the beginning of the Twenty-first Dynasty. The adytum and rearmost chambers of the temple were built by Ramses III and his immediate successors (§§ 214, 472). The hypostyle, the court before it, and the pylon were the work of Ramses XII and Hrihor, the hypostyle having been built by them both in common, and the court and pylon by Hrihor alone. Hence, in passing from the hypostyle outward to the court, the political change can be traced on the walls as one goes. We have seen the dedications of Ramses XII on the architraves of the hypostyle (§§ 601–3). The dedications around the base of the wall, however, as well as the scenes in the same hall, show the dominant position held by Hrihor and the subordinate rôle played by the king.

*Dedication*[c]

**609.** High Priest of Amon-Re, king of gods, commander in chief of the armies of South and North, the leader, Hrihor, triumphant; he made it as his monument for "House-of-Khonsu-in-Thebes-Beautiful-Rest;"

[a] *Etude sur une stèle égyptienne appartenant à la Bibliothèque impériale*, 195–202.

[b] *Momies royales*, 646 ff.

[c] Occupies the base of the wall (inside), and evidently extends around the right side of the hypostyle, from the door in front to the door in the rear; published by Maspero, *Zeitschrift für ägyptische Sprache*, 1883, 76–77; and again, *Momies royales*, 652.

making for him a temple for the first time[a] in the likeness of the horizon of heaven, extending his temple as an eternal work, enlarging his monument (more than) before.[b] He increased the daily offerings, he doubled that which was before, while the gods of Thebes are possessed of joy, and the great house is in festival, the house of Khonsu, (⌈because⌉) he repeated the august things, being great and beautiful monuments ——— Lord of the Two Lands: Menmare-Setepneptah; Lord of Diadems: Ramses (XII)-Khamwese-Mereramon-Nuterhekon, given life. Lo, the desire of his majesty was to enlarge the house of his father, "House-of-Khonsu-in-Thebes-Beautiful-Rest," in order that his shrine might be covered, by doing benefactions for his ka; that[c] which the Son of Re, Ramses XII, beloved of Khonsu, made for him.

### *Dedication*[d]

**610.** High Priest of Amon-Re, king of gods, Hrihor, triumphant. He made (it) as his monument for "House-of-Khonsu-in-Thebes-Beautiful-Rest;" making for him (the hall called): "Wearer-of-Diadems," for the first time, of fine white sandstone, exalting his Great Place, with electrum, adorned with every splendid costly stone, enlarging his house forever with labor, making it to be like the horizon of the great gods at the feast when he appears born again; an august [house] of fine gold and every genuine costly stone, like the [⌈horizon of⌉] Re when he is born again. — — many offering-tables of silver and gold, in order to satisfy thy ka, every day.

### *Scene*[e]

**611.** The great barque or sacred shrine[f] of Amon is borne by the priests into the temple of Khonsu (as the inscriptions

[a]Or merely "*anew*"? [b]Or: "*which was before.*"

[c]The antecedent is the building (understood), as commonly.

[d]In the hypostyle, around the base of the wall of the left side, being the pendant of the preceding. It is published by Rougé, *Inscriptions hiéroglyphiques*, 204; see also Maspero, *Momies royales*, 652 (where Rougé's publication is, however, not referred to).

[e]In hypostyle (Lepsius E) immediately behind court, at right of door *h* below; published, without reliefs, by Champollion, *Notices descriptives*, II, 230, 231; Maspero, *Zeitschrift für ägyptische Sprache*, 1883, 75, 76; and again, *Momies royales*, 651.

[f]It is followed by two others, doubtless those of Mut and Khonsu; the same is true of the following scene.

show). Walking backward before it, the High Priest Hrihor offers incense to it. The inscriptions are significant:

*General*

It is the procession of Amon-Re, king of gods, lord of —, to the "House-of-Khonsu-in-Thebes-Beautiful-Rest," to behold the beauty of his son (Khonsu).

*Over Hrihor*

Offering incense before this god, [Amon-Re], king of gods, by the companion, [⌜who presents⌝] the Two Lands to the lord of gods, the High Priest of [Amon-Re], king of gods, Hrihor, triumphant.

*Over Amon*

Utterance of Amon . . . . .:[a] O my son, Lord of the Two Lands: Menmare-Setepneptah (Ramses XII), I have seen this beautiful, pure and excellent monument which thou hast made for me; the reward thereof is all life and prosperity, all health, like Re, forever.

*Scene*[b]

**612.** The same sacred barque has been deposited upon its base, doubtless in the temple court. Hrihor offers incense and a libation before it. The accompanying inscriptions are:

*Over Hrihor*

Offering of incense and a libation to Amon . . . . . ,[a] that thou (sic!) mayest grant long life, beholding thy ⌜—⌝, and a good old age in thy city, Thebes; by the hereditary prince, over the Two Lands, great noble[c] in the whole land, High Priest of Amon-Re, king of gods, commander in chief of the army of the North and South, the leader, Hrihor, triumphant.

---

[a]Titles of the god.

[b]On the left of the door *h*, as pendant to the preceding scene; published *Zeitschrift für ägyptische Sprache*, 1883, 76; and *Momies royales*, 651.

[c]Possibly: "*companion* (*smr*), *great noble* (*wr* ᶜ ᵓ);" the last being the designation common in the Twenty-second Dynasty.

*Over Amon*

Utterance of Amon . . . . : O my son, of my body, my beloved, Menmare-Setepneptah (Ramses XII), my heart is glad, rejoicing — [in] thy monument, etc. . . . . . .

613. In other scenes which follow, Hrihor officiates while the name of Ramses XII appears behind him. The High Priest thus performs the official religious functions in which hitherto only the Pharaoh has been portrayed on temple walls, while the name of the Pharaoh, and the promises of the god to him, usual on such occasions, are still inserted.

614. The door leading out from this hypostyle to the court in front shows the power of Hrihor still increasing; he has become overseer of the granaries, the source of Egypt's greatest wealth, and viceroy of Kush. These titles appear side by side beneath the name of Ramses XII, in a date (unfortunately now lost) at the head of a very interesting, but fragmentary, inscription which narrated a prodigy in favor of Hrihor, doubtless connected with his advance in power. He appeared before Khonsu with a petition for "*life, prosperity, health, and many good things*," the blessings usually desired; but it is evident that some great event in Hrihor's favor was to take place within a year; though it is not clear what that event was. Khonsu's approval was expressed by numerous nods of the god's head, and news of this was taken to Amon, who also nodded violently in approval, adding the audible promise that he assured Hrihor twenty years, meaning, of course, twenty years more of power; but whether as king or High Priest is not stated in the scanty fragments preserved. However, it is highly probable that this is the narrative of the divine oracle declaring Hrihor king. In any case, he was very anxious to make the whole event a matter of record, and immediately secured Amon's approval of recording the prodigy "*upon stone*." The place

where the incident is recorded on the door, between the portion of the temple erected by Hrihor in conjunction with Ramses XII, and the court erected by Hrihor alone, suggests that in it we have the divine sanction of the transition which takes place at that point. The record[a] is as follows:

*Date*

**615.** 1——— Ramses XII,[b] beloved of Amon-Re, king of gods, given life forever.

*Hrihor before Khonsu*

2——— High Priest of Amon-Re, king of gods, king's-son of Kush,[c] overseer of the granaries 3———. Then the High Priest of Amon-Re, king of gods, repeated to him: 4"——— [Thebes], thy city." Then the god nodded with his head. 5"——— of Thebes, thy city." Then the god nodded — 6——— 7"——— 8honor to me, life, prosperity, health, and many good things in Thebes, thy city 9——— which thou givest, and thou shalt give them to me." Then nodded the 10[god] ——— within a year, the space that thou givest to me; those who are in 11——— within the year which thou givest me, which thou spendest to give them to me, besides the — 12——— Hrihor ([*Ḥry*]-*Ḥr*), triumphant.

*Amon's Confirmation*

**616.** The city went forth as messengers ⌜to⌝ him to tell that which Khonsu said 13——— [Amon-Re], king of gods, turning his face northward to Karnak. Then he arrived at the — 14——— Amon-

[a]Brugsch, *Recueil de monuments*, Pl. XXI; Lepsius, *Denkmäler*, III, 248, *b;* see also Text, III, 64. Lepsius, *Denkmäler*, is hardly readable; Brugsch is much better. See also Maspero, *Momies royales*, 671. The inscription is on the doorpost of the door leading from Hrihor's court to the hypostyle; it is marked *g* in Lepsius' plan (Text). Only the ends of twenty-eight horizontal lines are preserved.

[b]So read by Brugsch, by Lepsius (Text) and by Maspero (*Momies royales*, 671).

[c]There is not the slightest doubt that these titles belonged to Hrihor. He is the only High Priest of Amon known under Ramses XII, and his name occurs in this inscription below as the chief actor. From now on, the high priests during their ascendancy, are also viceroys of Kush; see, among other examples, a statue recently found by Legrain at Karnak (*Annales*, IV, 9). We are therefore to supply the name of Hrihor in the above lacunæ following the titles.

Re, king of gods, the ⌜father⌝ — — [15]——— [Then the god nodded his head] exceedingly, exceedingly, saying: "⌜A space⌝ of 20 years is [⌜that which⌝] Amon-Re, king of gods, [⌜gives⌝] to thee [16]——— [⌜because of⌝] the good deeds which thou hast done for Mut, Khonsu, and ⌜her⌝ children formerly [17]———."

*Record of the Prodigy*

**617.** Then the High Priest of Amon-Re, king of gods, Hrihor, triumphant, repeated it to him, saying: "O my good lord [18]——— [⌜Shall we record⌝ these] marvels upon stone?" The god nodded (his) head exceedingly, exceedingly. Then repeated to him [19][the High Priest of Amon-Re, king of gods, Hrihor, saying]: "——— [Khonsu-in-Thebes]-Beautiful-Rest, thy saying; grant that they make a stela— [20]——— [Khonsu-in]-Thebes-Beautiful-Rest, which he made." The god nodded (his) head exceedingly, exceedingly.

*Hrihor's Gratitude*

**618.** [21]——— eternity shall come to thee, and millions of years shall be in — — [22]——— generations shall come to talk of these marvels of — [23]——— generations, ⌜c[hildren⌝] shall make — [24]——— the words ⌜which⌝ came, ⌜shall be⌝ [25]——— [⌜which⌝] thou sayest to me, that givest to me the space[a] of twenty years [26]———." [The god] nodded (his) head exceedingly, exceedingly — — — [27]———. Then Hrihor gave [⌜command to erect this stela⌝] — — — — [28]——— in putting it, a copy — — — —.

**619.** With the outer court, then, begins the sole rule of Hrihor, the divine approval of which is doubtless narrated in the preceding document, recorded on the door where we leave Ramses XII behind. Here only Hrihor's name appears, and here he only is the recipient of the blessings of the gods, which up to this time, and in the hypostyle behind, were always accorded the Pharaoh alone. Hence in the relief scenes in the court, Khonsu addresses Hrihor thus:[b]

---

[a]Read *ᶜḥᶜ*, as in l. 10.

[b]Maspero, *Momies royales*, 653.

**620.** "I give to thee very many jubilees, like thy father, Re; I give to thee every land together; while the Nine Bows fall down to thy power."

Utterance of "Khonsu-in-Thebes-Beautiful-Rest:" "O my son, my beloved, Lord of the Two Lands, Siamon-[a]Hrihor; how beautiful is this beautiful, pure, and excellent monument which thou hast made for me! My heart is satisfied in seeing them (sic!), and I give to thee reward for them, even life, stability, satisfaction, and the kingdom of the Two Lands in peace, like Re."

**621.** As king, therefore, Hrihor built the forecourt and the pylon before it, as is amply borne out by the following dedications on the architraves and the pylon, giving him the full Pharaonic titulary. In this he boldly published his real office, putting the title "*High Priest of Amon*" into the first cartouche, as if it were his given name, before he gained the throne.

**622.** [b][1]Live Horus: Mighty Bull, Son of Amon, Maker of Monuments, Establishing for Him Who Begat Him, King of Upper and Lower Egypt, Great Ruler of Egypt, Lord of the Two Lands: High Priest of Amon. He made (it) as his monument for his father, Amon-Re, king of gods, making for him a colonnade, for the first time; it is made like the beauty of the horizon; all people are in joy at seeing it, the lord[c] of silver and mistress[c] of gold, comprehending[c] every splendid, costly stone; the deed of a son in love of him who [placed] him on his throne, giving to him eternity as King of the Two Lands, King of Upper and Lower Egypt, Lord of the Two Lands: High Priest of Amon, beloved of Amon-Re, king of gods, lord of heaven, ruler of the gods; that he might be given life forever.

**623.** [2]Live the Favorite of the Two Goddesses: Satisfying the Gods, Building their House, Furnishing the Satisfaction of their ka's; Son of Re, Amiable Lord of the Palace, Lord of Diadems: Siamon-Hrihor,[d] divine seed of the lord of gods, his splendid emanation, whom

---

[a]"*Son of Amon;*" both the names are now inclosed in a cartouche.

[b]Court, architrave over western colonnade; Lepsius, *Denkmäler*, III, 243, *a* = Champollion, *Notices descriptives*, II, 222, 223.

[c]Epithets of the temple.

[d]In cartouche.

Mut bore to be ruler of the circuit of the sun. All lands are under his authority, doing that which his ka wills. The chiefs of Retenu do obeisance to his fame every day, while he sits upon the Horus-throne, which all the living magnify for him, the Son of Re, of His Body, Lord of Diadems: Siamon-Hrihor, beloved of Mut the great, mistress of Ishru; given life like Re.

**624.** [3]Live Golden Horus: Doing Benefactions in Karnak for his father, Amon, Creator of his Beauty, King of Upper and Lower Egypt, Beloved of the Great Divine Ennead, Lord of the Two Lands: High Priest of Amon; king amiable, like Re, making festive Karnak, protecting it for the gods, setting the lords of Thebes to rejoicing, their hearts glad, when they see the "House-of-Khonsu-in-Thebes-Beautiful-Rest," like the horizon in heaven. All people, they praise its beauty, they acclaim [to] heaven. King of Upper and Lower Egypt, Beloved, Lord of the Two Lands: High Priest of Amon, beloved of Khonsu-Re; that he may be given life.

**625.** [a][1]...... He made (it) as his monument for his father, Amon-Re, king of gods, making for him a broad-hall (called): "Hall-of-the-High-Priest-of-Amon,-Siamon-Hrihor,-Great-in-Love-in-the-House-of-Khonsu;" for the first time, of fine white sandstone, as [a work] of eternity by the hand of Ptah, who furnished the plan.

### *Scene*[b]

**626.** Relief represents the pylon of the Khonsu-temple, with four flagstaves on either side of the portal. The inscriptions under the architrave and beside the flagstaves, though fragmentary, show the name of Hrihor.[c] Above the pylon is the following:

---

[a]First court, eastern architrave. Three lines corresponding to the triple dedication on the western architrave, translated above (§§ 622–24). The titles at the beginning of the line I have omitted; also the other two lines which add nothing. Published by Champollion, *Notices descriptives*, II, 223 (partially); Lepsius, *Denkmäler*, III, 244, *a;* Text, III, 61.

[b]In the court, right (east) colonnade; Lepsius, *Denkmäler*, III, 243, *b;* Text, III, 61.

[c]These are the dedications in the usual form taken from the actual pylon, Lepsius, *Denkmäler*, III, 248, *i*, *h*.

### *Inscription*[a]

Horus: Mighty Bull, Son of Amon, King of Upper and Lower Egypt, Lord of the Two Lands: [b]High Priest of Amon;[b] Son of Re, of his Body: [b]Siamon-Hrihor.[b] He made (it) as his monument for his father, Amon-Re, king of gods, restoring for him, and making Thebes to shine anew (for him), whose name is hidden in ⌈—⌉, establishing for him the "House-of-Khonsu-in-Thebes-Beautiful-Rest," for eternity.

---

[a]Lepsius, *Denkmäler*, III, 243, *b;* Champollion, *Notices descriptives*, II, 226.

[b]In cartouche.

## REIGN OF NESUBENEBDED

### GEBELÊN INSCRIPTION[a]

**627.** This, the only surviving inscription of King Nesubenebded (Smendes), the founder of the Twenty-first Dynasty, narrates some catastrophe at Thebes, due to the partial collapse of a wall around the Luxor temple, built by Thutmose III. Exactly what happened is not, however, certain. The king sent his officials with 3,000 men to the quarry at Gebelên, to secure stone for repairing the damage, and one reference (l. 16) may indicate that the king himself finally came.

The document shows that Nesubenebded ruled at Thebes, and, of course, controlled all Egypt. Hrihor must, therefore, have died before the close of Nesubenebded's reign.

**628.** [b]Lo, his majesty was in the city of Memphis, his august residence of might and victory, like Re ——— [Ptah], [4]lord of "Life-of-the-Two-Lands," Sekhmet the great, beloved of Ptah, — —, Montu and the great gods residing in Memphis. Lo, his majesty sat, in the hall [⌈of his palace, when there came messengers, informing⌉] [5]his majesty, that the canal-wall, forming the limits of Luxor, which King Menkheperre (Thutmose III) had built, had begun [to fall to ruin] ——— [6]forming a great flood, and a powerful ⌈current⌉ therein, on the great ⌈pavement⌉ of the house of the temple. It encircled ⌈the front⌉ ——— [Said his majesty] [7]to them: "As for this matter reported to me, there has been nothing in the time of my majesty from of old, like it. . . . . ."

---

[a]Engraved on a pillar in the quarry at Gebelên; over one-third of a line is lost at the beginning of each line; published by Daressy, *Recueil*, X, 136, 137. The portion preserved is often so uncertain, and has been so inaccurately published, that some omissions have been necessary.

[b]I have omitted the titulary.

**629.** His majesty [⌜dispatched master-build⌝]⁹ers, and 3,000 men with them, of the choicest of the people of his majesty. The command of his majesty to them: "Hasten to ——— [10]the mountain — people[a] of his majesty as the companions of (his) feet ⌜— — —⌝ ——— [12]⌜—⌝ — ⌜— —⌝ this quarry, from the time of the ancestors to the present day, Gebelên ——— [13]. . . . . ."

**630.** They engraved this decree, which perpetuates his majesty [forever] ——— [14]. . . . . . . His command arrived to beautify the work on the stela . . . . . . [Never] [16]was done the like of it in the time of the ancestors. Lo, his majesty passed by, in excellent virtues like Thoth ——— [17]. . . . . . The reward therefor is might and victory, and to appear upon the Horus-throne [of the living, forever] ———.

---

[a]*Ḫnty*, evidently the same class as are mentioned in the Paynozem II inscription (§ 671, l. 8).

# REIGN OF THE HIGH PRIEST AND KING PAYNOZEM I

## I. Paynozem I as High Priest

### BUILDING INSCRIPTIONS

631. On Hrihor's death his family were unable to maintain their royalty. His eldest son, Payonekh, followed him as High Priest of Amon, but evidently died soon after gaining the office. Hrihor's second son, Paynozem, succeeded to the high priesthood, but, as we have said, not immediately to the throne. He continued the unfinished portions of the Khonsu-temple, especially the pylon of his father, as recorded in the following building inscriptions:

632. [a]Live the High Priest of Amon-Re, king of gods, lord of offering, Paynozem, triumphant, son of the High Priest of Amon. . . . . . Payonekh, triumphant. He made (it) as his monument for his father, "Khonsu-in-Thebes-Beautiful-Rest," making for him a great and august pylon, over against his temple. The great flagstaves approach heaven, their [tops] are of electrum; all people rejoice when they see (it). . . . . .

[b]. . . . . . . making for him a very great pylon anew, in the likeness of his horizon in heaven. The great gods are possessed of joy and satisfaction of heart, because of what he has made in the great house. They give millions of years of satisfying life, to the High Priest, etc. . . .[c]

[d]Live, the Horus: Mighty Bull, Son of Amon; King of Upper and Lower Egypt, Satisfying the Gods, Doing Benefactions for their ka's;

---

[a]Pylon; Lepsius, *Denkmäler*, III, 251, *a;* another broken dedication on the pylon (Champollion, *Notices descriptives*, II, 220; Lepsius, *Denkmäler*, III, 248, *i*=Text, III, 57) also attributes it to him.

[b]As in the preceding; it is also on the pylon; Lepsius, *Denkmäler*, III, 251, *b;* Champollion, *Notices descriptives*, II, 215, 216.

[c]Usual name and parentage.

[d]On door of first pylon, Brugsch, *Recueil de monuments*, Pl. 57, 2.

High Priest of Amon-Re, king of gods, Paynozem, triumphant, son of Payonekh, triumphant. He made (it) as his monument for his father, Khonsu, making for him a pylon anew. ———

*Scene*[a]

633. A priest stands before Amon, presenting flowers. The inscriptions are these:

*Over Priest*

Presentation of all beautiful flowers by [the High Priest] of Amon-Re, king of gods, doing benefactions — — —, Paynozem, triumphant, son of the High Priest of Amon, Payonekh, triumphant; doing the pleasure of his ka, building [the temples] of all gods, fashioning (statues of) their majesties of ⌜electrum⌝; he supplies their offerings ———.

*Over Amon*

Utterance of Amon . . . . . "O my son, of my body, my beloved, Lord of the Two Lands, Paynozem,[b] triumphant, I have seen the monuments which thou hast made for me; my heart is satisfied because of them. Thou makest festive my house anew, thou buildest a ⌜dwelling⌝ of electrum, thou increasest the daily offering, thou multipliest that which was formerly. The reward therefore is the satisfying life of Horus."

634. Paynozem also restored the Eighteenth Dynasty temple of Medinet Habu, and left the following record of his work there:

[c]Live, the Good God, son of Amon, who came forth from his loins, to equip the Two Lands, whom Mut nourished, to fashion (statues of) the gods, to build their adyta; doing benefactions for all the gods of Thebes; while they are satisfied in heart [because of][d] what he has

---

[a]Entrance of pylon, Khonsu-temple; Lepsius, *Denkmäler*, III, 250, *a*. Behind Amon are Mut and Khonsu, and a figure of the "*divine votress Makere,*" inserted by Queen Henttowe.

[b]Not in cartouche.

[c]East side of Eighteenth Dynasty Medinet Habu temple, under similar restoration record of Ramses III; Lepsius, *Denkmäler*, III, 251, *e-g;* better, Text, III, 164.

[d]The preposition (*ḥr*) has dropped out; see Lepsius, *Denkmäler*, III, 251, *b*, for the same phrase.

done, and their hearts are glad; High Priest of Amon-Re, king of gods, governor of the city, vizier, commander of the army,[a] satisfying ⌜—⌝, Paynozem, triumphant, son of the High Priest of Amon . . . . . Payonekh, triumphant. He restored the monument of his father, "Amon-Re-of-the-Splendid-Throne," when he came to see the house of his father, and found it beginning to fall to ruin ———in order to restore his temple and his wall anew, in order to satisfy the heart of all the gods and goddesses, in order to shelter —— the divine — of the region of Themet (*Ṯ ᵓ -mw ͑ t*),[b] in order to cause the palace to be like the horizon of heaven. . . . . . .[c]

635. To work in Karnak he refers vaguely in the following record, repeated on the rams of Ramses II:

[d]High Priest of Amon-Re, king of gods, lord of offering, Paynozem, triumphant, son of Payonekh, triumphant; he says: "I am great in monuments and mighty in marvels in Karnak, victorious lord. I have enlarged monuments greater than (for) any gods. I made for him very great monuments in silver and gold, engraved with my name forever."

## RECORDS ON THE ROYAL MUMMIES

636. As High Priest Paynozem gave much attention to the restoration and preservation of the violated royal mummies. His successive efforts to this end are recorded on the coffins and wrappings. These records are all dated, and such dates, while not mentioning the name of the king, evidently belong to the reign of Pesibkhenno I, the successor of Nesubenebded in Tanis. Of these, perhaps, the most important is the note of the year 17, recording the transfer of Ramses II's body to the tomb of Seti I.

---

[a]Another short inscription near by (Lepsius, *Denkmäler*, III, 251, *d*) contains only the usual restoration formula, but it gives him the title: "*Commander in chief of the armies of the South and North.*"

[b]Name of Medinet Habu region; Coptic, Dshēme.

[c]Here follows a prayer of no historical content.

[d]On the rams of Ramses II connecting the front of the Karnak temple with the river; *Recueil*, XIV, 30.

### *Mummy of Thutmose II*

**637.** [a]Year 6, third month of the second season, day 7. On this day, the High Priest of Amon-Re, king of gods, Paynozem, son of the High Priest of Amon, Payonekh, sent the chief overseer of the White House, Payneferhir, to reinter King Okhepernere (ᶜᵓ-[*ḫpr*]-*n*-*R*ᶜ,[b] Thutmose II).

### *Mummy of Amenhotep I*

**638.** [c]Year 6, fourth month of the second season, day 5. On this day the High Priest of Amon-Re, king of gods, Paynozem, son of the High Priest of Amon, Paynozem,[d] son of Payonekh, sent to reinter[e] King Zeserkere, Son of Re, Amenhotep (I), L. P. H., by the hand of the overseer of the treasury, Pay————.

### *Mummy of Seti I*

**639.** [f]Linen, which the High Priest of Amon-Re, king of gods, Paynozem, triumphant, son of Payonekh, triumphant, made for his father, Khonsu, in the year 10.

### *Mummy of Ramses III*

**640.** [g]Year 13, second month of the third season, day 27. On this day the High Priest of Amon-Re, king of gods, Paynozem, son of the High Priest of Amon, Payonekh, sent: the scribe of the temple, Zosersukhonsu, and the scribe in the Theban necropolis, Butehamon, to give a place to King Usermare-Meriamon (Ramses III), L. P. H., established and abiding forever.

### *Mummy of Ramses III*

[g]High priest of Amon-Re, king of gods, Paynozem, triumphant, son of Payonekh, triumphant [made] (it) for his father, Amon, in the year 9.

---

[a]On the breast of the mummy; Maspero, *Momies royales*, 545, 546.

[b]The scribe in his hasty note has omitted the *ḫpr*-sign.

[c]On the breast of the mummy; *op. cit.*, 536.

[d]This is a dittography, as shown by the preceding docket, which records similar work by the same official about a month earlier under Paynozem, son of Payonekh.

[e]Lit., "*to repeat the burial of.*"

[f]On inner wrappings renewed by Twenty-first Dynasty; *op. cit.*, 555. The date, year 10, when this linen was made, is of course not necessarily the year when it was used.

[g]On the wrappings; *op. cit.*, 564.

*Mummy of Ramses III*

**641.** [a]The — matron, singer of Amon-Re, king of gods, Fetonemut (*F*ꜣ*t-*ꜥꜣ*t-nt-Mwt*), triumphant, daughter of the High Priest of Amon, Payonekh, triumphant, made and brought (it) for her lord, "Amon-Possessed-of-Eternity,"[b] residing in the temple; in order to crave life, prosperity and health from him.

*Mummy of Ramses II*

**642.** [c]Year 17, third month of the second season, day 6, day of bringing Osiris, King Usermare-Setepnere (Ramses II), L. P. H., to bury him again, (in) the tomb of Osiris, King Menmare-Seti (I), L. P. H.: by the High Priest of Amon, Paynozem.

## II. Paynozem I as King

**643.** On succeeding Pesibkhenno I as king, Paynozem I continued his pious works in the royal necropolis. The dates accompanying the records now refer to the reign of Paynozem I himself; and in the year 16 the care of the necropolis was assumed by his son, Masaheret, then High Priest of Amon.

*Mummy of Sitkamose*

**644.** [d]Year 7, fourth month of the first season, day 8. On this day a place was given to the king's-daughter, great king's-wife, Ahmose-Sitkamose, who liveth.

*Mummy of Ahmose I*

**645.** [e]Year 8, third month of the second season, day 29. The majesty of the King of Upper and Lower Egypt, Lord of the Two Lands, Kheperkhare-Setepnamon, Paynozem-Meriamon, L. P. H., sent to give a place to King Nebpehtire (Ahmose I).

---

[a]On the wrappings; *op. cit.*, 565.

[b]This is evidently the temple of Medinet Habu (see its name, §§ 5 ff.); it was the Amon of Ramses III's temple whom she thought to propitiate by making the shroud for Ramses III. He himself is also shown on the wrappings offering to the same god.

[c]On one of the bandages near the outside; *op. cit.*, 560.

[d]On the breast of the mummy; *op. cit.*, 541; probably by the same hand as the next record on wrappings of Ahmose I (*op. cit.*, 534) from year 8 of Paynozem I.

[e]Across the breast of the mummy; *op. cit.*, 534.

*Mummy of King's-Son, Siamon*

**646.** [a]Year 8, month 3, of the second season, day 29. His majesty, L. P. H., sent to give a place to the king's-son, Siamon.

*Mummy of Amenhotep I*

**647.** [b]Year 16, fourth month of the second season, day 11. The High Priest of Amon-Re, king of gods, Masaheret, son of King Paynozem, L. P. H., sent to reinter this god, by the hand of the scribe of the White House, scribe of the temple, Penamon, son of Sutimose.

---

## BUILDING INSCRIPTIONS

**648.** Paynozem I, as king, continued in the Khonsu-temple at Karnak the works which he had begun as High Priest, although only one record of them is preserved. His queen, Henttowe, also left a record of the removal of older sculptured rams to the Khonsu-temple.

**649.** [c]——— temple anew of fine white sandstone, as an excellent eternal work, even that which a son does who does benefactions for his father, who placed him upon his throne; King of Upper and Lower Egypt: Kheperkhare-Setepnamon;[d] Son of Re, of his body, his beloved: Paynozem-Meriamon.[d]

[e]Mistress of the Two Lands, Henttowe; she made (it) as her monument for her mother, Mut, when the King of Upper and Lower Egypt, Kheperkhare-Setepnamon, brought the rams to the house of Amon.

---

[a]*Op. cit.*, 538.

[b]On the breast of the mummy; *op. cit.*, 536, 537.

[c]Frieze outside west wall: Champollion, *Notices descriptives*, II, 230, 231; Lepsius, *Denkmäler*, III, 251, *c*.

[d]In cartouche.

[e]On the back of a sphinx belonging to Amenhotep III (according to Champollion, *Notices descriptives*, II, 263, 264, "léontocèphales") in the Khonsu-temple; published by Champollion, *Notices descriptives*, II, 264; Lepsius, *Denkmäler*, III, 249 f.; Maspero, *Momies royales*, 687.

# HIGH PRIESTHOOD OF MENKHEPERRE

## STELA[a] OF THE BANISHMENT

650. Masaheret, Paynozem I's son, whom we find restoring the royal mummies as High Priest of Amon, in his father's sixteenth year (§ 647), must have died before the king's twenty-fifth year, when, according to our present document, the king's son, Menkheperre, was High Priest of Amon. Another son of Paynozem I, Zekhonsefonekh, must have held the high priesthood, and died also before the twenty-fifth year. But it is yet impossible to determine certainly the order of these two sons.

We find Menkheperre coming from the north, supposedly from Tanis, to Thebes in Paynozem I's twenty-fifth year, and the remarkable errand which brought him thither is intentionally narrated in such veiled language that it is impossible to determine exactly what its nature was. He came to put down certain unknown enemies, and to restore affairs in Thebes to their ancient status (ll. 6 and 7). This probably indicates a rising of some sort among the Thebans. When this had been quelled Menkheperre appeared before Amon, and with the usual prodigies, customary, at least since the time of Hrihor, he secured an oracle from the god permitting the return to Egypt of all those who had been banished to the Southern Oasis. Furthermore, he also obtained the god's consent to a decree forever forbidding

[a]The Maunier stela, now in the Louvre; I was unable to secure the number. It is a black granite stela, very difficult to read; published by Brugsch, *Recueil de monuments*, I, Pl. XXII, 39 f.; and again, *Reise nach der Grossen Oase*, Pl. XXII (much better). I had my own copy made from the original, which I then collated with a squeeze.

such banishment in the future, and our stela is the permanent record of that decree. The interview with Amon closed with the god's consent that all murderers should be slain.

651. The interesting question as to the identity of the banished, who are thus pardoned, is one on which our document is studiously silent. Were they Thebans, on whose behalf the city had risen in insurrection (ll. 6 and 7)? And were they recalled to appease and quiet the turbulent city? And is the last grim enactment of the god a reminder to the violent of what they might expect in case of further insurrection?

*Date and Introduction*

652. Year 25, third month of the third season, day 29, corresponding to the feast of Amon-Re, king of gods, at his [beautiful] feast[a] ————.

———— [2]Nesuhor[b] in their increase thereof. The majesty of this august god was ———— [3]Thebes. Then he took (his) way to the scribes, inspectors, people ————.

*Departure for Thebes*

[4]Year 25, first month of the — [season, day] —. ⌈Then spake his majesty⌉ to the people: "Amon-[Re], lord of Thebes ———— [5]their heart is firm — — — their multitude —— the High Priest of Amon-Re, king of gods, commander in chief of the army, Menkheperre,[c] triumphant, son of King Paynozem-Meriamon ———— [6]his — — — — companion of his footsteps, while their hearts rejoiced because he had

[a]This cannot be the Feast of Opet, as restored by Brugsch (*Geschichte*, 645), for that feast took place in the second month. About two-thirds of a line are lost here, and the same is true of ll. 2-4.

[b]This man's connection with the events narrated is entirely obscure.

[c]This is the first mention of Menkheperre in the inscription, and he here bears his title of High Priest. Hence there seems to me no support for the supposition that he was nominated as High Priest on this visit to Thebes.

desired to come to the South in might and victory, in order to make satisfied the heart of the land, and to expel his enemies, that he might give ——— ⌈as] [7]they were in the time of Re.

### *Arrival at Thebes*

**653.** He arrived at the city (Thebes) with a glad heart; the youth of Thebes received him, making jubilee, with an embassy before him. The majesty of this august god, lord of gods, Amon-Re, [lord of] Thebes, appeared (in procession) — — — [8]that he might ⌈—⌉ him very greatly, very greatly, and establish him upon the throne of his father, as High Priest of Amon-Re, king of gods, commander in chief of the armies of the South and North. He (the god) decreed to him many gracious wonders, (such as) had never been seen since the time of Re.

### *New Year's Feast*

**654.** [⌈Now, after⌉] [9]the fourth month of the third season, on the fifth[a] day of the (feast), "Birth of Isis," corresponding to the feast of Amon at the New Year, the majesty of this august god, lord of gods, Amon-Re, king of gods, appeared (in procession), came to the great halls of the house of Amon, and rested before the ⌈inclosure wall⌉[b] of Amon. [10]The High Priest of Amon-Re, king of gods, commander in chief of the army, Menkheperre, triumphant, went to him and praised him exceedingly, exceedingly, many times, and he founded [⌈for him⌉] his offering, even [⌈every] good thing⌉.

### *Recall of the Banished*

**655.** Then the High Priest of Amon, Menkheperre, triumphant, recounted to him, saying:

"O my good lord, (when) there is a matter, shall one recount it — ?" [11]Then the great god nodded exceedingly, exceedingly. Then he went again to the great god, saying: "O my good lord, (it is) the matter of these servants, against whom thou art wroth, who are in the oasis, whither they[c] are banished." Then the great god [12]nodded exceedingly, while this commander of the army, with his hands uplifted was praising

[a]The fifth intercalary day is of course meant.

[b]*D̲ ͗ d̲ ͗ w*, the word which I have rendered "*courses*" in Papyrus Harris.

[c]Or: "*one*" (impersonal), meaning: to which people are customarily banished.

his lord, as a father[a] talks with his own son: "Hail to thee, [maker] of all [that is], creator of all that exists, father of the gods, fashioner of goddesses; who equips them in the cities and districts; begetter [13]of men, and fashioner of women, maker of the life of all men. He is Khnum, building excellently, [giving] the breath of life; the north wind — —. Men live from his provision, who supplies the necessities of gods and men; the sun by day, the moon by night, sailing the heavens without [14]ceasing. Great in fame, he is mightier than Sekhmet, like fire — — — — for him that prays to him; he is healthy to heal the sick, when the people look [⌜to him⌝] ⌜————⌝ [15]⌜————⌝.[b] Thou shalt hearken to my voice on this day, and thou shalt [⌜relent⌝] toward the servants, whom thou hast banished [16]to the oasis, and they shall be brought (back) to Egypt." The great god nodded exceedingly.

### *Abolishment of Banishment*

**656.** Then he (the High Priest) spake again, saying: "[O my good lord], as for any writing which any ⌜—⌝ makes, in order to bring it, let it be said — — —." Then the great god nodded exceedingly. Then he went [17]again to the great god, saying: "O my good lord, thou shalt make a great[c] decree in thy name, that no people of the land shall be [banished] to the distant region of the oasis, nor — — — — — from this day on." [18]Then the great god nodded exceedingly. He spake again, saying: "Thou shalt say that it shall be made into a decree upon a stela — — — — in thy ⌜—⌝,[d] abiding and fixed forever."

### *Thanksgiving to Amon*

**657.** Then the High Priest of Amon, Menkheperre, triumphant, spake again, saying: "O my good lord, then my ⌜—⌝ is ⌜for⌝ myriads of times, and the command is for father and mother in every family. My every word shall please the heart in [thy] presence, I am thy faithful servant, profitable to thy ka. [20]I was a youth in thy city, I produced thy provision and thy ⌜—⌝, while I was in the womb, when thou didst

[a]The inversion of the members of the comparison is in the original.

[b]Very much broken; it is only general praise, and the particular petition begins with the following.

[c]Or: "*good;*" the reading is uncertain.

[d]Brugsch read here: "and be set up in thy cities," but this is no longer visible on the stone.

form (me) in the egg, when thou didst bring me forth ⌜to the great joy⌝ of thy people. Grant that I may spend a happy life [21]as a follower of thy ka. There is purity and health wherever thou tarriest. Set my feet in thy way, and direct me on thy path. Incline my heart ⌜— —⌝ to do —. [22]Grant that I may pass a happy ⌜old age⌝ in peace, while I am established, living in thy august house, like every favorite ⌜— —⌝ —."

*Slaying of Murderers*

**658.** [23]Then the High Priest of Amon, Menkheperre, triumphant, went to the great god, saying: "As for any person, of whom they shall report before thee, saying, 'A slayer of living people ⌜— —⌝ (is he);' thou shalt destroy him, thou shalt slay him." Then the great god nodded exceedingly, exceedingly.

---

## RECORD OF RESTORATION[a]

**659.** Menkheperre was the author of works extending over a wide territory,[b] but they are accompanied only by his name and titles. A restoration in the temple of Luxor is, however, recorded as follows:

Restoration of the monument, which the High Priest of Amon-Re, king of gods, Menkheperre, triumphant, son of the Lord of the Two Lands, Meriamon-Paynozem I, made, in the house of his father, Amon of Luxor.

---

## KARNAK GRAFFITO

**660.** This is a record of an inspection of the Karnak temples by Menkheperre in the year 40, which must still be of the reign of Paynozem I, his father.

[c]Year 40, third month of the third season, day of inspection of the house of Amon-Re, king of gods, the house of Amen[em]opet (Luxor),

---

[a]On a wall in the Luxor temple; Maspero, *Momies royales*, 702.

[b]See Maspero, *ibid.*

[c]Fallen granite pillar, Middle Kingdom portion of Karnak Amon-temple; *Recueil*, 22, 53, No. 3 A.

the house of Mut, the house of Khonsu, the house of Ptah, "South-of-His-Wall-in-Thebes," the house of Montu, lord of Thebes, and the house of Mat; by the High Priest of Amon-Re, king of gods, Menkheperre, son of King Paynozem-Meriamon, when command was given to the fourth prophet of Amon-Re, king of gods, prophet of Montu-Re, lord of Thebes, chief censer-bearer, Hetamenthenofer (*Ḥ ᵓ˙ t-Ymn-ṯ ᵓ-nṯr*), triumphant, son of the fourth prophet of Amon, prophet of Montu, lord of Thebes, Nesupehernemut (*Ns-sy-p ᵓ-ḥr-n-Mw˙ t*), triumphant, ———.[a]

---

## RECORDS ON THE ROYAL MUMMIES

**661.** Menkheperre continued the care of the royal necropolis, and we find him renewing the wrappings of Seti I in the seventh year of a king not mentioned, who can only be the successor of his father, Paynozem I, Amenemopet of Tanis. It was probably in the interim between the two reigns that he gained royal privileges and the throne-name Pesibkhenno, which he never employed in his father's time. We are unable to determine whether he ever reigned alone or not.

### *Mummy of Seti I*

[b]Year 7, second month of the second season, day 26; day of entombing King Menmare (Seti I), L. P. H.

[c]Linen, which the High Priest of Amon-Re, Menkheperre, made for his father, Amon, (in the) year 6.

---

[a]Amount of loss is uncertain.

[b]On inner wrappings, just under the outside wrappings renewed by the Twenty-first Dynasty; *Momies royales*, 555.

[c]On inner wrappings renewed by Twenty-first Dynasty.

## HIGH PRIESTHOOD OF PAYNOZEM II

### RECORDS ON THE PRIESTLY MUMMIES[a]

**662.** The 153 mummies of the priests of Amon, found at Thebes in 1891 bore a few inscriptions of historical value. They show that Menkheperre was succeeded in the high priesthood by a certain Nesubenebded, who is known from the Karnak decree to be a son of Menkheperre.[b] Nesubenebded was early succeeded by another son of Menkheperre named Paynozem, the second of the name, in the high priesthood of Amon, which he entered upon under the Tanite king Amenemopet, probably before that king's twenty-second year, as the following records show. They likewise carry his administration at Thebes to the year 10[c] of Siamon.

**663.** [d]King of Upper and Lower Egypt, Usermare-Setepnamon (Amenemopet). Linen which the High Priest of Amon, Paynozem, son of Menkheperre, made for his father, Amon, in the year —.

[e]King of Upper and Lower Egypt, Lord of the Two Lands, Meriamon-Amenemopet. Linen which the High Priest of Amon, Paynozem, son of Menkheperre, made for his lord, Amon, in the year 22.[f]

[g]King of Upper and Lower Egypt, Amenemopet, year 49.

[h]Linen which the High Priest of Amon, Paynozem, son of Menkheperre, made for his lord, Khonsu, in the year 3.

---

[a]On the straps, bandages, and linen; Daressy, *Revue archéologique*, 28 (4–7 of the *tirage à part*). The numbers used in my notes are those of the mummies.

[b]Daressy, *op. cit.*, 28 (9, 10, of the *tirage à part*).

[c]A graffito at Karnak (Legrain, *Recueil*, 22, 61, No. 33) gives the year 14 of a king whose name is lost. It began with Amen, and may therefore be either Amenemopet or Siamon, very probably the latter.

[d]No. 17. [e]No. 134.

[f]Daressy adds (?) to this numeral without indicating how much of it is affected by the uncertainty.

[g]Loose piece of linen, detached. [h]No. 143.

[a]Linen which the High Priest of Amon, Paynozem, son of Menkheperre, made for his mistress, Mut, year 7 of King Siamon.

[b]———— Mut, year 8 of King Siamon.

[c]Linen which the High Priest of Amon-Re, king of gods, Paynozem, son of Menkheperre, made for his lord, Amon, in the year 10.

## RECORDS ON THE ROYAL MUMMIES

**664.** These rough notes, hurriedly recorded on the royal mummies, offer graphic testimony to the insecurity of the times at Thebes.

In Paynozem II's time, though his name is not mentioned in the records on the coffins, the bodies of Ramses II and Ramses I, which had been removed to the tomb of Seti I, as well as that of Seti I himself, were again transferred and deposited for safety in the tomb of Queen Inhapi. This was done in the sixteenth year of the Tanite king Siamon.

### *Coffin of Ramses II*

**665.** [d]Year 16, fourth month of the second season, day 17, day of bringing King Usermare-Setepnere (Ramses II), the Great God, out from the tomb of King Menmare-Seti-Merneptah (Seti I), in order to bring him into the tomb (*ḳ ᵓ y*) of (Queen) Inhapi which is (in) the "Great Place,"[e] by the hand of the prophet of Amon-Re, king of gods, Enkhofnamon, son of Beki; the divine father of Amon-Re, king of gods, third prophet of "Khonsu-in-Thebes-Beautiful-Rest,"[f] scribe of the administration of the house of Amon-Re, king of gods, servant of

[a]No. 16. Another piece from the Amon-temple bears the same year without the king's name.

[b]No. 134. The lost beginning was, of course, like the preceding.

[c]No. 134.

[d]On the lid of the coffin; *op. cit.*, 558.

[e]A particular part of the necropolis.

[f]*Nfr ḥtp*, which Maspero reads as the man's name; but this phrase is the usual one after Thebes in Khonsu's title, and the determinative is the divine person in all three texts. Hence, however long the man's titles, they do not stop here.

"The-House-of-King-Usermare-Setepnere (Ramses II)-in-the-House-of-Amon," chief treasurer of the necropolis, Merithoth; the scribe, and chief inspector, Nesupekeshuti, son of Beknekhonsu; after Mut, the guardian goddess of the Great Place, had said:

"That which is in good condition before me, no harm shall befall it, through my[a] bringing them (sic!) out from the tomb in which they rest, and they shall be taken into the tomb (ḳ ͗ y) of (Queen) Inhapi, which is in the 'Great Place,' wherein King Amenhotep rests."

*Coffin of Seti I*

**666.** [b]Year 16, fourth month of the second season, day 17, of King Siamon, the day of bringing King Menmare-Seti (I)-Merneptah, L. P. H., out from his tomb, in order to bring him into the tomb (ḳ ͗ y) of Inhapi, which is (in) the "Great Place;" by the hand of, etc. . . . .

Here follows a list of the same men as on the coffins of Ramses I and Ramses II (*q. v.*).

*Coffin of Ramses I*

**667.** [c][Year 16, fourth month of the second season, day 17[d]] of King Siamon, [day of bringing King Men]pehti[re] (Ramses I) out from the [tomb of King Menmare]-Seti (II)-Merneptah, ⌈in order to⌉ [bring him into the tomb (ḳ ͗ y) of Inhapi, which is in the "Great Place," wherein King Amenhotep rests; by the hand of the prophet of Amon-[Re, king of] gods, Enkhofnamon, son of Beki, etc.

Here follows the same list of men as on Seti I's and Ramses II's coffins.

---

RECORD OF PAYNOZEM II'S BURIAL

**668.** I have included the preceding documents under the high priesthood of Paynozem II, although he was evidently lying dead in the hands of the embalmers when they were written; for three days later he was buried in the rough

[a]Or: "*their.*" [b]On the lid of the coffin; *op. cit.*, Pl. XII.

[c]On the lid of the coffin; *op. cit.*, Pl. X A; 551.

[d]Maspero's restoration (*op. cit.*, 551), giving the first season and the thirteenth day, must be an inadvertence; the parallel texts have it as above.

receptacle excavated in the cliffs of Der el-Bahri, which had served as the tomb of Amenhotep I. The place was sealed up, and the following record was written with the pen on the doorpost by one of the accompanying scribes. The date of year 16 is the highest which we have from the reign of the Tanite Siamon.

[a]1Year 16, fourth month of the second season, day 20, day of the burial 2of the Osiris, the High Priest of Amon-Re, king of gods, governor [of the city][b] and vizier, prince and leader ⌜—⌝, Paynozem 3by the divine father of Amon, overseer of the White House, Zekhonsefonekh; the divine father of Amon, scribe of the vizier, the inspector, Nesupekeshuti; the ⌜—⌝ of Amon — — — —; 4the divine father of Amon, Wennofer; the king's-scribe of the Theban necropolis (*ysˑt-m ᵓ ᶜ ˑt*), Bek; the chief of workmen, Pediamon.

[c]Linen which the High Priest of Amon, Paynozem II [son of] Menkheperre, made for [his] lord, Khonsu, in the year 9.

---

## STELA OF THE "GREAT CHIEF OF ME," SHESHONK[d]

**669.** In this document we gain our first glimpse of the Libyan ancestors of the great family of the Twenty-second Dynasty. Sheshonk, the grandfather[e] of Sheshonk I, the

[a]On the left doorpost, at the bottom of the Der el-Bahri shaft; Maspero, *Zeitschrift für ägyptische Sprache*, 1882, 134; better, *Momies royales*, 523.

[b]Omitted, either in the publication or by the ancient scribe.

[c]On wrappings of the mummy; *op. cit.*, 572. The same records for years 1, 3, and 7 were found on the wrappings.

[d]A red granite stela, 1.20 by 1.50 m., found by Mariette "southward from the western entrance gate of the Kum-es-Sultan in Abydos" (Brugsch, *Zeitschrift für ägyptische Sprache*, 1871, 85 f.). He states that it was left by him in situ, although Wiedemann (Wiedemann, *Aegyptische Geschichte*, 543), places it in the Boulak Museum ("Salle historique de l'est, No. 93"), and seems to have copied it. Published by Mariette, *Abydos*, II, 36, 37; Mariette, *Catalogue général d'Abydos*, No. 1225. The upper portion is wanting, and an unknown amount of the inscription is lost. The copy of Mariette is very incomplete and inaccurate; a better copy was impossible, as the present location of the stone is unknown.

[e]See the long genealogy on the Serapeum stela, § 787, where the Sheshonk, with his wife Mehetnusekhet, is unquestionably the Sheshonk of our inscription, whose wife is also Mehetnusekhet.

first king of the Twenty-second Dynasty, was a powerful chief of the Meshwesh[a] who had achieved place and influence in Egypt. His great-grandfather, Musen, had gained control at Heracleopolis (§ 787, No. 2), and five generations later the family had seized the throne, as the Twenty-second Dynasty. The family retained their old native titles or an Egyptian rendering of them, but our Sheshonk was so thoroughly Egyptianized that he buried his deceased son, Namlot, in Abydos, with all the accompaniments of Egyptian mortuary belief. He later found that the officials in charge of his son's mortuary endowment had been appropriating the income. He went to Thebes, under the jurisdiction of which the crime fell, and from some unnamed king, who must have been either Amenemopet or Siamon, he obtained redress. The case, like all other matters of the kind in this period, was carried before Amon, and the stela, of which the first lines are lost, begins the middle of an address to the god by the king. As it continues, the god renders an oracle condemning the guilty officials to death. Sheshonk then conveyed his son's statue to Abydos, where full record of his son's mortuary endowment was entered in the temple archives, with their value in silver, furnishing useful data for determining the ancient values of various property in modern standards.[b]

**670.** The decree of Amon in this criminal case is of the greatest interest, and characteristic of the time. The case of those banished to the oasis, who are pardoned by the god at the High Priest Menkheperre's request (§§ 650–58), is more or less political, but such is not the character of this case. A similar case, also under the high priesthood of

[a]Abbreviated, as frequently in the inscriptions of this time, to Me.

[b]The data from our document have never been so employed; see Spiegelberg, *Rechnungen*, Text, 87 ff., for the data from the earlier documents.

Paynozem II, is that of certain temple officials who were slain for dishonesty in the temple accounts. Recorded with it is the remarkable acquittal of a certain major-domo named Thutmose, the method of whose trial is sufficiently evident from the following translation,[a] without further explanation.

*Appearance of Amon*

**671.** ————[b] [1]On this day in the house of Amon-Re, king of gods, on the sixth day of the month, appeared the august god, [2]the lord of gods, Amon-Re, king of gods; Mut the great, mistress of Ishru; and "Khonsu-in-[3]Thebes-Beautiful-Rest;" on the silver pavement of the house of Amon — —. The High Priest of Amon-Re, [4]king of gods commander in chief of the army, Paynozem, triumphant, son of Men-[kheper]re [triumphant], took counsel of the affairs of [5]this land, before the great god.

*Condemnation of the Guilty*

In the second month, on the sixth day, — the great god [6]who is far from injustice, had not (yet) been taken up to Opet at [⌜the Feast of⌝][c] Opet in this year. [7]Lo, this great god determined ⌜that⌝ which the scribes, [8]inspectors and administrators had done, who committed [9]fraudulent acts in Thebes, his city. [10]Then the great god condemned the scribes, [11]inspectors, and administrators, because of the acts of [12]fraud which they had committed.

*The Two Writings*

**672.** This great god appeared upon the pavement of silver in the house of Amon at the morning hour. The High Priest of Amon-Re, king of gods, Paynozem, triumphant, came [13]before this great god.

[a]This inscription, of which only the first part is translated above, was found on one of the southern pylons at Karnak in Maspero's excavations there in 1881. It was published and treated by Naville, *Inscriptions historiques de Pinodjem III* (our Paynozem II), Paris, 1883. See Maspero, *Zeitschrift für ägyptische Sprache,* 1882, 135.

[b]Naville numbers this line 1; at least one line, containing the date, is lost before it. In the long inscription below it, oracles of the god in the years 2 (ll. 8 and 10), 3 (l. 12), and 5 (l. 13) are recorded; hence this date will not be less than year 5.

[c]So also Naville; this was not long before the beginning of the Feast of Opet (see note on Papyrus Harris, § 237).

This great god saluted violently. He placed two tablets of writing before the great god; one writing said: [14]"O Amon-Re, king of gods, my good lord; it is said that there are matters which should be investigated[a] in the case of Thutmose, triumphant, son of Sudiamon (*Sw-dy-Ymn*), triumphant, the major-domo;" the other writing [said: "O Amon-Re, king of gods], my good lord; it is said that there are no matters which should [16]be investigated in the case of Thutmose, triumphant, the son of Sudiamon, triumphant, the major-domo." The [High Priest] of Amon-Re, king of gods, Paynozem, triumphant, repeated before this great god, saying: "O [17]my good lord, thou shalt judge — — —, thou prosperest beyond all wonders." [The] great god saluted violently.

*The Acquittal*

**673.** [18]These two tablets of writing were placed before the [great god]. The great god took the writing[b] which said: "O Amon-Re, my good lord; [19]it is said that there are no matters [which should] be investigated in the case of Thutmose, triumphant, son of Sudiamon, triumphant, the major-domo." The great god [20][⌜rejected⌝ the other writing which said: "O Amon-Re, king of gods], my good lord; it is said that there are matters which should be investigated in the case of [21][Thutmose, triumphant, son of Sudiamon, triumphant, the major-domo."]

[Then the High Priest of Amon-Re, king of gods, went again] to this great, great god, to put his two tablets of writing the second time before the great god. [The great god[c]] took [22][⌜the same writing as before⌝] ———. They bore witness, saying: "There are no matters which should be investigated [23][in the case of Thutmose, triumphant, son of Sudiamon, triumphant, the[d]] major-domo."[e]

**674.** The legal functions assumed by Amon at this period will be sufficiently illustrated by this and the following ex-

---

[a]Lit., "*which should be sought for with Thutmose.*"

[b]Lit., "*the one writing.*"

[c]Omitted by the ancient scribe or in the publication.

[d]These words hardly fill the lacuna.

[e]Some 8 lines are here lost; below these follows a long series of legal decisions by Amon, which lead to the acquittal above recounted.

ample. Even the wills and the property conveyances of the numerous relatives of the high priests are issued as oracles and decrees of the god. They form a remarkable class of legal documents by themselves, which will be treated later in this series.[a] We can understand, therefore, why the case of the Libyan chief Sheshonk was brought by the king before Amon. It is as follows:

### *Speech to Amon*

**675.** "——— [1][b]great chief of chiefs, Sheshonk, triumphant, his[c] son in the glorious place by his father, Osiris, ⌜that he might⌝ lay his beauty ⌜to rest⌝ in the city of Abydos (*Nf-wr*), over against — —. Thou wilt let him survive to attain old age, while his ⌜heart[2]— — —⌝. Thou wilt let him join the feasts of his majesty, receiving full victory." This great god saluted exceedingly.

### *Amon Condemns the Thieves*

**676.** Then his majesty spake again before this great god: "O my good lord, thou shalt slay the [3]⌜—⌝,[d] the administrator, the scribe, the inspector, every one who was sent on any commission to the field, of those who stole of his ⌜things⌝ from the offering-table of the Osiris, the great chief of Me, Namlot, triumphant, son of Mehetnusekhet, who is in Abydos; [4]all the people who plundered from his divine offerings, his people, his cattle, his garden, his every oblation and all his excellent things. Thou wilt do according to thy great spirit throughout; fill them up and fill up (⌜the number of⌝) the women [5]and their children." The great god saluted exceedingly.

### *Final Prayer to Amon*

**677.** His majesty smelled the earth before him; his majesty said; "Make to triumph, Sheshonk, triumphant, the great chief of Me, chief

---

[a]In the volume devoted to legal documents.

[b]In the lost portion of uncertain length preceding this, there was doubtless some verb of which Sheshonk was the subject and "*his son*" the object.

[c]This shows that the Sheshonk of the inscription is the father, not the son, of Namlot, as Wiedemann concludes (Wiedemann, *Aegyptische Geschichte*, 543, 544).

[d]A military officer.

of chiefs, the great ⌜—⌝, and all who are ⌜before thee⌝, [6]all the troops ———." [⌜Said to⌝] him, Amon-Re, king of gods: "⌜—⌝ I will do ⌜—⌝ for thee, thou shalt attain old age, abiding on earth; thy heir shall be upon thy throne forever."

*Statue of Namlot Sent to Abydos*

**678.** His majesty sent the statue of Osiris, the great chief of [7]Me, great chief of chiefs, Namlot, triumphant, northward to Abydos. There were — — — — — a great army, in order to protect it, having [⌜numerous⌝] ships, — — without number, and the messengers of the great chief of Me, in order to deposit[a] it in the august palace, [8]the sanctuary of the right eye of the sun, in order to make his offerings belonging in Abydos, according to the stipulations for making his offerings, incense ⌜— —⌝ in the hall of petition.

*Records of Endowment*

**679.** His contract was recorded [9]in the hall of writings,[b] according to that which the lord of gods (Amon) had said. A stela was erected for him of granite of Elephantine,[c] bearing the decree — in his name, in order to deposit it in the divine sanctuary to the end of eternity, (even) forever. Then was established the offering-table of Osiris, the great chief of Me, [10]Namlot, triumphant, son of Mehetnusekhet, who is in Abydos.

*People of Endowment*

**680.** There were brought the [people] of the — of the great chief of Me, who came with the statue: a Syrian servant (named) Ikhamon ⌜—⌝,[d] [11]a Syrian (named) Ekptah; ⌜the price of the first⌝ was 14 deben of silver; his majesty gave ⌜for the second⌝ 20 deben of silver; total, 35[e] deben of silver, the tale thereof.

---

[a]Lit., "*cause it to rest.*"

[b]Temple archives.

[c]Only one letter (*b*) of this word (ʾ *bw*) with the determinative, is preserved, but as the stela is of red Elephantine granite, there can be no doubt of the rendering. Brugsch's "in der Schrift des Landes Ba[bel]" is pure imagination. The text has: "*of stone of — b —*" (foreign determinative). Wiedemann reads "Ba-sut" (adding "so ist auf dem monumente zu lesen"), and says the material is porphyry (Wiedemann, *Aegyptische Geschichte*, 544).

[d]The end of the name is uncertain.

[e]The first number is doubtless misread by Mariette. These two numbers, making a total of 35, must be the prices of the two slaves.

### *Lands of Endowment*

**681.** That which was paid for 50 stat (of land) which are in the high district south of Abydos, called, "Eternity-[12]of-the-Kingdom:" 5[a] deben of silver.

That which is in ⌜— —⌝ of the pool which is in Abydos, (viz.,) 50 stat of land; amounting to 5 deben of silver.

Total of citizen-lands ⌜—⌝ two places being: the high district south of Abydos, and the high district [13]north of Abydos: 100 [stat], amounting to 10 deben of silver.

### *List of Men*

**682.** His [slave], Pewer, son of —f; his slave, Ebek[b] (ʾ-*bk*); his slave, Bupenamonkha (*Bw-pn-Ymn-ḫ*ʾ[c]); his slave, Neshenumeh (*N*ʾ*y-šnw-mḥ*);[c] his slave, Dene (*Dn*ʾ); total [14]of slaves: 6; amounting (⌜at) 3⌝ deben, 1 kidet of silver ⌜for each⌝, to 1[⌜8⌝] deben [⌜6 kidet⌝] of silver.

### *Children*

The child of — — son of Harsiese, triumphant; amounting to $4\frac{2}{3}$ kidet of silver.

### *Garden*

The garden which is in the high district ⌜—⌝[d] of Abydos, amounting to 2 deben of silver.

### *Gardeners*

The gardener, Harmose, triumphant, son of Pen —; [15]amounting to —$\frac{2}{3}$ kidet of silver; Pene —, triumphant, his —, Harnepe—r—, triumphant, [amounting to] $6\frac{2}{3}$ kidet of silver.

### *Men and Women*

⌜—⌝ Nesitetat, triumphant, whose mother is Tedimut, the female slave, Tediese, daughter of Nebethapi; her mother, Ero — [16]ekh; [the female slave], ⌜Tepiramenef⌝, daughter of Paynehsi, triumphant;

---

[a]Mariette has 6, but Brugsch has 5 (*Zeitschrift für ägyptische Sprache*, 1871, 86), which is in agreement with the second 50 stat for 5 deben of silver; 10 stat (= $6\frac{3}{4}$ acres) of land were thus worth 1 deben (1,404 grains) of silver.

[b]Brugsch: "Ari-bek."

[c]Meaning: "*The Full Trees.*"

[d]Brugsch: "north."

——— for each one; $5\frac{2}{3}$ kidet of silver being the price of the man; amounting to $3\frac{2}{3}$ deben.[a]

*List of Supplies*

**683.** Honey; [an expenditure amounting to — deben of silver][b] payable to the treasury, for a hin of honey issued from the treasury [17]of Osiris [for the divine offerings of Osiris], the [great] chief [of Me], great chief [of chiefs, Namlot], son of the [great] chief of [Me, Sheshonk] — — — — —. The money therefor has been made payable to the treasury of Osiris, no more, no less.

**684.** Incense; [18][an expenditure amounting to] 4 deben of silver, payable to the treasury of Osiris, for 4 kidet of incense, issued from the treasury of Osiris daily, for the divine offerings of Osiris, the great chief of Me, Namlot, triumphant, whose mother is Mehetnusekhet, forever and ever [19][from that which is issued from] the — — incense. The money therefor is payable to the treasury of Osiris, no more, no less.

**685.** Myrrh; [an expenditure] amounting to $5\frac{2}{3}$ kidet of silver, payable to the treasury of Osiris, for [20]—$\frac{2}{3}$ kidet of [myrrh], issued from the treasury of Osiris daily, for the censer of Osiris, the great chief of Me, Namlot, triumphant, whose mother is Mehetnusekhet, forever and ever; from that which is issued, of the myrrh — —. The money therefor has been made payable to the treasury of Osiris, no more, [21][no less].

**686.** [Grain] — — per man — — per man, an expenditure amounting to ⸢3⸣ kidet of silver — with 1 kidet of silver, payable to the treasury of Osiris, for this grain of the field[c] that is issued daily from — — — — — — [22][from] the treasury of Osiris and the — of Osiris, for the altar of Osiris, the great chief of Me, Namlot, triumphant, whose mother is Mehetnusekhet, forever and ever; from the impost of the — — of the cake-baking ⸢—⸣. The money therefor is made payable to the treasury of Osiris, [23]the treasury of the grain of the field ⸢— —⸣. [⸢The money therefor is payable to the treasury⸣] of Osiris — —, no more, no less.

[a]I am uncertain whether this total is to be connected with the preceding or the following paragraph. It is similar in form to the beginnings of the following paragraphs. There is evident confusion in the copy, and probably an omission.

[b]This is the formula which should introduce this paragraph; but see preceding note.

[c]See l. 23.

*Summary*

**687.** Total of the silver of these people, which is payable to the treasury of Osiris [24]— — — — 13[a] men ——— issued from — — to the ⌈—⌉ of Osiris, the great chief of Me, chief of chiefs, Namlot, triumphant, son of Sheshonk, triumphant, whose mother is Mehetnusekhet; in order to give [25]— — — — to Osiris, the great chief of Me, Namlot, triumphant, son of Mehetnusekhet, who is in Abydos:

| | |
|---|---|
| Lands | 100 stat |
| Men and women | 25 |
| Garden | 1 |
| Silver | 100[b] [deben] |

Abydos ———.

[a]The number is not certain.

[b]And probably more, but how much is uncertain.

## HIGH PRIESTHOOD OF PESIBKHENNO

### RECORDS ON MUMMY-WRAPPINGS

**688.** We have no records of this High Priest beyond the usual note on the temple linen used in swathing the bodies of the Amon priests found in 1891. These show that he was a son of Paynozem II, and that he was in office at least from the year 4 to the year 12 of a king who must be Pesibkhenno II, under whose predecessor, Siamon, he must have succeeded his father, on the latter's death in Siamon's sixteenth year (§ 668).

[a]Linen which the High Priest of Amon, Pesibkhenno, son of Paynozem (II), made for his lord, Amon, in the year 4.

Linen which the High Priest of Amon, Pesibkhenno, son of Paynozem (II), made for his lord, Amon, in the year 12.

---

### BURIAL OF NESIKHONSU

**689.** Nesikhonsu, wife of Paynozem II, died in the fifth year of a king, who must be Pesibkhenno II of Tanis. Her husband's tomb, originally that of Amenhotep I, was opened, and she was likewise buried there. When the door was sealed again, one of the scribes recorded the burial on the doorpost. It contains the names of some of the same officials who had buried her husband, not less than five years before.

[a]Mummy No. 17 of the cache of priests' mummies discovered at Der el-Bahri in 1891; published by Daressy (*Revue archéologique*, 28, p. 6 (of the *tirage à part*).

*Nesikhonsu*

[a]1Year 5, fourth month of the third season (twelfth month), day 21, 2day of the burial of the chief of favorites, Nesikhonsu, 3by the divine father of Amon, overseer of the White House, Zekhonsefonekh, ⌜together with⌝[b] Paynozem, 4the prophet of Amon-Re, king of gods, Enkhofamon (*ˁnḫ·f-Ymn*); 5——— Nesipai — —; 6the divine father of Amon, the chief treasurer, Nesupekeshuti (*Ns-sw-pꜣ-ḳꜣ-šwty*). The seals which are upon ⌜—⌝ of this place ⌜—⌝;[c] the seals of the overseer of the White House, Zekhonsefonekh; the seals of the scribe of the White House, Nesu————.

## RECORDS ON THE ROYAL MUMMIES

**690.** With these two records the history of the royal mummies in ancient times, so far as we know it, closes. The bodies of Seti I and Ramses II were taken from the tomb of Queen Inhapi in the tenth year of Pesibkhenno II, and deposited in the great cache at Der el-Bahri, in the tomb of Amenhotep I, where Nesikhonsu had been buried five years earlier. In all probability the other royal mummies were brought to the same place at this time also. The door was sealed up for the last time, not earlier than the eleventh year of Sheshonk I (§ 699); the shaft leading to it was soon filled with detritus from the cliffs above, and all knowledge of the place was lost. Thus the great kings of Egypt at last found undisturbed rest for three thousand years. Then, some time in the early seventies of last century, they were discovered by the native tomb-robbers of modern Thebes, the descendants of those who were prosecuted under Ramses IX

[a]At the bottom of the entrance shaft leading to the great cache of royal mummies, on the right door-jamb; it is written in ink in hieratic; *Zeitschrift für ägyptische Sprache*, 1882, 134; better, *Momies royales*, 520.

[b]Or: "*son of*."

[c]Maspero reads the numeral 40 here, but this seems to me improbable. He found fragments of these seals among the rubbish around the door, and among them one with the title "*High Priest of Amon*" in a cartouche.

and X (§§ 499 ff.) Under pressure of much the same legal methods as those employed by their ancestors, not forgetting the bastinade, they finally revealed the place which they had been plundering, and the ancient rulers of Egypt were, in 1881, again brought to the light of day.[a]

*Coffin of Seti I*

**691.** [b]Year 10, fourth month of the second season, day 20, the day of bringing in the god into his place, in order to cause him to rest [in] the eternal house of Amenhotep[c] — — — —; by the hand of the divine father of Amon, overseer of the White House, Zekhonsefonekh; divine father of Amon, ⌜—⌝; divine father of Amon, third prophet of Khonsu —.

*Coffin of Ramses II*

**692.** [d]Year 10, fourth month of the second season, day 20, day of bringing in the god into his place, to cause him to rest in the eternal house of Amenhotep, the ⌜— of Amon⌝, in life, prosperity, and health; by the hand of the divine father of Amon, overseer of the White House, Zekhonsefonekh; the divine father of Amon, third prophet of [Khonsu],[e] Efnamon, son of Nesupekeshuti; the divine father of Amon, Wennofer, son of Mentem⌜wese⌝; the divine father of Amon, —.

---

[a]On the discovery and rescue of the royal mummies, see Maspero, *Momies royales*, 511, 516.

[b]On the lid of the coffin; *op. cit.*, 554, and Pl. XII.

[c]This can hardly be anything else than the tomb of Amenhotep I; on the construction of the whole place, see Maspero, *op. cit.*, 517, 518.

[d]On the lid of the coffin; *op. cit.*, 559.

[e]From duplicate; text has *f*.

# THE TWENTY-SECOND DYNASTY

## RECORDS OF NILE-LEVELS AT KARNAK[a]

693. These records are of primary importance in the history of the Nile and its inundations. Further than this, the records of successive reigns furnish valuable data for the chronology and history of the dark period from the Twenty-second to the Twenty-sixth Dynasty.[b] From these and other contemporary documents, especially the Apis stelæ, the Twenty-second Dynasty may now be reconstructed as follows:

| | | | |
|---|---|---|---|
| Sheshonk I | 21[c] | years | (+$x$) |
| Osorkon I | 36[d] | " | " |
| Takelot I | 23[e] | " | " |
| Osorkon II | 30[f] | " | " |
| Sheshonk II | 00 | " | " |
| (Died during coregency with Osorkon II) | | | |

[a]Engraved on the quai of the great Karnak temple; published by Legrain, *Zeitschrift für ägyptische Sprache*, 1896, 111 ff. Unfortunately, Legrain says nothing about the order in which the records are arranged. When I have rearranged to introduce chronological sequence, I have added Legrain's number in parenthesis.

[b]For convenience, the records of the other dynasties have not been added here. They will be found in their chronological places later.

[c]§ 706.

[d]Petrie, *History*, III, 241.

[e]§ 695, No. 4; has year 6; the next higher known date is year 7 (*Recueil*, XVIII, 5 = Lepsius, *Denkmäler*, III, 258, *c*); but he would have reigned at least 8 years for his son, Osorkon II, celebrated his 30-years' jubilee in his twenty-second year. But Daressy has perceived that a stela at Florence (*Catalogue*, No. 1806; see *Recueil*, XV, 174, 175), dated in the year 23, belongs to Takelot I. Legrain's omission of a Takelot at this point in the dynasty (*Recueil*, 27, 76) is, of course, an error, as shown by the genealogy of Harpeson (§ 792).

[f]§ 696, No. 15. The High Priest Harsiese, son of the High Priest Sheshonk, and grandson of Osorkon I (§ 739), assumed royal honors as vassal king under Osorkon II (Legrain, *Recueil*, 27, 76). He must have died or been supplanted when Sheshonk II was made coregent.

| | |
|---|---|
| Takelot II | 25[a] years (+*x*) |
| (Seven years, coregency with Osorkon II) | |
| Sheshonk III | 52[b] years |
| Pemou[c] | 6[d] " (+*x*) |
| Sheshonk IV | 37[e] " " |
| Total | 230 years (+6*x*) |

or deducting 30 years of possible coregencies,[f] the total is 200 + 6*x* years.

**694.** The dynasty thus reigned not less than 200 years in round numbers. But it should be noted that between the twenty-first year of Sheshonk I and the eleventh year of Takelot II, or a period of 93 years according to the above table, there ruled seven high priests of Amon. This is giving about 13 years to each, and would indicate that the table is within the truth for this period. The second half of the dynasty is nearly certain as to length; the period from the accession of Sheshonk III to that of Pemou is exactly known, and the uncertainty chiefly concerns the last two kings, especially Pemou. It should be noted that from the reign of Osorkon II (probably toward its end), to the year 37 of Sheshonk IV, there were six generations of high priests at Heracleopolis (§ 787, Nos.

[a]§ 755. There is no year 29 of Takelot II as given by Maspero (*Empires*, 165, note 2); the year 29 belongs to Sheshonk III, as correctly seen by Maspero formerly (*Momies royales*, 741).

[b]§ 778.

[c]This name means "*the cat*," as is shown by the determinative of a cat in the case of a private individual (e. g., Ser. stela No. 276, noticed by Lepsius, *Zweiundzwanzigste Dynastie*, 290, although transliterated: Peχi). Hence I give it the vowels of the Coptic form, rather than perpetuate the impossible forms: Pimai, Paymi, Pimi, etc.

[d]§ 698, No. 24; not quite certain

[e]§ 791.

[f]Petrie, *History*, III, 227.

11–16), who thus correspond to four generations of kings. The reigns of Pemou and Sheshonk IV, especially the former, may thus have been much longer, notwithstanding the long reign of Sheshonk III. The descent from father to son is certain from the beginning, only down to and including Takelot II.

The omission in the publication of all indication of the relative positions of the following records on the wall, precludes some of the important conclusions which might otherwise be drawn from them:

*Reign of Sheshonk I*

**695.** 1. (3) The Nile. Year 5 of King Sheshonk I.[a]

2. (1) The Nile. Year 6 of King Sheshonk I.[a]

*Reign of Osorkon I*

3. (2) The Nile. Year 12 of King Osorkon I.

*Reign of Takelot I*

4. The Nile. Year 6 of King Takelot I; his mother, Tentsey (*Tnt-s* ͗ *y*).

*Reign of Osorkon II*

**696.** 5. The Nile. Year 3[b] of King Osorkon II; his mother, the Great King's-Wife ——— (cartouche).

6. The Nile. Year 5 of King Osorkon II; his mother, Great King's-Wife, Keromem (*Mr-Mw*ʿ*t-K* ͗ *-m* ͗ *-m* ͗ sic!).

7. Same, year 6.

8. The Nile. Year 12[c] of King Osorkon II.

9. The Nile. Year 12 (sic!)[c] of King Osorkon II.

10. The Nile. Year ⌈1⌉3 of King Osorkon II.

11. The Nile. Year 20 of King Osorkon II.

[a]This name is out of place as published, as it follows Osorkon I; it may also be Takelot II, who would also be out of place.

[b]This is the year of the high water recorded at Luxor (§§ 742–744); it was 62 cm. deep on the temple pavement at Luxor.

[c]At different levels.

**697.** 12. The Nile. Year 22 of King Osorkon II.

13. The Nile. Year 28 of King Osorkon II, the god, ruler of Thebes; which is the year 5 ⌜of his⌝[a] son Takelot (II), the god, ruler of Thebes, living forever.

14. The Nile. Year 29 of King Osorkon II.

15. [The Nile. Year 30 (+$x$) of King] Osorkon II.[b]

*Reign of Sheshonk III*

**698.** 16. (23) The Nile. Year 6 of King Usermare-Setepnamon, Son of Re, Meriamon-Sheshonk (III). Time of the High Priest of Amon-Re, king of gods, Harsiese.[c]

17. (22) The Nile. Year 39 of King Sheshonk III. Time of the High Priest of Amon-Re, king of gods, Osorkon.

*Reign of Pemou?*

18. (24) The Nile. Year 12,[d] which is year 6 of King Usermare-

---

[a]Reading the *n* as a genitive and the *f* as a possessive. It can hardly be doubted that Takelot II was the son of Osorkon II. The ephemeral reign of Osorkon II's son Sheshonk (II) was thus a coregency with the father, followed, on Sheshonk II's death, by a second coregency of the father (Osorkon II) and the deceased Sheshonk II's brother, Takelot II, which perhaps lasted at least 7 years (No. 15).

[b]The traces that remain make the name of Osorkon II certain. The year is, of course, not less than 30, if Legrain's arrangement be correct.

[c]We know that Takelot II's son, Osorkon, was High Priest of Amon in the years 11, 12, and 15 of Takelot II, and 22, 26, 28, 29, and 39 of Sheshonk III (§§ 756 ff.). Hence the High Priest Harsiese must have displaced Osorkon for a time, as explained below (§ 758). The occurrence of a Harsiese in the sixth year of Pemou (No. 24) is uncertain. If accepted, it must either be another Harsiese, or his term was interrupted at least from the year 22 to the year 39 of Sheshonk III.

[d]This cannot be a year of Sheshonk III, as it would involve a coregency with Pemou of some 46 years; nor can it be year 12 of the High Priest Harsiese, if he be the same as the Harsiese of Sheshonk III's sixth year (No. 22). Hence I am inclined to doubt the reading of Harsiese here which Legrain himself questions. If, however, we accept it, then there must be another king between Sheshonk III and Pemou—the Sheshonk with the new prenomen, of No. 25? This would not increase the length of the dynasty, as we know from the Apis stela (§ 778) that there were 26 years from the twenty-eighth year of Sheshonk III to the second year of Pemou. Thus, according to No. 25, the new Sheshonk would have reigned at least 6 years, and the Sheshonk III not more than 46 years (the highest recorded date of Sheshonk III is year 39, § 777); or if No. 24 belongs to the new Sheshonk, he reigned at least 12 years, and Sheshonk III not more than 40 years

Setepnamon, Meriamon-Siese-⌜Pemou⌝[a] High Priest of Amon-Re, king of gods, ⌜Harsiese⌝.

*Reign of Sheshonk IV?*

19. (25) The Nile. Year 6 of King Usermare-Meriamon, Son of Re, Meriamon-Sheshonk (⌜IV⌝).[b] Time of the High Priest of Amon, Takelot.

---

[a]Legrain is not certain of this name; the prenomen agrees, but unfortunately coincides with one form (No. 22) of Sheshonk III's prenomen. If Harsiese were certain, Wreszinski's remark (*Die Hohenpriester des Amon*, p. 35, note) would prove the king to be Pemou.

[b]If this name be considered a variant of Sheshonk III, we then have two Niles of the year 6, of very different levels, with two different high priests! We are therefore certainly dealing with a Sheshonk to be distinguished from Sheshonk III. His name differs greatly from that of Sheshonk IV.

## REIGN OF SHESHONK I

### RECORDS ON MUMMY-BANDAGES OF ZEPTAHEFONEKH[a]

**699.** The Der el-Bahri cache of royal mummies was opened for the last time, in so far as we know, not earlier than the year 11 of Sheshonk I, to insert the body of the "*third prophet of Amon, chief of a district* (ᶜ ᵓ *-n-ḳ* ᶜ *ḥ*[b]), *king's-son of Ramses, Zeptahefonekh.*" The dedications on the temple linen, used for his bandages, are of importance, as they show that Sheshonk I was in control at Thebes in his fifth year, when he had already installed his son Yewepet as High Priest of Amon, thus at last interrupting the hereditary succession to that office, and securing the control of the priestly principality of Thebes for his own family.

**700.** Fine linen which the King of Upper and Lower Egypt, Lord of the Two Lands, Kheperhezre-Setepnere; Son of Re, Lord of Diadems, Meriamon-Sheshonk I, made for his father, Amon, year 10. Fine linen which the High Priest of Amon-Re, commander in chief of the army, Yewepet, triumphant, king's-son of the Lord of the Two Lands, Sheshonk (I), made for his father, Amon, year 10.

Another bandage has the same inscription of year 11 and a third of the year 5.[c]

---

### BUILDING INSCRIPTION[d]

**701.** The great temple at Karnak had received no essential additions since the close of the Nineteenth Dynasty, the Ramessids of the Twentieth, and the priests of the Twenty-

[a]Maspero, *Momies royales*, 573.

[b]Doubtless miscopied in the publication.

[c]The name of the High Priest is lost; but as it was introduced by exactly the same formula, it is undoubtedly also to be attributed to Yewepet.

[d]Cut in the walls of the sandstone quarry at Silsileh; published by Champollion,

first Dynasty having given their attention to the temple of Khonsu. Sheshonk I, when he had ruled twenty years and firmly established his dynasty, determined to adorn the Karnak temple with a worthy memorial of his family. He therefore built a triumphal gate between the small Amon-temple of Ramses III and the then front of the Karnak temple, the present second pylon. It formed a westward extension of the south wall of the great hypostyle hall, and it covered up historical reliefs of Ramses II on the west end of that wall, as well as on the south end of the second pylon, which are still covered. This gate, commonly called the Bubastite gate, bears the records of the Bubastite family in Thebes. It immediately received the triumphal relief commemorating Sheshonk I's campaign in Palestine (§§ 709 ff.), and the high-priestly sons of the dynasty recorded their temple annals upon it. The designation of Sheshonk I's projected building in the Silsileh inscription (§ 707) is such as to show clearly that he planned also the entire first court at Karnak, including the first pylon before it.[a]

**702.** The priestly chief of works, Haremsaf, whom Sheshonk dispatched to Silsileh to procure the stone for the new gate, left in the quarry a stela recording his work there, and its purpose. While the king is credited with the initiation of the enterprise, his son Yewepet, High Priest of Amon, is given almost as prominent a place on the stela as the king himself; while his titles increase the impression that he enjoyed the power of a semi-independent ruler of Upper Egypt. At the top is the king led by Mut into the presence

*Monuments*, II, 122 *bis;* Lepsius, *Denkmäler*, III, 254, *c*, and partially Brugsch, *Thesaurus*, VI, 1242. I had also a collation of the Berlin squeeze, by Mr. Alan Gardiner, which he kindly placed at my disposal. From this I published the building portion (§ 706) of the inscription, in the *American Journal of Semitic Languages and Literatures*, XXI, 24.

[a]See my remarks, *ibid.*, 25.

of Amon, Harakhte, and Ptah. Behind the king, his son, the High Priest of Amon, Yewepet, represented with the same stature as the king, offers incense. His titles in the side columns occupy as much room as those of his father. Below the relief is an inscription (§§ 703–5) attributing the opening of this part[a] of the quarry to the king, and again in the same words to Yewepet. Below all, Haremsaf has had his own kneeling figure depicted, before which is an inscription (§§ 706–8) recording his commission and its execution.

*Royal Titulary*

**703.** [1]Favorite of the Two Goddesses: Shining-in-the-Double-Crown-like-Horus-Son-of-Isis, Satisfying-the-Gods-with-Truth; Golden Horus; Mighty-in-Strength, Smiting-the-Nine-Bows, Great-in-Victory; Good God, Re in his form, shape of the likeness of Harakhte, whom Amon placed upon his throne, to establish that which he had begun, to set in order Egypt anew; [2]the king of Upper and Lower Egypt, Kheperhezre-Setepnere.

*Sheshonk I, Opener of the Quarry*

**704.** [3]He made the opening of the quarry anew, as a beginning of the work, which the Son of Re, Meriamon-Sheshonk (I) made; who makes monuments for his father Amon-Re, lord of Thebes; that he may celebrate the jubilees of Re, and (pass) [4]the years of Atum, living forever. "O my good lord, mayest thou cause those who come during myriads of years, to say: 'Excellent is that which has been done for Amon!' Mayest thou bear witness that I have reigned a great reign."

*Yewepet, Opener of the Quarry*

**705.** He made the opening of the quarry anew, as a beginning of the work, [5]which the High Priest of Amon-Re, king of gods, commander in chief of the army, Yewepet (*Yw-w*ᵓ*-p-ty*), triumphant, who is leader of the great army of the whole South, the royal son of the Lord of the Two Lands, Meriamon-Sheshonk (I), made for his lord, for Amon-Re, king of gods; that he may obtain life, prosperity, health, long life,

[a]The part in which the stela is.

might, victory, and advanced old age[a] in Thebes, "O my good lord, mayest thou cause those who come during myriads of years, to say: 'Excellent is that which has been done for Amon!' Mayest thou bear witness that I have done a great deed."

*Dispatch of Haremsaf*

**706.** [1]Year 21, second month of the third season, — —.[b] On this day his majesty was in the house of Isis (named): "The-Great-Ka-of-Harakhte." [2]His majesty commanded that command be [3]given to the divine father of Amon-Re, king of gods, master of ⌈secret things⌉ [4]of the house of Harakhte, chief of works of the Lord of the Two Lands, Haremsaf (*Ḥr-m-s*ʾ*f*), [5]triumphant, to conduct every work ⌈— —⌉ [6]the choicest — of Silsileh, to make very great monuments for the house of his august father, [7]Amon-Re, lord of Thebes.

*Plans for Bubastite Gate*

**707.** His majesty gave stipulations for [8]building a very great pylon[c] of ⌈—⌉, in order to brighten Thebes; [9]erecting its double doors of myriads of cubits (in height), in order to make a jubilee-court[d] [10]for the house of his father, Amon-Re, king of gods; and to surround it with a colonnade.

*Return of Haremsaf*

**708.** [11]There returned in safety to the Southern City (Thebes), to the place where his majesty was, the divine father of Amon-Re, [12]king of gods, master of ⌈secret things⌉ of the house of Harakhte, chief of works in "House-of-Kheperhezre-Setepnere-in-Thebes,"[e] [13]great in the love of his lord, the king, Haremsaf, [14]triumphant. He said: "All that thou didst say has come to pass, O [15]my good lord; none sleeping at night, nor slumbering by day, but building the eternal work without [17]ceasing."

*Reward of Haremsaf*

The favors of the king's-presence were given him, his reward was things of [18]silver and gold. . . . . . . .[f]

[a]Not "(as) a great chief;" see *Recueil*, 15, 84, l. 6.

[b]Not a lacuna; the day has been omitted by the scribe.

[c]Written as a clearly made representation of a pylon.

[d]*Wsḫ-ḥb-śd*.

[e]The name of the great Karnak temple under Sheshonk I.

[f]The conclusion of fifteen words is unintelligible.

## GREAT KARNAK RELIEF[a]

**709.** The campaign of Sheshonk in Palestine in the fifth year of Rehoboam of Judah (1 Kings 14:25), probably about 926 B. C., must have taken place in the latter half of the reign of the founder of the new dynasty. He possessed no monument in Thebes, upon which he might record the achievement until his twenty-first year (about 924 B. C.), when he built the Bubastite gate in the Karnak temple and the first court to which it leads (§§ 701–8). Its wall then received a victorious relief of the conventional character, the inscriptions in which are made up of stereotyped phrases drawn from earlier monuments of the same kind, which are, therefore, too vague, general, and indecisive to furnish any solid basis for a study of Sheshonk's campaign. Had we not the brief reference in the Old Testament to his sack of Jerusalem, we should hardly have been able to surmise that the relief was the memorial of a specific campaign. However, as it is the only monumental record of the campaign[b] which we possess, it has been given in full below.

---

[a]On the outside of the south wall of the great Karnak temple, between the Bubastite gate and the south wall of the hypostyle, adjoining the reliefs of Ramses II. It is published by Champollion, *Monuments*, 284, 285; Rosellini, *Monumenti Storici*, 148; Lepsius, *Denkmäler*, III, 252, 253, *a;* Mariette, *Voyage dans la haute Egypte*, II, 42. Besides these, the list alone has been published: Brugsch, *Geographische Inschriften*, II, XXIV; Champollion, *Notices descriptives*, II, 113–19; and a collation by Maspero, *Recueil*, VII, 100, 101. I had also several photographs. The list is rapidly perishing; four names in the seventh row (Nos. 105–8) long ago fell out and are in Berlin; No. 27, Megiddo, has either fallen out or been removed; many names once legible are no longer so. And yet this priceless monument has never been exhaustively copied and published, in such a manner as a classical monument of its character would be. The best of the publications (apart from Mariette's photograph in *Voyage*) is Lepsius'.

[b]There are two other monumental references to the campaign. (1) the record of Syrian tribute at Karnak (§§ 723, 724); (2) the title attached to the name of an official of the time: "*[follow]er of the king on his campaigns in the countries of Retenu*" (fragment of coffin from the Ramesseum; Petrie, *Ramesseum*, Pl. XXX *a*, No. 1; Müller, *Orientalistische Litteraturzeitung*, IV, 280–82). There is some question as to the date of the second reference; nor is it the only reference to the Asiatic war of this period, as stated by Müller (*ibid.*, 281).

710. Fortunately for us, the relief is accompanied by a list of the towns and localities plundered by Sheshonk, and as this list is our sole source for determining the limits of his campaign, we must briefly note the extent of territory which it involves. It enables us to control the statement of Amon in the relief (§ 722, l. 19), crediting Sheshonk with having captured Mitanni. No towns so far north can be found on the list. The reference to Mitanni is unquestionably drawn from older inscriptions, and the Egyptian scribes of this period probably knew little more of the vanished Euphrates kingdom than the authors of the Bentresh stela (III, §§ 429 ff.), a little later, knew of the same distant region.

711. The list[a] is introduced as usual by the Nine Bows, and the names which follow are unquestionably arranged in two main groups: first, the towns of Israel, and second, those of Judah. The main line of cleavage is probably somewhere between Nos. 50 and 60 or 65, but that this line is exclusive, or that the groups themselves are exclusive, is by no means certain. Roughly stated, the list devoted between fifty and sixty names to Israel, and about a hundred to Judah. Of the total of seventy-five or so that are preserved, only seventeen can be located with certainty, and two more with probability.[b] Fourteen of these belong to Israel; they are mostly important towns; while the remaining five in Judah are, with one exception, obscure villages. This may be an accident of preservation. The southernmost town captured is Arad, in southern Judah, and the northernmost is possibly Beth Anath, in northern Galilee, which, with Adamah, west of the Sea of Galilee, would stand alone, well north of the group of towns in the Kishon valley, which

[a] On its arrangement and extent, see the description of the relief (§ 718).

[b] Of these nineteen, sixteen are found in the Old Testament.

are more likely to mark the limit of Sheshonk's northern advance.

**712.** Let us now notice the names in the list which may be identified and located.[a] Leaving the Nine Bows, which introduce the list, the following three names (10–12)[b] are mutilated and unrecognizable, the list then proceeds with towns of Israel in the Kishon valley and vicinity: No. 13, Rabbith (*Rw-b* ᵓ *-ty* = רַבִּית); No. 14, Taanach (*T* ᵓ *-* ᶜ *-n-k-* ᵓ = תַּעְנָךְ); No. 15, Shunem (*Š* ᵓ *-n-m-* ᵓ = שׁוּנֵם);[c] No. 16, Bethshean (*B* ᵓ *-ty-Š* ᵓ *-n-r-* ᵓ = בֵּיתשְׁאָן);[d] No. 17, Rehob (*Rw-ḥ* ᵓ *-b* ᵓ *-* ᵓ = רְחֹב);[e] No. 18, Hapharaim (*ḥ* ᵓ *-pw-rw-m-* ᵓ = חֲפָרַיִם);[f] No. 22, Machanaim (*M-ḥ* ᵓ *-n-m* = מַחֲנַיִם);[g] No. 23, Gibeon (*ḳ-b* ᵓ *-* ᶜᵓ *-n* ᵓ = גִּבְעוֹן);[h] No. 24, Beth-

[a]A number of important names in the list had already been identified by Champollion; many are due to Brugsch (*Geographische Inschriften*, II, 56–71); a study by Maspero *Zeitschrift für ägyptische Sprache*, 1880, 44 ff.), a useful treatment by Müller (*Asien und Europa*, 166–72), and another fuller essay by Maspero, in *Transactions of the Victoria Institute*, 27, 63–122, followed by a discussion by Conder, 123–30). The following numbers all refer to Lepsius, *Denkmäler;* Champollion, *Notices descriptives*, has inserted a lost oval between 41 and 45, omitted two between 48 and 51, omitted one between 59 and 61, and misplaced 65 behind 68. The second and last of these errors were noted by Maspero in collating the original (*Recueil*, VII, 100), but his study (*Zeitschrift für ägyptische Sprache*, 1880, 44 ff.) employs the hopelessly confused numbering of Champollion, *Notices descriptives*, which makes it difficult to follow. Much could still be done with the list by a thorough Semitist. I have treated only those names calculated to elucidate the list as a whole, or those which can be geographically placed. The customary juggling with Semitic roots, taken from a Hebrew dictionary, may be made to fill many pages, but is, historically, totally valueless.

[b]The identification of two of them, as Gaza and Megiddo, is a guess; the occurrence of Megiddo later (27) shows that we cannot look for it here.

[c]These three all in Issachar.

[d]Manasseh; *n-r* = *n*, as commonly.

[e]Probably not Rehob by the Sea of Galilee; see Müller, *Asien und Europa*, 153.

[f]Issachar. No. 19, ᵓ*-d-rw-m* ᵓ*-m*, that is, אדרם, is perhaps אֲדוֹרַיִם, Adaroim in Judah. We should then necessarily conclude that the list has mixed the towns of the two kingdoms. No. 20 is lost, and No. 21 (*Š* ᵓ*-w* ᵓ*-d*) is unknown.

[g]East of Jordan, Gad.

[h]Benjamin.

horon (*B ͗ -ty-ḥ-w ͗ -rw-n* = בֵּית חֹרוֹן);[a] No. 26, Ajalon (*͗ -yw-rw-n*=אַיָּלוֹן);[b] No. 27, Megiddo (*M-k-d-yw*=מְגִדּוֹ).[c]

**713.** Next follows the much-discussed *Yw-d-h-m-rw-k* or ידהמלך (No. 29), which is, of course, not to be rendered "the king or kingdom of Judah."[d] With No. 32,[e] *ᶜ ͗ -r ͗ -n ͗*, ערן, we are again in the vicinity of southern Carmel; for this place is the Aruna, passed by Thutmose III on his march to Megiddo (II, 425). No. 34,[f] *ḏ ͗ -d-p-t-ṯ-rw*, זדפת־אל or צדפתל, was probably a city of central Palestine,[g] while the next recognizable name,[h] No. 38, *S ͗ -yw-k ͗*, is phonetically exactly equivalent to Socoh (שׂוֹכֹה),[i] and it would carry us into Judah.

---

[a]Ephraim; No. 25, *ḳ ͗ -d-ṯ-m*, is unknown.

[b]Dan, but in Israel.

[c]Issachar (though held by Manasseh). No. 28, *͗ -d-rw* = אדר (or אדל) agrees phonetically exactly with אַדָּר in Judah (Josh. 15:3; Numb. 34:4), but, again we should have a long leap from Israel into Judah; and Addar is well reproduced in No. 100, certainly in Judah.

[d]The impossibility of this rendering was long ago shown by Brugsch (*Geographische Inschriften*, II, 62, 63). He also proposed rendering *h* as the article; so also Müller (*Asien und Europa*, 167; *Proceedings of the Society of Biblical Archæology*, X, 81), who proposed "Hand of the King." The difficulty is that this involves the transliteration of the Semitic article by the Egyptian scribe, whereas in the lists regularly, and in this list everywhere, the article is translated (see Nos. 71, 77, 87, 90, 92, 94, etc.). The location of the place is unknown.

[e]No. 30 is lost; and No. 31, *Ḥ ͗ -y ͗ -n-m*, חינם or חאנם, is unknown.

[f]No. 33, *B ͗ -rw-m ͗ -m*, בלמם, is unknown.

[g]It is not known from the Old Testament, but it is mentioned in Papyrus Anastasi, I, 22, 5, where it appears to be between northern Israel and Benjamin (see Müller, *Asien und Europa*, 167).

[h]No. 35 is too broken for use; No. 36, *B ͗ -ty-t ͗ -rw-m ͗ m* (*m ͗ m*=*m* in this list), or בֵּית־תֶּלֶם, "House of the furrow," is unknown. In the collation (*Recueil*, VII, 100, No. 36), the *ty* has been overlooked, but it is perfectly clear on the photograph. Hence the long paragraph on the word (*Transactions of the Victoria Institute*, 27, 102, 103) falls away. No 37, *K ͗ -ḳ ͗ -rw-y*, perhaps a כִּכָּר (with ק in the middle for כ ?), is unknown.

[i]There are two cities of this name in Judah, one in the valley of Elah toward the Shephelah, and the other in the highlands southwest of Hebron. See the objections of Müller (*Asien und Europa*, 161).

**714.** The entire next row (40–52) is lost,[a] except the first name, which began with an Abel, "meadow;" and the next row (53–65) is in little better condition. It contains three familiar names, No. 56, ᵓ-*d-m*-ᵓ or אדמא, perhaps Edom;[b] and No. 57, *ḏ*ᵓ-*rw-m*ᵓ*m* (read *m*?) or צורים, "Rocks," which, however, are of slight geographical value; and No. 59, *Y-rw-ḏ*ᵓ-ᵓ, Yeraza[c] of the Annals (II, 326, l. 12), in northwestern Judah.

**715.** Nos. 65, 66, *P*ᵓ-ᶜᵓ-*m-ḳ* ᶜᵓ-*y*ᵓ-*ḏ*-ᵓ,[d] "The[e] Valley of עיזא, or עצא," form the first example of a long series of compound names (each occupying two rings), of which the first member is a well-known Semitic word, like שִׁבֹּלֶת, "Stream" (73 and 75), נֶגֶב, "South-country" (84, 90, 92), and חקל, "Field" (68, 71, 77, 87, 94, 96, 101, 107). But, unfortunately, these names, while often capable of translation, cannot be geographically located. The most interesting is (Nos. 71, 72) *P*ᵓ[e]-*ḥw-ḳ-rw*-ᵓ-ᵓ-*b*ᵓ-*r*ᵓ-*m*, or חקל[f]

[a]A few fragments in Maspero's collation.

[b]But names of countries do not appear in this list. There was an אֲדָמָה in Naphtali, and Müller proposes "Edumia-Dôme" in eastern Ephraim (Müller, *Asien und Europa*, 168).

[c]See Müller, *Asien und Europa*, 152, note 1.

[d]There is no *m* at the end according to Maspero's collation (*Recueil*, VII, 100, No. 63, confirmed by photograph); hence there was no basis for the identification with עַצְמוֹן in Judah (Müller, *Asien und Europa*, 168). Why it is still read with *m* by Maspero (*Transactions of the Victoria Institute*, 27, 108, 109) in 1892, I do not know.

[e]*P*ᵓ is the Egyptian article.

[f]Even if this word be Aramaic, it would not militate against the identification of the second part of the name with Abram. But its frequent occurrence in this list, quite justifies Bondi's conclusion that, although not found in the Old Testament, חקל is an old Canaanite word. The strange ending ᵓ in which Müller would see the Aramaic status emphaticus, is of no significance here, for it is added to many names in the list, which we know existed in Palestine many centuries before the Aramaizing of the Palestinian dialects began. It is not unlikely that it is a feminine ending (for the undoubted feminine termination ת exists in the list only in those words in which is is still preserved in Hebrew. The ת elsewhere was therefore lost between the time of Thutmose III and Sheshonk I). That the

אברם,[a] which can be nothing else than "*The Field of Abram.*"[b] That the name of the traditional ancestor of the Hebrews should be found among the towns of southern Palestine, while of great interest, is not remarkable. We already have the name of Jacob in the lists of Thutmose III, and probably also that of Joseph. We might, therefore, expect to find the name of Abram, especially at this time, when we know that the traditions of their ancestors were especially cherished and daily current among the Hebrews, and were beginning at last to take permanent form. But the narratives of Genesis are all later than this list of Sheshonk; hence this is the earliest mention of Abram's name in an historical document—his first appearance in history.

**716.** The remainder of the list, as we have stated, offers very little which can be geographically determined. No. 100, ᵓ-*d-r*ᵓ-ᵓ,[c] is doubtless אַדָּר in Judah, while of two

---

ending ᵓ is a feminine ending in this list is indicated by the fact that this very word חקל, while four times written with the ending ᵓ, is once written with no ending, and once with *t* and the land-determinative. Such a *t* was at this time, exactly as in modern Arabic, not pronounced, but indicated merely the vowel *ă* or *ĕ*, the connection between the lost feminine *t* and the word to which it belonged. Finally it should be noticed that the plural of the word in this list is חקלם (107), which I need hardly state is a Hebrew and not an Aramaic plural. While masculine, it may still belong to a feminine noun like שׁנה, pl., שׁנים.

[a]This word is explained by Maspero (*Transactions of the Victoria Institute*, 27, 83) as a plural of אָבֵל, which he gives as "אֲבֵלִים." This equivalence is phonetically perfect, but nevertheless impossible. This plural is given its vowel-points as if it were an existent form, but the plural of אָבֵל, "meadow," does not occur. The word is used in Hebrew only as the first member of an annexion in geographical names, e. g., אָבֵל כְּרָמִים, and never occurs in any other combination. This is also its use in all of the other names in which it occurs in our list. Moreover, if this were not so, we must demand for the second number some specific term, name, or epithet.

[b]On showing this identification to Erman, he looked up his own studies on this list, and to his own surprise he found in his manuscript that he had made the same identification in 1888. It was also made independently by Schaefer.

[c]Repeated in No. 117.

Arads (Nos. 108, 110, ᶜ ͻ -*rw-d-* ͻ), one must be עֲרָד in the desert of Judah. No. 124 is possibly to be emended to Beth Anoth,[a] and No. 125 is probably Sharuhen of southern Judah.[b] We look in vain for Jerusalem, which (according to 1 Kings 14:25) was also plundered by Sheshonk. It must have been lost in one of the lacunæ.

Professor Sayce has kindly sent me the following note on the list:

"In the newly recovered portion of the list, Legrain has discovered the name of Jordan (*Yw-r-d-n*), and after *Raphia* and *L-b-a-n* we have ᶜ*-n-p-rw-n*, עין־פרן (see Gen. 21:19, 21), and finally *H-* ͻ *-m* (as in the list of Thothmes III)." He doubtless refers to readings in the bottom lines, which are not yet published.

**717.** The historical conclusions to be drawn from the peculiarities in the language and writing of the list seem to me to have been misunderstood. The alleged Aramaisms are very doubtful; but even if they be admitted, their use by the hieroglyphic scribe is so utterly opposed to the usage of Aramaic that they would prove only the personal peculiarity of an Egyptian scribe, slightly acquainted with Aramaic, and absolutely nothing as to the pronunciation of the name of a given town current in Palestine. The conclusion that this list shows that Aramaic had already become the leading language of Syria, therefore, seems to me, to be without basis.

---

[a]BethAnath (Josh. 19:38; Judg. 1:33) is in Naphtali; we may equally well read, with Müller, BethAnoth (Josh. 15:59), which was in Judah (modern Bêt-ᶜ Anûn ?).

[b]No. 118, *P* ͻ *-b* ͻ *-y-* ͻ, should be compared with the land *B* ͻ which Schaefer tells me occurs on Seti I's stela at Tell-esh-Shehab in the Hauran. From the squeeze he read: "*Mut, mistress of B* ͻ (*nb*ᵓ*t-B* ͻ, with *b* ͻ -bird and hill-country)." If BethAnath of Napthali occurs in the second half of the list, a place in the Hauran might also be there.

The arrangement and content of the famous relief and its inscriptions will be found in the following description.

*Scene*

718. The king[a] on the right gathers in his left hand the hair of a group of kneeling Asiatics, who raise their hands appealing for mercy, as he brandishes his war-mace over their heads. On the left, Amon approaches, extending to the Pharaoh a sword, and leading to him by cords five lines of sixty-five captives. Below these are five lines more, containing ninety-one captives, led by the presiding goddess of Thebes. There are thus one hundred and fifty-six captives, each symbolizing a Palestinian town, the name of which is inclosed in a crenelated oval, above which appear the shoulders and head of the captive in each case.[b] Of these names, the fourth and tenth rows have almost entirely perished, involving the loss of thirty-one names; while twelve more, in different places, have also disappeared. Omitting badly mutilated examples, allowing for at least fifteen names which occupy two ovals each, and eliminating the Nine Bows, some seventy-five names of ancient Palestinian cities have here survived.

719. The accompanying inscriptions are the following:

*Over the Kneeling Captives*

Smiting the chiefs of the Nubian Troglodytes, of all inaccessible countries, all the lands of the Fenkhu, the countries — —.

---

[a]This figure has now totally disappeared, as it evidently was only painted and never hewn in relief. From similar scenes we are able to restore the conventional figure of the Pharaoh, as above described.

[b]Compare the similar lists of earlier times; Thutmose III (II, 402, 403); Seti I (III, 113, 114); Ramses III (IV, 130, 131).

*Before the King*

Sheshonk I,[a] king, great in fame, smiting the countries that assail him, achieving with his sword, that the Two Lands may know that he has smitten the chiefs of all countries.

*With Amon*

**720.** [1]Welcome! my beloved son, Sheshonk,[b] —— mighty in strength. Thou hast smitten the lands and the countries, [2]thou hast crushed the Nubian Troglodytes, [thy] sword was mighty among the Asiatics; they were made fragments every moment. Thy victorious fame — all lands. [3]Thou wentest forth in victory, and thou hast returned in might; ⌈thou hast united⌉[c] —; I have ⌈—⌉[d] for thee the countries that knew not Egypt, that had begun to invade [thy] boundaries, in order to cut off their heads. [4]Victory is given into thy hands, all lands and all countries are united ——, the fear of thee is as far as the four pillars [of heaven], the terror[e] of thy majesty is among the Nine Bows: thou hast ⌈—⌉ the hearts of the countries. Thou art Horus over the Two Lands, [5]thou art ⌈—⌉ against thy enemies, when thou hast smitten the foe. Take thou my victorious sword,[f] thou whose war-mace has smitten the chiefs of the countries.

**721.** [6]Utterance of Amon-Re. . . . . . . .[g] [7]"My heart is very glad, when I see thy victories, [8-11]my son, Meriamon-Sheshonk, my beloved, who camest forth from me, in order to be my champion. I have seen the excellence of thy plans; which thou hast executed, the — of my temple, which thou hast established [for] me, in Thebes, the great seat to which my heart [inclines]. [12]Thou hast begun to make monuments in Southern Heliopolis, Northern Heliopolis, and every city —— thereof for the ⌈sole⌉ god of its district. Thou hast made my temple of millions

---

[a]Threefold titulary.

[b]Some epithets omitted in translation.

[c]*Sm*ꜣ *?* Or: "*thou hast explored*" (*wb*ꜣ *?*).

[d]The *p* before the *s*, given by Lepsius, is probably an accidental fracture or chisel mark (photograph); but it may be the *wsḫ*-vessel, although *wsḫ*, "*extended, enlarged,*" does not fit the context.

[e]*Nhm*, "*battle-cry?*"

[f]Referring, of course, to the sword which he is represented as extending to the king.

[g]Titles of the god.

of years, — — of electrum, wherein I —. [13]Thy heart is satisfied over ⌜———⌝ ————. Thou hast — [14]more than any king of them all. Thou hast smitten every land, my mighty sword was the source of the victories which I have given — — — — all the Asiatics [15](*Mntyw-Sṯt*). Thy fire raged as a flame behind them, it fought against every land, which thou didst gather together, which thy majesty gave to it, (being) Montu [16]the mighty overwhelming his enemies. Thy war-mace, it struck down thy foes, the Asiatics of distant countries; thy serpent-crest was mighty among them."

**722.** "I made thy boundaries [17]as far as thou desiredst; I made the Southerners come in obeisance to thee, and the Northerners to the greatness of thy fame. Thou hast made a great slaughter among them without number, [18]falling in their valleys, being multitudes, annihilated and perishing afterward, like those who have never been born. All the countries that came —⌜—⌝; [19]thy majesty has destroyed them in the space of a moment. I have trampled for thee them that rebelled against thee, overthrowing [for] thee the Asiatics of the army of Mitanni (*M-ṯ-n*); [20]I have humbled them ⌜—⌝ beneath thy feet. I am thy father, the lord of gods, Amon-Re, lord of Thebes, sole leader, whose remnant[a] escapes not, that I may cause thy valor to be [⌜remembered⌝] in the future[b] through all eternity."

---

## PRESENTATION OF TRIBUTE[c]

**723.** This fragmentary inscription in all likelihood accompanied a relief depicting the presentation of tribute to Amon; for it represents Sheshonk addressing Amon, and delivering to him the tribute of Syria (*ḫ ᵓ rw*) and Nubia. The date is unfortunately lost, but it is, of course, after the Palestinian campaign. Sheshonk evidently controlled lower Nubia,

[a]The remnant whom he has not slain.

[b]Text has *m nḫt* (with the legs); but we must read either *m ḫt* or *n m ḫt*, that is, "*hereafter*," or "*for the hereafter*."

[c]Wall inscription in great temple of Karnak, in a chamber immediately on the northwest of the sanctuary (Champollion, "Cour U"); published: Champollion, *Notices descriptives*, II, 142–44; Lepsius, *Denkmaler*, III, 255, *c* (royal name only).

as the tribute of that country is too specifically enumerated to be considered as a conventional boast. This fact is in harmony with the claim in the great relief, that Sheshonk I smote Nubia (§ 720, l. 2).

**724.** [Year] — under the majesty of King Sheshonk[a] (I) ——— [⌜in⌝] "The-House-of-Millions-of-Years-of-King-Kheperhezre-Setepnere-(*Ḫpr-ḥḏ-Rᶜ Stp-n-Rᶜ*),-Son-of-Re,-Meriamon-Sheshonk (*Šꜣ-šꜣ-n-ḳ*)-I,-Which-is-in-Memphis (*Ḥ·t-kꜣ-Ptḥ*)" ——— O Amon, thou maker of the land of the Negro ———[b] tribute of the land of Syria (*Ḫꜣ-rw*) ——— I bring it to thee from the land of the Negro ——— red cattle, thy firstlings[c] ——— thy gazelles, thy panther-skins.

---

## KARNAK STELA[d]

**724A.** On this stela Sheshonk I recorded a very interesting account of his Asiatic campaign, but it is now in such a fragmentary state that very little can be discerned beyond the fact that some incident, possibly a battle of the campaign, occurred on the shores of the Bitter Lakes in the Isthmus of Suez. At the top of the stela Sheshonk I and his son Yewepet are shown in a relief offering wine to Amon-Re. Of the inscription below them, only the following fragments are intelligible:

——— Said his majesty to the court: "——— the evil things which they have done." Said they: ——— his horses after him, while they knew (it) not. Lo ——— His majesty made a great slaughter among them ——— he —ed them upon the ⌜dyke⌝ of the shore of Kemwer[e] (*Km-wr*). He it was ———.

---

[a]Full fivefold titulary.

[b]The length of the lacuna is uncertain.

[c]With determinative of cattle.

[d]Fragments of a stela of gritstone, found by Legrain, in hall K, at Karnak; *Annales*, V, 38, 39.

[e]See I, 493, l. 21, and note.

## DAKHEL STELA[a]

725. This monument is dated under a Sheshonk whose prenomen is not given. As his nineteenth year is mentioned he cannot be Sheshonk II; so that the uncertainty lies between Sheshonk I and Sheshonk III. Of the two, Sheshonk I seems to me the more probable, as the document mentions a revolt in the oasis, and a reorganization, which would be especially likely to occur at the advent of a new dynasty, and we find Dakhel under the control of Sheshonk I's successor, Osorkon I.

The document is really the record of the successful claim of a certain priest of the Southern Oasis, Nesubast, to a well alleged to belong to his family. The case is tried before Khonsu, the god of the oasis, and a legal decision sought from him, in the manner customary since the Twenty-first Dynasty. As a legal document it will be taken up in a later volume of this series, devoted exclusively to such documents. The stela interests us here, because Nesubast presented his claim on the arrival of the new governor of the oasis, Wayeheset,[b] a priest of Diospolis Parva, whom Sheshonk sent to reorganize the oasis, then in a state of rebellion, and probably plundered and wasted. The oasis was used as a place of banishment for political exiles, and such an outbreak, as we have stated, might be expected at the accession of a new dynasty.

The name of the new governor is Libyan, like the new

[a]Limestone stela, 37 inches high, 26 inches wide, 4½ inches thick, with inscription of 20 lines in hieratic; found by Captain H. G. Lyons, in 1894, at the village of Mut, in the oasis of Dakhel. Published by Spiegelberg, *Recueil*, 21, 12–21, with an excellent pioneer study, and transcription, upon which my own treatment is essentially based.

[b]A relief at the top of the stela shows the governor and Nesubast praying, probably before one of the wells involved. Two women, probably their wives, appear with them.

dynasty he served, and the stela, both in its form and language, plainly betrays its half-barbarous origin at the hands of partly Egyptianized Libyans, in the distant oasis.

*Date*

**726.** [1]Year 5, fourth month of the second season, day 16, of the king, the Pharaoh, L. P. H., Sheshonk, L. P. H., beloved of Amon-Re.

*Arrival of Wayeheset*

On this day ⌈went up⌉ the son of the chief (*ms*) of the Me; [2]chief (ᶜ ᵓ) of a district (*ḳ ᶜ ḥ*);[a] prophet of Hathor of Diospolis Parva; prophet of Horus ⌈of the South⌉, lord of Perzoz (*Pr-ḏ ᵓ ḏ ᵓ*), prophet of Sutekh, lord of the oasis; chief of irrigation, [3]overseer of ⌈—⌉;[b] the chief of the two lands[c] of the oasis, and the two towns[d] of the oasis, Wayeheset (*W ᵓ -yw-h ᵓ -s ᵓ -t ᵓ*); when Pharaoh, L. P. H., sent him to organize the land of the oasis, [4]after it had been found to be in a state of rebellion, and desolate, on the day of arrival to inspect the wells and cisterns [5]which are behind the oasis (*nty s ᵓ wt*), *ḥbs*-wells, and *ww*-wells, which ⌈lie behind, and look eastward⌉, (even) the cisterns and wells, [6]when the prophet of Sutekh, Nesubast (*Ns-sw-b ᵓ-yś˙t*), son of Peheti (*P ᵓ ḥ ᵓ ty*), spake before him, saying:

*Claim of Nesubast*

**727.** "Behold, a ⌈flowing⌉ spring, lying here toward the east (⌈named⌉): 'Rising-of-Re,' which this [7][cistern][e] of Re sees, before which thou art; it is a citizen's-cistern belonging to Tewhenut (*T ᵓ yw-ḥnw˙t*), whose mother is Henutenter (*Ḥnw˙t-ntrw*), my mother." The prophet and chief Wayeheset; he said: "Stand before Sutekh [8][⌈and tell⌉] it, this day, when the prophet brings out in procession this august [god], Sutekh, the great in strength, son of Nut, the great god, in the year 5, fourth month of the second season, day 25, at his beautiful feast of Urshu (*Wršw*)."

---

[a]Besides the will of Yewelot (§ 741, l. 23), this title is found on the coffin of Zeptahefonekh (Maspero, *Momies royales*, 573), also of the Twenty-second Dynasty.

[b]Agriculture or gardening of some sort is indicated by the word (*št ᵓ y*).

[c]Viz., el-Khargeh and Dakhel, which together form the Southern Oasis, known to the ancients as *Oasis Major;* see Spiegelberg, *loc. cit.*, 18.

[d]Viz., el-Hibe and Dakhel; see Spiegelberg, *ibid.*

[e]Restored from l. 9.

*Claim Referred to Sutekh*

**728.** The chief Wayeheset stood in the presence (of the god), saying: [9]"O Sutekh, thou great god! If it be true as to Nesubast, son of Peheti, that the northwestern spring of this well, the cistern (⌜called⌝): 'Rising-of-Re,' this cistern of Re, which is behind the oasis, belongs to Tewhenut, his mother, [10](then) confirm thou it to him this day."

The remainder of the text is of a purely legal character, narrating how, after this first interview with the god, the decision was not rendered by him for fourteen years, during which the suit must have continued. Then, in the year 19, the god confirmed Nesubast's title to the well (ll. 11 ff.).

# REIGN OF OSORKON I

## RECORD OF TEMPLE GIFTS[a]

729. In his fourth year Osorkon I, for some reason, compiled a record of all the statues, images, vessels, utensils, and the like, which he had presented to the temples of Egypt. The amounts of gold and silver involved are sufficiently large to be of economic importance. The smaller items of gold amount to 20,538 deben, or about 5,005 pounds troy; and those of silver reach a total of 72,870 deben, or over 17,762 pounds, troy. The weight of many articles is, however, not indicated. On the fragments we find mentioned 2,000,000 deben, or about 487,180 pounds troy, of silver, and again 2,300,000 deben, or about 560,297 pounds troy, of gold and silver. How far these last amounts include the others, of which they might be the totals, is not determinable. That such sums could be given to the temples, evidently in addition to their fixed incomes, is important evidence of the great wealth and prosperity of the Twenty-second Dynasty kings. These records also show that Osorkon I controlled the oases of Dakhel and Khargeh (l. 5) and hence, of course, the other oases also.

*Address to the King*[b]

730. [1]——— their bodies repose in all their favorite places; ⌈there is none hostile toward them —⌉, since the time of former kings;

---

[a]Found by Naville in a small temple beyond the outskirts of the tell of Bubastis, dating from the time of Ramses II. The inscriptions are engraved on four sides of a red granite pillar, now in twenty-nine small fragments, of which two may be put together, giving the beginnings (from one-fourth to two-thirds of the line) of six lines. Now in Cairo Museum, No. 675 (*Guide*, 177, without name of king). They are published by Naville (*Bubastis*, I, Pls. 51, 52), from drawings by Madame Naville, made from squeezes.

[b]It is not clear who is here speaking to the king.

there is none like thee in this land. Every god abides upon his throne, and enters his abode with glad heart, ⸢since⸣ thou art installed[a] to be ²[⸢king⸣] ——— thee, building their houses, and multiplying their vessels of gold, silver, and every genuine costly stone, for which his majesty ⸢gave⸣ instructions, in his capacity as Thoth (*Ḫnty-ḥsr·t*).

*Heading of List*

**731.** List of monuments which the King of Upper and Lower Egypt, Lord of the Two Lands [Osorkon I][b] made ³[for all the gods and goddesses of][c] all the cities of the South and North; from the year [1], first (month) of the [second season],[d] day 7, to the year 4,[e] fourth month of the third season, day 25; which makes 3 years, 3 months, and 16 days.

*Re-Harakhte*

**732.** His majesty gave to the house of his father, Re-Harakhte:

Beaten gold: an august chapel of Atum-Khepri, lord of Heliopolis.

| | | |
|---|---|---|
| Hammered gold | | a sphinx |
| Real lapis lazuli | | 10 sphinxes[f] |
| Amounting to: | gold | 15,345 deben |
| | silver | 14,150 deben |
| | genuine lapis lazuli | ⁴——— — |
| | ——— | 4,000 (+x) [deben] |

— vessel, amounting to 100,000 deben, presented before Re-Harakhte-Atum, begetter of his two fledgelings.

A *sḥ*[g]-⸢vessel⸣, amounting to:

| | |
|---|---|
| Gold | 5,010 deben |
| Silver | 30,720 " |
| Genuine lapis lazuli | 1,600 " |
| Black copper | 5,000 " |

---

[a][*ym-tw ḥr*] *hs·k*.

[b]Restored from other fragments, where the name several times occurs.

[c]The amount lost is probably not great, and the restoration is almost certain.

[d]Restored by computing from the total of three years, etc. There is a discrepancy of two days, which is undoubtedly due to the modern copy.

[e]Another fragment (Pl. 52, C 1) bears the date: "*year 4, second month of the second season, day 10* (+x)."

[f]Both of these statues may be figures of the king on one knee with the other limb extended behind; but the drawing is too imperfect to determine.

[g]Mistake in the copy; the same word is written with *s* and the vessel (?) a little farther on in this line. It looks like the *ḥn*-sign; should we read *sḥn?* Models of this object were presented by the king to the god; see e. g., Naville, *Festival Hall of Osorkon II*, Pl. XI.

*Hathor*

**733.** A chapel, amounting to 100,000 deben, presented before Hathor, mistress of Hotep-em-hotep.

*Mut*

Gold and silver: a *sḥ*-⸢vessel⸣, presented before Mut, the sistrum-bearer.

*Harsaphes*

Gold and silver: a *sḥ*-⸢vessel⸣.

Beaten silver: a chapel presented before[a] Harsaphes, lord of Heliopolis.

*Thoth*

Gold and silver: a *sḥ*-⸢vessel⸣. presented before Thoth, lord of Hermopolis.

*Bast*

**734.** Gold and silver: a *sḥ*-⸢vessel⸣ presented before Bast, mistress of Bubastis.

*Thoth*

Gold: a *sḥ*-⸢vessel⸣ presented before Thoth, residing in ⸢—⸣.

Gold and silver: [5]————

*Uncertain God*

———— [amounting to:]

| | |
|---|---|
| Gold | — — |
| Silver | 9,000 deben |
| Black copper | 30,000 " |

His[b] tribute is (the oases of) Dakhel and Khargeh, being wine[c] and shedeh; Hemy wine, and Syene[d] wine likewise, in order to maintain ⸢—⸣ his house according to the word thereof.

---

[a]Of course, the copy is here wrong; read *rdy·t m bꜣḥ* as elsewhere *passim;* a Harsaphes of Heliopolis is not otherwise known, as far as I have observed.

[b]What god is meant is unfortunately uncertain, owing to the lacuna at the beginning of the line.

[c]On the wines of these two oases, see Brugsch, *Reise nach der Grossen Oase,* 79–81. Brugsch's remark (*ibid.*, 92) that the wines of these two oases are not mentioned before Græco-Roman times was made before our inscription was discovered. See also Dümichen, *Oasen,* 25, 26.

[d]Not to be confused with Syene at the first cataract. These two cities (*Ḥmy* and *Swny,* misread *Nwny* by Naville) were in the western Delta, the former in the vicinity of Lake Mareotis, the latter also probably not far from it. See Brugsch, *op. cit.*, 91, Nos. 2 and 5.

*Re*

**735.** His majesty gave to the house of Re and his divine ennead:

| | |
|---|---|
| Silver: | 3 candelabras[a] |
| Gold: | ⌜—⌝. |
| Silver: | 3 *dw*-vessels. |
| | 3 offering-tablets. |
| | 17 small altars. |
| | 1 flat dish (⌜*dd·t*⌝) |
| | 1 cartouche-vessel. |
| | 2 bowls. |
| | 10 altars. |
| | 1 ⌜hin⌝-vessel. |
| | 1 spouted vessel. |
| | 1 pitcher. |
| Gold: | 3 *dw*-altars. |
| | 1 pitcher. |
| | 2 Thoth-apes. |
| | 2 large censers. |
| | 6 altars. |
| | — ————. |
| | 1 fourfold censer. |
| Gold: | — ————. |
| Lapis lazuli | — ————. |
| 6———— | 332,000 deben. |

⌜In all⌝ 594,300 deben.

*Amon-Re*

**736.** His majesty gave to the house of Amon-Re, king of gods:[b]

His majesty wrought a standing statue offering incense ⌜— —⌝, its body was of gold and silver in beaten work, amounting to:

| | |
|---|---|
| Gold | 183[c] deben |
| Silver | 19,000[d] " |
| Black copper | —— " |
| Gold[e] | a ⌜— — —⌝ |

its chapel, a censer ⌜of⌝ gold of —.

[a] *Ḥry-sḏ·t*, lit., "*fire-bearer;*" it occurs elsewhere only in the Stela of Nastesen, l. 49 (ed. Schaefer, 126).

[b] The introductory formulary, ordinarily followed by a series of nouns, is here followed by a verb.

[c] Possibly 184 or 185.

[d] The hundreds, tens, and units are lost.

[e] It is uncertain whether this continues the description of the statue or begins a new article.

Silver: an altar.

⌜———⌝.

————.

**737.** The remaining fragments contain little available material, but they have preserved several data of importance. Among these are: "*4 chapels, 3 altars of silver, a processional image of Amon of fine gold;*"[a] "*2,000,000 (+x) deben of silver;*"[b] "*2,300,000 (+x) deben of gold and silver.*"[c]

[a]*Op. cit.*, Pl. 52, M 1.

[b]*Ibid.*, C 2.

[c]*Ibid.*, I 2.

## REIGN OF TAKELOT I

### STATUE OF THE NILE-GOD DEDICATED BY THE HIGH PRIEST SHESHONK[a]

738. Maspero's surprise[b] that this monument should formerly have been so strangely misunderstood, was well grounded. The monument is one of a common class, dedicated to a god, for the sake of the well-being of the donor, which he craves from the god in a prayer inscribed upon it. The character of the donor, his origin, and his prayer are, in the case of this statue, of great historical importance. He is the High Priest of Amon, Meriamon-Sheshonk, son of Osorkon I. As his mother, Makere, is stated to be the daughter of King Pesibkenno, this king can be no other than the second of that name, the last king of the Twenty-first Dynasty.

739. It thus appears that Sheshonk I strengthened his dynasty by an alliance with the old ruling house, the Twenty-first Dynasty of Tanis, by marrying his son, Osorkon I, to the daughter of Pesibkhenno II. As High Priest of Amon at Thebes, the son of this marriage, Sheshonk, assumed royal honors, placed his name in a cartouche, and commanded all the military of Egypt. Characteristic of the turbulent conditions of the time is his prayer for "*all valiant might, to take captive his land.*" His power again shows how truly Thebes

[a]British Museum; published: Yorke and Leake, *Les principaux monuments Egyptiens du Musée Britannique*, Londres, 1827, Pl. I, Fig. 3 (translated from *Royal Society of Literature*, I; statue and cartouches only); Arundale and Bonomi, *Gallery of Antiquities*, Pl. XIII; Lepsius, *Auswahl der wichtigsten Urkunden*, XV, *a-g;* Maspero, *Momies royales*, 734–36.

[b]*Op. cit.*, 734.

had become a semi-independent principality. He finally shook off the power of the north sufficiently to make his own son his successor at Thebes.[a]

**740.**[b] Made it the High Priest of Amon-Re, king of gods, Meriamon-Sheshonk, for his lord, Amon-Re, lord of Thebes, presider over Karnak, in order to crave life, prosperity, health, long life, an advanced and happy old age, might and victory over every land and every country, ⸢—⸣ — —, all valiant might, to take captive his land; lord of South and North, the leader, Meriamon-Sheshonk, who is great leader of the army of all Egypt, king's-son of the Lord of the Two Lands, Lord of Offering, Meriamon-Osorkon (I); his mother being Makere, king's-daughter of the Lord of the Two Lands, Meriamon-Horus-Pesibkhenno (II), given life, stability, satisfaction, like Re, forever.

[a]*Ibid.*, § 44.

[b]One section number (741) is intentionally omitted.

# REIGN OF OSORKON II

## FLOOD INSCRIPTION[a]

**742.** As in the days of Nesubenebded, some two hundred years earlier, the inundation again flooded the temple of Luxor in the third year of Osorkon II, and the water rose to a depth of over two feet[b] on the temple pavement. "*All the temples of Thebes were like marshes.*" Amon was brought forth from the temple in his sacred barque, and the priests prayed that he might abate the flood.

**743.** [1]Year 3, first month of the second season, day 12,[c] under the majesty of the King of Upper and Lower Egypt, Lord of the Two Lands, Usermare-Setepnamon, L. P. H.; Son of Re, Lord of Diadems, [2]Osorkon (II)-Siese-Meriamon, given life forever.

The flood[d] came on, in this whole land; [3]it invaded the two shores as in the beginning. This land was in his power like the sea, there was no dyke[e] of [4]the people to withstand its fury. All the people were like birds upon its ⌜—⌝, the tempest — his —, suspended — — like the heavens. [5]All the temples of Thebes were like marshes.

On this day Amon caused to appear in Opet, the [barque] of his (portable) image —; [6]when he had entered the "Great House"[f] of his barque of this temple.

**744.** Then one of the prophets of Amon addressed to the

---

[a]Hieratic inscription on the inner wall, in the northwest corner of the hypostyle of the Luxor temple. Published, in transcription only, by Daressy, *Recueil*, 18, 181–84.

[b]Exactly 62 cm.; Daressy, *Recueil*, 20, 80, CLIX. Its height is determined by the record on the quai at Karnak (§ 696, No. 5).

[c]This calendar date for the high level of the inundation does not at all correspond to the place of the calendar in the seasons at this time as fixed by well-authenticated dates in other periods. Hieratic dates are usually very cursive, and there is little doubt that the transliteration is here incorrect.

[d]*Nw* or *nwn*. [e]Or: "*canal*" (ᶜ*-mw*).

[f]This is the shrine which occupies the middle of the sacred barque, the whole being borne on the shoulders of priests.

god a long hymn of forty-two lines, consisting mainly of conventional phrases common in such compositions, but it contained, of course, an appeal to moderate the inundation, which is, however, too fragmentary to be intelligible.

---

## STATUE INSCRIPTION[a]

**745.** This inscription contains only a prayer of the king, but the blessings for which he prays are of great political significance. He desires that his descendants may rule over the high priests of Amon, the chiefs of the Meshwesh, and the prophets of Harsaphes. The power of the last is evident from the long genealogy of Harpeson, whose ancestor, Namlot, a son of Osorkon II, was appointed by this king as High Priest of Harsaphes at Heracleopolis and governor of the South, with military command (§ 787, No. 11).[b]

**746.** The distribution of territory among these nobles was evidently thus: Thebes controlled at least from lower Nubia to Siut;[c] Heracleopolis, probably from Siut to the Delta; and the Meshwesh chieftains held the Delta cities, as formerly. Egypt was thus clearly divided at this time into feudal principalities, more or less responsible to the Bubastite Pharaoh. It is for the control of this tottering state by his descendants, that Osorkon II prays as follows:

---

[a]Granite stela, held by a kneeling statue of Osorkon II, at Tanis, doubtless the one published by Petrie (*Tanis*, XIV, No. 3; VI, 41, A.C.D.), as Daressy has noticed (*Recueil*, 18, 49); although Petrie thought the statue was one of Ramses II usurped by Osorkon II (*op. cit.*, 25). It was seen and copied by de Rougé (*Inscriptions hiéroglyphiques*, 71, 72), and published again by Daressy (*loc. cit.*).

[b]The same Namlot was High Priest of Amon, and thus ruled at Thebes also (§ 789).

[c]The northern boundary is fixed by the will of Yewelot (§ 741); the southern is probable from the mention of "*gold of Khenthennofer*" given by the High Priest of Amon, Osorkon (§ 770), although this gold might have been secured in trade. For Heracleopolis we have no data as to its boundaries, except that it probably began control where that of Thebes ended, viz., at Siut.

**747.** May my issue —, the seed that has come forth from my limbs, rule[a] — [8]the great — of Egypt, the hereditary princes:[b] the high priests of Amon-Re, king of gods, the great chiefs of Me and — [9]— —,[c] the prophets of Harsaphes, king of South and North, while I command that his servant come down to — —, [10]and he inclines their hearts toward the Son of Re, Meriamon-Sibast-Osorkon (II); may he put them — [11]— ⌜—⌝. Thou shalt establish my children in the [offices] [12]which I have given to them; let not the heart of brother be exalted [⌜against⌝] his brother. [⌜As [13]for⌝] Queen Kerome, may he grant that she stand before me at these ⌜my⌝ feasts. [May he [14]grant] that her male children and her —[d] may live, [15]that they may go at the head of the army, and that they bring back to me [⌜their⌝] report [16][⌜concerning⌝] the —.[e]

---

## JUBILEE INSCRIPTIONS[f]

**748.** In his twenty-second year Osorkon II celebrated his first jubilee. At Bubastis the king erected a hall in the temple for the celebration of this feast, which he therefore called the "*jubilee-hall.*" One of the surviving blocks carries the following record[g] of the erection of the building:

Appearance[h] of the majesty of this august god, beginning the way, to rest in the jubilee-house, which his majesty made anew,[i] of — —; all its walls are of electrum, the columns — —.

---

[a]Lit., "*command*" (*ṯs*).

[b]I take it that, in apposition with the preceding, three classes are enumerated: (1) high priests of Amon; (2) chiefs of the Meshwesh and ——— (?); (3) prophets of Heracleopolis.

[c]According to Daressy, this word ends in *tyw* and has the determinative of foreigners; but Rougé gives it the ending *ḳ*ɔ, with the same determinative. It may therefore be the Libyan Kehek (*ḳhḳ*).

[d]One would expect "female children" in the lacuna, but there is hardly room, and the restoration would not fit the following context.

[e]A name of foreigners ending in *ywd!* The fragments of the remaining five lines I do not understand.

[f]Blocks from the jubilee-hall of the great temple at Bubastis, published by Naville, *The Festival Hall of Osorkon II* (London).

[g]Naville, *op. cit.*, Pl. VI.

[h]The appearance of the procession bearing Amon in his shrine; this was depicted in a relief which the inscription accompanied.

[i]Or possibly: "*for the first time.*"

**749.** The walls of this building bore a long series of reliefs depicting the elaborate ceremonies accompanying the celebration of the jubilee. These are almost all of religious significance and connection; but one of the ceremonies is of great historical importance. It was, perhaps, the opening rite of the jubilee, for it commemorated the assumption of power by the king. He is shown in a relief[a] seated on a portable throne, of the greatest simplicity, and borne on the shoulders of his servants. The scene is accompanied by the words:

Carrying the king, sitting upon the portable throne; procession of the king to the palace.

Beneath the throne are inscribed the words:

All lands, all countries, Upper Retenu, Lower Retenu, all inaccessible countries are under the feet of this Good God.[b]

**750.** Above the scene is an inscription which indicates clearly the nature of the particular event commemorated, viz., the assumption by the king of the responsibility for the protection of the land. That this was a characteristic, if not the chief, ceremony of the jubilee (*ḥb-śd*) is shown by the words of the conquered Hermopolitans to Piankhi: "*Celebrate for us a jubilee* (*ḥb-śd*), *even as thou hast protected the Hare nome*" (§ 848, l. 61). It is not evident why the ministering women of the Theban temple should be given so much attention. The prominence of Amon, who dominates the ceremony, is noteworthy. Probably the most important fact furnished by the inscription is the statement that Thebes is exempt from inspection by the royal fiscal officers, who do not even go thither. It would thus appear that Thebes was

[a] *Ibid.*

[b] The identification of Osorkon II, because of this inscription, with Zerah the Ethiopian, who, according to 2 Chron. 14:8, invaded Judah in Asa's time, hardly needs any refutation.

not taxed by the Bubastites, at least not by Osorkon II. This conclusion is substantiated by the long list of offerings to Amon, recorded by the High Priest of Amon, Osorkon, in his own name, under Takelot II and Sheshonk III (§§ 756 ff.).

**751.** The inscription is as follows:

*Assumption of Government*

Year 22, fourth month of the first season (occurred) the appearance of the king in the temple (*ḥ·t-ntr*) of Amon, which is in the jubilee-hall, resting on the portable throne; and the assumption of the protection of the Two Lands by the king, the protection of the sacred women of the house of Amon, and the protection of all the women of his city, who have been maid-servants since the time of the fathers, even the maid-servants in every house,[a] who are assessed for their service yearly.

*Royal Offerings*

Lo, his majesty sought great benefactions for his father, Amon-Re, when he (Amon) decreed the first jubilee for his son, who rests upon his throne, that he might decree for him a great multitude (of jubilees) in Thebes, mistress of the Nine Bows.

*Exemption of Thebes*

Said the king in the presence of his father, Amon: "I have protected Thebes in her height and in her breadth, pure, delivered to her lord. No inspectors of the king's-house (*pr-stny*) journey to her; her people are protected forever,[b] in the great name of the Good God."

---

[a]Temple.

[b]Lit., "*two sixty-year periods.*"

# REIGN OF TAKELOT II

## GRAFFITO OF HARSIESE[a]

**752.** This document, while furnishing some data of importance regarding hereditary claims among the priests of Amon, is valuable also for its confirmation of the arrival of Osorkon as High Priest at Thebes in the eleventh year of Takelot II. It is dated four months and eleven days after the date of the beginning of his annals (§ 760), and furnishes us the exact day of his arrival in Thebes.[b] The occasion is the feast of Khonsu, and a priest in the Karnak temple of Thutmose III, probably named Harsiese, improved the opportunity of the new High Priest's presence to present a family claim. The document is as follows:

*Date*

**753.** Year 11 under the majesty of the king, the Lord of the Two Lands, Meriamon-Siese-Takelot (II), given life forever; the first month of the third season, day 11.

*Arrival of the High Priest*

On this day there arrived at Thebes, the victorious, the eye of Re, mistress of temples, bright dwelling of Amon of the hidden name, his city of ⌜—⌝, the High Priest of Amon-Re, king of gods, commander in chief of the army, Osorkon, triumphant, royal son of the Lord of the Two Lands, Takelot II, living forever; at his beautiful feast[c] of the first (month) of the third season.

---

[a]Cut on one of the roofing-blocks of the rear of the great Karnak temple built by Thutmose III. Now in the Louvre; published: Champollion, *Notices descriptives*, II, 162–64; Lepsius, *Denkmäler*, III, 255, *i;* Brugsch, *Thesaurus*, V, 1071–73. I had also my own copy of the original.

[b]As the bulk of his term of office fell in the reign of Sheshonk III, the five years of his annals falling under Takelot II are herein placed with the reign of Sheshonk III (§§ 756–70).

[c]The Feast of Khonsu, after whom the month is named.

*Claim of Harsiese*

There came the great priest ($w^c b$) of the house of Amon, serving his month in "Glorious-in-Monuments,"[a] in the third phyle, Harsi[⌜ese⌝] — — — — —[b] triumphant, before the governor of the South, saying: "I am the ⌜ *ḳ*-priest of Karnak, I am the son of the great prophets of Amon, through my mother."

754. Harsiese then presents some hereditary claim, the nature of which is not entirely clear, but probably he claimed the hereditary right to cleanse the temple, its utensils, or the wardrobe of the god. The High Priest granted him his claim; whereupon he immediately exercised his family privilege, and, to prevent any further question as to his rights, he engraved the above record of the facts on the roof of the great Karnak temple.

## STELA OF KEROME[c]

755. This monument is primarily important because it furnishes the highest known date of Takelot II's reign, year 25. It records the gift of 35 stat of land to a princess, and singer of the temple of Amon, Kerome; but whether for her tomb or for her support in the temple, does not appear. A relief at the top shows Amon and Khonsu on the left, before whom, emerging from a chapel or possibly a sarcophagus on

[a]*y ᵓ ḫw mnw;* evidently a designation of the Amon-temple; the same building is mentioned on a mummy of the Twenty-first Dynasty (Daressy, *Annales*, IV, 10 of *tirage à part*); and as early as Haremhab the goddess Amonet (feminine of Amon) is once called "*Resident in 'Glorious-in-Monuments'*" (*Recueil*, 23, 64) on her statue found in the great temple of Karnak. The place of our inscription on the roof of the hall of Thutmose III shows what part of the temple was so called. The name is therefore clearly the one which he gave it, shortened by the omission of his name at the beginning. See II, p. 237, n. f., and II, 560.

[b]The name and titles of his father filled the lacuna.

[c]Found in an Osiris-chapel by the pylon of Thutmose I at Karnak, by Legrain in 1902; published by him in *Annales*, IV, but without data as to size and material.

the right, appears Kerome, holding a roll of papyrus, and praying to the said gods. The roll is probably to be considered as the deed for the land. Below is the following:

Year 25 of the King of Upper and Lower Egypt, Takelot (II),[a] living forever; the High Priest of Amon, Osorkon.

On this day were confirmed the 35 stat of citizen-lands, to the singer of the temple of Amon, the king's-daughter, Kerome.

---

[a]The name as written contains no indication by which we can determine which of the two Takelots is meant; but as there is no known High Priest of Amon, Osorkon, under Takelot I, it is evident that we are dealing with Takelot II, under whom we know from other monuments (§§ 752 ff.) that there was a high priest Osorkon. Legrain's statement that this High Priest Osorkon became King Osorkon II, is thus an error.

## REIGN OF SHESHONK III

### ANNALS OF THE HIGH PRIEST OF AMON, OSORKON[a]

**756.** This High Priest is better known to us than any of the princes of the Bubastite family who held that office, although the remarkable records which he left, owing to their mutilated condition, have never been studied or understood in their entirety. He began his term in the eleventh year of Takelot II, and was still in office in the thirty-ninth year of Sheshonk III (§ 698, No. 17); he thus served at least fifty-four years. He left a series of temple records in the great Karnak temple, which may be fairly termed his annals.[b] They cover fifteen years of Takelot II's reign, and much of the following reign of Sheshonk III; but they cannot be conveniently divided, and are, therefore, treated here under the reign of Sheshonk III. They begin with Osorkon's appointment to the office of High Priest of Amon; or, if not his appointment, at least some significant date (the first of Tybi), four months and eleven days before his arrival at Thebes to take up the duties of his office (§ 753). This took place at the Feast of Khonsu, in his father's eleventh year, and was accompanied by rich offer-

---

[a]These records are the longest inscriptions on the Bubastite gate. They are all on the inside (north side) of the gate on both sides of the door, and begin at the east side of the door (year 11), jump to the west wall at right angles to the door-wall west of the door (years 12–15), and, turning the corner, proceed on the door-wall, west of the door (year 11 of Takelot II to 29 of Sheshonk III). The vertical lines of the inscriptions are surmounted by a relief on each side of the door. The inscriptions are in a frightfully mutilated state, and no modern copy from the original has been published. The publications and materials at my disposal will be found with the translations.

[b]They are in such a fragmentary condition and so insufficiently published that of many parts only a summary could be given, in the following translations. Closer study would bring out some facts not noted in the following sketch.

ings, many signs of the god's favor, and the acclamations of all Thebes. In response to the flattery of the priests, he introduces a new calendar of offerings.

**757.** In the year 15 there occurred a remarkable prodigy of uncertain nature, but in some way connected with the moon. This natural phenomenon was accompanied by a long and serious civil war. Osorkon left Thebes and, as we afterward find him with his father's courtiers, we might suppose that he went to Bubastis, but for the fact that his return journey to Thebes was northward. With some of his father's court, therefore, he withdrew to the south. One of his sisters, Shepnesopdet, had married Zekhonsefonekh, a great noble of Thebes, who bore all the titles of power except those of the king and the High Priest,[a] and the presence of such a son-in-law of the king at Thebes would be a fruitful source of jealousy and friction. Years of hostility between the former followers of Osorkon's father passed; Osorkon's part in these events is not entirely clear, but he at last constrains his father's followers to peace, and some compromise with his enemies must have been effected. The unhappy events passed are attributed to the displeasure of the god, Osorkon orders his people to prepare a great propitiatory offering, and with many ships and a numerous following he returns amid great rejoicing to Thebes.

**758.** Here he consults Amon, as the offering is presented, regarding the god's purposes toward Thebes. Osorkon's question, "*Dost thou do to Thebes as thou hast done to them?*" shows that not only other revolters, already punished, but also Thebes had been implicated in the hostility against himself. It is evident that the compromise involved the exemption of the Thebans from punishment, for, in response

[a]See the genealogy and connections of this powerful family, Legrain, *Recueil*, 27, 75–78, especially 77–78.

to Osorkon's question, the god delivered an oracle in their favor; whereupon the Thebans broke out in praise of their magnanimous High Priest. Although not recorded in his annals, Osorkon's struggles to maintain himself were not yet passed; for in the sixth year of Sheshonk III we find another High Priest named Harsiese at Thebes (§ 698, No. 16). How and when Osorkon regained his power at Thebes the second time[a] it is not possible to determine.

759. Osorkon's annals pass on from his first return to a long list of offerings to the Theban temples, beginning in the eleventh year of Takelot II, and continuing to the twenty-eighth year of Sheshonk III. A final line adds those of the year 29. This table is important, for it shows that the temples of Thebes were supported at this time by the High Priest, and his offerings were recorded in his name alone, with no reference to the Bubastite king. From a graffito in the temple (§ 753), as already stated, we know that Osorkon ruled at least ten years longer at Thebes. That is, until the thirty-ninth year of Sheshonk III.

### I. EAST OF DOOR[b]

760. A relief in duplicate at the top shows Takelot II, accompanied by his son, the High Priest of Amon, Osorkon, before Amon. The accompanying inscriptions, containing

[a]Should it turn out that the stela of Kerome of year 25 (§ 755) belongs to Takelot I, and not to Takelot II (which would give us another high priest Osorkon under Takelot I), then the civil war and Osorkon's withdrawal from Thebes in the year 15 were caused by the death of Takelot II, and the intervening rule of the other high priest, Harsiese, till year 6 of Sheshonk III, is an incident in the same series of events. In that case Osorkon was expelled but once from Thebes.

[b]Published: Lepsius, *Denkmäler*, III, 257, *a*; Lepsius, *Auswahl der wichtigsten Urkunden*, 15; Champollion, *Monuments*, 277, 1; Champollion, *Notices descriptives*, II, 20, 21 (last three containing only reliefs or accompanying inscriptions, "Beischriften").

the titles of those depicted, add nothing to the content of the inscription below, which is as follows:

*Appointment of Osorkon*

[1]Year 11, first month of the second season, day 1, under the majesty of King Takelot II ——— . . . . . . .[a] [⌜went⌝ the High Priest of Amon-]Re, commander in chief of the whole army, the leader, Osorkon, born of the hereditary princess, great in favor, great king's-wife [Kerome], ———.

Here follows the same long series of epithets of praise, belonging to the High Priest Osorkon, as in the inscription of the year 12 (§ 762). These merge into the acclamations of Thebes, as in l. 5: "*Thebes betakes herself to thee.*" Osorkon then apparently entered the city and offered sacrifice to Amon (l. 6). Then, probably on a second appointed day, he entered the temple (l. 8), and performed the ritual of Amon, at the same time presenting an offering (l. 9), which was the first installment of a new and richer calendar of offerings (l. 10).

**761.** The god then appeared in procession (l. 11), and the High Priest in his capacity as "*Pillar-of-his-Mother*" (*yn-mw˙t˙f*) presented himself (l. 11). The god visibly expressed his satisfaction, as when a father receives marks of affection from a son (l. 12), whereupon the whole priesthood of the temple, of all ranks, came forward (l. 12), and all together, with one accord, joined in praising Osorkon as him whom Amon had appointed to his high office (l. 13). Their speech continues probably to l. 17, and apparently contained no more than the phraseology usual on such occasions. In l. 18 Osorkon is speaking, and announcing the new and rich calendar of offerings, which he is founding. The content of his further address (ll. 18–25?) is uncertain,

[a]Epithets of the king.

but it probably concludes with an exhortation to the officers of the temple faithfully to administer his foundations. He then enumerates the lists of the new calendar of offerings (ll. 26–35), which is very fragmentary, but shows the usual items where preserved. It concluded with the customary curse:

As for him who shall injure this stela, which I have made, he shall fall under the blade of Amon-Re.

### II. WEST OF DOOR[a]

**762.** A relief at the top showing Osorkon offering before Amon, surmounts the following inscription:

*Date*

[1]Year 12, first month of the first season, day 9, under the majesty of Horus: Mighty Bull, [Shining] in Thebes, King of Upper and Lower Egypt, Lord of the Two Lands, Lord of Offering: Kheperhezre-Setepnere; Son of Re, of his body: Meriamon-Siese-Takelot (II). . . . . . . . ———. Lo, his eldest son was ⌜in the land⌝ [the High Priest of Amon-Re], king of gods, commander in chief of the army, Osorkon — — —.

Lines 2–5 then proceed with a series of conventional epithets of praise and laudation, usually applied to kings, which, owing to the mention of the High Priest Osorkon at the end of l. 1, must refer to him.[b]

---

[a]On the arrangement of this inscription, see § 756, note; published: Lepsius, *Denkmäler*, III, 256, *a*, 258, *a*, *b;* Brugsch, *Thesaurus*, V, 1225–30 (only upper ends of lines). The passage regarding the alleged eclipse, is in confusion in Lepsius, *Denkmäler*, two sheets of the squeeze having exchanged places. This error was corrected by Goodwin (*Zeitschrift für ägyptische Sprache*, 1868, 25 ff.) from the rough copy in Young's *Hieroglyphics*. I had a collation of the Berlin squeezes by Mr. Alan Gardiner, who kindly placed it at my disposal; it covered the first half of the monument (Lepsius, *Denkmäler*, III, 256, *a*).

[b]The same occur in the corresponding place in the inscription of year 11 (§ 760, ll. 2–5). Mr. Gardiner noticed that they express Osorkon's favor and power with the king, in successive phrases, taking up the latter's titles in the order of the fivefold titulary.

### *Arrival of Osorkon*

**763.** Then l. 6 narrates that

He came in our time, in the year [1]1,[a] ⌜— —⌝ bearing her[b] festal offerings, that he might set her in festivity ———. They rejoiced at seeing him, making festive her offerings, and supplying her altars with every good, pure, and pleasant [thing], in order to increase the daily offerings.

### *Civil War*

**764.** [7]Now, afterward, in the year 15, fourth month of the third season, day 25, under the majesty of his august father,[c] the divine ruler of Thebes, before heaven devoured the moon,[d] ⌜great⌝[e] wrath arose in this land like — — the ⌜hated⌝ and the rebels. They set warfare in the South and North ——— not ceasing to fight against those who were therein and those who[f] followed his father; while years passed[g] [in] hostility (*ḫsf-ᶜ*) (each) one seizing upon his neighbor, [⌜not⌝] [8]remem-

---

[a]There is no doubt about this restoration, which corresponds with the statement of the graffito (§ 753), that the High Priest Osorkon came to Thebes in the year 11. The restoration also fits the space in the lacuna exactly; but it should be said that this space on the squeeze shows no trace of 10.

[b]Referring to Thebes.

[c]See the passage as read from the squeeze by Lepsius (*Zeitschrift für ägyptische Sprache*, 1868, 29, note). The long discussions regarding the king here meant might have been avoided, had the consecutive narrative ever been worked out. The adverb "*afterward*" is of itself sufficient to show that the date must be later than the last preceding date, which as we have seen, is year 11. "*His august father*" is therefore clearly the High Priest Osorkon's father, Takelot II, the then reigning king.

[d]Lit., "*heaven not having devoured the moon.*" There is no word or phrase in Egyptian for "not yet;" see my *New Chapter*, 11, (5). This is the famous passage supposed by Brugsch to record an eclipse of the moon. This seems to me possible only on the basis of the rendering I have adopted, according to which the meaning may be: "just before new moon;" or possibly: "just before an eclipse of the moon." The controversy on the subject will be found in *Zeitschrift für ägyptische Sprache*, 1868 (Goodwin, 25 ff.; Brugsch, 29 ff.; Chabas, 49 ff.); but the above rendering was not there discussed.

[e]The squeeze shows *n* and a papyrus roll; the frequency of the phrase, *nšn* ᶜ *ꜣ*, suggested to Chabas the emendation of our *nšn n* (which is grammatically impossible), and the emendation is probably correct.

[f]Read *nty m ḫt*, as at the beginning of l. 12.

[g]Gardiner's collation.

bering his ⸢son⸣[a] to ⸢protect⸣ him who came forth from him. He[b] was satisfied in his heart, leading excellent — to his every beautiful hall.

*Osorkon's Address to the Court*

**765.** Said this governor[c] of the South to his nobles, the companions ⸢of⸣ his father who were by his side: "........"

The details of this speech are totally obscure, but it is evident that Osorkon is exhorting them to peace.[d] He appeals (l. 9) to his authority in Thebes,[e] and apparently attributes the disturbance to Re, who must be appeased with offerings.

*Fidelity of the Court*

**766.** "[*Now,*] [10]*when he had finished speaking these words to his hearers, their hearts* [⸢*rejoiced*⸣]." They assured him: "*All thy* [*designs*], *they come to pass. Now, when we offer to the god, he will* ⸢*restore*⸣ *the land.*" The remainder of the speech is again uncertain, but the fragments show that they were faithful to him (l. 11).

*Return to Thebes*

**767.** Then said to them this governor of the South: "— — [⸢gather⸣] this army into one place, that we may build for him a ⸢colonnade⸣."[f]

---

[a]Gardiner's collation. This son may be the heir to the throne at Bubastis, or Osorkon, the High Priest.

[b]From here to the close of the paragraph I have no idea of the connection or meaning.

[c]The High Priest, Osorkon.

[d]I can make out: "*Ye were* (*wn·tn*) *the counselors of him who begat me* ——— *ye shall not fight* ⸢———⸣" (l. 8).

[e]He says: "*I found not a way of knowing her welfare.*"

[f]Mr. Gardiner read the determinative as the legs; but after the verb "*build,*" "*colonnade*" is the only noun that can possibly be rendered for the consonants *wḏy·t*. One naturally thinks of the Bubastite colonnade at the gate bearing this inscription, but its architraves bear the name of Sheshonk I. Its continuation, however, on the same side of the forecourt, and the entire opposite side, are uninscribed. The remainder of our inscription, moreover, does not refer to the collection of building material, but the gathering and bringing of offerings. But it must be remembered that much of the inscription is lost.

Then it was done according to that which [he] had said. They brought their — to the ships, even all his things that were numbered as his property. [⸢Then came⸣] [12]those who followed him, both men and women, the court of his father,[a] the troops of his following, without number. Moreover, there were many ships, every one thereof [bearing] their offerings.

All these people brought their gifts and came with [13]"*heart rejoicing, because he was justified in their hearts like the son of Osiris.*"

*Arrival at Thebes*

**768.** "*Then he stationed people before his advance and behind him, rejoicing to heaven.*" They proceeded on the voyage toward Thebes in festivity,

like Horus sailing north[b] at the Feast of Rekeh (*Rkḥ*) . . . . . . . [14]⸢— —⸣ his troops were like a flock of wild fowl. He arrived at the time of verdure, they came before him, with a heart of love to his victorious ⸢city⸣. Then they found Thebes rejoicing and Karnak in [jubilee] — — because of the arrival in her ———— in Southern Heliopolis.

*Presentation of the Offering*

Then he made a great oblation ——— [15]bulls, gazelles, antelopes, oryxes, fattened geese in tens of thousands and thousands ——— . . . . . . . ——— a flood of wine ———, flowers, honey, and shedeh likewise, — measures (*ḏdmt*) of incense. Then he presented — these [things to] the great god in Thebes. . . . . . . . [16]. . . . . This august god was brought forth in procession, to adorn this his oblation, while his divine ennead, with rejoicing heart, were receiving it.

*Amon Pardons Thebans*

**769.** "*The High Priest of Amon, Osorkon, spake to the great god, and his army spake in praising* [*him*]: '. . . . . .' " They now address appealing questions to the god, among

---

[a]Lit., "*of him that begat him*," as in l. 8 (§ 765).

[b]This evidently indicates the direction of Osorkon's voyage, not that of Horus only.

which can be discerned: [17]"*Dost thou do to Thebes as thou hast done to them?*"[a] But the following three lines (18–20), containing but a few scattered signs, fail to reveal the nature of their further address. Their appeal was successful, for the god responded (l. 1)[b] with the usual signs of favor and acquiescence. Thebes was thus spared, and the Thebans joined in praise of Osorkon and Amon, promising the god the most plentiful offerings (ll. 2–4).

### *Summary of Osorkon's Offerings*

**770.** The narrative now passes over a long period and begins a retrospect of Osorkon's benefactions from the beginning of his rule at Thebes, which Osorkon himself states as a

"list of all the benefactions which I did for them for the first time, from the year 11 under [the majesty of Takelot II][c] [7]to the year 28, under the majesty of Sheshonk III."

After a list of myrrh, incense, honey, and oil (l. 7) follows a statement of precious metals given to Amon, Mut, and Khonsu, among which "*fine gold of Khenthennofer*" twice appears (ll. 8 and 9). Later are offerings of "*the High*

[a]Meaning: "wilt thou punish Thebes as thou hast punished them?" for the preposition is *r*, lit., "*against*." Who is meant by "*them*" is uncertain, but it would appear that other revolters had been severely punished, and that Thebes, being implicated, appeals to Amon for mercy.

[b]The inscription now passes from the west to the south wall, and Lepsius begins a new numbering of lines (Lepsius, *Denkmäler*, III, 258, *a*, *b* = Brugsch, *Thesaurus*, V, 1227–30); but he knew that the inscription of the south wall was the continuation of that of the west wall (Text, III, 11).

[c]As we know that Osorkon arrived in Thebes in the year 11 of Takelot II, and that he made his first offering calendar in that year (§ 753), there can be no doubt about the restoration. Osorkon's term of office at that time, from year 11 of Takelot II to year 28 of Sheshonk III, thus rests on better evidence than that heretofore drawn from this inscription (Maspero, *Momies royales*, 741, 742). Of course, the interruption by the civil war just narrated is taken for granted, and not referred to in giving the chronological limits of his term of office, at the time when the record was made.

*Priest of Amon-Re, king of gods, Osorkon, from the year 22*[a] *to the year 26*"[b] (l. 12), among which appears the income of the goddess Mat (l. 15); after which the income of Amon in the year 25 is itemized (l. 17), followed by that of Mut (l. 17). The last line (22), perhaps added later, contains the income of Amon and Hathor in the year 29.[c]

### FIRST SERAPEUM STELA OF PEDIESE[d]

**771.** This Libyan commander was a great-grandson of Osorkon II, who lived in the time of Sheshonk III, in whose twenty-eighth year he erected, in the Serapeum, the votive stela under discussion. He gives his genealogy, which is as follows (adding his two sons):

1. King Osorkon II

2. Hereditary Prince Sheshonk

3. Great Chief of Me, Takelot—King's daughter,[e] Thesperebast

4. Great Chief of Me, Pediese—Tere (sister-wife)

5. High Priest of Ptah, Pefnefdibast    Sem priest of Ptah, Takelot

---

[a]It is not evident why he should begin a subsection with the year 22. This is his earliest date under Sheshonk III. Does it mark the beginning of Osorkon's restoration to office after the rule of Harsiese, who was High Priest in his absence?

[b]So Lepsius and Maspero, *Momies royales*, 741 (collation of original); Brugsch has 28.

[c]The mention of Sheshonk III in l. 7 shows clearly that this date belongs to his reign. Maspero's attribution of it to Takelot II (*Empires*, 165, note 2) is therefore an inadvertence. He attributed it correctly, *Momies royales*, 741.

[d]Found by Mariette in the Serapeum; now in the Louvre (No. 18); published by Mariette, *Fouilles*, Pl. 36 (not seen); Mariette, *Le Sérapéum de Memphis*, III, Pl. 24; Chassinat, *Recueil*, 22, 9, 10. I had also my own copy of the original.

[e]Not on our stela, but on another of the second year of Pemou (§ 781), as noticed by Lepsius, *Zweiundzwanzigste Dynastie*, 276, note.

772. As the Sheshonk mentioned (No. 2) is distinctly called "*great first hereditary prince,*" it can hardly be doubted that he is the prince who became Sheshonk II; but as his name is not inclosed in a cartouche, we may regard this as another evidence that he was never more than coregent, as indicated by the quai-records at Karnak (§ 696, No. 13). His son Takelot cannot be Takelot II; otherwise we should expect him to be called king. The above quai-record, furthermore, calls Takelot II son of Osorkon II.

773. The burial of an Apis in the twenty-eighth year of Sheshonk III having given Pediese opportunity to erect this stela, he took part in the search for the new Apis in the same year, and conducted its burial twenty-six years later in the second year of Pemou, when he erected a second stela (§§ 778–81).

774. The first stela is as follows:

Year 28, King of Upper and Lower Egypt: Usermare-Setepnamon; Son [of Re], Lord of Diadems: Meriamon-Sibast-Sheshonk (III)-Nuterhekon.

Below, three men are praying before the sacred bull. They are accompanied by the following inscriptions,[a] showing them to be father and two sons:

1. His beloved favorite, the great chief of Me, Pediese, triumphant, son of the great chief of Me, Takelot, triumphant; his mother was Thesperebast (*Ṯs-B*ᵓ*s*ˑ*t-pr*ˑ*t*), triumphant; son of the great first hereditary prince of his majesty, Sheshonk,[b] triumphant, royal son of the Lord of the Two Lands, Usermare-Setepnamon (Osorkon II),[c] given life like Re.

2. His beloved favorite, High Priest of Ptah, Pefnefdibast, trium-

[a]These are repeated in horizontal lines below the figures. Both versions are combined in the translation.

[b]Who became coregent as Sheshonk II.

[c]The prenomen does not differ from that of Sheshonk III, but the variant gives Osorkon.

phant, son of the great chief of Me, Pediese, triumphant; his mother was Tere (*T*ᵓ-*yry*), triumphant, daughter of the great chief of Me, Takelot,[a] triumphant.

3. His beloved favorite, sem priest of Ptah, Takelot, triumphant, son of the great chief of Me, Pediese, triumphant.

Heretibsuten, triumphant, made it.

---

## RECORD OF INSTALLATION[b]

**775.** This brief document is a graffito such as the officials of this age were wont to cut upon the walls at Karnak, in commemoration of their installation or promotion in office. It bears the latest surviving date of the High Priest Osorkon, and also informs us that his brother, Bekneptah, was commander at Heracleopolis in the year 39 of Sheshonk III. Bekneptah must, therefore, have interrupted the succession of Harpeson's family in that office at Heracleopolis.[c] Osorkon and Bekneptah are here making common cause, "*overthrowing all who fought against them.*"

**776.** This can hardly be a reminiscence of the trouble which interrupted Osorkon's rule at Thebes (§ 758). The interim in the power of the ruling family at Heracleopolis, by the installation of Osorkon's brother, Bekneptah, doubtless explains the origin of the trouble referred to. Osorkon and Bekneptah, sons of Takelot II, probably expelled from Heracleopolis the line established there by Osorkon II. This offers an interesting parallel to the expulsion from Thebes of the High Priest Osorkon himself, and suggests, at least, that he may have owed his expulsion to the Heracleopolitans, on whom he has now retaliated. Did their recov-

---

[a]Hence his mother was both sister and wife of his father.

[b]Graffito on one of the Middle Kingdom blocks behind the sanctuary of the great temple of Karnak; published by Legrain, *Recueil*, 22, 55, No. 7.

[c]He would fall in the generations Nos. 12–14 or thereabout (§ 787).

ery of Heracleopolis then bring Osorkon's long career at Thebes to a close?

**777.** Year 39, — month of the third season, day 26, under the majesty of King Sheshonk III, living forever.

Behold, the High Priest of Amon-Re, king of gods, governor of the South, the chief Osorkon, [son of King] Takelot II, living forever, was in Thebes, celebrating the feast of Amon with a single heart, with his brother, chief commander of the army of Heracleopolis, Bekneptah, ——— overthrowing all who fought against them. On this day was installed the chief judge, governor of the city, and vizier, —hor—[a] . . . . in the great and august throne of Amon . . . . . . .[b]

[a]The man's name, of which beginning and end are lost; his parentage followed.

[b]The remainder is an address of the installed official, mostly unintelligible as published.

## REIGN OF PEMOU

### SECOND SERAPEUM STELA OF PEDIESE[a]

**778.** Pediese, who had erected a stela at the burial of an Apis in the twenty-eighth year of Sheshonk III (§§ 771–74), records the successful search for another in the same year, and the death of the sacred animal twenty-six years later, in the second year of Pemou. Pediese has, meantime, become High Priest of Ptah; as such he conducted the burial of this Apis, and recorded the whole in this second stela. The length of life of the animal, given as twenty-six years, enables us to establish the length of Sheshonk III's reign, thus:

Apis born in year 28 of Sheshonk III.

Apis died in year 2 of Pemou.

Apis lived 26 years.

Length of Sheshonk III's reign, 52 years.[b]

**779.** The stela is surmounted by a relief showing the Apis in human form, with head of a bull, accompanied by the goddess of the west. Three people, praying before them, are designated as:

1. Great chief of the Me, Pediese, triumphant, son of the great chief of the Meshwesh,[c] Takelot, triumphant.

---

[a]Found by Mariette in the Serapeum; now in the Louvre (No. 34); published by Mariette, *Le Sérapéum de Memphis*, III, Pl. 26; Brugsch, *Thesaurus*, 967; Chassinat, *Recueil;* I had also my own copy of the original. The monument exists in duplicate; the second (Louvre, No. 36): Mariette, *Le Sérapéum de Memphis*, III, Pl. 27. Two other stela, of value in corroborating the dates, commemorate this Apis: Louvre, No. 35; Mariette, *Le Sérapéum de Memphis*, III, Pl. 28; and Louvre, No. 276, not published by Mariette.

[b]For the possibility of another Sheshonk, between Sheshonk III and Pemou, thus shortening the reign of Sheshonk III (though without lengthening the dynasty), see quai-records (§ 698, No. 18, n. d).

[c]This proves that Me is an abbreviation for Meshwesh, for this Takelot, the father of Pediese, occurs as "*chief of Me,*" on the preceding stela (§ 774).

2. Sem priest of Ptah, Harsiese ———.
3. ———.

**780.** Below them is the following inscription:

[Year] 2,[a] second month of the second season, under the majesty of the King of Upper and Lower Egypt, Lord of the Two Lands: Usermare-Setepnamon, given life; Son of Re, Lord of Diadems: Meriamon-Pemou,[b] given life, stability, satisfaction, like Re, forever, beloved of Apis, son of First of the Westerners, the great god.

On this day the god was conducted in peace to the beautiful west, (to) his burial in the cemetery, to lay him to rest in the eternal house, in his everlasting seat. Now, he was born in the year 28 in the time of the majesty of King Sheshonk III, triumphant. They sought his beauty in every place of the Northland, and he was found at the temple of Shedebod[c] (*Šd-ybd*), after three months, when they had gone around the regions of the Delta, and every district of the Northland.

**781.** He was conducted to Memphis, to his father, "Ptah-South-of-his-Wall," by the High Priest of Ptah, sem priest in the house of Ptah, great chief of the Meshwesh, Pediese, son of the High Priest of Ptah, sem priest, [great chief of] the Meshwesh, Takelot, born of the king's-daughter, of his body, his beloved Thesperebast; in the year 28, second month of the first season. The beautiful life[d] of this god was 26 years.

---

[a]I read a fragmentary first stroke immediately following the lacuna, making three; but another stela (No. 276, my own copy) gives the date as "*year 2, second month of the second season, day 1.*" The two other stelæ relating the burial of this Apis have lost still more, and do not aid in restoring the number.

[b]The first half of this part of the name is broken out, but is perfectly preserved on one of the duplicates (No. 35).

[c]Unknown place.

[d]Corrected from Mariette, *Le Sérapéum de Memphis*, III, Pl. 27, l. 7 (*ᶜ ḥ ᶜ nfr*).

# REIGN OF SHESHONK IV

## STELA OF WESHTEHET[a]

**782.** This interesting stela records Weshtehet's gift of land to the temple of Hathor in an unknown town, probably in the western Delta, called Pesebek. The importance of the monument lies in Weshtehet's office as chief caravaneer of Pharaoh, controlling the intercourse with the oases of the Libyan desert; and that of his immediate superior, who was the great chief of Libya, Hetihenker, the Pharaoh's governor of a portion of the western Delta, and, perhaps, some uncertain extent of Libyan country also, including the oases. These arrangements are doubtless only the continuation of the organization of Sheshonk I. The barbarous names borne by these men are, of course, Libyan, but the chief caravaneer's mother bore a name of Egyptian formation, and he himself conveyed an endowment of land to the Hathor of the town, which doubtless lay at the Egyptian terminus of his caravan route to the oases.

**783.** A relief at the top of the stela shows two scenes: on the left a man praying before Hathor, with the inscription: "*May she give life, prosperity, health, to the great chief of Libya* (*R-b*ᵓ);" on the right a similar scene, with the inscription: "*May she give life, prosperity, health, to the chief caravaneer of Pharaoh.*" These two men are the donator of the land, and his superior, as shown in the following inscription:

[a]Rough limestone stela, with round top broken off, 53 by 31 cm., in possession of Daninos Pacha; published from a squeeze by Maspero, *Recueil*, XV, 84, 85.

*Date*

784. [1]Year 19, under the majesty of the King of Upper and Lower Egypt, Okheperre (*ᶜ ͗-ḫpr-Rᶜ*, Sheshonk IV), given life.

*Donation*

The chief caravaneer [2]of Pharaoh, Weshtehet (*W ͗-š ͗-ty-h ͗-t ͗*), son of Newsetrekenye (*N-w ͗-s ͗-ty-rw-k ͗-n ͗-yw*), [3]whose mother is Tentseherye (*Tynt-S ͗-h ͗-rw-yw*), has presented five stat of land to the house of Hathor, [4]mistress of Malachite, under charge[a] of the chief of the door-keepers, Pese ͗eke (*P ͗-s ͗-ᶜḳ ͗*), son of [5]Pekenu (*P ͗-ḳnw*), whose mother is the divine votress of Soped, Hernofer (*Hr-nfr*); in order to crave for him life, prosperity, health, long life, [6]and an advanced and happy old age, under the favor of his lord, the great chief of Libya (*R-b*), great chief of Me, Hetihenker (*Ḥ ͗-ty-*[7]⌜*ḥn*⌝*-k-r*); in the house of Hathor, mistress of Malachite, abiding and permanent, forever.

*Curse*

As for any man, or [8]any scribe who is sent on a commission to the district of the town of Pesebek (*P ͗-Śbk*), who shall injure [9]this stela; they shall come under the blade of Hathor. (But) the name of him who shall establish it shall abide.

---

## SERAPEUM STELA OF HARPESON[b]

785. This remarkable stela, while of the usual form of votive stela in the Serapeum, contains facts of fundamental importance in the study of the origin and internal affairs of the Twenty-second Dynasty. It was erected by one Harpeson, the military commander and High Priest of Harsaphes

[a]This is undoubtedly the rendering here, although the determinative of the preposition (*r ḫt*) is not usually the legs. To render it "*after*" (*m ḫt*) and connect it with the verb "*crave*" (*dbḥ*), ignoring the preposition, "*in order to*" (*r*), as the editor of the text has done, is not a solution of the difficulty which need be discussed.

[b]Discovered by Mariette in the Serapeum, now in the Louvre (No. 278); published by Lepsius, *Die Zweiundzwanzigste ägyptische Königsdynastie*, 267–69; Mariette, *Le Sérapéum de Memphis*, III, Pl. 31. I had also my own copy of the original.

at Heracleopolis in the thirty-seventh year of Sheshonk IV; that is, practically at the close of the Twenty-second Dynasty.

**786.** After recording, in the usual manner, the interment of an Apis-bull in that year, Harpeson appends the customary prayer on his own behalf, adding to his name his genealogy, ascending through fifteen generations. We thus have enumerated sixteen generations of an important family, extending from the close of the Twenty-second Dynasty back through the entire dynasty (ten generations), and six generations preceding it. The ten generations of this family thus correspond in length to the nine kings of the Twenty-second Dynasty. More important than this, however, is the fact that with the sixth generation back of Harpeson, his genealogy merges with the royal line in the person of Osorkon II. This will be clearer from the following table:[a]

[a]The names of kings are in spaced capitals.

**787.** 1. The Libyan, Buyuwawa

2. Divine father of Harsaphes, great chief, Musen

3. Divine father of Harsaphes, great chief, Nebneshi

4. Divine father of Harsaphes, great chief, Pethut

5. Divine father of Harsaphes, great chief, Sheshonk—king's-mother, Mehetnuskhet

6. Divine father of Harsaphes, great chief, Namlot—Divine mother, Tentsepeh

7. King Sheshonk I—Divine mother, Kerome

8. King Osorkon I—Divine mother, Temehkhonsu

9. King Takelot I—Divine mother, Kepes

10. King Osorkon II—Uzmutenkhos

11. Count, governor of the South, High Priest of Heracleopolis, commander of the army, Namlot—Priestess of Harsaphes, Tentsepeh

12. (Same titles), Uzptahenkhof—King's-daughter, Tentsepeh

13. (Same titles), Henptah—Priestess of Harsaphes, Thenekemet

14. (Same titles), Harpeson—Priestess of Harsaphes, Petpetdedes

15. (Same titles), Henptah—Prophetess of Hathor, Ireteru

16. (Same titles), Harpeson (year 37 of Sheshonk IV)

**788.** Back of Osorkon II, therefore, the genealogy of Harpeson becomes that of the Twenty-second Dynasty, and the Libyan, Buyuwawa, the father of his line is, therefore, the ancestor of the Twenty-second Dynasty. His immediate descendants (Nos. 2–5) also bear Libyan names, and among them is that chief of the Meshwesh, Sheshonk (No. 5), whom we found endowing his deceased son Namlot's (No. 6)[a] tomb at Abydos (§§ 669 ff.). Their ancestor, Buyuwawa, bears no Egyptian title, but his son, Musen, became priest of Harsaphes at Heracleopolis, and was a "*great chief*," of course, of the Meshwesh, like his great-grandson, Sheshonk[b] (No. 5). These warlike chiefs of the Libyan mercenaries so husbanded their power that after five generations at Heracleopolis they seized the throne. There is no intimation in this document of any connection with Bubastis.[c]

**789.** It is evident, therefore, that for at least a hundred years before the Twenty-second Dynasty, Heracleopolis had been the seat of a powerful family. Of the fortunes of its rulers during the first three reigns of the dynasty we learn nothing; but our genealogy shows Osorkon II appointing his son Namlot as High Priest and military commander there, with the title of governor of the South, like the High Priest of Amon. Indeed, this Namlot became also High Priest

[a]As the name of Namlot's mother, Mehetnusekhet, and the name of his father, Sheshonk, are the same in our genealogy and in the Abydos stela, there can be no question about their identity.

[b]On the Abydos stela, § 677.

[c]We can only suppose that during the Twenty-first Dynasty the family had gained control of Bubastis, and that Sheshonk I, perceiving the necessity of a stronghold in the eastern Delta, took up his residence there, thus gaining for his family the name Bubastites; but the family was clearly not of Bubastite origin.

of Amon, as Lepsius long ago saw.[a] The principality of Thebes, added to that of Heracleopolis, gave to one man the control of all Upper Egypt, from the Delta into Nubia, creating a dangerous rival of the royal house. How long Namlot held both principalities is uncertain,[b] but the family held possession of Heracleopolis for five generations more, six in all (§ 787, Nos. 11 and 16).

**790.** But in the thirty-ninth year of Sheshonk III, Bekneptah, a son of Takelot II, not appearing in our genealogy, was in control at Heracleopolis (§§ 775, 776) and making common cause with Osorkon, High Priest at Thebes. Namlot's descendants[c] must therefore have lost and recovered control at Heracleopolis. The support of their enemy, Bekneptah, by the High Priest of Amon at Thebes, suggests earlier hostility between the two principalities, and is evidently only one example of the petty wars in which the dynasts of Egypt were now constantly embroiled. Thus, while Thebes did not succeed in maintaining a dynasty under the Bubastites, that of Heracleopolis, beginning early in the Twenty-first Dynasty, continued for fifteen generations, interrupted for four generations by the accession of the line to the throne as the Twenty-second Dynasty, and by the probably short usurpation of Bekneptah (see §§ 745, 746). The power and importance of Heracleopolis continued through the Ethiopian and Saitic periods. It is mentioned in the annals of Ashurbanipal and Isaiah saw the envoys of Judah going to Tanis and Heracleopolis (חנס, Isaiah 30:4) for assistance.

---

[a]*Zweiundzwanzigste Dynastie*, **Pl.** I.

[b]Evidently not into the reign of Takelot II; see Wreszinski's list (*Die Hohenpriester des Amon*, § 47), where a high priest of Amon, Amenhotep, is between Namlot and the High Priest Osorkon, who was appointed in year 11 of Takelot II (§ 760).

[c]About Nos. 12–14.

*Apis Record*

**791.** [1]This god was introduced to his father, Ptah, in the year 12,[a] fourth month of the second season, fourth day, of King Okheperre, [2]Son of Re, Sheshonk (IV), given life. He was born in the year 11 of his majesty; he rested in his place [3]in Tazoser (the cemetery) in the year 37, third month of the first season, day 27, of his majesty.

*Sixteenth Generation*

**792.** May he grant life, prosperity, health, and joy of heart to [4]his beloved son, the prophet of Neit, Harpeson;

*Fifteenth Generation*

Son of the count, governor of the South, chief prophet in Heracleopolis, commander of [5]the army, Henptah; born of the prophetess of Hathor of Heracleopolis, his sister, the matron, Ireteru (*Yr˙t-rw*);

*Fourteenth Generation*

[7]Son[b] of the like,[c] Harpeson; born of the chief sistrum-bearer of Harsaphes, king of the Two Lands, ruler of the two shores, [8]Petpetdedes;

*Thirteenth Generation*

Son of the like, Henptah; born of the like, Thenekemet (*Ṯ*ᵓ*-n-ḳm˙t*);

*Twelfth Generation*

Son of the like, [9]Uzphatenkhof (*Wḏ-Ptḥ-*ᶜ*nḫf*); born of the prophetess of Hathor of Heracleopolis, king's-daughter, the matron, Tentsepeh (*Tnt-spḥ*);

*Eleventh Generation*

Son of the like, Namlot, [10]born of the chief sistrum-bearer of Harsaphes, king of the Two Lands, ruler of the two shores, Tentsepeh;

*Tenth Generation*

Son of the Lord of the Two Lands: Osorkon (II), born of Uzmutenkhos;

*Ninth Generation*

Son of King Takelot (I), [11]and the divine mother, Kepes;

---

[a]His predecessor was buried in the year 11, the twenty-eighth of Paophi (Mariette, *Le Sérapéum de Memphis*, Pl. 30).

[b]The genealogy ascends from father to grandfather here; I have indicated each generation by a paragraph.

[c]Meaning that the father bore the same titles and filled the same offices as the son. "*The like*" may also be applied to the females of the line, as in l. 8.

*Eighth Generation*

Son of King Osorkon (I) and the divine mother, Temehkhonsu;

*Seventh Generation*

Son of King Sheshonk (I) and the divine mother, [12]Kerome;

*Sixth Generation*

[a]The divine father, the great chief, Namlot, and the divine mother, Tentsepeh;

*Fifth Generation*

Son of the like, Sheshonk, born of the king's-mother, Mehetnusekhet;

*Fourth Generation*

Son of the like, Pethut (*P* ᵓ -*ṯwt*);

*Third Generation*

Son of the like, Nebneshi (*Nbnšy*);

*Second Generation*

Son of the like, Musen (*M* ᵓ *w* ᵓ *sn*);

*First Generation*

Son of the Libyan (*Tyḥn*), Buyuwawa (*Bw-yw-w* ᵓ *-w* ᵓ).

Abiding, abiding, remaining, remaining, enduring, enduring, flourishing, flourishing, in the temple of Harsaphes, king of the Two Lands, ruler of the two shores, one man the son of another man, without perishing, forever and ever, forever and ever, in Heracleopolis.

---

[a]The omission of "*Son of*" is noticeable, but might easily happen in such a long series. Petrie (*Proceedings of the Society of Biblical Archæology*, XXVI, 284) thinks this couple the same as that of the eleventh generation, so that the genealogy stops at the seventh and goes back to begin again with the eleventh ( = sixth) and carries it back (6 to 1) parallel with 11 to 7; 11 to 7 being the ancestry of Namlot, and 6 to 1 the ancestry of his wife Tentsepeh. To this reconstruction there are three fatal objections: (1) If 6–1 is the genealogy of Tentsepeh alone, why has her husband's name been inserted before hers in 6? (2) If 6–1 is the genealogy of a woman, why does it proceed (fifth generation) with "*son*" and not *daughter?* (3) The titles in 6 and 11 are not the same, but in 6 we have the old Libyan title of Namlot, whereas in 11 (carried back from 15) we have the Egyptian titles which we should expect after the Egyptianization of the family. It is unfortunate that the above possibility of evading the Libyan origin of the Twenty-second Dynasty should be used as an argument for the Assyrian origin of that dynasty; although we have proof positive that at the rise of the Twenty-second Dynasty, Assyria was in a state of decline, and had absolutely no power in the west.

# THE TWENTY-THIRD DYNASTY

## RECORDS OF NILE-LEVELS AT KARNAK[a]

**793.** These records, continuing those of the Twenty-second Dynasty (§§ 695–98), are of great importance. They show that the new Twenty-third Dynasty controlled Thebes, probably from its accession (about 745 B. C.), but at least twenty-three years thereafter. Its conquest by Piankhi must, therefore, fall after this period and after the reign of Pedibast, which concluded those twenty-three years. The interruption of the Twenty-third Dynasty at Thebes by Piankhi was, therefore, not earlier than 722 B. C., and his campaign not earlier than about 720 B. C. (see §§ 812, 813). The remainder of the Twenty-third Dynasty will be found discussed in the notes and introduction to the Piankhi Stela (§§ 811–13). The question whether it may have been parallel with the Twenty-second Dynasty is also taken up there (§ 813). See also Appended Remark, p. 404.

*Reign of Pedibast*

**794.** 1. (26)[b] The Nile. Year 16 of King Meriamon-Pedibast, which is year 2 of King Meriamon-Yewepet (*Yw*-[*p*][c]-*ty*).

2. (27) The Nile. Year 19 of King Meriamon-Pedibast; time of the High Priest of Amon, [⸢Harsiese⸣], triumphant.

3. (28) The Nile. Year 19 (sic!) of King Meriamon-Pedibast, time of the High Priest of Amon, [Harsi]ese.

4. (29) The Nile. Year 23 of King Meriamon-Pedibast; time of the High Priest of Amon, Takelot.

---

[a]On the quai of the great Karnak temple; published by Legrain, *Zeitschrift für ägyptische Sprache*, 1896, 113 f.

[b]Legrain's number.

[c]The *p* has, of course, been omitted in the publication. This Yewepet is the same as the Yewepet mentioned in the Piankhi inscription, §§ 830, 878.

*Reign of Osorkon III*

5. (16) The Nile. Year 5.[a] High Priest of Amon, Yewelot (*Yw-w*ͻ*-r*ͻ*-ṯ*), triumphant, son of the Lord of the Two Lands, Osorkon III.

6. (17) The Nile. Year 8. High Priest of Amon-Re, king of gods, Nesube[neb]ded, triumphant, king's-son of the Lord of the Two Lands, Osorkon III.

7. (18) The Nile. Year 14. High Priest of Amon-Re, king of gods, Nesubenebded, triumphant, son of the Lord of the Two Lands, Osorkon III.

8. (19) The Nile. Year — (same as 18).

9. (20) [The Nile. Year] ——— triumphant, king's-son of the Lord of the Two Lands, Osorkon III.

10. (21) [The Nile. Year] ——— (conclusion like 20).

---

## Appended Remark

After these pages were in type, and as they go to press, I have received from Mons. Legrain, a letter in which he has had the great kindness to review the evidence from his brilliant excavations at Karnak, relating to the chronology of the Twenty-third Dynasty. He concludes from this evidence that the Twenty-third Dynasty was contemporary with the end of the Twenty-second. I wish to thank him very cordially here for the labor and time which he has so kindly devoted to this valuable letter, and to congratulate him upon the remarkable success of his work at Karnak, although I am as yet unable to see that the evidence adduced proves the alleged contemporaneity.

---

[a]The following records (Nos. 5–21) cannot belong to Osorkon I, whose second name is Meriamon-Osorkon, as here; nor are they of Osorkon II, whose second name is Meriamon-Sibast-Osorkon. Hence they evidently belong to Osorkon III, whose second name was likewise Meriamon-Osorkon, as here. This also relieves us of an impossible series of otherwise unknown High Priests of Amon, who cannot be made sons of Osorkon I.

# REIGN OF OSORKON III

## WILL OF YEWELOT[a]

795. The introduction to this will contains historical facts, too important to be omitted here, even though this series is not designed to include legal documents. I have, therefore, given below the introduction and the conclusion which furnish the framework of the document. According to the custom since the Twenty-first Dynasty, at least, all such legal instruments are decrees of Amon. Yewelot, son of Osorkon III and High Priest of Amon at Thebes, had founded a landed estate there in his youth, in the tenth year of his father's reign. He wills this estate to his son, Khamwese. In the introduction he indicates the northern limit of his military command as Siut.

[1]Said Amon-Re, king of gods, the great god, great in the beginning of being: "As for the landed estate, which the High Priest of Amon-Re, king of gods, commander in chief of the army, who is at the head of the great army of [2]the South as far as the region of Siut, Yewelot, triumphant, founded; which lies in the district of the highland northwest of ⌜Thebes⌝, and is called 'Beautiful Region;' while he was a youth in the time of his father, King Meriamon-Osorkon (III), [3]in the year 10, fourth month of the third season, last day . . . . . . . [22]. . . . in all 556 ⌜stat⌝ of various land, and 35 men and women, their dykes, their [23]trees, their large and small cattle; I confirm them to the prophet of Amon-Re, king of gods, the chief of a district,[b] Khamwese, triumphant, his son, whom the daughter of a king's-daughter, [24]Tedenetnebast (*Tᵓ dnʿ t-n-Bᵓ sʿ t*), bore to him, forever."

---

[a]Red granite stela, round top, 2.67 m. high, 1.25 m. wide, 38 cm. thick, discovered by Legrain in the great Karnak temple; published by him, *Zeitschrift für ägyptische Sprache*, 35, 13–16, and translated by Erman, *ibid.*, 19–24. A relief at the top in two parts shows: on the right a priest with panther-skin offering a statuette of Truth to Amon and Khonsu; on the left, the same person in the same ceremony before Amon and Mut. Below is the text in thirty-two horizontal lines.

[b]See Dakhel Stela (§ 726, l. 2) for the same title.

## REIGN OF PIANKHI

### THE PIANKHI STELA[a]

**796.** This stela is the most instructive surviving document in respect of the internal political condition of Egypt in a time when no strong central power and no aggressive monarch controlled the whole country. The conditions pictured in this record are undoubtedly typical of similar periods throughout the historic age in Egypt, and in reading it the student clearly perceives why certain epochs in the history of the Nile-dwellers have left us no monuments. That we consequently know almost nothing of such periods is, in view of the revelations of the Piankhi Stela, probably no great loss, as far as political conditions are concerned. We may safely picture them to ourselves as essentially like this period first revealed to us by our great stela.

The Piankhi Stela discloses the Nubian kingdom

---

[a]Large and splendid stela of pink granite, with rounded top, 180 cm. high, 184 cm. wide, and 43 cm. thick; in the Museum of Cairo (No. 160, *Guide*, 111, *b*). It was discovered in the temple at Gebel Barkal (Napata) by a native Egyptian officer of the Sudanese government in 1862, and a rude copy made by him was used by de Rougé for his essay on the stone in 1863 (*Revue archéologique*, 1863,[2] n. s. VIII, 94 ff.). The original having arrived in Cairo in 1864, a copy was made by Devéria, and published in 1867 (*Fouilles exécutées en Egypte, en Nubie et au Soudan, d'après les ordres de son Altesse le Vice-Roi d'Egypte*, par Auguste Mariette-Bey; folio; Paris: Franck, 1867; I (texte), 1–2; II (planches), Pls. 1–14). This work was for some reason withdrawn from sale a few days after publication, and only the few copies sold now exist. It was then published from the copies of Devéria in Rougé's *Chrestomathie*, fasc. IV (1876), and in Mariette, *Monuments divers*, Pls. I-VI. The publications are very good; I had also a collation of the original by Schaefer, and my own collation of the Berlin squeeze, from both of which sources a few corrections have been inserted. The best and most recent translation is that of Griffith (*A Library of the World's Best Literature*, 5275–95). See bibliography of older treatments, by Maspero (Mariette, *Monuments divers*, 1, 2, and Maspero, *The Passing of the Empires*, p. 166, n. 6). The geographical notes which I have appended are chiefly drawn from Brugsch, *Dictionnaire géographique*.

already in existence as a full-fledged power. King Piankhi must have come to the throne in Napata about 741 B. C., but his records offer no hint of the development of the kingdom which must have preceded him. Its character as an Amonite theocracy or hierachy sufficiently indicates its Theban origin. When, moreover, we remember that the Nubian "*gold-country of Amon*," with its own governor, already existed toward the close of the Nineteenth Dynasty;[a] that the Theban High Priest of Amon became viceroy of Kush at the end of the Twentieth Dynasty;[b] and, finally, that the sacerdotal princess of Thebes in the Twenty-first Dynasty was "*viceroy of Kush, and governor of the Southern Countries*,"[c] it will be seen that over four hundred years before Piankhi's reign the Theban hierarchy had a strong hold on Nubia, and that some two hundred years later this had strengthened into full possession of the country.

**797.** The transfer of the Pharaonic seat of power to the Delta and the prominence of Ptah in the family of the Twenty-second Dynasty, had alienated the Amon priests from the northern dynasties. What was the specific occassion of the priests' withdrawal and the foundation of a new government at Napata, the old Eighteenth Dynasty seat of Amon worship by the fourth cataract, we do not know. As the later generations of the Twenty-second Dynasty weakened, petty dynasts arose throughout the Delta and as far south as Hermopolis. The Twenty-third Dynasty, at Bubastis,[d] although acknowledged for at least twenty-three years at Thebes during the reign of its first king, Pedibast (§§ 793,

---

[a]III, 640. [b]§ 615.

[c]E. g., on the Canopic jars and stela of Nesikhonsu, A. B. Edwards, *Recueil* IV, 80–85, and Maspero, *Momies royales*, 712.

[d]Although Manetho gives the twenty-third as a Tanitic dynasty, it is clearly Bubastite, according to the Piankhi inscription.

794), brought no order out of the chaos; for, as the Nubian kingdom now (about 722 B. C.)[a] suddenly emerges upon our view, we find it in possession of Thebes and Upper Egypt, as far north as Heracleopolis just south of the mouth of the Fayûm.[b]

**798.** The occasion of the Nubian conquest of the farther North, narrated in our document, was a disturbance in the situation just described, occasioned by the aggressiveness and rapid rise of Tefnakhte, a local dynast of Sais in the western Delta, whose career at this point illustrates that of almost every founder of a Pharaonic dynasty. Had the Nubian conquest not put an end to his brilliant career, he, too, like Ahmose of Thebes, and Sheshonk of Heracleopolis (later Bubastis), would have headed a dynasty of Pharaohs. In Piankhi's twenty-first[c] year, in the first month of the calendar year, his vassals in Upper Egypt reported to him that Tefnakhte had defeated the dynasts of the entire western Delta, and of both shores of the Nile above the Delta, almost as far south as the vicinity of Benihasan. Besides these, he had also gained control of all the eastern and middle Delta princes (l. 19), so that he was practically king of all lower Egypt, and of the lower portion of Upper

---

[a]Or possibly a little later. The reasons why Thebes could not have fallen much later will be found at the close of this discussion, § 813. The correctness of this dating of Piankhi's appearance in Lower Egypt some fifty years later than has been heretofore done by other historians, is not only rendered certain by the chronological data of the preceding period (dead reckoning from accession of Eighteenth Dynasty), but also by the fact that Piankhi was the father of Taharka, who began to reign in 690 or 691 B. C.; the fact that Bocchoris, the son of Tefnakhte, Piankhi's enemy, was the opponent of Shabaka; so that Piankhi and Shabaka cannot have been far apart.

[b]The Ethiopian period in Egypt thus includes Dynasties 23 (excepting the first reign), 24, and 25, the last of which only, is called Ethiopian by Manetho, because it was not until the overthrow of the ephemeral Twenty-fourth Dynasty, in the Delta that the Ethiopians established themselves permanently there.

[c]As he must have been holding Upper Egypt for some time before this, we must place his occupation of Thebes a year at least before these reports.

Egypt. Only Heracleopolis was holding out against him, and was suffering a siege at his hands, all his vassal princes lending him aid against it.

**799.** The wily Piankhi, desirous of drawing his enemy far southward, away from the safety of the impenetrable Delta swamps, quietly awaited developments. A second appeal from the north (§ 819) then informed Piankhi of the submission of Namlot, king of Hermopolis, to Tefnakhte (§ 820). Piankhi thereupon sent his commanders, with the troops then in Egypt, northward to check Tefnakhte's further southern advance, and besiege Hermopolis (§ 821). This they did, while Piankhi was, at the same time, dispatching from Nubia a second army for their support (§ 822). Having left Thebes, the second army met Tefnakhte's fleet coming up, and defeated it, capturing many ships and prisoners (§ 825). Continuing northward, probably down the Bahr Yusuf,[a] they struck Tefnakhte's army, which was besieging Heracleopolis, with the assistance of the Delta dynasts, as we have already stated. The northerners were defeated, both by land and water, and fled to the west side of the Bahr Yusuf (§ 831), whither they were pursued by the Nubians the next morning, again discomfited and forced to retreat toward the Delta.

**800.** Namlot, king of Hermopolis, escaped from the disaster, and returned southward to protect his own city, Hermopolis, which had not yet surrendered; whereupon the Nubian commanders returned up the Bahr Yusuf to Hermopolis which they closely beset (§ 833).

**801.** On receiving reports of these operations, Piankhi was enraged that the northern army had been allowed to escape to the Delta. It was now late in the calendar year,

[a]See p. 424, n. f.

and Piankhi determined, after the celebration of the New Year at home, to proceed to Thebes to celebrate there the great Feast of Opet in the third month, and then to lead the campaign against the North in person (§§ 835, 836). Meanwhile, his commanders in Egypt captured Oxyrhyncus, Tetehen, and Hatbenu (§§ 837–39), although Hermopolis still held out against them.

**802.** Piankhi then proceeded northward early in the calendar year, celebrated the Feast of Opet at Thebes in the third month, and went on to assume charge of the siege of Hermopolis, which had now been going on for certainly four, and probably five months (§ 840). He pressed the siege so vigorously that the city was soon at his mercy, and Namlot, finding that gifts, even his own royal crown, availed nothing with Piankhi, sent out his queen to plead with Piankhi's women that they might intercede with him in Namlot's behalf (§§ 842–44). This move was successful and, assured of his life, Namlot surrendered and turned over all his wealth to Piankhi, who immediately entered the city (§§ 845–50). One of the most remarkable touches in this remarkable inscription is the wrath of Piankhi as he visits Namlot's stables and finds that the horses have suffered hunger (§ 850). All of Namlot's wealth was assigned to the royal treasury of Piankhi and the sacred fortune of Amon (§ 851).

**803.** Heracleopolis, being already exhausted after a siege at the hands of Tefnakhte, its king, Pefnefdibast, now came to greet Piankhi and praise him for his deliverance (§ 852). The advance to the Delta, sailing down the Bahr Yusuf, was then begun, and all the chief towns of the West surrendered one after another on seeing Piankhi's force, except Crocodilopolis, in the Fayûm, which would have carried him too far from his course by Illahun. On the other hand, he did not touch Aphroditopolis, which lay on the east side of the river, equally far removed from his route, past Medûm and Ithtowe to Memphis (§§ 853–57). Piankhi offered sacrifice to the gods in all the cities which he passed, and took possession of the available property for his own treasury and the estate of Amon.

804. On reaching Memphis, it was found to be very strongly fortified and, in answer to Piankhi's demand to surrender, the Memphites closed the gates and made a sortie, which was evidently not very effective (§§ 857, 858). Under cover of night, Tefnakhte entered the city, and exhorted the garrison to rely on their strong walls, their plentiful supplies, and the high water which protected the east side from attack, while he himself rode away north for reinforcements (§§ 859, 860). Having landed on the north of the city, Piankhi was surprised at the strength of the place. Some of his people favored a siege, others desired to storm the walls upon embankments and causeways raised for the purpose (§ 861). Piankhi decided to storm, devising a shrewd plan of assault which speaks highly for his skill as a leader.

805. The lofty walls on the west side of the city had been recently raised still higher, and it was evident that the east side, protected by high waters (artificially raised ?), was being neglected. Here was the harbor, where the ships now floated so high that their bow-ropes were fastened among the houses of the city. Piankhi sent his fleet against the harbor, and quickly captured all the shipping. Then, taking command in person, he rapidly ranged the captured craft and his own fleet along the eastern walls, thus furnishing footing for his assaulting lines, which he immediately sent over the ramparts and captured the city before its eastern defenses could be strengthened against him (§§ 862–65). A great slaugh-

ter ensued, but the sanctuaries were, of course, respected and protected, and Ptah recognized Piankhi as king (§§ 865, 866).

**806.** The entire region of Memphis then submitted (§ 867), whereupon the Delta dynasts also came to Memphis with gifts for Piankhi, and signified their submission (§ 868). After dividing the wealth of Memphis between the treasuries of Amon and of Ptah, Piankhi crossed the river, worshiped in the ancient sanctuary of Khereha-Babylon, and followed the old sacred road thence to Heliopolis, where he camped by the harbor. Among the important religious ceremonies here was his entrance alone into the holy of holies of the Re-temple, that he might view the god and be recognized by him as king, according to the immemorial custom[a] (§ 871).

**807.** Before he left Heliopolis, King Osorkon III of Bubastis surrendered and visited Piankhi. Having moved his camp to a point just east of Athribis, by a town called Keheni, he there received the submission of all the petty kings, princelets, chiefs, and dynasts of the Delta (§§ 872, 873). Among these, Pediese of Athribis showed himself especially loyal to Piankhi and invited him thither, placing all his wealth at the Nubian's disposal. Piankhi, therefore, entered Athribis, received the gifts of Pediese, and, in order to choose for himself the best horses, especially entered the stables, which the shrewd Athribite, observing his love of horses, had particularly invited him to do. Fifteen Delta dynasts were here dismissed, at their own request, that they might go back to their cities and return to Piankhi with further gifts, in emulation of Pediese (§§ 873–76).

**808.** Meantime the desperate Tefnakhte had garrisoned

[a]See II, §§ 134, 221 ff.

Mesed, a town of uncertain location, but probably somewhere on his frontier. Rather than have them captured by Piankhi, he burned the ships and supplies which he could not save. Piankhi then sent a body of troops against Mesed, and they slew the garrison. Tefnakhte had, meanwhile, taken refuge on one of the remote islands in the western mouths of the Nile. The season was far advanced; many miles of vast Delta morass, and a network of irrigation canals, separated Piankhi from the fugitive. It would have been a hazardous undertaking to have dispatched an army into such a region. When, therefore, Tefnakhte sent gifts and a humble message of submission, requesting that Piankhi send a messenger with whom he might go to the neighboring temple and take the oath of allegiance to Piankhi, the Nubian king was very ready to accept the proposal (§ 880). In this less humiliating, not to say much less dangerous manner, Tefnakhte then accepted the suzerainty of Piankhi, and when the two kings of the Fayûm and Aphroditopolis, whom he had not molested on his way northward, appeared with their gifts (§ 882), a Nubian Pharaoh was lord of all Egypt.

**809.** The vassals, having paid Piankhi a last visit, he loaded his vessels with the wealth of the North and sailed away for his southern capital, amid the acclamations of the people. Arrived at Napata, he had erected in the temple of Amon our magnificent granite stela, recording how he, the son of Amon, had humiliated the rivals of that god in the North. The language of the inscription is good, and clear Egyptian in the narrative portions; but in the speeches, especially those of Piankhi himself, it is in places quite unintelligible, and produces the impression of a composition by one not perfectly familiar with the language. Apart from the Annals of Thutmose III, and possibly the documents of Ramses II on the Battle of Kadesh, the inscription of Piankhi is the clearest and most rational account of a campaign which has survived from ancient Egypt. It displays a good deal of literary skill, and an appreciation of dramatic situations which is notable, while the vivacious touches found here and there quite relieve it of the arid tone usual in such hieroglyphic documents. The imagination endues the personages appearing here more easily with life than those of any other similar historical narrative of Egypt; and the humane Piankhi especially, the lover of horses, remains a man, far removed from the conventional companion and equal of the gods, who inevitably occupies the exalted throne of the Pharaohs in all other such records, except, possibly, the Annals of Thutmose III.

**810.** Tefnakhte, while he had nominally submitted to Piankhi, only awaited the withdrawal of the Ethiopian to resume his designs. He eventually assumed the Pharaonic titles; and a gift of land near Sais by a priest of Neit, to this goddess, is dated in Tefnakhte's eighth year as Pharaoh.[a] He must have greatly increased the power and prestige of Sais, for his son Bocchoris[b] was the founder of the Twenty-fourth Dynasty (about 719–713 B. C.).

**811.** In Upper Egypt, Piankhi's rule continued for an uncertain but brief period. In the temple of Mut, at Thebes, he left a relief[c] representing a festal voyage of his ships, perhaps his return from the North. Among the ships appears

[a]Stela in hieratic in the museum of Athens, first noticed and partially published by Mallet (*Recueil*, 18, 4 ff.); then fully by Spiegelberg in transcription (*ibid.*, 25, 190–93); the relief at the top by Maspero (*Empires*, 181).

[b]Diodorus, I, 45.

[c]Benson and Gourlay, *The Temple of Mut in Asher*, Pls. XX–XXII, and pp. 370–79. These blocks may belong to some other Piankhi.

the state barge[a] of Sais, of course captured from Tefnakhte's fleet in the northern war. Osorkon III of Bubastis finally recovered Thebes, perhaps about 720 B. C., and together with an otherwise unknown Takelot (III) ruled there for a few years.[b] Some years later[c] Tefnakhte's son Bocchoris (*W* ᵓ *ḥ-k* ᵓ *-R* ᶜ) ascended the throne as the first and, as far as we know, the sole king of the Twenty-fourth Dynasty (see following table).

---

[a]The Somtu-tefnakhte, who appears here as a naval commander of Piankhi and prince of Heracleopolis, cannot possibly be the same as the Saite Tefnakhte, who, besides the difference in the name, was not prince of Heracleopolis.

[b]See note, § 872, l. 106.

[c]Who ruled at Thebes during these years we do not know. Osorkon III's, coregent, Takelot III, may have continued there. As Osorkon III's successor Africanus and Syncellus give a certain Psammus, with ten years, and Africanus follows Psammus with one Zet (thirty-one years); but neither of these two kings has been found on the monuments.

**812.**

| | Ethiopians | | Saites | | | Bubastites Twenty-third Dynasty | | |
|---|---|---|---|---|---|---|---|---|
| | | | | | | 745 | Pedibast | |
| Piankhi | 741 | Accession in Napata | | | | | | |
| | | | 726 | Tefnakhte | Ruled at least 8 years as Prince of Sais and Memphis and as King in Western Delta | | | |
| | 722 | Control of Thebes and Lower Egypt | | | | | Takelot III–Osorkon III | |
| Uncertain | 720 | Campaign | | | | 718 | | Rule of Psammus and Zet of Africanus, here? |
| | | | 718 | Bocchoris | Beginning of Twenty-fourth Dynasty | End of Twenty-third Dynasty | | |
| | 717 | Thebes probably lost | 712 | | | | | |
| Shabaka | 712 | Beginning of Twenty-fifth Dynasty | End of Twenty-fourth Dynasty | | | | | |
| | 700 | | | | | | | |

700

**813.** The preceding table will show how the complicated history of the time is probably to be restored. The Twenty-third Dynasty ruler, Osorkon III, is a Bubastite, and not a Tanite, as Manetho states.[a] Hence the Twenty-third Dynasty, being clearly Bubastite, could not have been parallel with the close of the Bubastite Twenty-second Dynasty, but must have followed it. Again, both Pedibast and Osorkon III of the Twenty-third Dynasty, controlled Thebes (§§ 793, 794) as did all the later kings of the Twenty-second Dynasty. Hence they could not have been contemporary.[b] There are two other possible parallels: first, the last few years of the Twenty-third Dynasty, with the reign of Bocchoris,[c] but Bocchoris could not have been regarded as the founder and sole king of a new dynasty, if he had not ruled the country as a whole for a time; second, the early years of Shabaka may have been parallel with the close of Bocchoris's reign. The whole period involved by these two parallels could not have been more than ten years, and was probably less, if it existed at all.

**814.** Returning now to the Piankhi Stela, it is crowned by a relief, showing Amon of Napata[d] enthroned, with Mut standing behind him. Before the divinities stands Piankhi. Approaching him a king, wearing upon his forehead the royal serpent-crest (*uraeus*), leads a horse with the left hand, and in the right hand carries a sistrum; above him the words: "*King Namlot.*" This incident is afterward

[a]On the position of Osorkon III and his relation to Thebes and Piankhi, see § 872, l. 106, note; and § 941.

[b]The new materials found by Legrain in the great cache at Karnak (*Recueil*, 27, 78, 79) have led him to think that the old conclusion of the contemporaneity of the Twenty-second and Twenty-third Dynasties is supported by them. In so far as published, they do not prove this conclusion. [Later: See Appended Note, p. 404.]

[c]On date of Bocchoris, see § 884.

[d]The fragmentary words inscribed beside him, refer to the "*pure mountain,*" or Gebel Barkal, by Napata.

described in the great inscription (l. 58). A woman, standing with uplifted right hand, preceding Namlot, represents "*the king's-wives,*" the women of Namlot, who appeared before Piankhi in the palace at Hermopolis (ll. 62–64). Three kings, with the royal uraeus upon their foreheads, are kissing the earth at Piankhi's feet. They are designated as: (1) *King Osorkon;* (2) *King Yewepet;* (3) *King Pefnefdibast.*

**815.** Five other princes approach Piankhi, of whom one, without the uraeus, but wearing the sidelock of youth, was "[⌜*Prince*⌝] *Teti.*" The other four, who are also without the uraeus, but wear the feather plume on the head, are:

(1) The prince (*ḥ ͗ ty-ᶜ*),[a] Pethenef (*P ͗ -ṯnfy*); (2) The prince (*ḥ ᶜ ty-ᶜ*), Pemou (*P ͗ -m ͗*); (3) Great chief of Me, Akenesh (*͗ -k ͗ -n-š ͗*); (4) Great chief of Me, Zeamamefonekh.

The words of these conquered dynasts, or at least of Namlot, inscribed before them, are too fragmentary for restoration, but they began: "*Be appeased, Horus, lord of* [*the palace*]," in which we recognize the opening words of Namlot's speech before Piankhi (ll. 55, 56). The figure of Piankhi has been chiseled away by his political enemies.

Beneath the relief the great inscription then follows, as translated below:

*Date*

**816.** [1]Year 21,[b] first month of the first season, under the majesty of the King of Upper and Lower Egypt, Meriamon-Piankhi[c] (*P-ᶜ nḫy*), living forever.

---

[a]The old "*counts*" have now become practically independent "*princes,*" and the old title, *ḥ ͗ ty-ᶜ*, should generally be so rendered in this age.

[b]This date may be either that of the first events in the following record, or that of the return of Piankhi and the erection of the stela. Piankhi, having celebrated the New Year's feast at Napata, departed for Thebes, which in turn he left in the third month, for his campaign in the north. The above date, nine months later, would allow enough for his campaign and the return to Napata. Again, if it be the date of the first report of Tefnakhte's aggressions, Piankhi's departure was a year later (his commanders operating in Egypt meanwhile), so that his departure and campaign fell in the year 22.

[c]For this name I have retained the traditional spelling, although it is evident

### *Introduction*

**817.** Command which my majesty speaks: "Hear of what I did, more than the ancestors. I am a king, divine emanation, living image of Atum, who came forth from the womb, adorned as a ruler, of whom those greater than he were afraid; whose father knew, ²and whose mother recognized that he would rule in the egg, the Good God, beloved of the gods, achieving with his hands, Meriamon-Piankhi."

### *Announcement of Tefnakhte's Advance*

**818.** One came to say to his majesty: "A chief of the west, the great prince in Neter,[a] Tefnakhte (*Tꜣ f-nḫt·t*)[b] is in the nome of —,[c] in the nome of Xois, in Hapi (*Ḥ ꜥ p*),[d] in — ³in Ayan,[e] in Pernub,[f] and in Memphis. He has seized the whole west from the back-lands to Ithtowe, coming southward with a numerous army, while the Two Lands are united behind him, and the princes and rulers of walled towns are as dogs at his heels. No stronghold has closed [⌜its doors⌝ in] ⁴the nomes of the South: Mer-Atum (Medûm), Per-Sekhemkheperre,[g]

---

from the two reed-leaves at the end that the vowel followed the *ḫ*. The *p* or *py* is certainly the demonstrative "pay." The name of Hrihor's son, Payonekh, owing to the lack of the *y* at the end, evidently had nothing to do with Piankhi. Hence the political connection between Thebes and Napata, however probable on other grounds, cannot be based on the supposed identity of these two names, as is commonly done.

[a]A region in the central Delta near modern Behbeit, the Iseum or Isidis oppidum of classic geographers; see also § 878, No. 5, note.

[b]This name is an abbreviation, the full form being: *X* (divine name)-*tꜣ f-nḫt·t* = tefnakhte, "*(the god) X is his Strength.*" See Schaefer, *Festschrift für Georg Ebers*, 93, note 2. The full form occurs on the Theban blocks of Piankhi (Benson and Gourlay, *The Temple of Mut in Asher*, 375). Feminine form *X*-tesnakhte (§ 918).

[c]The sign above the nome standard is omitted in the original.

[d]Lit., "*Nile*," a Nilopolis supposed by Brugsch to be somewhere in the western Delta.

[e]Uncertain.

[f]There was a Per-Nub near Sais (Brugsch, *Dictionnaire géographique*, 325) in the western Delta. The following generalization, "*the whole west, etc.*," shows that all these places are to be distributed in the western Delta from Memphis to the coast. Ithtowe was between Medûm and Memphis.

[g]Lit., "*House of Osorkon I;*" the place was therefore a foundation of this king. Its exact site is no longer known, but it must have been near Illahûn at the mouth of the Fayûm.

the temple of Sebek,[a] Permezed,[b] Theknesh[c] (*Ṯ-k*ᵓ*-n-š*); and every city of the west;[d] they have opened the doors for fear of him. He turned to the east, they opened to him likewise: Hatbenu,[e] Tozi[f] (*T*ᵓ *ywḏ*ᵓ*˙t*), Hatseteni[g] (*Ḥ˙t-stny*), Pernebtepih[h] (*Pr-nb-tp-yḥ*). Behold, [5][he] besieges Heracleopolis, he has completely invested it,[i] not letting the comers-out come out, and not letting the goers-in go in, fighting every day. He measured it off in its whole circuit, every prince knows his wall;[j] he stations every man of the princes and rulers of walled towns over his (respective) portion."

*Piankhi's Indifference*

**819.** Then [his majesty] heard [the message] [6]with courageous heart, laughing, and joyous of heart.

*Second Appeal of the North*

These princes and commanders of the army who were in their cities sent to his majesty daily, saying: "Wilt thou be silent, even to forgetting the Southland, the nomes of the ⸢court⸣?[k] While Tefnakhte advances his conquest and finds none to repel his arm."

---

[a]Crocodilopolis, capital of the Fayûm.

[b]Oxyrhyncus-Behnesa, capital of the nineteenth nome of Upper Egypt.

[c]Coptic Takinash of the nome of Pemdshe (Oxyrhyncus); see Brugsch, *Dictionnaire géographique*, 669.

[d]This means the west side of the Nile, above the Delta.

[e]The capital of the eighteenth nome of Upper Egypt, perhaps the Hipponon of the classic times. It literally means: "*House of the Phœnix*" (Brugsch, *Dictionnaire géographique*, 670–96).

[f]A town in the nineteenth nome of Upper Egypt, perhaps the Coptic Tôdshi (Brugsch, *Dictionnaire géographique*, 182).

[g]A town of the eighteenth nome of Upper Egypt, probably the classic Alabastronopolis. It was "*Horus, lord of Hatseteni*," who conducted Harmhab to Thebes for his coronation (III, 27). See Brugsch, *Dictionnaire géographique*, 669–71.

[h]Atfih (Aphroditopolis) of the twenty-second nome of Upper Egypt; and as we find this city (called Metenu) surrendering to Piankhi later (l. 145), it is evident that Tefnakhte had taken it.

[i]A remarkable expression, literally meaning: "*He has made himself into a 'tail-in-the-mouth;'*" viz., he lay around the city like a serpent with its tail in its mouth.

[j]The section of wall assigned to him by Tefnakhte.

[k]Or: "*the nomes of the court of the Southland*," like "*Elephantine of the South* (*tp rśy*)."

*Submission of Hermopolis to Tefnakhte*

**820.** "Namlot[a] — —, ⁷prince of Hatweret[b] (*Ḥ·t-wr·*[*t*]), he has overthrown the wall of Nefrus[c] (*Nfrws*), he has demolished his own city, for fear of him who might take it from him,[d] in order to besiege another city. Behold, he goes to follow at his (Tefnakhte's) heels,[e] having cast off allegiance to his majesty[f] (Piankhi). He tarries with him (Tefnakhte) like one of [his vassals in] ⁸the nome of Oxyrhyncus, and gives to him (Tefnakhte) gifts, as much as he desires, of everything that he has found."

*Piankhi Commands the Capture of the Hare Nome*

**821.** Then his majesty sent to the princes and commanders (*mr*) of the army who were in Egypt: the commander (*ṯś*), Purem[g] (*P-w ᵓ-r-m ᶜ*); and the commander (*ṯś*), Lemersekeny (*Rw- ᶜ-mr-s-k-n-y*);[h] and every commander (*ṯs*) of his majesty who was in Egypt (saying): "Hasten into battle line, engage in battle, surround —, ⁹capture its people, its cattle, its ships upon the river. Let not the peasants go forth to the field, let not the plowmen plow, beset the frontier of the Hare nome, fight against it daily." Then they did so.

*Piankhi Sends His Army; His Instructions*

**822.** Then his majesty sent an army to Egypt, charging them earnestly: "[⌜Delay⌝] not [day nor] ¹⁰night, as at a game of draughts;[i] (but) fight ye on sight. Force battle upon him from afar.[j] If he says

---

[a]In cartouche.

[b]Lit., "*Great House,*" a designation of a town in the sixteenth nome of Upper Egypt, perhaps the same as Hebenu (*Ḥbnw;* cf. Harris, 61*b*, 6, § 367).

[c]Town in the same nome as Hatweret.

[d]Or: "*for fear that he* (*Tefnakhte*) *might take it.*" As he submitted to Tefnakhte immediately afterward, the motive for the act is not clear in either case.

[e]Lit., "*to be the companion of his feet,*" the figure of the dog, as above in l. 3. It is a common figure applied to followers of a king.

[f]Piankhi's rule had thus extended as far north as Hermopolis.

[g]Lit., "*The Negro,*" from a Nubian word "urum" = "black" and the Egyptian article.

[h]Or Lesmersekeni (*Rw- ᵓ -s-mr-s-k-n-y*).

[i]Perhaps a reference to the slowness of the game.

[j]Judging from the context, this certainly means, not that they are to fight at long range, avoiding close quarters, but that they are to seek battle at the earliest opportunity, and begin the attack from afar.

to the infantry and chariotry of another city, 'Hasten;' (then) ye shall abide until his army comes, that ye may fight as he says. But if his allies be in another city, [11](then) let one hasten to them;[a] these princes, whom he has brought for his support: Libyans (*Tḥnw*) and favorite soldiers, force battle upon them ⌈first⌉.[b] Say, 'We know not what he cries in mustering troops.[c] Yoke the war horses, the best of thy stable; [12]draw up the line of battle! Thou knowest that Amon is the god who has sent us.'"

*Instructions as to Thebes*

**823.** "When ye arrive at Thebes, before Karnak, ye shall enter into the water, ye shall bathe in the river, ye shall dress in ⌈fine linen⌉; unstring the bow, loosen the arrow. Let not the chief boast [13]as a mighty man; there is no strength to the mighty without him (Amon). He maketh the weak-armed into the strong-armed, so that multitudes flee from the feeble, and one alone taketh a thousand men. Sprinkle yourselves with the water of his altars, sniff the ground before him. Say [14]ye to him, 'Give to us the way, that we may fight in the shadow of thy sword. (As for) the generation[d] whom thou hast sent out, when its attack occurs, multitudes flee before it.'"

*Reply of the Army*

**824.** Then they threw themselves upon their bellies before his majesty (saying): "It is thy name which endues us with might, and thy counsel is the mooring-post of thy army; thy bread is in our bellies on every march, thy beer [15]quenches our thirst. It is thy valor that giveth us might, and there is strength at the remembrance of thy name; (for) no army prevails whose commander is a coward. Who is thy equal therein? Thou art a victorious king, achieving with his hands, chief of the work of war."

---

[a]If Tefnakhte should send his allies to fight them, they are to await the attack; but if the allies remain in some city, Piankhi's forces are to seek them.

[b]*Tpy-*ᶜ, evidently parallel with *m w*ᵓ ("*from afar*") in l. 10.

[c]The meaning is uncertain; possibly: we are indifferent to his battle-cry, in encouraging his troops. The remainder is a defiance to Tefnakhte, to be spoken by Piankhi's army.

[d]*Ḏ*ᵓ*m*, lit., "*young men,*" or, in the military organization of the country, a "*class,*" as they successively fall due for military service (see § 402).

### *Advance to Thebes*

**825.** They sailed [16]down-stream, they arrived at Thebes, they did according to all that his majesty had said.

### *Battle on the River*

They sailed down-stream upon the river;[a] they found many ships coming up-stream bearing soldiers, sailors, and commanders;[b] every valiant man of the Northland, equipped with weapons of war, [17]to fight against the army of his majesty. Then there was made a great slaughter among them, (whose) number was unknown. Their troops and their ships were captured, and brought as living captives (sic!) to the place where his majesty was.[c]

### *Arrival at Heracleopolis*

They went to the ⌈frontier⌉[d] of Heracleopolis, demanding battle.

### *List of the Northern Enemy*

**830.**[e] List of the princes and kings of the Northland,[f] namely:

1. King Namlot and
2. [18]King Yewepet (*Yw-w*ʾ*-p-ṯ*).[g]
3. Chief of Me, Sheshonk,[h] of Per-Osiris (Busiris), lord of Ded.

---

[a]The addition is significant; the advance through Nubia had been largely by land. The exact place of the battle is uncertain; but as Piankhi's commanders were already besieging Hermopolis, it could hardly have been south of that city.

[b]Or perhaps "*troops*" (*ṯs·t*). [c]Napata.

[d]The meaning of this word (*ẖn·t*) is here uncertain; it is possibly "*houn*" (of *ehoun*), "*into*." As the troops of Tefnakhte were besieging Heracleopolis, the battle which now took place must have been by the city far from the Nile; and the capture of ships would indicate that the Nubians had descended the Bahr Yusuf, as Schaefer has suggested to me. See § 831 and note.

[e]Omission of Nos. 826–29 in the section numbering is intentional.

[f]The term is loosely used here, for Namlot, the first king, was king of Hermopolis, the second nome south of the Fayûm. A fuller list of the Delta dynasts is given later (§§ 878, ll. 114–17).

[g]See § 794; p. 437, n. d; and § 878.

[h]This mercenary commander from Busiris is subordinate to Pemou, prince of that city (l. 116). They are contemporary, and neither bears royal titles; hence they cannot have been identical with Pemou and Sheshonk IV, the last kings of the Twenty-second Dynasty. Moreover, both Pemou and Sheshonk IV held Memphis to the end of their reigns, but Memphis has now long been held by Tefnakhte, who was sem priest of Ptah there.

4. Great chief of Me, Zeamonefonekh, of Per-Benebded (Mendes), together with

5. His eldest son,[a] who was commander of the army of Per-Thutup-rehui (*Pr-Ḏḥwty-Wp-rḥwy*).[b]

6. The army of the hereditary prince, Beknenef (*Bk-n-nfy*), together with

7. His eldest son, chief of Me,[19] Nesnekedi[c] (*Ns-n*ᵓ-ᶜᵓ*y*, sic!) in the nome of Hesebka (*Ḥsb-k*ᵓ).[d]

8. Every chief wearing a feather who was in the Northland;[e] together with

9. King Osorkon, who was in Per-Bast (Bubastis) and the district of Ranofer (*R*ᶜ-*nfr*).

10. Every prince, the rulers of the walled towns in the West, in the East, (and) the islands in the midst, were united of one mind as followers of the great chief of the West, ruler of the walled towns of the Northland, prophet of Neit, mistress of Sais, [20]sem priest of Ptah, Tefnakhte.

### *Battle Opposite Heracleopolis*

**831.** They went forth against them; then they made a great slaughter among them, greater than anything. Their ships were captured upon the river.[f] The remnant crossed over and landed on the west side before Per-Peg.[g]

---

[a]His name, Enekhhor, will be found in the other list (§ 878, No. 4).

[b]Hermopolis Parva, in the western Delta.

[c]L. 116 has *Ns-n*ᵓ*-ḳd-y*.

[d]Eleventh nome of Lower Egypt.

[e]How many names this term may include is uncertain, but doubtless the chiefs of Me, enumerated in the second list, are meant.

[f]This word (*ytr*) has a common plural, referring to the canals of Egypt, and does not necessarily designate the Nile. Schaefer suggested to me that the Bahr Yusuf is meant here. It then occurred to me that all the cities taken by Piankhi as he went north, were far from the Nile, on the west side, until he reached Khereha-Babylon, and that he left the Fayûm on one side and Atfih-Aphroditopolis on the other side untouched, passing north between them, as is shown by the later surrender of their kings (l. 145, note). This would have been almost impossible in the case of Atfih, had Piankhi been descending the Nile. He probably reached the river again below Atfih by the ancient connection between Heracleopolis and Alexandria (Wilcken, *Archiv für Papyrusforschung*, II, 317; see also Papyrus Harris, § 224, note), of which we do not know the exact course. See also l. 76 (§ 853, n. a), which is the main proof of this hypothesis.

[g]This town is uncertain; but seeing that the Nubians had already reached

### *Battle at Per-Peg*

**832.** When the land brightened early in the morning, the army of his majesty crossed over [21]against them. Army mingled with army; they slew a multitude of people among them; horses of unknown number; a rout[a] ensued among the remnant. They fled to the Northland, from the blow, great and evil beyond everything.

List of the slaughter made among them:

People: —[b] men.

### *Hermopolis Besieged*

**833.** [22]King Namlot fled up-stream southward, when it was told him: "Hermopolis (*Ḫmnw*) is in the midst of the foe from the army of his majesty, who capture its people and its cattle." Then he entered into Hermopolis (*Wnw*), while the army of his majesty was upon the river, in the harbor [23]of the Hare nome.[c] Then they heard of it, and they surrounded the Hare nome[c] on its four[d] sides, not letting the comers-out come out, and not letting the goers-in go in.

### *Report to Piankhi*

**834.** They sent to report to the majesty of the King of Upper and Lower Egypt, Meriamon-Piankhi, given life, on every conflict which they had fought, and on every victory of his majesty.

### *Piankhi Determines to go to Egypt Himself*

**835.** Then his majesty was enraged thereat like a panther (saying): "Have they allowed [24]a remnant of the army of the Northland to remain? allowing him that went forth of them to go forth, to tell of his campaign?

---

the vicinity of Heracleopolis (l. 17), it must have been on the west side of Bahr Yusuf close to that city, and almost certainly further north. Maspero's identification with الفقاعى hardly seems phonetically possible, and hardly fits the conditions (*Proceedings of the Society of Biblical Archæology*, 20, 123–25).

[a]See Piehl, *Zeitschrift für ägyptische Sprache*, 1887, 124 f.

[b]The sculptor has omitted the numeral, although he left room for it.

[c]The nome names are commonly used in this inscription as here, for the chief city of the nome. The harbor was evidently on the Bahr Yusuf, on the east side of which Heracleopolis lies (see Schaefer's plan, *Archiv für Papyrusforschung*, II). They must therefore have returned up the Bahr Yusuf.

[d]Text has five.

not causing their death, in order to destroy the last of them? I swear: as Re loves me! As my father Amon favors me! I will myself go northward, that I may destroy [25]that which he has done, that I may make him turn back from fighting, forever."

### *Piankhi Would Visit Thebes*

**836.** "Now, afterward when the ceremonies of the New Year are celebrated, I will offer to my father, Amon,[a] at his beautiful feast, when he makes his beautiful appearance of the New Year, that he may send me forth in peace, to behold Amon[b] at the beautiful Feast of Opet; that I may bring his image[c] forth in procession [26]to Luxor at his beautiful feast (called): "Night of the Feast of Opet," and at the feast (called): "Abiding in Thebes," which Re made for him in the beginning; and that I may bring him in procession to his house, resting upon his throne, on the "Day of Bringing in the God," in the third month of the first season, second day;[d] that I may make the Northland taste the taste of my fingers."

### *Capture of Oxyrhyncus*

**837.** Then the army, which was there in [27]Egypt, heard of the wrath which his majesty felt toward them. Then they fought against Per-Mezed[e] of the Oxyrhynchite nome, they took it like a flood of water, and they sent to his majesty; (but) his heart was not satisfied therewith.

### *Capture of Tetehen*

**838.** Then they fought against Tetehen,[f] great in might. They found it filled [28]with soldiers, with every valiant man of the Northland. Then the battering-ram was employed against it, its wall was overthrown, and a great slaughter was made among them, of unknown number; also the son of the chief of Me, Tefnakhte. Then they sent to his majesty concerning it, (but) his heart was not satisfied therewith.

### *Capture of Hatbenu*

**839.** [29]Then they fought against Hatbenu (*Ḥ·t-Bnw*), its interior was breached, the army of his majesty entered into it. Then they sent to his majesty, (but) his heart was not satisfied therewith.

---

[a]Of Napata. [b]Of Thebes. [c]Lit., "*him as* (*or in*) *his image.*"

[d]This is one of the days of the long "Feast of Opet;" see § 237, note; and de Rougé, *Mélange d'archéologie égyptienne et assyrienne*, I, 133.

[e]Oxyrhyncus. [f]Modern Tehneh.

### *Piankhi Goes to Hermopolis*

**840.** First month of the first season, ninth day; his majesty went northward to Thebes, and completed the Feast of Amon at the Feast of Opet. His majesty sailed [30]northward to the city of the Hare nome (Hermopolis); his majesty came forth from the cabin of the ship, the horses were yoked up, the chariot was mounted, the terror of his majesty reached to the end of the Asiatics, every heart was heavy with the fear of him.

### *Piankhi Rebukes His Army*

**841.** Then his majesty went forth ⌈— —⌉ to [31]hate his soldiers, enraged at them like a panther (saying): "Is the steadfastness[a] of your fighting this slackness in my affairs? Has the year reached its end, when the fear of me has been inspired in the Northland? A great and evil blow shall be smitten them."

### *Siege of Hermopolis*

**842.** He set up for himself the camp on the southwest of Hermopolis (*Ḫmnw*), and besieged it [32]daily. An embankment was made, to inclose the wall; a tower[b] was raised to elevate the archers while shooting, and the slingers while slinging stones, and slaying people among them daily.

### *The City Pleads for Mercy*

**843.** Days passed,[c] and Hermopolis (*Wnw*) was foul to the nose, without her (usual) [33]fragrance. Then Hermopolis (*Wnw*) threw herself upon her belly, and plead before the king. Messengers came forth and descended bearing everything beautiful to behold: gold, every splendid costly stone, clothing in a chest, and the diadem which was upon his[d] head, the uraeus which inspired the fear of him; [e]without ceasing during many days,[e] pleading with his[f] diadem.

---

[a]Read *mn* and the roll, for *mn* and *s*.

[b]The determinative shows that a wooden construction of some sort is meant by the word (*bk*).

[c]The city had already been besieged many months: three months in the new year, and long enough in the old year for news of it to reach Piankhi at Napata before the New Year's feast (l. 25). Five months is therefore not improbable as the length of the siege.

[d]Namlot's.

[e]These adverbs belong to "*came forth and descended.*"

[f]Piankhi's? Or do they use Namlot's diadem as a ransom or bribe?

### *Namlot's Queen Intercedes*

**844.** Then they sent [34]his[a] wife, the kings'-wife, and king's-daughter, Nestent (*Nsṯnt*), to plead with the king's-wives, king's-concubines, king's-daughters, and king's-sisters, to throw herself upon her belly in the harem,[b] before the king's-wives (saying): "We come to you, O king's-wives, king's-daughters, and king's-sisters, that ye may appease Horus,[c] lord of the palace, whose fame is great and his triumph mighty. Grant [35]that he — — — me; lo, he ———— [36]him. Lo, ⌜— —⌝ ———— [⌜Speak⌝] [37]to him, that he may incline to the one that praises him ———— [38]— ⌜—⌝ ————[d].

### *Piankhi Addresses Namlot*[e]

**845.** [51]"Lo, who has led thee? who has led thee? Who, then, has led thee? Who has led thee? — — [52]thou didst [⌜forsake⌝] the way of life. Did heaven rain with arrows? I am [⌜content⌝] [53]when the Southerners do obeisance and the Northerners (say): 'Put us in thy shadow.' Lo, it is evil ⌜—⌝ — — [54]bearing his food. The heart is a steering-oar; it capsizes its owner through that which is from the god. It seeth flame as coolness ⌜in⌝ the heart[f] — —. [55]There is no old man, ⌜————⌝. Thy nomes are full of youths."

### *Namlot's Reply to Piankhi*

**846.** He threw himself upon his belly before his majesty (saying): "[Be appeased],[g] [56]Horus, lord of the palace, it is thy might which has done it. I am one of the king's slaves, paying impost into the treasury ⌜— [57]—⌝ their impost. I have brought for thee more than they."

---

[a]Namlot's. [b]Lit., "*house of women* (*pr-ḥm·wt*)." [c]The king.

[d]Four signs are legible in l. 39; ll. 40–49 are entirely lost, and three signs are clear in l. 50. Beginning with l. 35, we pass to the short lines of the left edge, or thickness of the stela.

[e]The plea of Namlot's wife must have been successful; the surrender was accepted by Piankhi, and Namlot has presented himself before him. All this is lost in the long lacuna, and the narrative resumes with Piankhi's obscure address to Namlot.

[f]Or: "*The flame seemeth to it as coolness ⌜in⌝ the heart,*" the heart itself being so hot?

[g]Restored from the relief, where the utterance of Namlot is also partially recorded (§ 814).

*Namlot's Gifts*

**847.** Then he presented much silver, gold, lapis lazuli, malachite, bronze, and all costly stones. [58]Then he filled the treasury with this tribute; he brought a horse in the right hand and a sistrum in the left hand,[a] of gold and lapis lazuli.

*Piankhi's Triumphant Entry into Hermopolis*

**848.** Then his [majesty] appeared in splendor [59]in his palace,[b] proceeded to the house of Thoth, lord of Hermopolis (*Ḫmnw*), and he slew bulls, calves, and fowl for his father, lord of Hermopolis (*Ḫmnw*), and the eight gods in the house of [60]the eight gods. The army of the Hare nome acclaimed and rejoiced, saying: "How beautiful is Horus, resting in [61]his city, the Son of Re, Piankhi! Celebrate for us a jubilee (*ḥb-ŝd*), even as thou hast protected the Hare nome."[c]

*Piankhi Visits Namlot's Palace*

**849.** His majesty proceeded to [62]the house of King Namlot, he entered every chamber of the king's-house, his treasury and his magazines. He caused that there be brought to him; [63]the king's-wives and king's-daughters; they saluted his majesty in the fashion of women,[d] (but) his majesty turned not his face to [64]them.

*Piankhi Visits Namlot's Stables*

**850.** His majesty proceeded to the stable of the horses and the quarters of the foals. When he saw that [65]they had suffered hunger, he said: "I swear, as Re loves me, and as my nostrils are rejuvenated with life, it is more grievous in my heart [66]that my horses have suffered hunger, than any evil deed that thou hast done, in the prosecution of thy desire. It has borne witness of thee to me, the fear of thy associates for thee. [67]Didst thou not know that the god's shadow is over me? and that my fortune never perishes because of him? Would that another had done it to me! [68]I could not but ⌜condemn⌝ him on account of it. When I was being fashioned in the womb, and created in the divine egg [69]the

[a]The relief shows the horse led by the left hand and the sistrum in the right (§ 814).

[b]This must mean Piankhi's tent, for he does not reach Namlot's palace until later (ll. 61, 62).

[c]See §§ 750, 751

[d]Lit., "*with the things of women.*"

seed of the god was in me. By his ka, I do nothing without him; he it is who commands me to do it."

### *Disposal of Namlot's Property*

**851.** Then his[a] possessions were assigned to the treasury, [70]and his granary to the divine offerings[b] of Amon in Karnak.

### *Loyalty of Heracleopolis*

**852.** The ruler of Heracleopolis Pefnefdibast[c] (*Pf-nf-dyy-B᾽s·t*) came, bearing tribute [71]to the palace: gold, silver, every costly stone, and horses of the choicest of the stable. He threw himself upon his belly before his majesty; he said: "Hail to thee, Horus, [72]mighty king, Bull subduer of Bulls! The Nether World[d] had seized me, and I was submerged in darkness, [73]upon which the light has (now) shone. I found not a friend in the evil day, who was steadfast in the day of battle; but thou, O mighty king, thou hast expelled [74]the darkness from me. I will labor together with (thy) subjects, and Heracleopolis shall pay taxes [75]into thy treasury, thou likeness of Harakhte, chief of the imperishable stars.[e] As he was, so art thou king; as he perishes not [76]so thou shalt not perish, O King of Upper and Lower Egypt, Piankhi, living forever.

---

[a]Namlot's. [b]Temple income (*ḥtp nṯr*).

[c]A fragment of a wooden coffin belonging to a great-granddaughter of this king (Lepsius, *Denkmäler*, III, 284, *a*) was found at Thebes by Lepsius. It is now in Berlin (No. 2100, *Ausführliches Verzeichniss des Berliner Museums*, 238). Combined with an inscription found by Daressy at Medinet Habu (*Recueil*, 19, 20), we may construct the following genealogy of Pefnefdibast's great-granddaughter, whom we call *X*, as her name is lost:

King Pefnefdibast — King Osorkon III
———— ha — King Amenrud
[Pediamon]nebnesttowe (father) — Irbastuzenefu (mother)
Princess *X*

The Heracleopolitan house and the fallen house of Bubastis, were thus later connected by marriage.

[d]The following description refers to the struggle of his city with Tefnakhte, and the relief brought by Piankhi.

[e]Lit., "*those which cannot perish* (*yḫm·w-šk*);" an epithet applied to the stars of the northern heavens (Brugsch, *Aegyptologie*, 321).

### *Per-Sekhemkheperre is Summoned to Surrender*

**853.** His majesty sailed north to the opening of the canal[a] beside [b][77]Illahun (*R˒-ḥn·t*); he found Per-Sekhemkhperre[c] with its wall raised, and its stronghold (*ḥtm*) closed, filled with every valiant man of the Northland. Then his majesty sent to them, saying: "Ye living in death! Ye living in death! Ye insignificant [78]— and miserable ones! Ye living in death! If an hour passes without opening to me, behold, ye are of the number of the fallen; and that is ⌜painful⌝[d] to the king. Close not the gates of your life, to be brought to the block this day. Love not death, nor hate life ⌜—⌝ [79]— — ⌜—⌝ before the whole land."

### *Surrender of Per-Sekhemkheperre*

**854.** Then they sent to his majesty, saying: "Lo, the shadow of the god is over thee; the son of Nut, he gives to thee his two arms; the thought of thy heart comes to pass immediately, like that which comes forth from the mouth of a god. Lo, thou art fashioned as the face of a god; we see by the decree of thy hands. Lo, thy city, his stronghold; [80][⌜do⌝] thy [⌜pleasure⌝] therewith. Let the goers-in go in there, and the comers-out come out. Let his majesty do what he will." Then they came out, with the son of the chief of Me, Tefnakhte. The army of his majesty entered into it, without slaying one of all the people. He found [81]— — —[e] and treasurers to seal his possessions. His treasuries were assigned to the Treasury, and his granaries to the divine offerings of his father, Amon-Re, lord of Thebes.

### *Surrender of Medûm*

**855.** His majesty sailed northward; he found that Mer-Atum (Medûm), the house of Sokar, lord of Sehez, had been closed, and was inaccessible. It had set fighting in its heart, taking [82]— — Fear [⌜seized⌝] them; terror sealed their mouth. Then his majesty sent to

---

[a]I read *mr*, "*canal*," on the squeeze in place of Mariette's 𓈙 (so also Schaefer), "*lake*." The irrigation canal leading into the Fayûm is meant, and the "*opening*" is the gap in the hills, through which it still flows. It would have been impossible for him to "*sail north*" to this gap, unless he was descending the Bahr Yusuf.

[b]The text here passes to the back of the stela, and the lines increase in length.

[c]The name means "*House of Osorkon I*," who must therefore have built a town in the vicinity of Illahun.

[d]The same word occurs in l. 131, where I render "*wretched*."

[e]The determinative shows that some other class of officers preceded.

them, saying: "Behold, two ways are before you; choose ye as ye will: open, and ye shall live; close, and ye shall die. My majesty will not pass by a closed city." Then they opened immediately; his majesty entered into this city, and offered 83— — —[a] [to] Menhy of Sehez. His treasury was assigned [to the Treasury],[b] his granaries to the divine offerings of Amon of Karnak.

### *Surrender of Ithtowe*

**856.** His majesty sailed north to Ithtowe (*Yṯy-tʾwy*); he found the rampart closed, and the walls filled with the valiant troops of the Northland. Then they opened the stronghold, and threw themselves upon [their] bellies 84[before] his majesty (saying): "Thy father has assigned to thee his inheritance. Thine are the Two Lands, thine is what is therein, thine is all that is on earth." His majesty entered to cause a great oblation to be offered to the gods residing in this city, consisting of bulls, calves, fowl, and everything good and pure. Then his treasury was assigned to the Treasury, and his granaries to the divine offerings 85[of Amon].

### *Piankhi Demands the Surrender of Memphis*

**857.** [His majesty sailed north to] Memphis; then he sent to them, saying: "Shut not up, fight not, thou abode of Shu in the beginning. As for him that would go in, let him go in; as for him that would come out, let him come out; and let not them that would leave be hindered. I would offer an oblation to Ptah and to the gods dwelling in Memphis (*Ynbw ḥḏ*), I would sacrifice to Sokar in the mysterious place (*Štʾ·t*), I would behold 'Him-Who-is-South-of-His-Wall,' that I may sail north in peace. 86[The people] of Memphis [shall be] safe and sound; not (even) a child shall weep. Look ye to the nomes of the South (*Tp-rśy*); not a single one has been slain therein, except the enemies who blasphemed against the god, who were dispatched as rebels."

### *Memphis Resists and Makes a Sortie*

**858.** Then they closed their stronghold; they sent forth an army against some of the soldiers of his majesty, being artisans, chief builders and sailors 87— — — the harbor of Memphis.

---

[a]The lacuna contained either the objects offered, or possibly "*to Sokar,*" the other god mentioned at Sehez (l. 81).

[b]Omitted in original.

### *Tefnakhte Enters Memphis*

**859.** Lo, that chief of Sais (Tefnakhte) arrived at Memphis in the night, charging his infantry and his sailors, all the best of his army, a total of 8,000 men, charging them very earnestly: "Behold, Memphis is filled with troops of all the best of the Northland; (with) barley and spelt and all kinds of grain, the granaries are running over; (with) all weapons of [88][war. ⌈It is fortified with⌉] a wall; a great battlement has been built, executed with skilful workmanship. The river flows around the east side, and no (opportunity of) attack is found there.[a] Cattle yards are there, filled with oxen; the treasury is supplied with everything: silver, gold, copper, clothing, incense, honey, oil."

### *Tefnakhte Goes for Reinforcements*

**860.** "I will go, and I will give something to the chiefs of the North, and I will open to them their nomes.[b] I will be [89]— — [⌈There will be but a few⌉] days[c] until I return." He mounted upon a horse, he asked not for his chariot, he went north in fear of his majesty.

### *Plans for Taking Memphis*

**861.** When day broke, at early morning, his majesty reached Memphis. When he had landed on the north of it, he found that the water had approached to the walls, the ships mooring at [90][⌈the walls of⌉] Memphis. Then his majesty saw that it was strong, and that the wall was raised by a new rampart, and battlements manned with mighty men. There was found no way of attacking it. Every man told his opinion among the army of his majesty, according to every rule of war. Every man said: "Let us besiege [91][it] —; lo, its troops are numerous."[d] Others said: "Let a causeway be made against it;[e] let us elevate the ground to its walls. Let us bind together a tower;[f] let us erect masts

---

[a]The alleged mention of this fact by Tefnakhte is one of the numerous rhetorical devices of the author of the inscription; for it was on this very side that Piankhi stormed the city (ll. 95, 96).

[b]Tafnakhte intends to marshal reinforcements among the Delta chiefs. What he means by opening their nomes is not clear; Griffith suggests that he means: relinquish his claims upon them as suzerain.

[c]Possibly three days.

[d]So numerous that the city could not be assaulted, but, in the opinion of these men, it should be besieged.

[e]Or: "*to it.*"

[f]*Bk*, the same device employed at Hermopolis (l. 32).

and make the spars into a bridge to it. We will divide it on this (plan) on every side of it, on the high ground and 92— on the north of it, in order to elevate the ground at its walls, that we may find a way for our feet."[a]

*Piankhi Decides to Assault*

**862.** Then his majesty was enraged against it like a panther; he said: "I swear, as Re loves me, as my father, Amon ⌜who fashioned me⌝, favors me, this shall befall it, according to the command of Amon. This is what men say: 93'[⌜The Northland⌝] and the nomes of the South, they opened to him from afar, they did not set Amon in their heart, they knew not what he commanded. He (Amon) made him (Piankhi) to show forth his fame, to cause his might to be seen.' I will take it like a flood of water. I have commanded 94— — —."

*Harbor of Memphis Captured*

**863.** Then he sent forth his fleet and his army to assault the harbor of Memphis; they brought to him every ferry-boat, every ⌜cargo⌝-boat, every ⌜transport⌝,[b] and the ships, as many as there were, which had moored in the harbor of Memphis, with the bow-rope fastened among its houses. 95[There was not] a citizen (*nḏs*) who wept, among all the soldiers of his majesty.[c]

*Piankhi Orders Assault of Memphis*

**864.** His majesty himself came to line up[d] the ships, as many as there were. His majesty commanded his army (saying): "Forward against it! Mount the walls! Penetrate the houses over the river. If one of you gets through upon the wall, let him not halt before it, 96[so that] the (hostile) troops may not repulse you.[e] It were vile that

---

[a]The second party therefore desired to assault the city, as against the first who desired to besiege it.

[b]The exact character of these two kinds of boat (*mḫn* and *šhry*) is unknown.

[c]Either all were considered in the distribution of the spoil, or no man was injured in the assault.

[d]This word (*sk*), used of ranging troops in line of battle, is here applied to lining up ships. The king in person ranged the captured ships, and his own fleet under the walls on the inundated (east) side of the city. This arrangement gave his troops footing for the assault. The nature of the attack is quite evident.

[e]They are not to stop on the wall, but to press over it immediately into the city.

we should close up the South, should land [in] the North and lay siege in 'Balances of the Two Lands.'"[a]

*Capture of Memphis*

**865.** Then Memphis was taken as (by) a flood of water, a multitude of people were slain therein, and brought as living captives to the place where his majesty was.

*Protection of Memphis*

Now, afterward, [97]when it dawned, and the second day came, his majesty sent people into it, protecting the temples of the god. He[b] ⌜—⌝ the holy of holies of the gods, offered to the community of gods of Hatkeptah (Memphis), cleansed Memphis with natron and incense, installed the priests in their places.

*Piankhi's Recognition by Ptah*

**866.** His majesty proceeded to the house of [98][Ptah], his purification was performed in the Dewat-chamber, and every custom that is practised upon a king was fulfilled upon him. He entered into the temple, and a great oblation was made for his father, "Ptah-South-of-His-Wall" (*Rśy-ynb˙f*), consisting of bulls, calves, fowl, and everything good. His majesty proceeded to his house.[c]

*Region of Memphis Surrenders*

**867.** Then all the nomes which were in the district of Memphis, heard (of it): Herypedemy,[d] Penineywe (*Pny-*[99]*n*ɔ *yw*ᶜ), the Tower of Beyew (*Byw*), the Oasis of Bit; they opened the strongholds, and fled away; none knew the place whither they had gone.

---

[a]Evidently a name for the locality dividing Upper from Lower Egypt, where Piankhi now was. The same phrase (*mḫ*ɔ˙*t*ɔ*wy*) occurs in a hymn to Amon (Berlin Papyrus, 3048, Band II, Taf. 45, l. 6), where the god is called: "*One whose word is the balances of the Two Lands.*" I owe the reference to Schaefer. Piankhi means that, having cut off the South from Tefnakhte, it would be humiliating, after reaching the North, to sit down for a siege on its threshold.

[b]The text is not in order here.

[c]Evidently a palace in Memphis, now taken possession of by Piankhi.

[d]Or: "*Hery the city.*" These places in the region of Memphis, cannot be exactly placed at the present day.

*Submission of Delta Dynasts*

**868.** King Yewepet came, and the chief of Me, Akenesh (*ʾ-kʾ-n-šw*), and the hereditary prince, Pediese, [100]together with all the princes of the Northland, bearing their tribute, to behold the beauty of his majesty.

*Wealth of Memphis Assigned*

Then the treasuries and granaries of Memphis were assigned to the divine offerings of Amon, of Ptah, and of the gods dwelling in Hatke-ptah (Memphis).

*Piankhi Worships in Khereha*

**869.** When the land brightened, very early in the morning, his majesty proceeded eastward, and an offering was made for Atum in Khereha, [101]the divine ennead in the house of the ennead, the cavern and the gods dwelling in it; consisting of bulls, calves, and fowl; that they might give life, prosperity, and health to the King of Upper and Lower Egypt, Piankhi, living forever.

*Piankhi Goes to Heliopolis*

**870.** His majesty proceeded to Heliopolis (*Ynw*), upon that mount of Khereha, on the highway of (the god) Sep to Khereha. His majesty proceeded to the camp, which was on the west of Eti.[a] His purification was performed, and he was cleansed in [102]the pool of Kebeh, and he bathed his face in the river of Nun, in which Re bathes his face.

*Ceremonies in Heliopolis: the "Sand-hill"*

Proceeding to the Sand-hill in Heliopolis, a great oblation was made upon the Sand-hill in Heliopolis, in the presence of Re, at his rising, consisting of white oxen, milk, myrrh, incense, and [103]every sweet-smelling wood.

*Temple of Re*

**871.** He came, proceeding to the house of Re, and entered into the temple with great praise. The chief ritual priest praised the god, that rebels might be repelled from the king. The Dewat-chamber was visited, that the sedeb-garment might be fastened on; he was purified

[a]This is the name of the Heliopolitan canal; it here has the determinative of a city, and probably the settlement on the harbor of Heliopolis is meant; see Harris 28, 6 (§ 266).

with incense and libations; garlands for the pyramidion-house were presented to him, and flowers were brought to him. He ascended [104]the steps to the great window,[a] to behold Re in the pyramidion-house. The king himself stood alone, he broke through[b] the bolts, opened the double doors, and beheld his father, Re, in the glorious pyramidion-house, the Morning-Barque of Re, and the Evening-Barque of Atum.[c] He closed the double doors, applied the clay, and sealed (them) [105] with the king's own seal. He charged the priests: "I have proved the seal; no other shall enter therein, of all the kings who shall arise." They threw themselves upon their bellies before his majesty, saying: "To abide, to endure, without perishing, O Horus, beloved of Heliopolis."

*Temple of Atum*

872. He came and entered into the house of Atum, following the image [106]of his father, Atum-Khepri the Great, of Heliopolis.

*Submission of Osorkon*

King Osorkon[d] came to see the beauty of his majesty.

*Piankhi Camps near Athribis*

873. When the land brightened, very early in the morning, his majesty proceeded to the harbor, and the ⌜best⌝ of his ships crossed over to the harbor of the nome of Athribis (*K*ʾ*-km*). The camp of his

[a]The front of the god's shrine is compared with the balcony-like window (*sšd*) of the palace, where the king shows himself.

[b]Meaning the seal upon the bolts.

[c]See Wiedemann, *Orientalistische Litteraturzeitung*, VI, No. 2, 49 ff.

[d]This Osorkon can be no other than Osorkon III of the Twenty-third Dynasty. For the invasion of Piankhi was later than Pedibast. Another connection is: that King Yewepet, one of the Delta kings who submitted to Piankhi, is mentioned as coregent with Pedibast at Thebes. Yewepet must therefore have survived Pedibast. Osorkon III survived the conquest of Piankhi, and together with an otherwise unknown Takelot (III) recovered Thebes, where they built an Osiris chapel together, the remains of which were found by Legrain at Karnak (*Recueil*, 22, 128–34). That their control of Thebes did not begin at the death of Pedibast and precede the invasion of Piankhi, is evident from the fact that Yewepet, who ruled in Thebes with Pedibast, survived him, and would have continued there. Osorkon III must therefore have ruled several years, a conclusion corroborated by the dates of the Nile-levels at Karnak in the years 5, 8, and 14 of his reign. It is evident, then, that the whole occupation of Lower Egypt by Piankhi must fall within the reign of Osorkon III.

majesty was set up on the south of Keheni[a] (*K*ͻ*-h-ny*), on the east [107]of the nome of Athribis (*K*ͻ*-km*).

*Submission of Delta Dynasts*

Then came those kings and princes of the Northland, all the chiefs who wore the feather, every vizier, all chiefs, and every king's-confidant, from the west, from the east, and from the islands in the midst, to see the beauty of his majesty.

*Piankhi is Invited to Athribis*

**874.** The hereditary prince, Pediese, threw himself upon his belly [108]before his majesty, and said: "Come to Athribis (*K*ͻ*-km*),[b] that thou mayest see Khentikhet (*Ḫnt-ḫty*), that thou mayest worship Khuyet[c] (*Ḫwy·t*), that thou mayest offer an oblation to Horus in his house, consisting of: bulls, calves, and fowl; and that thou mayest enter my house. My treasury is open to thee, to ⸢—⸣ thyself with my paternal possessions. I will give to thee gold, as much as thou desirest; [109]malachite shall be heaped up before thee; many horses of the best of the stable, and the first of the stall."

*Piankhi in Athribis*

**875.** His majesty proceeded to the house of Harkhentikhet, and there were offered bulls, calves, and fowl to his father, Harkhentikhet, lord of Kemwer (*Km-wr*). His majesty went to the house of the hereditary prince, Pediese; he (Pediese) presented to him silver, gold, [110]lapis lazuli, and malachite, a great heap of everything; clothing of royal linen of every number;[d] couches laid with fine linen; myrrh and ointment in jars (*ḥbḥb*); horses, both stallions and mares, of all the best of his stable.

*Speech of Pediese of Athribis*

**876.** He (Pediese) purified himself by a divine oath, before these kings and great chiefs of [111]the Northland (saying): "Every one of

---

[a]A town midway between Cairo and Benha bears the name Kaha, which is suggested by Daressy (*Recueil*, 20, 85, CLXIII) as possibly our Keheni, but it does not suit the location "*east*" of Athribis.

[b]It is evident that the city is meant here, and probably also above (l. 106).

[c]A goddess.

[d]As Griffith suggests, this is doubtless a reference to the fineness determined by the number of threads in a given measure.

them, if he conceals his horses and hides his obligation shall die the death of his father. So be it to me, till ye[a] bear witness of the servant there,[b] in all that ye know of me; say ye, (whether) I have concealed (aught) from his majesty, of all the possessions [112]of my father's house: [of] gold, silver; of costly stone; of all kinds of vessels, ⌜—⌝; of golden bracelets, of necklaces, and collars wrought with costly stones; amulets for every limb, chaplets for the head, rings for the ears: all the adornments of a king; all the vessels of the king's purification, in gold and — all costly stones. All these I have presented [113]in the (royal) presence: garments of royal linen by thousands of all the best of my house, wherewith I knew thou wouldst be pleased. Go to the stable that thou mayest choose as thou desirest, of all the horses that thou willst." Then his majesty did so.

*Delta Dynasts Dismissed*

**877.** Said these kings and princes to his majesty: "Dismiss us to our cities, that we may open [114]our treasuries, that we may choose as much as thy heart desires, that we may bring to thee the best of our stables, the first of our horses." Then his majesty did so.

*List of Delta Dynasts*

**878.** List of names belonging thereto:

1. King[c] Osorkon in Bubastis, the district of Ranofer (*R*ᶜ-*nfr*).

2. King[d] Yewepet in Tentremu (*Ṯnt-rmw*) and Tayan (*T*ᵓ-ᶜ*yn*).[e]

3. The prince (*ḥ*ᵓ*ty*-ᶜ), Zeamonefonekh [115]in "The Granary[f] of Re," of Per-Benebded (Mendes).

---

[a]He addresses the Delta princes.

[b]A circumlocution for "me," or "thy servant."

[c]On this Osorkon, see above, l. 106, § 872.

[d]This king had ruled in Thebes together with the now deceased Pedibast, beginning with the latter's sixteenth and his own second year (§ 794). He had thus been ruling some eleven or twelve years at this time, and, as he survived Pedibast, he had probably continued in Thebes, and was expelled by Piankhi about 722 B. C.

[e]The reading of ᶜ *yn* is not quite certain; both these places are of uncertain location. In the case of ᶜ *yn*, I am inclined to identify it with Ayan of l. 3. Brugsch identifies with "Daneon Portus" of Pliny (Brugsch, *Dictionnaire géographique*, 124).

[f]Identified by Foucart (*Recueil*, 20, 163 f.) with a modern Shuneh Yusuf, about 16 kilometers from Tell Tmai (Mendes), though he does not consider his identification as certain.

4. His eldest son, commander of the army, in Per-Thutuprehui (*Pr-Ḏḥwty-wp-rḥwy*), Enekhhor.

5. The prince (*ḥ* ͗ *ty-* ͨ), Akenesh (͗ *-k* ͗ *-n-š*) in Sebennytos, (*Ṯb-ntr*), in Per-heby[a] (*Pr-ḥby*), and in Samhudet[b] (*Sm* ͗ *-ḥwd*).

6. The prince (*ḥ* ͗ *ty-* ͨ), chief of Me, Pethenef (*P* ͗ *-ṯnf*), in Per-Soped[c] and in "Granary[d] of Memphis."

7. [116]The prince (*ḥ* ͗ *ty-* ͨ), chief of Me, Pemou[e] (*P* ͗ *-m* ͗), in Per-Osiris (Busiris), lord of Ded.

8. The prince (*ḥ* ͗ *ty-* ͨ), chief of Me, Nesnekedy[f] (*Ns-n* ͗ *-ḳdy*) in the nome of Hesebka[g] (*Ḥsb-k* ͗).

9. The prince (*ḥ* ͗ *ty-* ͨ), chief of Me, Nekhtharneshenu (*Nḫt-Ḥr-n* ͗ *-šnw*) in Per-Gerer[h] (*Pr-G-rw-rw*).

10. The chief of Me, Pentewere.

11. The chief of Me, Pentibekhenet (*Pnty-Bḫn·t*).

12. The prophet of Horus, lord of Letopolis (*Sḫm*), [117]Pediharsomtous (*P* ͗ *-dy-Ḥr-sm* ͗ *-t* ͗ *wy*).

13. The prince (*ḥ* ͗ *ty-* ͨ), Hurabes (*Ḥw-r* ͗ *-b* ͗ *-s*) in the house of Sekhmet, mistress of Sais (*S* ͗), and the house of Sekhmet, mistress of Rehesu[i] (*Rḥš* ͗ *wy*).

14. The prince (*ḥ* ͗ *ty-* ͨ) Zedkhiyu (*Ḏd-ḫy-yw*) in Khentnofer[j] (*Ḫnt-nfr*).

---

[a]This place is identified by Brugsch (*Dictionnaire géographique*, 489) with Iseum, modern Behbeit, which is probably correct. But in that case, Neter, the home of Tefnakhte (l. 2) cannot also be wholly identified with Iseum, for it is here held by Prince Akenesh.

[b]See II, 935.

[c]The name of this well-known city of the eastern Delta (Arabian nome) is not preserved by the classic geographers, but occurs in the annals of Ashurbanipal as Pi-saptu.

[d]The reading, although uncertain on the original, is rendered certain by a stela found at el Awasgeh, district of Sawaleh, in the region of Saft-el-Henneh (Per-Soped), on which "*Granary of Memphis*" (*Šnw·t Ynbw ḥḏ*) twice occurs. See Daressy, *Recueil*, 10, 142, IV.

[e]See note on his subordinate, Sheshonk, l. 18 (§ 830).

[f]See l. 19. [g]Eleventh nome of Lower Egypt.

[h]Probably the Phagroriopolis of Strabo, as Brugsch has shown (Brugsch, *Dictionnaire géographique*, 858). It was in the region near the northern terminus of the Gulf of Suez.

[i]A city near Letopolis (Brugsch, *Dictionnaire géographique*, 660).

[j]Entirely uncertain: Brugsch's suggestion (Brugsch, *Dictionnaire géographique*, 612) does not seem probable.

15. The prince (*ḥʾty-ʿ*) Pebes (*Pʾ-Bʾ-š*) in Khereha (*Ḫr-ʿḥʾ*) in Per-Hapi (*Pr-ḥʿp*).

Bearing all their good tribute: [a][118]gold, silver, —. —, couches laid with fine linen, myrrh in [119]jars (*ḥbḥb*), — — — —, as goodly dues; horses [120]of ———.

*Revolt of Mesed*

**879.** [⸢Many days⸣ after] this, came one to say [121]to his majesty: "The — — army — — — — his wall [122]⸢for fear⸣ of thee; he has set fire to [his] treasury [and to the ships][b] upon the river. He has garrisoned Mesed[c] (*Mšd*) [123]with soldiers and — — —. Then his majesty caused his warriors to go [124]and see what had happened there, among the force[d] of the hereditary prince, Pediese. One came to report [125]to his majesty, saying: "We have slain every man whom we found there." His majesty gave it as a reward [126]to the hereditary prince, Pediese.

*Tefnakhte's Message of Submission*

**880.** Then the chief of Me, Tefnakhte, heard of it[e] and caused [127]a messenger to come to the place where his majesty was, with flattery, saying: "Be thou appeased! I have not beheld thy face for [128]shame;[f] I cannot stand before thy flame, I tremble at thy might. Lo, thou art Nubti, presiding over the Southland, Montu, [129]the Bull of mighty arm. To whatsoever city thou hast turned thy face, thou hast not found the servant there,[g] until[h] I reached the islands [130]of the sea, trembling before thy might, and saying, 'His flame is hostile to me.' Is not [131]the

---

[a]The text here proceeds from the back to the right edge or thickness of the stela, the last of the four inscribed surfaces.

[b]Restored from the same phrase, l. 9.

[c]The place is unknown, but in view of the effect of its fall on Tefnakhte, it must have been on his frontier in the western Delta.

[d]Either there was a force of Pediese's at Mesed, or the troops dispatched by Piankhi were taken from Pediese's forces, according as "*among*" is construed with "*happened*" or with "*warriors*."

[e]Judging from this, the preceding incident is the last hostile enterprise of Tefnakhte.

[f]Lit., "*because of occasions of shame*" (*m sp n šp*), meaning that he has been ashamed to appear before Piankhi.

[g]See above, l. 111, note.

[h]He fled from place to place, as Piankhi advanced, "*until*" he reached the sea.

heart of thy majesty appeased,[a] with these things that thou hast done to me? For I am verily a wretched man. Thou shouldst not smite me according to the measure of the crime; weighing with [132]the balances, knowing with the kidet-weights. Thou increasest it to me threefold; leave the seed that thou mayest ⌜spare⌝ it in ⌜time⌝; do not hew down [133]the grove to its ⌜root⌝. By thy ka, the terror of thee is in my body, and the fear of thee in my bones. I have not sat in [134]the beer-hall,[b] nor has the harp been played for me; but I have eaten bread in hunger, and I have drunk water in [135]thirst,[c] since that day when thou heardest my name. ⌜Disease⌝ is in my bones, my head is bare, my clothing [136]is rags, till Neit is appeased toward me. Long is the course which thou hast brought to me; ⌜thy face is against me — [137]the year has undone me⌝. Cleanse (thy) servant of his fault, let my possessions be received into the Treasury, of [138]gold and every costly stone, and the best of the horses, (even) ⌜payment[d] for⌝ everything. Send to me [139]a messenger quickly, that he may expel fear from my heart. Let me go forth before him to the temple, that I may cleanse myself with a divine oath."

### *Tefnakhte Takes Oath of Allegiance*

**881.** [140]His majesty dispatched the chief ritual priest, Pediamenest-towe (*Pʾdy-Ymn-nsʾt-tʾwy*), and the commander of the army, Purme (*P-wʾ-r-mʾ*). [141]He[e] presented him with silver and gold, clothing and every splendid, costly stone. He went forth to the temple, he worshiped the god, [142]he cleansed himself with a divine oath, saying: "I will not transgress the command of the king, I will not overstep [143]that which the king saith. I will not do a hostile act against a prince (*ḥʾty-ʿ*)

[a]Lit., "*cooled.*"

[b]See § 451, note.

[c]There is probably a reminiscence of this in Diodorus (I, 45), where it is related that Tefnakhte was on a campaign, εἰς τὴν Ἀραβίαν, and, being without supplies, was obliged to resort to the coarsest food from the hands of common people. Upon finding it very appetizing, he cursed Menes (who had introduced luxury) and thereafter ate only simple food.

[d]*Dbʾ*; the same word means "*to clothe,*" but, so far as I know, it applies only to people, or gods; hence "*accoutered with everything*" (Griffith) is also uncertain.

[e]The uncertainty in the pronouns is equally bad in the original; the most probable interpretation, in view of the situation, is that Tefnakhte made presents to Piankhi.

without thy knowledge; I will do according to that which [144]the king says, and I will not transgress that which he has commanded." Then his majesty was satisfied therewith.

### *Submission of the Fayûm, Atfih, and the Last Kings of the Delta*

**882.** One came to say [145]to his majesty: "The temple of Sebek,[a] they have opened its stronghold, Metenu[b] (*Mtnw*) throws itself upon its belly, there is not [146]a nome closed against his majesty of the nomes of the South and North; the west, the east, and the islands in the midst are upon their bellies in fear of him, [147]causing that their possessions be presented at the place where his majesty is, like subjects of the palace." When the land brightened, very early in [148]the morning these two[c] rulers of the South and two rulers of the North, with serpent-crests (uraei), came to sniff the ground before the fame [149]of his majesty, while, as for these kings and princes of the Northland who came to behold the beauty of his majesty, their legs [150]were as the legs of women. They entered not into the king's-house, because they were unclean[d] [151]and eaters of fish; which is an abomination for the palace. Lo, King Namlot, he entered [152]into the king's-house, because he was pure, and he ate not fish. There stood three [153]upon their feet, (but only) one entered the king's-house.

### *Piankhi's Return to the South*

**883.** Then the ships were laden with silver, gold, copper, [154]clothing, and everything of the Northland, every product of Syria (*Ḫ*ꜣ*-rw*), and all sweet woods of God's-Land. [155]His majesty sailed up-stream, with

---

[a]The Fayûm, mentioned in l. 4 as having submitted to Tefnakhte.

[b]Aphroditopolis (Atfih), the capital of the twenty-second nome of Upper Egypt. Its surrender to Tefnakhte is probably mentioned in l. 4. As Piankhi passed northward along the western side of the Nile valley between the Fayûm on the west and Aphroditopolis on the east, neither of these was then touched by him. Hence they both come in and surrender of themselves afterward.

[c]As Namlot is one of the two kings of the South (l. 151), the Fayûm king or the king of Atfih must be the other. Who the two kings of the North were is not indicated.

[d]*M*ʿ*m*ʿ with determinative of a phallus; sometimes rendered "*uncircumcised.*"

glad heart, the shores on his either side were jubilating. West and east, they seized the ⌜—⌝, [156]jubilating in the presence of his majesty; singing and jubilating as they said: "O mighty, mighty Ruler, [157]Piankhi, O mighty Ruler; thou comest, having gained the dominion of the Northland. Thou makest bulls [158]into women. Happy the heart of the mother who bore thee, and the man who begat thee. Those who are in the valley give to her praise, the cow [159]that hath borne a bull. Thou art unto eternity, thy might endureth, O Ruler, beloved of Thebes."

# THE TWENTY-FOURTH DYNASTY

# REIGN OF BOCCHORIS

## SERAPEUM STELÆ

**884.** Bocchoris, the only king of the Twenty-fourth Dynasty, the son of Tefnakhte,[a] has left only a few Serapeum stelæ,[b] and a wall inscription, which record the burial of an Apis in his sixth year. It was interred in the same chamber as the one which died in the thirty-seventh year of Sheshonk IV. These documents give his name as: *King of Upper and Lower Egypt, Wohkere*[c] (*W* ᵓ *ḥ-k-* ᵓ *R* ᶜ), *Son of Re, Bekneranef.* As Africanus also gives his reign as six years,[d] he probably did not reign longer. Counting back from 663, the beginning of the Twenty-sixth Dynasty, his accession was about 718 B. C.

---

[a]Diodorus, I, 45.

[b]Louvre, 298, 299; Mariette, *Le Sérapéum de Memphis*, Pl. 34.

[c]This is the origin of the classic form Βόκχορις (Diodorus, I, 45, 65).

[d]Syncellus has 44.

# THE TWENTY-FIFTH DYNASTY

## RECORDS OF NILE-LEVELS AT KARNAK[a]

885. Like those of the preceding dynasties, these records of the Twenty-fifth Dynasty are of great chronological value. They enable us, for the first time, to arrange the kings of the Ethiopian dynasty in order of succession, the position of Shabaka having heretofore been uncertain. The record here (No. 4) shows that Shabataka's third year was near 700 B. C., and, as it is impossible in that case to insert Shabaka between Shabataka and Taharka, the only other possible order is: Shabaka, Shabataka, Taharka—an order which is confirmed by the datum of Manetho, that Shabaka overthrew the Twenty-fourth Dynasty, having defeated and slain Bocchoris. If Shabataka's third year was near 700 B. C., and he was the predecessor of Taharka, whose accession was in 688 B. C.,[b] then Shabataka must have begun to reign, at the latest, about 700, and his reign lasted some twelve years, which is exactly what Syncellus gives him. The whole dynasty may then be restored thus:

| | | |
|---|---|---|
| Shabaka | 12[c]+$x$ years | 712–700 B. C. |
| Shabataka | 12 years | 700–688 " |
| Taharka | 26 years | 688–663[d] " |
| Total | 50 years | |

[a]Engraved on the quai before the great Karnak temple; published by Legrain, *Zeitschrift für ägyptische Sprache*, 1896, 114–16.

[b]§§ 959 ff.

[c]Lepsius, *Denkmäler*, V, 1, *e;* Syncellus also gives him twelve years.

[d]§ 1026.

*Reign of Shabaka*

**886.** 1. [a](30) [b]Year 2, under the majesty of Horus: Sebektowe (*Šbk-tˀwy*); Favorite of the Two Goddesses: Sebektowe; Golden Horus: Sebektowe; King of Upper and Lower Egypt: Neferkere; Son of Re: [Shabaka], living forever, beloved of Amon-Re, lord of Thebes, beloved of Montu-Re, lord of Thebes. The Nile, father of gods, was 20 cubits, 1 palm, 1 finger.

2. (31) [The Nile] Year — [under] the majesty of King Shabaka ———.

3. (32) [Year] — [under] the majesty of King Shabaka ———.

*Reign of Shabataka*

**887.** 4. (33) Year 3, first month[c] of the third season, day 5, under the majesty of King Shabataka.[d] When his majesty was crowned as king in the house of Amon, he granted him that he should splendidly appear as Favorite of the Two Goddesses, like Horus upon the throne of Re. (The Nile) which his father Amon the great, Hapi the great, great in Niles, granted him in his time: 20 (cubits), 2 palms.

*Reign of Taharka*

**888.** 5. (34) Year 6 of King Taharka (*Tˀ-h-rw-ḳ*), beloved of Amon the great.

6. (35) The Nile. Year 6 under the majesty of the King of Upper and Lower Egypt: Nefertem-Khure (*Nfr-tm, Ḫw-Rᶜ*); Son of Re: Taharka, living forever, beloved of Nun the great, Amon the great, the Nile, father[e] of gods, and the (divine) community upon the flood. (The Nile), which his father, Amon, gave to him, that his time might be made prosperous.

---

[a]The numbers in parenthesis are those of Legrain's publication.

[b]The latest preceding date is the fourteenth year of Osorkon III.

[c]Meyer has shown that this date for the highest point of the inundation must have fallen somewhere about 700 B. C. (*Zeitschrift für ägyptische Sprache*, 40, 124 f.; and 41, 93).

[d]The scribe attempted to give the full titulary of the king, but it is very confused.

[e]The whole series is perhaps one composite god; see, e. g., No. 36 (*Zeitschrift für ägyptische Sprache*, 34, 116).

7. (36) The Nile. Year 7 under the majesty of King Taharka, living forever, beloved of Nun the great, Amon the great, the Nile, father of gods, and the divine (community) upon the flood. (The Nile) which his father, Amon, gave to him, that his time might be made prosperous.

8. (37) The Nile. Year 7 (sic!) under the majesty of King Taharka. . . . . . . . .[a]

9. (38) The Nile. Year 9[b] of King Taharka, living forever, beloved of Nun the great, and Amon the great.

---

[a]Like No. 7, except the height, which is different. The year is doubtless an error for 8, as it is preceded by 7 and followed by 9.

[b]Followed by year 10 of Psamtik.

# REIGN OF SHABAKA

## BUILDING INSCRIPTION[a]

**889.** As a memorial of his rule in Thebes, Shabaka left the following record of a restoration by him on the fourth pylon of the Karnak temple:

[King Shabaka; he made (it) as his monument for his father], Amon-Re, lord of Thebes, presider over Karnak, restoring the great and august gate[b] (*šbꜣ*): "Amon-Re-is-Mighty-in-Strength," making for it a great overlay of fine gold, which the majesty of King Shabaka,[c] living forever, brought from the victories, which his father, Amon, decreed to him; the great hall[d] (*hy·t*) being overlaid with fine gold, the south column and the north column[e] being wrought with gold, the two lower lips being of pure silver, made ———.

---

[a]On the north side of the door of the fourth pylon of the great Karnak temple; published by Champollion, *Notices descriptives*, II, 129, 130; Lepsius, *Denkmäler*, V, 1, *b;* Brugsch, *Thesaurus*, VI, 1316; see Lepsius, *Denkmäler*, Text, III, 152.

[b]This is, of course, the main door or gate of the pylon (IV) in which the inscription is. See the name again, Brugsch, *Thesaurus*, VI, 1315.

[c]Double name.

[d]This is the colonnaded hall of Thutmose I, behind Pylon IV.

[e]This pair must have been like the two beautiful pillars of Thutmose III, a little farther back, just in front of the sanctuary. "*The two lower lips*" are perhaps the two bases or their edges.

# REIGN OF TAHARKA

## TANIS STELA[a]

892.[b] This unfortunately fragmentary stela was erected by Taharka at Tanis to commemorate the coming of his mother thither from Napata, after his coronation in Lower Egypt. He narrates how he came north from Nubia as a youth of twenty years with some king. This would have been on the invasion of Lower Egypt by Shabaka. Many years then elapsed before he became king, during which he did not see his mother, and must, therefore, have spent these years in the north. As a son of Piankhi, he must have occupied a prominent position. When it is recollected that the Hebrew records (2 Kings 19:9) state that the enemy of Sennacherib at Altaqû in 701 B. C. (some thirteen years before Taharka's accession) was Taharka, the conclusion cannot be resisted that Shabaka sent Taharka in command of the Egyptian and Ethiopian forces, against the Assyrians. It is evident, therefore, that the Hebrew writer, reporting the matter at a later date, long after Taharka's reign, supposes him to have been already king in 701.[c]

893. The beginning of the stela is too fragmentary for

---

[a]Fragmentary stela in two parts, left lying as found in the ruins of Tanis. The lower fragment, containing 19 lines, was first seen and copied by de Rougé, (*Inscriptions hiéroglyphiques*, 73; and "Etudes sur des monuments du règne de Tahraka," *Mélanges d'archéologie égyptienne et assyrienne*, I, 21–23); again published by Birch, *Zeitschrift für ägyptische Sprache*, 1880, 22 ff. Petrie then found the upper part, and published both parts in his *Tanis* (II, Pl. IX, No. 136). It was first understood historically by Schaefer (*Zeitschrift für ägyptische Sprache*, 1900, 51, 52).

[b]The omission of two in numbering the sections is intentional.

[c]See also Griffith, *Stories of the High Priests*, 10, 11.

translation, but it is evident that someone, of course the king, gave the young Taharka, who narrates it all in the first person, a fine field (l. 1), which the gods protected against grasshoppers (l. 2), so that Taharka reaped (ᶜ*w*ᵓ) from it (l. 3) a plentiful yield of all grain and fruit of the ground. Meanwhile he was brought up among the royal children (l. 5) and someone, again of course the king, loved him more than the royal children (l. 6). Taharka then says:

My father, Amon, [⌜vouchsafed⌝] to me to place all lands under my feet [10]——— [⌜the east as far as⌝] the rising of Re, and the west [11][⌜as far as his setting⌝].

**894.** Whether the restorations are correct or not it is evident that Taharka is here relating his accession in the conventional terms, which always make such a usurpation an act of the gods. Immediately thereupon, Taharka narrates the coming of his mother from Napata, which leads him to revert to the long separation from her, caused by his departure for the North years before. He says:

**895.** [a][⌜The queen-mother⌝] was in Napata[b] as King's-Sister, amiable in love, King's-Mother [12]———. Now, I had been separated from her as a youth (*ḥwn*) of twenty years, [13][⌜accompanying his majesty⌝] when he[c] came to the Northland (Delta). Then she went north to [14][⌜the Northland where I was⌝] after a long period (*ḥnty*) of years, and she found me crowned [15][⌜as king upon the throne of Horus⌝]. I had taken the diadems of Re, and I had assumed the double serpent-crest, as [16]——— as the protection of my limbs. She rejoiced greatly [17][when she saw] the beauty of his majesty,[d] as Isis saw her son, Horus, crowned upon the throne [18]——— while he was a youth in the marsh of [19]——— all countries. They bowed to the ground to this King's-

---

[a]This would connect directly with the above beginning of l. 11.

[b]This reading, first noticed by Schaefer (*Zeitschrift für ägyptische Sprache*, 1900, 51, 52), is certain.

[c]This "*he*" can only refer to the king under whom the youth Taharka was serving, when separated from his mother; see Schaefer, *loc. cit.*

[d]Taharka.

Mother, while she [20]——— ⸢greatly⸣. Their old as well as their young ones [21][⸢gave praise to⸣] this King's-Mother, saying: "Isis hath received [22]———, she hath — her son, King of Upper and Lower Egypt, Taharka, living forever [23]———.

**896.** Here follow four lines of conventional praise addressed to Taharka, closing with a comparison of his kindness toward his mother with that of Horus to his mother, Isis:

[26]——— for his mother, Isis, when thou wast crowned upon the throne.

## BUILDING INSCRIPTION IN LARGE CLIFF-TEMPLE OF NAPATA

**897.** The following dedications in the larger temple at Napata record Taharka's building activity there:

[a]Taharka, living forever; he made (it) as his monument for his mother, Mut of Napata; he built for her a temple anew, of fine white sandstone, his majesty having found this temple built of stone,[b] by the ancestors, of bad workmanship. His majesty caused that this temple should be built of excellent workmanship, forever.

**898.** The same hall as the above conclusion has:

[c]He made (it) as his monument for his mother, Mut, mistress of heaven, queen of Nubia (*Tˀ pd·t*); he built her house, he enlarged her temple anew, of fine white sandstone.

**899.** A cella beside the main adytum has:

[d]He made (it) as his monument for [his] mother, Mut, Eye of Re, Mistress of Heaven, queen of gods, residing in Napata; building her house of fine white sandstone.

---

[a]Lepsius, *Denkmäler*, V, 5: frieze inscription in the first hall.

[b]The inscription as published stops abruptly here, and the frieze inscription of the next hall as published (Lepsius, *Denkmäler*, V, 7, *a*) begins with equal abruptness, and fits the inscription of the first hall exactly. Whether this is an accident of preservation, or was originally intended, is immaterial.

[c]Lepsius, *Denkmäler*, V, 7, *c*. [d]*Ibid*., 12, *a*.

**900.** An altar in the Amon-temple bears the dedication:[a]

He made (it) as his monument for his father, Amon-Re, lord of Thebes (*Nswt-tꜣwy*), great god, residing in Nubia (*Tꜣ-pd·t*); (of) granite ⌈—⌉, in order to offer upon it in his palace (*ꜥḥꜥ*). Never happened the like.

## INSCRIPTION OF MENTEMHET[b]

**901.** The history of the principality of Thebes after the middle of the Twenty-second Dynasty, until the latter part of the Ethiopian period is almost entirely unknown. We see it in the possession of Piankhi toward the end of the Twenty-third Dynasty, but its local history is still totally obscure until the reign of Taharka, when we find a certain "*prophet of Amon, prince of Thebes, Nesuptah,*"[c] ruling there. His son Mentemhet succeeded him, and evidently maintained himself during Taharka's reign in power and wealth.[d] His titles are of importance. Although he was prince of the Theban principality, he was only fourth prophet of Amon. At the same time, he was "*chief of the prophets*

[a]Lepsius, *Denkmäler*, V, 13, *b, d*.

[b]In a niche-like chamber of the temple of Mut at Karnak. It had contained a statue of Mentemhet (Mariette, *Karnak*, Texte, 64), probably one of those found by Miss Benson (*Recueil*, XX, 188–92; Benson and Gourlay, *The Temple of Mut in Asher*, 261–63, Pl. XXIII-XXIV, 350–57). Our inscription is published by Dümichen, *Historische Inschriften*, II, 48 (without relief), and Mariette, *Karnak*, 42–44; both are very inaccurate, and an exhaustive publication is much needed.

[c]Krall, *Studien*, III, 77 A. The genealogy of the family is carried back four generations beyond Nesuptah by the statues in the great Karnak cache. See Legrain, *Recueil*, 27, 80; but he does not indicate whether or not these four generations were already princes of Thebes.

[d]Besides those above referred to, numerous monuments of this man are known. His tomb in the Assasîf at Thebes was excavated by Eisenlohr (*Zeitschrift für ägyptische Sprache*, 1885, 55), and its inscriptions (only titles and family) were published by Krall (*Studien*, III, 76–80). Two neighboring tombs of his family were found beside it, and the inscriptions bearing on Mentemhet also published by Krall (*ibid.*, 80–82). A list of his smaller monuments is given by Wiedemann (*Recueil*, VIII, 69) and by Newberry (Benson and Gourlay, *The Temple of Mut in Asher*, 356, 357).

*of all gods of South and North.*"[a] He, therefore, held the sacerdotal primacy of Egypt without being High Priest of Amon. The High Priest of Amon had, therefore, been deprived of his temporal power as prince of the Thebaid, as well as of his sacerdotal supremacy. This is confirmed by the relative position of Mentemhet and the High Priest of Amon in the Adoption Stela (§§ 949–52).[b] As Mentemhet's father was prince of Thebes before him, these changes may have taken place at the advent of the Ethiopian dynasty under Shabaka.

**902.** The activity of Mentemhet in the building and restoration of the monuments under Taharka at Thebes renders his rule there notable. This work was all done before Taharka's death, and the renewal of so many costly cultus images of the gods, besides references to the purification of all the temples in the South, and vague allusions to a great catastrophe, make it extremely probable that the mooted capture and sack of Thebes (667 B. C.) in Ashurbanipal's first campaign, although not certain from his confused records, actually took place. The restoration recorded by Mentemhet must have been done, therefore, between 667 and 661 B. C. The wealth which he was able to devote to restoring his plundered city must have been considerable; but it all fell a prey to the Assyrians at the second capture of the city by Ashurbanipal in 661 B. C., when it was frightfully laid waste. Of any attempted restoration by Mentemhet after this we hear nothing. He continued as ruler of the Thebaid, survived the rise of the Twenty-sixth Dynasty, and

[a]Benson and Gourlay, *The Temple of Mut in Asher*, 356.

[b]For the current and widespread conclusion that the high priesthood of Amon was now held by the Ethiopian kings themselves, I find no support. It is evident from the Adoption Stela that the High Priest of Amon had been stripped of his power; and this fully explains why we have no records of him at this time.

maintained his position into the reign of Psamtik I (§ 945). But his son Nesuptah did not succeed him,[a] and the family cannot be traced any farther.

**903.** Mentemhet's record consists of a relief on the rear wall of the temple chamber, and an inscription occupying the two side walls. The relief shows Taharka worshiping the goddess Mut, while behind him are Mentemhet, the latter's father Nesuptah, and son Nesuptah. Above these figures are depicted the statues and images replaced or restored by Mentemhet. On the right of the relief his narrative begins thus:

*Titles of Mentemhet*

**904.** [1]——— all gods, fourth prophet of Amon, prince of Thebes, governor of [the Southland], Mentemhet, son of the prophet of Amon, prince of Thebes, Nesu[ptah];[b] he saith:

*Sacred Barge*

I fashioned [2][the sacred barge of ⌈Amon⌉] of 80 cubits in its length, of new cedar of the best of the terraces. The "Great House" was of electrum, inlaid with every genuine costly stone — — ⌈of the last day⌉ — equipped [3]———.

*Purification of Temples*

**905.** I purified all the temples in the nomes of all Patoris, according as one should purify [⌈violated⌉] temples, — after there had been [4][⌈an invasion of unclean foreigners in⌉] the Southland. ⌈— — — —⌉ — ⌈—⌉ all these things which I have brought before you, there is no [lying] speech therein, no contradiction [5]——— deceit. There is no lie in the place of my mouth.

---

[a]A relief in Abydos (Mariette, *Abydos*, I, Pl. 2, *b*) shows Psamtik I before Orisis and Horus. He is accompanied by the "*Divine Votress, Nitocris,*" and "*the prince* (*ḥ*ᵓ*ty*-ᶜ) *of Thebes, governor of the South,* — , *chief steward of the Divine Votress, Pedihor.*" It is thus clear that Nesuptah did not succeed his father, Mentemhet, although it is barely possible also that Pedihor was another son, and that Nesuptah had died.

[b]The name of the father is preserved in the relief.

### *Prosperity and Plentiful Offerings*

**906.** My mistress is satisfied with all that I have done ⌜for ⌝Thebes, [the Horizon of] him of the hidden name, Eye of Re, Mistress [6][of temples][a] ——— I satisfied her lord with the things of his desire, bulls of the largest, and calves of the best. I gave — — my lord, of good things [7]——— satisfied with food, and divine offerings, like that which he receives at the beginning of all the seasons, at th[eir] times, — — I multiplied the amount [8]———. His granaries swelled with the first fruits[b] [⌜which came to⌝] him down-stream in their season, and up-stream in their time. They made festive [9]——— in his totals, to celebrate the feasts; that he might provision the prophets, priests, — and lay priests of the temples[10]——— in the nomes, great and small — — making for me an overflow for my city, the land having moisture, the cities and nomes fatness.

### *Foreign Invasion*

**907.** [11]——— it being divine chastisement. [⌜In⌝] the protected Southland in its divine way, while the whole land was overturned, because of the greatness of [12]——— ⌜———⌝ coming from the South. I satisfied my — coming from [13]——— in — [in] going in and in going out by night and by day[c] [14]——— an excellent refuge for my city. [⌜I⌝] repelled the wretches from the southern nomes — — — ⌜time⌝.

### *Family Prosperity and Conclusion*

**908.** [15]——— following his god without ceasing, — the temple, seeing that which was in it. Every shrine was sealed with [⌜my⌝] seal [16]——— belonging thereto. I was in the temple —, following the footsteps of my lord. My son was with me [17]——— priest of his ka, chief prophet of — in Thebes, chief of the phyle, Nesuptah. My children were healthy ——— [18]the prophets knew his counsel —. I spent the day in searching and the night in seeking, searching [19]——— ⌜summoning⌝ them that passed, calling them that —, and revising the rules that had begun to be ⌜obsolete⌝.

---

[a]See § 753, l. 1, for similar epithets of Thebes, from which this is restored.

[b]Or possibly the "*best*" of the grain.

[c]This is evidently a reference to a siege, as in Piankhi, e. g., § 854, l. 80.

The inscription proceeds to praise of his son (ll. 21 and 22), and concludes with a prayer in the first person plural, of no historic interest (ll. 24–29).

**909.** On the other side of the relief, Mentemhet then continues an enumeration of his buildings and other works for the temples, as follows:

*Works for Min-Amon*

I brought forth Min-Amon to his stairway in the southern house (Luxor) at his beautiful feast [3]——— plenty. I presented the oblations of the eight gods in the second month of the third season, twenty-eighth day, in order that [4]——— of electrum and every splendid costly stone. I fashioned the august image of Khonsupekhrod overlaid with gold (called): "His-Every-Emanation-is-[5]——— - Crowns."[a] I made a throne for this god, the legs of pure silver, inlay-figures [6]——— of his stipulations — — them after a long space (*ḥnty*) of years, beginning to decay. [7]——— ⌜———⌝ according as a thorough inspection should be made.

*Temple of Mut?*

**910.** I built her temple of stone [8]——— [the doors were of] new[b] cedar, and kedet (*ḳd·t*) wood, mounted with Asiatic copper; the inlay-figures thereon were of electrum, the bolts and fastenings [9]——— gold inlaid with every costly stone. I erected for her a hall with thirty-four[c] columns of fine white sandstone ⌜—⌝ [10]———. I constructed her pure and beautiful lake of fine white sandstone; I erected for her, her storehouse for the storage of her divine offerings therein; I multiplied the offering-tables [11]———.

*Works for Khonsu*

**911.** I restored the august image of "Khonsu-in-Thebes-Beautiful-Rest" (called): "Wearer-of-the-Divine-Diadem," with gold and every

---

[a]Two Amon crowns, and one Khonsu crown.

[b]Correct *m* ᵓ ᶜ to *m* ᵓ *w*, as commonly.

[c]So Mariette; Dümichen has 23; no such hall is now discoverable in the temple of Mut. Mentemhet probably means restoration, although he makes a similar claim on his statue (Benson and Gourlay, *The Temple of Mut in Asher*, 353, l. 10): "*I erected the temple of Mut, mistress of heaven, of fine white sandstone.*"

genuine costly stone. I multiplied their offering-tables of silver, gold, and copper. [12]——— ⌜I clothed⌝[a] Khonsu (called): "The-Plan-Maker-is-an-Emanation," with electrum, as formerly.

### *Works for Montu*

**912.** I constructed the pure lake of Montu, lord of Thebes, of fine white sandstone like [13]——— illuminating his great and august house therewith. I multiplied his offering-tables of silver, gold, and bronze.

### *Theban Divinities*

I fashioned individual vessels. I equipped Wes and Weset,[b] Victorious Thebes, Mistress of Might, as an emanation[c] [14]———.

### *Image of Bast*

I fashioned the august image of Bast, residing in Thebes; with staves[d] of electrum and every genuine costly stone.

### *Works for Ptah*

**913.** I fashioned the august image of Ptah (called): "⌜Thebes⌝-is-Bright-at-His-Appearance," of gold [15]——— their offering-tables more beautiful than before.

### *Images of Hathor*

I fashioned [the image] of Hathor, Mistress of the Valley (called): "— - — - —-Bright;" as their glorious emanation, according as a thorough inspection should be made [16]——— every one thereof had two staves.

### *Images of Amon*

I fashioned the august image of Amon, lord of Thebes (*Ns·wt-t*ʾ *wy*), residing in Thebes (*W*ʾ *s·t*); the august image of Khonsu (called): "Numberer-of-Life;" the august image of Amon, lord of Thebes [17]——— every one thereof had two staves.

---

[a]Or: "*the protection of K., etc., was of electrum.*"

[b]Apparently a male and female divinity, each apotheosizing Thebes. The goddess is well known, but this is the only occurrence of the god with which I am acquainted.

[c]*M ty·t;* it is not always certain what this phrase means in this inscription, e. g., l. 18 after "*Themet.*"

[d]For carrying.

*Statue of Amenhotep I*

I fashioned the statue of Zeserkere (Amenhotep I), triumphant; of electrum and every costly stone; with two staves, as it had been before 18———.

*Khonsu of Themet*

**914.** [⌜I fashioned the image of⌝] Khonsu, residing in Themet (*Ṯ*ᵓ-*mw*ˁ*t*) ⌜— —⌝ of electrum, with two staves.

*Image of "The Great One"*

I fashioned "The-Great-One (feminine)-of-the-Garden" as her glorious emanation; I restored her temples, that it might be as formerly.

*Wall of Karnak*

19——— it of fine white sandstone, to keep off the flood of the river from ⌜it when it came⌝. I hewed a ⌜—⌝ 20——— at his beautiful feast of the fourth month of the first season, twenty-fifth day. I restored the wall of the temple of Amon in Karnak ⌜—⌝ 21——— ⌜— — —⌝. I built a ⌜—⌝ of brick, according as I found it good to make the ancestors 22———.

*Works for the Sacred Bull*

**915.** I [⌜fashioned⌝] the bull of Mad[a] (*M*ᵓ *d*), as his glorious emanation; I built his house; it was more beautiful than what was therein 23[⌜before⌝] ———.

*Temple of Montu*

I built the temple of Montu, lord — — — — — its gates shone beautifully 24———.

*Works for Uncertain Gods*

[I fashioned the image of] — upon his stairway (called): "— - — - of-the-Field-in-Thebes;" of gold, more beautiful than it was before 25——— who is lord of the hill-country, residing in Khemkhem (*Ḫmḫm*).

*Image of Horus*

I fashioned the august image of Horus (called): "The-God-Abides-26———."

[a]A sacred precinct near Karnak.

*Image of Min?*

**916.** I [fashioned] (the image of) ⌈Min⌉ (called): "⌈Chief⌉-of-Heaven," as his glorious emanation, overlaid — — [27]————.

*Image of Thoth*

I fashioned the august image of Thoth, presiding over Hatibti (*Ḥ·t-ybty*), residing in ————.

*Works for Isis*

[28]———— I — the emanation of Isis. I fashioned — upon them — — my whole city ⌈— —⌉ — ⌈—⌉ — [29]———— more beautiful than formerly. I constructed a sacred lake for the temple of Isis ⌈— —⌉ — [30]————.

*Works for Osiris*

I fashioned the barge of Osiris in this district, of — cubits — — — — of new[a] cedar, according to the accustomed stipulations, ⌈after I had found it of acacia⌉ ———— [31]———— of brick, after I had found it beginning to fall to ruin ————.

---

## SERAPEUM STELA[b]

**917.** This stela, recording the burial of an Apis at Memphis in the twenty-fourth year of Taharka, is important as showing that in 664 B. C. the priests of Memphis regarded Taharka as still reigning there, although he had been driven out by Ashurbanipal in 668. As the stela was hidden far down in the subterranean passages of the Serapeum, the priests could have safely so dated the monument, even though the city was under Assyrian government. Hence,

---

[a]Correct *m ᵓ ᶜ* to *m ᵓ w*.

[b]Louvre, No. 121; published by Mariette, *Le Sérapéum de Memphis,* III, Pl. 35; *Revue égyptologique,* VII, 136; Chassinat, *Recueil,* 22, 18. I had also my own copy of the original.

it is not safe to conclude, from this stela, that Taharka actually held Memphis in 664 B. C.

**918.** Year 24, fourth month of the second season (eighth month), day 23, under the majesty of the King of Upper and Lower Egypt, Taharka, living forever.

The god was conducted in peace to the beautiful West, by the hereditary prince, sem priest, master of all wardrobes, prophet of Ptah, divine father, Senbef, son of the divine father, of Sekhetre (*Sḫt-R*ᶜ), Enekhwennofer; born of Neatesnakhte (*N*ᵓ-ᶜᵓ-*t*ᵓ *ys-nht·t*). His brother, divine father of Sekhetre, Ptahhotep.

# REIGN OF TANUTAMON

## STELA OF TANUTAMON[a]

919. This stela brings us to the close of Ethiopian rule in Egypt. Lower Egypt was in control of Assyrian vassals, resulting from the defeat of Taharka by Ashurbanipal's army, not long after the latter's accession in 668 B. C. The Delta vassals had been discovered in their subsequent plotting with Taharka against their Assyrian overlord. Necho, the Saitic dynast, after being sent to Ninevah, was pardoned and reinstated at Sais. His son, likewise, was made vassal king in Athribis, and at this juncture, according to the records of Ashurbanipal,[b] Taharka died.

920. The stela of Tanutamon records the course of political events in Upper Egypt during the last days of Taharka, and the short reign of Tanutamon over all Egypt. It shows us Tanutamon coregent with Taharka during the latter's last year (663 B. C.), which was the first of Tanutamon;[c] and narrates how he proceeded from some place in Upper

---

[a]Gray granite, round-topped stela, 1.32 m. high and 0.72 m. wide, now in Cairo (No. 162, *Guide* of 1902, 112); discovered at Napata with the Piankhi Stela in 1862; published by Maspero, *Revue archéologique*, 1868, XVII, 329 ff.; *tirage à part, Didier*, 8vo, 11 pp. and 2 Pls.); and by Mariette (*Monuments divers*, Pls. 7, 8). I had also a squeeze and a copy of squeeze by Schaefer, and he and I together went over the copy again with the squeeze. This copy brought out a number of important readings filling up several lacunæ. I am also indebted to Schaefer for several valuable suggestions.

[b]Winckler, *Untersuchungen zur altorientalischen Geschichte*, 103–5, ll. 36–69.

[c]The proper relation of Tanutamon and Taharka in this narrative was first explained by Schaefer (*Zeitschrift für ägyptische Sprache*, 1897, 67 ff.). As he did not come to the throne even as coregent until 663 B. C., Winckler's explanation of Ashurbanipal's confused records (*Altorientalische Forschungen*, 480–83), in which he makes Tanutamon the final opponent of Ashurbanipal in the campaign of 668–7, is impossible.

Egypt (probably Thebes), of which he was king, to Napata, where he was crowned sole king, so that Taharka's death must have been the occasion of his assumption of sole power.[a] He had been summoned by a dream, before going to Napata to seize also the Northland, then in Assyrian hands, and, leaving Napata, he then undertook the recovery of the North. He captured Memphis, perhaps slew Necho of Sais in battle,[b] and, although unable to subdue the Delta dynasts, accepted what he construed as their submission, which they offered in person. He then ruled in Memphis as nominal king of all Egypt, and at this point the narrative of his stela closes. The presence of the Assyrians in the land is ignored throughout, and the inglorious conclusion of his reign in Egypt at the approach of Ashurbanipal's second great invasion in 661 B. C. is naturally not added at the end.

*Introduction*

**921.** [1]"Good God"[c] on the day when he was born; Atum is he for the people (*rḫy·t*), lord of two horns, ruler of the living, prince, seizing every land, victorious in might on the day of battle, facing the front on the day[d] [2]⌈of conflict⌉, lord of valor, like Montu, great in strength, like a fierce-eyed lion, wise-hearted, like Thoth; crossing the sea[e] in pursuit

---

[a]Ashurbanipal calls Tanutamon the son of Taharka's sister, and the son of Shabaka (Winckler, *op. cit.*, 105); hence Shabaka must have married Piankhi's daughter, which explains his claim to the throne. Tanutamon was thus Piankhi's grandson.

[b]The battle is recorded by Tanutamon (ll. 16, 17), but he does not mention the slaying of Necho. This is probable from the remark of Herodotus (as Eduard Meyer first perceived, *Geschichte des alten Aegyptens*, 353) that Necho was slain by an Ethiopian king, who, Herodotus thought, was Shabaka. But, according to Manetho, Necho's death must have occurred in 663 B. C., that is, the year of Tanutamon's expedition against Memphis.

[c]That is, "*king*."

[d]There is possibly, but probably not, a lost word at the end of l. 1.

[e]*D̠ ᵓ wᵓ d̠-wr.*

of his opponent, carrying off the ends of[a] ⌜—⌝ —. He has [taken] this land; none fighting and none standing before him, (even) the King of Upper and Lower Egypt, Bekere (*B ͗ -k ͗ -R ͗*), Son of Re, Tanutamon (*T ͗ n-w ͗ -ty-Ymn*), beloved of Amon of Napata.

### *The Dream*

**922.** In the year 1, of his coronation as king — — 4his majesty saw a dream by night: two serpents, one upon his right, the other upon his left. Then his majesty awoke, and he found them not. His majesty said: 5"Wherefore [has] this [come] to me?" Then they answered[b] him, saying: "Thine is the Southland; take for thyself (also) the Northland. The 'Two Goddesses'[c] shine upon thy brow, the land is given to thee, in its length and its breadth. [No] 6other divides it with thee."

### *Journey to Napata*

**923.** When his majesty was crowned upon the throne of Horus in this first[d] year, his majesty went forth from the place[e] where he had been, as Horus went forth from Khemmis. He went forth from—, while there [came] 7to him millions and hundreds of thousands coming after him. Said his majesty: "Lo, the dream is true! It[f] is profitable for him who sets it in his heart, (but) evil for him who understands [it] not." His majesty went to Napata, while none stood 8before him.[g]

### *Coronation in Napata*

**924.** His majesty arrived at the temple of Amon of Napata, residing in the Pure Mountain. As for his majesty, his heart was glad when he saw his father, Amon-Re, lord of Thebes (*Nswt-t ͗ wy*), residing in the Pure Mountain. Garlands for this god were brought to him; 9then his

[a]Possibly: "*carrying away the rear of his foe* (*pḥ sw*)." The *pḥ* is very probable.

[b]Read *whm˙šn nf*, but the scribe has omitted the second *n*.

[c]The double diadem of Upper and Lower Egypt.

[d]This remark can refer only to his second coronation as sole king. It is here referred to at the beginning of his journey to Napata, in anticipation of what happened on his arrival there, viz., his said coronation as sole king. His joint reign with Taharka thus lasted less than a year.

[e]This must have been some place in Upper Egypt, of which he was then king; it was therefore probably Thebes.

[f]A dream.

[g]In a hostile sense.

majesty brought forth in splendor Amon of Napata; and he made for him a great festival offering, founding for him a ⌜feast⌝: 39 oxen, 40 jars (ᶜ š) of beer, and 100 *šw*.

*Departure for the North*

**925.** His majesty sailed down-stream toward the Northland, that he might behold [10]Amon, whose name is hidden from the gods.

*Ceremonies at Elephantine*

His majesty arrived at Elephantine; then his majesty sailed across to Elephantine, he arrived at the temple of Khnum-Re, lord of the cataract, [11]and he caused this god to be brought forth in splendor. He made a great festival offering, and he gave bread and beer for the gods of the two caverns. He appeased ⌜Nun⌝ in his cavern.

*Ceremonies at Thebes*

**926.** Then his majesty sailed down-stream to the city Thebes of Amon. His majesty sailed to the frontier[a] of Thebes (*Wᵓ s·t*), and he entered the temple of Amon-Re, lord of Thebes. There came to his majesty the servant of the great —,[b] and the lay priests of the temple of Amon-Re, [13]lord of Thebes, and they brought to him garlands for Amon, whose name is hidden. As for his majesty, his heart rejoiced when he saw this temple. He brought forth Amon-Re, lord of Thebes, in splendor, and there was celebrated a great feast in the whole land.

*Departure for the Delta*

**927.** [14]His majesty sailed down-stream to the Northland, while the west and the east made great jubilee, saying: "Welcome is thy coming, and welcome thy ka! To sustain alive the Two Lands; [c][15]to erect the temples which have begun to fall to ruin; to set up their statues in their shrines; to give divine offerings to the gods and goddesses, and mortuary offerings to the glorified (dead); [16]to put the priest in his place; to

[a]Or: "*into*" (*r ḫn ehoun*), as in the Piankhi inscription.

[b]Evidently a priestly title.

[c]The following evidently refers to the ruin and disorganization resulting from the Assyrian invasions.

furnish all things of the sacred property." As for those who had fighting in their hearts,[a] they became rejoicers.

*Capture of Memphis*

**928.** When his majesty arrived at Memphis, there came forth [17]the children of rebellion, to fight with his majesty. His majesty made a great slaughter among them; their number being unknown. His majesty took Memphis, and he entered into the temple of [18]Ptah, "South-of-His-Wall;" he made a great festival oblation for Ptah-Sokar; he appeased Sekhmet, the great, who loves him.

*New Buildings in Napata*

**929.** As for his majesty, his heart was glad in giving ⌜—⌝ to his father, Amon, of Napata. His majesty issued a command concerning it, [19]to Nubia (*T ͗ pd·t*), to build for him a hall anew; it was not found built in the time of the ancestors. His majesty caused it to be built of stone, mounted with gold;[b] [20]its panel[c] was of cedar [21]incensed with myrrh of Punt. The double doors thereof were of electrum, [22]the two bolts (*ḳrty*) of ⌜tin⌝ (*Tyḥty*). He built for him another hall at the rear exit, for furnishing his milk [23]of his numerous herds, in tens of thousands, thousands, hundreds, and tens; the number of the young calves [24]with their mothers was unknown.

*Campaign in the Delta*

**930.** Now, after these things, his majesty sailed north, to fight with the chiefs of the North. [25]Then they entered their strongholds [⌜as beasts crawl into⌝] their holes. Then his majesty spent many days before them, (but) there came not forth one [26]of them to fight with his majesty. Then his majesty sailed southward to Memphis.

*Arrival of the Delta Dynasts*

**931.** He sat in his palace deliberating and counseling with [27]his heart how to cause his army to reach and to ⌜—⌝ them. Then his army said that one had come to report to him, saying: "These chiefs come

---

[a]Lit., "*Those (wnn) in whose hearts was to fight, they, etc.*"

[b]Here begins the back of the stela.

[c]Or tablet.

to the place [28]where his majesty is, [O king], our lord." Said his majesty: "Come they to fight? Come they to submit,[a] they shall live from this hour." They said [29][to] his majesty: "They come to submit to (*bk*) the king, our lord." Said his majesty: "As for my lord, this august god, Amon-Re, lord of Thebes, residing in the Pure Mountain, great and ⌈excellent⌉ god, whose name is ⌈known⌉, vigilant ⌈—⌉ [30]for his beloved, and giving valor to him who serves him; he who possesses his plans does not go astray; nor doth he whom he leads err. Behold, he told (it) me by night, [31]and I behold (it) by day."[b] Said his majesty: "Where are they in this hour?" Said they before his majesty: "They are here, waiting at the hall (*ᶜry·t*)."

### *Submission of the Delta Dynasts*

**932.** Then his majesty went forth [32]from his [⌈palace⌉] to —, as Re shines in his bright dwelling. He found them prostrate upon their bellies, kissing the ground to his majesty. Said his majesty: "Lo, it is true that which he uttered, [33]the word ⌈of his design. Lo, he knows what⌉ shall happen. It is the decree of the god; (hence) it comes to pass. I swear as Re loves me, as Amon favors me in his house, ⌈behold, I saw⌉ this august god, Amon [34]of Napata, residing in the Pure Mountain, while he was standing[c] by me, he said to me: 'I am thy leader in[d] every way. Thou mayest not say: "Would that I had[e] . . . ."' [35]. . . ." Then they answered him, saying: "Lo, this god, [36]he hath [revealed] to thee the beginning; he hath completed for thee the ⌈end⌉ in prosperity. Lo, thou dost not ⌈— —⌉[f] that comes out of his mouth, O king, our lord." Then the hereditary prince of Per-Soped, Pekrur[g] (*Pꜣ-ḳrr*), arose to speak, saying: [37]"Thou slayest whom thou wilt; and lettest live whom thou wilt ⌈————⌉." They answered him with one accord, saying:

---

[a]Lit., "*to serve*," or "*labor*" (*bk*), the word for pay taxes. The second question is likewise a protasis.

[b]Schaefer suggests: "*That which he told me by night, I have seen by day.*"

[c]Compare the dream of Merneptah, III, 582.

[d]Lit., "*to every way.*"

[e]The conclusion of Tanutamon's speech is fragmentary, and hopelessly obscure. Enough remains to show that it consisted only of pious phrases of no historical importance. It is evident that he is telling the subject chiefs that their submission is only the fulfilment of Amon's promise to him.

[f]The text is uncertain.

[g]Lit., "*The Frog*," the same as Coptic "Pekrour;" see Steindorff, *Zeitschrift für ägyptische Sprache*, 1892, 63.

"Give to us breath, O lord of life, [38]without whom there is no life. Let us serve (*bk*) thee[a] like the serfs who are subject to thee, as thou[b] saidest at the first on the day when thou wert crowned as king." The heart of his majesty rejoiced when he heard this word, [39]and he gave to them bread, beer, and every good thing.

*Dismissal of the Delta Dynasts*

**933.** Now, when some days had passed, after these events, and ⌜everything had been given in plenty⌝ — —, they said: "Wherefore are we (still) here, O king, our lord?" Said [40]his majesty: "Wherefore!" Said they to his majesty: "Let us go to our cities, that we may command our peasant-serfs that we may bring (*f ᵓ y˙n*) our impost (*bk*) to the court." His majesty (let) them go [41]to their cities, and they became ⌜subjects⌝.[c]

*Brief Reign at Memphis*

**934.** The Southerners went north, and the Northerners went south to the place where his majesty was, bearing every good thing of the Southland, and all provision [42]of the Northland, to satisfy the heart of his majesty, (⌜when⌝) the King of Upper and Lower Egypt, Bekere, Son of Re, Tanutamon, L. P. H., appeared upon the throne of Horus, forever.

---

[a]Lit., "*labor for (pay taxes to) him*" (*bk˙ n nf*).

[b]The change of person is in the original.

[c]Schaefer read *ḥsfy(w)*.

# THE TWENTY-SIXTH DYNASTY

## REIGN OF PSAMTIK I

### ADOPTION STELA OF NITOCRIS[a]

935. This document has thrown a flood of light on the dynastic connections in the Ethiopian and Saitic period, and its discovery was especially welcome, in view of the paucity of contemporary monuments from this age. It may be described as a decree of adoption and property-conveyance. It records the adoption of Nitocris, the daughter of Psamtik I, by a Shepnupet, daughter of Taharka, the Divine Votress, or sacerdotal princess, at Thebes. Shepnupet transfers all her property to Nitocris, and the purpose of the adoption was that the family of Psamtik I might legally gain control of this property, as well as the position which it entailed at Thebes.

936. The beginning of the document is lost, and it now commences in the middle of a speech of Psamtik I to his court, announcing his purpose to have his daughter Nitocris adopted by Shepnupet. The court responds with the usual encomiums. In the ninth year of Psamtik I, therefore, Nitocris proceeds to Thebes, where she is received with acclamation, and the property of Shepnupet is formally conveyed to her, a full invoice of her estate being appended.

937. The stela shows that Psamtik had gained full control of Thebes by his ninth year, and that Tanutamon had, therefore, lost Upper Egypt before that time. The status of Thebes is much the same as under the Ethiopians, Men-

[a]Red granite stela, nearly 6 feet high, and 4½ feet wide, found by Legrain at Karnak in 1897; now in Cairo. The top is broken off and missing; published by Legrain (*Zeitschrift für ägyptische Sprache*, 35, 16–19); translated by Erman (*ibid.*, 24–29), on whose rendering the present translation is largely based

temhet, the favorite of Taharka,[a] was still its prince, showing that some of the old feudal dynasts still survived under Psamtik I.[b] The High Priest of Amon occupies a completely subordinate position; he possesses no political influence, and his subordinate, the third prophet of Amon, contributes as much as he to the revenues of Nitocris.

**938.** The adoption of Nitocris, and the similar adoption of her predecessor, Shepnupet, as well as the adoption of Amenirdis by the same Shepnupet, render it clear that this was the usual method of succession in the Ethiopian and Saitic periods, and much simplifies the royal family connections of the time. Already, as early as 1885, Erman had noticed that Nitocris was but the adoptive mother of Enekhnesneferibre.[c] A stela, recounting this adoption, which is a second Adoption Stela (§§ 988A–988J) has now been discovered at Karnak. They furnish the following chronology of the Theban princesses:

Adoption of Nitocris: year 9 of Psamtik I, 654 B. C.

Death of Shepnupet II: Unknown date ———.

Induction of Nitocris: unknown date ———.

Adoption of Enekhnesneferibre: year 1 of Psamtik II, 593 B. C.

---

[a]That this is the same Mentemhet as the one under Taharka, is shown by the name of his eldest son, Nesuptah, the same whom we find in the records of Mentemhet under Taharka (§ 903).

[b]The old principality of Heracleopolis also still survived, at least into the third generation of the Saite line; for there was a prince of Heracleopolis named Hor, son of Psamtik. The father must have been born not earlier than the time of Psamtik I. Hor built considerably on his own account at Heracleopolis; cf. statue inscription in Louvre (see §§ 967 ff.). A chapel was also built by one *P'-drps* (in the year 51 of Psamtik I at Pharbæthus), who may also have been a local prince; cf. Berlin stela (No. 8438); Brugsch, *Thesaurus*, IV, 797 = Revillout, *Revue égyptologique*, I, 33). Compare also the buildings or temple works of Nesuhor at Elephantine (§§ 989 ff.).

[c]In Schweinfurth, "Alte Baureste im Uadi Gasûs" (*Abhandlungen der Berliner Akademie*, 1885).

Death of Nitocris: year 4 of Apries, 584 B. C.

Induction of Enekhnesneferibre: year 4 of Apries, 584 B. C.

Death of Enekhnesneferibre: after Psamtik III, not earlier than 525 B. C.

**939.** These stelæ and other contemporary monuments enable us to reconstruct the following genealogy,[a] tracing the succession of these sacerdotal princesses from the Twenty-third to the Twenty-sixth Dynasty. Incidentally, this reconstruction discloses important relationships among the Ethiopian rulers.

[a]Names of princesses are in italics; dotted lines indicate adoption. Essentially the same table in so far as the princesses are concerned was drawn up by Daressy, *Recueil*, XX, 84; then by Erman, *Zeitschrift für ägyptische Sprache*, 35, 29.

**940.**

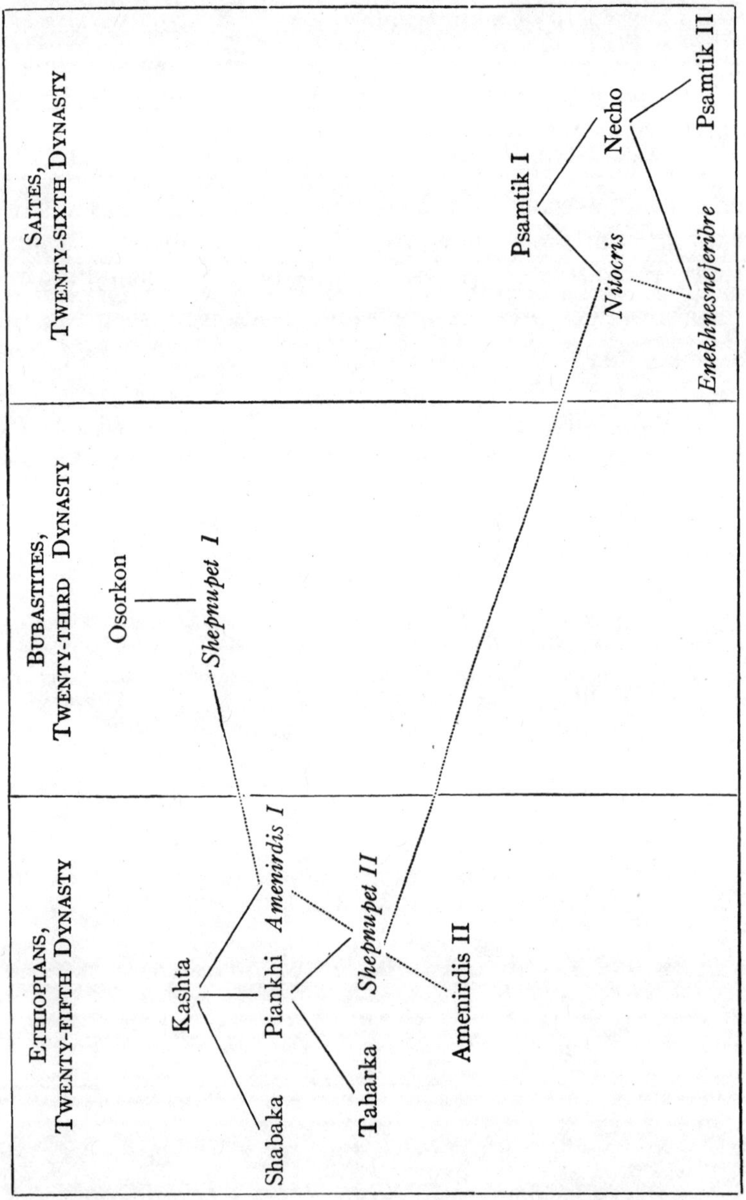
Ethiopians,
Twenty-fifth Dynasty
Bubastites,
Twenty-third Dynasty
Saites,
Twenty-sixth Dynasty
Kashta
Shabaka
Piankhi
Taharka
*Amenirdis I*
*Shepnupet II*
Amenirdis II
Osorkon
*Shepnupet I*
Psamtik I
Necho
*Nitocris*
*Enekhnesneferibre*
Psamtik II

941. In this table the most important difficulty is the identity of Piankhi, a question not raised in Erman's discussion.[a] There were at least three Piankhis,[c] and nowhere is Piankhi, brother of Amenirdis I, identified by his throne-name; nor do we know the throne-name of the great Piankhi. In view of the fact that Piankhi, brother of Amenirdis I, appointed her to succeed the daughter of an Osorkon, and we know that Piankhi the Great overthrew an Osorkon of the Twenty-third Dynasty (§ 872), it can hardly be doubted that Amenirdis I's brother is the great Piankhi. The chronological considerations (§§ 810 ff.) also demand that the great Piankhi shall be dated in the same general period involved in the position occupied by Piankhi, brother of Amenirdis I in the table.

### *Psamtik's Declaration of Adoption*

942. [b]2"I am his son, first in the favor of the father of the gods, offering to the gods; whom[c] he begat for himself, to satisfy his heart. I have given to him my daughter, to be Divine Consort, that she ⌈may invoke protection for the king⌉ more than those who were before her; that he may indeed be satisfied with her prayers, and that he may protect the land of 3him who gave her to him."

"Lo, I have now heard saying, a king's-daughter of Taharka,[d]

---

[a]*Zeitschrift für ägyptische Sprache*, 35, 29.

[c]1. *Wsr-m*ˀᶜ*·t-R*ᶜ*-P-*ᶜ*nḫy* (Lepsius, *Denkmäler*, V, 14, *a-d*).

2. *Snfr-R*ᶜ*-P-*ᶜ*nḫy* (Lepsius, *Denkmäler*, V, 14, *l*).

3. *Mn-ḫpr-R*ᶜ*-P-*ᶜ*nḫy* (Louvre Stela, 100; Rougé, *Notice*, 116). One of these must have been the great conqueror Piankhi. See fuller list, Petrie, *History*, III, 267 f.

[b]Several lines are lost at the beginning; of the line numbered 1, the first half is lost, and the second is unintelligible.

[c]Refers to "*son.*"

[d]Horus-name, *Ḳ*ˀ *ḫ*ᶜ *w*, followed by "*Good God*" and erased cartouche. This daughter of Taharka, as Erman has observed, is doubtless the same as the Amenardis of l. 16, who had already shared in the property of the sacred office. But as her predecessor, Shepnupet, was not yet dead, she had not yet succeeded to the office. This Amenardis is now supplanted as "*Great Daughter*" by Nitocris, daughter of Psamtik I.

triumphant, is there whom he gave to his sister to be her 'Great Daughter,' who is there as 'Divine Votress' (*Ntr-dw*ʾ·*t*). I am not one[a] to expel an heir from his place, for I am a king who loves [4]truth; my particular abomination is lying; (I am) a son protecting his father, taking the inheritance of Keb, uniting the two portions as a youth. Hence I give her[b] to her,[c] to be her 'Great Daughter' as her[c] father[d] (once) conveyed her[c] to (his) sister."[e]

*Response of the Court*

**943.** Then [5]they bowed to the ground, they gave thanks to the King of Upper and Lower Egypt, Wahibre (Psamtik I), living forever; and they said: "Abiding and enduring through eternity! Thy every command shall abide and endure. How beautiful is this which the god doeth for thee! How excellent is that which thy father doeth for thee! ....[6]..... He loves to remember thy ka, and he rejoices at the mention of thy name, O Horus, 'Great-of-Heart,' King of Upper and Lower Egypt, Psamtik I, living forever. He has done this as his monument for his father, Amon, lord of heaven, ruler of gods. He hath given his beloved eldest daughter, Nitocris (*Nt-yḳr*·*t*), [7]whose 'beautiful name' is Shepnupet, to be Divine Consort, to play the sistrum before his (Amon's) beautiful face."

*Nitocris Proceeds to Thebes*

**944.** In the year 9, first month of the first season (first month), day 28, went forth his eldest daughter from the king's family apartments, clad in fine linen, and newly adorned with malachite. The attendants conducting her were legion in number, [8]and marshals cleared the path, for beginning the goodly way to the harbor, to turn up-stream for Thebes. The vessels bearing her were very numerous, the crews were mighty men; and they were deeply laden ⌜to the decks⌝ with every good thing of the king's-palace. [9]The commander thereof was the sole companion, nomarch of Heracleopolis, commander in chief of the army,

---

[a]The sense is clear, but the construction is entirely uncertain.

[b]Nitocris.

[c]Shepnupet, sister of Taharka.

[d]Piankhi.

[e]Piankhi's sister, Amenardis, as shown by Berlin 7972; Greene, *Fouilles*, 8, 1, and Lieblein, St. Petersburg, II, 7. See Erman, *Zeitschrift für ägyptische Sprache*, 35, 29.

chief of the harbor, Somtous-Tefnakhte.[a] Messengers sailed to the South, to make splendid provision before her. Sail was set ⸢— — — — —⸣. [b]10The great men took their weapons, and every noble ⸢had⸣ his provision, supplied with every good thing: bread, beer, oxen, geese, ⸢—⸣, dates, herbs, and every good thing. One transferred (her) to his neighbor, until she reached Thebes.

*Reception in Thebes*

**945.** 11In the year 9, second month of the first season (second month), day 14,[c] they arrived at the city of the gods, Thebes. As she advanced, she found (all) Thebes, men and women alike, standing, rejoicing at her approach, surrounding her 12with great offerings, a multitude in number. Then they said: "The daughter of the King of Upper Egypt, Nitocris, comes to the house of Amon, that he may receive her and be satisfied with her. The daughter of the King of Lower Egypt, Shepnupet, comes to Karnak, that the gods therein may honor her. Every monument of 13the King of Upper and Lower Egypt, Psamtik (I), abides and endures forever and ever. Amon, lord of heaven, king of gods, hath received what his son, Horus, 'Great-of-Heart,' living forever and ever, made for him. Amon, ruler of gods, hath praised that which his son, Favorite of the Two Goddesses, Nebe (*Nb-* ᶜ), living forever and ever, made for him. . . . . . 14. . . . . The reward therefore is with Amon,[d] and with Montu,[d] even a million years of life, a million years of stability, a million years of satisfaction. All health and joy of heart are with them for their beloved son, the King of Upper and Lower Egypt, Lord of the Two Lands, Wahibre, 15Son of Re, Psamtik (I), living forever and ever. . . . . . . . . ."[e]

*Conveyance of the Fortune*

**946.** Now, afterward when she came to the Divine Votress, Shepnupet, 16she saw her, was satisfied with her, and loved her beyond every-

[a]A Heracleopolitan of the same name and the same office appears under Piankhi after the conquest, at Thebes (Benson and Gourlay, *The Temple of Mut in Asher*); as the ninth year of Psamtik is some seventy-five years later, the two men are not the same, but probably father and son.

[b]The text as published is not in order, but it is evident that the fleet here sails away from Sais.

[c]Only sixteen days after leaving Sais.

[d]Epithets omitted above.

[e]The gods have given him the kingship.

thing. She conveyed to her the fortune (*ymy-pr*) which her father and her mother had conveyed to her and to her 'Great Daughter,' Amenardis, king's-daughter of King —, triumphant. It was put into writing concerning them, saying: "We[a] have given to thee[b] all our property in field and in town. Thou abidest upon our throne, abiding [17]and enduring forever and ever." The witnesses concerning them were the prophets, the priests and all the adherents of the temple.

*Inventory of the Fortune*

**947.** List of all the property given to her ⌜by [them⌝] in the towns and nomes of the South and North:

*Lands*

**948.** That which his (sic!) majesty gave to her in seven nomes of the Southland:

| | |
|---|---|
| 1. In the district of Heracleopolis, the nome [18]called Yuna (*Yw-n*ˀ), which is in the district thereof | lands, 300 stat |
| 2. In the district of Oxyrhyncus, the estate of Putowe (*Pw-t*ˀ *wy*), which is in the district thereof | lands, 300 stat |
| 3. In the district of Sep, the estate of Kewkew (*K*ˀ *w-k*ˀ *w*), which is in the district thereof | [19]lands, ⌜300⌝ stat |
| 4. In the district of the Hare nome, (Hermopolis), the estates of Nesumin, which are in the district thereof | 600 stat |
| 5. In the district of Aphroditopolis, (the town of) Kay (*Ḳ*ˀ *y*), which is in the district thereof | 300 stat |
| 6. [c]In the district of ⌜—⌝, the estate of Harsiese, which is in the district thereof | [20]200 stat |
| All this added together | lands, 1,800[d] stat |

together with all the income thereof from field and town; with their arid lands, and their canals.

[a]The pronoun refers to Shepnupet (II) and Amenardis.

[b]Feminine.

[c]There should be seven nomes, according to the heading. The lacking nome, which was omitted by error of the scribes, has been added at the end of the inscription.

[d]The total is 2,000, but the discrepancy is, perhaps, explained by the uncertainty of the third item.

*Revenues*

**949.** Bread and beer given to the temple of Amon for her:

*From the Prince of Thebes*

That which the fourth prophet of Amon, prince of [21]the city (Thebes), governor of the whole South, Mentemhet, gives to her:

| | |
|---|---|
| Daily: | |
| Bread | 200 deben |
| Wine | 5 hin |
| ⌜Cakes⌝ (*š* ᶜ) | 1 |
| Vegetables | 1 bundle (*ḥtp*) |
| Monthly: | |
| Oxen | 3 |
| Geese | 5 |

*From His Son*

**950.** That which his eldest son, chief of the prophets of Thebes, Nesuptah, gives to her:

| | |
|---|---|
| Daily: | |
| Bread | 100 deben |
| Wine | 2 hin |
| Vegetables | 1 bundle (*ḥtp*) |
| Monthly: | |
| [22]⌜Cakes⌝ (*š* ᶜ) | 15 |
| Beer | 10 jars (*hbn*) |
| Lands of the region (*ḳ* ᶜ *ḥ* ˙ *t*) of Wawat | 100 stat |

*From His Wife*

**951.** That which the wife of the fourth prophet of Amon, Mentemhet (named): Uzarenes (*Wḏ* ᵓ *-rns*), gives to her:

| | |
|---|---|
| Daily: | |
| Bread | 100 deben |

*From the High Priest of Amon*

**952.** That which the High Priest of Amon, Harkheb (*Ḥr-ḫb*), gives to her:

| | |
|---|---|
| Daily: | |
| Bread | 100 deben |
| Wine | 2 hin |
| Monthly: | |
| ⌜Cakes⌝ (š ʿ) | 10 |
| [23]Beer | 5 jars (*hbn*) |
| Vegetables | 10 bundles (*ḥtp*) |

*From the Third Prophet of Amon*

**953.** That which the third prophet of Amon, Pediamennebnesttowe, gives to her:

| | |
|---|---|
| Daily: | |
| Bread | 100 deben |
| Wine | 2 hin |
| Monthly: | |
| Beer | 5 jars (*hbn*) |
| ⌜Cakes⌝ (š ʿ) | 10 |
| Vegetables | 10 bundles (*ḥtp*) |

*Summary*

**954.** Combined total:

| | |
|---|---|
| Daily: | |
| Bread | 600 deben |
| Wine | 11 hin |
| ⌜Cakes⌝ (š ʿ) | $2\frac{1}{6}$[a] |
| Vegetables | $2\frac{2}{3}$[a] bundles |
| [24]Monthly: | |
| Oxen | 3 |
| Geese | 5 |
| Beer | 20 jars |
| Lands | 100 stat |

*From the King*

**955.** That which his majesty gives to her in the nome of Heliopolis in the temple of Atum, of the divine offerings (temple income), which his majesty founded:

| | |
|---|---|
| Spelt | 2 khar |

[a]Including also the monthly quota reduced to days.

after it has been offered in the (divine) presence daily, and the god has been satisfied therewith.

*From the Temples*

**956.** That which is given to her from the temples:

| | | |
|---|---|---|
| Sais | Bread | 200 deben |
| [25]Buto | " | 200 " |
| House of Hathor of the Malachite | " | 100 " |
| ⌜Memphis⌝ (*Pr-ynbw*) | " | 50 " |
| Kom el-Hisn | " | 50 " |
| Per-Manu | " | 50 " |
| The house (*ᶜ·t*) of Tharu | " | 50 " |
| Tanis | " | 100 " |
| House of Hathor | " | 100 " |
| [26]Bubastis | " | 100 " |
| Athribis | " | 200 " |
| Mesta (*Mś-t*ᵓ) | " | 50 " |
| Bista (*Byᵓ s-t*ᵓ) | " | 50 " |
| House of Harsaphes, lord of Heracleopolis | " | 100 " |
| Per-Seped (Saft-el-Henneh) | " | 100 " |
| Combined total | Bread | 1,500 deben |

*Further Lands*

**957.** That which was given to her in four[a] nomes of the Northland:

| | |
|---|---|
| 1. [27]In the district of Sais, the estates (*pr*) of the southern Bedwin, which are in the district thereof: lands | 360 stat |
| 2. In the district of Bista (*Byᵓ s-t*ᵓ), the house (*ᶜ·t*) of Neferher (*Nfr-ḥr*), which is in the district thereof: lands | 500 stat |
| 3. In the district of Thebu (*Ṯbw*), [28]— in the Barque of the Sycamore, which is in the district thereof | 2⌜4⌝0 stat |
| 4. In the middle district of Heliopolis, "The-Wall-of-Hori," son of Zedti (*Ḏdty*), which is (also) "The-Wall-of-Psenmut," born of [29]Meretubekhet (*Mr·t-wbḫ·t*), which is in the district thereof | 200 (+*x*) stat |
| Total lands of four nomes | 1,400 stat |

[a]Miscopied 3 in the publication; see l. 29, and l. 30.

together with all the income thereof, from field and town; with their arid lands and their [30]canals.

Combined total:

| | |
|---|---|
| Bread | 2,100 deben |
| Lands in eleven nomes | 3,300 stat |

Abiding, abiding, conveyed, conveyed, imperishable and ineffaceable, forever and ever, forever and ever!

*Land Omitted Above*[a]

**958.** In the district of — ⌈pep⌉, with all its people, all its lands, and all its possessions in field and town.

---

## STATUE INSCRIPTION OF THE CHIEF STEWARD, IBE[b]

**958A.** This inscription records part of the career of Ibe, one of the nobles in attendance upon Nitocris, the daughter of Psamtik I, after her appointment as sacerdotal princess of Thebes. Ibe describes her installation (year 9), at the ceremonies of which he was present (§§ 958D–958E); and then narrates his appointment by the king as her chief steward [seventeen years later, in the year 26 (§ 958G)], for the purpose of restoring her palace. He arranged the affairs of the princess, and she spent a day with him in the temple, looking over her papers. He then conducted the restoration of her palace, involving the erection of one building a hundred cubits high (over 172 feet!). This is the only literary reference to the height of a dwelling in earlier Egypt. Ibe also built a palace-chapel of Osiris, assisted in the celebration of the feasts of Amon, and aided in the restoration of the Osirian tomb at Thebes.

---

[a]The scribe omitted this piece of land from the list in seven nomes (§ 948).

[b]Limestone statue bought at Luxor by Legrain in 1903; it represents a standing figure broken off at the waist, the upper portion missing. A stela held before the figure bears the inscription. Published by Daressy, *Annales*, V, 94–96. The stone is friable and the surface much eroded, so that the text is very uncertain.

*Introduction*

958B. [1]——— chief steward of the Divine Consort, Ibe (*Yb*ʾ), son of the priest (*mry·ntr*), Enekhhor (ʿ*nḫ-Ḥr*) [2]——— . . . [3]. . . .[a] ——— [4]chief [⌜steward⌝] of my queen, his daughter, the Divine Consort ———.

*Appointment of Nitocris*

958C. A lacuna at this point evidently contained the statement that Psamtik I commanded the appointment of his daughter,

[5]His beloved, the great favorite of Amon, the sweet —, [⌜daughter of⌝] the beloved of Mut, Mehetnusekhet (*Mḥ·t-m-wsḫ·t*) to be Divine Consort, Divine Votress of Amon in Karnak.

*Installation of Nitocris*

958D. [6]The chief ritual priest, divine scribe, prophets, divine fathers, priests (*w*ʿ*b*), and the great companions of his majesty, were the suite of their queen. The whole land was in great festivity; an oblation — [7]filled with every offering, ⌜jubilating⌝ to him, satisfying the heart; ⌜by⌝ the glorious one, great among the great, his beloved, the Divine Votress, Nitocris, who liveth; while the lay priesthood of the temple were following [her] [8]⌜— —⌝. There was performed for her every customary ceremony, like the fashion of the coronation of her good lord, Amon — — radiance, like the sun (*Šw*). She caused — — [9]that there be presented a great oblation; the lay priesthood brought the incense of favor, love, life,[b] prosperity, and health for her father, Wahibre (*W*ʾ *ḥ-yb-R*ʿ, Psamtik I).

*Nitocris Arrives at Her Theban Palace*

958E. Her majesty proceeded — — [10]to the palace, seated in her palanquin (*dnṯ*ʾ·*t*), the poles (thereof) being made anew, of silver and gold, inlaid with every genuine costly stone,[c] and she caused ⌜that there be offered⌝[c] — —.

[a]Fragments of a mortuary prayer for Ibe, whose title is, perhaps, partially preserved at the beginning of l. 4.

[b]See II, 960.

[c]Or: "*given to her* ⌜*beside them*⌝ — —."

### *Decay of the Palace of Nitocris*

**958F.** [11]Year 26, second month of the first season, day 3. [a]⌜On this day⌝,[a] his majesty ⌜— — — —⌝. His majesty sent those who were in his suite, — — [12]of the Southland, prophets, and priests (*w*ᶜ*b*) of Amon, and sacred women of Amon. They came, saying: "His majesty has heard that the house of the Divine Votress of Amon [13]is beginning to fall to ruin."

### *Appointment of Ibe as Chief Steward of Nitocris to Carry Out Restoration*

**958G.** These people also bring with them a command of the king that

There should be appointed [14]the king's-confidant, Ibe, as chief steward of the Divine Consort, and that there should be collected for him all his things which should go ⌜for the payment⌝ of the works, [15][an]d that they should be delivered to all the scribes and inspectors sent with the business of the house of the Divine Votress, as many as they were. The list of every day — — — [16]⌜————⌝ utensils of silver, gold, copper, ⌜—⌝, [everything] of the White House.

### *Ibe's Administration*

**958H.** [17]I ⌜filled⌝ her granaries with ⌜wheat⌝, spelt, and all fruits. I multiplied her cattle yards with bullocks, [⌜obliged⌝] her officials to pay dues — — [18]all of them. I conserved everything by exaction in — throughout.

### *Nitocris Spends a Day Inspecting Her Affairs*

**958I.** — — he ⌜went⌝ to receive her in the temple of Amon — —. [19]She spent the day sealing ⌜— —⌝ of the house.

Here she seems to have inspected

[20]All her affairs of the myriad of years which every excellent king lives.

### *Ibe Conducts the Restoration of the Palace of Nitocris*

**958J.** I built her refectory (*w*ᶜ*b·t*) by the side of the king's-house (*pr stny*), (⌜called⌝): "Khonsu-of-⌜—⌝,"[b] as an eternal work, everything

---

[a]Or: "⌜*the coronation day*⌝ *of his majesty.*"

[b]Amon ?

was a work of — [21]— in it, — her house (*ḥ·t*) in the pure house (*pr*) of her father, Amon, which her father, Re, made for her in the first beginning (*sp tpy*), 100 cubits high, and 100 cubits wide — — — — [22]built in all its —. Its — was of stone, its pavement was of stone, every ⌜altar⌝ found in it, its tables — [23]without ⌜number⌝. Its ceiling (lit., heaven) was of electrum, inlaid with every genuine costly stone.

### *Ibe Builds a Palace-Chapel of Osiris*

958K. I erected a temple (*ḥ·t-ntr*) beside it for her lord, Osiris-Wennofer, of ⌜all⌝ excellent work. His barque — [24]— like Re in his horizon. The portable image of his majesty was fashioned of electrum, inlaid with every genuine costly stone, together with statues of her[a] body of electrum — — — [25]— — to her palace in her ⌜barge⌝ before the — place.

### *Celebration of Amon's Feasts*

958L. Ibe then narrates how the god (Amon) was brought forth in procession, with his sacred women who accompanied Nitocris,

At his feast which the land celebrated for him on the sixth of the month; ⌜whereof the like was done⌝ beside the upper gate of Amon-Re ⌜— —⌝ with her father at his feast of the first month of the third season (Pakhons) [26]—.

### *Restoration and Furniture of the Osirian Tomb?*

958M. She filled his secret cavern[b] with brick, with [⌜all⌝] ⌜genuine things⌝ that he desired. Its doors were of cedar, the pavement of ⌜— — — — —⌝ which the queen (*ḥn·t*), L. P. H., ⌜—⌝, Divine Votress, Nitocris, fashioned ⌜————⌝ [27]— — Great Divine Consort, Mehetnusekhet, likewise in everything; ⌜in order[c] to bury⌝ a multitude of their vessels, even all their[d] offering-tables of the temple, of silver, gold, and every costly stone. I founded their divine offerings, of bread, beer, cattle, fowl, linen, ointment, wine, milk, ⌜—⌝, and vegetables as daily [offerings ⌜without⌝] [28]number. . . . . .[e]

---

[a]Nitocris. [b]The Osirian tomb of Amon?

[c]*Yw* for *r*, both being pronounced "*e*."

[d]It is not certain to whom this "*their*" (and again in this line) refers.

[e]The remainder of the line is chiefly an obscure asseveration of faithfulness by Ibe.

## FIRST SERAPEUM STELA[a]

959. This is the important stela which shows that Taharka immediately preceded Psamtik I. The deceased Apis died just before the beginning of Psamtik I's twenty-first year, having lived twenty-one years, two months, and seven days. As the animal was born in the twenty-sixth year of Taharka, it is evident that Taharka was the predecessor of Psamtik I, with a possible interval between them of not more than one or two months. The stela is further important as indicating that the years of the king's reign coincided with the years of the civil calendar. The Apis died on the twenty-first of the twelfth month in Psamtik's twentieth year. At the expiration of the ceremonial seventy days, the burial took place on the twenty-fifth of the second month in the king's twenty-first year. The transition from year 20 to year 21 evidently fell on New Year's Day (see also § 984).

*Death of Apis*

960. Year 20, fourth month of the third season (twelfth month), day 21; under the majesty of the King of Upper and Lower Egypt, Wahibre (*Wꜣ ḥ-yb-Rꜥ*); Son of Re, of his body, Psamtik (*Psmṯk*) I; went forth the majesty of Apis, the Living Son, to heaven.

*Burial of Apis*

961. This god was conducted in peace to the Beautiful West in the year 21, second month of the first season (second month), (on) the twenty-fifth day.

*Birth and Age*

962. Now, he was born in the year 26 of King Taharka; he was received into Memphis in the fourth month of the second season (eighth month), (on) the ninth day; which makes 21 years, 2 months ⌈7 days⌉.[b]

---

[a]Louvre, No. 190; published: Mariette, *Le Sérapéum de Memphis*, III, Pl. 36; Piehl, *Inscriptions*, I, XXII, C; Revillout, *Revue égyptologique*, VII, 138; Chassinat, *Recueil*, 18, 19. I had also my own copy of the original.

[b]After the "*2 months*" there is a hieratic 7, and before it a half-circle, which is probably the sign for day.

## SECOND SERAPEUM STELA[a]

963. This inscription has heretofore been understood as recording both repairs in the Serapeum or a sanctuary of Apis,[b] and the burial of an Apis deceased under Psamtik I. The true import of the inscription is totally different. There is no reference to an Apis which died in Psamtik I's reign, but only the record of the restoration by him, of an old interment, on receiving a report that the coffin was so fallen to pieces that the body of the sacred animal was exposed to view.

### *Date*

964. In the year 52 under the majesty of this Good God (Psamtik I),[c] came one to say to his majesty:

### *Message*

965. "The temple[d] of thy father, Osiris-Apis, and the things therein are beginning to fall to ruin. The divine limbs are visible in his coffin,[e] decay has laid hold of his (mortuary) chests."

### *Restoration*

966. His majesty commanded restoration in his temple,[d] and that it should be more beautiful than that which was there before. His majesty caused that there be done for him all that is done for a god on the day of interment. Every office had its duties, that the divine limbs might be splendid in ointment, wrappings of royal linen, and all the

---

[a]Large stela found by Mariette in the Serapeum, now in the Louvre (No. 239); published by Mariette, *Renseignements*, 11 f. (not seen); I had my own copy of the original.

[b]Brugsch (*Geschichte*, 741, 742) and Wiedemann (*Aegyptische Geschichte*, 619, 620).

[c]His fivefold titulary immediately precedes.

[d]As the context shows, "*temple*" (*ḥ˙t-nṯr*) is here the sepulcher of an Apis, and must mean an alcove of the Serapeum, in which an Apis was entombed. If this stone had not been found in the Serapeum, we should think such a burial chapel as that erected by Amenhotep III for an Apis, was meant.

[e]This (*wn*) must have been a wooden coffin, which was so decayed that the body of the Apis could be seen.

raiment of a god. His (mortuary) chests were of ked wood, meru wood, and cedar wood, of the choicest of every wood. Their ⸢troops⸣[a] were subjects of the palace,[b] while a king's-companion stood over[c] them, levying their labor for the court,[d] like the land of Egypt.

May he be given life, stability, satisfaction, like Re, forever and ever.

---

## STATUE INSCRIPTION OF HOR[e]

**967.** This fragmentary inscription, like that of Pefnefdineit (§§ 1015 ff.) and Nesuhor (§§ 989 ff.) illustrates the excessively religious spirit of the Saitic age. Hor was military commander at Heracleopolis, where he executed considerable additions, or at least restorations, in the temple of Harsaphes.[f] These he has recorded upon his votive statue in some detail. His reference to the use of cedar from the royal domain would be more important if the king under whom he served were mentioned,[g] as it shows that the forests of Lebanon were under the control of the Pharaoh at this time.

### *Introduction*

**968.** ——— [1]benefactions in Heracleopolis, watchful in restoring Ner (*N*ᶜ*r*), making Heracleopolis prosper, repelling her obstructors

---

[a]This word is written with three standing men with feathers upon their heads. The reference to "*Egypt*" at the end would indicate that they were not Egyptians, and the feathers point to Libyans. The antecedent of "*their*" is also in doubt.

[b]Read ᶜ *ḥ* ᶜ.

[c]Spiegelberg's interpretation (*Recueil*, 26, 43, 1) involves making "*kings-companion*" plural, while the text shows a singular.

[d]Or: "*collecting their impost into the court.*"

[e]On his black granite statue, now in the Louvre (A 88); published by Pierret (*Recueil d'Inscriptions*, I, 14–21); and partially by Brugsch, *Thesaurus*, VI, 1251, 1252. I had a copy of the Berlin squeeze, kindly made for me by Schaefer.

[f]Other examples of nobles building temples will be found in the Northern Oasis (Steindorff, *Königlich-Sächsische Gesellschaft der Wissenschaften*, 1900, 226).

[g]Our insertion of the inscription in the reign of Psamtik I is conjectural.

when the ⌈filthy⌉[a] lay in her streets as in a stable; repelling ⌈—⌉ from her district, chief of Heracleopolis, commander of the army, Hor, son of the chief of ⌈militia⌉ (*šš*) in the district of Busiris, Psamtik, born of the matron, Nefrusebek; he saith:

*Prayer*

**969.** "O divine lord, Khnum, king of the Two Lands, ruler of lands, sole god, whose qualities none possesses;[b] I am ⌈zealous⌉, showing allegiance to thee. I have filled my heart with thee, the prosperous way of him who follows thy majesty. Thou hast made my heart, that my heart might be vigilant in pursuit of genuine things[c] ————."

*Temple Court*

**970.** "———— [2]in the great forecourt of Harsaphes, as a great work without its like; a colonnade of pink granite, the doors of fine cedar of the (royal) domain, many — of gold like the horizon of heaven. Its south and north walls are of fine limestone of Ayan, the lintels of pink granite, overlaid with gold, the door with electrum."

*Temple Hall*

**971.** "I restored the southern aisle (*Ytwr*), and the northern aisle, and the southern and northern aisle in this place, besides the house of Nehebkau."

*Temple Lake and Furniture*

**972.** "I built the rear wall of the pool ⌈of⌉ the shore, I seized the place ———— [3]I beautified the broad-hall of the ⌈militia⌉ (*šš*) behind the tomb,[d] in order to make for me a great work in the house (*pr*) of Harsaphes, lord of gods, ⌈— —⌉. I gave two pieces of land (*ḥsp*) before the great god ⌈— — — — —. I gave⌉ wine ⌈—⌉ every day; I rewarded ⌈—⌉ with goods from my house, I beautified them, (for) I knew that the abomination of a god is withholding. I made their two offering-tablets

[a]Is this a term of contempt for a foreign foe, referring to the expulsion of an Assyrian garrison?

[b]This is the phrase applied to the sun-god, Aton, in the great hymn (see my *De Hymnis in Solem sub Rege Amenophide IV Conceptis*, 47, l. 50, where the end is to be amended thus: *ntr wꜥ nn ky ḥr sp·w·f*).

[c]For the god's temple.

[d]*Ḥbš-bg·t*; see Brugsch, *Wörterbuch*, 456.

of white stone (*ds*), in order to present the divine offerings upon them: one being in the pit of the coffin, the place where Atum, the old man, goes to rest; the other in "None-Prospers-Against-Him,"[a] ⌈before⌉ King Wennofer ——— [4]his gods, I filled up what was found empty[b] in his house."

*Feast of Bast*

**973.** "I brought out Bast in procession to her barge, at her beautiful feast of the fourth month of the second season (eighth month), the fifth day until ⌈—⌉."

*Concluding Prayer*

"I have done these things with a glad heart, without — —. I have opened ⌈to thee⌉ my arms and extended my embrace ⌈before [thee]⌉ — work ⌈— —⌉ which was in my heart, while making monuments in thy house. Endue me with life, prosperity, and health ⌈— —⌉ which is in my heart in thy temple. Give me revered old age, spending a long life in happiness, possessing all favor of the ruler of lands (the king), while my name endures in Heracleopolis until the coming of eternity."

[a]Name of a place.

[b]Referring to broken inscriptions which he restored.

## REIGN OF NECHO

### SERAPEUM STELA[a]

974. This stela furnishes the data for computing the exact length of Psamtik I's reign. Having lived sixteen years, seven months and seventeen days, this Apis died in the sixteenth year of Necho, on the sixth of the second month. The bulk of his life fell in the reign of Necho, and he was only one year, six months, and eleven days old at the accession of Necho. This period of his life thus coincided with the last year, six months and eleven days of Necho's predecessor, Psamtik I. Now, the Apis was born in the fifty-third year of Psamtik I, on the nineteenth of the sixth month; hence the total length of Psamtik I's reign was the sum of

| | | | |
|---|---|---|---|
| | 52 years, | 5 months, | 19 days |
| and | 1 " | 6 " | 11 " |
| or | 54 years, | 0 months, | 0 days. |

975. This would indicate that Psamtik ruled an even number of complete years,[b] but we cannot suppose that Psamtik I died on the last day of the year; it is evident that he died in the fifty-fifth year of his reign, and that the fraction of that incomplete year was, after his death, included in the first year of his successor, Necho. It is thus clear that the years of the king's reign in the Twenty-sixth Dynasty began on New Year's Day. We have already reached the same conclusion from the first Serapeum Stela of Psamtik I (§ 959).

[a]Louvre, No. 193; published by Piehl, *Inscriptions*, I, XXI, A; Chassinat, *Recueil*, 22, 21. I had also my own copy of the original.

[b]The scribe's computation ignores the 5 epagomenæ; the Apis was really 16 years, 7 months, and 22 days old.

*Date*

**976.** [1]Year 16, fourth month of the first season (fourth month), day 16, under the majesty of Horus: Wise-hearted (*Śyʾ-yb*); King of Upper and Lower Egypt;[a] Favorite of the Two Goddesses: Triumphant; Golden Horus: Beloved-of-the-Gods; [2]Uhemibre; Son of Re, of his body, his beloved: Necho, living forever, beloved of Apis, son of Osiris.

*Burial of Apis*

**977.** [3]The day[b] of the interment of this god. This god was conducted in peace to the necropolis, to let him assume his place in his temple in the western desert of [4]"Life-of-the-Two-Lands," after there had been done for him all that is done in the pure house, as it was done formerly.

*Life of Apis*

**978.** He was born [5]in the year 53, second month of the second season (sixth month), day 19, under the majesty of the King of Upper and Lower Egypt: Wahibre; Son of Re: Psamtik (I), triumphant. [6]He was [rece]ived into the house of Ptah in the year 54, third month of the first season (third month), day 12. He departed from life [7][in the year] 16, second month of the first season (second month), day 6. The total of his length of life was 16 years, 7 months, and 17 days.

*Tomb and Equipment of Apis*

**979.** The majesty of [8]the King of Upper and Lower Egypt, Necho, living forever, made all the coffins and every thing excellent and profitable for this august god. [9]He built for him his place in the necropolis, of fine limestone of Ayan, of excellent workmanship. Never happened the like [10]since the beginning. That he might be given all life, stability, satisfaction, health, and joy of heart, like Re, forever and ever.

---

[a]This title has been inserted by the scribe in the wrong place after the Horus-name.

[b]The date at the top; it is just 70 days after his death, as dated in the document (l. 7).

## BUILDING INSCRIPTION[a]

**980.** The inscription shows that Uzahor superintended the quarries at Assuan during the building operations of Necho. Like the old officials stationed at this place from the Sixth Dynasty on, he was "*governor of the door*," or frontier post, of the southern countries.

Revered by the King of Upper and Lower Egypt, Uhemibre (Necho), like Re. Hereditary prince and count (*rpᶜ ty*, *ḥ*ᵓ *ty*-ᶜ), governor of the door of the countries, Uzahor (*Wḏ*ᵓ-*Ḥr*), he says: "I was commander of works upon the mountain ———, to make great obelisks of granite, and all monuments of diorite (*bḫn*) and granite for the ———."

[a]From a statue bought by Petrie at Memphis; published, *Season*, XXI, 5, and 26.

## REIGN OF PSAMTIK II

### STATUE INSCRIPTION OF NEFERIBRE-NOFER[a]

**981.** This fragmentary document contains a few references to the building activity of Psamtik II, of whose reign we know so little. Neferibre-nofer was a "*magazine overseer*," who can have been no other than the Neferibre-nofer, of another statue[b] at Cairo, who held the same office under Psamtik II, and bore also the name Irhoro (*Yry-ḥr-*ᶜ ᵓ). Besides being tutor and guardian of the king, he also held the rank of "*hereditary prince, count, wearer of the royal seal, and sole companion.*"

Omitting unessential and fragmentary self-praise, the building references are these:

**982.** . . . . . Neferibre-[3]nofer, to whom the Two Lands recount their hearts, and repeat to him all their thoughts; [⌜who [4]pleases⌝] King Neferibre (Psamtik II) by doing that which is his desire, when he commands to protect their[c] holy places, beautifying the Two Lands — [5]. . . . . . . . . [7]. . . . He built the temple of the lord of eternity, [8]erecting a pyramidion (*bnbn*[*·t*]) in Mehenet of Sais, in work ⌜——⌝ fine limestone of Ayan; [9]obelisks of Elephantine granite, houses for the first time for Neit; a (portable) barque-shrine (*wṯs-nfr·t*) of fine gold, inlaid with every splendid costly stone [10]. . . . . . . .

**983.** The very fragmentary remainder (ll. 10–16) contains references to liberal offerings to the gods, "*for the sake of the life, prosperity and health of King Psamtik* (*II*), *living like Re.*"

---

[a]Black granite statue in Cairo; published by Daressy, *Recueil*, XVI, 46, 47 (C).

[b]Gray granite statue; published by Mariette, *Monuments divers*, 29, *a*, 1–5 = Piehl, *Zeitschrift für ägyptische Sprache*, 1887, 120–22.

[c]The gods?

# REIGN OF APRIES

## SERAPEUM STELA[a]

984. From this stela we can compute the length of the combined reigns of Necho and Psamtik II. The Apis commemorated died on the twelfth day of the eighth month in the twelfth year of Apries, being seventeen years, six months, and five days old; hence his life began five years, ten months, and twenty-three days before the accession of Apries. As the animal's birth fell on the seventh of the second month in the sixteenth year of Necho, the lapse of time from the accession of Necho to that of Apries (or to the death of Psamtik II) is the sum of

| | | | |
|---|---|---|---|
| | 15 years, | 1 month, | 7 days |
| and | 5 " | 10 months, | 23 " |
| or | 21 years, | 0 months, | 0 days. |

The combined reigns of Necho and Psamtik II, therefore, lasted exactly twenty-one years.[b] It is noticeable, also, that, as above (§ 975), the fraction of Psamtik II's last or incomplete year is not counted, but his reign is concluded with the end of his last complete year, as if Apries had begun to reign on New Year's Day.

985. Since the above was written the conclusion reached has received interesting confirmation by the discovery of the

---

[a]Louvre, No. 240; published by Mariette (*Choix de monuments du Sérapéum*, Pl. VII); thence by Bunsen (*Egypt's Place*, 2d ed., V, 738–40); Piehl, (*Inscriptions*, I, XXI, B); Birch (*Egyptian Texts*, 39–41); Chassinat (*Recueil*, 18). I also had my own copy of the original.

[b]The scribe has ignored the 5 epagomenæ at the end of the year, as in § 975, note; the Apis really lived 17 years, 6 months, and 10 days.

second Adoption Stela (§§ 988A-988J) at Karnak.[a] It furnishes the two following data for the length of Psamtik II's reign:

1. In the first year of Psamtik II's reign, in the eleventh month, on the twenty-ninth day, his daughter, the princess Enkhnesneferibre, arrived at Thebes to be adopted by the Divine Consort, Nitocris.

2. In the seventh year of his reign, in the first month, on the twenty-third day, Psamtik II died.[b]

The adoption was a political device which would be carried out by the Pharaoh without delay; hence we are safe in concluding that Enekhnesneferibre arrived in Thebes not long after Psamtik II's accession,[c] which thus fell late in the calendar year. His first regnal year thus consisted of no more than a month or two. Of his last year (the seventh), but twenty-three days had elapsed when he died. He thus actually reigned but five years and two or three months. From the twenty-one years above obtained as the total length of the successive reigns of Necho and Psamtik II, combined, we may then deduct the latter's reign of a little over five years, furnishing practically sixteen years as the length of Necho's reign. This coincides with the fact that our highest known date of Necho is the sixteenth year[d] (when the Apis of the following stela was born), and with Herodotus, who gives Necho sixteen years, and Psamtik II six years.

---

[a]Legrain, *Recueil*, 27, 81, 82. See above, § 938.

[b]The stela also states that his son Apries then succeeded him.

[c]The late date (year 9) for the adoption of Nitocris under Psamtik I was, of course, due to the fact that he did not gain control of Thebes immediately.

[d]This date is the 106th day of the sixteenth year (§ 976); hence there is plenty of margin for the few months in excess of the five years reigned by Psamtik II.

*Date*

**986.** [1]Year 12, second month of the third season (tenth month), day 21, under the majesty of King Apries[a] (*Ḥ ʿʿ-yb-Re*), [2]beloved of Apis, son of Osiris.

*Interment of Apis*

The god was conducted in peace to the Beautiful West, [3]to let him assume his place in the necropolis, the western desert of Memphis; after there had been done for him all that is done in [4]the pure house. Never was done the like before.

*Life of Apis*

**987.** The majesty of this god went forth to heaven [5]in the year 12, fourth month of the second season (eighth month), day 12. He was born in the year 16, second month of the first season (second month), day 7, under the majesty of [6]King Necho, living forever. He was installed in the house of Ptah [7]in the year 1, third month of the third season (eleventh month), day 9, under the majesty of Psamtik II. [8]The beautiful life of this god, was 17 years, 6 months, 5 days.

*Mortuary Equipment*

**988.** The Good God, Wahibre (Apries), made all the coffins, [9]everything, excellent, and every profitable thing, for this august god; that he (the king) might be given life and health therefore, forever.

---

## STELA OF THE DIVINE CONSORT ENEKHNESNEFERIBRE[b]

**988A.** This new monument furnishes several important facts in the history of the Twenty-sixth Dynasty, enabling us to confirm our reconstruction of the chronology and family history of this dynasty. These new facts are:

1. The final proof that Psamtik II was the father of Enekhnesneferibre.

2. The date of Psamtik II's death, and thus the exact length of his reign.

---

[a]Full fivefold titulary.

[b]Stela of alabaster, 0. m. 74 c. high, 0. m. 42 c. wide, 0. m. 13 c. thick, now in the Cairo Museum. It was discovered by Legrain in the great cache at Karnak, and was published by Maspero, with translation in *Annales*, V, 84–90.

3. Apries was the son of Psamtik II.
4. The date of the adoption of Enekhnesneferibre.
5. The date of the death of Nitocris.
6. The date of the accession of Enekhnesneferibre.

**988B.** The stela narrates the arrival of Enekhnesneferibre at Thebes in the first year of her father, Psamtik II, and her adoption there by Nitocris, as Nitocris herself had once been adopted by Shepnupet II, at the decree of Psamtik I (§§ 935 ff.). At this adoption she received the title of High Priest of Amon. Five years and fifty-nine days after her arrival at Thebes, Enekhnesneferibre's father, Psamtik II, died,[a] and was succeeded by his son, Apries. In the fourth year of this king, just eight years, four months, and ten days after Enekhnesneferibre's adoption, Nitocris died, and twelve days later Enekhnesneferibre succeeded to her office. This she held into the reign of Psamtik III, when she was at least eighty years old (see table, § 938).

*Arrival of Enekhnesneferibre at Thebes*

**988C.** [1]Year 1, third month of the third season, day 29, under the majesty of Horus: Menekhib (*Mnḫ-yb*); Favorite of the Two Goddesses: Mighty of Arm; Golden Horus: Beautifying the Two Lands; King of Upper and Lower Egypt: Neferibre; Son of Re: [2]Psamtik II, given life. On this day the king's-daughter, Enekhnesneferibre, arrived at Thebes.

*Adoption of Enekhnesneferibre by Nitocris*

**988D.** Her mother, the Divine Consort, Nitocris, who liveth, came forth [3]to behold her beauty, and they went together to the House (*pr*) of Amon. Then was conducted the [⌜divine⌝] ⌜image⌝[b] from [⌜the House of⌝] ⌜Amon⌝, to — — [4]⌜—⌝ in order to make her titulary as follows:

"The Greatly Praised in ⌜—⌝,[c] Flower in the Palace, ⌜—⌝ of the ⌜—⌝

[a]Having thus reigned five years and two or three months; see § 985.

[b]*Ḫnty*?

[c]Possibly "*House of Amon.*"

of [5]Amon, High Priest of Amon, King's-Daughter, Enekhnesneferibre. She shall be[a] in the Presence of her Father, Amon-Re, Lord of Thebes, Presider over Karnak."

*Death of Psamtik II*

988E. [6]Year 7, first month of the first season, day 23, went forth this Good God, Lord of the Two Lands, Psamtik II to heaven. He joined the sun, the divine limbs mingling with him who made him (*yr-sw*).

*Accession of His Son Apries*

988F. Then was crowned [7]his son, in his place, (even) Horus: Wahib; Favorite of the Two Goddesses: Lord of Might; Golden Horus: Making Verdant the Two Lands; King of Upper and Lower Egypt: Apries (*Ḥ* ᶜᶜ *-yb-R* ᶜ); Son of Re: Wahibre (*W* ᵓ *ḥ-yb-R* ᶜ), who liveth.

*Death and Burial of Nitocris*

988G. Year 4, fourth month of the third season, [8]day 4, of this king; went forth the Divine Votress (*Dw* ᵓ ˙*t-ntr*), Nitocris, triumphant, to heaven. She joined the sun, the divine limbs mingling with him who made her. Her daughter, the High Priest, Enekhnesneferibre, [9]did for her all that is done for every excellent king.

*Induction of Enekhnesneferibre*

988H. Now, when twelve days had elapsed after these events, (in) the fourth month of the third season, day 15, went the king's-daughter, [10]the High Priest, Enekhnesneferibre, to the House of Amon-Re, king of gods; while the prophets, the divine fathers, the priests (*w* ᶜ *b*), ritual priests and lay priests of the temple of Amon [11]were behind her, and the great companions were in front thereof. There were performed for her all the customary ceremonies of the induction of the Divine Votress (*Dw* ᵓ˙*t-ntr*) of Amon into the temple, by the divine scribe [12]and nine priests (*w* ᶜ *b*) of this house (*pr*). She fastened on all the amulets and ornaments of the Divine Consort (*Ḥm*˙*t-ntr*), and the Divine Votress (*Dw* ᵓ˙*t-ntr*) of Amon, crowned with the two plumes, the diadem of [13]her forehead,[b] to be queen (*ḥn*˙*t*) of every circuit of the sun.

---

[a]Or possibly the titulary closes with her name, and the following should be rendered: "*While she was, etc.*"

[b]It is possible that the word rendered "*forehead*" (*dhn*) may be the verb "*appoint*" (*dhn*).

*Titulary of Enekhnesneferibre*

**988I.** Her titulary was made as follows:

"Hereditary Princess, Great in Amiability, Great in Favor, Mistress of Loveliness, Sweet in Love, Queen (*ḥn·t*) of all Women, Divine Consort, [14]Divine Votress, Heknefrumut[a] (*Ḥḳ᾽·t nfr·w-Mw·t*), Divine Hand, Enekhnesneferibre, who liveth, King's-Daughter of the Lord of the Two Lands, Psamtik (II)."

*Reign of Enekhnesneferibre*

**988J.** There were done for her all the customary rites and all the ceremonies as [15]was done for Tafnut in the beginning.[b] The prophets, the divine fathers, and the lay priests of the temple came to her at all times when she went to the House of Amon, at his every festal procession.[c]

## INSCRIPTION OF NESUHOR[d]

**989.** The remarkable, and often misunderstood, narrative contained in this document furnishes an interesting corroboration of the tale of the mutiny of Psamtik I's troops, as narrated by Herodotus (II, 30, 31). Our Nesuhor was commander of the fortress and garrison at Elephantine, where he had assumed the responsibility for many pious works for the local divinities, in accordance with the increased religious spirit of the Saitic age. On one occasion the foreign mercenaries of the garrison mutinied and, like the Automoloi of Herodotus, planned to migrate to Upper

[a]Her alabaster statue (*Annales*, V, 90–92) gives as the reading of this name: *Ḥḳ᾽(t)-nfr·w-mry·(t)-Mw·t.*

[b]Lit., "*at the first time*" (*m-sp-tpy*).

[c]Lit., "*at his every feast of the appearance*" (*m ḥb·f nb n ḫ ᶜ*).

[d]On his statue in the Louvre (A 90); published by Maspero (*Zeitschrift für ägyptische Sprache*, 1884, 88, 89), with corrections by Brugsch (ibid., 93–97). I had also my own copy of the original which added a number of corrections, and a collation of the Berlin squeeze by Schaefer, which furnished the proper reading of the name of Nesuhor's mother. The inscription was first properly understood by Schaefer (*Beiträge zur alten Geschichte*, IV, 152–63), who also gives a final text (*ibid.*, Tafel, I–II).

Nubia, to a region called Shas-heret. Nesuhor succeeded in dissuading them and delivered them to Apries, who accordingly punished them. Believing that the gods had delivered him from his dangerous predicament among a horde of turbulent foreign soldiery, Nesuhor did not fail to narrate the event on his statue as a motive for his good works to the divinities of the first cataract. It thus furnishes graphic contemporary evidence of the dangerously unstable character of the military, of which the power of the Saite kings consisted. A similar but more widely-spread disaffection was the occasion of the overthrow of Apries by Amasis.

### *Qualities of Nesuhor*

**990.** [1]————[a] as his lord — his equal; whom his majesty appointed to a very great office, the office of his eldest son,[b] governor of the Door of the Southern Countries, to repel the countries that rebel against him. When he hath spread the fear of him in the southern countries, [2]they flee into their valleys for fear of him. Who did not ⸢relax [vigilance in⸣] seeking benefits for his lord; honored of the King of Upper and Lower Egypt, Apries (*Ḥ ʿʿ-yb-R ʿ*), favored by the Son of Re, Wahibre (*W ʾ ḥ-yb-R ʿ*), Nesuhor, whose beautiful name is Ib-Psamtik-menekh ("The-Heart-of-Psamtik-is-Excellent"), son of Ifrer (*Ywfrr*), born of the mistress, Tesenethor (*T ʾ-sn·t-Ḥr*), triumphant.

### *Nesuhor's Prayer*

**991.** He says: "O lord of might! Fashioner of gods and men! Khnum, lord of the Cataract, Satet, [3]and Anuket, mistress(es) of Elephantine! I rejoice in your names, I praise your beauty. I am free from laxity in doing that which you[c] desire; I fill my heart with you[c] in every design which I carry out. May my ka be remembered because of that which I have done in your house.

[a]The upper half of this (vertical) line is lacking; the document begins with epithets of praise applied to Nesuhor.

[b]The southern country under the empire was governed by a viceroy, who was originally the king's eldest son. This old tradition is now applied to the governor of Elephantine.

[c]Lit., "*your ka's*."

### *Good Works for the Gods*

**992.** I have splendidly equipped your temple with vessels of silver; numerous cattle, ducks, and geese; I have made secure their maintenance by (an endowment of) lands, as well as [4](that of) their custodians forever and ever. I built their shelters in your city. I gave very fine wine of the Southern Oasis, spelt and honey into your storehouses, which I built anew in the great name of his majesty. I gave illuminating oil for lighting the lamps of your temple. I appointed weavers, maid-servants and launderers for the august wardrobe of the great god [5]and his divine ennead. I built their quarters in his temple, established forever by decree of the Good God, Lord of the Two Lands, Apries, living forever.

### *Requital of Good Works*

**993.** Remember ye him in whose heart was the beautification of your house, (even) Nesuhor, whose name is abiding in the mouth of the citizens; as a reward for (all) this. Let my name abide in your house, let my ka be remembered after my life, let my statue abide and my name endure upon it imperishably in your temple.

### *Rescue of Nesuhor*

**994.** [6]For ye rescued me from an evil plight, from the mercenaries ⌈Libyans⌉,[a] Greeks, Asiatics, and foreigners, who had it in their hearts to —, and who had it in their hearts to go to Shas-heret (*Š*ᵓ *yš-ḥr·t*).[b] His majesty feared because of the evil which they did. I re-established their heart in reason by advice, not permitting them to go to Nubia (*T*ᵓ*-pd·t*), (but) bringing them to the place where his majesty was; and his majesty executed their [⌈punishment⌉].

**995.** Here follows a mortuary prayer, containing the following titles of Nesuhor:

Hereditary prince, count, wearer of the royal seal, beloved sole companion, great in his office, grand in his rank, official at the head of the people, governor of the Door of the Southern Countries.

---

[a]One is inclined to read *Ṯmḥw* here; for if we read ᶜᵓ *mw*, "Asiatics," then the Asiatics appear twice.

[b]Schaefer has shown that this region was in upper Nubia (*op. cit.*, 158–63).

# REIGN OF AMASIS (AHMOSE II)

## ELEPHANTINE STELA[a]

996. This, perhaps the most important document of the Saitic period, is, unfortunately, so badly preserved that a consecutive translation is totally impossible.[b] In the following I have rendered only what is capable of safe translation, and have then connected the few scattered translatable passages, by statements of their probable relation to each other, as indicated by the intervening uncertain context.

997. The drift of the historical facts furnished by the document is thus, in the main, discernible, in spite of the uncertainties and obscurities in details. In his third year as king of Egypt, Amasis finds Apries advancing against him from the north with a force of Greeks and a fleet. Apries assumed the offensive, and advanced to the vicinity of Sais, where Amasis, having mustered his forces, met and defeated him. The army of Apries was scattered, but the dethroned king escaped, and his troops continued to rove the North, infesting the roads and, of course, living by plunder. Meantime, Apries was a fugitive, with a few Greek (?) ships. When four or five months had passed in this way, Amasis was obliged to dispatch his forces, to exterminate the remnant of Apries' army, and while this went on, Apries was slain.

998. The narrative of Herodotus begins at an earlier

[a]A large stela of rose granite, 5 feet 9 inches high and three feet wide, found as part of a doorway in a house in Cairo, now in the Cairo Museum. Published by Daressy (*Recueil*, XXII, 2, 3). The stone is much worn, and so illegible that sometimes not a single sign is certain for half a line or more.

[b]The rendering by Daressy (*ibid.*) is nine-tenths conjecture, and the English version of Hall (*Oldest Civilisation of Greece*, 323, 324) is chiefly a translation of Daressy's French.

point in the usurpation of Amasis than does our stela. It would seem that after the defeat of Apries, and his dethronement by Amasis, as related by Herodotus, Apries had taken advantage of Amasis' kindness, had after some three years made his escape and had gathered an army of Greeks, who were again defeated by Amasis, as recorded on our stela. If this reconstruction be correct, then this second battle, as being much like the first, was not properly distinguished by Herodotus, who says nothing of it. This seems to me more probable than to identify the battle of our stela with that of Herodotus, in which case Amasis had ruled over two years, at least, before he was attacked by Apries; and there would also be no sojourn of Apries in the custody of Amasis, as so particularly related by Herodotus.[a] The account of Apries' death, as given by Herodotus, is difficult to harmonize with that on our stela on any hypothesis; but both sources agree in the statement that Amasis gave Apries honorable burial, according to Herodotus, among his ancestors at Sais.

**999.** There is contemporary evidence of the gradual rise of Amasis; for long after his assumption of the royal cartouche he continued to use his titles as a noble and a powerful palace official. Thus he inscribed his mother's sarcophagus[b] as follows:

**1000.** Revered by her husband, royal confidante of Wahibre (*W*ˀ *ḥ-yb-R*ᶜ, Apries), Teperet. Her lifetime was 70 years, 4 months, 15 days. The name of her mother was Mer-Ptah-Si-Hapi. It was her son who made it for her, the wearer of the royal seal, sole companion, chief of

[a]Unless we suppose that Apries was captured in the battle on our stela (which does not mention the fact), sojourned with Amasis four or five months, and then escaped to the Greek ships, there to be slain.

[b]Now in the Museum of Stockholm; published by Piehl (*Petites Etudes*, 32, and *Zeitschrift für ägyptische Sprache*, 28, 10); and Revillout (*Revue égyptologique*, II, 97).

the palace, prophet of Isis, master of the judgment-hall, [a]Ahmose (Amasis),[a] — Si-Neit.

**1001.** His mother was thus associated with, and perhaps related to, Apries, and Amasis' powerful connections thus aided him in usurping the throne. Herodotus' stories of his low birth are, therefore, unfounded.

**1002.** Year 3, second month of the third season (tenth month), under the majesty of King Amasis,[b] beloved of Khnum, lord of the Cataract, and Hathor, residing in Zeme (*Ḏ*ᵓ*-mw*˙*t*), given all life, stability, satisfaction, like Re, forever. ²........[c]

**1003.** Here follows the statement that his majesty was in the palace-hall, deliberating the affairs of the land, when one came to say to his majesty: "Apries (*Ḥ*ᶜᶜ*-yb-R*ᶜ), ³he has sailed ⌜southward —⌝ ships of ⌜—⌝, while Greeks without number are coursing through the Northland ⌜———— ⁴— —⌝.[d] They are wasting all Egypt; they have reached Malachite-Field,[e] and those who are of thy party flee because of them."

**1004.** Then his majesty caused the royal companions and ⌜—⌝ to be called, and informed them of what had happened.

He addressed them with reassuring exhortations (ll. 5–7), and they replied with praise of Amasis, declaring that Apries had acted like a dog at a carcass (ll. 7–10).

---

[a]In cartouche. A libation basin in the Louvre (Pierret, *Recueil d'inscriptions*, I, 82; Revillout, *Revue égyptologique*, I, 51, and II, 69 ff.); Piehl, *Zeitschrift für ägyptische Sprache*, 28, 12, enumerates his titles, before he assumed the cartouche, thus: "*Prince, sole companion, chief of the palace, master of the throne* ⌜—⌝, *chief of temples, master of secret things of all affairs of the king, favorite of his lord, strong in mind for his lord, chief of the royal council-halls, master of the judgment-hall, Ahmose-Si-Neit-Wahibre, born of Teperet.*" It is, perhaps, to his mother's connection with Wahibre-Apries that the addition "*Wahibre*" to his name is due. Daressy's suggestion of another woman as the mother of Amasis (*Recueil*, 22, 143, 144) is without support in the monument adduced.

[b]Full fivefold titulary. [c]Epithets belonging to the royal name.

[d]Possibly: "*Now he hath remembered their place* ⁴*in Pḥ-*ᶜ*n*." *Pḥ-*ᶜ*n* is a part of the Andropolite nome in the western Delta, but the reading of the name is quite uncertain.

[e]*Sḫ*˙*t-mfk* (sic!) is probably the same as *Pr-Ḥ*˙*t-ḥr-Mfk*, near Sais and Buto; see Daressy's note, *Recueil*, XXII, 8.

Said his majesty: "Ye shall fight tomorrow! Every man (*ḥr-nb*) to the front!" His majesty mustered his infantry and his cavalry[a] ———⌉. His majesty mounted [11]upon his chariot; he took arrows and bow in his hand, ⌈he arrived⌉ (⌈*spr-nf*⌉) at ⌈—⌉, he reached Andropolis, the army jubilating and rejoicing on the road.

**1005.** The introduction to the battle is totally unintelligible. Then follows (l. 12):

His majesty fought like a lion, he made a slaughter among them, whose number was unknown. Numerous ships ⌈took⌉ (⌈ᶜ *w* ᵓ⌉) them, falling into the water, whom they saw sink [13]as do the fish.

Amasis triumphed.

**1006.** [14]Year 3, third month of the first season (third month), day 8, ⌈came⌉ one to say to his majesty: "The enemy infest the ways, there are thousands there, invading the land; they cover every road. As for those who are in the ships, ⌈they bear hatred of thee in their hearts⌉ [15]without ceasing."

**1007.** Amasis then gave his troops instructions to scour "*every road, not letting a day pass,*" without pressing the enemy (ll. 15, 16); whereupon the army greatly rejoiced, and proceeded to their task (l. 16). The enemy's ships were taken (l. 17), and Apries was probably surprised and slain while taking his ease on one of the vessels. "*He (Amasis) saw his favorite*[b] *fallen in his — which he had made* [18]*before the water.*" Amasis had him buried as befitted a king, forgot the "*abomination of the gods,*" which he had committed, and "*he (Amasis) founded divine offerings in great multitude,*" for the mortuary observances of the fallen Apries.

---

[a]The word is uncertain; *ḥf nfr* is impossible. I translate from the determinative. The Greeks must have had horsemen at this time.

[b]*Mḥ-yb*ᶜ *f*, lit., "*one filling his heart,*" common term for the favorite or friend of a king.

## SERAPEUM STELA[a]

**1008.** As this stela records the life of an Apis, the duration of which fell entirely in Amasis' reign, it furnishes no data as to the exact length of his reign.

### *Date*

**1009.** [1]Year 23, first month of the third season (ninth month), day 15, under the majesty of the King of Upper and Lower Egypt, Khnem-ibre (Amasis), given life forever.

### *Burial of Apis*

**1010.** [2]The god was conducted in peace to the Beautiful West, to let him assume his place in the necropolis, [3]in the place which his majesty made for him, the like of which never was made before; after [4]there had been done for him all that is done in the pure house.[b]

### *Mortuary Equipment*

**1011.** Lo, his majesty had in his remembrance how [5]Horus did for his father, Osiris, and he made a great sarcophagus[c] of granite. Behold, his majesty [6]found it good to make it of costly stone ⌜—⌝ all kings of all times. [7]He made a shroud of mysterious linen of Resenet and Mehenet,[d] to attach [8]to him his amulets, and all his ornaments of gold, and every splendid, costly stone. They were more beautiful than [9]what was done before,[e] for his majesty loved Apis, the Living Son, more than any (other) king.

### *Life of Apis*

**1012.** [10]The majesty of this god went forth to heaven in the year 23, third month of the second season (seventh month), day 6. He was

---

[a]Louvre, No. 192, published by Piehl, *Inscriptions*, I, XX, H (good translation, 23, 24); Chassinat, *Recueil*, 22, 20. I had also my own copy of the original.

[b]The place of embalmment.

[c]This sarcophagus is still in the Serapeum (Brugsch, *Geschichte*, 743, 744). Inscription upon it (Brugsch, *Thesaurus*, V, 966, 967): "*Amasis; he made* (*it*) *as his monument for Apis, the living son* (*even*) *a great sarcophagus of granite because his majesty found it good to make it of costly stone* (*c ɔ· t*)." The last part is verbatim the same as on the stela above.

[d]The two parts of the sacred district of Sais; see Piehl, *Inscriptions*, I, 24, note 2.

[e]By earlier kings.

born in the year 5, [11]first month of the first season (first month), day 7. He was installed in the house of Ptah in the second month of the third season (tenth month), day 18. [12]The beautiful lifetime of this god was 18 years, 1 month, 6 days.

Ahmose (II)-Sineit, given satisfying life forever, made (it) for him.

## STATUE INSCRIPTION OF THE GENERAL AHMOSE[a]

**1013.** The titles and epitheta borne by this officer are the only contemporary evidence for the foreign campaigns of the latter part of the Saitic age. Ahmose's "*beautiful name*" shows that he was born under Psamtik II. He could hardly have become a general, therefore, before the reign of Ahmose II, under whom his duties in Nubia doubtless fell. His titles in the inscription are as follows:

**1014.** Commander of the army, Ahmose, whose beautiful name is Neferibre-nakht.

King's-messenger, fighting for his lord's sake in every country, doing what his majesty desires in Nubia (*Tʾ-pd·t*), governor of the two doors[b] in the northern countries, prophet of Soped, lord of the East, Ahmose, etc. (as above).

## STATUE INSCRIPTION OF PEFNEFDINEIT[c]

**1015.** The monuments left by this noble disclose the interesting fact that he was Apries' "*chief physician*," and a prominent member of the treasury administration who was among those won over to the cause of Amasis. He held the

[a]Found near Zagazig, now in Cairo; published by Daressy, *Recueil*, XX, 77.

[b]Two forts on the Asiatic frontier in the eastern Delta, as is shown by the man's priesthood of Soped, a god of that region.

[c]Louvre, A 93; published by Pierret, *Recueil d'inscriptions du Louvre*, II, 39 = Brugsch, *Thesaurus*, VI, 1252–54 (incomplete); from these two by Piehl, *Zeitschrift für ägyptische Sprache*, 32, 118–22; collation of last by Baillet, *Zeitschrift für ägyptische Sprache*, 1895, 127 ff. (a number of glaring errors); I had also my own copy of the original.

same offices under the latter, becoming, likewise, his "*chief physician*."[a] The Louvre statue was erected in Abydos, and bears an inscription narrating Pefnefdineit's notable achievements in support of Osiris and his temple. He claims the consideration of the god and his priesthood, because he constantly presented the needs of Abydos to King Amasis and secured wealth and buildings for the Abydos temple. Some of this work he personally superintended at Abydos, and he participated in the presentation of the Osirian drama there. His incessant activity for the cult of Osiris, although he was not a member of the royal family, is a striking example of the excessive religious zeal of the age, pictured so graphically by Herodotus.

**1016.** One of his achievements on behalf of Osiris is striking. A descendant of the ancient Thinite family, whose counts we still find in the Eighteenth Dynasty, was dispossessed of his income from the Great Oasis and from the local ferry, and Pefnefdineit had these revenues diverted to the treasury of Osiris. The income from the oasis was then devoted to meet the funeral expenses of the people of Abydos.

### *Titles of Pefnefdineit*

**1017.** [1]The hereditary prince, count, sole companion, chief of the palace (*ḫrp-ᶜ ḥᶜ*), chief physician, overseer of the gold-treasury, great one of the hall, great revered one in the king's-house, chief steward. Pefnefdineit, begotten of the chief of strongholds, local governor of Dep, prophet of Horus of Pe, Sisebek, says:

### *Mortuary Prayer*

**1018.** "O every priest (*wᶜb*), who shall perform divine offices; the First of the Westerners (Osiris) shall favor you, as ye recite for me

[a]Pefnefdineit erected another statue in the temple at Heliopolis which bears record of his rank under Apries. Now in British Museum: Sharpe, *Egyptian Inscriptions*, I, 111=Piehl, *Zeitschrift für ägyptische Sprache*, 31, 88–91. An offering-tablet of his is also in the Mosque of Bibars, Cairo (Wiedemann, *Recueil*, VIII, 64; Piehl from W., *Zeitschrift für ägyptische Sprache*, 31, 87 f.).

the prayer for mortuary offerings, with prostrations to the First of the Westerners; so shall ye behold the glories before your god; because I was more honored by the majesty [2]of my lord than any noble of his. I was one distinguished by reason of what he had done, an excellent craftsman, establishing his house."

*Attention to Abydos*

**1019.** "I transmitted the affairs of Abydos to the palace, that his majesty might hear (them). His majesty commanded that I do the work in Abydos, in order that Abydos might be furnished. I did greatly in improving Abydos, I put all the things of Abydos in order; (whether) sleeping (or) waking, seeking the good of Abydos there-with. [3]I besought favor from my lord every day, in order that Abydos might be furnished."

*Temple and Equipment*

**1020.** "I built the temple of the First of the Westerners in excellent and eternal work, as was commanded me from his majesty. He saw the prosperity in the affairs of the Abydos nome. I surrounded it with walls of brick, and the necropolis with granite, an august shrine[a] of electrum, the adornments[a] and the divine ⌜amulets⌝, all the tables[a] of the divine offerings (*yḥ˙t-ntr*) were of [4]gold, silver, and every costly stone. I built *Wpg*, I set up its altars (ᶜ *ḥ*), I dug its lake, planted with trees."

*Temple Income*

**1021.** "I provisioned the temple of the First of the Westerners, increasing that which came in to him, established as daily income. His magazine was settled with male and female slaves. I gave to him 1,000 stat of lands, of the fields of the Abydos nome; equipped with people and all small cattle; its name was made: 'Establishment (*grg˙t*)-of-Osiris,' [5]in order that the divine offerings might be furnished from it throughout eternity. I renewed for him the divine offerings more plentifully than what was formerly there. I made for him arbors,[b] planted with all date[c] trees, and vineyards (with) people therein of

---

[a]These nouns are enumerated as if in a list, without any verb of which they are the objects.

[b]ᶜ*t nt ḥt;* the same phrase occurs twice in Papyrus Harris (see §§ 194 and 264).

[c]Or: "*sweet trees.*"

foreign countries, [6]brought as living captives, yielding 30 hin of wine therefrom every day upon the altar of the First of the Westerners; and offerings shall be brought thence throughout eternity."

### *Temple Archives*

**1022.** "I restored the house of sacred writings when ruined; I recorded the offerings [7]of Osiris, I put in order all his contracts."

### *Osiris Drama*

**1023.** "I hewed from cedar (ʿš) the sacred barge[a] which I found (made) of acacia. I repelled the chief of the devastators[b] from Abydos, I defended Abydos [8]for its lord, I protected all its people."

### *Confiscation of Count's Property*

**1024.** "I gave to the temple the things that issued from the desert (*ḫʾš·t*)[c] of Abydos, which I found in the possession of the count, in order that [9]the people of Abydos might be buried. I gave to the temple the ferry-boat of Abydos which I took from the count; (for) Osiris desired that his city should be equipped. [10]His majesty praised me because of what I had done."

### *Prayer for King*

**1025.** "May he[d] grant life to his son, Ahmose (Amasis)-Sineit; may he grant favor before his majesty and honor before [11]the great god. O priest, praise the god for me; O every one coming forth, praise ⌈ye⌉ in the temple. Speak my name, the [12]chief steward, Pefnefdineit, born of Nenesbast [13]([*Nʿ*]-*nš*-*Bʾs·t*)[e]. . . . . . ."

---

[a]This temple barge was used in the Osiris drama; compare II, 183.

[b]In the dramatic enactment of the incidents of the Osiris myth.

[c]These can only be the income from the Great Oasis, which from the time of the Eighteenth Dynasty had belonged to the counts of Abydos (II, 763). This income then seems to have been devoted to paying the expenses of burying the people of Abydos.

[d]Osiris.

[e]Restored from the other monuments of this man (*Zeitschrift für ägyptische Sprache*, 31, 87, 88).

## MORTUARY STELÆ OF THE PRIEST PSAMTIK[a]

**1026.** The historical value of these stelæ consists solely in the chronological data which they furnish. From these data it is possible to establish the exact length of the Twenty-sixth Dynasty, and also the length of the reign of Apries, otherwise uncertain. The calculation is as follows:

Psamtik was sixty-five years, ten months, and two days old at his death in the twenty-seventh year of the reign of Amasis, on the twenty-eighth day of the eighth month. He was, therefore, born thirty-nine years, two months, and four days before the accession of Amasis. Now, the date of his birth is given as the first day of the eleventh month in year 1 of Necho; hence, Necho's accession was exactly forty[b] years before that of Amasis. The length of the dynasty is, then, the total of the following items:

| | |
|---|---|
| Psamtik I | 54 years |
| Necho } | |
| Psamtik II } | 40 " |
| Apries } | |
| Amasis | 44 " |
| Total | 138 " |

[a]Small stelæ in Leyden (V, 18 and 19), written with ink and rapidly becoming illegible; published by Piehl, (*Inscriptions*, III, XXVIII, G and H). I had also my own copy of the original which I collated with an old manuscript copy of Leemanns, made while the stelæ were more legible than at present.

[b]The computation is as follows:

| | | |
|---|---|---|
| Lifetime, | 65–10– 2 | |
| Date of death, | 26– 7–28 | |
| From birth to accession of Amasis, | 39– 2– 4 | |
| | 10– 1 | Date of birth in reign of Necho. |
| | 40– 0– 5 | |

The five days are, of course, the five epagomenæ.

As the fall of the dynasty occurred in 525 B. C., its accession took place in (525+138) 663 B. C.

**1027.** The length of the reign of Apries may also be determined from the same data, thus: the total of all the other reigns in the dynasty is as follows:

| | | |
|---|---|---|
| Psamtik I | 54 | years |
| Necho } Psamtik II } | 21 | " |
| (Apries omitted) | — | |
| Amasis | 44 | " |
| Total | 119 | " |

This total deducted from the 138 years' duration of the dynasty leaves nineteen years for the reign of Apries.[a] From the Elephantine Stela of Amasis we know that Apries lived over two years (i. e., into the third year) after the accession of Amasis, but these two years fall within the reign of the latter, and are not included in the nineteen years of Apries' sole reign. The text is as follows:

**1028.** Year 1, third month of the third season, day 1, under the majesty of the King of Upper and Lower Egypt, Uhemibre (*Wḥm-yb-R* ᶜ), Son of Re, Necho (*N-k* ᵓ *w*).

**1029.** On this good day was born the divine father, Psamtik, begotten of Ahuben (*Y* ᶜ *ḥ-wbn*), born of Enkhetesi (ᶜ *nḫts*). His good life was 65 years, 10 months, 2 days. Year 27, fourth month of the second season, day 28, was his day of departure from life. He was introduced into the Good House,[b] and he spent 42[c] days under the

[a]A stela in Berlin (No. 15393) is dated in the seventeenth year of Apries.

[b]This was the place of the embalmers, where he spent 42 days in process of embalmment, as is evident from the following context, Anubis being the embalmer. For a clear narrative of such mortuary proceedings, see the Miramar stela (Bergmann, *Hieroglyphische Inschriften*, VI, l. 10).

[c]Leemanns read 42; I could see only 30 and a stroke, with room between for another 10, and at the end for several strokes (units). Piehl read 30+*x*. The duplicate has clearly 42; but see next note.

hand of Anubis, lord of Tazoser. He was conducted in peace to the Beautiful West in the first month of the third season (ninth month), day ⸢—⸣;[a] and his life in the necropolis is forever and ever.

---

[a]Merely the day-sign with no numeral. On the duplicate I could not read the numeral; Leemanns gives 2, and Piehl read 1. None of these numerals fits the case; 42 days after his death would bring the burial on the tenth of the tenth month. As our texts both give ninth month, the 42 is evidently an error. It cannot be more than 32.